Comparative Employment Relations in the Global Economy

'Employment Relations' is widely taught in business schools around the world. Increasingly, however, more emphasis is being placed on the comparative and international dimensions of the relations between employers and workers. It is becoming ever more important to comprehend today's work and employment issues alongside a knowledge of the dynamics between global financial and product markets, global production chains, national and international employment actors and institutions and the ways in which these relationships play out in different national contexts.

Comparative Employment Relations in the Global Economy is the first to present a cross-section of country studies, including all four BRIC countries, Brazil, Russia, India and China, alongside integrative thematic chapters covering all the important topics needed to excel in this field. The textbook also benefits from the editors' and contributors' experience as leading scholars in Employment Relations.

The book is an ideal resource for students on advanced undergraduate and postgraduate comparative programmes across areas such as Employment Relations, Human Resource Management, Political Economy, Labour Politics, Industrial and Economic Sociology, Regulation and Social Policy.

Carola Frege is Professor of Employment Relations at the London School of Economics, UK.

John Kelly is Professor of Industrial Relations at Birkbeck, University of London, UK.

Comparative Employment Relations in the Global Economy

Edited by
Carola Frege and John Kelly

LONDON AND NEW YORK

First published 2013
by Routledge
2 Park Square, Milton Park, Abingdon, Oxon OX14 4RN

Simultaneously published in the USA and Canada
by Routledge
711 Third Avenue, New York, NY 10017

Routledge is an imprint of the Taylor & Francis Group, an informa business

British Library Cataloguing in Publication Data
A catalogue record for this book is available from the British Library

Library of Congress Cataloging in Publication Data
Comparative employment relations in the global economy / edited by Carola Frege and John Kelly.
pages cm
Includes bibliographical references and index.
ISBN 978-0-415-68662-4 (hbk)—ISBN 978-0-415-68663-1 (pbk)—
ISBN 978-0-203-76664-4 (ebk) 1. Industrial relations. I. Frege, Carola M., 1965- II. Kelly, John E., 1952-
HD6971.C66 2013
331—dc23

2012050456

ISBN: 978–0–415–68662–4 (hbk)
ISBN: 978–0–415–68663–1 (pbk)
ISBN: 978–0–203–76664–4 (ebk)

Typeset in Times New Roman
by RefineCatch Limited, Bungay, Suffolk

To Matteo Felli Frege
To Jo, Alex and Sarah Kelly

Contents

Figures

Tables

Contributors

Mark S. Anner is Director of the Center for Global Workers' Rights and an Associate Professor of Labor Studies and Political Science at Pennsylvania State University. He has a PhD in government from Cornell University and an MA in Latin American Studies from Stanford University. His research interests include industrial restructuring in the apparel and auto industries, labour law reform and labour solidarity in the Americas. He is the author of 'Industrial structure, the state, and ideology: shaping labor transnationalism in the Brazilian auto industry', *Social Science History*, 2003, and *Solidarity Transformed: Labor Responses to Globalization and Crisis in Latin America* (Cornell University Press, 2011).

Eileen Appelbaum is Senior Economist at the Center for Economic Policy and Research, Washington, DC. She was previously Professor of Economics at Temple University and Professor of Labor Studies and Employment Relations at Rutgers University. Her research focuses on the implications of company practices for organizational effectiveness and employee outcomes, and she is currently examining the effects of private equity ownership on managers, workers, unions and companies. Her books include the co-edited *Low Wage America* (Russell Sage, 2003) and the co-authored *Manufacturing Advantage* (ILR Press, 2000) and *The New American Workplace* (ILR Press, 1994), which were all selected by Princeton University as Noteworthy Books in Industrial Relations and Labor Economics.

Sarah Ashwin is a Professor of Industrial Relations at the London School of Economics and Political Science. She has been researching the Russian labour movement since 1991. Her publications include *Russian Workers: The Anatomy of Patience* (Manchester University Press, 1999) and (with Simon Clarke) *Russian Trade Unions and Industrial Relations in Transition* (Palgrave, 2003) as well as many journal articles.

Vidu Badigannavar is a Senior Lecturer in Human Resource Management at Royal Holloway, University of London. He holds an MSc and PhD in industrial relations from the London School of Economics. Prior to joining academia, he worked as an HR professional in the IT industry and later as a policy researcher with an international trade union federation. His main research interests are in the areas of economic policies and labour regulation, labour–management cooperation and international employment relations. He has published in leading journals such as the *British Journal of Industrial Relations, Economic and Industrial Democracy* and the *International Journal of Human Resource Management*.

Martin Behrens is Programme Director at the Institute of Social and Economic Research in the Hans Böckler Foundation (WSI) and lecturer at the Institute for Sociology at the University of Göttingen. His research focus is on comparative industrial relations and on German employers associations, works councils and labour unions. Recent publications include *Das Paradox der Arbeitgeberverbände [The Paradox of Employers Associations]* (Edition Sigma, 2011) and 'Still married after all these years? Union organizing and the role of works councils in German industrial relations', *Industrial and Labor Relations Review*, 2009.

João Paulo Cândia Veiga is Professor of Political Science and International Relations at the University of São Paulo (USP). He is a senior researcher at the Center of International Negotiations (Caeni), and earned his PhD and MA degrees in Political Science from USP. His research interests include labour and environmental standards, corporate social responsibility, non-state actors in world affairs, and private governance in commodity chains. His publications include (with K.A. Jakobsen) *The Orange and Yellow-Green Cooperation: The FNV and CUT Partnership* (2011), and *The Question of Child Labor* (1998).

Cynthia Estlund is the Catherine A. Rein Professor at the New York University School of Law. She has written extensively on workplace regulation and governance; worker voice and participation; freedom of expression and procedural fairness at work; diversity, integration and affirmative action; and many aspects of collective labour law. Her current research is primarily comparative, with a major focus on Chinese labour law and labour relations. She is the author of *Regoverning the Workplace: From Self-Regulation to Co-Regulation* (Yale University Press, 2010), and *Working Together: How Workplace Bonds Strengthen a Diverse Democracy* (Oxford University Press, 2003).

Keith D. Ewing has been Professor of Public Law at King's College, London, since 1989, and is President of the Institute of Employment Rights and Vice President of the International Centre of Trade Union Rights.

Michael Fichter completed his PhD in political science at the Freie Universität Berlin (FU Berlin), where he was a senior lecturer and researcher, specializing in German and European labour relations until his retirement in 2011. Since 2005, he has been an adjunct faculty member of the Global Labour University in Germany. His publications on labour relations include 'German trade unions and right extremism: understanding membership attitudes', *European Journal of Industrial Relations* (2008) and (with M. Helfen) 'Going local with global policies: implementing international framework agreements in Brazil and the United States', in K. Papadakis (ed.) *Shaping Global Industrial Relations* (Palgrave Macmillan, 2011).

Carola Frege is Professor of Comparative Employment Relations at the London School of Economics and Political Science. Frege's research has focused on the transformation of workplace democracy and labour unions in Western and Eastern Europe as well as in the USA. She has also written about the social science traditions of employment research and is currently working on racism across European labour markets. She is the author of *Employment Research and State Traditions: A Comparative history of Britain, Germany and the United States* (Oxford University Press, 2007), *Varieties of Unionism: Strategies for Union Revitalization in a Globalizing Economy* (Oxford University Press, 2004) (with John Kelly) and *Social Partnership at Work* (Routledge, 1999).

Gerald Friedman is a Professor of Economics at the University of Massachusetts Amherst, and a labour economist. In addition to his 1998 book, *State-Making and Labor Movements: The United States and France, 1876–1914*, he is the author of *Reigniting the Labor Movement: Restoring Means to Ends in a Democratic Labor Movement* (Routledge, 2007), and many articles on the labour history of the United States and Europe, as well as on economic theory and economic policy. He is currently working on an intellectual biography of Richard Ely, an early American economist, as part of a larger study of the decline of institutionalism in American economics.

Rebecca Gumbrell-McCormick is a Senior Lecturer in the Department of Management at Birkbeck, University of London. She specializes in European and international industrial relations, trade unions and equality. Her most recent publications include 'Trade unions and atypical workers', *Industrial Relations Journal*, 2011, and 'The international trade union confederation: from two (or more?) identities to one', *BJIR*, 2012. Her book, *Trade Unions in Western Europe: Hard Times; Hard Choices* (with Richard Hyman), will be published by Oxford University Press in 2013.

Anke Hassel is Professor of Public Policy at the Hertie School of Governance in Berlin. After studying political science, economics and law in Bonn and at the London School of Economics and Political Science, she joined the Max Planck Institute for the Study of Societies in Cologne before moving to the Hertie School. She is also a Professor at the Berlin Graduate School of Transnational Studies. Recent publications include 'The evolution of a global labour governance regime', *Governance: An International Journal of Policy, Administration and Institutions* (2008), and *Wage Setting, Social Pacts and the Euro: A New Role for the State* (Amsterdam University Press, 2006).

Richard Hyman is Emeritus Professor of Industrial Relations at the London School of Economics and Political Science, and founding editor of the *European Journal of Industrial Relations*. He has written extensively on industrial relations, trade unionism, industrial conflict and labour market policy, and is author of a dozen books as well as numerous journal articles and book chapters. His comparative study, *Understanding European Trade Unionism: Between Market, Class and Society* (Sage, 2001) is widely cited by scholars working in this field. His latest book, *Trade Unions in Western Europe: Hard Times, Hard Choices* (with Rebecca Gumbrell-McCormick), will be published by Oxford University Press in 2013.

Monika Ewa Kaminska is a researcher at the Centre for Social Science and Global Health, and was previously at the Amsterdam Institute for Advanced Labour Studies (both University of Amsterdam). Her research interests include employment relations, social policies, healthcare systems and their reforms in the European Union. She has recently published on the emergence of industrial relations in regional trade blocs (*British Journal of Industrial Relations*), healthcare governance in post-1989 East-Central European countries (*Journal for Comparative Policy Analysis*), and privatization, managerialization and decentralization of Polish healthcare (in an edited volume on healthcare restructuring and retrenchment in Europe, forthcoming, for Palgrave).

John Kelly is Professor of Industrial Relations in the Department of Management, Birkbeck, University of London. His main research interests revolve around trade unions, labour movements and collective action, and his recent publications include *Parties, Elections and Policy Reforms in Western Europe* with Kerstin Humann (Routledge, 2011), *Ethical Socialism and the Trade Unions* (2010), *Varieties of Unionism* with Carola Erege (Oxford University Press, 2004), *Rethinking Industrial Relations* (Routledge, 1998) as well as several recent articles on general strikes in Western Europe since 1980.

Irina Kozina is Head of the Department of Sociological Research Methods in the Faculty of Sociology at the Higher School of Economics, Moscow. Her research areas are gender equality, employment law, trade unions, labour markets and social policy. Recent publications in English include: (with E. Vinogradova and L. Cook) 'Russian labor: quiescence and conflict', *Communist and Post-Communist Studies* (2012) and (with V. Yakubovich) 'Recruitment at Russian enterprises' in M. Domsch and T. Lidokhover (eds) *Human Resource Management in Russia* (Ashgate, 2007).

Sarosh Kuruvilla is currently Professor of Industrial Relations, Asian Studies and Public Affairs at Cornell University, and a Visiting Professor of Employment Relations and Organizational Behaviour at the London School of Economics. He joined Cornell's faculty in 1990 after obtaining a doctorate in business administration from the University of Iowa in 1989. His research interests focus broadly in the area of comparative industrial relations and specifically on the linkages between industrial relations policies and practices, national human resource policies and practices and economic development policies. His research has informed government policy and practice in Asia, particularly in relation to Singapore, Malaysia, Philippines, South Korea, Taiwan and, more recently, in China and India. He serves as a consultant to international agencies and global corporations, and has authored a large number of refereed journal articles on labour and human resource policies and practices. His current research focuses on the analysis of employment relations in global value chains, and on the globalization of professional labour markets, particularly the linkages between labour markets for lawyers in the USA, the UK and India.

Tashlin Lakhani is a PhD candidate at the ILR School at Cornell University. Her research focuses on understanding how differences in economic organization shape employment systems and outcomes. In addition, she has conducted research on union strategies and the distribution of bargaining power in labour–management relations. Her work has been published in the *British Journal of Industrial Relations*.

Mingwei Liu is Assistant Professor of Labor Studies and Employment Relations in the School of Management and Labor Relations at Rutgers University, USA. His research interests fall into two broad areas. The first is Asian industrial relations, with a specific focus on Chinese labour relations, trade unions and human resource issues. The second is high performance work practices, with a specific focus on the healthcare sector. He has recently published articles in leading journals such as *Industrial and Labor Relations Review* and the *British Journal of Industrial Relations*, as well as chapters in books such as *From Iron Rice-Bowl to Informalization* (ILR Press, 2011), *The Role of Collective Bargaining in the Global Economy* (ILO, 2011), and *China's Changing Workplace* (Routledge, 2011).

Patrick McGovern worked as a farm labourer, factory operative, painter and decorator, and mechanic before starting life as an academic, and continues to be fascinated by both manual and non-manual labour. Currently a Reader in Sociology at the London School of Economics and Political Science, his major research interests are in the sociology of work and labour markets, employment relations and international migration. His book, *Market, Class and Employment* (OUP, 2007), examined the marketization of the employment relationship, the decline of class-based forms of inequality, and the individualization of employment relations. He finds academic work much more rewarding than 'lapping hay' in the Irish summer rain.

Nick Parsons is a Reader in French in the School of European Languages, Translation and Politics, Cardiff University. He has written extensively on French and European employment relations and social policy, including *French Industrial Relations in the New World*

Economy (Routledge, 2005) and *Economic Globalisation and Employment Policy* (2004, edited with Yuan Zhigan, Fudan University, Shanghai). Recent publications have addressed issues such as 'bossnapping' in France, postap worker disputes in the UK and the European social model during the economic and financial crisis that began in 2008.

John Schmitt is a Senior Economist at the Center for Economic and Policy Research in Washington, DC. His research focuses on economic inequality in the United States and comparative labour market performance in OECD countries. He is the co-editor of *Low-Wage Work in the Wealthy World* (Russell Sage Foundation, 2009) and has co-authored three editions of *The State of Working America* (Cornell University Press).

Roger Southall is Professor of Sociology and a Research Associate in the Society, Work and Development Institute (SWOP) at the University of Witwatersrand, Johannesburg. His books include *South Africa's Transkei: The Political Economy of an 'Independent' Bantustan* (Heinemann and Monthly Review Press, 1982), *Imperialism or Solidarity? International Labour and South African Trade Unions* (University of Cape Town Press, 1995) and *Liberation Movements in Power: Party and State in Southern Africa* (James Currey and University of KwaZulu-Natal Press, forthcoming, 2013). He is also the author of numerous articles in journals and edited books in diverse areas of African politics and political economy, as well as editor or co-editor of more than a dozen collections, including the *New South African Review* volumes published by Wits University Press.

Torsten Svensson is Professor of Political Science in the Department of Government, Uppsala University. His research interests include labour market relations, interest organizations, civil society, party strategy and welfare politics. He is the editor of *Power and Institutions in Industrial Relations Regimes: Political Science Perspectives on the Transition of the Swedish Model* (2005) and the author of many articles in journals such as *West European Politics, Rationality and Society, Economic and Industrial Democracy, Political Studies, Government and Opposition* and *European Political Science Review.* His current research is focused on trust and on civil society.

D. Hugh Whittaker is Professor in the Department of Management and International Business and Director of the New Zealand Asia Institute at the University of Auckland, as well as a Visiting Professor at Doshisha University, Kyoto, Japan. His research interests encompass comparative employment relations, corporate governance, management of innovation, and small businesses and entrepreneurship. His books include *Comparative Entrepreneurship: The UK, Japan and the Shadow of Silicon Valley*, and (co-edited with Simon Deakin) *Corporate Governance and Managerial Reform in Japan* (both Oxford University Press, 2009).

Stephen Wood is Professor of Management and Director of Research in the School of Management at the University of Leicester. His current interests include high involvement management, workplace aggression and discrimination, job quality, work–life balance and family-friendly management. His publications include: (with A. Gamble, S. Ludlam and A. Taylor), *Labour, the State, Social Movements and the Challenge to Neo-Liberal Globalisation* (Manchester University Press, 2006); (with H. Gospel), *Representing Workers: Trade Union Recognition and Membership in Britain* (Routledge, 2003); *The Transformation of Work?* (Unwin Allen, 1989); and recent articles in *Human Relations*, the *Journal of Business Ethics, Industrial and Labor Relations Review* and *Personnel Psychology*.

Acknowledgements

We would like to thank the following for permission to reproduce material: Taylor and Francis for Table 8.2; Klaus Armingeon and colleagues, University of Bern, for the Comparative Political Dataset used in Table 11.1; Lyle Scruggs, University of Connecticut, for the Comparative Welfare Entitlements Dataset used in Table 13.3; the Institute for Labour and Social Research (Fafo), Oslo, for Table 15.7; HSRC Press, South Africa, for Figure 19.1; and Sage Publications for Figure 20.3.

Abbreviations

ACAS	Advisory, Conciliation and Arbitration Service
Acemo	*Activité et Conditions d'Emploi de la Main d'œuvre*
ACFIC	All China Federation of Industry and Commerce
ACFTU	All China Federation of Trade Unions
AFL-CIO	American Federation of Labor and Congress of Industrial Organizations
AFTA	ASEAN Free Trade Area
AITUC	All India Trade Union Congress
ALMPs	active labour market policies
AMCU	Association of Mineworkers and Construction Union
AMSA	Apparel Manufacturers of South Africa
ANC	African National Congress
ASEAN	Association of Southeast Asian Nations
ASSOCHAM	Associated Chambers of Commerce and Industry of India
ATL	Association of Teachers and Lecturers
BAVC	German Chemicals Employers Association
BDA	Confederation of German Employers
BDI	Confederation of German Industry
BIFR	Board of Industrial and Financial Reconstruction
BIR	Bombay Industrial Relations Act
BMS	Bhartiya Mazdoor Sangh
BRIC	countries of Brazil, Russia, India and China
BSA	Business South Africa
BUSA	Business Unity South Africa
BWI	Building and Wood Workers' International
CACB	Confederação das Associações Comerciais e Empresariasis do Brasil
CBDT	Central do Brasil Democratica de Trabalhadores
CBA	collective bargaining agreements
CCMA	Commission for Conciliation, Mediation and Arbitration
CDU	Christian Democratic Union
CEC	China Enterprise Confederation
CEO	Chief Executive Officer
CER	comparative employment relations
CFTC	*Confédération Française des Travailleurs Chrétiens*
CFTUI	Confederation of Free Trade Unions of India
CGB	Christian Trade Union Confederation of Germany
CGTB	Central Greral dos Trabalhadoreas do Brasil

CGT	*Confédération Générale du Travail*
CII	Confederation of Indian Industry
CIO	Congress of Industrial Organizations
CITU	Centre of Indian Trade Unions
CLC	Commission of Labor Cooperation
CLS	Core Labour Standards
CLT	Consolidação das Leis do Trabalho
CME	coordinated market economy
CNA	Confederación Nacional de Agricultura
CNC	Confederación Nacional de Comercio, Bienes, Servicios y Turismo
CNF	ConfederaçãoNacional das Instituições Financeiras
CNI	Confederação Nacional de Indústria
CNPF	*Conseil National du Patronat Français*
CNT	Confederación Nacional de Transporte
Codesa	Convention for a Democratic South Africa
COE	collective-owned enterprise
COSATU	Congress of South African Trade Unions
CSO	civil society organization
CSR	Corporate Social Responsibility
CTB	Central dos Trabalhadores e Trabalhadoras do Brasil
CUT	Central Única dos Trabalhadores/Central Workers Union
dbb	Deutscher Beamtenbund
DGB	Deutscher Gewerkschaftsbund
EAP	Economically Active Population
EC	European Commission
ECB	European Central Bank
ECJ	European Court of Justice
ECOWAS	The Economic Community Of West African States
ECtHR	European Court of Human Rights
EEOC	Equal Employment Opportunity Commission
EES	European Employment Strategy
EFI	Employers Federation of India
EMCEF	European Mine, Chemical, and Energy Workers Federation
EMF	European Metalworkers' Federation
EMU	Economic and Monetary Union
EPZ	export processing zone
ET	Employment Tribunal
ETI	Ethical Trading Initiative
ETUC	European Trade Union Confederation
EU	European Union
EWCs	European Works Councils
FDI	foreign direct investment
FEDUSA	Federation of Unions of South Africa
FICCI	Federation of Indian Chambers of Commerce and Industry
FIE	foreign-invested enterprise
FIESP	Federação das Indústrias do Estado de São Paulo
FLA	Fair Labour Association
FNPR	Federation of Independent Trade Unions of Russia

FO	*Force Ouvrière*
FS	Força Sindical (cedilla)
FSA	*Fédération des Syndicats Autonomes*
FTA	free trade agreement
GDP	gross domestic product
GDR	German Democratic Republic
GE	General Electric
GEAR	Growth, Employment and Redistribution
GFA	Global Framework Agreement
GM	General Motors
GMB	General and Municipal Workers Union
GPN	Global Production Network
GRI	Global Reporting Initiative
GSEE	Greek Confederation of Trade Unions
GUF	Global Union Federation
GVC	Global Value Chain
HIM	high involvement management
HLM	High Level Mission
HME	Hierarchical market economy
HMIL	Hyundai Motors India Ltd
HMS	Hind Mazdoor Sabha
HRM	Human Resource Management
ICEM	International Chemical, Energy, Mining and General Workers' Federation
ICFTU	International Confederation of Free Trade Unions
ICT	information and communications technology
IDA	Industrial Disputes Act
ILO	International Labour Organization
IMF	International Metalworkers' Federation
IMF	International Monetary Fund
IMF-JC	Japanese Chapter of the International Metalworkers' Federation
INTUC	Indian National Trade Union Congress
IPE	International Political Economy
IR	investor relations
IR	industrial relations
ISCO	International Standard Classification of Occupations
ISO	International Organization for Standardisation
ITGLWF	International Textile, Garment and Leather Workers' Federation
ITS	International Trade Secretariat
ITUC	International Trade Union Confederation
IUF	International Union of Foodworkers
IWP	Institute of Work Psychology
JILPT	Japan Institute for Labour Policy and Training
JIT	just in time
KGB	security police
LDAC	labour dispute arbitration committee
LDMC	Labor Dispute Mediation Committee
LME	liberal market economy

LO	Swedish Confederation of Trade Unions
LPMIC	Labor Protection Monitoring Inspecting Committee
LRA	Labour Relations Act
MEDEF	*Mouvement des Entreprises de France*
MEXT	Ministry of Education, Culture, Sports, Science, and Technology
MHRSS	Ministry of Human Resources and Social Security
MIT	Massachusetts Institute of Teachnology
MNC	multinational corporation
MNE	multinational enterprise
MRTU&PULP	Maharastra Recognition of Trade Unions and Prevention of Unfair Labour Practices
MSI	multi-stakeholder initiative
NAALC	North American Agreement on Labor Cooperation
NACTU	National African Congress of Trade Unions
NAFCOC	National African Federated Chambers of Commerce and Industry
NAFTA	North American Free Trade Agreement
NAO	National Administrative Offices
NASUWT	National Association of Schoolmasters/Union of Women Teachers
NBF	National Bargaining Forum
NBS	Nippon Broadcasting System
NCP	National Contact Point
NCST	Nova Central Sindical de Trabalhadores
NEDLAC	National Economic, Development and Labour Council
NEF	National Economic Forum
NGO	non-governmental organization
NLRA	National Labour Relations Act
NLRB	National Labour Relations Board
NP	National Party
NPG	Independent Miners' Union
NRA	National Industrial Recovery Administration
NUM	National Union of Mineworkers
NUMSA	National Union of Metalworkers of South Africa
NUT	National Union of Teachers
OECD	Organization for Economic Co-operation and Development
OT	*ohne Tarifbindung*
PAC	Pan-Africanist Congress
PCF	French Communist Party
POE	private-owned enterprise
PR	proportional representation
PT	Workers' Party
QE	quantitative easing
RDP	Reconstruction and Development Programme
RMMS	Rashtriya Mazdoor Mill Sangh
RSPP	Russian Union of Industrialists and Entrepreneurs
RTK	Tripartite Commission for the Regulation of Social-Labour Relations
SACO	Swedish Confederation of Professional Associations
SACP	South African Communist Party
SACTU	South African Congress of Trade Unions

SACTWU	South African Textile Workers' Union
SADC	South African Development Community
SAF	Swedish Employers' Confederation
SAI	Social Accountability International
SAIRR	South African Institute of Race Relations
SAP	Social Democratic Party
SE	European Company Directive
Seta	sector and education training authorities
SEWA	Self-Employed Women's Association
SEZs	Special Economic Zones
SN	Confederation of Swedish Enterprise
SNMW	statutory national minimum wage
SOE	state-owned enterprise
SPD	Social Democratic Party
SUD	*Solidaires, Unitaires, Démocratiques*
SWRC	Staff and Workers' Representative Congress
TCO	Swedish Confederation for Professional Employees
TEU	Treaty on European Union
TFEU	Treaty of the Functioning of the European Union
TNC	transnational corporation
TQM	total quality management
TUC	Trades Union Congress
TVE	township and village enterprises
UCU	University and College Union
UGT	União Geral dos Trabalhadores
UNI	Uni Global Union
UNSA	Union nationale des syndicats autonomes
USDAW	Union of Shop, Distributive and Allied Workers
VKP	General Confederation of Trade Unions
VoC	varieties of capitalism
VPI	voluntary private initiative
VTsSPS	All-Union Central Council of Trade Unions
WAP	Working Age Population
WERS	Workplace Employment Relations Survey
WPR	welfare production regime
WRC	Workers' Rights Consortium
WTO	World Trade Organization

Part 1

Comparative employment relations

1 Introduction

Global challenges at work

John Kelly and Carola Frege

The structure and content of this textbook are based on four main premises: first, the study of comparative employment relations (CER) has to be set in the context of the global economy and its impact on regional, national and sub-national regulation of the employment relationship. Second, the study of CER must be firmly grounded in theory and that is the subject of Chapter 2 where we set out and discuss in detail the theories that will recur throughout the book. Third, a successful CER textbook must include not only accounts of employment relations in selected countries – Part 3 of the book – but also must include genuinely comparative analyses of the main aspects of the employment relationship, hence the five chapters in Part 2. Finally, in order to understand contemporary employment relations in the context of the global economy, we must also analyze forms of employment regulation above the level of the nation state, whether they emanate from multinational corporations (MNCs), regional bodies or international agencies, and these are the topics that comprise the fourth and final part of the book.

We begin, however, with the global economy and, in order to appreciate its significance, it is helpful to go back in time to the so-called 'Golden Age of Capitalism', from the late 1940s until the mid-1970s. This period was characterized by unprecedented rates of economic growth, dramatic rises in consumption and levels of unemployment lower than at any time before or since (Marglin and Schor 1990). The advanced economies of Western Europe and the USA dominated world manufacturing production, trade and investment, a fact reflected in the composition of the labour force. For example, in 1960, almost 50 per cent of the workforces in Britain and Germany was employed in industry and the figures for the USA and France were about 34 per cent (Glyn *et al.* 1990: 44). The output from what were often large industrial plants was intended primarily for the domestic market: in 1950, only 6 per cent of the European market for manufactured goods was supplied from outside of Europe, and most of that was from the United States (Glyn 2006: 97). The workforce in these plants was predominantly male and employed on full-time, open-ended contracts with wages and conditions mostly regulated by collective bargaining (Marglin and Schor 1990). The mid-1970s was both the tail end of the long post-war economic boom, marked by rising unemployment and inflation, and the zenith of trade union power and militancy with its strong upward pressure on wages. Many governments responded to union militancy, rising inflation and unemployment by attempting to negotiate wage restraint and industrial peace with trade unions (Pizzorno 1978).

The intervening years have witnessed a far-reaching and fundamental transformation of employment relations, even before the financial and economic crises that erupted in 2008 (Nolan 2011). Widespread changes in employment relations have occurred both in the advanced capitalist world as well as in the major new economic powers such as in the BRIC countries of Brazil, Russia, India and China, as well as others (Dicken 2011). Manufacturing employment has declined in Western Europe and North America but expanded in the Southern Hemisphere, especially in the BRIC countries (ibid.). Trade union membership and strike activity have declined in many countries around the world (Phelan 2007; van der Velden *et al.* 2008). The management of employment relations has become the responsibility of human resource management departments but the decline of trade unionism has also allowed a resurgence of a more authoritarian approach to labour management and an increased reliance by employees on individual legal remedies for their employment problems (cf. Colling 2010). Multinational corporations have become increasingly influential in shaping the labour policies of governments around the globe (Sklair 2002) while at the same time government intervention has increasingly been directed to retrenching welfare and pension systems and weakening employment protection laws (Hamann and Kelly 2011). Although two of the core institutions of employment relations – high collective bargaining coverage and works councils – have remained largely intact in most of Western Europe as of 2011, there is clear evidence of a decline in the membership and effectiveness of trade unions within collective bargaining (Nolan 2011). Collective regulation of employment relations has been significantly eroded in 'liberal market economies' such as the UK and the USA and remains weak in many developing economies (Hall and Soskice 2001; Morley *et al.* 2006).

The economic background to this transformation has often been encapsulated under the umbrella term 'globalization', a series of processes involving the geographical spread of production, trade and investment and the ubiquitous upheaval of the organization of work, in part through the impact of micro-computer technologies (Dicken 2011). The new configuration of the global economy is best epitomized by the rise of China as a major economic power. With annual growth rates from the 1980s of around 10 per cent, China had by 2008 become one of the world's largest manufacturing economies, second only to the USA in the total value of its production. In the same year it also held the world's second largest share of exports (behind Germany) and the third highest share of imports (behind Germany and the USA). Other large economies too were transformed during this period, notably the other BRIC countries – Brazil, Russia and India. In 2008, these three, plus China, were responsible for almost one-fifth of the world's manufacturing production, only a fraction less than that of the USA (ibid.: 36). China's labour force alone, estimated at 750 million around 2005, is 1.5 times greater than the workforce of the whole of the Organization for Economic Co-operation and Development (OECD) (Glyn 2006: 88).

The expansion of manufacturing output and employment in the BRIC countries, but especially in China, went hand in hand with a sharp decline in industrial employment in the advanced capitalist economies. In Britain, for example, there were almost eight million industrial workers in 1960 but just three million by 2010. In the 27 member countries of the European Union, just over 70 per cent of employees worked in private services in 2009, a broad category that includes retail, leisure, hotels and tourism, and business and financial services. Some 45 per cent of the European labour force is female and approximately 19 per cent of employees – mostly women – work part-time while 14 per cent are on fixed-term contracts (European Union 2010).

The intellectual challenge for employment relations scholars has been, and remains, how best to think about these ongoing changes in the forms and outcomes of the regulation of the employment relationship. Insights from the study of comparative employment relations (CER) continue to be necessary for social science and business students in the twenty-first century; in fact, they are more important than ever because of the immense changes to the global economy since the 1970s. Yet for all the changes that have taken place in the world of work, paid employment is still the dominant activity for most citizens between the end of their education and their retirement, and the social, family and personal lives of most adults depend on the income derived from paid work (Colling and Terry 2010: 5–7). However, paid employment retains its importance in a context where patterns of work, the rewards of work and even its availability have become increasingly precarious and subject to the turbulent forces of the global economy and the actions of governments and employers.

The structure of the book

As previously mentioned, the aim of this textbook is to introduce students to the comparative study of employment relations in a global economy. Unlike many texts in the field which provide detailed descriptions of employment relations in different national settings, this text aims to be both more analytical and more comparative. It is analytical because we set out a number of major theoretical approaches to comparative employment relations (Chapter 2) and aim to deploy these throughout the book. It has become a truism in the study of comparative employment relations that intensified and global product market competition has contributed to far-reaching changes in the world of work. Yet it is also the case that the impact of markets is refracted through a variety of institutions, such as those covering collective bargaining, employment protection and welfare payments, for example. Within these institutions the actors themselves have some degree of choice over how to operate within existing institutions, how to bypass them or how to reconfigure them (Thelen 2009). Each of these perspectives is brought to bear in the analysis of substantive issues across countries (Part 2) and in the discussion of employment relations within each of the countries that feature in Part 3 of the book.

The book is comparative in two ways: first, we include chapters on substantive topics related to employment regulation, such as employee rights and the employee experience of work, that include data from a variety of countries, and second, we include material on regulation above the national level of employment relations, on the European Union and on the International Labour Organization (ILO), for example. Our selection of substantive issues is rooted in our understanding of the employment relationship and its context. The employer pays a wage or salary in order to hire the capacity of the employee to work, usually for a fixed number of hours per week. Yet the precise amount of work to be performed remains unspecified and it is the responsibility of the employer to organize rewards, sanctions, training and controls in order to ensure maximum job performance. These tasks are complicated by the differences in interests between employer and employee. If we consider the firm as a profit-maximizing unit of capital, then wages and salaries represent a deduction from profits. To this conflict of interests we can add an imbalance in power because, typically, the employer can replace a difficult worker more readily than the worker can find alternative employment (Colling and Terry 2010). These properties of the employment relationship raise complex and difficult issues about how the relationship is to be regulated and about the consequences of different forms of regulation. In many non-union workplaces throughout the UK and the USA, employees may be able to exercise legal rights, if they know about them and if the costs of doing so are not prohibitive. Historically, employees have almost invariably formed collective organizations, trade unions, in order to counterbalance the power of the employer (who was often in turn backed up by the state). Chapters 4 and 5 therefore look in turn at these two modes of regulation, through individual rights and through collective organization.

We then turn to the consequences of different modes of regulation, starting with the employee experience of work and we include here issues under the broad rubric of quality of work life, in particular work intensity, skill use, job satisfaction, work–family balance and equal opportunities (Chapter 5). We then turn our attention to the links between the regulation of the employment relationship and the interests of employers, looking at the spread and impact of Human Resource Management (HRM) and its consequences for both employers and employees (Chapter 6). Chapter 7 focuses on the links between employment practices and regulations, on the one hand, and macro-economic outcomes, on the other, including gross domestic product (GDP) growth, employment and unemployment and income distribution. Finally, in this part of the book, Chapter 8 examines the connections between different varieties of welfare regime, electoral and party political systems, civil society and employment relations. The period since 1980 has witnessed widespread government attempts to reform welfare and pension systems, often through tripartite negotiations with unions and employers, raising important questions about the capacities of the 'social partners' to engage in radical reforms.

Part 3 contains 11 national studies of a wide range of countries, varying in the ways in which they regulate the employment relationship. We chose the UK and the USA as the world's leading exemplars of 'liberal market capitalism'. Within Western Europe we then selected three countries that vary significantly in their systems of employment relations, structure of trade unions and employers, welfare regimes and party political systems: one Scandinavian country (Sweden), one 'statist' economy (France), Europe's largest exemplar of coordinated market capitalism (Germany), and Japan as Asian's largest coordinated market economy. Further afield, we have included four of the world's largest and fastest growing economies, the so-called BRIC countries of Brazil, Russia, India and China. Finally, in order to complete our coverage of the world's continents, we include South Africa as a particular example of the African continent which is currently experiencing a notable economic transition. Each of these chapters has a set of common features: there is a brief historical introduction that describes the origins of the national system of employment relations; the next section then describes the main actors in employment relations, the trade unions, employers and government. It also describes the main processes in employment relations, including collective bargaining, unilateral decision-making by the employer and the role of legal regulation. The third section looks at the far-reaching changes in contemporary employment relations from a number of theoretical perspectives and weighs up competing arguments about the roles of markets, institutions and actors' strategic choices.

In the concluding part of the book (Part 4), we discuss globalization and the need for regulation of the employment relationship above the national level, a topic of growing importance but one whose significance is rarely reflected in comparative employment relations textbooks. From a political economy perspective, we first examine the role and significance of the value chains that increasingly stretch across the globe, linking raw materials suppliers in one country, assembly factories in a second, to storage and retail facilities in a third (Chapter 20). Value chains create both opportunities as well as threats for the firms that organize them and for trade unions and other employee organizations searching for ways of exerting leverage over large multinational corporations. We then examine different forms of regulation above the national level, starting with voluntary codes of practice and voluntary framework agreements (Chapter 21). Both have been pursued by trade unions and a variety of non-governmental organizations (NGOs) as an alternative to the legal regulation that has often evoked hostility from MNCs. We then examine the regulation of employment relations issues within two sets of countries, comprising the European Union (EU) and the North American Free Trade Agreement (NAFTA) (Chapter 22). Under the various treaties that regulate EU membership, the member states are obliged to enact into national law the various

Directives approved by the EU's governing institutions. Many of these Directives have covered core issues of employment such as working time, equal pay and fixed term contracts. Finally, we turn to the largest international body in the field of employment (measured by country membership), namely, the International Labour Organization (ILO) (Chapter 23). Created in the early twentieth century, it remains an active participant in policy debates about work and employment and has been at the forefront of discussions about the global economy.

References

Colling, T. (2010) 'Legal institutions and the regulation of workplaces', in T. Colling and M. Terry (eds) *Industrial Relations: Theory and Practice*, 3rd edn, Chichester: John Wiley & Sons, Ltd.

—— and Terry, M. (2010) 'Work, the employment relationship and the field of industrial relations', in T. Colling and M. Terry (eds) *Industrial Relations: Theory and Practice*, 3rd edn, Chichester: John Wiley & Sons, Ltd.

Dicken, P. (2011) *Global Shift: Mapping the Changing Contours of the World Economy*, 6th edn, London: Sage.

European Union (2010) *Employment in Europe 2010*, Luxembourg: Office for Official Publications of the European Communities.

Glyn, A. (2006) *Capitalism Unleashed: Finance, Globalization, and Welfare*, Oxford: Oxford University Press.

——, Hughes, A., Lipietz, A. and Singh, A. (1990) 'The rise and fall of the Golden Age', in S. A. Marglin and J. B. Schor (eds) *The Golden Age of Capitalism: Reinterpreting the Postwar Experience*, Oxford: Clarendon Press.

Hall, P. A. and Soskice, D. (2001) 'An introduction to varieties of capitalism', in P. A. Hall and D. Soskice (eds) *Varieties of Capitalism: The Institutional Foundations of Comparative Advantage*, Oxford: Oxford University Press.

Hamann, K. and Kelly, J. (2011) *Parties, Elections, and Policy Reforms in Western Europe: Voting for Social Pacts*, London: Routledge.

Marglin, S. A. and Schor, J. B. (eds) (1990) *The Golden Age of Capitalism: Reinterpreting the Postwar Experience*, Oxford: Clarendon Press.

Morley, M. J., Gunnigle, P. and Collings, D. G. (eds) (2006) *Global Industrial Relations*, London: Routledge.

Nolan, P. (2011) 'Money, markets, meltdown: the 21st century crisis of labour', *Industrial Relations Journal*, 42(1): 2–17.

Phelan, C. (2007) 'Worldwide trends and prospects for trade union revitalisation', in C. Phelan (ed.) *Trade Union Revitalisation: Trends and Prospects in 34 Countries*, Bern: Peter Lang.

Pizzorno, A. (1978) 'Political exchange and collective identity in industrial conflict', in C. Crouch and A. Pizzorno (eds) *The Resurgence of Class Conflict in Western Europe Since 1968*, Vol. 2, London: Macmillan.

Sklair, L. (2002) *Globalization: Capitalism and its Alternatives*, 3rd edn, Oxford: Oxford University Press.

Thelen, K. (2009) 'Institutional change in advanced political economies', *British Journal of Industrial Relations*, 47(3): 471–98.

van der Velden, S., Dribbusch, H., Lyddon, D. and Vandaele, K. (eds) (2008) *Strikes Around the World, 1968–2005: Case-Studies of 15 Countries*, Amsterdam: Aksant.

2 Theoretical perspectives on comparative employment relations

Carola Frege and John Kelly

Introduction

Research in the area of work and employment, traditionally described in Anglophone countries as Employment, Industrial or Labour Relations, or Labour Studies, was established as an independent field of study in the 1920s in the USA and subsequently after the Second World War in Britain and other Anglophone countries. Though originally established by US institutional labour economists, it soon came to be seen as an interdisciplinary field incorporating labour economists, industrial psychologists, personnel management scholars, industrial sociologists, and other social scientists working on labour issues. In continental Europe, and indeed in the rest of the world, research on work and employment has remained multidisciplinary and thus a component of various social science disciplines, in particular political science and sociology (Frege 2007: 2).

The inter-disciplinarity of the field is seen as one of the defining characteristics of Anglophone employment relations research (Kochan 1998) and was always recognized as a major advantage of the field. Yet, doubts have been raised over the extent to which employment relations research remains truly inter-disciplinary. Lewin and Feuille (1983: 357) had already concluded in the early 1980s that 'in reality little employment research is truly interdisciplinary, for specialists in particular disciplines rarely combine research forces with specialists in other disciplines'. Scholars have in particular criticized the increasing dominance of labour economics. Employment has been increasingly perceived as primarily a labour market outcome, accompanied by a paradigm of contractual *laissez-faire* framed by legal regulations on private property and individual rights (Frege 2007: 173).[1]

Scholars have also pointed to the subsequent narrowing of methodologies, as well as the increasingly a-theoretical empiricist nature of employment relations research. Thus, the field, which has traditionally focused on its achievements in empirical research, has struggled to offer much by way of conceptual development or theoretical innovation (Lewin and Feuille 1983: 357; Marshall 1998: 355–6; Hyman 2001a; Mitchell 2001: 387). Hyman has defined employment relations research by a focus on institutional description, governmental policy and 'good industrial relations', with surprisingly little interest in theory. Marsden (1982: 235) argues that employment research has been a-theoretical from its beginning and has been trapped within the confines of empiricist epistemology since then. And Hyman (2004: 266) observes damaging consequences in that 'the field detaches analysis from broader social science traditions, trivialises its conceptual apparatus and privileges pragmatism over theoretical imagination. If theories are used, they are mainly mid-range, thus hypotheses-testing of psychological (behaviourist) or economic theories.'

One promising development in rectifying these weaknesses can be seen in the growth of comparative research in employment relations (CER) since the late 1980s (marked by the first publication of leading comparative textbooks by Bamber *et al.* in 1987 and Ferner and Hyman in both 1992 and 1998; also Hyman and Ferner 1994). One of the potential benefits of comparative research is that it can help to advance a more inter-disciplinary and theoretical understanding of employment relations and thus provide an important opportunity to rectify the empiricist bias of past research. Yet, until now, much of the recent comparative research has presented even less theoretical ambition and frequently remained within empirical comparisons of national employment models.

In our understanding, CER is not just about a more international scope of research on work and employment, or a particular scientific method (comparison), but ideally should also be advancing specific paradigms and theories about the nature and processes of employment relations systems. Cross-national comparative methodology is in many ways the fundamental laboratory for employment relations. Without the ability to compare across countries, it is virtually impossible to understand and explain the scientific importance of findings in one particular economy. Moreover, one of the core functions of comparative research is to link conceptually micro- and macro-levels of analysis (for example, employees' job happiness with collective representation systems) and to compare across different national settings. In other words, while most theoretical attempts in employment relations have essentially focused at the micro-level, for example, attempting to understand the logic of actors' preferences and behaviour (e.g. managerial or union strategies), CER theory should advance our understanding of how actors' strategies are channelled through national institutions but also actively shape institutions and regulations. As Crouch (2005: 208) concludes, comparative research raises the awareness of academics that:

> features of one's native environment which one had thought to be distinctive and had attributed to rather specific, local causes are in fact more general or in turn that features of relationships between variables which one thought to be of universal meaning are in fact locally embedded and not transferable to other countries.

This textbook aims to contribute therefore towards a more inter-disciplinary and theoretically informed analysis of the issues and debates in CER. The present chapter starts by discussing existing theoretical approaches relevant for CER, followed by an outline of a conceptual framework, which will be used as a broad guide for subsequent chapters.

We start from the basic assumption that labour markets – like all markets in capitalist economies – are in need of some kind of regulation. The nature and functioning of these regulations are a core part of the study of employment relations, and the most basic form of regulation is a labour contract between an employer and an employee. Colling and Terry (2010: 7) highlight three core characteristics of the employment relationship that we want to discuss: (1) the indeterminacy of the labour contract; (2) the inequality or asymmetry of power resources of the actors involved; and (3) the dynamic nature of the relationship and the co-existence of conflict and cooperation. First, in contrast to the original neo-classical belief that all markets and contracts are complete, modern contract theory starts from the basic observation that in reality all labour contracts are by nature incomplete (Fox 1974; Grossman and Hart 1986; Hart and Moore 1990). Thus, no labour contract can be written which is complete (except in slavery where full ownership replaces incompleteness). Hence, by default, markets or contracts cannot exist without regulation or institutions. Moreover, it might not be in the interest of the involved parties to pursue maximum contractual completeness. For example, it is not clear whether employers have a preference to pursue maximum contractual completeness or incompleteness. It depends on the existing bargaining power of both sides at the time of contract writing, as well as on actors' predictions about how markets, and hence their power position, might develop in the future. If employers hire someone before the start of a recession, they might want to keep the contract as incomplete as possible to allow future re-negotiations once employers' bargaining power increases, and vice versa. The same logic (just the other way around) can be applied to workers' preferences in the completeness of the contract. The degree of incompleteness is also influenced by the nature of the job. The more unforeseen conditions exist and the more discretion the job entails, the more difficult it is to write a complete contract. A call centre employee typically has a very specific job description, whereas an investment banker has not. Consequently, in most scenarios, employers and employees are interested in engaging in a certain amount of bargaining exchange going beyond the established minimum contract. The incompleteness or indeterminacy of the employment relationship is therefore open to negotiation and therefore results in a dynamic interplay of conflict and cooperation between the actors, conditional on their preferences and their power resources. This might develop into collective bargaining in circumstances where the labour movement has effective power resources (Crouch 1993: 56), which moves the original individual employment contract to a collective level. It can also lead to employers adopting non-market strategies (e.g. high performance HR strategies) to extract work effort from their workers since they cannot fully control them.

This brings us to the second point of Colling and Terry (2010), which is widely accepted in employment relations research, that in capitalist economies the power resources of employers and workers are inevitably asymmetric (see also Hyman 1975; Offe and Wiesenthal 1980). In other words, workers (sellers of labour power) are asymmetrically dependent on employers (buyers), and that makes labour inseparable from its seller. Workers' livelihoods and well-being are closely connected to maintaining an employment relationship with their employer. Unemployment for a worker usually involves substantial loss in income and in social status and the costs of finding a new job can be high (Western 1998: 226). In contrast, employers are not as dependent on a particular employee. If an employee leaves the firm, the employers' livelihood is not threatened. In other words, because of the asymmetric dependence of workers on employers, there is never real equality between buyers and sellers in the labour market and hence their relationship and the employment contract inevitably express a power relationship in which the costs to workers of lost employment are generally far higher than for employers (ibid.). This imbalance or, as Edwards (1986) called it, 'structured antagonism', shapes any employment negotiation or regulation. It is also a main source of the dynamic nature of the employment relationship and the co-existence of conflict and cooperation, which is Colling and Terry's third point. However, according to Hyman (1975: 11), most research focuses on how conflict is contained and controlled rather than on the complex processes through which imbalances, disagreements and disputes are produced.

There have been various overviews of social science theories used in employment relations research (Adams and Meltz 1993; Müller-Jentsch 2004). One of the best and most comprehensive summaries is by Müller-Jentsch (2004), who distinguishes ontologically between system theory, Marxist theory, institutionalism, action theory and economic approaches.[2] Rather than providing another comprehensive review, we want to concentrate here on two underlying 'philosophies', which cut across all theories, and are particularly important for a comparative understanding of employment relations issues. Both trajectories offer alternative accounts of the main driving forces in employment regimes: the first, based on economic functionalism, focuses on market forces and firms (in particular corporate business) and advocates the primacy of the market. It assumes that the development of political economies is driven by 'economic imperatives for higher efficiency in the use of scarce resources' (Streeck 2009: 172). For example, a major assumption is that efficiency-driven capitalist firms will collectively convince the state to behave in the best interests of their international competitive advantage; and thus the state behaves essentially as an agent of market forces. In the following section we introduce Dunlop's systems theory, which emphasizes market forces and shaped much subsequent Anglophone research, Kerr's convergence theory, and the efficiency-theoretical approaches of the 'varieties of capitalism' and 'globalization' theories. The latter approaches have in common that they combine economic and institutional analysis but ultimately adhere to a functionalist understanding of capitalist (employment) models.

The second, political economic, approach highlights the historical and institutional embeddedness of employment regimes and focuses on the opportunities available to social and political forces, which are seen as equally important to market forces, and which can shape and constrain the labour market. In other words, the labour market is seen as a political as well as an economic forum (Western 1998: 226). The state is regarded as an independent actor and not subordinate to the market. The approach also highlights the fluid power relations and potential of conflict between employment relations actors (Edwards 1986; Korpi 2006). It is historically informed rather than functionalist and acknowledges the dynamic processes and changes of employment relations models rather than their static equilibria (Streeck 2009: 19). We discuss approaches centred on politics at workplace level, power resource theory, trade unions as political actors, the role of the state in employment relations, corporatism and historical institutionalism.

Market-driven theories

The pluralist Anglophone employment relations school and its main protagonist Dunlop (1958) focus on the substitution of open contestational conflicts between employers and workers by collective bargaining. Dunlop's systems theory defines three core 'actors'– employers and managers, workers and their representatives, and governmental agencies–and three 'contexts'–echnology, markets, and the distribution of power in society. The pluralist theory was progressive in that it amended classical market liberalism by allowing organized collective groups to be analyzed as actors (Crouch 1993). Essential ingredients of the Dunlop model are relatively decentralized collective bargaining, a plurality of mutually competing unions, and an avoidance of union political entanglements (ibid.: 57). Politics, and government, are thus treated as peripheral; collective bargaining is central. Dunlop's core independent variables are the strategies of the 'industrializing elites'.

In short, Dunlop's main focus is on the rules negotiated between employers and unions and on the economic and (in particular) technological factors which influenced these rules. He devoted two central chapters of his book to a comparison of work rules in coal mining and construction, arguing that cross-national similarities reflected common technical requirements. Stability and a common or at least compatible ideology are core ingredients; little attention is paid to the internal dynamics and conflicts of the actors. Thus, Dunlop and his followers placed a premium on the stable functioning of the economy (Crouch 1993) and focused on market forces and employers as the driving forces within employment relations. The dimensions of conflict and change were, however, underrated (Müller-Jentsch 2004: 3). In part, this perspective reflected the realities of the North American institutional framework at the time Dunlop was writing, together with an assumption that these would become the universal model elsewhere. Thus, the dominant approach in Anglophone employment relations analysis for much of the post-war period assumed that common technologies and cross-national markets would create convergence towards a common model of employment regulation.

Convergence theories

The first attempt to formulate an explicit theory of such a convergence is usually traced to Kerr *et al.*'s seminal work *Industrialism and Industrial Man* (1960). Their main argument was that the world's employment regimes would experience a certain convergence to greater uniformity. The central driving force was seen to be the homogenizing pressure of new technologies, which was thought to be central to the logic of industrialism. Other forces were the push of progress, education, equality and the 'compulsion of comparisons'. The underlying assumption was that structure follows functions. Thus, employment relations were thought to change in line with technological and developmental requirements. Kerr further argued (e.g. 1983) that the emerging common model would match the Anglo-American pattern of the time, which they called 'pluralistic industrialism'. This they defined as a system in which employers and unions developed increasingly effective and non-conflictual bargaining relationships, making detailed state regulation unnecessary. Hence in their view, 'mature' employment relations systems became detached from the political process.

It is worth noting that Kerr *et al.* (1960) conceded that a range of different employment relations patterns within the rubric of 'pluralistic industrialism' could co-exist for some time. They identified certain factors promoting continued diversity such as the persistence of particular actor strategies, the imprint of national culture and existence of distinctive industrial cultures. However, in the end, the logic of industrialism would override these diversities and produce a homogeneous set of labour market institutions and regulations. Uniformity draws on technological imperatives and management's authority, divergence on individuality and workers' rebellion (ibid.: 277).

This 'convergence theory' has been much debated ever since. Scholars have criticized their work as excessively functionalist, technologically deterministic, and ethnocentric:

> It reflected the ethnocentrism pervasive in Anglo-American social science of the [Cold War] period in that the US was seen as the technological world leader and therefore its institutions and practices were defined as 'best practice' for other nations to emulate. Patterns in other countries were seen as derivative of, or deviations from, the US model.
>
> (Locke *et al.* 1995: xvi)

Moreover, as Traxler *et al.* (2001: 7) pointed out, their theory remains ultimately based on the (neo-classical or neo-liberal) assumption that markets are superior, while non-market institutions constitute performance-inhibiting rigidities. Consequently, the theory concludes that the model best designed to succeed in the global economy is the US model. However, empirical research from the 1970s onwards has challenged this core assumption and suggests that rather than converging, 'national patterns of employment relations are increasingly diverging' (Wailes *et al.* 2011: 12). In particular, empirical studies revealed that technology cannot be seen as exogenous to economy and society but instead is shaped by economic and societal forces (Sabel 1982). Furthermore, the historical transformation of the American labour market in the 1980s with the decline of collective bargaining rendered the Dunlop and Kerr approaches less relevant. The preconditions for the consensual creation of bargaining rules were vanishing. Finally, the frequently observed proactive role of management argued for a stronger focus on the strategic choices of all actors as determinants of action rather than on potentially exogenous factors, such as technology (Müller-Jentsch 2004: 22).

The focus on firms and market forces remained but was modified by an action theoretical extension of Dunlop's systems approach. The influential textbook by Kochan, *et al.* (1986) developed a strategic choice theory, which argued that, although markets and institutional factors influence and shape actors' behaviour, there remains a degree of latitude within which the actors can make significant policy choices. Although all employment actors are mentioned, their main focus remains almost exclusively on management's strategic choices and management–union relations. Thus, the relatively autonomous strategic decisions of managers are seen as an intervening variable between environmental conditions and company structures. Moreover:

> the empirical basis remains the USA, which continues to be characterized by state abstinence from issues of employment relations, by the existence of company level unions, and the use of human resource management, which prefers individual solutions to collective ones.
>
> (Müller-Jentsch 2004: 23)

And so it comes as no surprise that strategic choice theory has seldom been applied to the analysis of employment relations outside of the USA or Britain (ibid.).

More recently, attempts have been made to upgrade the strategic choice approach and to make it less functionalist. For example, Locke, *et al.* (1995: xxvii) compare the strategic choice and institutionalist approaches in order to 'address whether a focus on the competitive strategies of firms or one that emphasizes the role of public policy and legal institutional arrangements (or some combination of these two approaches) best explains recent shifts in employment relations'. Their framework distinguishes between two core explanatory forces: 'national, industry and firm governance, institutions and structures', and 'firm strategies' (competitive strategies, technology/production, strategies). Their empirical answer is, however, vague and ultimately points to a combination of both. Other studies have also promoted a more nuanced argument that convergence might be taking place in two ways at the firm level due to increased international competition, thus narrowing managerial strategic choices to a 'high road' or 'low road' option. 'High road' functionally flexible workplaces produce complex goods and services, mainly in advanced economies, and are characterized by high pay and team-based work, whereas 'low road', numerically flexible workplaces produce simple goods and services, mainly in the developing countries, and are characterized by non-unionization and Taylorist work practices (see Frenkel and Kuruvilla 2002: 388).

Globalization theories

In the meantime, an increasing number of studies of globalization have come to the fore, fostering a new discussion on a global market-driven convergence of employment regimes towards the US model. This time the impact on employment relations arises from major economic and financial characteristics of globalization, in particular:

> the integration of product markets as a consequence of removing trade barriers; internationalization of financial markets stimulated by deregulating restrictions on capital

> flows; cross-border spread of technological advances; and transnational organization of production by multinational companies.
>
> (Traxler *et al.* 2001: 4)

Globalization is seen as a threat to any nationally based governance institution, in particular, for employment institutions, which are deeply embedded in national traditions. As a consequence, employment models are assumed to inevitably change and converge in line with economic requirements. According to Gereffi (2005: 170), a leading scholar in the field, the competition among firms from different business systems in overseas markets tends to diminish the influence of national institutions on firms' behaviour (see also Herrigel and Wittke 2005). Gereffi notes the increase of 'global production networks' as resulting from a growing fragmentation of the production value chain, which used to be located in hierarchically integrated companies. The concept of production value chains assumes that every stage in the production and delivery of goods and services adds economic value. And the argument is that these stages are increasingly separated both organizationally and geographically (see also Dicken *et al.* 2001). For example, sections of the value chain can more easily than in the past be outsourced to independent contractors abroad and can lead to an international division of labour that allows producers to form cross-border networks of production (Lane and Probert 2009: 24). According to Gereffi (2005), in many industries (e.g. textiles), the centre of production has moved to developing countries although the power remains in the hands of large retailers in the developed world.

Globalization theories have been criticized for continuing a functionalist approach to the explanation of social and economic structures and processes. Their arguments make sense only in a world of perfect market competition (Elster 1982). But critics of globalization theories find it questionable that global markets have become so powerful that national employment regimes are necessarily subject to performance-driven convergence (Traxler *et al.* 2001). This claim is supported by a large set of comparative studies indicating that national economies can stay competitive and efficient through a diverse set of employment relations solutions, which are functionally equivalent (e.g. Piore and Sabel 1984; Hollingsworth and Boyer 1997). The argument was picked up and further developed by the 'varieties of capitalism' literature (see below). For example, a recent study of the global clothing industry by Lane and Probert (2009: 292) agrees with Gereffi *et al.* that global production networks do exist and they shape global work and employment patterns. But they also find that these networks remain substantially shaped by both national institutional ensembles and domestic markets, evidence that supports the continuing variety of capitalist employment regimes and the core distinction into coordinated and liberal market economies.

Varieties of capitalism

The 'varieties of capitalism' (VoC) literature (Hall and Soskice 2001; Amable 2003) continues the focus on the primacy of market forces. It identifies firms and financial markets as the core actors within capitalist economies, and suggests less prominent, less strategic roles for both state and organized labour (Howell 2005: 27). It portrays a firm-centred political economy where firms establish relationships with other actors by strategic interaction (Hall and Soskice 2001: 6). At its core the theory combines several theoretical approaches (game theory, transaction costs, institutionalism) with a functionalist equilibrium model (Streeck 2009: 18). In particular, national models of capitalism are characterized by distinctive institutional arrangements supporting specific kinds of strategies on the part of firms in international markets (Thelen 2004: 2).

Institutions enter the analysis because they are seen as helping firms to solve several coordination problems in five spheres: employment relations, vocational training and education, corporate governance, inter-firm relations and the workforce. Different institutions deal with these different spheres but they are not isolated but interconnected and produce 'institutional complementarities' whereby different institutions reinforce and complement one another (Hall and Soskice 2001: 9). A core argument is that these institutional arrangements provide the foundation on which the competitive advantage of firms and their national economies rest, so that employers as key actors, who have organized their strategies around these institutions, will be reluctant to change them. One implication of this argument is that institutions possess a significant degree of resilience even in the face of strong market pressures and that institutional changes that do occur are likely to be incremental, revealing a strong degree of 'path dependency' (Kelly 2011: 64). These interlocking and mutually reinforcing institutions are thought to co-vary systematically, yielding two major ideal-typical capitalist models: liberal market economies (LMEs) and coordinated market economies (CMEs). Thus, both models solve their coordination problems with a different set of institutions. In LMEs, firms tend to coordinate their activities via market relations and hierarchies and, in CMEs, firms depend more on additional political and societal institutions.

Not surprisingly, the VoC theory has become the most popular vehicle for comparative employment research in the last decade. According to Streeck (2009: 17): 'VoC theory must be applauded for its recognition of the importance of institutions, its emphasis on the significance of national contexts even in times of globalization, and its rejection of a neoliberal convergence-on-best-practice model of political economies.' At the same time, VoC theory has been criticized on a number of grounds: for reducing the diversity of national capitalist regimes to two types;[3] for ultimately rooting both models in efficiency-theoretical, functionalist premises; and for its underdeveloped account of change which may be linked to the underlying idea that, conceptually, stability takes precedence over change (Streeck 2009: 18; Baccaro and Howell 2011; Heyes *et al.* 2012). Critics also argue that the theory falls short in explaining what brought these regimes into being in the first place, what holds them together, and 'how we should characterize the dynamics of change and weigh these against the forces of institutional reproduction' (Thelen 2004: 3).

The political economy of employment relations

Alternatively, scholars more influenced by political science traditions have focused their attention on the political and social nature of employment relations and have interpreted the incompleteness of employment contracts as a political and not just a market problem. The starting assumption is that labour markets are inherently different to other (product or financial) markets in that they deal with human beings and citizens of, in most cases, political democracies. Early scholars primarily focused on the dynamic political nature of work and workplace relations. They analyzed power relations at workplace level between individuals and groups and understood the concept of politics primarily as a means to achieve power (Machiavelli's or Max Weber's definition of power). For example, Burawoy (1985) establishes the important concept of 'the politics of production', arguing that work and employment inevitably form a power relationship, since the employer has to compel, persuade or motivate the employee to work diligently and productively. Kelly (1998) takes this further and underlines the importance of a social movement perspective on employment relations by emphasizing the crucial role of workers' perceived injustice at their workplace in explaining social unrest and collective action in the employment relationship. Hyman (1975: 11) argues that employment relations should not be exclusively defined in terms of rules and regulations because to do so is to foster the maintenance of stability and regularity rather than recognizing the inevitability of conflict and control. Interpreting collective bargaining as economic regulation was already contested by Flanders, who saw it as primarily a political process, modifying power relations in order to impose rules, which constrain management discretion. Trade unions, he argued, were therefore more significant in establishing rights than in obtaining economic benefits for workers. In other words, trade unions provide a 'sword of justice' (Flanders 1975; Kelly 2010). The political nature of trade unions and their relationship to the state and political parties are topics that have been of longstanding research interest (e.g. Marks 1989; Burgess 2004).

Other, more recent approaches, dominated by political scientists and economic sociologists, discuss the political character of work and employment in a more institutional sense, focusing on political regimes and power resources. They discuss labour policies of national states and integrate other political and civil society actors (such as NGOs – non-governmental organizations – or lobbying associations), which impact on work and employment. Labour markets and employment relations are thus inevitably embedded not just in the economic but also in the political sphere. They are located at the intersection of the economy and politics. Employment regimes are therefore regarded as fluid social orders, shaped by multiple actors with differing interests and power resources as well as by institutional path dependencies, long-standing norms, political and economic cultures and traditions (Gallie 2007). This requires a theoretical understanding of the underlying power structures in capitalist economies, which have been somewhat neglected in previous employment relations research.

In particular, the 'power resources theory' essentially claims that power differences between major social actors, grounded in the social (capitalist) structure of society, are the basis for the development of social institutions, among them the welfare state (e.g. Korpi, 1978: 37–54; 2001: 242–50). In short, power resources theory: (1) involves claims as to what kinds of power resources are basic in capitalist societies, and consequently, who are the most important (dominant and dominated) actors in politics; and (2) suggests a set of causal and intentional mechanisms resulting in hypotheses regarding the institutional consequences of these power differences, namely, the development of the welfare state (Sommer Harrits 2006: 7). According to this theory, the two main power resources in capitalist societies are the control over the means of production and the control over labour power or human capital. The most effective power resource is the former, and hence capitalists or employers are expected to be, at the outset, the dominant actors. However, these different power resources can be affected by changes in institutional surroundings, and specifically, the effectiveness of labour power can be enhanced by collective mobilization. Thus, the working class, in possession only of labour power, will tend to organize collectively, whereas capitalists or employers will not. This tendency will be ideally supported by political institutions, assuming that labour within the arena of politics (as distinct from the economy) will be relatively stronger. Second, institutions that reduce the need for the continuous activation of power will be built, and as such, the welfare state (as well as collective bargaining) can be seen as a strategic attempt of the mobilized working class, that is, unions and social democratic parties, to include more and more areas of conflict within a political context. Hence, this theory assumes that strong welfare states and strong employment regimes will be built in countries with a strong and mobilized working class (ibid.: 8). As a consequence, markets and employment institutions are interpreted as 'less inherently coherent and not self-equilibrating' (Thelen 2004: 4, but *pace* Hall and Soskice 2001).

Related to the power resources model is the work of some comparative political scientists who have taken a more institutionalist approach to employment relations. They have concentrated on legal, regulatory or organizational frameworks as comprising both constraints and opportunities on the actions of employment actors. In addition, they have tried to map the different preferences and logics of actions of the various actors while acknowledging some degree of path dependency (Sommer Harrits 2006: 3). In particular, these scholars focus on the importance of the nation state and employment institutions. The state is not just seen as the guardian of economic well-being but also of individual well-being and is seen as a potential representative of not just employers but also workers' interests in society. More radically, Esping-Andersen *et al.* (1976) define the state as the 'locus for class struggle'. Arguably, the state's task is not only to introduce regulations, which help to make labour contracts more efficient and to support the economic performance, productivity and competitiveness of its industries ('accumulation'), but also to ensure dignified working conditions, social justice and human rights for its citizens at their workplaces. Some authors have called this 'legitimation', maintaining popular consent by pursuing social equity (which may require 'market correcting' interventions) and fostering citizenship and voice at work (industrial democracy). Involving the 'social partners' in economic and social policy-making may also be a means of enhancing government legitimacy. For example, Hamann and Kelly (2011) found that social pacts are partly driven by competition between political parties in proportional representation (PR) electoral systems with fragmented party systems. Moreover, the state has an ultimate interest in reducing conflicts, which challenge social harmony and are costly for society at large ('pacification'). Historically, the boundaries between industrial conflict and social and political disorder have been uncertain and frequently overlapping, as in the case of general strikes (Hamann *et al.* 2013), and governments are usually eager to avoid industrial conflicts becoming political (see Ost 2005).

Finally, employment lawyers have pointed to the government's involvement in many countries in establishing collective employee rights and minimum working standards that have fundamentally shaped employment contracts over the last two centuries. Arguably they have also helped to reduce, in particular during the twentieth century, the need for negotiation between individual employers or employer associations and trade unions. In particular, more recently, as employees' ability to bargain collectively for rights and improved labour standards has declined, we can observe a parallel growth of states' engagement in the field of individual employment laws, such as anti-discrimination, anti-bullying and privacy laws. One could argue that the development of individual rights and minimum work standards increasingly substitutes for collective employment laws (Estlund 2010: 75). The verdict is out on the extent to which collective labour rights can be fully replaced by individual rights.

Corporatism

A particular topic of interest for comparative political scientists has been the capacity of the state to enable intermediary, private interest governance of employment relations, namely corporatist arrangements, to regulate the potentially conflictual employment relationship (Korpi 1978; Esping-Andersen 1985; Streeck and Schmitter 1985). This approach analyzes the state 'as a medium in institution-building processes, particularly between parties with diverging interests, for their capacities to build intermediating institutions (ones that bridge conflicting interests) on their own are limited' (Müller-Jentsch 2004: 28). Corporatist arrangements have been characterized by an all-encompassing scope of political governance and a high degree of organizational centralization. Typical examples are the Scandinavian countries, as well as Austria, Switzerland and Germany. These corporatist political economies have long been admired as models of economic efficiency and social equality (Thelen 2004: 1). For example, Streeck and Schmitter (1985: 14) examine the self-regulation of intermediary associations (besides family, community, market or state actions) that shape and coordinate private interests in societies. They argue that employment regulation in corporatist countries is governed by the concerted coordination of the state and non-state ('private') institutions and interest organizations (trade unions and employer associations), also called tripartism. This coordination is embedded in an institutional system, often created and changed with the aid of the state, without which the associative arrangement of relevant interests would not work (Müller-Jentsch 2004: 18). Necessary preconditions for a functioning corporatist governance are 'active economic policy-making of the state, social democratic political parties that are part of the government and that are supported by unions, and encompassing interest organizations that have bargaining power and centralized representation structures' (ibid.: 18). Many authors have interpreted corporatism as a high point of workers' power in society (Esping-Andersen 1985; Rothstein 1987; Glyn 1991) and view large centralized political unions' bargaining over national economic policy aspects as revealing the ultimate strength of labour movements in democratic societies.

Moreover, a major underlying assumption is that non-market institutions in the labour market (such as collective labour market regulations) are not necessarily performance decreasing but, on the contrary, can enhance performance (Schmitter 1979). Strong corporatist institutions (characterized by an all-encompassing scope of governance and a high degree of internal centralization) can even outperform market-based regimes (Traxler *et al.* 2001: 7). In fact, in the heyday of corporatist thinking, some scholars even predicted a universal trend toward 'corporatist intermediation' (Schmitter and Lehmbruch 1979; Lehmbruch and Schmitter 1982). Later on, from the mid-1980s, corporatism fell into abeyance, given the widespread decline of trade union density and the decentralization of collective bargaining (e.g. Lash and Urry 1987). A major force behind these changes towards disorganizing corporatist employment relations was, arguably, increasing international product market competition (Traxler *et al.* 2001: 9), as well as increasing strains on welfare states and pension systems. Liberal market economic models re-emerged onto the research agenda, ironically supported by Hall and Soskice's (2001: 30) prediction that LMEs will adapt more easily to globalization, given 'their preference for more flexible and loose relations, both within and between firms' (and see also Baccaro and Howell 2011). However, empirical studies have remained more ambiguous, revealing that the increasing processes of disorganization and disintegration in national employment regimes remain complex. Tendencies towards convergence on the LME model are accompanied by increasing cross-national diversity (Ferner and Hyman 1992, 1998; Crouch 1996; Visser 1996; Traxler *et al.* 2001) and corporatist arrangements have been revived in many countries under the rubric of 'social pacts' (Avadgic *et al.* 2011; Hamann and Kelly 2011).

Historical institutional theories

Finally, building on the corporatist literature, there has been a growing body of work in the 1990s and 2000s which revives an historical and institutionalist approach to the comparative study of capitalism (Thelen 2004; Thelen and Streeck 2005; Hollingsworth *et al.* 1994). The ambitious aim was to combine the insights of institutionalism concerning the constrained nature of strategic action, with an account of social change and innovation (Crouch 2005: 2) and thus contribute to the understanding of varieties of capitalism with a more dynamic political economic approach. Thus, it attempts to advance the varieties of capitalism theory by moving away from the original functionalist equilibrium model to a more historically informed theory of social action, which is conceptually open to change. Streeck (2009: 237) calls it an 'action-theoretical microfoundation for an institutionalist theory of capitalism as a social system' or 'action-centered institutionalism' or 'a theory of institutional action'. In short, it advocates a more political understanding of the varieties of capitalism. Such a theory aims to explain 'processes like the parallel, endogenous, dialectical, and mutually reinforcing institutional change' in employment regimes (ibid.).

For example, Thelen (e.g. 2004, 2010) aims to explore the continuing diversity of employment institutions (such as vocational training) across countries through a historical perspective. She calls her approach the 'political economy of skills in comparative-historical perspective' and focuses on 'where these institutions come from, what has sustained them, and the ways in which they have changed over time' (Thelen 2004: 4). A similar theme can be found in Streeck (2001, 2009), who stresses the institutional complementarities of political economies but at the same time downplays the functional and economic logic of the varieties of capitalism in favour of a more singularly political analysis (Thelen 2004: 3). National employment regimes are seen as the product of past and current political interventions designed both to maintain but also to recalibrate institutions. Political economies are 'not the product of a grand design, and ex-post accommodation . . . seems to have been at least as important . . . as a priori calculations of the advantages of compatibility and complementarity under conditions of interdependence' (Streeck 2001: 31). From this perspective, political economies are more open to change than in Hall and Soskice's analysis. 'While stability is a temporary product of social and political construction, change is endemic and in fact may be largely endogenous, external shocks notwithstanding' (Streeck 2009: 2).

Streeck reconstructs 'capitalist development as a conflictual interplay between the individual pursuit of economic advantage and collective political efforts at restoring and protecting social stability rather than as a negotiated rearrangement of meso-level institutions in pursuit of national competitiveness'. He argues that capitalist developments have been fundamentally misconstrued in the former market-driven theories as a collective and consensual quest for higher levels of efficiency, i.e. as a collective effort at 'economizing' on transaction costs. In reality, according to him, capitalism must be understood as an outcome of a permanent struggle between pressures for the expansion of markets and increasing commodification of social and political relations, on the one hand, and social demands for the political stabilization of relative prices and extant social structures (based on non-market values such as communities or trust relations), on the other.

To conclude: we have summarized selected theories from diverse disciplines, which were found to be influential in the analysis of comparative employment relations in a global economy. We broadly distinguished between approaches focusing on markets and firms, highlighting an economic functionalism as the main driving force in employment regimes with the potential to reach a stable equilibrium, and approaches that foster the historical and institutional embeddedness of employment regimes in the wider political economy highlighting processes and change rather than a stable social order. Our subsequent country chapters will reveal the inherent dynamics between periods of social stability and of transformation and change in selected employment regimes. We favour the political economic approach but acknowledge that both approaches are interrelated and both provide deep insights into the making of employment relations. In the last section of this chapter, we want to provide a heuristic framework, which outlines the major variables to be taken into account in analyzing country specific employment relations regimes.

Conceptual framework

One of the major challenges for comparative empirical researchers is to specify the conditions under which certain sets of variables are more or less successful in explaining attributes of work and employment and in particular how they can account for change. Here we develop a broad conceptual framework, which focuses on five core variables, based on Peters' famous framework of comparative politics (2008): 'actors' interests', 'power resources', 'institutions', 'international environment', and 'ideas, ideologies and identities'.

1 *Employment actors* should be defined broadly, integrating not only the three traditional agents (employers, workers, state), but also non-traditional actors such as worker centres (Fine 2006) or NGOs. As we have seen above, actors' interests, preferences and their subsequent strategic choices can be based on rational choice explanations, as in the basic neo-classical assumption that employers or employees are utility maximizers, or, as the new institutional economists (Williamson 1985) would argue, that they are minimizing their transaction costs (e.g. information costs, negotiating and decision-making costs, controlling and monitoring costs). However, as institutionalist theory in political science reminds us, reality is often more complex. For example, employers are not necessarily only interested in short-term profit-maximizing but also in long-term sustainability. Moreover, in corporatist countries, employers and workers are given the right to participate in making economic and employment policies, but in return have to be reliable partners, with their membership abiding by agreements, avoiding, for example, wildcat strikes (Peters 2008: 51). A good example is German-style works councils, which have, by law, the dual task of representing workers' interests and cooperating with management. And governments as employment actors tend to pursue a complex mix of complementary and sometimes conflicting goals and interests which can also change over time. The state is also not autonomous in its decision-making but influenced by various actors such as national constituencies, lobbyists and supranational bodies. Recent network theorists have also propagated the importance of networked groups, thus 'surrounding almost all policy areas there is a constellation of actors and groups (e.g. lobbyists) who seek to influence that policy, and who are increasingly connected formally to one another and to the relevant policy-making institution' (ibid.: 51). These examples modify the traditional, self-interested rational choice assumption of employment actors, in favour of a mixture of individual and collective preferences and actions.
2 The main emphasis of our textbook is a focus on the *power resources of the employment actors*, a topic that has been neglected or underestimated in traditional theoretical approaches. In particular, the importance of power as an institution-building and institution-preserving force has usually been underplayed by most market-oriented approaches. Yet, as outlined above, capitalist labour markets can be convincingly characterized by 'structural antagonism' and power therefore plays an important role. We strongly agree with Müller-Jentsch (2004: 27) that 'the building of employment institutions by two or more actors in conflictual interactions cannot be explained without the notion of power and counterpower'. In employment relations, actors' power is inevitably influenced by a variety of factors, in particular by market forces (the state of the economy), by political forces (political parties and policies), but also by internal

organizational capacities of the actors (e.g. degree of centralization of unions or employer associations), and by the changing nature of work and technology and group relations at the production level. Power resources are therefore dynamic and in constant flux.

3 *Employment institutions* are generally interpreted as norms and rules, which enable markets to operate but can also constrain markets. Employment institutions are usually taken to comprise labour laws, collective bargaining institutions and arbitration bodies, but can also include broader economic institutions such as free trade zones or trade agreements; and political institutions such as different forms of democracy (for example, direct or representative electoral systems) and their path dependencies, which have an impact on employment regimes. Institutions do not rigidly determine individual actions but rather establish trajectories for possible actions. Those trajectories have 'conditioning effects on the goals, strategies, and interest definitions of the actors as well as on the power relations between them' (ibid.: 12). Thus, actors are seen as being embedded in a rich institutional context consisting of social ties, organizations, and disparities in social power (Western 1998: 224). Moreover, as the historical-institutionalist theorists have rightly reminded us, institutions have an inherent tendency to persist over long periods of time, even in the face of their potential dysfunctionality (Peters 2008: 49). The difficulty is therefore not so much to explain institutional stability but institutional change.

4 *The international environment* is increasingly important in the understanding of employment relations. Much recent work has focused on comparing national actors and institutions in two or more employment regimes and this is very valuable research. However, as our introductory chapter revealed, global financial and product markets, patterns of labour migration, global politics and institutions (such as the European Union [EU], the World Bank and the International Monetary Fund [IMF]) increasingly shape national employment regimes. For example, there is an increasing number of studies on the links between national labour laws and regulations and supranational bodies such as the WTO (Hepple 2005).

It is an obvious point to make that individual countries function in a globalized environment and cannot be understood as isolated systems. An excellent example is the member states of the EU or eurozone, which have to conform to precise economic and political membership conditions and witness increasing homogenization and convergence tendencies (sometimes reluctantly as with the case of the UK). A dramatic example is provided by the institutions of Greek employment relations, which are now subject to scrutiny and intervention by the European Central Bank, the European Commission and the IMF institutions. Or again, with regard to the transformation of post-communist Central Eastern Europe, the EU as well as the IMF and the World Bank has had a significant impact on the development of their employment relations. The World Bank has also played a major role in influencing employment relations institutions in Asia and South America (Evans 1995).

5 Finally, the concept of *ideas, ideologies or identities* (to use Hyman's 2001b phrase) refers to the historical path dependencies or inherited normative or ideational traditions as well as to new ideas that shape actors' interests as well as institutions. The concept broadly refers to the 'economic culture' of a country,[4] thus to the prevalent societal ideas on private property, ownership, employment at will, industrial democracy, workers' dignity, justice, privacy, trust or social capital. Dominant social actors might have very different understandings of what defines social justice in the labour market or what entails private property and ownership in a capitalist society across countries, and the struggle of different ideologies and discourses certainly shapes the institutional architecture of employment regimes. Of course, concepts such as ideas or economic

cultures might not be as easily measured as institutional constraints since they have a more subtle or indirect effect. One option is therefore to analyze actors' legitimation for certain strategic choices (such as companies' corporate social responsibility claims) or the social and discursive (de)construction of political agendas in the media or public arena (e.g. Schroeder's Hartz reforms, Merkel's policy on minimum wages in Germany or Obama's 'American Jobs Act').

Last, but not least, every comparative analysis of employment relations needs to be specific about its dependent variables, that is, which outcomes are to be explained. Different theories tend to concentrate on different outcomes; Part 2 of our book will discuss the major outcomes of employment regulation. Market-driven theories are usually interested in performance indicators, for example, which employment regime yields the highest labour productivity, highest skills or highest employment rates. Political economic theories tend to include the outcomes for society as a whole such as the quality of their welfare states, strike levels, social unrest, the quality of their civil societies or the well-being of individual workers (happiness) and their social and political engagement levels. Relatedly, different national employment regimes might focus on different employment outcomes.[5] Moreover, not all five variables will prove equally important in different country settings. It remains an empirical task to analyze the importance each factor plays in a particular historical and national setting. This will be illustrated in the country studies in Part III.

Notes

1 For example, with regard to the increasing influence of economics in the field of labour law, see Schwab (1997).

2 In more detail: Systems theory (Dunlop), Marxist approaches (political economy, labour process debate, regulation theory), institutionalism (historical institutionalism, neo-corporatism), action theory (micro politics, labour politics, negotiation of order, strategic choice), and economic approaches (rational choice, transaction costs).

3 Note, however, that Hall and Soskice acknowledged there might be a third type, the Mediterranean economy, a theme developed in Hancké, *et al.* (2007) through the concept of the 'mixed market economy'.

4 Note that legal scholars are discussing a similar concept, 'legal cultures', across countries (Finkin 2004; Nelken 2004; Whitman 2004).

5 Interestingly, on the international policy level, the recent Stiglitz Commission on the Measurement of Economic Performance and Social Progress, initiated by former French President Sarkozy in 2008, is trying to combine both.

References

Adams, R. and Meltz, N. (eds) (1993) *Industrial Relations Theory: Its Nature, Scope and Pedagogy*, Metuchen, Canada: Scarecrow Press.

Amable, B. (2003) *The Diversity of Modern Capitalism*, Oxford: Oxford University Press.

Avdagic, S., Rhodes, M. and Visser, J. (eds) (2011) *Social Pacts in Europe: Emergence, Evolution and Institutionalization*, Oxford: Oxford University Press.

Baccaro, L. and Howell, C. (2011) 'A common neo-liberal trajectory: the transformation of industrial relations in advanced capitalism', *Politics and Society*, 39(4): 521–63.

Bamber, G. J., Lansbury, R. D. and Wailes, N. (eds) ([1987] 2011) *International and Comparative Employment Relations*, 5th edn, London: Sage.

Burawoy, M. (1985) *The Politics of Production: Factory Regimes under Capitalism and Socialism*, London: Verso Books.

Burgess, K. (2004) *Parties and Unions in the New Global Economy*, Pittsburgh, PA: University of Pittsburgh Press.

Colling, T. and Terry, M. (2010) 'Work, the employment relationship and the field of industrial relations', in T. Colling and M. Terry (eds) *Industrial Relations: Theory and Practice*, 3rd edn, Oxford: Wiley-Blackwell.

Crouch, C. (1993) *Industrial Relations and European State Traditions*, London: Clarendon Press.

—— (1996) *The Social Contract and the Problem of the Firm*, Florence: European University Institute.

—— (2005) *Capitalist Diversity and Change: Recombinant Governance and Institutional Entrepreneurs*, Oxford: Oxford University Press.

Dicken, P., Kelly, P. F., Olds, K., and Yeung, H. (2001) 'Chains and networks, territories and scales: towards a relational framework for analysing the global economy', *Global Network*, 1(2): 89–112.

Dunlop, J. (1958) *Industrial Relations Systems*, New York: Henry Holt.

Edwards, P. K. (1986) *Conflict at Work*, Oxford: Blackwell.

Elster, J. (1982) 'Marxism, functionalism, and game theory', *Theory and Society*, 11(4): 453–82.

Esping-Andersen, G. (1985) *Politics Against Markets: The Social-Democratic Road to Power*, Princeton, NJ: Princeton University Press.

——, Friedland, R. and Wright, E. O. (1976) 'Modes of class struggle and the capitalist state', *Kapitalstate*, 4–5: 184–220.

Estlund, C. (2010) *Regoverning the Workplace: From Self-Regulation to Co-Regulation*, New Haven, CT: Yale University Press.

Evans, P. (1995) *Embedded Autonomy: States and Industrial Transformation*, Princeton, NJ: Princeton University Press.

Ferner, A. and Hyman, R. (eds) ([1992] 1998) *Industrial Relations in the New Europe: Changing Industrial Relations in Europe*, 2nd edn, Oxford: Blackwell.

Fine, J. (2006) *Worker Centers: Organizing Communities at the Edge of the Dream*, Ithaca, NY: Cornell University Press.

Finkin, M. (2004) 'Menschenbild: the conception of the employee as a person in Western law', *Comparative Labor Law and Policy Journal*, 23(2): 577–637.

Flanders, A. (1975) *Management and Unions*, 2nd edn, London: Faber and Faber.

Fox, A. (1974) *Beyond Contract: Work, Power and Trust Relations*, London: Faber.

Frege, C. (2007) *Employment Research and State Traditions: A Comparative History of Britain, Germany and the United States*, Oxford: Oxford University Press.

Frenkel, S. and Kuruvilla, S. (2002) 'Logics of action, globalization and changing employment relations in China, India, Malaysia, and the Philippines', *Industrial and Labor Relations Review*, 55(3): 387–412.

Gallie, D. (2007) 'Production regimes and the quality of employment in Europe', *Annual Review of Sociology*, 33: 85–104.

Gereffi, G. (2005) 'The global economy: organization, governance and development', in N. J. Smelser and R. Swedberg (eds) *The Handbook of Economic Sociology*, Princeton, NJ: Princeton University Press.

Glyn, A. (1991) 'Corporatism, patterns of employment and access to consumption', in J. Pekkarinen, M. Pohjola and B. Rowthorn (eds) *Social Corporatism: A Superior Economic System?*, Oxford: Oxford University Press.

Grossman, S. J. and Hart, O. (1986) 'The costs and benefits of ownership: a theory of vertical and lateral integration', *Journal of Political Economy*, 94(4): 691–719.

Hall, P. A. and Soskice, D. (2001) 'An introduction to varieties of capitalism', in P. A. Hall and D. Soskice (eds) *Varieties of Capitalism: The Institutional Foundations of Comparative Advantage*, Oxford: Oxford University Press.

Hamann, K. and Kelly, J. (2011) *Parties, Elections and Policy Reforms in Western Europe: Voting for Social Pacts*, London: Routledge.

Johnston, A. and Kelly, J. (2013) 'Unions against governments: general strikes in Western Europe 1980–2006', *Comparative Political Studies*, 46(9). Available at; http://eprints.bbk.ac.uk/4247.

Hancké, B., Rhodes, M. and Thatcher, M. (eds) (2007) *Beyond Varieties of Capitalism: Conflict, Contradictions, and Complementarities in the European Economy*, Oxford: Oxford University Press.

Hart, O. and Moore, J. (1990) 'Property rights and the nature of the firm', *Journal of Political Economy*, 98(6): 1119–158.

Hepple, B. (2005) *Labour Laws and Global Trade*, Oxford: Hart Publishing.

Herrigel, G. and Wittke, V. (2005) 'Varieties of vertical disintegration: the global trend toward heterogeneous supply relations and the reproduction of difference in US and German manufacturing', in G. Morgan, E. Moen and R. Whitley (eds) *Changing Capitalisms: Internationalisation, Institutional Change and Systems of Economic Organization*, Oxford: Oxford University Press.

Heyes, J., Lewis, P. and Clark, I. (2012) 'Varieties of capitalism, neoliberalism and the economic crisis of 2008–?', *Industrial Relations Journal*, 43(3): 222–41.

Hollingsworth, J. R. and Boyer, R. (1997) 'Continuities and changes in social systems of production: the cases of Japan, Germany and the United States', in J. R. Hollingsworth and R. Boyer (eds) *Contemporary Capitalism: The Embeddedness of Institutions*, Cambridge: Cambridge University Press.

Hollingsworth, J. R., Schmitter, P. and Streeck, W. (1994) *Governing Capitalist Economies*, Oxford: Oxford University Press.

Howell, C. (2005) *Trade Unions and the State: The Construction of Industrial Relations Institutions in Britain, 1890–2000*, Princeton, NJ: Princeton University Press.

Hyman, R. (1975) *Industrial Relations: A Marxist Introduction*, London: Macmillan.

—— (2001a) 'Theorising industrial relations: Anglo-American individualism versus the European social model', Working Paper, London School of Economics.

—— (2001b) *Understanding European Trade Unionism: Between Market, Class and Society*, London: Sage.

—— (2004) 'Is industrial relations theory always ethnocentric?', in B. Kaufman (ed.) *Theoretical Perspectives on Work and the Employment Relationship*, Madison, WI: Industrial Relations Research Association.

—— and Ferner, A. (eds) (1994) *New Frontiers in European Industrial Relations*, Oxford: Oxford University Press.

Kelly, J. (1998) *Rethinking Industrial Relations: Mobilization, Collectivism and Long Waves*, London: Routledge.

—— (2010) *Ethical Socialism and the Trade Unions: Allan Flanders and British Industrial Relations Reform*, London: Routledge.

—— (2011) 'The political economy of comparative employment relations', in M. Barry and A. Wilkinson (eds) *Research Handbook of Comparative Employment Relations*, Cheltenham: Edward Elgar.

Kerr, C. (1983) *The Future of Industrial Societies: Convergence or Continuing Diversity?*, Cambridge, MA: Harvard University Press.

——, Dunlop J. T., Harbison F. H. and Myers, C. A. (1960) *Industrialism and Industrial Man*, Cambridge, MA: Harvard University Press.

Kochan, T. (1998) 'What is distinctive about industrial relations research?', in K. Whitfield and G. Strauss (eds) *Researching the World of Work*, Ithaca, NY: ILR Press.

——, Katz, H. C. and McKersie R. B. (1986) *The Transformation of American Industrial Relations*, New York: Basic Books.

Korpi, W. (1978) *The Working Class in Welfare Capitalism: Work, Unions and Politics in Sweden*, London: Routledge.

—— (2001) 'Contentious institutions: an augmented rational-action analysis of the origins and path dependency of welfare state institutions in western countries', *Rationality and Society*, 13(2): 235–83.

—— (2006) 'Power resources and employer-centered approaches in explanations of welfare states and varieties of capitalism: protagonists, consenters, and antagonists', *World Politics*, 58(2): 167–206.

Lane, C. and Probert, J. (2009) *National Capitalisms, Global Production Networks*, Oxford: Oxford University Press.

Lash, S. and Urry, J. (1987) *The End of Organized Capitalism*, London: Polity Press.

Lehmbruch, G. and Schmitter, P. (eds) (1982) *Patterns of Corporatist Policymaking*, Beverly Hills, CA: Sage.

Lewin, D. and Feuille, P. (1983) 'Behavioral research in industrial relations', *Industrial and Labor Relations Review*, 36(3): 341–60.

Locke, R., Kochan, T. and Piore, M. (eds) (1995) *Employment Relations in a Changing World Economy*, Cambridge, MA: MIT Press.

Marks, G. (1989) *Unions in Politics: Britain, Germany and the United States in the Nineteenth and Early Twentieth Centuries*, Princeton, NJ: Princeton University Press.

Marsden, R. (1982) 'Industrial relations: a critique of empiricism', *Sociology*, 16(4): 232–50.

Marshall, G. (1998) 'Labour relations', in J. Scott and G. Marshall (eds) *Oxford Dictionary of Sociology*, Oxford: Oxford University Press.

Mitchell, D. (2001) 'IR journal and conference literature from the 1960s to the 1990s: what can HR learn from it? Where is it headed?', *Human Resource Management Review*, 11(4): 375–93.

Müller-Jentsch, W. (2004) 'Theoretical approaches to industrial relations', in B. Kaufman (ed.) *Theoretical Perspectives on Work and the Employment Relationship*, Madison, WI: Industrial Relations Research Association.

Nelken, D. (2004) 'Using the concept of legal culture', *Australian Journal of Legal Philosophy*, 29(1): 1–26.

Offe, C. and Wiesenthal, H. (1980) 'Two logics of collective action: theoretical notes on social class and organizational form', *Political Power and Social Theory*, 1: 67–115.

Ost, D. (2005) *Defeat of Solidarity: Anger and Politics in Post-Communist Europe*, Ithaca, NY: Cornell University Press.

Peters, B. G. (2008) 'Approaches in comparative politics', in D. Caramani (ed.) *Comparative Politics*, Oxford: Oxford University Press.

Piore, M. and Sabel, C. (1984) *The Second Industrial Divide: Possibilities for Prosperity*, New York: Basic Books.

Rothstein, B. (1987) 'Corporatism and reformism: the social democratic institutionalization of class conflict', *Acta Sociologica*, 30 (3–4): 295–311.

Sabel, C. (1982) *Work and Politics*, Cambridge: Cambridge University Press.

Schmitter, P. (1979) 'Interessenvermittlung und Regierbarkeit', in U. von Alemann and R. G. Heinze (eds) *Verbände und Staat*, Opladen: Westdeutscher Verlag.

—— and Lehmbruch, G. (eds) (1979) *Trends Towards Corporatist Intermediation*, Beverly Hills, CA: Sage.

Schwab, S. (1997) 'The law and economics approach to workplace regulation', in B. Kaufman (ed.) *Government Regulation of the Employment Relationship*, Madison, WI: Industrial Relations Research Association.

Sommer Harrits, G. (2006) 'The class thesis revisited: social dynamics and welfare state change', Conference paper, ESPAnet, University of Bremen.

Streeck, W. (2001) 'Introduction: explorations into the origins of nonliberal capitalism in Germany and Japan', in W. Streeck and K. Yamamura (eds) *The Origins of Nonliberal Capitalism: Germany and Japan*, Ithaca, NY: Cornell University Press.

—— (2009) *Re-Forming Capitalism: Institutional Change in the German Political Economy*, Oxford: Oxford University Press.

—— and Schmitter, P. (1985) 'Community, market, state and associations? The prospective contribution of interest governance to social order', in W. Streeck and P. Schmitter (eds) *Private Interest Government: Beyond Market and State*, London: Sage.

Thelen, K. (2004) *How Institutions Evolve: The Political Economy of Skills in Germany, Britain, the United States and Japan*, New York: Cambridge University Press.

—— (2010) 'Beyond comparative statics: historical institutional approaches to stability and change in the political economy of labor', in G. Morgan, J. L. Campbell, C. Crouch, O. K. Pedersen and R. Whitley (eds) *The Oxford Handbook of Comparative Institutional Analysis*, Oxford: Oxford University Press.

—— and Streeck. W. (eds) (2005) *Beyond Continuity: Institutional Change in Advanced Political Economies*, Oxford: Oxford University Press.

Traxler, F., Blaschke, S. and Kittel, B. (2001) *National Labour Relations in Internationalized Markets: A Comparative Study of Institutions, Change, and Performance*, Oxford: Oxford University Press.

Visser, J. (1996) 'Traditions and transitions in industrial relations: a European view', in J. van Ruysseveldt and J. Visser (eds) *Industrial Relations in Europe: Traditions and Transitions*, London: Sage.

Wailes, N., Bamber, G. J. and Lansbury, R. D. (2011) 'International and comparative employment relations: an introduction', in G. J. Bamber, R. D. Lansbury and N. Wailes (eds) *International and Comparative Employment Relations*, London: Sage.

Western, B. (1998) 'Institutions and the labor market', in M. Brinton and V. Nee (eds) *New Institutionalism in Sociology*, New York: Russell Sage Foundation.

Whitman, J.Q. (2004) 'The two Western cultures of privacy: dignity versus liberty', *The Yale Law Journal*, 113: 1151–221.

Williamson, O. (1985) *The Economic Institutions of Capitalism: Firms, Markets, Relational Contracting*, New York: Free Press.

Part 2

The content of employment regulation

3 Individual employee rights at work

Cynthia Estlund

Introduction

There have been laws regulating the employment relationship for as long as there have been employment relationships. Throughout the industrialized world, societies have claimed a significant stake in workers' terms and conditions of employment, and have been unwilling to leave them entirely to the vagaries of private bargaining within unregulated labour markets. For much of the twentieth century, the primary mode of societal intervention into the employment relationship took the form – or a variety of forms – of frameworks for collective representation and bargaining. But even when and where collective bargaining was the dominant mode of workplace governance, the collective freedom of contract was either constrained by legislation (e.g. setting a floor on labour standards), coordinated through (corporatist) institutions accountable in some manner to the wider public, or both. Work has long been deemed too important to leave its regulation entirely to the decisions of workers and employers alone.

So alongside the development of legal frameworks for collective bargaining – which aim to reform the bargaining *process* between workers and employers – modern industrial societies have also regulated the *substantive* terms of employment. With few exceptions, they have done so in response to the demands of workers and their allies for protection from employer treatment that is deemed unfair, exploitative, arbitrary, or otherwise contrary to societal norms of decent work. To that end, legislatures, and sometimes courts, have imposed mandatory rights and minimum terms or conditions of employment that are more generous to employees than those which the latter might otherwise have agreed to, individually or collectively, under prevailing labour market conditions. (To be sure, many of these employment mandates also correct for collective action problems, information asymmetries, or other impediments to efficient contracting; but they still operate largely in favour of employees, as constraints on employers, and as floors rather than ceilings on what the parties may agree to on their own.) By contrast, employers are generally thought capable of protecting their own interests in the employment relationship, and are rarely given the benefit of mandatory terms of employment more favourable than those they can exact for themselves through voluntary agreements.

Of course, the type and extent of laws regulating the substantive terms of employment have varied greatly across nations and across time. Still, by the end of the twentieth century, nearly all developed nations and most developing nations had enacted one or more employment mandates from each of the following four categories:

1 *minimum labour standards* applicable to all employees *qua* employees (albeit sometimes varying by sector), including minimum wages, maximum hours of work, health and safety standards, minimum vacation time, and protection against unjust dismissal;

2 *equal status rights* against discrimination on the basis of certain identity traits, such as sex, race, religion, national origin, and sexual orientation;
3 *individual rights of dignity, privacy, and autonomy* that aim to insulate employees' personal and civic lives from employer power; and
4 *protections against retaliation* for engaging in certain socially valued activity related to work, such as disclosing illegal or harmful conduct within the employing organization or asserting employment rights.

These rights and mandates are distinct from those that support each nation's particular system of collective bargaining (such as protection of union activists against employer reprisals), and from those that may be secured through individual or collective bargaining (such as unjust dismissal protections in the USA).

The four categories above are neither exhaustive nor mutually exclusive. One emerging area of employment mandates, which aims to afford employees greater flexibility and work–life balance, does not fit neatly into the foregoing taxonomy. (Indeed, some legal frameworks for accommodating work–family conflicts even challenge the boundaries of the term 'mandates' as they call upon employers to meet with and seriously consider individual employee requests for accommodation.[1]) Some employee rights straddle two or more of the above categories. For example, parental leave provisions may be understood variously as minimum labour standards or as equality-promoting provisions for women; the prohibition of genetic testing may be seen as a privacy protection or as an anti-discrimination law. Yet the four categories of employment rights will help to organize our discussion.

We will begin with some reflections on the rationales for the legislative imposition of mandates within what is essentially a voluntary contractual relationship. We find that some major types of employment mandates – especially those in support of equal employment and employee speech and privacy interests – are loosely analogous to the constitutional rights that constrain democratic politics. If private contracting (and especially collective contracting) can be seen as the 'ordinary politics' of the workplace, then it is perhaps not surprising that some of the outside constraints on ordinary politics are designed to respond to the latter's perceived deficiencies (e.g. the tendency to neglect minority interests), much as constitutional rights often protect interests that are likely to be undervalued in majoritarian politics. This does not explain the imposition of minimum economic terms, which one might think would be well suited to resolution through 'ordinary politics' and majoritarian institutions. But of course both the absence of those majoritarian institutions of collective bargaining in large swathes of the labour market and the interests of those majoritarian institutions, when they are present, in supporting their bargaining positions are likely to be powerful explanations for the growth of minimum standards legislation. After developing these broader arguments, we will take up each of the four categories of employee rights briefly below, focusing chiefly on the first two, and by far the largest, categories of employment mandates: minimum labour standards and equal status rights.

Preliminary observations on the rationales for employment mandates

Before turning to the different types of employment mandates, it is worth considering what they may all have in common. At the risk of tautology, we may say that the rights and labour standards that have been mandated in each country are meant to establish a minimum and non-negotiable set of entitlements that are too important or too basic to leave to the vagaries of either individual or collective bargaining. For the developed nations that relied for much of the twentieth century on collective bargaining as the primary corrective for the deficiencies of individual bargaining, we might hypothesize that employment mandates covered terms and conditions of employment that were not satisfactorily addressed through collective bargaining.

But already we face a puzzle that will require us to distinguish among the categories of employment mandates in discerning their rationales. That is because the first category of mandates – minimum labour standards – concerns matters that have been the 'bread and butter' of collective bargaining throughout its history and across the world. In principle, democratically accountable, occupationally-based trade unions should be well suited to enabling workers to bargain for their own sector-wide or workforce-wide labour standards – their own wage and hour standards, vacations, job security, and even health and safety. Historically, that is exactly what trade unions have done. So the rationale for taking these matters off the bargaining table (up to the minimum standards) must be quite different from the rationale for taking, for example, equal status rights off the bargaining table. This suggests that, in attempting to discern the rationales for employment mandates, it will be useful to have in mind a very general understanding of the nature of trade unions and of collective bargaining, and of their institutional limitations, both in principle and in fact. That is a challenging task, given the diversity of collective bargaining systems across the world. A broadly comparative assessment of those systems occupies Chapter 4 and some more specific comparative points will emerge in the remainder of this chapter as we review each of the four categories of employment mandates. So, for present purposes, a few general observations will suffice. First, trade unions are to varying degrees democratic and occupationally-based. 'Democratic' here has the usual majoritarian connotations; unions thus tend to represent the 'median' worker's interests (Freeman and Medoff 1979). That is a crucial counterweight to the labour market pressures that may lead employers to cater to the demands of the 'marginal' worker – the most attractive new recruits, or the most valued incumbent employees who might leave for greener pastures. Trade unions are thus reasonably well suited to addressing many issues that confront all workers, or all workers in a particular sector or job category. We will return below to the reasons why even some of those issues are often addressed by legal mandates and are removed from the give-and-take of collective bargaining, at least up to a minimum level.

But not all important interests of workers have been adequately addressed by collective bargaining, even in those sectors and workplaces in which it exists. As foreshadowed above, we may think of collective bargaining as the 'ordinary politics' of the workplace, and as the default process for addressing issues of shared concern among employees, much as democratically elected legislatures are presumptively empowered to address the shared concerns of the citizens of a polity (Estlund 2010). But of course nearly all democratic polities remove certain issues from the domain of 'ordinary politics' and of plenary legislative control, and impose some constitutional, and often judicially-enforced, limitations on majority rule; those include rights-based limitations. Along similar lines and for some similar reasons, legislatures (or courts) may remove certain issues from the domain of collective bargaining – the 'ordinary politics' of the workplace. Indeed, it would not be surprising to see some parallels between the two domains – the democratic polity and the collective bargaining relationship – in the kinds of issues that are removed from the realm of majoritarian decision-making.

So, for example, the converse of unions' majoritarian virtues are the difficulties that unions often face, and the shortcomings they may display, in dealing with the concerns of discrete minority groups within an occupational group (Frymer 2007). This is an obvious rationale for addressing problems of identity-based employment discrimination through legislation, and through mandatory equal status rights, rather than through the give-and-take of collective bargaining. Employment discrimination legislation is thus the workplace analogue of constitutional equality rights. Both bodies of law constrain political majorities from actions that harm or neglect the interests of discrete minority groups or other subgroups (including women) that are disadvantaged in the political process, whether by their small numbers and voting strength, a history of exclusion and prejudice, or both (Ely 1980).

The problem of employment discrimination gained salience first in nations with long histories of demographic heterogeneity in the labour force, and of identity-based subordination, stratification, and social unrest. In particular, the USA, with its historical legacy of slavery and a long aftermath of *de jure* and *de facto* segregation, was eventually forced to take a leading role in this arena of employment law. But with globalization and increased cross-border migration, both diversity and discrimination within national labour markets have become more widely recognized phenomena, and equal status rights have become a major area of employment legislation across much of the world. One important question, beyond the scope of this chapter, is whether growing workforce diversity erodes the ability of unions to effectively address even shared workplace concerns. Demographic diversity may generate divergent and conflicting interests among workers, as well as intergroup friction, and may undermine the solidarity on which trade unions are founded and on which they depend for their efficacy. If that is so, then workforce diversity might be one factor in both the relatively low union density of the USA and the decline of union density across the increasingly diverse societies of the developed world. (That may be true even though diversity among co-workers and among union members helps to build intergroup bonds and break down intergroup divisions (Estlund 2003). In any event, it is clear that majoritarian unions are not ideally structured, and historically have not always functioned, to protect the interests of minority groups within the workforce.

Majoritarian unions also face institutional limitations in addressing the most personal of workers' concerns, such as interests in privacy and autonomy in one's life outside the workplace. Although these interests may be widely shared among workers at some abstract level, their specific content is bound to vary from person to person. Majoritarian institutions may not be expected to deal satisfactorily with rights to be different and rights to be left alone. As in the case of equal status rights, the development of autonomy and privacy rights at work has its obvious parallel in the constitutional realm. Democratic polities have often elevated some individual rights of citizens to the constitutional domain rather than leaving them to the give-and-take of ordinary legislative politics. Such rights are often denominated as 'fundamental' – either as inherent and inalienable attributes of personhood, or as a foundation for individuals' ability to participate in democratic politics, or both (Dworkin 1978; Ely 1980; Elster and Slagstad 1988). For analogous reasons, those rights may be injected into the employment relationship and protected against employer power as well. Of course, just as societies vary in the extent and content of citizens' constitutional rights of privacy, liberty, and autonomy, they vary in the degree to which such rights are extended into the workplace. (And societies do not always follow parallel paths in the two domains, as we will see.) But some of the basic rationales for addressing those rights through legislation that is binding on individual employers, rather than through bargaining between unions (or individuals) and employers, echo the arguments for recognizing individual constitutional rights in democratic societies.

Another significant category of mandates consists of protections against retaliation for employees' engagement in socially valued activities. Most importantly, this includes protection of 'whistleblowers' – those who disclose (to managers, to regulators, or to the public) harmful or illegal activity within the employing organization, such as dangerous products, financial misconduct, or tax evasion – from employer retaliation. We will not devote much attention to this category below (though it is important in the USA, given the background rule of employment at will – the employer's presumptive right to terminate employment without cause). Still, it is worth noting one distinct rationale for embodying these protections in mandates rather than deferring to the parties and their individual or collective bargains. The benefits of such activity by employees are mostly external to the parties to the employment relationship; they flow to the public generally, or to some subset of third party beneficiaries of regulation, but usually not to the employee who decides to speak up or even to employees as a group. The logic of mandates here is clear: there is no particular reason to expect such societal benefits to be secured through individual or even collective contracts between employers and employees (Schwab 1996).

That brings us back to the question identified above: why are ordinary minimum labour standards not left to collective bargaining, given that they address matters of shared interest to workers within a given occupation or workplace, to which unions' majoritarian processes would seem well suited? At a very general level, two sorts of reasons suggest themselves: substitution for collective bargaining where it does not exist, and support for collective bargaining where it does exist. Both ultimately rest on societal judgements about what terms and conditions of work are too 'fundamental' to relegate to the contingencies of labour market competition and bargaining power, even collective bargaining power. To some degree minimum standards laws serve as a substitute for collective bargaining where it does not exist. Even in the heyday of collective bargaining, some workers at the bottom of the labour market lacked union representation. As union density declines, especially in the liberal market economies, the union substitution rationale reaches a growing segment of the labour market. That would suggest one reason why minimum standards mandates have proliferated in recent decades, and why that trend is likely to continue in the future.

Minimum standards mandates may also support collective bargaining – and strengthen the union hand in collective bargaining – by putting a floor on certain terms and conditions of employment. Minimum terms limit the extent of cost-based competition that unions and unionized firms face. Moreover, if unions can shift issues from the industrial relations agenda to the legislative agenda, they can conserve their bargaining power for the issues that remain. To some degree, then, a nation's labour standards legislation reflects the political power of organized labour. But whether labour standards laws are meant as a substitute or a support for collective bargaining, the normative case must still be made to the broader polity that some terms and conditions of employment should not depend on the fortuities of labour market competition or on workers' individual or collective bargaining power, but should be enjoyed by all workers.

That nearly-tautological assessment glosses over important national variations. For in some countries, minimum standards legislation serves as an extension of collective bargaining; and in others, collective bargaining does much of the work that minimum standards legislation does elsewhere. There are, in short, important differences across nations and regions in both the nature of labour standards and the mechanisms by which they are set.

So let us proceed to examine each of the four basic categories of employment mandates, with an eye to some of the major variations across societies and over recent history. The primary focus here will be on the liberal market economies of the USA and the UK and on the coordinated market economies of Western Europe.

Minimum labour standards

All industrialized countries maintain some minimum labour standards – regulation of minimum wages, maximum hours and overtime premiums, breaks, holidays, parental leaves, workplace safety, and dismissals and redundancies, among other matters – that apply in all or nearly all workplaces and that are meant to protect workers *qua* workers. We will discuss the regulation of wages, of hours of work and leaves, and of dismissals and redundancies, where the differences across the leading market economies are especially stark.

Wages

In the coordinated market economies of Northern Europe, labour standards and especially wages are relatively high and are generally set at the national and sectoral level – either instead of across-the-board minima or in addition to and above such minima – through some form of 'peak bargaining' between trade unions and employer associations. Such bargaining is fairly comprehensive, and its results are often extended, by legislation or otherwise, beyond the members of the peak federations of employers and employees. The results of 'peak bargaining' typically encompass workers and jobs at the bottom of the labour market as well as more skilled workers and jobs that have historically been the core constituencies of the trade unions (Malmberg 2002). By contrast, in liberal market economies like the USA and the UK, minimum standards are set solely through legislation, and they are largely uniform across the economy rather than sector-specific. Almost inevitably, those uniform minimum economic standards are lower than sectoral standards would be. Trade unions are free to seek higher wages, and to attempt to set sectoral standards; but they must do so through 'voluntarist' and decentralized collective bargaining and collective self-help, and without the aid of corporatist-style mechanisms for extension of collectively bargained wage levels throughout the sector. Workers at the bottom of the labour market may be especially difficult to organize in these decentralized systems because of their weak labour market position. Trade union organizing and collective bargaining efforts in the liberal market economies thus directly confront labour market headwinds that are stiffened by increasingly transnational competition in product markets. Firms that can escape higher unionized wages and labour standards by avoiding collective bargaining will predictably resist both union organizing and bargaining concessions (Rogers 2006; Wachter 2007).

These differences in labour relations systems are historically rooted, but they also reflect in part a crucial philosophical divide. To what degree should wages, hours of work, and other economically salient labour standards be 'taken out of competition'? In the liberal market economies, labour market competition is generally regarded as legitimate and functional for society as a whole, and is understood to determine most material terms and conditions of employment for most workers. Market forces are constrained only by a legally established floor that is meant roughly to keep full-time workers out of poverty. In the coordinated market economies, by contrast, competition among firms that is based on lower labour costs is highly suspect, and is constrained not only by what workers need to support themselves and their families but by what employers in different sectors of the economy are capable of delivering (Hall and Soskice 2001; Rogers 2006).

Hours, vacations, and leaves

This philosophical difference is also reflected in dramatically different approaches to the regulation of hours of work. The USA and the UK have tended to impose only minimal legal constraints on the number of hours that employers can require employees to work in a given week. The law intervenes, and modestly discourages long hours, largely by 'taxing' overtime – that is, by requiring employers to pay a premium wage rate for hours beyond a normal work week (e.g., 150 per cent of the normal wage for hours in excess of 40). In the USA, even those overtime requirements do not apply to many salaried professionals and managers. In the USA and the UK, 'maximum hours' laws are exceptional, 'freedom of contract' is given wide scope, and employers are generally allowed to impose take-it-or-leave-it demands for overtime. This may induce employees – especially salaried employees who are exempt from overtime requirements – to 'compete' among themselves by putting in long hours. It also allows employers to ramp up production in market upswings by exacting more hours from the existing workforce before hiring new (or even temporary) workers.[2] By contrast, the coordinated market economies of Northern Europe regulate working hours more tightly. The labour market forces that might impel employers to demand or employees to accept longer hours are seen social evils to be restrained by law. An individual's choice to work longer hours is deemed either illusory or harmful to the promotion of the greater collective good, and no more worthy of accommodation than an individual's 'choice' to work at less than the minimum wage. If employers want to increase production, they must either hire more workers (perhaps temporary workers) or get more productivity out of their existing workforce.

These differences extend to the analogous issue of vacations and leaves (including parental leave). Such matters are largely left to the market and individual or collective bargaining in the USA and the UK, while they are subject to comparatively generous minimum standards in the rest of Europe. The unsurprising result of these different approaches to labour market regulation is that workers in the USA and the UK work significantly longer hours – both more hours per week and more weeks per year – than their counterparts in much of Europe, especially in Germany and Scandinavia.[3] The former look with a mix of envy and disbelief at heated public debates in the latter over whether to reduce the maximum work week to 40 hours or less, or to extend minimum vacation periods to more than five weeks per year. And the latter look with alarm at the prospect that competition within and beyond Europe's enlarged boundaries – as well as controversial judicial interpretations of European Union (EU) principles of free movement of persons, establishments, goods, and services[4] – will erode high labour standards and undermine corporatist mechanisms for maintaining high sectoral labour standards.

Job security

The contrast between the liberal market economies and the coordinated market economies extends to the distinct realm of job security, or regulation of dismissals and redundancies. In the coordinated market economies, workers are entitled as a matter of basic fairness and economic security to protections against unjustified dismissal or layoff. Both disciplinary and economic grounds for termination are regulated (although remedies for unjust dismissal may consist largely of monetary awards that reflect job tenure).

The greater cost and difficulty of shedding workers in an economic downturn tend to inhibit new hiring in upturns; on some accounts, it tends to reduce employment levels overall (Minford 1985; Baker *et al.* 2005). This tendency is countered to some degree by employers' inability to simply demand more hours of work from current workers. Strong job security protections tend to go hand in hand with relatively generous social welfare benefits for the unemployed. Both encourage workers to invest in firm- and sector-specific job skills by reducing their need to switch firms or sectors in a downturn (Hall and Soskice 2001). Strong job security protections also tend to go hand in hand with regulation of temporary employment arrangements, which employers might otherwise use to circumvent dismissal restrictions (Houseman and Osawa 2003: 8). At the same time, restrictions on dismissal tend to induce employers to invest in training and retraining of existing employees. That fact may help to explain some empirical results showing little or no net impact of unjust dismissal protections on employment levels, and some positive productivity effects (Deakin 2012).

In the liberal market economies of the UK and the USA, job security was traditionally governed by the presumption that employment was terminable at will, and in the private sector was left to individual and collective bargaining.[5] In recent decades, all of the liberal market economies other than the USA now provide some sort of remedy for 'unfair dismissals', although they still tend to define 'unfair dismissals' rather narrowly by EU standards (Collins 2004). One recent assessment of employment protections in the Organization for Economic Co-operation and Development (OECD) as of 2008 finds that the six least protective legal regimes are all in Anglo-American liberal market economies (the USA, Canada, the UK, New Zealand, Australia, and Ireland) (Venn 2009: 8).

The USA is a special case. It famously adheres to the employment-at-will presumption, under which employers do not need to justify discharge decisions except for employees who have gained job security protections by individual or collective contract (or, in the public sector, by statute). Yet the reality of employment-at-will in the USA is powerfully shaped by a large and growing collection of wrongful discharge laws and doctrines, some of which will be discussed below (Estreicher and Hirsch, 2013). Under the shadow of these wrongful discharge laws, and the costly litigation and liabilities that they can generate, many employers have developed internal review and grievance procedures and informal norms of fairness that offer some protection against arbitrary dismissal (Estlund 1996; Wachter 2012). It is noteworthy that even sophisticated comparative assessments of employment protection regimes fail to take into account the indirect effects of these exceptions to employment-at-will on both workers' job security and employers' dismissal costs (Venn 2009). It remains true, however, that most non-union private sector workers in the USA have no legal entitlement to keep their job without good cause for their termination. US employers are thus comparatively free to respond to product market fluctuations by hiring or shedding workers, and the external labour market is accordingly more active. Because there is no formal unjust dismissal regime for employers to circumvent, US law does not regulate employers' use of temporary workers (Clauwaert 2000). And because employers often fill their demand for new skills by resort to the external labour market, both employers and the state tend to invest less in training and retraining of existing workers.[6] Employees, too, have less incentive in the US and the UK to invest in firm- and industry-specific skills (Hall and Soskice 2001).

The European commitment to job security for incumbent employees and generous welfare benefits for the unemployed has come under pressure from changes in technology, firm structure, and the boundaries of product and labour markets. Many voices have urged a shift along the spectrum from strong job *security* toward greater emphasis on employability and employer *flexibility* in the labour market (Deakin 2012). The ubiquitous concept of 'flexicurity'[7] has been deployed to press for liberalization of unjust dismissal regimes, and has met stiff, even violent, resistance from workers in some countries. The proposition that employees are entitled to continue in their jobs unless there is a persuasive justification for their dismissal has become deeply embedded in many Europeans' sense of social justice. That notion of job security as a basic entitlement is reflected in an International Labour Organization (ILO) convention on the matter,[8] and has been taken up as well by many developing countries. US-style employment-at-will looks to much of the world like an abomination.

For their part, many US workers would surely prefer greater job security, just as they would prefer guaranteed four-week vacations. But that preference has never ripened into a powerful political demand for mandatory protections, even at the state level.[9] That may be partly because many US workers appear to believe incorrectly that the law does prohibit arbitrary dismissals (Kim 1997, 1999). It may also reflect the availability of legal remedies against the worst kinds of unfair dismissals, as well as the tendency of those multiple wrongful discharge remedies to discourage most arbitrary dismissals (Estlund 1996). The lack of political demand for unjust dismissal protections in the USA may also reflect divergent views of the relative value of security and stability, on the one hand, and freedom, flexibility, and mobility, on the other, as well as more fractured and sceptical views of both the efficacy and the legitimacy of government regulation of labour market outcomes. A romanticized sympathy for the entrepreneur, and especially small business owners, provides a predictable reservoir of political resistance to new minimum standards laws and other restrictions on managerial flexibility. The historical, cultural, and political roots of those attitudinal differences are, however, beyond the scope of the present chapter.

Equal status rights

When we move from minimum labour standards to individual employee rights, and especially to equal status rights, the picture changes dramatically. The USA, with its long history of racial subordination and segregation, was dragged to the forefront in crafting legal rights and remedies against identity-based discrimination. Title VII of the Civil Rights Act of 1964 prohibited discrimination on the basis of race, sex, colour, religion, and national origin; subsequent statutes extended the discrimination ban to age, pregnancy, disability, and genetic endowment. As migration has grown and labour markets around the world have become increasingly heterogeneous, the anti-discrimination norm in some form has become nearly universal (at least on paper). The ILO has declared the right to be free from discrimination in employment as one of the four 'core labour standards' to which all ILO member nations are bound.[10] Countries and regions differ, of course, in their articulation and implementation of the anti-discrimination norm. In some countries, equal employment rights are not backed by meaningful remedies (de Búrca 2011). But the basic idea that it is wrong for employers to discriminate against workers on the basis of certain identity traits – especially race, sex, national origin, religion, age, and disability – has gained remarkable currency.

In tracing the logic of anti-discrimination law and its expansion, it is useful to begin with the paradigm case of discrimination against African-Americans in the USA. Racial discrimination was widespread in the USA when it was first prohibited by federal law in 1964. Yet the wrongfulness of race discrimination was not hard to grasp. Race is not only irrelevant to an individual's job qualifications and performance, but is also immutable and inheritable. The immutable, inheritable, and non-job-related nature of race may have sufficed to establish the unfairness (and inefficiency) of allocating employment opportunities on that basis. But the dreadful historical legacy of slavery and centuries of segregation and discrimination, both public and private, had also produced massive social injustice in the form of group subordination and disadvantage, shared within families and communities and across generations. Those group harms became a source of national embarrassment, a foreign policy liability, and a source of internal unrest and even violence that lent urgency to the political case for anti-discrimination legislation.

The historical pattern of group subjugation on the basis of heritable, immutable, and non-job-related identity traits was not strictly limited to discrimination against African-Americans in the USA. But not all of these dimensions were present in all forms of discrimination. Discrimination because of national origin was perhaps the closest analogy. In the USA, for example, a history of discrimination against Mexican-Americans, Puerto Ricans, and Asian-Americans had created patterns of segregation and communal disadvantage in some regions. But 'national origin' as such, especially when it was detached from 'race' – for example, French or Norwegian ancestry – was not a basis for historically entrenched, state-backed discrimination or segregation or even systematic private discrimination. That does not mean that such discrimination is not unfair; but it is not unfair in the same way as discrimination against racial minorities.

Other forms of discrimination departed further from the paradigm case of race. For example, sex discrimination and segregation do not translate as directly into socio-economic disadvantage, nor do they transmit trait-based disadvantages from one generation to the next, because men and women do not live in separate families and communities; men's economic advantages are to some degree enjoyed by their wives and daughters. Age discrimination is different because everyone gets older (if they are lucky); the harms of age discrimination, like other disadvantages of aging, are eventually borne more or less by everyone. Many physical disabilities are neither immutable nor inheritable, nor are they the basis for community and familial disadvantage or segregation; moreover, some disabilities are clearly related to job performance (or are costly to accommodate).

So the proliferation of protected classes under anti-discrimination law has required a shift in the nature of the arguments against discrimination, and a de-emphasis of historical group disadvantage, stratification, and segregation. Discrimination at its core came to mean subjecting individuals to adverse treatment on the basis of identity traits rather than individual merit, qualifications, or performance. This simple, thin version of the anti-discrimination idea has proven to be highly adaptable and politically popular, and its simplicity and universality have facilitated its extension to a still-expanding list of traits and groups. Yet the extension of the anti-discrimination principle beyond its paradigm setting of race is not without cost. It tends to divert attention from the history, sociology, and economics of accumulated group disadvantage that had so powerfully oppressed certain racial minorities. If race discrimination is wrong simply because race is irrelevant to job performance, then all forms of discrimination on the basis of non-job-related identity traits are roughly equivalent (whether or not associated with historically entrenched group disadvantage). Indeed, if race discrimination is wrong simply because race is irrelevant to job performance, then it may also be wrong to discriminate *in favour* of historically disadvantaged minority groups. Thus did anti-discrimination law in the USA become an obstacle to 'affirmative action' initiatives that favoured historically disadvantaged groups.

The symmetrical conception of discrimination is hardly inevitable, nor is it relentlessly applied, even in the USA.[11] Some race- or gender-conscious 'affirmative action' – where demonstrably aimed at remedying a history of discrimination by the same actor – is permissible. But the boundaries of such remedial efforts are policed lest they license 'reverse discrimination' and infringe upon the individual right to be treated at work without regard to one's race or gender. It is certainly possible to devise and apply anti-discrimination laws in a way that is tilted more heavily toward redressing historical patterns of discrimination. The point is that this choice is in tension with the thin, individualistic conception of discrimination, and what makes it wrong, that has helped to underwrite the expansion of the anti-discrimination ideal far beyond its initial paradigm cases. The symmetrical, 'colour-blind' (or 'trait-blind') version of the anti-discrimination ideal is particularly influential in the USA, perhaps because it is the concept of anti-discrimination that is easiest to identify as an individual right, rather than as a collective right against group disadvantage. The competing idea of group rights, or of anti-discrimination as anti-subordination, is well developed in the US academic literature (Fiss 1976; Lawrence 1987), though it has met resistance within the courts and mainstream legal and political discourse. But the tension between a symmetrical, 'trait-blind' conception of anti-discrimination and workplace equality, on the one hand, and a more historically and sociologically sensitive group anti-subordination conception, on the other, may be inescapable. The first view aspires to purge decision-making processes of certain considerations; the second view, which is more influential in Europe, aims to achieve greater equality of results, sometimes by taking explicit account of race and gender. 'Quotas' and proportional hiring are anathema under the former view, but often appropriate under the latter view. Mandatory maternity leave and mandatory retirement are *prima facie* discriminatory and unlawful under the former view but may be crucial public policy tools for advancing substantive equality under the latter view (Suk 2012). Probably no country's anti-discrimination laws follow one or the other of these views to the complete exclusion of the other; yet this is one important dimension along which national approaches to employment discrimination vary.

Another crucial dimension on which countries' anti-discrimination laws vary is their reach: how far does the law extend beyond the core of explicit or intentional refusal to hire members of a particular group? The law may extend beyond that core in several ways. It may (and usually does) extend to a larger set of employment decisions, such as promotions. It may also extend to intangible forms of disparate treatment, such as harassment on the basis of sex or race (to which we will return briefly below). Anti-discrimination law may also extend beyond intentional discrimination to include employment decisions or criteria (such as written tests or job qualifications) that are race- or sex-neutral on their face, but that have the *effect* of disproportionately screening out minority or female candidates. (In the USA, this is known as 'disparate impact' discrimination; in the UK, it is 'indirect discrimination'.) Similarly, anti-discrimination law may require not just non-discrimination but the *accommodation* of certain differences, as in the case of women's pregnancy and childbearing needs or certain disabilities. On a number of these issues, US anti-discrimination jurisprudence has been quite influential – albeit sometimes as a cautionary tale rather than a positive model – in shaping the development of anti-discrimination law in other parts of the world.[12]

The US influence, as well as its limits, can be seen in the law of discriminatory harassment. The US courts long ago recognized that verbal and physical harassment was one powerful way to marginalize women or minorities at work, and that serious harassment was a form of unlawful discrimination in conditions of employment. This gloss on Title VII of the Civil Rights Act (1964) became particularly important for women, who often met hostility in traditionally male jobs, as well as sexualized working conditions – unwelcome sexual demands, propositions, verbal taunting, and even sexual assaults. The USA, in which a strong formal commitment to gender equality is coupled with conservative attitudes toward sexuality, provided relatively fertile ground for the development of the concept of sexual harassment as a form of sex discrimination. The attempt to purge the workplace of sexuality under the banner of gender equality has held less appeal in countries where sexuality is a more accepted fact of life (as in '*vive la différence*', in France) (Zippel 2008). The law of discriminatory harassment has also been shaped by the US law's failure to recognize any general right to be free from bullying or 'mobbing' as some European countries do (Yamada 2000). Indeed, the employee's right to quit – the other side of employment-at-will – has traditionally been seen as recourse enough against abuse. Bullied workers in the USA thus usually have no legal remedy unless they can prove a discriminatory motive for their victimization.[13] That gave greater urgency to the project of banning discriminatory harassment in the USA. (It also tends to make discrimination law a vehicle for generalized complaints of abuse, much as it does for complaints of unjustified dismissal.)

Apart from the conceptual basis and scope of anti-discrimination legislation, it is worth taking brief notice of the institutional context for the enforcement of equality rights (and other employee rights). The impact of anti-discrimination law on employer practices in the USA has been magnified by the ability of employees to bring private litigation (including class actions and other forms of aggregate litigation), to seek a jury trial, and to recover substantial monetary remedies (including attorney fees under one-way fee shifting provisions). Plaintiffs' success rate in these cases is rather low.[14] But for large reputation-conscious employers, the prospect of costly and embarrassing litigation, and the small risk of a large award, are well worth avoiding, and have helped to spur decades of internal reform, first under the rubric of 'equal employment opportunity' and 'affirmative action'. When 'affirmative action' and 'quotas' were attacked by the Reagan Administration (1980–88) and challenged in court as 'reverse discrimination', the reforms continued under the rubric of diversity and inclusion. And the 'business case for diversity', for better and worse, began to overshadow traditional justice-based arguments for increasing representation of minorities (Dobbin 2009). The high volume of employment litigation in the USA, for all its costs and problems, may give the anti-discrimination principle a potency that it lacks in countries with lower-powered remedial schemes (or no effective remedies at all, as in the case of China and, until recently, Japan).[15]

A final comparative point is worth underscoring. As we have seen, anti-discrimination law interacts with a country's basic approach to job security and unjust dismissal. One reason for the salience and potency of equal status rights in the USA is that they operate against the background of employment-at-will, which would otherwise have permitted employers to fire employees not only arbitrarily but discriminatorily. Where the background rules require 'good cause' for discharge, as they do in most of the world, unjust dismissal laws provide indirect protection against discriminatory discharge (though not, of course, against hiring discrimination). Similarly, as we have seen, a general right against bullying provides protection against some serious forms of discriminatory harassment. At the same time, as suggested above, the proliferation of high-powered private remedies against discrimination in the USA tends to afford some indirect protection against unjustified discharge, and softens and complicates the harsh simplicity of employment-at-will.

One reason the anti-discrimination principle has proven so politically popular and protean is that it requires virtually no public expenditures (except perhaps for the funding of enforcement agencies), and it imposes little tangible burden on private employers. Noncompliance may be costly, of course; but compliance is not, at least not in any obvious economic way. The anti-discrimination mandate at its core does not require hiring more workers, retaining them longer, or paying them more; it only requires that jobs and job-related goods be distributed without regard to race, sex, and the like.[16] Economic analysts of the law have identified some costs, especially in the case of explicit or implicit duties to accommodate differences (most obviously in the case of disability) (Jolls 2001). But by and large, the anti-discrimination principle is an almost magically costless mandate. To the extent that employers comply, its costs fall mainly on workers who would otherwise benefit from their privileged place in a social hierarchy that the law has declared illegitimate.

The evolution of the idea that discrimination is wrong, and that equal employment opportunity is a fundamental commitment of a decent society, is one of the law's great social engineering projects of the late twentieth century. The success of that project is incomplete, but few law reform movements have so transformed people's economic and social lives, as well as social norms and attitudes, over the course of a few decades. To be sure, history – the history of colonialism, patriarchy, slavery, and overt segregation and discrimination – has produced deep-seated inequalities of conditions and capacities that cannot be undone merely by enjoining employers from discriminating on the basis of race or national origin or sex. That requires other social policies and probably greater public budgetary outlays than the magically costless anti-discrimination principle.

Privacy and dignity rights

Societies vary dramatically, as we have already suggested, in the extent to which they protect workers' personal privacy and dignity, and their political and civic liberties, from employer invasion. Unjust dismissal laws outside the USA afford some indirect protection of these interests, for those laws require employers to justify efforts to dictate employees' off-work activities or political affiliations and activities, and that will usually be difficult to do. But some invasions of employee privacy, dignity, and liberty may have job-related justifications, and may be permitted or not, depending on the existence and strength of a countervailing legal right on the part of employees. Drug testing requirements, for example, may have some legitimate basis, and rise or fall depending on whether the employer's interests are weighed against or limited by employees' legally recognized privacy rights.

The USA has tended to anchor the least protective end of the spectrum. With scant exceptions, a private sector employer in the USA:

> has almost plenary power to control one's off-duty life – one's fraternization with others (including sex partners), what recreation one may enjoy, where one lives, where one shops, what charities one must contribute to, even one's political and civic expression and activities (except for union activity).
>
> (Finkin 2002)

One can see that position as a corollary to employment-at-will: the employer can fire the employee for any reason or no reason, including refusal to accept rules or practices that invade the employee's off-duty life or personal privacy (and the employee can quit at will if he or she rejects those conditions) (Kim 1996). But that begs the question of why US courts and legislatures have failed to created significant privacy and dignity-based exceptions to employment-at-will. Why did the harsh at-will background rule not underscore the need to affirmatively protect individual privacy rights (as it did with equality rights and, as we will see, whistleblower rights)? But we will leave the 'why' question aside here, for it would require a long detour into US politics. German law, by contrast, recognizes robust privacy and dignity rights of employees as restrictions on employer power (Finkin 2002). In part, this position, too, can be seen as a corollary of German law on job security: to the extent that employees are held to have a strong entitlement to job tenure, it makes sense to ensure that the job cannot be conditioned on employees' submission to unjustified intrusions into their off-duty lives. The German Constitution guarantees dignity and privacy rights that the courts have interpreted to limit the power of private employers as well as the state. Additional protections are conferred by statute, as in the case of data protection and the federal Works Constitution Act. These laws 'safeguard and protect the free development of the personality of the employees' unless exceptions can be argued on the grounds of business necessity. As a result, 'virtually all of an employee's life out of the workplace is out of an employer's hands' (ibid.). German law has strongly influenced EU law. For example, the EU Data Protection Directive, inspired by German conceptions of informational privacy, tightly regulates the collection, use, and transfer of personal information in both the private and public sectors (Bignami 2005).

As technology advances, and with it the capacity to expose ever more extensive and intimate information about individuals, the law of employee privacy is likely to become more salient politically, even in the USA. And as labour markets and information flows become increasingly transnational, especially within multinational corporations, conflicting approaches to employee privacy rights are putting pressure on the law in the least protective jurisdictions like the USA.[17] We will see an important example of this in the next section on whistleblower rights.

Whistleblower rights and anti-retaliation protections

A large and growing area of employment law, especially in the USA, concerns the rights or duties of workers to report wrongful conduct within the organization. That includes employees' right to complain about their own treatment, for example, to complain of failure to pay overtime or of discrimination. Those rights are necessary adjuncts to the underlying employment rights that are reportedly being infringed. But employees also have the right (or occasionally the duty) to report on violations that do not affect them personally, such as unlawful toxic emissions or securities fraud, free from employer retaliation.

As indicated above, the USA is at the forefront of this area of employment law, in part because the employment-at-will background rule would otherwise tolerate employers' conditioning of employment on employee silence about organizational misconduct. There are hundreds of state and federal statutes, and a large body of state common law, protecting employees who 'blow the whistle', internally or externally, on wrongdoing. Indeed, internal protection of employee whistleblowers and official channels for reporting of wrongdoing are a standard element of corporate compliance programmes, which are themselves virtually mandatory among large US corporations (Estlund 2010; Moberly 2011). Those laws have often been generously construed in favour of employee protection, even by a Supreme Court that has not otherwise been noted for its pro-plaintiff decisions. One can fairly speak of an 'anti-retaliation principle' that has become increasingly central to the law of employment in the USA (Moberly 2011).

European law is less expansive in protecting employee whistleblowers. In part, that is because such protection is less necessary, given the background protection afforded by unjust dismissal laws. Employers would rarely be able to justify dismissing or disciplining an employee for truthfully reporting employer misconduct. But the lack of special protections or inducements to whistleblowing is also traceable to ambivalent European attitudes toward whistleblowing that may stem from a traumatic twentieth-century history of government-sponsored informants in both Communist and fascist regimes (Lobel 2009). Here, too, contrasting legal principles and priorities between the USA and Europe are giving rise to acute legal controversies that will put pressure on legal divergences. In particular, internal corporate compliance structures that encourage employees' anonymous reporting on co-workers or managers – standard and virtually mandatory within US corporations' ethics codes – have been held by European courts to run foul of national laws protecting employee privacy and dignity (Pagnattaro and Peirce 2007). Specifically, the transmission of such anonymous complaints and reports within a multinational corporation's compliance system has been held to violate the rights of accused wrongdoers to privacy of personal data.

Conclusion

For many years, comparative law, including the law of employment, has been much occupied with dissecting the competing tendencies of convergence and divergence (Weiss 2007; Gahan *et al.* 2012). On the one hand, industrialization and economic integration (or 'globalization') are seen to exert pressure toward convergence in the law governing many fields of economic activity, including employment. On the other hand, several schools of thought, including the 'varieties of capitalism' and 'legal origins' theories, have sought to explain the persistence of differences across legal regimes, including in employment (Hall and Soskice 2001; Botero *et al.* 2004). Our own brief comparative venture, largely confined to the advanced Western economies and to the sphere of individual employee rights (broadly defined), has found signs of both convergence and continuing divergence, in a mix that is at least as complex as is suggested by Katz and Darbishire's (2000) evocative phrase, 'converging divergences'.

We have touched on at least two distinct sources of pressures toward convergence, both stemming from dynamics of economic integration, over the past several decades: first, the EU is an explicitly and formally integrative project that has gradually expanded its reach to include a growing array of employment rights. Second, large and powerful multinational corporations, with organizational cultures and structures that tend to favour uniformity of norms, may tend to homogenize the internal implementation of external law and to put pressure on nation states toward convergence. And yet these developments have not brought about any simple or unambiguous trend toward convergence. Most obviously, the EU's integrative project has brought about both convergence (within the EU) and divergence (from other countries, especially the USA). In particular, the UK's assimilation into the EU has begun to pull its labour market policies away from its liberal origins (though differences persist), thus ensuring that the 'legal origins' theory of the persistence of national divergence will increasingly have to reckon with one rather prominent outlier. More broadly, while both the USA and the various nations of the EU have had their economic ups and downs in recent decades, the labour market policies of the 'coordinated market economies' have given rather little ground to the liberalization movement that appeared to be in ascendancy a decade ago. Those labour market policies have obviously been highly influential in shaping EU policy in the labour arena. Moreover, there appear to be complementarities among the components of the more interventionist European labour market policies (only some of which are discussed here) that allow them to compete rather effectively, at least in some configurations, with the liberal alternative (Deakin 2012; Gahan *et al.* 2012).

As for the role of multinational corporations, we have seen that they may indeed become agents of convergence, though sometimes in a surprising direction. For example, multinational corporations may be a medium not only for spreading the corporate diversity practices that have developed under the shadow of US law, but also for spreading aspects of US-style anti-discrimination law beyond US boundaries. On the other hand, national divergence exerts pressure on corporate practices as well as vice versa. Multinational corporations have been compelled to submit to more protective EU and European legal norms, and may become the medium for carrying those more protective norms back to the USA (e.g., in the case of informational privacy). Corporations' interest in operating in European labour and product markets may sometimes override their preference for less fettered managerial power. It will be interesting to watch how these competing pressures shape the law governing 'whistleblowers', for example. Will other nations develop a US-style 'anti-retaliation principle'? Or will that principle be reshaped in its home country to accommodate

European values, sensibilities, and legal norms? Or will existing differences persist, perhaps through the development of legal 'safe harbours' from which corporations can manage to satisfy both sets of regulatory requirements?

The most important stakes in the 'competition' between the more liberal labour market policies of the USA and the more protective labour market policies of the EU may eventually emerge elsewhere, in the growing economies of the developing world, and especially in countries like China, India, and Brazil. China, for example, has recently enacted labour law reforms that resemble those in Europe more than the USA (notwithstanding the vocal efforts of US corporations to promote the latter model) (Cooney *et al.* 2007).

Perhaps one prediction is safe: legally mandated employee rights and labour standards appear to be gaining ground on, if not displacing, collective bargaining as the dominant source of protection for workers against harsh labour market forces. Ironically, that may be especially true in the liberal market economies, whose labour movements have been most battered by employer resistance and product market competition, *and* whose employment laws have historically been less protective as well. Whether it is possible to improve and enforce decent labour standards through regulatory mechanisms, and whether it is possible to do so without the support and involvement of strong institutions of collective worker representation, remain to be seen.

Notes

1 For a detailed discussion of the types of work–life accommodations offered in different countries within the European Union, see *Reconciliation of Work and Family Life and Collective Bargaining in the European Union* (2006).

2 The UK approach to regulation of working hours came under pressure from the EU's Working Time Directive; but the UK managed to insist on a provision in the Directive that permits individual waivers of the 48-hour maximum work week. UK law thus allows employers to demand such waivers, and they have become routine in much of the economy. The UK thus remains an outlier within the EU, in keeping with its historic liberal market traditions (Barnard *et al.* 2003).

3 In 2009, the average number of hours worked per year was 1,407 in Norway, 1,559 in Denmark, 1,602 in Sweden, and 1,390 in Germany compared with 1,768 in the USA and 1,643 in the United Kingdom (OECD 2012a). The data on average annual paid leave is similarly telling (though the UK is more similar to other European countries in this respect): in 2007, the average annual paid leave (including public holidays) was 34 days in Denmark and Sweden, 32 days in the United Kingdom, 29 days in Norway, 29 days in Germany, and only 10 days (all public holidays) in the United States. The United States is one of the few countries without a federal statutory minimum of annual paid leave (OECD 2010).

4 That is, the rulings of the European Court of Justice in the *Viking* and *Laval* cases and their progeny (Davies 2008; Reich 2008).

5 Collective bargaining agreements (CBAs) in the USA constrain disciplinary discharges through a robust 'just cause' principle (Elkouri *et al.* 2003). CBAs in the USA typically afford employers wide discretion over whether to eliminate jobs, while regulating the order of layoffs through a strong seniority principle (which prevents employers from using layoffs to single out disfavoured or highly-paid workers) and through a 'tax' in the form of unemployment compensation.

6 The United States ranks among the lowest of all OECD countries in public and mandatory private expenditures on active labour market programmes. For example, in 2007, such expenditures amounted to only 0.1 per cent of the United States' GDP. By contrast, Belgium, Denmark, Sweden, and the Netherlands spent upwards of 1 per cent of their respective GDPs on active labour market programmes; and Finland, France, Germany, Norway, and Switzerland spend between 0.6 per cent and 0.9 per cent of GDP on such programmes (OECD 2012b).

7 A 'flexicurity model' is one that provides employers with high *flexibility* in job mobility due to limited employment protection legislation, while also providing employees with a high degree of financial *security* in the form of social welfare programmes (Mploy 2011).

8 The Termination of Employment Convention, 1982 (No. 158), ILO.

9 With the one exception of Montana (Ewing *et al.* 2005).

10 International Labour Organization Declaration on Fundamental Principles and Rights at Work, International Labour Conference, 86th Session, Geneva, 1998 (Annex revised 15 June 2010). The other three ILO 'core labour standards' include freedom of association and the effective recognition of the right to collective bargaining, elimination of forced or compulsory labour, and effective abolition of child labour.

11 US age discrimination law, for example, is explicitly asymmetrical and does not prohibit discrimination against younger workers.

12 US law influenced many of the core concepts of EU anti-discrimination law such as the EU concept of 'indirect discrimination' (Hepple 2006). Similarly, EU disability discrimination law was strongly influenced by the Americans with Disabilities Act (Quinn and Flynn 2012). The creation of the Equal Employment Opportunity Commission (EEOC) in 1964 also played a prominent role in the proliferation of national equality bodies across Europe (de Witte 2012). On the other hand, the concept of 'reverse discrimination', the idealization of 'colour blindness' and the hostility to 'quotas' have not been followed in the EU, where it is common to encourage preferential treatment or numerical proportionality for historically disadvantaged or under-represented minorities. For example, many EU Member States mandate quotas for the disabled: France and Germany, for example, regard quotas 'as an intrinsic element of disability employment policy' (Waddington and Lawson 2009).

13 In extreme cases, bullying may amount to the tort of 'intentional infliction of emotional distress', but that tort is very narrowly defined in some jurisdictions. For one notorious case, see Hollomon v. Keadle, 931 S.W.2d 413 (1996).

14 Between 1979 and 2006, the plaintiff win rate in federal courts was 15 per cent for employment discrimination cases, compared with 51 per cent for all other civil cases (Clermont and Schwab 2009).

15 For a discussion of the problems of combating employment discrimination within the Chinese legal system, see Lu (2009). Similarly, see Gelb (2000) for a discussion of employment discrimination in Japan.

16 As a practical matter, employers who had been paying women or minority workers less may find it impossible to lower the wages of men or white workers, and may have to raise the wages of the former. That is a start-up cost of complying with anti-discrimination laws. But in fairly short order, employers are generally able to adjust the total wage package so that they are not spending more on labour after the anti-discrimination mandate takes effect.

17 This has particularly been an issue with regard to data protection. The European Union is currently pushing for American companies to adopt a new privacy system that would give internet users the 'right to be forgotten' – namely the right to control the dissemination of their personal information on websites (Bennett 2012). The fact that the American companies are even considering such a system when many of them rely heavily on such information to efficiently reach consumers belies the immense pressure the United States is facing due to the stricter privacy regulations adopted abroad.

References

Baker, D., Glyn, A., Howell, D. and Schmitt, J. (2005) 'Labour market institutions and unemployment: a critical assessment of cross-country evidence', in D. Howell (ed.) *Fighting Unemployment: The Limits of Free Market Orthodoxy*, Oxford: Oxford University Press.

Barnard, C., Deakin, S., and Hobbs, R. (2003) 'Opting out of the 48-hour week: employer necessity or individual choice? An empirical study of the operation of Article 18(1)(b) of the Working Time Directive in the UK', *Industrial Law Journal*, 32(4): 223–52.

Bennett, S. C. (2012) 'The "right to be forgotten": reconciling EU and US perspectives', *Berkeley Journal of International Law*, 30(1): 161–95.

Bignami, F. (2005) 'Transgovernmental networks vs. democracy: the case of the European information privacy network', *Michigan Journal of International Law*, 26: 807–68.

Botero, J., Djankov, S., La Porta, R., Lopez de Silanes, F. and Shleifer, A. (2004) 'The regulation of labor', *Quarterly Journal of Economics*, 119(4): 1339–82.

Clauwaert, S. (2000) *Survey of Legislation on Temporary Agency Work*, Brussels: European Trade Union Institute (ETUI).

Clermont, K. M. and Schwab, S. J. (2009) 'Employment discrimination plaintiffs in Federal court: from bad to worse?,' *Harvard Law and Policy Review*, 3(1): 3–35.

Collins, H. (2004) *Nine Proposals for the Reform of the Law of Unfair Dismissal*, Liverpool: Institute of Employment Rights.

Cooney, S., Biddulph, S., Zhu, Y., and Kungang, L. (2007) 'China's new labour contract law: responding to the growing complexity of labour relations in the PRC', *University of New South Wales Law Journal*, 30(3): 786–801.

Davies, A.C.L. (2008) 'One step forward, two steps back? The *Viking* and *Laval* cases in the ECJ', *Industrial Law Journal*, 37(2): 126–48.

Deakin, S. (2012) 'The law and economics of employment protection legislation', in C. Estlund and M. Wachter (eds) *Research Handbook on the Economics of Labor and Employment Law*, Northampton, MA: Edward Elgar.

de Búrca, G. (2011) 'The trajectories of European and American antidiscrimination law', Public Law and Legal Theory Working Paper, New York University. Available at: http://lsr.nellco.org/nyu_plltwp/315.

de Witte, B. (2012) 'New institutions for promoting equality in Europe: legal transfers, national bricolage and European governance', *American Journal of Comparative Law*, 60(Winter): 49–74.

Dobbin, F. (2009) *Inventing Equal Opportunity*, Princeton, NJ: Princeton University Press.

Dworkin, R. (1978) *Taking Rights Seriously*, Cambridge, MA: Harvard University Press.

Elkouri, F., Elkouri, E. A. and Ruben, A. M. (2003) *How Arbitration Works*, 6th edn, Washington, DC: Bureau of National Affairs.

Elster, J. and Slagstad, R. (1988) *Constitutionalism and Democracy*, Cambridge: Cambridge University Press.

Ely, J. H. (1980) *Democracy and Distrust: A Theory of Judicial Review*, Cambridge, MA: Harvard University Press.

Estlund, C. (1996) 'Wrongful discharge protections in an at-will world', *Texas Law Review*, 74(June): 1655–92.

—— (2003) *Working Together: How Workplace Bonds Strengthen a Diverse Democracy*, New York: Oxford University Press.

—— (2010) *Regoverning the Workplace: From Self-Regulation to Co-Regulation*, New Haven, CT: Yale University Press.

Estreicher, S. and Hirsch, J. (2013) 'Comparative wrongful dismissal law: reassessing American exceptionalism, north Carolina Law Review, 92 (Fothcoming). Available at: SSRN:http://ssrn.com/abstract=2238776.

European Foundation for the Improvement of Living and Working Conditions (2006) *Reconciliation of Work and Family Life and Collective Bargaining in the European Union*. Available at: http://www.eurofound.europa.eu/eiro/other_reports/work_family_life.pdf.

Ewing, B. T., North, C. M., and Taylor. B. A. (2005) 'The employment effects of a "good cause" discharge standard in Montana', *Industrial and Labor Relations Review*, 59(1): 17–33.

Finkin, M. W. (2002) 'Menschenbild: the conception of the employee as a person in Western law', *Comparative Labor Law and Policy Journal*, 23(4): 577–638.

Fiss, O. M. (1976) 'Groups and the equal protection clause', *Philosophy and Public Affairs*, 5(2): 107–77.

Freeman, R. B. and Medoff, J. L. (1979) 'The two faces of unionism', *The Public Interest*, 57(Fall): 69–93.

Frymer, P. (2007) *Black and Blue: African Americans, the Labor Movement, and the Decline of the Democratic Party*, Princeton, NJ: Princeton University Press.

Gahan, P., Mitchell, R., Cooney, S., Stewart, A., and Cooper, B. (2012) 'Economic globalization and convergence in labor market regulation: an empirical assessment', *American Journal of Comparative Law*, 60(3): 703–41.

Gelb, J. (2000) 'The Equal Employment Opportunity Law: a decade of change for Japanese women?', *Law and Policy*, 22(3–4): 385–407.

Hall, P. and D. Soskice (eds) (2001) *Varieties of Capitalism: The Institutional Foundations of Comparative Advantage*, Oxford: Oxford University Press.

Hepple, B. (2006) 'The European legacy of Brown v. Board of Education', *University of Illinois Law Review*, 2006(3): 605–24.

Houseman, S. and Osawa, M. (2003) *Nonstandard Work in Developed Economies: Causes and Consequences*, Kalamazoo, MI: W.E. Upjohn Institute for Employment Research.

Jolls, C. (2001) 'Antidiscrimination and accommodation', *Harvard Law Review*, 115(2): 643–99.

Katz, H. C. and Darbishire, O. (2000) *Converging Divergences: Worldwide Changes in Employment Systems*, Ithaca, NY: Cornell University Press.

Kim, P. T. (1996) 'Privacy rights, public policy and the employment relationship', *Ohio State Law Journal*, 57: 671–730.

—— (1997) 'Bargaining with imperfect information: a study of worker perceptions of legal protection in an at-will world', *Cornell Law Review*, 83(November): 105–60.

—— (1999) 'Norms, learning and law: exploring the influences on workers' legal knowledge', *University of Illinois Law Review*, 1999: 447–515.

Lawrence, C. R., III. (1987) 'The id, the ego, and equal protection: reckoning with unconscious racism', *Stanford Law Review*, 39(2): 317–88.

Lobel, O. (2009) 'Citizenship, organizational citizenship, and the laws of overlapping obligations', *California Law Review*, 97(2): 433–500.

Lu, J. (2009) 'Employment discrimination in China: the current situation and principle challenges', *Hamline Law Review*, 32: 133–90.

Malmberg, J. (2002) 'The collective agreement as an instrument for regulation of wages and employment conditions', *Scandinavian Studies in Law*, 43: 189–213.

Minford, P. (1985) *Unemployment: Cause and Cure*. 2nd edn, Oxford: Basil Blackwell.

Moberly, R. (2011) 'The Supreme Court's anti-retaliation principle', *Case Western Reserve Law Review*, 61(2): 375–452.

Mploy (2011) *Building Flexibility and Accountability into Local Employment Services: Country Report for Denmark*, Paris: OECD, Local Economic and Employment Development (LEED) Working Papers, 2011/12. Available at: http://dx.doi.org/10./5kg3mktsn4tf-en.

OECD (2010) *Gender Brief*. Available at: http://www.oecd.org/dataoecd/23/31/44720649.pdf.

—— (2012a) 'Average annual hours actually worked per worker', StatExtracts. Available at: http://stats.oecd.org/Index.aspx?DatasetCode=ANHRS# (accessed May 22, 2012).

—— (2012b) 'Social expenditure – aggregated data', StatExtracts. Available at: http://stats.oecd.org/Index.aspx?QueryId=4549# (accessed September 7, 2012).

Pagnattaro, M. A. and Peirce, E. (2007) 'Between a rock and a hard place: the conflict between U.S. corporate codes of conduct and European privacy and work laws', *Berkeley Journal of Employment and Labor Law*, 28(2): 375–428.

Quinn, G. and Flynn, E. (2012) 'Transatlantic borrowings: the past and future of EU non-discrimination law and policy on the ground of disability', *American Journal of Comparative Law*, 60(1): 23–48.

Reich, N. (2008) 'Free movement v. social rights in an Enlarged Union: the *Laval* and *Viking* cases before the ECJ', *German Law Review*, 9: 125–61.

Rogers, J. (2006) 'United States: lessons from abroad and home', in J. Rogers and W. Streeck (eds) *Works Councils: Consultation, Representation, and Cooperation in Industrial Relations*, Chicago: University of Chicago Press.

Schwab, S. J. (1996) 'Wrongful discharge law and the search for third-party effects', *Texas Law Review*, 74(June): 1943–78.

Suk, J. C. (2012) 'From antidiscrimination to equality: stereotypes and the life cycle in the United States and Europe', *American Journal of Comparative Law*, 60(Winter): 75–98.

Venn, D. (2009) *Legislation, Collective Bargaining and Enforcement: Updating the OECD Employment Protection Indicators*, Paris: OECD, Directorate for Employment, Labour and Social Affairs. Available at: www.oecd.org/els/workingpapers.

Wachter, M. L. (2007) 'Labor unions: a corporatist institution in a competitive world', *University of Pennsylvania Law Review*, 155(3): 581–634.

—— (2012) 'The striking success of the National Labor Relations Act', in C. Estlund and M. Wachter (eds) *Research Handbook on the Economics of Labor and Employment Law*, Northampton, MA: Edward Elgar.

Waddington, L. and Lawson, A. (2009) *Disability and Non-Discrimination Law in the European Union*, Luxembourg: Publications Office of the European Union.

Weiss, M. (2007) 'Convergence and/or divergence in labor law systems? A European perspective', in B.A. Aaron and K. Stone (eds) *Rethinking Comparative Labor Law*, Lake Mary, FL: Vandeplas Publishing.

Yamada, D. C. (2000) 'The phenomenon of "workplace bullying" and the need for status-blind hostile work environment protection', *Georgetown Law Journal*, 88(March): 475–536.

Zippel, K. (2008) 'Violence at work? Framing sexual harassment in the European Union', in S. Roth (ed.) *Gender Politics in the Expanding European Union: Mobilization, Inclusion, Exclusion*, New York: Berghahn Books.

4 Collective representation at work

Institutions and dynamics

Richard Hyman and Rebecca Gumbrell-McCormick

Introduction

This chapter examines the mechanisms through which workers obtain collective representation of their interests in the company and workplace. The most universal institutions for such representation are trade unions, defined more than a century ago by Sidney and Beatrice Webb (Webb and Webb 1894: 1) as 'continuous association[s] of wage-earners for the purpose of maintaining or improving the conditions of their employment'. Subsequently, they described trade union functions as comprising 'mutual insurance' (by which they meant the provision of financial benefits when members faced adversity); collective bargaining (a term which they themselves invented); and 'legal enactment' (pressure for favourable government action) (Webb and Webb 1897). The bulk of this chapter provides a comparative analysis of trade unionism, with the aim of developing an analytical understanding of the key dilemmas and contradictions involved in union organization and action. We focus on different models of trade unionism and on membership density, union structure and internal democracy. But we also discuss the role of works councils established independently of the employer. First, though, we need to explore the very meaning of collective representation, a concept heavily laden with ambiguity. To end the chapter, we discuss the future of collective representation in an era of economic crisis and labour weakness.

What is collective representation? Meanings and ambiguities

Both concepts in the term 'collective representation' are ambiguous. What constitutes a collective? In any workplace, employees differ in multiple respects, such as age, gender, ethnic origin, education, pay, type of employment contract, as well as social and political attitudes. Yet they are all also subject to the authority of the employer, whose interest it is to maximize their performance while containing the costs of their labour. Increasingly, all are to greater or lesser degrees vulnerable to the loss of their job if more profitable (or, in the public sector, more cost-saving) opportunities are available to the employer. Whether the diversity of individual circumstances or the broader commonality of interests takes priority in workers' conceptions of their own identities at work is an open question. *Creating* and *sustaining* a collective interest and identity is a task which representatives themselves struggle to accomplish, with varying degrees of success.

It is often argued that this is becoming more difficult today because the social identities and life-worlds of employees are increasingly diverse. How far, and how, can unions tailor their priorities and practices to workers as individuals (for example, offering personalized services or negotiating flexible agreements) without undermining their collective purpose?

An analogous issue is the relationship between particularism – the interests of a specific occupational group or of employees in a specific workplace – and broader class or social aggregation. The single-minded pursuit of purely local interests not only undermines solidarity, but can be self-defeating, encouraging a 'race to the bottom' in a harsh competitive environment. In the past, building national union movements which are more than the sum of their parts has been a major challenge. Today, transcending narrow nationalism in order to construct international solidarity is an even greater challenge, as we discuss below with reference to European Works Councils.

The notion of representation is just as problematic. In one sense, an individual is representative of a constituency by sharing the same basic characteristics. These may be demographic: for example, an important debate within trade unions is whether a middle-aged white male can effectively represent a workforce which is predominantly young, female and ethnic minority. They may be attitudinal: to be representative in this sense implies sharing orientations and expectations. But most workers have little interest in devoting the time and energy needed to representing their fellows, so in this sense a representative is usually different from the majority of the constituency. A second meaning of the notion is to express their immediate wishes (grievances and aspirations), and many representatives perceive their role in such terms. They see themselves as the mouthpiece of the workers they represent. But a third, somewhat different meaning, is to defend and advance their interests, on the basis of a reflective and strategic judgement which most constituents may fail to make: acting as a leader rather than a mere delegate.

We may identify four key aspects of strategic representation. First, it is necessary to *aggregate* the diverse grievances and aspirations of different groups into a common programme. Second, there have to be strategic *priorities*; it is usually impossible to pursue every demand simultaneously, so workers' power resources need to be focused on those issues of key importance and those which, perhaps, will lead to enhanced organizational influence if pursued successfully. Third, it is essential to be able to *mobilize* the rank and file in support of the demands adopted, a task which often involves sustained work of argument and motivation. Fourth, there is a task of *consolidating the organization* in order to strengthen the capacity for intervention in the future.

It is common to distinguish between 'single-channel' and 'dual-channel' systems of representation: in the former, workplace representative institutions are sub-units of trade unions; in the latter, they exist independently. In this chapter we therefore start by analyzing trade unions before considering independent works councils; but as we will see, the distinction between the two types of institution is often less clear in practice than in theory.

Varieties of trade unionism

The workplace, described by Marx as the hidden abode of production, can also be regarded as the primary unit of trade union organization, the arena of everyday trade unionism which was traditionally neglected by many students of industrial relations. There are major differences between (and indeed also within) countries in terms of the extent to which workplace trade union organizations operate and the influence which they exert; the existence of other institutions such as works councils which are not formally agencies of trade unionism but may be more or less competitive with or complementary to union structures; and in the degree to which national or sectoral trade unions integrate the workplace within their activities.

To an important extent, such differences connect to contrasting understandings of what trade unions are, what are their primary objectives and modes of action. Do they only recruit employees, or also the self-employed, the unemployed, pensioners? Do they only represent the interests of their members, or do they pursue the interests of a broader constituency, acting as a 'sword of justice' rather than a 'vested interest' (Flanders 1970)? Is the agenda which they pursue exclusively employment-related, or does it encompass broader social and political issues? Are the methods they adopt primarily those of peaceful bargaining (whether with employers or with governments), regarding strike action as the very last resort, or is there a frequent use of mobilization and militancy (reflecting a conception of trade unionism as a social movement rather than simply an organization)?

Trade unions have been described as 'intermediary organizations' (Müller-Jentsch 1985), since their main task as collective actors is to deploy workers' collective resources in interaction with those who exert power over them. This means that it is impossible to understand trade unions in isolation. They are embedded in four main types of relationship: first, with their own members and constituents, a relationship which generates a 'logic of membership' (Schmitter and Streeck 1981) and gives rise to issues of democracy and accountability; second, with employers, a relationship which gives rise to issues of recognition, and of the distribution but also production of profit; third, with governments, a relationship which gives rise to issues of the economic and juridical framework of industrial relations, the representative status of unions in policy-making and the 'social wage' constituted by public welfare provision. These two relationships involve a 'logic of influence', whereby action is adapted to the expectations of unions' interlocutors in order to deliver results. Fourth, unions have relations with 'civil society' (or 'public opinion'), a relationship which has become increasingly important as unions' intrinsic resources diminish and they seek external legitimacy and alliances with other non-governmental organizations. Here we may speak of the 'logic of legitimacy'.

We now outline three 'ideal types' of trade unionism (see also Hyman 2001). The definition provided by the Webbs, quoted above (though in later writing they broadened this significantly) conceived of trade unions as interest organizations representing occupationally-based membership constituencies. A century ago when Samuel Gompers – for several decades, the leader of the American Federation of Labor – was asked what were the objectives of his organization, he answered simply: 'More.' This 'business union' perspective has dominated the Anglophone analysis of industrial relations.

However, this type of unionism encounters serious problems. It is particularly exposed to 'collective actor' issues (Olson 1965). If the main appeal of union membership is self-interest, the prospect of improved wages and conditions through collective bargaining, then the rational individualist may choose the option of 'free-riding', since non-members also benefit from the results contained in collective agreements. And though the focus of union action is the individual employer (or groupings of firms within employers associations), and business unions have often proclaimed themselves as 'non-political', effectiveness depends on a favourable macroeconomic environment and a secure legal status, which can only be facilitated by government. In consequence, business unionism faces particular difficulties in hard times (such as economic recession, the erosion of traditional industrial strongholds or the growth of precarious forms of employment). This is clearly demonstrated in the USA, where union density has fallen to a mere 7 per cent in the private sector, and survival typically involves assent to concession bargaining. Increasingly, the union response has been to move towards political pressure and social mobilization.

One argument against the whole conception of business unionism, strongly asserted by Flanders (1970), is that unions are involved not only in substantive regulation (defining wages, hours of work, and so on) but more importantly, in his view, in *procedural* regulation (determining the rules and processes through which substantive conditions are determined).

Such a procedural role inevitably involves sensitive issues of rights and of power; in this sense, it is a political process and thus unions cannot be 'apolitical' actors. And as agencies of collective 'voice' (Freeman and Medoff 1984), unions may be viewed as protagonists of democracy (hence the title of the Webbs' second major book, *Industrial Democracy*).

A second conception of trade unions, which in a global perspective has certainly been more typical, views them as a social movement. Historically, unions in many countries (including a minority tendency in the USA itself) defined themselves as radical oppositional agencies of class struggle. A century ago, revolutionary socialist and Communist traditions were dominant in southern Europe, subsequently extending to Latin America. In many countries of Africa, Asia and the Caribbean, trade unions emerged as integral components of movements for national liberation, and were often radicalized as a result of repression by the colonial powers. In some countries, radical trade unionism had a religious inspiration, as with 'liberation theology' in Latin America.

Radical unionism, however, has its own distinctive problems and tensions. First, strong political and ideological identities, in many countries involving links to a political party, commonly gave rise to a fragmented trade union movement with rival political (or religious) movements competing for workers' allegiance. Such divisions have usually weakened labour as a whole (see Chapters 11 and 17 in this volume, on France and India respectively). Second, the imperatives of survival have commonly created pressures towards compromise and moderation, reinforced if unions gain some degree of acceptance and recognition by concerns with the 'logic of influence'. Often there develops a divorce between what are still defined as ultimate objectives, on the one hand, and everyday activity, on the other. In other words, the increasingly intermediary character of the union results in tensions between ideology and practice. Third, a distinctive set of dilemmas arises where political radicalism is successful. This was the case in post-revolutionary Russia, where unions became quickly subordinated to the demands of the state. Parallel dilemmas arose in post-colonial states (and most recently, by analogy, in South Africa, see Chapter 19 in this volume); as the new government struggles with the task of national reconstruction, unions face strong pressures to cooperate and often switch from militancy to moderation. Analogous pressures exist in countries where unions helped in the struggle against dictatorship (Italy in the 1940s, Spain in the 1970s), where the threat of reaction then casts them in the role of defenders of the new social order.

A third model could be termed 'corporatist': unions are agencies of social integration, partners in national socio-economic development or, where they are primarily enterprise-based (as in Japan), in the success of the company. In Europe, this conception was propagated by Catholic trade unionism from the 1890s, and was then embraced (in part as a reaction to the Communist revolutionary model) by social-democratic trade unionism in the twentieth century. Corporatist trade unionism was reinforced by the Cold War after 1948; at the same time, the Keynesian welfare state offered trade unions a new status as 'social partners', often with a privileged role in the formulation and administration of social and labour market policy. This was most developed in the export-oriented Nordic countries, notably with the consolidation of the 'Swedish model' in the 1950s: unions agreed to wage restraint in return for egalitarian social and fiscal policies and expanding welfare provision. From the 1970s there was a much more extensive development of 'political exchange' (Pizzorno 1978; Baglioni 1987) in response to economic crisis, and not only in Europe; the 'Accord' between government and unions in Australia in the 1980s was a notable example. Company-level 'productivity coalitions' (Windolf 1989) display a similar logic: not only in the case of Japanese company unionism (with other Asian parallels) but also with analogies in Western

Europe (notably German works councils, examined below) and the more general development of 'micro-corporatism' (Regini 1995) in response to economic adversity.

Integrative unionism is also beset by problems and dilemmas. What are the limits to partnership? How can unions maintain their independence and avoid takeover by management or by the state? To the extent that the logic of influence overrides the logic of membership, there is a serious risk of detachment from the rank and file, perhaps provoking exit or revolt. C. Wright Mills (1948), writing of trade unionism in the United States, described the role of the union representative or official as the 'management of discontent'. If workers are perfectly contented, they may see no need for union representation; but if they are too discontented, a union may be unable to satisfy their expectations. Union representatives have to walk a tightrope. This becomes all the more difficult in hard times: Keynesian demand management, economic growth and an expanding welfare state allowed unions to co-manage the distribution of affluence in a positive-sum game. In times of economic adversity and austerity, they struggle to minimize losses in a zero- or negative-sum game. Political bargaining of this type is exemplified by the 'social pacts' which became widespread from the 1990s (Avdagic *et al.* 2011): unions assented to packages which often entailed reductions in real incomes and cuts in social benefits. Cooperation no longer delivered positive results.

Both radical and integrative models of trade unionism possess an overtly political dimension. But the nature of this dimension varies considerably. Can unions best achieve their objectives, as traditionally in much of Europe, through close cooperation with a labour-friendly party (or even formal affiliation)? Or should they retain their party-political independence, or even abstain from direct intervention in the political arena? This issue remains hotly debated; and in Europe we can see a secular trend towards greater detachment between unions and parties (Hyman and Gumbrell-McCormick 2010).

These three contrasting types of unionism were historically conditioned, reflecting the structural conditions (different national varieties of capitalism and state traditions) under which unionism was constructed in the past and operates in the present. Among factors which were clearly important were the timing of economic development and the position of the national economy within the world market; the nature and timing of political democratization; national 'state traditions' (Crouch 1993); and the character of civil society (including the importance of religious and ideological divisions). Usually there is an elective affinity between a country's trade unions and its economic, social and political institutions: not surprisingly, since such institutions helped shape trade union development but unions in turn contributed to the shaping of these institutions, particularly those regulating welfare and labour market policy. Many such institutions acquire iconic status for trade unions, as symbols of their own achievement (Locke and Thelen 1995) which they defend with particular determination. This can create a powerful path-dependency, but trade unions (like all institutions) can and do change their character over time.

Some national examples of trade unionism

Some brief examples may illustrate how context has shaped national union identities, creating opportunity structures encouraging one set of strategies while inhibiting others. In *Britain,* early capitalist industrialization together with imperialist dominance in world markets for most of the nineteenth century created space for negotiating improvements in wages and conditions, at least for more skilled workers or those with a capacity to disrupt production. A democratic franchise was achieved incrementally, over many decades, as political elites responded pragmatically to popular pressure. The result was less intense popular radicalism than in much of continental Europe, where the struggle for the working-class right to vote was often bitter and insurrectionary. Despite an eventual rhetorical commitment to socialism, British trade unionism remained predominantly oriented to economic bargaining.

In the *USA*, a sheltered domestic market and the 'frontier tradition' encouraged belief in continuing economic expansion, inhibiting collectivist or socialist politics (though it is important to note also the severe and violent repression of radical trade unions and political organizations). The limited regulatory powers of the federal state also inhibited the political activism typical of unions in many countries.

Trade unionism in *Germany* was shaped by the key role of an authoritarian state in sponsoring the development of capitalist industry, its efforts (until the end of the nineteenth century) to suppress independent working-class organization and action, and the early construction of an (non-egalitarian) welfare state. Created initially as an arm of the Social Democratic Party, the main German unions were strong centralized organizations, for several decades riven (like the socialist movement itself) by antagonisms between reformists and revolutionaries. The post-war (and post-Nazi) realignment of German trade unionism, particularly during the Cold War (when the Communist Party was outlawed), embraced the principles of social partnership and the 'social market economy'. A further distinctive feature is that pre-capitalist traditions of collective regulation (the guild system) were carried over into modern industry; their influence can still be seen in a strong trade union commitment to apprenticeship-based skill formation, and involvement in institutions within and beyond the company which regulate its provisions.

Sweden, like Germany, developed a strong centralized trade union movement, closely linked to Social Democracy. But unlike in Germany, trade unionism was never affected by radical religious or ideological divisions, which assisted the gradual growth of unionization to the highest level in any Western country. From 1932 until the election of the current conservative coalition, there was almost uninterrupted Social Democratic government, facilitating the creation of an elaborate egalitarian welfare regime. The economy is heavily dependent on exports, and manufacturing industry is highly concentrated, with correspondingly strong employers organizations. For half a century from the 1930s, unions pursued peaceful concertation with employers and political exchange with governments, trading wage moderation for economic growth and welfare benefits. Despite more recent challenges, union identities in Sweden (as in other Nordic countries) have remained notably stable. However, a distinctive feature is the existence of separate confederations for white-collar and professional employees; the decline in manual occupations has reconfigured the geography of trade unionism and created new lines of internal conflict.

The case of *France* is radically different. Historically an interventionist state and authoritarian employers provoked the emergent union movement to favour demonstrative protests which could induce the government to redress grievances to which employers were unwilling to respond. In the absence of institutionalized 'industrial relations', trade unionism (at least until very recently) was thus unavoidably political in orientation. French society has also long been marked by sharp divisions between Catholicism and anti-clericalism, and in the twentieth century between Communism and anti-Communism, with the Communist Party for a time the strongest post-war force on the Left and its associated trade union confederation the most influential. The outcome was a weak and divided union movement, dependent on a cadre of rank-and-file militants for whom the whole idea of compromise was often suspect.

The historical background in *Italy* was in a number of respects similar, but union identities have changed substantially in recent decades. Gains achieved through mass militancy in the late 1960s were institutionalized in a new structure of industrial relations in the 1970s, facilitating a growing emphasis on collective bargaining as the core trade union function. At the same time, the powerful Communist Party moved towards an increasingly reformist position and loosened its organizational ties with the most important union confederation. Governments, often with flimsy popular legitimacy, proved willing to engage in political exchange with the unions; the result was a tense inter-linkage between economics and politics. Though trade unionism remains divided between three main confederations (with a number of smaller rivals), their post-war political identities have been diluted and more often than not they are able to act in concert.

In *Japan*, the political system was long marked by dynastic political authoritarianism, and even with post-war democratization a conservative, virtually one-party governmental regime persisted (partly sustained by US hegemony). Post-war unions were initially radical but suffered repression and a series of traumatic defeats. While national union confederations do exist, they are weak and divided (though there has been some consolidation in the past two decades). The main arena of industrial relations is the 'internal social market' of large firms, where company unions largely collaborate with management; the large peripheral workforce is barely touched by trade unionism.

South Africa is an example of the dilemmas which confront a successful insurgent labour movement. Trade unionism under apartheid articulated a complex combination of class, race and community issues (Seidman 1994), mobilizing a common struggle against the social, political and economic oppression of black workers. Industrial militancy was one element in a movement of resistance in which the main unions worked in concert with the African National Congress and the Communist Party. But the unions' role became more problematic in post-apartheid South Africa, when the new government sought to demonstrate that it was no threat to overseas investors and to the international financial institutions: trade unionists were divided between those whose priority was to support the government and those who wished to continue the struggle for emancipation from below. The departure of many former union leaders to (well-paid) positions in government or in private industry has compounded the tensions.

Union membership, structure, democracy and effects

Union membership and density

Trade unions are membership organizations – this is part of the meaning of 'continuous association'. Yet levels of membership vary dramatically across countries – far more than virtually any other socio-political indicator ('left' voting, for example). We present statistics for a number of countries in Table 4.1, also indicating the coverage of collective agreements. There are also marked variations within countries (between manual and white-collar workers, public and private sectors, male and female employees, for example). There is a growing fashion for econometric analysis of membership data in an attempt to account for these variations, or to explain changes over time, or both. However, such analysis does not always take adequate account of the limits of national statistics, since these typically derive from unions' own declarations, which may be exaggerated in order to enhance their own status, particularly in countries with rival union organizations seeking to assert their own representativeness. Data may also be drawn from social surveys, though their reliability may also be uncertain, at least for some countries.

Table 4.1 Trade union density and collective bargaining coverage, 1980 and 2010

	Union density		*Bargaining coverage*	
	1980	*2010*	*1980*	*2010*
Denmark	79	68	72	80
Sweden	78	69	85	91
Austria	57	28	95	99
Belgium	54	52	97	96
Germany	35	19	78	62
The Netherlands	35	21	79	82
France	18	8	85	90
Italy	48	33	85	80
UK	51	27	70	33
Ireland	64	37	64	44
USA	22	11	26	13
Japan	31	19	28	16
Brazil	21	29		35
India		7		60
South Africa		30		43

Source: Visser (2011) (ICTWSS Database).

Note: No realistic data available for China and Russia.

For the purpose of comparability, figures are usually presented as percentages of density: the proportion of eligible workers who are unionized. But who is eligible? Most often, the denominator consists of workers in employment; yet in some countries, unions may regard retired and unemployed workers as part of their constituency. In many countries, agricultural workers are barely unionized; hence the size of this sector will bias aggregate statistics. Where there is a high proportion of 'informal' employment, the difficulties are compounded. More elusively, the very meaning of union membership can vary cross-nationally. One reason why union density in Sweden was until recently 80 per cent, as against only 8 per cent in France, is that to become a formal union member in France has traditionally implied a commitment to active participation and engagement, in contrast with Sweden. In France, overall union support is better assessed by voting in workplace elections and by readiness to follow union calls for strike action. One should also add that deciding what collective organizations should count as a trade union is often contentious. Staff associations, or in Germany the federation for civil servants, possess some but not all of the characteristics of a union. As an extreme case, whether the 'official' organization is regarded as a *bona fide* union determines whether China has one of the highest, or one of the lowest, unionization rates in the world.

Despite these reservations, density is usually regarded as an important if imperfect indicator of union strength (Vernon 2006), even though unions may be able to mobilize alternative power resources (Sullivan 2010). Traditionally, the most influential analyses of density were economic in focus, treating changes in the levels of employment or unemployment, or movements in prices and wages, as key causes of fluctuations in union density. We may note such approaches fail to explain trends in the Nordic countries, which are often countercyclical. These trends can best be explained by the key union role in the administration of unemployment benefits (at least until recently), creating a particular incentive to membership in times of rising unemployment. Hence institutional factors are also important, and are the focus of many theories of cross-national differences in unionization, which highlight the effects of government policy and the legal framework, and more general institutional supports for 'union security'. Clegg (1976) stressed the impact of specifically industrial relations determinants, such as employer policies and the structure of collective bargaining. Another factor which recent research has highlighted is social attitudes and the importance of 'social custom' (Visser 2002): where the 'habit' of union membership becomes entrenched it can prove resilient even in an otherwise unfavourable environment. Price and Bain (1983) contrast phases of institutional stability (when econometric models fit) and phases of crisis and innovation (which they term 'paradigm breaks') when other factors are more important.

We must also ask how much unions themselves can influence their fate. Increasingly, the literature addresses how opportunity structures, even if overall unfavourable, nevertheless can offer space for positive outcomes. Reconstructing membership density may be a matter of 'resourcefulness' as well as resources (Ganz 2000).

Trade union structure

All trade union movements contain internal demarcations. These may reflect ideological pluralism (southern Europe and much of the global South); industrial or sectoral boundaries; and occupational status (with divisions between craft and general unions, or manual, white-collar and professional associations). Turner (1962), in a study of British trade unionism, presented a dynamic model in which some organizations based on narrow occupational groupings with a secure labour market status remained exclusive ('closed') whereas others became increasingly inclusive ('open'), creating a tendency towards 'general unionism'. Since he wrote, the latter tendency has been reinforced by structural changes in the economy and labour market: the number of protected occupational groups has dwindled, unions in declining sectors of the economy have been impelled to merge with others to form 'conglomerate' unions.

Historical origin is one important explanation of cross-national variations in structural patterns. For example, in countries which industrialized early, there were more likely to be self-confident craft groups which formed exclusive occupational unions; conversely, the early presence of an influential socialist movement encouraged industrial unionism. Employers organization and policies have also been important: strong sectoral employers associations encouraged integrated counterparts on the union side. Legal regulation of union recognition (certification) and rules on 'representativeness' have in some countries provided obstacles to small occupational unions and provided incentives to the rise of more encompassing organizations. Finally, we should note that powerful centralized union confederations may be able to regulate inter-union demarcations among their affiliates.

Union democracy

Most trade unions insist, with reason, that they are democratic organizations. However, there is great diversity in the formal decision-making structures in unions, both within and between countries: the relative powers of national officers, executive committees and conferences, the degree to which middle-range officials are elected from below, or appointed from above, the balance of authority between peak confederations and their affiliated unions. To some extent, cross-national differences reflect diverse understandings of the meaning of democracy, in general and specifically in the trade union context; but they may also derive from relatively contingent decisions made a century or more ago (for example, unions subject to state repression often adopted highly centralized, almost military methods) which have persisted despite changed circumstances. Unions in some countries (such as Germany or the USA) have a high ratio of paid officials to members, while others depend heavily on 'lay' activists (as in Britain and France); such differences have evident implications for the internal distribution of power.

There is, however, a problematic relationship between formal decision-making structures and the elusive and complex dynamics of real intra-union politics. Famously (or notoriously), Michels (1915: 32) argued (primarily on the basis of German experience) that trade unions and socialist parties, though formally democratic, were subject to an irresistible 'tendency to oligarchy'. Subsequent scholarship (and debate among trade union members themselves) have tended to focus on differences of power and interests within trade unions, but with two contrasting types of emphasis. One is hierarchical, giving primary attention to the roles and influence of leaders and other paid officials, rank-and-file activists and members more generally. This approach has often led to rather polemical arguments concerning the distorting effects of the 'trade union bureaucracy'. A second approach, particularly associated with feminist analyses, focuses on horizontal differences (occupation, sector, gender, age, ethnicity). From this perspective, trade unions not only redistribute power and resources between workers and capitalists but also *within* the working class. Since both paid officials and lay representatives typically derive disproportionately from relatively skilled male native-born sections of the workforce, their distinctive interests often shape the policies of the union as a whole. In recent years, unions in many countries have attempted to implement some form of 'proportionality' – aligning the proportions of women and ethnic minorities among the officers and the membership – in order to address this problem.

A related debate, particularly relevant to any discussion of workplace organization, concerns the issue of centralization as against decentralization in union policy-making. Are decentralized structures more democratic, in that they provide greater scope for membership involvement in decision-making? Such an argument is consistent with participative theories of democracy. But a counter-argument is that (at least beyond a certain point) decentralization precludes overall strategic direction, a particular problem when key employer strategies are increasingly centralized (Streeck 1988). For some analysts, efficiency and democracy in trade unions are incompatible (Child *et al.* 1973). More constructive approaches investigate how the democratic vitality of decentralization and the strategic coherence of centralization might be reconciled; for example, Kjellberg (1983) has argued that Swedish unions combine both authoritative national decision-making *and* workplace-level autonomy over key issues, with close articulation between the two levels providing a source of strength *and* democracy.

What do unions do?

In their US-based discussion, Freeman and Medoff (1984) asked: what do unions do? It is possible to propose a variety of different measures of union achievements. One is the share of wages and salaries in the national income (the division between labour and capital). On this index, unions in most countries have been losing effectiveness together with membership, since the wage share in national income has almost universally declined in the last three decades (Glyn 2006). Another measure is the union 'mark-up': the extent to which wages in firms covered by union organization and/or collective agreements exceed those without. Such a 'mark-up' tends to be greatest where company bargaining is the most important level of pay determination, and far less significant where multi-employer bargaining prevails and agreements are legally extended across whole sectors of the economy (Aidt and Tzannatos 2002).

In countries of the former type, such as the USA and Britain, the evidence suggests a significant decline in the union 'mark-up' in recent years (Metcalf 2005). A third, almost contrary measure is the degree of equalization in wages and conditions of employment. In many countries, unions have traditionally embraced an understanding of 'solidarity' which requires the minimization of differences in rewards based on sector, occupation, gender or employment status; and there is evidence that they have been successful in reducing such differentials, particularly where bargaining is centralized and unions are strong (Vernon 2011).

In some countries, unions may measure their achievements less in terms of collective bargaining outcomes than by the significance of the 'social wage'; here again, the trend to cutbacks in social benefits may be seen as a sign of union weakness. More insubstantial but perhaps no less important is the union role in securing employee rights at work and effective 'voice' over key decisions which affect their employment. Overall, can we conclude that union effectiveness has been declining? Not only are many of these outcomes difficult to measure quantitatively; we must also take account of unions' own objectives before we can measure outcomes against aspirations. We must also factor in the more difficult situations under which unions currently operate (a theme to which we return in the conclusion to this chapter): if the outcomes are unfavourable, would they have been even worse without union representation? Such a counterfactual is impossible to evaluate empirically.

To conclude this section, we should stress that it is risky to treat trade unions as 'actors' (though this can be a useful shorthand, which we ourselves employ in this chapter). Unions are social organizations within which *people* – who have different interests, objectives and power – act collectively. Union policies often emerge in an ad hoc and incremental manner. Cumulatively, the choices of decision-makers in any union (or more broadly, national union movement) shape its identity, the understanding by members, activists and officials of its character and purpose; and such understandings in turn shape future orientations and policies. As we have seen already, the logics of membership and of influence push union policy-makers in contradictory directions, in particular in shaping the balance between cooperation and conflict in collective bargaining and in political change. Their intermediary character also tends to make unions primarily reactive organizations, largely responding to the initiatives of the external actors with which they engage. Is it possible for unions to become proactive, setting the agenda rather than merely responding to one which is externally determined? In other words, can unions become genuinely strategic actors? This is perhaps the most fundamental issue with which trade unions are confronted.

'Non-union' collective representation

Trade unions are indeed not the only mechanism of employee representation. In this section, we focus on other representative institutions at company and workplace level. Analytically it is possible to distinguish two types of 'dual-channel' representation. The first is initiated and controlled by the employer. Since our concern is with institutions which allow employees an independent 'voice', we devote little space to this type. Second, there are mechanisms such as works councils which are at least formally independent of the employer and also separate from trade unions. In practice, however, there may be a close interdependence with union organization; for this reason we place 'non-union' in inverted commas in our section title.

Management-initiated mechanisms are particularly common in the Anglophone countries, where there is no tradition of mandatory works councils and where collective bargaining normally takes place – if at all – at enterprise level. Employers may perceive advantage in union exclusion tactics, and may face few legal obstacles in pursuing these, notably in North

America (Kaufman and Taras 2000). As just indicated, we do not discuss such mechanisms further because we do not consider them vehicles of independent voice, though we must also concede that the question of independence is not straightforward. Where there are competing unions, an employer may have considerable discretion in deciding with which to negotiate; a union may be willing to sign a 'sweetheart' deal as the price of recognition. In many countries, there exist systems in which the employer deducts trade union subscriptions directly from earnings or may even, as in the Netherlands, pay financial subsidies to recognized unions. Much more extensively, trade unions often obtain from an employer a range of facilities: time off work for representatives, office facilities, and so on. Does this compromise trade union independence? Much depends on whether the unions concerned have already achieved representative legitimacy.

Conversely, some workplace mechanisms are explicitly linked to trade unions, such as committees of shop stewards or staff representatives in the UK, and bodies with similar titles in other Anglophone countries. The same is the case in Scandinavia, where employees' workplace interests are typically represented by the unions' local organizations. Single-channel representation is the essence of the Swedish system, for example, the unions' workplace stewards and 'clubs' are the sole institutional intermediary between management and the workforce. However, in 'single-channel' countries there has in recent decades been a trend to the creation of parallel and overlapping 'non-union' structures. In the UK, joint consultation committees exist in 40 per cent of workplaces (Kersley *et al.* 2006: 127). In contrast to experience in North America, these are not typically mechanisms of union exclusion; they are far more likely to exist in workplaces with union recognition, and may serve in practice as a channel through which primarily trade union representatives discuss issues which are not part of the conventional collective bargaining agenda. In the Nordic countries, likewise, there has for some time been a spread of workplace 'cooperation committees'. For example, in Denmark, such committees were first established through a central agreement in 1947; in principle, non-unionists can be elected, but shop stewards typically play a leading role.

We now turn to works councils, defined by Rogers and Streeck (1995: 6) as 'institutionalized bodies for representative communication between a single employer ("management") and the employees ("workforce") of a single plant or enterprise ("workplace")'.

We are concerned with *generalized* systems, where participation structures exist largely independently of management wishes, and not with representative bodies established voluntarily through localized management (or union) initiatives. We also limit attention to bodies with the capacity to discuss a broad range of issues; this means, for example, that statutory health and safety committees, which exist in many countries, are not the focus of our discussion. On this definition, works councils are almost exclusively a phenomenon of continental Western Europe. Works councils differ substantially between countries in their status (established by law or by comprehensive collective agreement), their powers and functions (from information to consultation and – rather infrequently – codetermination) and hence their capacity to exert significant influence over management decision-making, their composition (employee-only, or joint management–worker), and their relationship with trade unions external to the company.

Varieties of works councils

It is common to see independent representation of employee interests within the company as one expression of the 'European social model' – a concept notoriously difficult to define

(Ebbinghaus 1999; Jepsen and Serrano Pascual 2006). An important principle is that firms are social institutions with a variety of stakeholders, not simply economic institutions accountable only to their shareholders; and that employees are thus in an important sense 'citizens' of the company in which they work. This principle is incompatible with the common-law models of company law which prevail in the Anglophone countries.

According to Sorge (1976: 284), works councils tend to be legally mandated where state repression long ago provoked the rise of a radical, indeed revolutionary, labour movement, and governments then had to create order by imposing institutions of workplace employee representation designed to bypass more militant class-wide mobilization. Hence, as Knudsen (1995: 18) suggests, 'the common ground for participation has emerged historically through social compromises which have crystallized from social struggles'; and as Ramsay (1977) argues, there appear to occur 'cycles of control' through which new institutions are created in response to phases of oppositional worker mobilization. We may also note that governments have more recently encouraged participative mechanisms in order to achieve employee support, or at least acquiescence, in productivity-enhancing changes in work organization. Hence there is an inherent ambiguity or contradiction underlying works council systems: they may be seen as designed in part to promote workers' rights by facilitating collective 'voice' over key aspects of the employment relationship, but often to a greater extent are intended to foster industrial peace and productive efficiency when these goals are considered problematic.

National works councils are as diverse as national trade unionisms: this is one reason why it has proved impossible to 'harmonize' representative mechanisms across the European Union (EU). The Information and Consultation Directive adopted in 2002 gives workers in larger companies a right to be informed about the undertaking's economic situation, and informed and consulted about employment prospects and about substantial changes in work organization; it does not, however, prescribe works councils as defined above. Below we summarize the institutional arrangements in a number of countries, explaining their historical evolution and outlining their actual functioning (for more details, see Gumbrell-McCormick and Hyman 2010).

In *Germany*, the rights assigned to employee representatives are usually considered the strongest of any national system. The so-called 'dual system' of employee representation assigns trade unions the right to bargain collectively over terms and conditions of employment, and the monopoly of the strike weapon, while establishing mechanisms of 'codetermination' in individual companies. Provisions in Austria are very similar. Though statutory workplace representation structures date back almost a century, the modern system stems from legislation in 1952. The significance of works councils has, however, altered over time, partly through legislative amendments but primarily through an evolution in the triangular relationship between councils, unions and managements. In all but the smallest companies there is a requirement to establish a works council; and in all firms with over 2,000 employees the latter are represented on the supervisory board, in practice, through a combination of works councillors and outside trade union officials. The public sector has a parallel system of personnel councils. In larger establishments, one or more works councillors have full-time release from their normal work. There are rights to information over a range of business and financial questions, consultation over a broader set of employment matters, and codetermination (giving at least a provisional veto) on hiring and firing, payment and grading systems and the regulation of working time. While councils are mandatory, there is no obligation on the employer to take the initiative to establish one; in practice, many firms, particularly the smallest, lack councils, and the proportion without them is growing.

In many respects the notion of a 'dual system' of industrial relations is a misnomer; in practice, 'the two levels in the dual system are mutually reinforcing' (Thelen 1991: 16). Most councillors (and an even higher proportion of council presidents) are unionists, typically elected on a union 'slate'. Given the (almost) unitary trade union structure in Germany, elections are not normally an arena of inter-union competition as in many other countries. Unions require the councils to provide a channel of information and communication, to monitor the application of collective agreements, and often to help with recruitment; councils need the union for training, information and advice, and as a source of legitimacy in defending broad collective principles against the particularistic interests of their constituents. Nevertheless, one should not assume that the strong works council functioning as the extended arm of the union is the norm. There is a growing 'exclusion zone' of firms covered neither by a collective agreement nor by a works council, encompassing a high proportion of workplaces, but (since the traditional institutions are still firmly established in larger firms) a far smaller proportion of employees.

In *the Netherlands*, works councils were legally constituted in 1950; after changes to the law in 1971 there was a considerable expansion in numbers, and today the Netherlands has one of the highest rates of coverage of works councils. In addition, one-third of establishments with fewer than 50 employees have a 'personnel delegation', according to a provision created in 1998. Works councils have considerable powers. Their right to information and consultation is very broad; they monitor the firm's implementation of legislation on equal opportunities, health and safety and other work-related areas; enjoy consultation rights on economic and financial matters; and they have codetermination rights over pension insurance, the arrangement of working hours and holidays, health and safety, and rules concerning hiring, firing, promotion, training and grievance handling. In disagreements over plans for restructuring or redundancies, the employer must postpone their implementation while an amicable solution is sought. This 'capacity to create negative dilemmas for management' is often used by councils as a bargaining chip in order to influence 'strategic policy issues', without actually having to invoke the formal power of appeal (Teulings 1989: 81). Recently, however, there has been concern that their effectiveness is under threat from the internationalization of ownership, which means that strategic decisions are increasingly taken outside the Netherlands; and from decentralization of decision-making *within* companies, including mechanisms for direct employee participation.

In *Belgium*, the main institutions of workplace employee representation were established by law in 1948. Works councils are strongly integrated into the system of industrial relations and are accepted by both sides of industry, although there are disagreements over their powers and the rules regulating them. Their powers include the right to receive information on economic and financial matters; consultation on work organization, working conditions, new technology, training, restructuring, collective redundancies, early retirement and closure; codetermination on criteria for dismissal and re-employment, work rules, annual holidays and paid study leave; and monitoring of the application of social legislation, re-deployment of disabled workers, vocational skills criteria and the employment of young workers. Following the closure of Renault's Vilvoorde plant without proper consultation, the 'Renault' law of 1998 tightened the mandatory consultation procedure and strengthened the sanctions against any breach (Delbar 2003). Since 1996, companies have been required to discuss detailed annual company reports or 'social balance sheets' with their councils. On some issues, councils often wield considerable influence. Their operation is rarely confrontational, and they concentrate on financial and economic information, consultation on work rules, hiring and dismissal procedures.

The Mediterranean countries are marked by a history of adversarial industrial relations and intense social and political cleavages, with fascist dictatorships in the cases of Italy, Portugal and Spain. In France, as in these other countries, Communist parties were for decades the strongest in Western Europe, and the trade unions linked to these parties were, at least for a period, the largest within ideologically divided labour movements. Some form of works council system is legally mandated in all four countries; not surprisingly, the context often makes their functioning problematic.

In *France*, the mechanism of 'personnel delegates' was established by the 'Popular Front' government in 1936: they represent employees (individually or collectively) with grievances regarding the application of legal or contractual rules, meeting the employer on a monthly basis (Tchobanian 1995: 117). They have no bargaining powers and no formal links to trade unions, though practice is often very different. Legislation was adopted in 1946 creating works committees as a forum for information and consultation on social and economic matters between the employer, who chairs the committee, and elected employee representatives. They lack formal bargaining powers and have no codetermination rights; often their main role is to manage social and welfare activities, with a budget provided by the company. The officially recognized 'representative' unions have a privileged role: they alone can nominate candidates in the first round of elections, and only if these fail to attract half the available votes is there a second round open to all. Following the mass social protests and general strike of May 1968, further legislation enabled unions to appoint workplace delegates and branches. Formally the coverage of these institutions is extensive – higher than in Germany, particularly in smaller firms. Even in small workplaces, formal trade union representation is the norm (Dufour *et al.* 2004: 15). Yet Andolfatto and Labbé (2000: 49–50, 111) report that workplace representatives are ageing, and fewer activists combine more tasks. This results in a 'professionalization of representation', with declining contact with the workforce. On this reading, the whole structure of collective representation has become a façade while workplace reality involves a new managerialism (Goyer and Hancké 2005: 176, 189–93).

In *Spain*, the institutions of workplace representation resemble those described below in the case of France: personnel delegates, works committees and trade union delegates, with relatively significant formal rights assigned by legislation in 1980 and 1986. While there is in principle a 'dual system', in practice, the former two institutions are closely integrated with the two main unions, and indeed provide a forum within which they can reconcile their different priorities (Martínez Lucio 1992: 501; Escobar 1995: 183).

In *Portugal*, the Constitution gives employees the right 'to create workers' commissions for the defence of their interests and democratic involvement in the workplace'. However, employers and unions have few incentives to make this right effective. Coverage is patchy, and most of those that exist on paper are inactive (Barreto and Naumann 1998: 415).

In *Greece*, with many background similarities to the other Mediterranean countries, the law provides for voluntary works councils; neither employers nor unions have shown any enthusiasm for the institution, and scarcely any have been established (Broughton 2005: 214–15).

In *Italy*, in contrast to the other Mediterranean countries, there exist functional equivalents of works councils which wield considerable codetermination capacity. After the 'hot autumn' of 1969, when rank-and-file factory councils became widespread, the 1970 Workers' Statute introduced the notion of a workplace trade union representative structure with an array of legal prerogatives and protections, but without defining the nature or composition of the new mechanisms. Following a tripartite national agreement in 1993 – a characteristically Italian process whereby collective bargaining gives detailed shape to legal prescription – the status of the workplace structures has been more clearly prescribed, under the revised title *rappresentanza sindacale unitaria.* Two-thirds of the members are directly elected by the workforce, but the other third is nominated, in effect, by the main confederations. Hence elements of single- and dual-channel systems are combined. In the public sector, however, all delegates are directly elected. There is a lack of official statistics on their extent, but there is a broad consensus that a large majority of employees in all but the smallest firms are covered (Muratore 2003). Even more than in other countries, a 'dual channel' system is effectively union-controlled; and the particularly strong rights enjoyed by union delegates under the 1970 legislation result in an unusually powerful representative mechanism.

As we have noted, works councils as defined above are widespread in continental Europe but extremely rare elsewhere. In the *USA*, where the Commission on the Future of Worker-Management Relations (the Dunlop Commission) was established in 1993 to propose solutions to the widening 'representation gap', its report did not even consider the possibility of legislation on works councils. In other non-European countries, where council-like structures have been established it has typically been in emulation of European models, often to little effect. Perhaps the one clear exception is *South Korea,* where labour-management councils have been obligatory in larger firms since 1980; they do appear to function relatively effectively (Kato *et al.* 2005; Kleiner and Lee 1997).

Even within Europe, councils are far from universal. British employers overwhelmingly regard mandatory councils as a challenge to their own managerial prerogatives – and lobbied powerfully against the adoption of any EU Directive on works councils; most unions have also considered them a threat to their 'single channel' of representation. In the countries of Central and Eastern Europe which joined the EU in 2004, the principle of joint employee–management structures was typically rejected after 1989; unfettered managerial prerogative was commonly regarded as an essential element in the invention of a market economy. One exception is Hungary, where mandatory works councils were introduced in 1992 under the influence of German experience; but their functions are purely informational and consultative, and most observers consider their significance limited (Tóth 1997; Frege 2002). In some other countries (for example, the Czech Republic), the law permits the formation of councils on a voluntary basis. Almost certainly the closest to a Western European 'strong' works council system is in Slovenia, in part, perhaps because of popular attachment to the former Yugoslav tradition of self-management (Stanojević 2003).

Comparing and contrasting

Works councils in Europe share largely similar origins, in the sense that most came about in response to major conflicts between labour and capital. Their aims were shaped by their origins: to restore or preserve industrial and social peace, by giving workers a stake in society and a voice at the workplace. But they differ greatly in terms of their composition, modes of selection, powers and responsibilities and links to the remaining institutions of the industrial relations system in each country. There are also important differences between formal provisions and actual practice, as well as in their actual coverage; as a recent survey concluded (Bryson *et al.* 2012: 58), 'one of the most striking findings . . . is the degree to which the incidence of workplace representation varies within and across EU countries'.

One simple distinction is between national systems established by law and those that are the outcome of peak-level collective agreement (which may in turn possess legally binding status), but reality is rather more complex. Certainly the Dutch, French and German systems are legislatively based (even if the law to some extent gave force to the wishes of the 'social partners'). But in Italy the two processes have interacted; likewise in Belgium, councils were established by law in 1948, but this resulted from a peak-level agreement, as did many subsequent amendments.

According to the definition we have adopted, works councils are *mandatory* bodies. However, there are at least four qualifications to be made. First, there is normally a size threshold for the requirement to take effect. As we have seen, in Germany it is only five, although councils take on additional functions and powers as the workforce grows; in Italy it is 15; in most other countries it is 50. Second, establishing a council often requires some form of 'trigger'. The Belgian and French systems put the onus on the employer to hold 'social elections', whereas there is no such automatic obligation in Germany and the Netherlands. Rather, the workforce (in Germany this requires only three employees to act) or a trade union must take the initiative. The same is the case in Italy. In smaller firms in particular, the 'default option' of no works council tends to prevail. There is a lack of reliable data for most countries, and it appears that patterns are highly uneven. The lower the size threshold, the higher the proportion of firms (though less so of employees) without works councils even though covered by the law. Germany is a striking example: councils exist in only 11 per cent of eligible firms and establishments (Carley *et al.* 2005: 24), though they cover roughly half the eligible workforce.

Third, works councils require the employer's cooperation in order to function effectively. It takes two to engage in meaningful information and consultation, let alone codetermination. Most legal prescriptions require that information on the specified issues be provided accurately and in good time, and that the employer consult in good faith before taking final decisions. But it typically takes a qualitative judgement to assess whether an employer has genuinely complied. Even more fundamentally, protection is needed for employees who initiate the creation of a works council, stand for election as councillor or some other type of delegate, and exercise their functions if elected. This leads to the fourth qualification: requirements have to be observed voluntarily or else enforced. What *sanctions* are available to persuade recalcitrant employers to establish a works council, subject to the necessary 'triggers'; to provide the specified information and engage properly in consultation; and more fundamentally, to refrain from victimization of employee representatives or those who seek to exercise their legal rights? More specifically, who is responsible for complaining if an employer breaches the law (or legally binding agreement)?; in what type of court?; what is the delay before a case is heard?; what penalties may be imposed if the employer is found guilty?; and what happens if the employer then fails to comply with the judgment of the court? In general, European countries possess labour inspectorates who can initiate prosecutions, but normally on individual rather than collective issues; hence typically it is up to aggrieved employees, or their union, to bring complaints. Most countries (though not, for example, the Netherlands) have specialized labour courts or tribunals which can often provide speedier decisions than the normal courts. In theory, penalties can be significant: for example, in France, Germany and Italy, an employer in serious breach of the law is liable not only to a substantial fine but even to a year's imprisonment. Some local magistrates in Italy may be prepared to utilize draconian powers, but in general it seems that the penalties for non-compliance are in practice relatively trivial, at least for a large and wealthy company.

The *composition* of the councils and the *number* of councillors are important variables. In Germany and Italy, all councillors, including the chair, are representatives of the employees. Belgium and France have joint councils, and the employer acts as chair; this was also the case in the Netherlands until the law of 1979 brought the Dutch system more into line with the German. *Election* by the workforce is the most common form of selection, although some employee representatives (for example, representatives of trade union confederations in Italy) are appointed, as are most management representatives. Elections are usually open to all employees, but this is often qualified by length of service (usually six months to one year), age (over 16 or 18), and sometimes by contractual status (full-time, or with permanent contracts).

We have already emphasized the complex relationship between *councils* and *unions*. It is common to distinguish where unions and councils have distinct bases of representation. As our national accounts show, the dichotomy between single- and dual-channel systems is by no means clear-cut in practice. There is usually an institutional separation, but this is qualified in different ways. In part, this is true even at the formal level, in particular as concerns electoral arrangements. In Belgium, nominations are restricted to union-sponsored lists; in France, the same is true unless the union nominees fail to obtain the votes of a majority of the electorate in the first round of elections (as often happens). In both Germany and the Netherlands, candidates may be nominated either by groups of employees or by unions with members in the workplace. The Italian system is a hybrid, since (in the private sector) the unions can directly appoint a third of the representatives as well as submitting lists of candidates for the other seats. The law may also prescribe working relationships between councils and unions, for example, in Germany an outside union official can participate in the activities of the *Betriebsrat* if a quarter of its members so request. Dufour and Hege have argued (2002: 171) that 'effective representation normally depends on resources extending well beyond formal rights'; and in terms of informal operation, the union—council link is typically intimate. In the day-to-day work of representation there is a general need for mutual support, which is one reason why, in France, many of those elected to *comités* as non-unionists subsequently affiliate with one or other confederation. As a corollary, the fear often expressed that works councils may supplant employees' attachment to trade unionism is probably misplaced. As Brewster *et al.* conclude (2007: 69):

> It is clear that a central concern for unions should not be whether the one form of representation erodes the other. Rather, it is what is *done* on these respective bodies that should be their main preoccupation.

This is certainly the case with European Works Councils (EWCs), which an EU Directive made mandatory in 1994 in 'Community-scale' enterprises (with at least 1000 employees across the EU, including 150 in at least two countries). This was, however, subject to a complex 'trigger' mechanism. There was no formal link to trade unions (though this was changed when the Directive was 'recast' in 2009). Calling EWCs 'works councils' is in many respects a misnomer (Streeck 1997): what is mandated is merely a 'transnational information and consultation procedure', which need be convened only once a year (apart from 'exceptional circumstances'). Either because of management resistance, lack of enthusiasm among national worker representatives, or the inability to coordinate an effective 'trigger', coverage is patchy: currently they exist in just under 1,000 of some 2,400 eligible enterprises – though these tend to be the larger companies.

Where EWCs do exist, are they mere token mechanisms, adjuncts to national procedures in the company's home country, or a basis for genuine transnational industrial relations? There is considerable diversity of experience in the limited period of their operation. However, most research has been sceptical, suggesting that most EWCs are either marginalized by management, or else incorporated in a process of instilling the 'company culture'; that problems of language and of different national industrial relations backgrounds inhibit cross-national unity among employee representatives; and in addition, that at times of restructuring and redundancy, representatives are often preoccupied with defending their 'national interests' (Fitzgerald and Stirling 2004; Whittall *et al.* 2007; Waddington 2010). The key issue is whether these are predictable 'teething problems' for any new institution, or whether they reflect fundamental design faults.

Institutional continuity and change

What is the future for collective representation in times of globalization and economic crisis? In general, the formal status of existing institutions – both trade unions and works councils – seems resilient. Yet it is clear that representative institutions operate today in a hostile environment. There has been an occupational and sectoral restructuring of employment towards situations which traditionally have been poorly organized (a continuation or acceleration of long-term trends). The coercive impact of international competitiveness has resulted in adverse labour markets and in major obstacles to real improvements in conditions of employment through collective bargaining. Privatization and budgetary restraints in the public sector have undermined the basis for once advantageous opportunities for employee voice and security. All these factors lie behind the almost universal decline in union membership.

At workplace level, works councils are engaged in a complex and problematic balancing act. First, their primary relationship is with the employees whom they represent: articulating their wishes and interests, and in the process redefining these. The very notion of representativeness, as we have seen, can be deeply ambiguous. Second, they are interlocutors of management; but this relationship can be precarious and contradictory. Third, those workplace representatives who are subject to external union authority nevertheless exercise some autonomy, while those who are in theory independent nevertheless typically depend on external union organization for support and legitimation. Negotiating this complex three-way relationship is difficult at the best of times; but it has become increasingly precarious in recent years, as a result of interlocking changes in work organization, the structure of employment, corporate ownership and the global economy.

The impact of economic globalization is pervasive: above all, in the overriding compulsion of competitiveness. Consensus in one workplace – the original official rationale of works council systems – is all too easily transformed into concession bargaining, as managements force local representatives into a competitive process of acquiescence in a drive for reduced labour costs. The implication is that the only employee interest which can be effectively defended is to avoid plant closure and minimize job losses.

In the last decades of the twentieth century, there were ambitious projects in many of the countries we have discussed for unions and works councils to articulate new, 'qualitative' demands and to engage proactively in reshaping the work environment and working life more generally. It would be a sad paradox if the trend in the twenty-first is towards more sophisticated mechanisms of employee voice but diminished influence over management decisions.

References

Aidt, T. and Tzannatos, Z. (2002) *Unions and Collective Bargaining*, Washington DC: World Bank.

Andolfatto, D. and Labbé, D. (2000) *Sociologie des syndicats*, Paris: La Découverte.

Avdagic, S., Rhodes, M. and Visser, J. (eds) (2011) *Social Pacts in Europe: Emergence, Evolution, and Institutionalization*, Oxford: Oxford University Press.

Baglioni, G. (1987) 'Constants and variants in political exchange', *Labour*, 1(3): 57–94.

Barreto, J. and Naumann, R. (1998) 'Portugal: industrial relations under democracy', in A. Ferner and R. Hyman (eds) *Changing Industrial Relations in Europe*, Oxford: Blackwell.

Brewster, C., Wood, G., Croucher, R. and Brookes, M. (2007) 'Are works councils and joint consultative committees a threat to trade unions? A comparative analysis', *Economic and Industrial Democracy*, 28(1): 49–77.

Broughton, A. (2005) 'European comparative practice in information and consultation', in J. Storey (ed.) *Adding Value through Information and Consultation*, Basingstoke: Palgrave Macmillan.

Bryson, A., Forth, J. and George, A. (2012) *Workplace Employee Representation in Europe*, Dublin: European Foundation.

Carley, M., Baradel, A. and Welz, C. (2005) *Works Councils: Workplace Representation and Participation Structures*, Dublin: European Foundation.

Child, J., Loveridge, R. and Warner, M. (1973) 'Towards an organizational study of trade unions', *Sociology*, 7(1): 71–91.

Clegg, H.A. (1976) *Trade Unionism under Collective Bargaining*, Oxford: Blackwell.

Crouch, C. (1993) *Industrial Relations and European State Traditions*, Oxford: Clarendon Press.

Delbar, C. (2003) *Works Councils and Other Workplace Employee Representation and Participation Structures: Belgium*. Available at: http://www.eurofound.europa.eu/eiro/2003/09/tfeature/be0309304t.htm (accessed 25 May 2012).

Dufour, C. and Hege, A. (2002) *L'Europe Syndicale: La représentation des salariés en France, Allemagne, Grande-Bretagne et Italie*, Brussels: P.I.E.-Peter Lang.

Dufour, C., Hege, A., Malan, A. and Zouary, P. (2004) *Post-enquête Réponse*, Noisy-le-Grand: IRES.

Ebbinghaus, B. (1999) 'Does a European social model exist and can it survive?', in G. Huemer, M. Mesch and F. Traxler (eds) *The Role of Employer Associations and Labour Unions in the EMU*, Aldershot: Ashgate.

Escobar, M. (1995) 'Spain: works councils or unions', in J. Rogers and W. Streeck (eds) *Works Councils: Consultation, Representation and Cooperation in Industrial Relations*, Chicago: University of Chicago Press.

Fitzgerald, I. and Stirling, J. (eds) (2004) *European Works Councils: Pessimism of the Intellect, Optimism of the Will?*, London: Routledge.

Flanders, A. (1970) *Management and Unions*, London: Faber.

Freeman, R.B. and Medoff, J.L. (1984) *What Do Unions Do?*, New York: Basic Books.

Frege, C. M. (2002) 'A critical assessment of the theoretical and empirical research on German works councils', *British Journal of Industrial Relations*, 40(2): 241–59.

Ganz, M. (2000) 'Resources and resourcefulness: strategic capacity in the unionization of California', *American Journal of Sociology*, 105(4): 1003–62.

Glyn, A. (2006) *Capitalism Unleashed: Finance, Globalization, and Welfare*, Oxford: Oxford University Press.

Goyer, M. and Hancké, B. (2005) 'Labour in French corporate governance: the missing link', in H. Gospel and A. Pendleton (eds) *Corporate Governance and Labour Management*, Oxford: Oxford University Press.

Gumbrell-McCormick, R. and Hyman, R. (2010) 'Works councils: the European model of industrial democracy?', in A. Wilkinson, P. Gollan, M. Marchington and D. Lewin (eds) *The Oxford Handbook of Participation in Organizations*, Oxford: Oxford University Press.

Hyman, R. (2001) *Understanding European Trade Unionism: Between Market, Class and Society*, London: Sage.

—— and Gumbrell-McCormick, R. (2010) 'Trade unions, politics and parties: is a new configuration possible?', *Transfer*, 16(2): 315–31.

Jepsen, M. and Serrano Pascual, A. (eds) (2006) *Unwrapping the European Social Model*, Bristol: Policy Press.

Kato, T., Lee, J., Lee, K.-S. and Ryu, J.-S. (2005) 'Employee participation and involvement in Korea: evidence from a new survey and field research', *International Economic Journal*, 19(2): 251–81.

Kaufman, B. E. and Taras, D. G. (eds) (2000) *Nonunion Employee Representation: History, Contemporary Practice and Policy*, Armonk, NY: M.E. Sharpe.

Kersley, B., Alpin, C., Forth, J., Bryson, A., Bewley, H., Dix, G. and Oxenbridge, S. (2006) *Inside the Workplace: Findings from the 2004 Workplace Employment Relations Survey*, London: Routledge.

Kjellberg, A. (1983) *Facklig Organisering I Tolv Länder*, Lund: Arkiv.

Kleiner, M. M. and Lee, Y.-M. (1997) 'Works councils and unionization: lessons from South Korea', *Industrial Relations*, 36(1): 1–16.

Knudsen, H. (1995) *Employee Participation in Europe*, London: Sage.

Locke, R. and Thelen, K. (1995) 'Apples and oranges revisited: contextualized comparisons and the study of comparative labor politics', *Politics and Society*, 23(3): 337–67.

Martinez Lucio, M. (1992) 'Spain: constructing institutions and actors in a context of change', in A. Ferner and R. Hyman (eds) *Industrial Relations in the New Europe*, Oxford: Basil Blackwell.

Metcalf, D. (2005) 'Trade unions: resurgence or perdition?', in S. Fernie and D. Metcalf (eds) *Trade Unions: Resurgence or Demise?*, London: Routledge.

Michels, R. (1915) *Political Parties*, New York: Hearst's.

Mills, C. W. (1948) *The New Men of Power*, New York: Harcourt Brace.

Müller-Jentsch, W. (1985) 'Trade unions as intermediary organizations', *Economic and Industrial Democracy*, 6(1): 3–33.

Muratore, L. (2003) *Works Councils and Other Workplace Employee Representation and Participation Structures: Italy*. Available at: http://www.eurofound.europa.eu/eiro/2003/09/tfeature/it0309304t.htm (accessed 10 June 2012).

Olson, M. (1965) *The Logic of Collective Action*, Cambridge, MA: Harvard University Press.

Pizzorno, A. (1978) 'Political exchange and collective identity', in C. Crouch and A. Pizzorno (eds) *The Resurgence of Class Conflict in Western Europe Since 1968*: vol. 2, *Comparative Analysis*, London: Macmillan.

Price, R. and Bain, G. (1983) 'Union growth in Britain: retrospect and prospect', *British Journal of Industrial Relations*, 21(1): 46–68.

Ramsay, H. (1977) 'Cycles of control: worker participation in sociological and historical perspective', *Sociology*, 1(3): 481–506.

Regini, M. (1995) *Uncertain Boundaries: The Social and Political Construction of European Economies*, Cambridge: Cambridge University Press.

Rogers, J. and Streeck, W. (1995) 'The study of works councils: concepts and problems', in J. Rogers and W. Streeck (eds) *Works Councils: Consultation, Representation and Cooperation in Industrial Relations*, Chicago: University of Chicago Press.

Schmitter, P. and Streeck, W. (1981) *The Organization of Business Interests: A Research Design to Study the Associative Action of Business in the Advanced Industrial Societies of Western Europe*, Berlin: WZB.

Seidman, G.W. (1994) *Manufacturing Militance: Workers' Movements in Brazil and South Africa, 1970–1985*, Berkeley, CA: University of California Press.

Sorge, A. (1976) 'The evolution of industrial democracy in the countries of the European Community', *British Journal of Industrial Relations*, 14(3): 274–94.

Stanojević, M. (2003) 'Workers' power in transition economies: the cases of Serbia and Slovenia', *European Journal of Industrial Relations*, 9(3): 283–301.

Streeck, W. (1988) 'Editorial introduction', *Economic and Industrial Democracy*, 9(3): 307–18.

—— (1997) 'Neither European nor works councils', *Economic and Industrial Democracy*, 18(2): 325–37.

Sullivan, R. (2010) 'Labour market or labour movement? The union density bias as a barrier to labour renewal', *Work, Employment and Society*, 42(1): 145–56.

Tchobanian, R. (1995) 'France: from conflict to social dialogue?', in J. Rogers and W. Streeck (eds) *Works Councils: Consultation, Representation and Cooperation in Industrial Relations*, Chicago: University of Chicago Press.

Teulings, A.W.M. (1989) 'A political bargaining theory of codetermination' in G. Széll, P. Blyton and C. Cornforth (eds) *The State, Trade Unions and Self-Management*, Berlin: de Gruyter.

Thelen, K. A. (1991) *Union of Parts: Labor Politics in Postwar Germany*, Ithaca, NY: Cornell University Press.

Tóth, A. (1997) 'The invention of works councils in Hungary', *European Journal of Industrial Relations*, 3(2): 161–81.

Turner, H.A. (1962) *Trade Union Growth, Structure and Policy*, London: Allen and Unwin.

Vernon, G. (2006) 'Does density matter? The significance of comparative historical variation in unionization', *European Journal of Industrial Relations*, 12(2): 189–209.

—— (2011) 'Still accounting for difference? Cross-national comparative joint regulation and pay inequality', *Economic and Industrial Democracy*, 32(1): 29–46.

Visser, J. (2002) 'Why fewer workers join unions in Europe: a social custom explanation of membership trends', *British Journal of Industrial Relations*, 40(3): 403–30.

—— (2011) *ICTWSS Database*. Available at: http://www.uva-aias.net/208 (accessed 10 June 2012).

Waddington, J. (2010) *European Works Councils and Industrial Relations*, London: Routledge.

Webb, S. and Webb, B. (1894) *History of Trade Unionism*, London: Longmans.

—— (1897) *Industrial Democracy*, London: Longmans.

Whittall, M., Knudsen, H. and Huijgen, F. (eds) (2007) *Towards a European Labour Identity: The Case of the European Works Council*, London: Routledge.

Windolf, P. (1989) 'Productivity coalitions and the future of European corporatism', *Industrial Relations*, 28(1): 1–20.

5 The experience of work in comparative perspective

Patrick McGovern

Introduction

'How was your day?' or 'Did you have a good day?' are familiar questions in our everyday lives. University students chatting about their part-time jobs on the way home from the library, young professionals commuting back to the suburbs or families sitting down to an evening meal regularly revisit their daily experience of work with all its frustrations, challenges and moments of achievement. Significantly, our interest in the experience of work has also spread into our leisure and consumption habits. Television companies now offer a regular diet of documentary-style reality TV series that follow the daily activities of a remarkably wide variety of occupations including airport check-in staff, ocean fishermen, lifeguards and, of course, police officers (e.g. *Airport*, BBC, UK; *Bondi Rescue*, Channel Ten, Australia; *Deadliest Catch*, Discovery Channel, USA; *COPS*, Fox TV, USA). Work and our reactions to the demands, dangers and dramas of the workplace seem to be more popular than ever.

There is, of course, a voluminous social science literature on the subjective experience of work. A now-dated review of quantitative research on the subject found that there were nearly 250 measures covering everything from alienation to work values (see Cook *et al.* 1981). However, what must be emphasized here is that the *experience of work* is a conventional term or phrase from everyday language rather than a formal social science concept. In other words, it has neither an agreed definition nor a common set of indicators, not to mention evidence from construct validity tests, to assure social scientists that they are indeed measuring a specific social phenomenon. Instead, the phrase is interpreted rather loosely so that it may, for example, include research by psychologists on job satisfaction, sociologists on skill levels and organizational behaviour specialists on group dynamics.

The field of enquiry traditionally known as industrial relations has had only a limited interest in the experience of work. For the most part, this was restricted to trade unions, collective bargaining and union–management relations (Kelly 1998; Frege 2007). Even then, the experience of work was only of interest in so far as it generated the kind of workplace discontent that led to the organization and mobilization of workers through trade unions. With the collapse in trade union membership across Europe and North America, notably in the private sector, and the rise of human resource management, the future of industrial relations as an academic area of enquiry has been questioned. In response, a number of prominent scholars have called for the subject to be recast with a more broadly conceived focus on the employment relationship and related labour problems. This change would be marked by the adoption of the new label of *employment relations* which would also help distinguish it from the earlier association with manufacturing and smoke-stack industries generally (Edwards 2003; Frege 2007). Such a recasting would also mean that the organization and the experience of work would play a more central role, such as in debates about high performance work systems (Godard and Delaney 2000).

Nevertheless, it is worth remembering that one of the characteristics of an applied area such as industrial relations is that it tends to engage with what governments or the general public deem to be a *social problem*, with one of the most well-known and controversial examples being that of strikes (Hyman 1984: 145–56). What this means is that the field of inquiry is occasionally broadened to address issues beyond the traditional agenda of trade union organization, collective bargaining and union–management relations. One such example is working time. Industrial relations researchers have, for instance, examined campaigns to reduce working hours, notably as a means of reducing unemployment by sharing work, as well as the use of flexible working hours policies that seek to promote greater work–life balance (Blyton 2008). Later in this chapter I shall examine the question of work–life balance because it raises an enduring problem that is central to the experience of work. Specifically, is it possible for workers to have children and raise a family, given the demands of their jobs? Or, as it is often expressed, do women have to choose between having a career and having children?

In the next section I shall review some of the arguments in psychology and sociology on the importance of work and on the changing nature of employment. Here I raise the troubling question of whether, and to what extent, employees can be satisfied by the kind of work that is produced within the constraints of a market economy. This leads to a discussion of different kinds of market economies, which I shall briefly explore through two of the major comparative perspectives on capitalism and employment relations. The second half of the chapter reviews the contemporary cross-national evidence on some select aspects of the experience of work. Specifically, I examine the emerging evidence on skill and occupational change, job satisfaction, effort, and finally the public policy-related problem of work–life balance.

Why work matters

Aside from the 'dismal science' of economics, where work is viewed as a sacrifice that people make in order to enjoy the benefits of an income, the importance of the experience of work has long been recognized across the social sciences. Jahoda's pioneering research on the unemployed during the 1920s found that work provides a sense of self-worth, a connection to the wider community, and a means for individuals to structure their time. Apart from suffering the hardship of being without an income, the unemployed were also more likely to experience a growing sense of social isolation and a loss of self-esteem while also being more prone to mental illness (Jahoda *et al.* 1972). Since then numerous studies have confirmed the overwhelming importance of work as a central life interest, as a source of identity and social status, and as an influence on general well-being (Treiman 1977; MOW International Research Team 1987; Marmot 2004).

For psychologists, the intrinsic content of work, notably in the form of task and job design, has been a major theme in some of the most influential contributions within industrial and organizational psychology. The most sophisticated recent example is probably the celebrated *job characteristics theory* of Hackman and Oldham which contends that employees are motivated by intrinsic satisfaction and, furthermore, that all jobs can be (re)designed to increase their motivational potential. To this end, they claim to have identified the five core characteristics that can be used to motivate employees in any job: skill variety, task identity, task significance, autonomy and job feedback. The first three, namely skill variety, task identity and task significance, help employees feel that their work is meaningful, while autonomy encourages a sense of responsibility. Job feedback should help employees appreciate the overall impact of their efforts. Hackman and Oldham's (1975, 1980) originality stems from the claim that these characteristics could be brought together to create a measure of motivational potential that would help design jobs with higher levels of satisfaction and performance. One of the obvious achievements of their theory was to place job design at the centre of the study of job satisfaction and motivation while simultaneously offering managers a theory with practical applications. Not surprisingly, it subsequently informed the job redesign movement of the 1970s and 1980s as it sought to create a happy marriage between job satisfaction and organisational performance (Kelly 1982; Parker and Wall 1998).

However, these theories and their associated research programmes, which had the explicit aim of helping employers raise productivity through increased satisfaction, have been challenged by both psychologists and sociologists. Psychologists argue that job satisfaction is an unnecessarily simplistic measure that captures a relatively narrow range of emotional responses to work. It fails, for instance, to measure the extent to which jobs even arouse an emotional response not to mention whether this might be one of 'displeasure' or 'pleasure' (Warr 1987). Moreover, the very relationship between satisfaction and job performance raises the old chicken-and-egg question of which came first: increases in satisfaction or increases in performance? Rather than satisfaction leading to higher performance, it might actually stem from relatively low levels of performance. For instance, employees may take satisfaction from the very fact that they occupy jobs that are not very strenuous but pay very well (Hodson 1991).

This takes us to one of the standard criticisms from sociologists, which is that job satisfaction does not consider what it is that workers want from work and the role that work plays in their lives. These expectations, or 'prior orientations', may mean that even assembly line workers doing tedious repetitive tasks may report relatively high levels of satisfaction precisely because they chose jobs with high wages to support their family-centred lifestyles (Goldthorpe *et al.* 1968). Or, to put it another way, those who work mainly for instrumental reasons may report greater levels of satisfaction than more career-minded colleagues with higher aspirations. This, indeed, is one of the explanations for the now well-established finding that women in part-time jobs have surprisingly high levels of job satisfaction compared with women or men in full-time employment. Many of these workers may see their primary identity as mothers and so their jobs are viewed positively as a welcome opportunity to provide a supplementary income for the household (Hakim 1991; Clark 1997).

The second major criticism directed at this well-meaning psychological humanism is that 'a fortuitous concurrence exists between individual and organizational needs' so that the interests of employers and employees are always perfectly aligned (Rose 1988: 193). The belief that both parties would gain equally from the satisfaction–performance relationship assumes that 'happy cows' would or should give more milk simply because they are being made to feel somewhat satisfied rather than because they are getting more fodder. While sociologists acknowledge that employers and workers share overlapping goals, such as the efficient functioning and survival of the organization, they also emphasize the existence of an enduring conflict over the distribution of income earned by the enterprise (i.e. the relative share of the economic cake to be divided between the employer and the employees). At the heart of this distributional conflict lies the concept of the *effort bargain*, which is the often implicit agreement about the level of effort to be exchanged for the level of reward (Baldamus 1961). Accordingly, schemes to improve satisfaction through job enrichment, for example, are both naïve in conceptualization and vulnerable in practice because they invariably mean that effort bargain is being altered so that workers are being asked to work harder without getting matching increases in pay (Kelly 1982: 170–203; Thompson 1983: 138–42).

For sociologists, one of the reasons the organization of work became a major interest was precisely because of its contested nature. Perhaps the best-known example is the debate about the *deskilling thesis* which the Marxist and former craft-worker Harry Braverman set out in his influential *Labor and Monopoly Capital* (1974). Aside from the fact that Braverman's background gave the book a ring of authenticity, one of the reasons for its remarkable success was that it resurrected some old questions with a vengeance. Can humans fulfil their potential within industrial society? Or do capitalist forms of work organization, which are derived from the dictates of profit-making, strip workers of their skills and pride? Above all, must capitalism inevitably lead to the degradation of labour? Braverman's basic premise is that employers are intent on establishing complete control over the workforce. While this desire may have started as a means of increasing profit, notably through Frederick 'Speedy' Taylor's system of *scientific management* (Rose 1988: 23–47), it became infused with the political aim of subduing the working class in order to remove any threat to the capitalist system. One of the key mechanisms used by employers was what Braverman termed the *separation of conception from execution*. In effect, this principle sought to remove all knowledge of work organization from the factory floor and place it in the hands of management who would specify precisely what needed to be done, how it should be undertaken, and the speed at which it should be completed. The result would be a highly simplified, sub-divided, and specialized set of tasks that, when allied to *time and motion* studies, would create what Taylor considered to be the 'one best way' of organizing work. For Braverman, however, it represented the deskilling and dehumanization of workers who would gradually be reduced from skilled artisans to little more than assembly line machines.

Though frequently overlooked, Braverman's Marxist analysis sought to relate these developments to changes in the class structure and within capitalism generally. He was convinced that the ranks of the working class would expand as the inherent tendency to deskill would create an ever more vulnerable proletariat whose jobs could easily be undertaken by the machines that they had come to resemble. Significantly, the rapidly growing white-collar occupations would also experience the same fate as their work became ever more routinized through the application of new technology. As these processes made it easier for employers to replace white-collar workers, their bargaining power would be eroded and so their loss of status and salary differentials would inevitably make them identify with the ranks of the manual working class.

In the voluminous literature inspired by 'Bravermania', the deskilling thesis was so heavily criticized that it could only be defended as a 'tendency within capitalism' rather than a general imperative or widespread feature (Thompson 1983: 118). Among other things, Braverman had overstated the employers' desire to control labour, the existence of a 'golden age' of craft work, and the prevalence of scientific management (Wood 1982). But perhaps one of the most telling criticisms of the deskilling thesis was that it was shaped more by the particularities of the American experience than Braverman may have appreciated. Above all, he failed to appreciate the possibility that there might be different types of capitalism in which different kinds of institutional arrangements, notably between employers, trade unions and the state, might sustain predominantly high-skill high-wage economies of the kind found in Germany and Japan (e.g. Littler 1982; Lane 1989).

A similar criticism could also be made of the more optimistic but equally universalistic theories of *post-industrialism* and the *informational society* that followed on the deskilling debate. Briefly, the theory of post-industrialism argued that knowledge would become the major source of economic growth and the critical factor in social change (Bell 1973). Consequently, education, which would be at the heart of the coming society, would expand massively. Elite higher education, for instance, would be replaced by a mass higher education system that would both make university places available for the wider population and provide a vehicle for social mobility. Instead of the preoccupation with mass production that was evident in the writings of Braverman and others, the post-industrial economy would be dominated by the rise of the service industries that would include a greater role for scientific and technical knowledge. Along with the expansion of the education system, this shift would be accompanied by a general upgrading of the occupational structure as the proportion of highly skilled, professional, technical and managerial workers would increase far beyond the decline in the old manufacturing-related occupations.

Echoes of this theory would reappear in claims about the advent of the *knowledge economy* and the *informational society* in the 1990s (e.g. Reich 1991; Castells 1996). Such theories would insist that developments in informational and communications technology, the spread of network forms of economic organization, and the demands of the global economy mean that even the major economic nations are compelled to invest in the new knowledge economy. In the first part of his celebrated trilogy on the information age, Castells states that the diffusion of information technology has revolutionized production which, along with the emerging network enterprise, has created a new kind of 'informational capitalism' that is redefining work processes, workers and employment. While a significant proportion of jobs are upgraded, a process that is accentuated by the use of information technology, Castells insists that a large number are either phased out through automation or moved overseas to low-wage economies. The result is a dualized society 'with a substantial top and a substantial bottom growing at both ends of the occupational structure' while the middle layers gradually shrink (see also Castells 1996: 279; Aoyama and Castells 2002).

In sum, the theories of post-industrialism and informationalism suggest that the evolution of capitalism would enable some sections of the labour force to achieve a greater degree of well-being than was possible in the days of mass manufacturing. But again the problem with these theories is that their universal claims make little allowance for the persistence of international differences, including those relating to the institutions of work, welfare and employment relations.

Institutions, labour markets and national diversity

The existence of institutional and cultural differences means that the question of whether or not humans can fulfil their potential within a market economy is no longer so straightforward because we cannot assume that there is a typical *market experience* (e.g. Lane 1991). Also, sociologists and other institutionally oriented scholars who work on employment relations insist that the market for labour is not like that for other commodities. Among other things, it is difficult to conceive of labour as a commodity when it cannot be bought and stored, when the employer hires only the capacity to work rather than an actual quantity of work, and when the exchanges between employers and employees are essentially part of a social relationship that is governed largely by institutional practices, social norms and feelings of trust rather than a simple economic transaction involving the exchange of work for pay (Fox 1974; Offe 1985; Kaufman 2010). In addition, the labour market cannot be viewed as an abstract entity governed by impersonal market forces when both the supply and demand for labour are clearly shaped by their social and political contexts (e.g. Maurice *et al.* 1986; Rubery and Grimshaw 2003).

Nonetheless, the danger for social scientists is that any attempt to explain international differences in skill levels and worker well-being, for instance, may descend into a lengthy list of national institutional peculiarities leavened with the occasional cultural stereotype. Fortunately, one of the major developments in the study of work and employment relations over the past couple of decades has been the emergence of a set of theories that seek to explain the persistence of the kind of cross-national differences that were either ignored or underestimated by the universalistic theories described earlier. As these theories are discussed in some detail in Chapter 2, I shall restrict this review to those aspects that relate directly to the experience of work.

The best-known of these theories is probably the *varieties of capitalism* perspective developed by a group of political economists led by Peter Hall and David Soskice (Hall and Soskice 2001). The theory draws a basic distinction between the liberal and coordinated market economies according to how they resolve a series of coordination problems in such areas as corporate governance, training and industrial relations. Obviously, the liberal market economy relies on the use of relatively unfettered markets to resolve these coordination problems while the coordinated market economy combines state intervention and agreements between the peak associations of employers and trade unions with a more regulated set of markets.

In terms of the experience of work, the coordinated economies place a greater emphasis on employment conditions and on employee well-being generally. According to Soskice, firms within these coordinated economies try to develop 'diversified quality products' which, along with the benefit of industry-based arrangements with trade unions, allow for greater job security, the provision of substantial vocational training, and the possibility of participating in co-operative industrial relations arrangements (Soskice 1999). Over time, trade unions continue to provide an effective form of representation for employees while wage bargaining is coordinated on an industrial or national basis. Within the liberal economies, by contrast, firms are more concerned with short-term market returns, relations with unions are generally adversarial (where they exist at all), jobs are less secure and wages are usually set at the workplace level. The education and training arrangements contribute to a highly polarized skill structure that is supplied by a competitive university system (for those who can afford it) alongside a low status vocational education system whose primary function is to enhance the employment opportunities of entry-level workers. Generally, the reliance on market forces means that conditions of employment and worker well-being are viewed as an additional and uncompetitive cost on business.

In contrast to the emphasis placed on firms in the varieties of capitalism perspective, the *power resources* perspective emphasizes the organizational capacity and power of labour relative to capital (Korpi 1978, 1983). The basic premise is that workers and employers mobilize through trade unions and employer associations that are invariably aligned with left-wing and right-wing political parties respectively. These then channel conflicting class interests through parliament, the state bureaucracy and the courts in the form of elections, legislation and executive decisions. One of the primary aims of the labour movement within this democratic class struggle is to de-commodify labour through the creation of a welfare state that will reduce the dependence on the labour market by providing workers with an income while unemployed, ill or retired. The power resources perspective also distinguishes between different types of employment regime. Generally, where organized labour enjoys a powerful position within an economy, then most of the labour force enjoys a wide range of employment and welfare rights, regardless of industry or occupation. Full employment tends to be a major policy goal and the state encourages women to enter and remain in employment through work–family policies. Within the market regime whose underlying philosophy is that of the 'small state', there is limited employment regulation and social welfare because the dominant ideology is that the unrestricted market is the best mechanism for promoting human welfare. Organized labour is generally excluded from decision-making both at the national and workplace levels which is one of the main reasons why there is little public interest in policies that might improve job quality or the work–life balance. The well-being of employees is instead the result of a market process that allocates the more satisfying and better paying jobs to those workers whose skills are in greatest demand (see also Gallie 2007a).

In sum, these theories suggest that the experience of work is likely to be mediated by the degree of labour market regulation, the size of the welfare state, and the relative power of trade unions. Once again, it seems that the question of whether or not labour can achieve its potential within the confines of market economies can only be answered by considering the social foundations and institutional dynamics of these same markets.

Skills, occupations and economic change

While these theories certainly help us to understand how differences in national institutions may shape the experience of work, they are rather silent on the nature of that work. So, before discussing the existing evidence on the experience of work, we need to describe the kind of work that is available within the contemporary economy. For this we need to examine some of the long-term changes in the structure of the economy and in the composition of the workforce.

Economic and occupational change

The most striking change in the distribution of employment by economic sector has of course been the much documented decline of manufacturing industries and the rise of services. While this shift was becoming evident in Britain and the USA during the 1970s, the proportion of the global labour force working in the services sector was almost twice that employed in industry by 2010 (43.9 per cent compared with 22.1 per cent). Even more dramatically, the proportion employed by the service industries sector within the world's more developed economies, including the European Union (EU), has risen to more than three times that employed in the industrial sector (73.8 per cent compared to 22.4 per cent) (ILO 2012: 98). Some early commentators insisted that this was a shift from 'good' unionized, male, manual, manufacturing jobs to 'bad', non-union, female, non-manual, service jobs. One strand of this debate on 'bad' service jobs examines the demands of dealing with people in 'in-person services', such as those provided by airlines, care homes and restaurants, and the likely consequences of this work for the well-being of employees. At the heart of the debate lies the concept of emotional labour, which according to Hochschild's original definition, may be defined as 'the management of feeling to create a publicly observable facial and bodily display' (1983: 7). This innovative concept, which captures the essence of 'in-person services', draws attention to the ways in which organizations try to control the feelings of their employees as they interact with customers. Even though the popular stereotype is that such work is somehow 'natural' for women, Hochschild argues that the constant management of emotional reactions has a human cost: workers may gradually feel estranged from their work and 'burn out' over time (see also Wharton 1999; Bolton and Boyd 2003).

Certainly, personal and protective service occupations, such as beauticians, hairdressers, nursery workers and security guards, which have been among the fastest growing occupations in Europe and the United States, are known for employing large numbers of women doing part-time work on low pay (Goos *et al.* 2009; Gautié and Schmitt 2010). Even so, it would be misleading to assume that most of the jobs in the service economy are of the 'McJob' variety so memorably described by the *Generation X* novelist Douglas Coupland as 'low-pay, low-prestige, low-dignity, low-benefits, low-future jobs that are considered a satisfying career choice by people who never held one' (Coupland 1991: 6). The service economy also contains a range of high-earning occupations that include some of the more prestigious professions such as medicine, law and accountancy as well as some of the newer and more lucrative occupations of consultancy (management and public relations), brokers (financial and insurance), and IT programmers. If anything, service sector employment is characterized by a marked polarization between elite professionals and low-end personal service workers (Hamnett 1994; Sassen 2001).

The emergence of a post-industrial economy dominated by the service industries has inevitably been accompanied by equally dramatic changes in the occupational structure. However, these changes have not led to the kind of expansion in working-class occupations predicted by Braverman. Instead, the employment of highly skilled service workers has increased substantially across Western economies while that of skilled and semi-skilled labour has fallen, with the sharpest declines being in the so-called 'hard industries' of mining and manufacturing. Within Europe and the United States, employment has expanded most at the top of the occupational hierarchy where the proportion of managerial, professional and technical workers has continued its long-term pattern of growth (Oesch and Rodríguez Menés 2011; Fernandez-Macias *et al.* 2012). In Britain, Germany, Spain and Switzerland, for instance, some of the strongest growth is among highly-qualified occupations in the private sector, notably among financial managers, legal professionals and computer specialists. Similar expansion is also evident in the public sector among nurses, teachers and social workers.

Though generally less well paid, the growth of sales and retail as well as personal and protective services work is also evident across most of Europe and North America (Goos *et al.* 2009; Fernandez-Macias *et al.* 2012). Unlike manufacturing, these 'in-person services' have the virtue of being the kind of work that cannot easily be outsourced to the emerging low-wage economies (Reich 1991). By contrast, substantial decline can be found in the traditionally male-dominated occupations of mechanics, maintenance fitters and assemblers (Oesch and Rodríguez Menés 2011). If assembly work was a classic setting for industrial relations activity during the twentieth century, then it is quite striking that fewer than 3 per cent of the British labour force worked on an assembly line by the end of that century (Gallie *et al.* 1998: 65).

Of course, much of the work in retail and personal services is undertaken by women. Despite increased entry into male-dominated occupations during the 1970s and 1980s, occupational segregation on the basis of sex is an enduring feature of contemporary labour markets. Of the 110 major occupational groups listed by the International Labour Organization (ILO) (ISCO), half of all women in the world's more advanced economies work in 11 or fewer of these occupations. Clerical, sales, and life science/health occupations as well as teaching, especially at the elementary level, are all heavily feminized (OECD 2002: 879). Discrimination, especially gender stereotyping of jobs as 'women's work', gender role socialization, women's educational choices, and recruitment practices all appear in explanations of this enduring phenomenon (e.g. Charles and Grusky 2004).

Comparative trends in skill levels

While there are many studies documenting trends towards greater proportions of higher-skilled occupations across the more affluent economies, there is still limited comparative research on changes in skill requirements within those occupations. Research of this kind is important because occupational skills may increase and decrease over time. For instance, the introduction of 'satnav' among taxi drivers is an obvious example of how the introduction of new technology can decrease the levels of skill and knowledge required for admission to a particular occupation (for further examples, see Clark *et al.* 1988: 28; Penn 1989: 110–12). Admittedly, capturing changes in job requirements across a whole range of occupations is not easy. Rather than attempt the herculean task of systematically observing the work, researchers use surveys to capture information about skill levels through self-reports from workers on the qualifications necessary to enter the job, the amounts of on-the-job training, as well as the actual requirements of the job (see Green 2006: 28–35). Using data from the European Social Survey, Tåhlin (2007) presents what is still a rare comparative investigation of this kind of evidence across five European countries: Germany, Great Britain, France, Spain and Sweden. As we might expect, he finds that that the upgrading of the occupational structure has led to a significant increase in the demand for skill in Britain, Germany and Sweden but not in France. Interestingly, his analysis finds that the long-term upgrading of the occupational structure has been more beneficial for women than men when it comes to the overall rise in the demand for skills. This is especially the case in Britain and Sweden where the skill demands have risen much faster than for men in the period between 1975 and 2004. More surprisingly he finds that the upgrading of occupations has been greatest in Britain even though the varieties of capitalism perspective views it as being locked into a low-skill low-wage equilibrium. Britain is, however, characterized by a distinct polarization of skill demand, among both men and women (which may partly explain the dramatic rise in wage inequality in that country).

Work intensification and job satisfaction

Earlier we saw that one of the criticisms of new forms of work organization is that they might change the effort bargain: workers may have to work harder without getting concomitant increases in pay. Obviously, the amount of effort that workers have to put into their jobs will influence their experience of work especially if it leads to excessive strain or 'burn-out'. Developments in information and communications technology (ICT) mean that the boundaries between work and home have become more porous as workers can be reached by emails and instant messages at any time of the day or night, including at weekends. Electronic forms of monitoring mean that employers also have the possibility of tracking how hard employees work (or spend time shopping on the internet or interacting with friends on social media). Even though electronic monitoring is still considered to be an emerging phenomenon, a recent British survey found that more than half of all employees reported some form of computerized monitoring while one quarter claimed that it was being used to check their performance (McGovern *et al.* 2007: 169–71).

By contrast, performance management through performance appraisals, merit-based payment systems and other kinds of human resource management policies are now quite common in most countries (Brown and Heywood 2002; Kersley *et al.* 2006: 87–9, 190-1). For employment relations scholars, one of the more intriguing features of these policies is the possibility that they may contribute to the individualization of the employment relationship as pay and other job rewards are based on individual performance and individual bargaining (Roche 2001; McGovern *et al.* 2007: 107–9, 120–2). Similarly, employer interest in various forms of high performance work systems also raises questions about effort levels and job satisfaction (White *et al* 2003; Godard 2004). Even if this new management rubric is not as prevalent as the hype suggests (Blasi and Kruse 2006; Kersley *et al.* 2006: 95–7), the general upgrading of the occupational structure still raises the question of whether more and more people have to work longer and harder because they have entered the potentially all-consuming world of professional and managerial work.

Effort at work

Using data from the European Survey on Working Conditions, Green and McIntosh found evidence from several countries pointing to an intensification of effort (Green and McIntosh 2001). Britain experienced the fastest rise in work effort, while in Germany, Denmark and Greece, there has been little change. Generally, effort increased faster in countries where there had been a substantial decline in trade union density. Subsequent research by Green found that work intensification was experienced by workers across the European Union, in Australia and the United States although to different degrees (Green 2006: 58–64).

Given the claims about the advent of informational capitalism, the earlier study by Green and McIntosh is of interest because it finds that effort levels were higher in jobs requiring intensive computer usage. This latter finding inspired further studies of technology use generally, with the hypothesis being that technological change might be effort-biased (i.e. new technology, such as ICT, is inclined to make employees work harder). Further research by Green confirmed an association between technology and work effort though the computer effect only remained when computer usage was a substantial part of the job (Green 2006). A more comprehensive set of analyses using evidence from a national sample of British workers also found that ICT had a significant impact while offering a possible explanation for this effect. In particular, computerized or automated monitoring of work was responsible for much of the increase in effort and in work strain. Furthermore, this effect was concentrated on employees who were below the professional and managerial level, especially among semi- and routine occupations, with the effect holding regardless of whether the employee thought it was merely a recording system or a means of checking performance. At the same time, appraisals and individual incentives raised reported effort levels across all employees (McGovern *et al.* 2007: 178–83).

Comparative trends in job satisfaction

If workers have generally been working harder, then it raises the obvious question of what that might mean for job satisfaction. Do they somehow feel more fulfilled by delivering a demanding day's work? Or are they more pressured and less satisfied by the sheer intensity of the work? Despite recent advances in cross-national research, the emerging evidence only allows us to offer some tentative arguments. As indicated earlier, measures of job satisfaction provide a relatively narrow account of employee responses to their jobs. Even so, the availability of comparable data makes it possible to examine general trends in subjective well-being in the absence of more comprehensive measures.

Before we examine changes in job satisfaction, it is important to recognize that employee surveys generally report relatively high levels of job satisfaction (Firebaugh and Harley 1995; Blanchflower and Oswald 1999). For instance, a recent study of 21 countries, mostly

European, finds that the majority of workers are more satisfied than dissatisfied with their jobs and, outside of Eastern Europe, between one-third and one half of all workers claim to be either 'very' or 'completely' satisfied. At the same time, only a tiny fraction claim to be dissatisfied with their jobs (Sousa-Poza and Sousa-Poza 2000). Taken together, these findings challenge the recurring journalistic claim that the working population has somehow been overwhelmed by stress, long hours, or some other source of dissatisfaction. But the big story from the research on job satisfaction is about change over time. In his path-breaking *Demanding Work* (2006), Green examines evidence from seven countries, namely Britain, Germany, Hungary, Italy, the Netherlands, Norway and the United States. What is particularly valuable about this analysis is that he is able to compare job satisfaction levels from the late 1980s through to 2000, which just happens to be a period in which each of these countries became increasingly affluent. Even so, the results, as Green acknowledges, are rather stark: the average job satisfaction reported in these countries is either stationary or falling. Job satisfaction declined sharply in Britain, Germany and the United States, and while it fell noticeably in Britain and Germany at different points during the 1990s, the US experience has been one of a steady long-term decline that goes back to 1973 (see also Blanchflower and Oswald 2004).

Given our earlier discussion, Green also provides some valuable analysis of the relationship between job satisfaction and effort, using British data, and the results are at least suggestive. Roughly half the decline in job satisfaction is due to the fall in job discretion that was evident in Britain across the 1990s. One-third of the fall in job satisfaction was attributed to increases in employee effort as those who had to put more effort into their work tended to be those with the greatest drop in job satisfaction (Green 2006: 162–4). Perhaps we should remind ourselves here that good research frequently tells us something we think we already know but for which we do not have the evidence. In this case, reducing worker independence and making them work harder without an increase in pay is likely to make them less satisfied.

But what accounts for cross-national differences in job satisfaction? A comprehensive study of all 27 European Union countries by Pichler and Wallace finds that differences in job satisfaction can be explained largely by objective working conditions such as occupational level, type of contract, provision of training and evaluations of various intrinsic and extrinsic factors. Those in the higher occupational classes tend to be more satisfied with their jobs as do those in permanent or long-term employment contracts and those with access to training. Pichler and Wallace's analysis also find that subjective evaluations of intrinsic and extrinsic factors have a substantial influence. If the job is well paid, offers the prospect of promotion, and is not considered to be boring, then employees will report higher levels of satisfaction than if this were not the case.

What this evidence also means is that a considerable amount of the variation in job satisfaction between countries can be explained by compositional and individual effects. In other words, employees in countries with large proportions of poor quality jobs, manual work and limited training will report less satisfaction. For Pichler and Wallace, this helps to explain why job satisfaction is generally lower in the new member states from Central and Eastern Europe where greater proportions of jobs have these characteristics. Finally, Pichler and Wallace (2009) report that institutional factors, such as levels of unionization, unemployment and wages are of less importance in predicting satisfaction than employment and job characteristics (occupation, type of contract, etc.). While these particular institutions may have a limited impact on job satisfaction, the striking differences between the experiences of those in Eastern and Western Europe cannot be fully understood without an appreciation of the historical differences in their economic, social and political institutions. Nonetheless, the challenge is to identify how, when, and to what extent institutional differences shape the experience of work. The next section provides some further examples.

Work–life balance

The issue of *work–life balance* is a good example of the kind of social problem that features regularly in applied areas such as employment relations. Conventionally understood to refer to the challenge of combining a job and a private life, especially one that involves caring for children or elderly relatives, it once again raises the question of the extent to which humans can achieve fulfilling lives within economies that are geared to the creation of profit rather than the satisfaction of human needs. The increased labour market participation of women, the demise of the male breadwinner family model and long working hours are frequently cited as reasons why the topic of the work–life balance came to prominence at the turn of the millennium. Of these, much of the focus has been on the supposed spread of a 'long hours culture' fuelled by excessive workloads and workplace norms of 'presenteeism' and 'face time': the need to impress the boss by being seen to work late. The best-known version of this thesis comes from the sociologist Juliet Schor who claims that changing social conditions and rising levels of consumerism have created a generation of overworked Americans. The demands of greedy employers and the ever more sophisticated advertising of 'must have' products are putting employees on a treadmill of longer hours at the expense of their private lives and family relationships (Schor 1991). Outside of the USA, however, it is widely acknowledged that working hours have been in decline for much of the twentieth century. Over the past 30 years, for example, average annual hours have fallen across most of Europe's leading economic nations (Faggio and Nickell 2007). Generally, as European nations become richer, their populations have chosen to work less.

Nonetheless, employment in 'long hours' occupations has been expanding over time. The obvious examples are of course the 'money-rich, time-poor' professional, technical and managerial occupations where seemingly endless hours of unpaid overtime await as a reward for those who have done well in higher education. But the danger of focusing exclusively on the working time of individuals rather than that of families or households would mean that some important social trends are overlooked. In particular, changes in family composition, notably the increasing prevalence of dual-earner couples and of single parents, means that families are increasingly squeezed for time, regardless of whether or not individual employees are working longer hours. While this trend was first identified in the United States (Jacobs and Gerson 2004: 43–8), recent research shows that the number of dual-earner families is also increasing across Europe. The demographic evidence strongly suggests that this trend is likely to continue (den Dulk *et al.* 2005: 13–14). Consequently, future research will need to pay greater attention to differences between households and the very different dilemmas that they face instead of simply focusing on the experience of individual workers.

Meanwhile, the rapidly emerging comparative European research on the work–life balance emphasizes the role of long hours, the effects of occupation and the presence of children (e.g. Crompton and Lyonette 2006; Scherer and Steiber 2007). Scherer and Steiber, for instance, find that women who are mothers and work in higher-level occupations have the highest levels of work–family conflict. Men tend to report higher levels of conflict when they are the sole breadwinner and work long hours to compensate for their partner's economic inactivity (see also White *et al.* 2003). The other critical factor is of course the presence of small pre-school age children, though this is generally more of a problem for women than men (Crompton and Lyonette 2006; Scherer and Steiber 2007). An interesting feature of these studies is the way that they capture cross-national differences in institutions. Crompton and Lyonette claim that 'societal effects' may serve to either increase or reduce the work–life balance. In the cases of Finland and Norway, the 'societal effect' consists of an encompassing welfare state that facilitates dual-earner families while encouraging men to assume a larger share of caring and domestic work. Together, these contribute to lower levels of work–life conflict being reported in these countries. In France, by contrast, the 'societal effect' has negative consequences. Despite having liberal gender attitudes and state support for working mothers, French families have a much more traditional division of domestic labour. The result is that French women experience significantly higher levels of work–life conflict (Crompton and Lyonette 2006). Scherer and Steiber also find that strong state support does not necessarily resolve the work–life balance problem in ways that would might seem consistent with either the 'varieties of capitalism' or power resources theories. They found that welfare policy measures, such as the kind of state-subsidized child-care provided in the Nordic countries, made a difference by boosting women's labour market participation, including after childbirth. But the irony is that enabling mothers to return to work does not of itself reduce work–family conflict since these women must then cope with the pressures of working while also being parents. Where there is less state support, such as in the more liberal economies of the United Kingdom and Ireland, as well as in Germany and the Netherlands, the preferred solution for many women is simply to work part-time (UN 2010: 94).

Conclusion

It should be clear from this review that the question of whether and to what extent employees can enjoy their jobs within the constraints of market economies immediately raises the issue of how cross-national differences affect the structure and experience of work. Even if this seems obvious, it is worth emphasizing that this was not always the case. Some of the early literature on human relations and industrial psychology, for instance, assumed that workers' needs were fixed and universal, regardless of social circumstances, work goals or societal norms. Similarly, theories of deskilling and post-industrialism assumed that the changes that occurred in the USA would follow inexorably in other countries. If the evidence on the direction of occupational change is now fairly clear, the situation with regard to the experience of work is more mixed.

Contrary to Braverman, there is now substantial and incontrovertible evidence of a general process of occupational upgrading across many of the world's advanced economies. Increasing proportions of the labour force are joining the expanding ranks of professional, technical and managerial employment. By contrast, the proportions of the labour force in semi-skilled and elementary occupations, such as plant and machine operators, clerical workers and assemblers, have been falling. In other words, more and more employees have the prospect of following a career rather than merely doing a job for the money. Consistent with this upgrading, the level of job skills has also been rising across Europe and North America (Green 2006: 29–32). Despite this occupational upgrading, the comparative evidence on job satisfaction indicates that satisfaction is falling while the problem of the work–life balance has become more pronounced. In other words, we have something of a paradox or puzzle. The expansion of employment in the higher occupations, where entry often requires tertiary-level education, should offer the prospect of greater fulfilment, yet the experience of work has, if anything, become more negative. Madeleine Bunting, a British journalist, seemed to capture an unspoken truth among a generation of high-achieving white-collar workers when she claimed that job-related stress, insecurity and work intensification were undermining the general well-being of otherwise successful people (Bunting 2004). Edwards' more systematic review of the British evidence also identifies a puzzle in which rising skill levels, greater levels of job autonomy and improvements in employer–employee communication go along with widespread reports of increases in working hours, stress and feelings of insecurity (Edwards 2005). Similarly, Green's (2006) comparative research sets out to examine the apparent paradox in which a widespread decline in job quality takes place in the context of economic growth and increasing material affluence.

How might we explain these puzzles? Edwards suggests that part of the answer is that different aspects of experience are being assessed and employee surveys are often unable to capture the nuances of experience. Employees may welcome the discipline of a new performance management system and report higher satisfaction but also think that the system could be improved while having little impact on their own behaviour (2005: 116–17). By contrast, Green argues that many of the premises that lead to the apparent paradox of declining job quality in an increasingly affluent economy break down on closer inspection. Perhaps the most striking example relates to wages, where he finds that in most industrialized countries, with the notable exception of the United States, real hourly wages have been rising and so adding to the affluence of these economies (2006: 123). Despite extensive commentary about rises in job insecurity, Green could find no evidence that the chances of job loss were out of synch with the business cycle. In other words, the risk of losing one's job had not risen relative to the rate of unemployment and so claims that widespread job losses were no longer just a feature of economic downturns could not be sustained (ibid.: 146–7). However, Green acknowledges that effort levels have indeed risen as a result of processes of work intensification induced by the introduction of new technology.

This pattern of mixed results also applies to the institutional theories that we considered earlier. The reviews of the trends in occupational change, skills, job satisfaction and the work–life balance did not produce findings that consistently favoured one theory over another. Obviously, the theories of post-industrialism and the informational society found support in the substantial increase in skill levels but they would not have anticipated the decline in job satisfaction, the increases in effort, or the emerging problem of the work–life balance. Gallie's review of the varieties of capitalism and welfare-state-centred approaches, which considers a more comprehensive range of empirical indicators, also yields a mixed scorecard. That said, he acknowledges that the power resources theory, which stresses the role of labour movements and the welfare state, fares best when it comes to accounting for the increasing polarization in employment conditions. For example, in Britain, where trade unions are in decline, there is a clear trend towards polarization in job quality. This trend is, however, much less evident in the Scandinavian countries where organized labour still holds considerable influence. In short, power resources theory, which stresses the organizational capacity and power of the labour movement relative to that of employers, is still an essential tool for understanding cross-national developments in the experience of work. At the same time, Gallie is right to acknowledge that it shares a limitation with the varieties of capitalism perspective which is that both are too broadly oriented to capture prominent national or societal effects as well as important differences between countries that are grouped together within a particular variety of capitalism (Gallie 2007b).

At this point, it is important to recognize that these theories have been developed primarily to explain institutional differences in work and employment relations in Europe and North America. The rapid emergence of the newly industrializing Asian economies, the rise of the so-called BRIC economies of Brazil, Russia, India and China, and the continuing market transitions in Central and Eastern Europe present a wide variety of institutional arrangements that will inevitably require changes to existing theories. At the same time, they will obviously require further consideration of what it means to work in a market economy, the relative influence of labour movements, the role of the state, and the impact of cultural notions of what it means to achieve fulfilment or success at work. On this basis it would seem that the comparative study of the experience of work has much to offer to the future development of employment relations as an area of enquiry.

References

Aoyama, Y. and Castells, M. (2002) 'An empirical assessment of the informational society: employment and occupational structures of G7 countries', *International Labour Review*, 141(12): 124–59.

Baldamus, W. (1961) *Efficiency and Effort: An Analysis of Industrial Administration*, London: Tavistock Publications.

Bell, D. (1973) *The Coming of Post-Industrial Society*, New York: Basic Books.

Blanchflower, D. G. and Oswald, A.J. (1999) *Well-Being, Insecurity and the Decline of American Job Satisfaction*, Coventry: University of Warwick, Department of Economics.

—— (2004) 'Well-being over time in Britain and the USA', *Journal of Public Economics*, 88(7–8): 1359–86.

Blasi, J. and Kruse, D. (2006) 'U.S. high-performance work practices at century's end', *Industrial Relations*, 45(4): 547–78.

Blyton, P. (2008) 'Working time and work–life balance', in P. Blyton, N. Bacon, J. Fiorito and E. Heery (eds) *The Sage Handbook of Industrial Relations*, London: Sage.

Bolton, S. C. and Boyd, C. (2003) 'Trolley dolly or skilled emotion manager? Moving on from Hochschild's managed heart', *Work, Employment and Society*, 17(2): 289–308.

Braverman, H. (1974) *Labor and Monopoly Capital: The Degradation of Work in the Twentieth Century*, New York: Monthly Review Press.

Brown, M. and Heywood, J. S. (2002) *Paying for Performance: An International Comparison*, Armonk, NY: M.E. Sharpe.

Bunting, M. (2004) *Willing Slaves: How the Overwork Culture Is Ruling Our Lives*, London: HarperCollins.

Castells, M. (1996) *The Rise of the Network Society*, Cambridge, MA: Blackwell.

Charles, M. and Grusky, D.B. (2004) *Occupational Ghettos: The Worldwide Segregation of Women and Men*, Stanford, CA: Stanford University Press.

Clark, A. E. (1997) 'Job satisfaction and gender: why are women so happy at work?', *Labour Economics*, 4(4): 341–72.

Clark, J., McLoughlin, I., Rose, H. and King, R. (1988) *The Process of Technological Change*, Cambridge: Cambridge University Press.

Cook, J. D., Hepworth, S., Wall, T. and Warr, P. (1981) *The Experience of Work: A Compendium and Review of 249 Measures and Their Use*, London: Academic Press.

Coupland, D. (1991) *Generation X: Tales for an Accelerated Culture*, New York: St Martin's Press.

Crompton, R. and Lyonette, C. (2006) 'Work–life "balance" in Europe', *Acta Sociologica*, 49(4): 379–93.

den Dulk, L., Peper, B. and Van Doorne-Huiskes, A. (2005) 'Work and family life in Europe: employment patterns of working parents across welfare states', in B. Peper, A. van Doorne-Huiskes and L. den Dulk (eds) *Flexible Working And Organisational Change*, Cheltenham: Edward Elgar.

Edwards, P. K. (2003) 'The employment relationship and the field of industrial relations', in P. K. Edwards (ed.) *Industrial Relations: Theory and Practice*, Oxford: Basil Blackwell.

—— (2005) 'The puzzle of work: insecurity and stress *and* autonomy and commitment', in A. Heath, J. Ermisch and D. Gallie (eds) *Understanding Social Change*, Oxford: Oxford University Press.

Faggio, G. and Nickell, S. (2007) 'Patterns of work across the OECD', *The Economic Journal*, 117(521): 416–40.

Fernandez-Macias, E., Hurley, J. and Storrie, D. (2012) *Transformation of the Employment Structure in the EU and USA, 1995–2007*, Basingstoke: Palgrave Macmillan.

Firebaugh, G. and Harley, B. (1995) 'Trends in job satisfaction in the United States by race, gender, and type of occupation', *Research in the Sociology of Work*, 5: 87–104.

Fox, A. (1974) *Beyond Contract: Work, Power and Trust Relations*, London: Faber and Faber.

Frege, C. (2007) *Employment Research and State Traditions*, Oxford: Oxford University Press.

Gallie, D. (2007a) 'Production regimes, employment regimes, and the quality of work', in D. Gallie (ed.) *Employment Regimes and the Quality of Work*, Oxford: Oxford University Press.

—— (2007b) 'The quality of work life in comparative perspective', in D. Gallie (ed.) *Employment Regimes and the Quality of Work*, Oxford: Oxford University Press.

—— and White, M., Cheng, Y. and Tomlinson, M. (1998) *Restructuring the Employment Relationship*, New York: Clarendon Press.

Gautié, J. and Schmitt, J. (2010) *Low-Wage Work in the Wealthy World*, New York: Russell Sage Foundation.

Godard, J. (2004) 'A critical assessment of the high-performance paradigm', *British Journal of Industrial Relations*, 42(2): 349–78.

—— and Delaney, J. T. (2000) 'Reflections on the "high performance" paradigm's implications for industrial relations as a field', *Industrial and Labor Relations Review*, 53(3): 482–502.

Goldthorpe, J., Lockwood, D., Bechofer, F. and Platt, J. (1968) *The Affluent Worker: Industrial Attitudes and Behaviour*, Cambridge: Cambridge University Press.

Goos, M., Manning, A. and Salomons, A. (2009) 'Job polarization in Europe', *The American Economic Review*, 99(2): 58–63.

Green, F. (2006) *Demanding Work: The Paradox of Job Quality in the Affluent Economy*, Princeton, NJ: Princeton University Press.

—— and McIntosh, S. (2001) 'The intensification of work in Europe', *Labour Economics*, 8(2): 291–308.

Hackman, J. R. and Oldham, G. R. (1975) 'Motivation through the design of work: test of a theory', *Organizational Behavior and Human Performance* 16(2): 250–79.

—— (1980) *Work Redesign*, Reading, MA: Addison-Wesley.

Hakim, C. (1991) 'Grateful slaves and self-made women: fact and fantasy in women's work orientations', *European Sociological Review*, 7(2): 101–21.

Hall, P. A., and Soskice, D. (eds) (2001) *Varieties of Capitalism: The Institutional Foundations of Comparative Advantage*, Oxford: Oxford University Press.

Hamnett, C. (1994) 'Social polarisation in global cities: theory and evidence', *Urban Studies*, 31(3): 401–24.

Hochschild, A. R. (1983) *The Managed Heart: Commercialization of Human Feeling*, Berkeley, CA: University of California Press.

Hodson, R. (1991) 'Workplace behaviors: good soldiers, smooth operators, and saboteurs', *Work and Occupations*, 18(3): 271–90.

Hyman, R. (1984) *Strikes*, London: Collins.

ILO (2012) *Global Employment Trends 2012: Preventing a Deeper Jobs Crisis*, Geneva: International Labour Office.

Jacobs, J. A., and Gerson, K. (2004) *The Time Divide: Work, Family, and Gender Inequality*, Cambridge, MA: Harvard University Press.

Jahoda, M., Lazarsfeld, P., Zeisel, H., Reginall, J. and Elsässer, T. (1972) *Marienthal: The Sociography of an Unemployed Community*, London: Tavistock Publications.

Kaufman, B. E. (2010) 'The theoretical foundation of industrial relations and its implications for labor economics and human resource management', *Industrial and Labor Relations Review*, 64(1): 74–108.

Kelly, J. (1982) *Scientific Management, Job Redesign and Work Performance*, London: Academic Press.

—— (1998) *Rethinking Industrial Relations: Mobilization, Collectivism and Long Waves*, London: Routledge.

Kersley, B., Alpin, C., Forth, J., Bryson, A., Bewley, H., Dix, G. and Oxenbridge, S. (2006) *Inside the Workplace: Findings from the 2004 Workplace Employment Relations Survey*, London: Routledge.

Korpi, W. (1978) *The Working Class in Welfare Capitalism: Work, Unions and Politics in Sweden*, London: Routledge and Kegan Paul.

—— (1983) *The Democratic Class Struggle*, London: Routledge and Kegan Paul.

Lane, C. (1989) *Management and Labour in Europe: The Industrial Enterprise in Germany, Britain and France*, Aldershot: Edward Elgar.

Lane, R. E. (1991) *The Market Experience*, Cambridge: Cambridge University Press.

Littler, C. (1982) *The Development of the Labour Process in Capitalist Societies*, London: Heinemann.

McGovern, P., Hill, S., Mills, C. and White, M. (2007) *Market, Class, and Employment*, Oxford: Oxford University Press.

Marmot, M. G. (2004) *Status Syndrome: How Our Position on the Social Gradient Affects Longevity and Health*, London: Bloomsbury.

Maurice, M., Sellier, F. and Silvestre, J-J. (1986) *The Social Foundations of Industrial Power*, Cambridge, MA: MIT Press.

MOW International Research Team (1987) *The Meaning of Working*, London: Academic Press.

OECD (2002) *Employment Outlook*, Paris: OECD.

Oesch, D. and Rodríguez Menés, J. (2011) 'Upgrading or polarization? Occupational change in Britain, Germany, Spain and Switzerland, 1990–2008', *Socio-Economic Review*, 9(3): 503–31.

Offe, C. (1985) 'The future of the labour market', in C. Offe (ed.) *Disorganized Capitalism*, Cambridge: Polity Press.

Parker, S. and Wall, T.D. (1998) *Job and Work Design: Organizing Work to Promote Well-Being and Effectiveness*, Thousand Oaks, CA: Sage Publications.

Penn, R. (1989) *Class, Power and Technology: Skilled Workers in Britain and America*, Oxford: Polity.

Pichler, F. and Wallace, C. (2009) 'What are the reasons for differences in job satisfaction across Europe? Individual, compositional, and institutional explanations', *European Sociological Review*, 25(5): 535–49.

Reich, R. B. (1991) *The Work of Nations*, New York: Alfred A. Knopf.

Roche, W. K. (2001) 'The individualization of Irish industrial relations?', *British Journal of Industrial Relations*, 39(2): 183–206.

Rose, M. (1988) *Industrial Behaviour: Research and Control*, London: Penguin.

Rubery, J. and Grimshaw, D. (2003) *The Organization of Employment: An International Perspective*, Basingstoke: Palgrave Macmillan.

Sassen, S. (2001) *The Global City: New York, London, Tokyo*, Princeton, NJ: Princeton University Press.

Scherer, S. and Steiber, N. (2007) 'Work and family in conflict: the impact of work demands on family life', in D. Gallie (ed.) *Employment Regimes and the Quality of Work*, Oxford: Oxford University Press.

Schor, J. (1991) *The Overworked American: The Unexpected Decline of Leisure*, New York: Basic Books.

Soskice, D. (1999) 'Divergent production regimes: coordinated and uncoordinated market economies in the 1980s and 1990s', in H. Kitschelt, P. Lange, G. Marks and J. D. Stephens (eds) *Continuity and Change in Contemporary Capitalism*, New York: Cambridge University Press.

Sousa-Poza, A. and Sousa-Poza, A. (2000) 'Well-being at work: a cross-national analysis of the levels and determinants of job satisfaction', *Journal of Socio-Economics*, 29(6): 517–38.

Tåhlin, M. (2007) 'Skills and wages in European labour markets: structure and change', in D. Gallie (ed.) *Employment Regimes and the Quality of Work*, Oxford: Oxford University Press.

Thompson, P. (1983) *The Nature of Work: An Introduction to Debates on the Labour Process*, Basingstoke: Macmillan.

Treiman, D. J. (1977) *Occupational Prestige in Comparative Perspective*, New York: Academic Press.

United Nations (UN) (2010) *The World's Women 2010: Trends and Statistics*, New York: United Nations, Department of Economic and Social Affairs.

Warr, P. B. (1987) *Work, Unemployment, and Mental Health*, Oxford: Oxford University Press.

Wharton, A. S. (1999) 'The psychosocial consequences of emotional labor', *The Annals of the American Academy of Political and Social Science*, 561(1): 158–76.

White, M., Hill, S., McGovern, P., Mills, C. and Smeaton, D. (2003) 'High performance management practices, working hours and work–life balance', *British Journal of Industrial Relations*, 41(2): 175–95.

Wood, S. (ed.) (1982) *The Degradation of Work? Skill, Deskilling and the Labour Process*, London: Hutchinson.

6 HRM, organizational performance and employee involvement

Stephen Wood

Introduction

Management in employment relations was dominated in the 1990s–2000s by human resource management (HRM). For some, this was part of a new, all-embracing approach to employment relations. For others, HRM drove a wedge through the subject matter of employment relations that required rebuttal, as HRM was perceived to undermine the significance of the core unit of past employment relations, the trade unions. In the extreme, HRM has been seen as an overt anti-union management strategy or as increasing workers' satisfaction such that their need for unions is reduced. Moreover, its beneficial effects on organizational performance should ensure workers' receive wage increases and other non-pecuniary gains. At the other extreme, HRM is centred on enhancing the direct involvement of workers, in contrast to the Taylorist model of management, with its tight division of labour and narrowly designed specialized jobs, which was the bedrock for much of the development of collective bargaining in the twentieth century. There is no reason why, as this bedrock changes, trade unions should not have roles, if only in ensuring that the benefits from performance gains are shared fairly. Given these competing perspectives, varied associations of HRM with unions and assumptions about positive performance effects, this chapter first outlines the nature of HRM, and then focuses on whether it is associated with performance, job satisfaction, trade unionism and national employment systems. In so doing, we aim to show how a comparative perspective can aid our understanding.

The concept of human resource management

Common to most characterizations of HRM is a set of practices that includes enriched job design, idea-capturing schemes, information disclosure and appraisal systems, intensive training and teamwork, and that identifies a specific approach to personnel management. Practices associated with HRM have been classified into three main groups: (1) a work organization element which is about the opportunities for employee involvement and participation; (2) a training and development component concerned with human capital or skill and knowledge acquisition; and (3) a motivation-enhancement component concerned with incentives to perform to ensure that employees are motivated to use their discretion in line with the organization's objectives (Appelbaum *et al.* 2000; De Menezes and Wood 2006).

Typically an orientation on the part of management towards their employees is assumed to underlie the use of these practices. This orientation is seen as entailing a commitment towards providing employees with security and opportunities for involvement and development, and, in accountancy terms, treating the workforce as an asset that can contribute to innovation and the long-term development of the organization, and not just a variable cost to be minimized. Such an approach is termed, following Walton (1985), high commitment management or, following Lawler (1986), high involvement management (HIM).

Most concepts of HRM begin with these terms and, for some, HRM is synonymous with them and thus centred on methods of involvement and developing employee commitment. However, as the term became more widespread, it was used more generally to characterize what is currently taken to be the sophisticated and modern approach to personnel management. Allied to this development, HRM specialists often advocate an integrated approach, in which the triad of high involvement, skill development and incentives are used in concert. The prescription is based on the assumption that there will be synergistic effects between the practices and hence the yield from greater use of practices will grow exponentially. By implication, piecemeal adoption is not likely to yield strong performance gains.

Both the specific high involvement and more general HRM perspectives may end up at the same point with an emphasis on the importance of involvement, development, sophisticated recruitment processes and payment systems that have some link to collective performance. However, in the high involvement perspective, employee involvement is the core element of the approach and the other elements are supports for achieving this, whereas in the more general approach the practices may be given more equal status. In reality, practices may not be used in conjunction with each other, even with the increasing publicity given to their holistic use. Moreover, if managements give differing emphases to the elements, then very different approaches to HRM are likely to materialize across the economy. If, for example, the emphasis within the organization is on intensive training and development, this might represent a skill acquisition approach to HRM, which we might label human capital HRM. Even then there may be an alternative human capital approach which relies on skill acquisition by recruitment through the external labour market at the expense of widespread training and development or involvement. In this case, the recruitment and selection processes might be the core of the HRM approach.

The extreme contrast is perhaps between the high involvement approach and HRM centred on the motivational elements such as performance-related pay. The fulcrum of the latter approach would be performance management that is centred on setting goals and linking pay to their achievement. Management thus targets high performance directly and through increasing pay satisfaction, not through involvement and attitudinal change. Huselid and Becker (1996: 407) characterize high performance management in these terms as they accord a pivotal role to 'performance-contingent incentive compensation systems'. The performance management approach is thus set apart from HIM, as performance-related pay is widely seen as unsupportive of involvement, teamworking and cooperation (Beer *et al.* 1984: 114; Wood 1996a). Gooderham *et al.* (1999) formally demarcated this approach from HIM, labelling it 'calculative', because matters relating to human resources are evaluated according to their direct contribution to the organization's strategy and performance; employees are also treated as individuals rather than collective entities. The contrasting high involvement approach is termed 'collaborative', as management evaluates HR issues against additional criteria to short-term economic ones, including the need for organizations to have social legitimacy and to create a cohesive workforce founded on a partnership between employers and employees.

Employee involvement

Employee involvement, especially direct involvement, is probably the HRM element of most interest to employment relations specialists, though pay systems are also significant.

Two types of opportunity for direct participation are associated with HRM: (1) role involvement through designing jobs that give their holders discretion, variety and high levels of responsibility; and (2) organizational involvement methods that extend beyond the narrow confines of the job, such as idea-capturing schemes, teamwork and functional flexibility. Involvement is very much on management's terms, unlike that through trade unions or works councils. A collective voice through management-promoted consultative bodies and financial involvement through share ownership or profit-sharing systems are also often thought to have a role in HIM, perhaps alongside indirect employee involvement through representative bodies. In this context, the skill acquisition and motivational elements have often been treated as supports for involvement. Theoretically, motivational systems can align an individual's motivations to organizational objectives regardless of the level of HIM in the organization. Although no single form of reward system will be uniquely associated with HIM, we would expect highly individualized systems of payment by results such as piecework systems to be eschewed by managements practising HIM.

In Walton (1985) and Lawler's (1986) original conceptions of HIM, good job design that creates enriching jobs is its bedrock. This provides lower-level employees with 'opportunities to make decisions concerning the conduct of their jobs'. Yet HIM entails going beyond the role level to include organizational involvement, so employees 'participate in the business as a whole' (Benson and Lawler 2003: 156). Lawler and Walton based their image of HIM on a mixture of: (1) what they observed to be leading-edge developments in the US and Japanese organizations as they forsook their traditional Taylorist methods; and (2) job design research in the 1960s which highlighted its decisive effect on job satisfaction and performance. The implication of both leading-edge practice and social science was the need to develop away from the Taylorist model, with its routinized jobs and consequent limited involvement and commitment of employees.

As the experiments in redesigning jobs developed, however, the need for wider changes that went beyond role involvement was identified. These were required to ensure the job design worked and to extend involvement beyond its limited scope. If job design was to work well, people needed to be more aware of the wider context of their jobs and trained accordingly, and so supervisory, appraisal and selection systems also needed to change. Furthermore, giving individuals more autonomy in their jobs would not necessarily guarantee innovation. Increasingly it became clear that new quality and logistic methods that were allied to continuous improvement methods – variously known as lean production, total quality management (TQM) and Toyotaism – required inputs from employees at all levels. A wider organizational involvement through teamwork and idea-capturing methods was needed.

Just as the triad of involvement, skill acquisition and incentives need not go together, so the two types of involvement may not coexist. Indeed many case studies on organizational involvement practices have been in assembly-line production systems, where the advent of more participative management had left the level of autonomy or variety in core manual jobs largely unaffected (e.g. Wood 1988; Womack *et al.* 1990). Organizational involvement may thus change the nature of work by increasing demands on employees, for example, when they are encouraged to participate in idea-capturing schemes, while the level of autonomy or variety when carrying out core functions is unaffected. A feature of the much-proclaimed Japanese model was that its origins in mass production manufacturing meant that jobs were designed in relatively conventional ways and its distinctiveness was in involving people in wider issues including the design of these jobs. The aim of high organizational involvement is best seen as encouraging greater flexibility, proactivity and collaboration between employees than was the norm in low involvement Taylorist systems. As Wood and De Menezes (2011: 1586) put it:

> High involvement management is concerned with the development of broader horizons among all workers so that they can think of better ways of doing their jobs, connect what they do with what others do, and react effectively to novel problems.

It therefore helps employees create and contribute to a continuous improvement culture.

In the remainder of this chapter the emphasis will be on HIM and we will use the following terms to label its core components: 'enriched jobs' to describe job designs that give employees a degree of variety and autonomy over their role, and 'direct organizational involvement' which centres on teamwork, information sharing, quality circles and other idea-capturing schemes. The focus of much HRM research has been on HRM's performance effects, and this is reflected in the use, by some, of the term high performance management or high performance work systems to capture or promote the HRM or HIM model. HRM research has been largely concerned with testing whether the model warrants this label. Given the emphasis on the benefits of the holistic or integrated use of practices to all types of organizations, research has centred on correlating measures of the total use of practices with organizational performance. Some attention has been paid to the extent to which this relationship is universal or contingent on the type of organization or business strategy; in some theories, for example, HIM is deemed more appropriate for organizations that are following a product differentiation or innovative strategy, to use Porter's (1980) terms, and will be less effective in those following a cost-minimization strategy.

The impact of HRM practices on organizational performance

Research on performance effects is dominated by single-country studies, most of which come from the USA or the UK, but there are examples from a number of other countries. The methodology has largely involved creating composite measures of HRM or HIM practices and then using regression analysis to establish if they are uniquely associated with organizational performance. Little attention has been paid to the extent to which the practices coexist; to the precise details of the practices; or to testing the mechanisms or intervening variables that explain any association between practices and performance.

The research originated in the USA with industry-specific studies, and most have found some association between HRM practices and performance. One of the first, a study by Arthur (1994) of small steel mills, concentrated on employee involvement, using Walton's (1985) high commitment management as its organizing principle. This was thought to be characterized by an underlying orientation on the part of management to develop committed employees, and it was measured by such practices as high levels of employee involvement in managerial decisions, formal participation programmes, and training in group problem-solving. Its opposite, the control or Taylorist model, was defined by its emphasis on 'enforcing compliance with specified rules and procedures and basing employee rewards on some measurable output criteria'. Using data on these practices from questionnaires completed by HR managers in a sample of 30 small steel mills, Arthur divided the sample into high commitment management and high control management plants. The 14 mills in the high commitment category were found to have higher labour efficiency (average number of labour hours required per ton of steel), lower scrap rates (tons of raw steel required per ton of finished product), and lower labour turnover (number of shop floor workers who had left in the last year), after controlling for such factors as plant size and degree of trade union membership.

Huselid's (1995) larger cross-industry study of 968 US private sector organizations with over 100 employees was the first major survey in the area. Having obtained information on the firms' HRM practices by a questionnaire mailed to the senior HRM professional, Huselid used the statistical method of principle component analysis to investigate the relationships among the practices, and found that they formed two identifiable factors. In broad terms, the first, entitled 'Skills and organizational structure', covered the involvement and skill-acquisition dimension of HRM, and the second covered the motivational element. Huselid measured the practices at the company level by asking managers at headquarters about the percentage of people involved in a practice across the whole company, an approach that may have created reliability problems. He found that employee motivation, but not employee skills and organizational structures, was significantly and positively associated with productivity. It was also related to Tobin's q measure of market value, but not to the gross rate of return on assets. In contrast, the employee skills and organizational structures index was strongly related to the gross rate of return on assets but only weakly associated with Tobin's q.

The only project that has covered a number of countries is MacDuffie's (1995) single-industry study of 62 final assembly plants in the major car-producing countries, using data from the MIT Future of the Auto Industry project, the birthplace of the lean production concept (Womack *et al.* 1990). The plants were in a range of countries, including the USA, Canada, Germany, France, the UK, Korea, Taiwan, Mexico, Brazil, Japan and Australia, as well as Japanese plants in the USA. MacDuffie differentiated two types of HRM practices: first, work system practices, which measure HIM as they include work teams, problem-solving groups, job rotation, decentralization of quality-related tasks and an effective system for employee suggestions. Second, there are HRM policies covering skill acquisition and other supports for HIM, including recruitment and hiring criteria geared towards openness to learning, interpersonal and teamworking skills, contingent pay systems, the minimization of status differentials, and training for both new and experienced employees. MacDuffie also measured the extent to which the production regime was lean, for example, by the average level of inventory stocks: the lower the figure, the leaner the plant. MacDuffie showed that plants with the triad of high involvement work systems, supporting HRM practices and lean methods, which he termed flexible production systems, had superior productivity and quality compared to traditional plants with little use of high involvement, HRM or lean practices. A third type of plant, which had traditional work systems, that is, little or no involvement, but medium levels of HRM and lean practices, also had superior productivity and quality. However, the quality levels in these plants were closer to the traditional rather than the lean plants, suggesting that HIM is especially decisive for quality.

While MacDuffie's study covered a range of countries, the only national comparison made was between Japanese and non-Japanese plants. Not all Japanese plants were of the integrated lean type, and the basic performance results were the same across both samples. In other words, lean plants were outperforming other types of plant in both the Japanese and non-Japanese groups. Any apparent Japanese effect was due to the greater use of HIM and lean methods in Japan itself.

Studies by Wood and colleagues, using the UK's Workplace Employee Relations Survey (WERS 2004) series, a representative sample of British workplaces across the whole economy, followed MacDuffie in distinguishing a core high involvement variable from other HRM practices. They have shown that practices associated with organizational involvement, such as quality circles and teamwork, as well as involvement-specific skill and knowledge practices, for example, information dissemination and training for groupwork, tend to be used together (De Menezes and Wood 2006; Wood *et al.* 2012). In contrast, motivational practices typically associated with HRM, such as performance-related pay and harmonized benefits, are not uniquely associated with involvement practices. Likewise, organizational involvement practices (HIM) are not strongly associated with enriched job design or general training. However, both enriched jobs and high organizational involvement management were related to productivity, quality and financial performance in the WERS surveys in both 1998 and 2004 (Wood and De Menezes 2008; Wood *et al.* 2012).

Using data from the WERS (2004) survey, Wood *et al.* also explored the mechanisms that may explain these relationships, and showed that many of the enriched jobs–performance relationships were explained by greater job satisfaction. In the case of high organizational involvement, however, the positive effects on performance were not explained by job satisfaction or by workers responding positively to higher job demands. In fact, high organizational involvement management reduced job satisfaction and in a way that actually depressed any positive effects on performance that involvement might have had. It also increased workers' anxiety, but this effect made no difference to organizational performance.

The majority of the other studies have remained the single-country type and have mostly been conducted in the USA or the UK. However, Guthrie (2001), using data from New Zealand, developed a composite measure that covered the work organization, skill acquisition and motivational elements of HRM. Two involvement measures were used, information sharing and employee participatory programmes, and they were positively associated with productivity. Bae and Lawler (2000) studied South Korea and included empowerment and broad job design in a measure of HRM strategy which was centred on involvement. HRM was positively associated with both a self-report measure of organizational performance and an objective measure based on the rate of return on investment. The same results were found with both concurrent and later measures of performance. A study in Russia by Fey *et al.* (2000) tested the individual effects of a broad range of 16 HRM practices, of which the only involvement measure was decentralized decision-making. They found that overall company performance was only associated with two of these practices: job security for non-managers and promotion on merit for managers. In contrast, a longitudinal study in Germany by Zwick (2003), which focused on employee participation, measured by teamwork, autonomous work groups and the reduction of hierarchies, did find a positive association with higher levels of productivity.

Most studies have remained focused on private sector organizations. But a good example to show how HRM effectiveness may extend to all areas of the economy is a study by West *et al.* (2006) which looked at its impact on mortality rates in 52 public hospitals in England. What was called the high performance system was measured by aggregating the use of six practices: training, performance management, participation, decentralization, teams and employment security. This measure was associated with a standardized mortality ratio, which indicates whether more or fewer patients have died than one would expect, taking into account the context of the hospital.

Evaluating the research on HRM and performance

In most summaries of the major studies of HRM and performance they are widely credited as showing a link between HRM and valued organizational outcomes (Becker and Gerhart 1996; Wood 2009a). Yet they also point to qualifications to this general conclusion, but much of the controversy focuses on whether a causal relationship has been established, and not so much on the strength of the association. A meta-analysis by Combs *et al.* (2006) of the relationship between a large range of individual HRM practices and both operational and financial performance indicators up to the mid-2000s, revealed a positive relationship with most practices, even though it covered a wider range than those used in many HRM studies. Only a small minority of studies tested the contingency argument that the success of HRM depends on the circumstances of the firm, and those that have tested this claim found little support for it (e.g. Huselid 1995; Delery and Doty 1996). However, as other reviews have shown (Godard 2004; Wall and Wood 2005), most studies – 21 out of 25 studies reviewed by Wall and Wood (2005) – do not show consistent results across all the performance measures they investigated. And three of the 12 commonly studied practices included in Combs *et al.*'s (2006) analysis that were found to be unrelated to performance are high involvement practices: teams, appraisal and information sharing.

Taken together, the studies do not provide a clear picture of which aspects of HRM systems are crucial for performance, especially as the practices investigated vary considerably. Wood's (2009b) narrative review compared those studies that allowed the effects of HIM to be isolated from other HRM practices with those that did not and found no difference in performance effects across the two groups. It may be that studies that excluded methods of employee involvement but which nonetheless found performance benefits are picking up indirect effects of unmeasured forms of employee involvement.

Moreover, the studies that use a single index of HRM which does not differentiate between types of HRM practices will assign the same score to organizations whose HRM practices are dominated by one or other of involvement, skill acquisition and motivational practices. For example, if an organization has merit pay, promotion on merit and profit-sharing but no involvement practices, and another has quality circles, teamwork and flexible job descriptions, they would both be given a score of three on the HRM index but could have very different HRM philosophies. At the top end of the index, organizations will be using all sets of practices, and thus a positive association between the index and performance implies that all practices are important. On the other hand, a positive association between performance effects and medium use of practices implies that the particular mix of practices does not matter: different configurations of practices may be equally effective. Alternatively those that use particular combinations may be correctly fitting their HRM policies to their circumstances, as contingency theory suggests they should. The McDonald's case, well documented in Royle and Towers (2002), suggests, for example, that a calculative approach to the management of labour could produce strong performance effects and may be well suited to a cost-minimization business strategy.

The implication of the linear positive relationship between the HRM index and performance is that the highest performers are using a truly holistic approach to HRM, in which one or other of the involvement or skill elements dominates. This is distinctive from the approaches that use only some practices, but which may not be as successful as the holistic approach or underpinned by the same HRM orientation. To use the McDonald's illustration again, a fast-food chain that adopts a more employee involvement approach in conjunction with the use of incentives and performance management may produce higher profits than McDonald's, not least because it will have lower labour turnover and absenteeism.

The study by Wood *et al.* (2012) based on the highly representative Workplace Employment Relations Survey (WERS) sample, coupled with previous work on job design, suggests that role and organizational involvement are crucial, if not uniquely decisive among

HRM practices, for organizational performance. Moreover, a meta-analysis by Subramony (2009) showed that combinations of empowerment practices (job design and HIM) or of motivational practices are more strongly related to various performance indicators than are combinations of all types of HRM practices. Skill acquisition practices are, in contrast, no more strongly related to performance than are the bundles of any type of HRM practice. This evidence implies that it is essential to be especially cautious about conclusions drawn from studies that do not include good measures of enriched jobs and high involvement practices. To draw a more positive conclusion: the involvement practices that are central to the concerns of employment relations specialists may, on close inspection, be what matter most for organizational performance, especially if they are linked to worker satisfaction as is implied in the theory of HIM. We now look at the studies of this linkage before turning to discuss employee involvement in relation to employment relations institutions, such as trade unionism and wider national systems of employment relations.

High involvement management and worker satisfaction

Enriched job design and HIM are widely assumed to create a 'better work environment for employees' (Barling *et al.* 2003: 277), and this has positive effects on workers' satisfaction, and perhaps other relevant outcomes such as their organizational commitment, enthusiasm and contentment with work. In turn, these outcomes may have positive consequences for organizational performance, including key HRM outcomes such as low absenteeism and labour turnover. This line of argument is consistent with a mutual gains perspective on employment relations (Kochan and Osterman 1994), which rests on the 'happy workers being productive' thesis (Wright and Cropanzano 2007): employers and employees can simultaneously benefit from increased employee involvement.

Enriched jobs have traditionally been associated with increased autonomy, meaningfulness of work and skill utilization, which are welcome rewards that lead to pleasurable and emotional states and job satisfaction. High involvement management with its broadening of people's roles and opportunities for participation may similarly increase variety at work, skill utilization and the meaningfulness of work, even if there is no concomitant increase in job discretion. Wood *et al.* (2012), however, offer several additional routes through which HIM impacts on employee outcomes. These include, first, that teamwork, functional flexibility, and group methods of capturing ideas may increase social contact, which is a source of job satisfaction and may reduce job anxiety. Second, information-sharing and workers' greater understanding of the organization's objectives and their role in the achievement of goals may reduce uncertainty in the work environment. Third, the encouragement to be involved in the organization may signal to employees that they are respected and acknowledged, which may increase their self-esteem. Finally, Wood *et al.*, following Mackie *et al.* (2001: 1070–1) argue that the increased meaningfulness, manageability and comprehensibility of work life associated with HIM enhance individuals' sense of coherence, which in turn improves their ability to withstand stress.

Enriched job design, work intensification and stress

Despite the plausibility of these routes to increased job satisfaction, a strong thesis, particularly voiced by employment relations specialists, is that job design and HIM represent a form of work intensification. This means that enriched job design and HIM have detrimental effects on workers' well-being; being essentially modern less-obtrusive forms of management control, they create stress among employees (Barker 1993; Ramsey *et al.* 2000). The negative effects on well-being means that better organizational performance is explained as the product of stress and coercion, driving workers to fulfil the enhanced demands placed on them. HRM may then generate conflicting outcomes for employers and employees, and not the mutual gains traditionally assumed in the mainstream literature. Wood *et al.* (2012) add a third line of argument that, insofar as enriched jobs or high involvement management do have negative effects, for example, on stress or satisfaction levels, these will have negative, not positive, effects on performance. Any performance gains from involvement are not dependent either on increased satisfaction or increased stress that creates pressures to perform. Job design and involvement may increase performance through making workers more proactive and through the implementation of their ideas for work reorganization and other efficiencies. In this third thesis, the negative effects on well-being reduce this positive performance effect. Hence Wood *et al.* (2012) call this a counteracting force argument, in contrast to the mutual gains and conflicting outcomes arguments.

Studies of the relationship between job design and satisfaction have covered a range of countries, and tend to confirm the link and hence are consistent with the mutual gains thesis (Cotton 1993; Van der Doef and Maes 1999). Studies on the link between the broader concept of HRM and well-being, which use general aggregate measures of HRM, have also yielded positive relationships with satisfaction or stress (e.g. Appelbaum *et al.* 2000; Harley *et al.* 2007; Kalmi and Kauhanen 2008). Mohr and Zoghi's (2008) study particularly focused on measuring HIM, as they used an index of participation in practices such as suggestion schemes and quality circles, and found that it was associated with job satisfaction. Macky and Boxall (2007) also found, in a New Zealand sample, that an index covering a broad spectrum of high performance work practices was associated with job satisfaction. Godard's (2010) study, in samples of Canadian and British workers, showed that participative methods (no measure of enriched job design was included in the study) were positively related to satisfaction and negatively associated with stress, measured in terms of people's perception of whether the job was a stressor. In the Wood *et al.* (2012) study that allowed the separate identification of enriched jobs and organizational involvement, worker satisfaction was found to only mediate the positive relationship between enriched jobs and organizational performance in a way that is consistent with the mutual gains thesis. In contrast, the negative relationship between HIM and worker satisfaction reduced organizational involvement's relationship with performance and supports Wood *et al.*'s (2012) counteracting effect model.

Wood *et al.*'s finding that organizational involvement is positively related to anxiety further shows HIM can have conflicting outcomes, but as this anxiety neither mediates the HIM–performance relationship nor is it associated with increased demands, it does not support the intensification thesis. Wood *et al.* suggest that any anxiety provoked by HIM reflects its encouragement of employees to be proactive and flexible, so its use may be accompanied by pressures to improve employee performance. These in turn may raise concerns among employees about their competencies, their relationships with others, and psychological (and not just job) security. As Wood *et al.* (ibid.: 437) conjecture, rather than high involvement:

> creating an increased sense of coherency or a feeling of being valued by the organization, . . . its introduction and on-going demands lead workers to question the organization's valuation of them and the comprehensibility and meaningfulness of what surrounds them.

HRM, trade unionism and voice

The link between HRM and employee satisfaction led some to treat HRM as an explanation for the decline of unionism in many countries as it was assumed that trade unionism would become increasingly irrelevant. Fiorito (2001: 335) argued that it was a deliberate form of union avoidance, and subtler than past confrontational methods that were used to reduce the success of unions' recruitment drives. In other words, HRM is a union substitution as opposed to a union suppression strategy. However, theoretical argument and evidence suggest the HRM–unionism relationship is more complicated.

First, some of the practices that fall under HIM or HRM are ones for which unions have either campaigned or which are consistent with their demands, the most obvious being involvement, training, job security and fair selection processes. Explicit demands for good quality jobs may not have been a feature of trade unionism over the years, as pay and other economic issues have dominated its orientation, but improved working conditions and the establishment of basic standards have been major achievements of trade unions throughout the world. During specific periods of history, job design aspects have been high on the union agenda, for example, in France with the advent of Taylorism (see Chapter 11 in this volume, on France). Currently there remain concerns for unsafe and dangerous working conditions that are a priority over demands for enriched job designs in many countries, particularly developing countries. Nonetheless, Gooderham *et al.* (1999: 511) suggest there is, 'no reason to suppose that [collaborative] practices would necessarily be met with resistance by unions or other collective bodies representing the interests of employees'. Where wholesale condemnation of HRM has been most pronounced (e.g. in the USA and the UK in the 1980s and early 1990s), this was largely based on associating HRM with work intensification or on doubts about the sincerity of management proposals to increase participation and devolve some power to lower-level organization members.

Second, cross-sectional data shows that the extent of HRM is not associated with union recognition in the USA and the UK; it is as common (or uncommon) in unionized as in non-unionized workplaces (Osterman 1994; Wood 1996b; Clegg *et al.* 2002; De Menezes and Wood 2006). More telling longitudinal evidence from the UK reinforces this point. Machin and Wood (2005) showed that the use of a limited number of practices associated with HRM (excluding enriched jobs and most high involvement practices) increased between 1980 and 1998 at the same time as trade union membership declined, but the two trends were not directly associated. Indeed, motivational supports, such as a preference for internal recruitment, job security guarantees and single status, were found to be positively related to union recognition in the UK (De Menezes and Wood 2006), which reflects the first point that some HRM practices reflect trade union goals.

Moreover, the rise of direct communication, associated with HRM, is also not necessarily a substitute for trade unionism. Wood and Fenton-O'Creevy (2005), for example, showed in a variety of European countries that direct communication methods could be used in conjunction with trade unions or other representative methods. Likewise, Brewster *et al.* (2007) compared Britain, Sweden and Germany and showed that, while direct methods of communication were on the increase, there was no convergence towards a heavy reliance on these at the expense of indirect or representational methods of involvement such as collective bargaining or joint consultation. Moreover, regardless of the combinations of direct methods with types of in-direct methods, the level of voice in Wood and Fenton-O'Creevy's (2005) study was no lower than in representative systems that were not supplemented with direct methods (where employee voice is measured on a graded scale, from negotiation through consultation and information provision to no voice). Only the use of direct communication alone, without any representative involvement, was associated with a lower level of voice, but there was no evidence that this is uniquely associated with the use of other HRM practices. Overall the evidence suggests that formal employee voice institutions matter for voice that goes beyond information sharing but that the level of voice is not necessarily reduced by HRM practices.

Third, there is no strong evidence that unions or other representative bodies affect the HRM–performance relationship, which implies that organizations are less likely to derecognize unions simply to install high involvement or other HRM practices. Evidence shows that the growth of HIM reflects changing operational or production methods rather than any anti-union, individualistic or humanistic values on the part of management. Particularly important as a major driver are lean production methods. Analysis of high involvement practices in the UK using data from a Sheffield Institute of Work Psychology (IWP) survey and the WERS 1998 showed relationships between HIM practices and lean methods such as total quality management (TQM) – making all staff responsible for quality and continuous improvement – and just in time (JIT) – making products in direct response to internal and external customer demands and not for stock (Wood *et al.* 2004; De Menezes and Wood 2006). A 22-year longitudinal study of lean production in manufacturing, using the IWP data, showed that two key HIM practices – teams and empowerment – which combined both enriched jobs and forms of organizational involvement such as idea capturing – were associated with lean operational methods (e.g. TQM and JIT), and moreover that the more integrated the use of HIM with these operational methods, the higher the levels of productivity (De Menezes *et al.* 2010).

More generally, Clegg *et al.* (2002), using IWP survey data from the UK, Australia, Japan and Switzerland, similarly found that high involvement and operational practices tended to be used together in manufacturing firms in all four countries. Consistent with Japan's greater use of lean methods, both Clegg *et al.*'s study and Wood's (1996c) study of Japanese-owned manufacturing workplaces in Britain in the mid-1990s found that, except for teamwork, high involvement practices were significantly more prevalent in Japanese workplaces than in others. Clegg *et al.* also showed that empowerment was lower in these plants, which reinforces the earlier point that role and organizational involvement need not go hand in hand.

De Menezes *et al.* (2010) found that the pioneers of the high lean approach continued to outperform even those who subsequently adopted it. These later adopters gained the performance advantages associated with the integrated approach, but their productivity growth was not sufficient to catch up with those who had adopted it earlier. This suggests that employee involvement is helping to achieve lean production's goal of continuous improvement. The development of HRM and particularly HIM has been and will continue to be an important part of diffusing lean and associated operational management ideas and, as such, part of the globalization of modern management methods (see Chapter 20). Nonetheless, HIM may be more readily adaptable in some nations, so while organizations adopting it may outperform others in an economy, they may still be performing on average lower than comparable (or even all) organizations in other national contexts. We now turn to these contexts and the limited literature on their links to HIM.

National employment relations systems

A fundamental element of comparative employment relations is the importance of institutions in managerial behaviour (see Chapter 2). Institutions may affect the extent of adoption of HRM practices, or the ways in which they are adopted or their success. National institutional systems represent sets of rules and resources that shape organizational goals and the use and effectiveness of management practices. Within the terms of neo-institutional organizational theory, organizations have to attend to more than economic or product market pressures; to survive they must conform to the rules and belief systems prevailing in the environment (DiMaggio and Powell 1983; Scott 1995). Organizations may sub-optimize economically for the sake of maintaining legitimacy. Legal and other regulatory agencies and business associations may constrain managements, but also they may, directly or indirectly, provide organizations with resources such as skilled workers or opportunities for relationships that facilitate innovation and learning.

In the long run there may not be a strong tension between adopting a practice for legitimacy purposes and maximizing one's economic or core performance objectives. Equally, in the case of HRM practices, if they are adopted for efficiency purposes, they are unlikely to conflict with the pursuit of legitimacy. For example, it would appear that extending either role or organizational involvement is unlikely to be seen as illegitimate in modern societies. Yet where management puts a large store on having a prerogative over work organization, technology and business decisions, the assumed advantages of HRM may not be so readily appreciated. Gooderham *et al.* (1999) suggested that where management has a significant degree of autonomy from institutions, they may opt for the calculative approach to HRM, as they would prefer to deal with employees individually. They may see employee involvement as reducing their control to levels that adversely affect performance or at least constrain or slow down their decision-making.

National contexts may affect: (1) the extent of adopting specific approaches and practices; (2) the form they take; and (3) the effects on organizational performance and employee well-being and behaviour. For example, when the use of high involvement practices was first identified as integral to the ascendancy of Japanese manufacturing, the significance of the surrounding employment relations institutions was widely acknowledged. Much discussion focused on the lifetime employment systems built on the complex segmentation of the labour markets, and the use of temporary and contract workers as buffers by employers. These mechanisms were thought to create job and psychological security for workers and an orientation towards efficiency and sharing the success of the company. But other elements were identified as equally, if not more important, particularly the *nenkō* wage system, in which the assessment, age and seniority of workers are important determinants of wages, and which creates keen competition for promotion within the company. The enterprise basis of trade unionism, in which the roles within the union either overlap with company roles (such as when the supervisor is a shop steward) or are integrated into the career system of the enterprise, is also important. Although jobs may not be designed with a great deal of individual autonomy and discretion, the Japanese context has enabled the development of a wide range of organizational involvement methods, including idea-capturing schemes and joint consultation processes in which workers' representatives are involved in planning and scheduling production, overtime, and work allocation.

More generally, commonly adopted categories for differentiating national institutional contexts are presented as implying that these influence managerial approaches to involvement. Differences in managerial prerogatives, skill formation systems and unionization are often embedded in the very definitions of key concepts such as the coordinated and liberal market economies so central to the Varieties of Capitalism approach (Hall and Soskice 2001, and see Chapter 2 in this volume). The capacity for coordinated economies to develop high levels of industry-specific skills and trust between employers and workers, as well as the institutional separation of wage bargaining from production and wider organizational issues, has been discussed in the HRM literature. In contrast, liberal market economies are characterized as having less coordinated training across the economy and a history of distrust between employers and workers based on a contractual rather than a partnership orientation towards each other. Based on the commonplace assumption that HRM is a unitary concept, namely, employers and workers having an overriding common interest, it is then argued that HRM is incompatible with the low trust liberal market economies with a history of conflicting relations (Godard 2010). HRM is less likely to reap the performance gains or be readily institutionalized and survive in the long-term in liberal market economies as, for example, firms make redundancies or overtly control and monitor the performance of workers. In contrast, the alignment of interests and trust within coordinated economies makes high involvement practices in particular more readily applicable.

However, the root of this argument is weak, as it rests on a long-standing association of management theories with an assumed unitary philosophy. In fact, the foundations of these theories have always rested on an acceptance of a structural conflict between employers and employees and the desire to develop methods that would bring economic prosperity through aligning competing interests, not reducing them to one common interest (see Wagner-Tsukamoto 2007, on the case of Taylorism). Second, intra-national data suggests that the union factor *per se* is less important than other variables. As we have seen, union presence is no more or less likely to inhibit the spread of HRM practices in the USA and the UK, or to impact on their performance effects, and there is, as yet, no evidence of their declining use over time in unionized sectors of the economy. Moreover, although unions in liberal market economies have expressed some resistance to HRM, subsequent trade union positions acknowledged that HIM was a more circumscribed approach and that the quality of work came higher up people's evaluations of what they want from work than was previously acknowledged. Third, the works council dimension, which particularly differentiates coordinated economies, was not found to be associated with a greater use of high involvement practices in Germany or with a greater voice in their design or implementation (Frick 2002; Zwick 2004). Moreover, any role works councils play in HRM does not appear to arise from its cooperative orientation; Frick (2002) found a greater use of high involvement practices when management rated the works council as 'antagonistic'.

Nonetheless, it is possible that unions in liberal markets have been less involved in the introduction of HRM practices than in coordinated economies, and as Thelen (1991: 225) puts it, their historical marginalization from work reorganization issues 'only reinforces their more defensive role in the process'. In contrast, in coordinated economies there are already adjuncts to collective bargaining in the form of works councils and a higher level of trust between workers and manager, so this may mean that involvement methods are not seen by unions as encroaching on their role. The national coverage of unions and collective bargaining and the legally backed rights of works councils allow the councils to 'participate positively in work reorganization from a position of relative strength' (Thelen 1991: 225).

Even so, national employment relations institutions may not be fundamental drivers of HRM. They may have the capacity to constrain managers' willingness to experiment or workers to fully embrace these experiments. But the relative differentiation in HRM practices between liberal market economies and coordinated economies may reflect differences in national institutions other than systems of collective employee representation. In particular, national training systems create different levels of skills and types of orientation among workforces, while employment protection legislation may affect the expected returns on HIM (Doellgast 2008: 292). In addition, both training and employment protection systems may increase the level of trust between employers and employees.

Studies in call centres involving Germany and the USA support such arguments. Call centres are a good case for testing whether HIM is more likely to be adopted and successful in coordinated economies, especially when there is a highly skilled and trusted workforce, because the jobs in such centres are generally seen as highly structured and based on technologies that constrain enriched job design. Moreover the recent introduction of call centres means the effects of bargaining institutions may be weaker compared to older workplaces. Doellgast (2008) showed that the prevalence of self-managed teams, quality circles, flexible job descriptions and task discretion was higher in Germany than in the American call centres. The use of these practices was independent of the bargaining institutions in both countries and, in the case of Germany, independent of the presence of a works council. Intensive performance management, associated with the calculative approach to HRM, was more prevalent in the USA. Other national institutions that generate job security and a highly skilled workforce are decisive for the adoption of HRM practices in Germany compared with the USA, where there is less protection and less formalized extra-company training systems for workers. However, the extent of intensive performance management was influenced by employment relations institutions because it was less common in call centres with both collective bargaining and a works council.

A second study of call centres, by Holman *et al.* (2009), focused on job design in 17 countries, including liberal and coordinated market economies as well as a third type, newly industrializing countries. They also assessed the importance of national institutional settings relative to the call centres' market strategy (in Porter's 1980 terms). The study showed that the coordinated economies, such as Germany and Sweden, were indeed more likely to have jobs with higher levels of discretion but also – reflecting greater levels of trust – less intensive performance monitoring compared to liberal market economies, such as the UK and the USA. The research showed that national institutional systems explained much of the variation in performance monitoring, which was most common in the liberal market economies. However, in the case of job discretion, the call centre's market strategy was more significant than national institutional systems. Job design in call centres in industrializing countries such as India and Poland was more similar to that in liberal market economies than to the coordinated market economies.

In both these call centre studies, job design was shown to have significant implications for organizational outcomes. In Doellgast's (2008) study, HIM was significantly associated with lower quit rates in both countries, a result that was not moderated by intra-country differences in employment relations institutions. In the Holman *et al.* (2009) study, the effects on performance also did not vary according to the national system. Job discretion was negatively associated with quit rates and labour costs, and a more intensive, potentially punitive monitoring was negatively associated with call abandonment rates, and positively associated with quit rates and sales growth. Consistent with these results, a study by Brookes *et al.* (2011) attempted to assess if Gooderham *et al.*'s (1999) calculative approach was more likely to be used in liberal market economies. In a study of 3,027 firms with more than 100 employees in 14 countries (12 European plus New Zealand and Australia), they found that institutional closeness to the USA was positively related to the use of calculative HRM. The association of the calculative approach with the USA was consistent with the observation that US multinationals insisted that their subsidiaries abroad used merit pay, the fulcrum of this approach (Almond *et al.* 2006).

We should, however, avoid labelling the calculative approach as American HRM, whether this is counterposed to a continental European collaborative approach or not, and more generally be wary of attaching any approach to a particular region. First, there is considerable diversity in HRM practices within countries, as illustrated by the range in the data using the measures of HRM in the studies we have reviewed. Moreover, the diversity may be greater in liberal market economies as management has more autonomy from institutions (Turner 1991). Second, in Gooderham *et al.*'s (1999) terms, the calculative approach can be used in conjunction with the collaborative, as in the holistic approach to HRM based on involvement. The combined use of these approaches may not fall into neat geographical categories. Thus, Gooderham *et al.*'s study showed that, at least in the 1990s, use of the collaborative and calculative approaches was greater in the UK than in Germany, France or Spain, while use of the collaborative approach was lower in the UK than in Norway and Denmark. Studies assessing convergence in Europe, which focused on voice mechanisms (Brewster *et al.* 2007) or aspects of personnel other than HIM (Brewster *et al.* 2008; Mayrhofer *et al.* 2011), found no strong support for any convergence in HRM or employment relations. Studies are needed that measure all elements of HRM, both separately and in combination, and gauge the management orientations underlying the different configurations.

Conclusion

This chapter has introduced the concept of HRM and overviewed the studies that have assessed its relationship with organizational performance, job satisfaction and well-being, direct forms of involvement and national employment relations systems. HRM is concerned with a set of practices – enriched job design, idea-capturing schemes, information disclosure, appraisal systems, intensive training, teamwork, performance-related pay – which may be classified into three main elements – work organization, training and development, and motivation enhancement practices. Approaches to HRM may vary depending on which of these is emphasized, though the focus in the literature has been on their holistic use. The high involvement approach is centred on role and organizational involvement, and the forms of motivational support that are compatible or used with high involvement may not be limited to one type such as performance-related pay. Studies of the HRM–performance relationship have yielded results that suggest a positive link. It is nonetheless unclear which practices or underlying approaches are decisive in accounting for this link. However, from studies that focused on enriched jobs and high organizational involvement, these would appear to be important contributory factors.

What evidence we have on the relationship between HRM practices and worker attitudes also suggests a generally positive relationship between job satisfaction and enriched jobs although, in some cases, the relationship may be negative. Nonetheless, the positive aspects of direct involvement do not seem to account for the widespread decline in trade unionism and are not associated with a decline in overall voice or the availability of indirect representative forms of involvement. New operational management methods anchored in Japanese-inspired lean philosophy are major factors behind the growth of HRM and HIM. The limited comparative studies of HRM have been largely confined to HIM and performance management, and suggest that enriched jobs are more prevalent in coordinated market economies. These studies suggest the performance effects of such practices seem to be universal and are not strongly affected by national context. There is also little to suggest that the pursuit of HRM or HIM is inevitably at the expense of trade unions and other formal representative bodies. We have no evidence on whether job satisfaction and particularly the negative effects on well-being are contingent on the national context. Overall, too few studies have assessed different configurations of HRM practices across countries to permit us to draw any firm conclusions about which practices are decisive for performance or well-being, which relationships are universal and which reflect different varieties of capitalism. We certainly need more studies akin to the call centre studies we showcased; and comparative analysis may be a significant means of answering key questions surrounding HRM and HIM. Nonetheless, the most pressing need is to clearly differentiate types of involvement and other aspects of HRM and this entails being particularly cautious about, or even forsaking, the simple aggregation of practices to form global HRM indexes.

Within industrial relations it has long been recognized that the collective bargaining system in the USA was founded on the bedrock of the Taylorist system of work organization. Yet the initial development of the subject focused on the former in isolation of the latter. Its proponents also sought to differentiate themselves from the work organization and interpersonal focus of the human relations movement (Dunlop 1950), and thus accentuated the narrowly circumscribed nature of industrial relations. The increased saliency of HIM has contributed to an increased concern about interpersonal relations in the workplace, covering issues such as bullying and discrimination and their construction as mainstream employment relations phenomena. The saliency of HIM should be viewed not as driving a wedge through the field of employment relations but rather as heightening the need for an integrated employment relations in which the core remains centred on various types of involvement and voice. Integration also implies the *simultaneous* pursuit of understanding *inter*-national and *intra*-national differences. Pursuing this agenda should ensure that the need for comparative analysis – as well as conceptual clarity – will take care of itself.

References

Almond, P., Muller-Camen, M., Collings, D. and Quintanilla, J. (2006) 'Pay and performance', in P. Almond and A. Ferner (eds) *American Multinationals in Europe: Managing Employment Relations across National Borders*, Oxford: Oxford University Press.

Appelbaum, E., Bailey, T., Berg P. and Kalleberg, A. L. (2000) *Manufacturing Advantage: Why High Performance Work Systems Pay Off*, Ithaca, NY: Cornell University Press.

Arthur, J. B. (1994) 'Effects of human resource systems on manufacturing performance and turnover', *Academy of Management Journal*, 37(3): 670–87.

Bae, J. and Lawler, J. J. (2000) 'Organizational and HRM strategies in Korea: impact on firm performance in an emerging economy', *Academy of Management Journal*, 43(3): 502–17.

Barker, J. R. (1993) 'Tightening the iron cage: concertive control in self-managing teams', *Administrative Science Quarterly*, 38(3): 408–37.

Barling, J. E., Kelloway, K. and Iverson, R. D. (2003) 'High-quality work, job satisfaction, and occupational injuries', *Journal of Applied Psychology*, 88(2): 276–83.

Becker, B. E. and Gerhart, B. (1996) 'The impact of human resource management on organizational performance: progress and prospects', *Academy of Management Journal*, 39(4): 779–801.

Beer, M., Spector, B., Lawrence, P. R., Mills, D. Q. and Walton, R. E. (1984) *Managing Human Assets*, New York: The Free Press.

Benson, G. S. and Lawler, E. E. III (2003) 'Employee involvement: utilization, impacts and future prospects', in D. Holman, T. Wall, C. Clegg, P. Sparrow and A. Howard (eds) *The Essentials of the New Workplace*, London: Wiley.

Brewster, C., Brookes, M., Croucher, R. and Wood, G. (2007) 'Collective and individual voice: convergence in Europe?', *International Journal of Human Resource Management*, 18(7): 1246–62.

Brewster, C., Wood, G. and Brookes, M. (2008) 'Similarity, isomorphism or duality? Recent survey evidence on the human resource management policies of multinational corporations', *British Journal of Management*, 19(4): 320–42.

Brookes, M., Croucher, R., Fenton-O'Creevy, M. and Gooderham, P. (2011) 'Measuring competing explanations of human resource management practices through the Cranet survey: cultural versus institutional explanations', *Human Resource Management Review*, 21(1): 68–79.

Clegg, C. W., Wall, T. D., Pepper, K., Stride, C., Woods, D. and Morrison, D., (2002) 'An international survey of the use and effectiveness of modern manufacturing practices', *Human Factors and Ergonomics*, 12(2): 171–91.

Combs, J., Liu, Y., Hall, A. and Ketchen, D. (2006) 'How much do high-performance work practices matter? A meta-analysis of their effects on organizational performance', *Personnel Psychology*, 59(3): 501–28.

Cotton, J. L. (1993) *Employee Involvement*, Thousand Oaks, CA: Sage.

Delery, J. E. and Doty, D. H. (1996) 'Modes of theorizing in strategic human resource management: tests of universalistic, contingency, and configurational performance predictions', *Academy of Management Journal*, 39(4): 802–35.

De Menezes, L. M. and Wood, S. (2006) 'The reality of flexible work systems in Britain', *International Journal of Human Resource Management*, 17(1): 1–33.

De Menezes, L., Wood, S. and Gelade, G. (2010) 'A longitudinal study of the latent class clusters of modern management practices and their association with organizational performance in British manufacturing', *Operations Management*, 28(6): 405–71.

DiMaggio, P. J. and Powell, W. W. (1983) 'The iron cage revisited: institutional isomorphism and collective rationality in organizational fields', *American Sociological Review*, 48(2): 147–60.

Doellgast, V. L. (2008) 'Collective bargaining and high involvement management in comparative perspective: evidence from US and German call centers', *Industrial Relations*, 47(2): 284–319.

Dunlop, J. T. (1950) 'Framework for the analysis of industrial relations: two views', *Industrial and Labor Relations Review*, 3(3): 383–412.

Fey, C. F., Björkman, I. and Pavlovskaya, A. (2000) 'The effect of human resource management practices on firm performance in Russia', *International Journal of Human Resource Management*, 11(1): 1–18.

Fiorito, J. (2001) 'Human resource management practices and worker desires for union representation', *Journal of Labor Research*, 22(2): 335–54.

Frick, B. (2002) '"High performance work practices" und betriebliche Mitbestimmung: komplementär oder substitutiv? Empirische Befunde für den deutschen Maschinenbau', *Industrielle Beziehungen*, 9(1): 79–102.

Godard, J. (2004) 'A critical assessment of the high-performance paradigm', *British Journal of Industrial Relations*, 42(2): 349–78.

—— (2010) 'What is best for workers? The implications for workplace and human resource management practices revisited', *Industrial Relations*, 49(3): 406–88.

Gooderham, P. N., Nordhaug, O. and Ringdal, K. (1999) 'Institutional and rational determinants of organizational practices: human resource management in European firms', *Administrative Science Quarterly*, 44(3): 507–31.

Guthrie, J. P. (2001) 'High involvement work practices, turnover and productivity: evidence from New Zealand', *Academy of Management Journal*, 44(1): 180–90.

Hall, P. A. and Soskice, D. (eds) (2001) *Varieties of Capitalism: The Institutional Foundations of Comparative Advantage*, Oxford: Oxford University Press.

Harley, B., Allen, B. C. and Sargent, L. D. (2007) 'High performance work systems and employee experience of work in the service sector: the case of aged care', *British Journal of Industrial Relations*, 45(3): 607–33.

Holman, D., Frenkel, S., Sørensen, O. and Wood, S. (2009) 'Work design variation and outcomes in call centers: strategic-choice and institutional explanations', *Industrial and Labor Relations Review*, 62(2): 510–32.

Huselid, M. A. (1995) 'The impact of human resource management practices on turnover, productivity, and corporate financial performance', *Academy of Management Journal*, 38(3): 635–72.

—— and Becker, B. E. (1996) 'Methodological issues in cross-sectional and panel estimates of the human resource-firm performance link', *Industrial Relations*, 35(3): 400–22.

Kalmi, P. and Kauhanen, A. (2008) 'Workplace innovations and employee outcomes: evidence from Finland', *Industrial Relations*, 47(3): 430–59.

Kochan, T. A. and Osterman, P. (1994) *The Mutual Gains Enterprise: Forging a Winning Partnership among Labor, Management and Government*, Cambridge, MA: Harvard Business School Press.

Lawler, E. E. (1986) *High Involvement Management*, San Francisco: Jossey-Bass.

MacDuffie, J. P. (1995) 'Human resource bundles and manufacturing performance: organizational logic and flexible production systems in the world auto industry', *Industrial and Labor Relations Review*, 48(2): 197–221.

Machin, S. and Wood, S. (2005) 'HRM as a substitute for trade unions in British workplaces', *Industrial and Labor Relations Review*, 58(2): 201–18.

Mackie, K. S., Holahan, C. K. and Gottlieb, N. H. (2001) 'Employee involvement management practices, work stress, and depression in employees of a human services residential care facility', *Human Relations*, 54(8): 1065–92.

Macky, K. and Boxall, P. (2007) 'The relationship between "high performance work practices" and employee attitudes: an investigation of additive and interaction effects', *International Journal of Human Resource Management*, 18(4): 537–67.

Mayrhofer, W., Brewster, C., Morley, M. J. and Ledolter, J. (2011) 'Hearing a different drummer? Convergence of human resource management in Europe – a longitudinal analysis', *Human Resource Management Review*, 21(1): 50–67.

Mohr, R. D. and Zoghi, C. (2008) 'High involvement management work design and job satisfaction', *Industrial and Labor Relations Review*, 61(3): 275–96.

Osterman, P. (1994) 'How common is workplace transformation and who adopts it?', *Industrial and Labor Relations Review*, 47(2): 175–88.

Porter, M. E. (1980) *Competitive Strategy: Techniques for Analyzing Industries and Competitors*, New York: Free Press.

Ramsey, H., Scholarios, D. and Harley, B. (2000) 'Employees and high-performance work systems: testing inside the black box', *British Journal of Industrial Relations*, 38(4): 501–31.

Royle, T. and Towers, B. (2002) *Labour Relations in the Global Fast-Food Industry*, London: Routledge.

Scott, W. R. (1995) *Institutions and Organizations*, Thousand Oaks, CA: Sage.

Subramony, M. (2009) 'A meta-analytic investigation of the relationship between HRM bundles and firm performance', *Human Resource Management*, 48(5): 745–68.

Thelen, K. (1991) *Union of Parts: Labor Politics in Postwar Germany*, Ithaca, NY: Cornell University Press.

Turner, L. (1991) *Democracy at Work: Changing World Markets and the Future of Labor Unions*, Ithaca, NY: Cornell University Press.

Van der Doef, M. and Maes, S. (1999) 'The job demand–control(–support) model and psychological well-being: a review of 20 years of empirical research', *Work and Stress*, 13(2): 87–114.

Wagner-Tsukamoto, S. A. (2007) 'An institutional economic reconstruction of scientific management: on the lost theoretical logic of Taylorism', *Academy of Management Review*, 32(1): 105–17.

Wall, T. D. and Wood, S. (2005) 'The romance of human resource management and business performance and the case for big science', *Human Relations*, 58(4): 1–34.

Walton, R. E. (1985) 'From "control" to "commitment" in the workplace', *Harvard Business Review*, 63(2): 77–84.

West, M. A., Guthrie, J. P., Dawson, J. F., Borrill, C. S. and Carter, M. (2006) 'Reducing patient mortality in hospitals: the role of human resource management', *Journal of Organizational Behaviour*, 27(7): 983–1002.

Womack, J., Jones, D. T. and Roos, D. (1990) *The Machine that Changed the World*, New York: Rawson.

Wood, S. J. (1988) 'Between Fordism and flexibility? The US car industry', in R. Hyman and W. Streeck (eds) *New Technology and Industrial Relations*, Oxford: Blackwell.

—— (1996a) 'High commitment management and payment systems', *Journal of Management Studies*, 33(1): 53–77.

—— (1996b) 'High commitment management and unionization in the UK', *International Journal of Human Resource Management*, 7(1): 41–58.

—— (1996c) 'How different are human resource practices in Japanese "transplants" in the UK?', *Industrial Relations*, 35(4): 511–25.

—— (2009a) 'Human resource management and organizational performance', in D. G. Collins and G. Wood (eds) *Human Resource Management: A Critical Introduction*, London: Routledge.

—— (2009b) 'High involvement management and performance', in A. Wilkinson, P. Gollan, M. Marchington and D. Lewin (eds) *The Oxford Handbook of Participation in Organizations*, Oxford: Oxford University Press.

—— and De Menezes, L. (2008) 'Comparing perspectives on high involvement management and organizational performance across the British economy', *International Journal of Human Resource Management*, 19(4): 639–83.

—— and De Menezes, L. (2011) 'High involvement management, high performance work systems and well-being', *International Journal of Human Resource Management*, 22(7): 1585–608.

—— and Fenton-O'Creevy, M. P. (2005) 'Direct involvement, representation and employee voice in UK multinationals in Europe', *European Journal of Industrial Relations*, 11(1): 27–50.

——, Stride, C. B., Wall, T. D. and Clegg, C. W. (2004) 'Revisiting the use and effectiveness of modern management practices', *Human Factors and Ergonomics in Manufacturing*, 14(4): 415–32.

——, Van Veldoven, M., Croon, M. and De Menezes, L. M. (2012) 'Enriched job design, high involvement management and organizational performance: the mediating roles of job satisfaction and well-being', *Human Relations*, 65(4): 419–46.

Workplace Employment Relations Survey 2004 (WERS 2004). Online. Available at: http://www.wers2004.info (accessed 25 September 2012).

Wright, T. A. and Cropanzano, R. (2007) 'The happy/productive worker thesis revisited', *Research in Personnel and Human Resources Management*, 26: 269–307.

Zwick, T. (2003) *Works Councils and the Productivity Impact of Direct Employee Participation*, Mannheim: Centre for European Economic Research (ZEW), ZEW Discussion Papers 03–47.

—— (2004) 'Employee participation and productivity', *Labour Economics*, 11(6): 715–40.

7 Employment relations and economic performance

Eileen Appelbaum and John Schmitt

Introduction

Employment outcomes in the Organization for Economic Co-operation and Development (OECD) European countries in the middle of the last century were enviable: European unemployment rates were consistently below that of the USA through the 1970s and into the early 1980s. Unemployment rates in 1980 in continental Europe's largest economies – Germany and France – were 2.6 and 5.8 per cent respectively, compared with 7.1 per cent in the USA. Between 1980 and 2000, however, the unemployment rate in the USA fell while unemployment rates in continental European countries diverged, falling in some countries and rising in others. Notably, the unemployment rates in Germany and France rose to 8 and 9 per cent respectively while the US unemployment rate fell to 4 per cent. Meanwhile, the share of the working age population that is employed – the employment-to-population ratio – moved in the opposite direction, rising in the USA and falling in Germany and France.[1] Thus, the USA experienced a falling unemployment rate even as a larger share of the population entered the workforce seeking – and finding – jobs.

The gap between the USA and several of Europe's largest economies in job creation and unemployment led to a search for an explanation of these differences. What followed was a spate of econometric cross-country studies built on the notion that, in the absence of labour market 'rigidities' that interfere with the functioning of market mechanisms, full employment would prevail. These studies sought the causes of variations across countries in the unemployment rate in differences in labour market institutions. This chapter examines the theory underlying this approach and critically examines the empirical evidence mustered in support of it. We find the evidence unpersuasive. Our review of the labour market institutions most important for comparative employment relations leads us to two main conclusions: first, that institutions interact in complex ways, so that constellations of labour market institutions are more than just the sum of their parts; and second, that – with some notable exceptions – trade unions, their centre-left political allies, and academics who study employment relations have tended to ignore or downplay the role played by macro-economic institutions such as central banks (the Federal Reserve in the USA and the European Central Bank), currency regimes and macro-economic policies in determining budget deficits and sovereign debt; and the role of interest rates and exchange rates in determining growth and employment outcomes.[2]

The chapter is organized as follows. In the next section we examine the dominant view that labour market, institutions primarily act to distort competitive outcomes in the labour market, thereby increasing the unemployment rate, lowering employment levels, and lowering gross domestic product (GDP). In this section, we primarily review econometric analyses of the connection between labour market institutions and employment. We find the evidence for this view unpersuasive and emphasize the lack of robust empirical support for the standard claims. The following section goes beyond the econometric evidence to take a more fine-grained look at economies with different constellations of labour market institutions. We demonstrate that there are few systematic connections between individual characteristics of labour markets and macro-economic performance. In particular, labour market institutions do not systematically affect inflation, GDP growth, unemployment rates, or employment-to-population ratios. The next section argues that there is no strong relationship between labour market institutions and macro-economic outcomes because the relevant institutions interact in complex ways, creating more than one path to full employment. Coordinated bargaining institutions that moderate wage demands of strong unions may be as effective as weak unions in promoting low unemployment and high rates of growth. In the penultimate section we show that differences in macro-economic policy – that is, fiscal and monetary policies – affect the pattern of unemployment across countries. Tight monetary policy and fiscal austerity in the face of external shocks, for example, can constrain growth and raise the unemployment rate, despite much of the orthodox thinking about macro-economics over the last three decades. The final section concludes with a review of the period since the onset of the Great Recession and examines the lessons for policy that can be gleaned from the very different policy responses and experiences across the OECD countries.

Labour market institutions and unemployment

Following the experience of the Great Depression of the 1930s, the publication of John Maynard Keynes' (1936) analysis of the causes of high unemployment had a great influence on policy-makers. The lesson drawn in the USA and, to a lesser extent, in Europe, was that employment is determined primarily by aggregate demand – the sum of the demand by households for consumption goods, by business for investment goods, by the rest of the world for a country's exports, and the level of government spending on the purchase of goods and services. In periods when private sector demand flags and net exports (exports minus imports) is weak, it is up to the government to increase its spending and run deficits to take up the slack. The role of the monetary authorities is to support expansionary fiscal policy by increasing the money supply and taking actions designed to keep interest rates low. In the USA, this approach to fiscal and monetary policy moderated the business cycle. It led to long periods of expansion and to contractions that were short and, for the most part, mild. By the early 1970s, Republican President Richard Nixon could declare, as he removed the USA from the gold standard: 'I am now a Keynesian in economics.'[3] A second school of macro-economics, based on the work of Milton Friedman, held that fiscal policy was ineffective and that the role of monetary policy was to maintain price stability. This monetarist approach to macro-economic policy was a minority view in the USA in the decades after World War II. It was more popular in Europe, where the German central bank, the Bundesbank, played the leading role in macro-economic policy and memories of German hyperinflation in the 1920s remained strong. The oil price shocks of the 1970s led to high inflation and high unemployment in the USA and to a greater focus by policy-makers on price stability. In the 1970s and 1980s, a new approach to macro-economic policy, building on the monetarist views of Milton Friedman, became prominent. Today, the dominant explanation for differences in employment and unemployment across countries derives from this approach to macro-economic theory (known as New or Classical theory), which emerged in the mid-1970s (Lucas 1972; Sargent 1973; Barro 1976).[4] According to this theory, institutional arrangements in labour markets interfere with what would otherwise be perfectly competitive markets and it is these distortions, rather than a deficiency of aggregate demand, that lead to unemployment. In the absence of 'labour market rigidities' that reduce competition in labour markets, such as a legally mandated minimum wage, the presence of unions, the size of the public sector, generous unemployment insurance benefits, and employment protection laws, the economy, according to this view, would experience full employment (see, for example, Siebert 1997). In perfectly competitive labour markets, wages would simply adjust and full employment would prevail. The argument is that institutional arrangements in each country's labour markets determine a unique level of 'equilibrium' unemployment, to which that country's economy will tend to return. Efforts by policy-makers to use fiscal or monetary policy to reduce the unemployment rate below this 'natural' rate of unemployment will only cause inflation to accelerate. In this framework, the only way policy-makers can sustainably lower the unemployment rate is by removing 'market imperfections' (such as unions, minimum wages, and unemployment benefits) that raise the 'natural rate' of unemployment.

This argument rests on two pillars: on faith in the possibility of perfectly competitive labour markets in which employers have no more power than employees to determine wages; and on changes in labour market institutions that can explain the reversal in unemployment experience in countries such as Germany and France. Nickell (2003) and Layard *et al.* (2005) contend that changes in key labour market institutions can explain changes in unemployment across countries. But identifying such institutional changes has proved difficult. For example, Nickell's (1997) simple but influential 'scorecard exercise' sought to link institutions, including unions, unemployment benefits, and employment protection legislation to employment outcomes, but failed to explain the high unemployment in France, Germany, Italy, and Spain in the 1990s.[5] As Howell observes:

> according to Nickell's scorecard, both Austria and Switzerland – two consistently low unemployment countries – should have shown the same dismal performance as France. The three other high unemployment countries (Germany, Spain and Italy) get the same scores in the middle of the distribution as Norway and the U.S.
>
> (Howell 2010: 13)

Although a direct relationship between labour market rigidities and the unemployment rate has been difficult to establish, an important variation on this theme has emerged (OECD 1994; Blanchard and Wolfers 2000). While acknowledging that changes in labour market institutions cannot explain the increase in unemployment in some European countries after the early 1980s, this view argues that the more rigid institutions in some European countries, as compared with the USA, had the effect of slowing growth, following adverse shocks to the economy. Thus, as Siebert (1997) notes, both Europe and the USA experienced oil shocks in the early and late 1970s, but the USA did not experience an ongoing rise in unemployment over the next 25 years. Similarly, any shocks from trade or technology were also experienced by the United States. Proponents of this view argue that, as a result of more rigid labour market institutions, employment in countries such as Germany and France did not fully recover following such external shocks, and unemployment remained high. Divergence among European countries in rates of unemployment was attributed to differences in the extent of labour market rigidities (Siebert 1997; Saint-Paul 2004).

Proponents point to various differences between US and European labour markets. Thus, the statutory minimum wage in France rose from about 40 per cent of the average wage in the 1960s to about 60 per cent in the 1990s. In the USA, in contrast, the minimum wage fell from more than 50 per cent of the median wage in the 1960s to about a third of the median wage in the 1990s. The codetermination law passed in Germany in 1976 provided workers with representation on the supervisory boards of large companies and placed limits on, among other things, firms' ability to lay off workers. Plans to dismiss workers have to be discussed with works councils and severance pay became standard. In the USA, in contrast, employers have far greater freedom to lay off or fire workers at will. Unemployment benefits are far more generous in many European countries than in the USA. Drawing on OECD data, Siebert notes that in the mid-1990s the ratio of unemployment benefits to previous after-tax income was 'in the range of 41 to 60 percent in Germany and the United Kingdom and 81 to 100 percent in Denmark and Sweden, whereas it ranges from 21 to 40 percent in the United States' (1997: 50). More generally, low unionization and low coordination of industrial relations in the USA – as compared with the relatively high unionization and union coverage rates in much of Europe – were interpreted as meaning that wage formation in the USA 'comes close to being a market process' (Siebert 1997: 46).

The OECD's 1994 Jobs Study was particularly influential in arguing that these differences in labour market institutions account for the variation in countries' responses to external shocks. In the Introduction to that report, the OECD summarized its view of the cause of higher unemployment in OECD Europe as follows:

> After having considered the available evidence and the various theories which have been advanced to explain today's unemployment, the basic conclusion was reached that it is an inability of OECD economies and societies to adapt rapidly and innovatively to a world of rapid structural change that is the principal cause of high and persistent unemployment. Consequently, the main thrust of the study was directed towards identifying the institutions, rules and regulations, and practices and policies which have weakened the capacity of OECD countries to adapt and to innovate, and to search for appropriate policy responses in these areas.
>
> (OECD 1994: vii)

Thus, the Jobs Study acknowledges that the OECD economies faced important shocks and structural changes that are relevant for policy-makers, but it shifts the blame for high unemployment to economic and social institutions that it maintains cannot adapt to these changes. Also notable is the OECD's negative view in this study of macro-economic policy responses to high unemployment: 'The use of fiscal policy in response to a more or less permanent supply shock . . . weakened the incentives of people to make the necessary adjustments' (ibid.: 63).

A large empirical literature has grown up to address the claim that variations in labour market institutions – especially 'protective' institutions such as trade unions, employment protection legislation and unemployment benefits – that shelter less-skilled workers from the full brunt of employers' actions, explain, differences in unemployment and employment-to-population rates across countries (Scarpetta 1996; Nickell 1997; Elmeskov *et al.* 1998; Belot and van Ours 2004; and other studies cited in OECD 2006). These studies have had a strong influence on the policies promoted to reduce unemployment and improve labour market outcomes. The policies that follow from the diagnosis that labour market rigidities lead to high unemployment and low employment-to-population ratios have stark and profound implications for workers. In a theme that was echoed in 2012 in the demands made on Greece, Spain, Ireland, Portugal, and Italy during the Eurozone crisis, the International Monetary Fund (IMF) proclaimed in 2003 that:

> . . . The European Commission, the [OECD] and the [IMF] have argued that the causes of unemployment can be found in labour market institutions. Accordingly, countries with high unemployment have been repeatedly urged to undertake comprehensive structural reforms to reduce 'labour market rigidities'.
>
> (IMF 2003: 129)

The IMF estimated that adopting the right reforms (i.e. the US model) would increase output by 5 per cent and reduce unemployment by 3 per cent.

We take a different view. As we demonstrate in the next section, the cross-country pattern of unemployment has varied over the decades of the 1980s, 1990s, and the 2000s. Large swings in unemployment have occurred in countries with very different institutional settings, suggesting that one-to-one relationships between labour market institutions and outcomes may not hold. Indeed, from the early 1990s, doubts have been raised about the persuasiveness of empirical work examining the effects of individual labour market institutions on employment and unemployment outcomes across countries (Bean 1994; Fitoussi 2003; Freeman 2000, 2005). While many of the influential studies of these effects found strong support for a relationship between one or another of the suspect labour market institutions and poor employment performance, results varied widely – even across studies using the same data or by the same author.

The most important challenge to the mainstream view that protective labour market institutions are responsible for the high levels of unemployment in continental Europe came from Baker *et al.* (2005).[6] These authors explored the sensitivity of the main results in the most influential of these studies to the choice of the measures used to represent labour market institutions and to the specification of the relationship that was estimated. Their findings indicate the lack of robustness of results of these studies. To take one example: Baker *et al.* examined how sensitive the results of Nickell's influential (1997) paper were to the choice of variables used to measure labour market institutions. They replaced six of the eight measures of institutional variables in the 1997 paper with improved measures used by Nickell and colleagues (2003, 2005) in later studies. They used the improved measure of union coverage employed by Blanchard and Wolfers (2000) and the OECD's measure of active labour market policies. The results are striking. In the 1997 analysis, seven of the eight institutional variables – all but the employment protection variable – had the predicted sign and were significant. With the new measures, only union coverage is significant, but only marginally so.

Baker *et al.* are not the only researchers to note the lack of robustness of empirical results. Blanchard and Wolfers (2000) note the sensitivity of their results to the specification employed. Examining several prominent studies, Howell *et al.* (2007) point out that only bargaining coordination is significant in every regression, regardless of specification – and this variable *reduces* the rate of unemployment. Baccaro and Rei (2005) examine the relationship between labour market institutions and unemployment using many different estimation techniques and specifications for the key variables. They find that changes in employment protection, unemployment insurance benefit replacement rates, and payroll taxes do not have a significant effect on unemployment and, in any case, the coefficients on these variables have the opposite sign to the mainstream predictions. Only change in union density is found to be positively associated with change in unemployment. The lesson they draw from their work is that:

> [U]nemployment is mostly increased by policies and institutions that lead to restrictive macroeconomic policies . . . [T]he claim that systematic deregulation of labour markets

would solve the unemployment problem faced by several advanced countries appears unwarranted based on our results.

(ibid.: 44)

In its 2006 Employment Outlook, the OECD returned to the question of the relationship between labour market institutions and unemployment it had raised in its 1994 Jobs Study. Chapter 7 of this report (OECD 2006) summarizes the results of an internal study by Andrea Bassanini and Romain Duval, commissioned by the OECD. Using the better and more consistent measures of the key variables across countries that were available at the time of their study, the authors fail to confirm the prediction of mainstream theory that increases (decreases) in protective labour market institutions – generosity of unemployment benefit levels, stringency of employment protections, and union density – increase (decrease) unemployment (Howell *et al.* 2007). The institutional variables that did have a significant effect on unemployment in this analysis were active labour market policies and the level of coordination of wage bargaining, both of which reduced unemployment. Apart from labour market institutions, they found that strict product market regulation and the 'tax wedge' (the difference between what employers pay and workers receive due to payroll taxes), which increased unemployment, were also significant. The study also suggests that macro-economic policies can affect the extent of unemployment. The main finding is that 'cyclical unemployment patterns can be explained by aggregate demand and supply developments – and not only by labour- and product-market policy settings' (OECD 2006: 213).

Our review of the evidence suggests that the often-posited connection between labour market institutions and national unemployment is either not robust or non-existent; in some cases, labour market institutions may even help to reduce unemployment.[7] In a later section, we will explore two alternative possibilities: (1) that labour market institutions may interact in complex ways to increase or decrease unemployment; and (2) that macro-economic institutions and policies have important effects on unemployment that should not be ignored. But first we take a closer look at the available national level data on institutions and employment outcomes.

Labour market institutions and macro-economic outcomes

The preceding section reviewed some of the econometric research on the relationship between labour market institutions and unemployment, but a closer look at the underlying data can shed additional light on both the weak relationship between labour market institutions and outcomes and the important role that macro-economic policy plays in explaining the observed differences in employment performance across the OECD countries. We present a series of tables with data for the rich OECD countries, organized according to four broad political regimes: social-democratic (Denmark, Finland, Norway, and Sweden), continental market (Austria, Belgium, France, Germany, Italy, the Netherlands, and Switzerland), liberal market (Australia, Canada, Ireland, Japan, New Zealand, the United Kingdom, and the United States), and ex-dictatorships (Greece, Portugal, and Spain).[8]

Key labour market institutions related to comparative employment relations generally cluster together across these four categories. As Table 7.1 demonstrates, union density (the share of employees who are members of a union) and collective bargaining coverage (the share of employees covered by a union contract, regardless of whether they belonged to the union) were both high across the social-democratic countries. In these same countries, density typically fell only slightly in the three decades between 1980 and the end of the first decade of the 2000s, while union coverage was basically flat or even rising over the same period. In the

Table 7.1 Union density and collective bargaining coverage, 1980–2007

	Union density		*Union coverage*	
	1980	*2007*	*1980*	*2007*
Social-democratic				
Denmark	78.6	69.1	82.0	80.0
Finland	69.4	70.3	77.0	90.0
Norway	58.3	53.3	70.0	74.0
Sweden	78.0	71.1	85.0	91.0
Average	71.1	66.0	78.5	83.8
Continental market				
Austria	56.7	29.9	95.0	99.0
Belgium	54.1	51.9	97.0	96.0
France	18.3	7.6	85.0	90.0
Germany	34.9	19.9	87.0	62.8
Italy	49.6	33.5	85.0	80.0
the Netherlands	34.8	19	85.0	82.3
Switzerland	27.7	18.2	50.0	48.0
Average	39.4	25.7	83.4	79.7
Liberal market				
Australia	48.5	18.2	85.0	40.0
Canada	34.0	29.4	37.1	31.5
Ireland	63.5	34.9	63.5	44.0
Japan	31.1	18.3	28.0	16.1
New Zealand	69.0	21.3	70.0	17.0
United Kingdom	51.6	28.3	71.0	34.6
United States	22.3	11.6	25.7	13.3
Average	45.7	23.1	54.3	28.1
Ex-dictatorships				
Greece	39.0	24.0	70.0	65.0
Portugal	54.8	20.5	70.0	65.0
Spain	18.7	15.0	76.3	84.5
Average	37.5	19.8	72.1	71.5

Source: Based on Visser (2011), ICTWSS dataset, version 3.0

Notes: For union density and collective bargaining coverage, data for New Zealand and the UK for 1980 refer to 1979; data for Norway, Belgium, France, the Netherlands, Switzerland, Greece, Portugal, and Spain for 2007 refer to 2008.

continental market economies, union coverage is generally as high as in the social-democratic countries, but union density tends to be significantly lower. Between 1980 and 2007, union density generally fell sharply, while coverage changed little (except in Germany, which saw a steep decline). In the liberal market economies, density rates were similar, if generally lower, than in the continental market economies, but coverage rates were much lower and fell steeply after 1980. The ex-dictatorships all had relatively high coverage rates and relatively low density rates at the end of the 2000s, but without common trends since 1980.

The size and strength of unions are only one of many institutions defining differences in employment relations across these countries. Table 7.2 provides data on a selection of other relevant institutional features. Employment protection legislation (as judged by a scale created by the OECD) tends to be highest in the ex-dictatorships, relatively high in the

Table 7.2 Labour market policies, 2007–2010

	Employment protection legislation (EPL)	*Active labour market policies (ALMP)*	*Generosity of unemployment insurance benefits (UI)*	*Work-sharing*
	OECD Index, 1–6, 2008	*Percent of GDP per percentage point of unemployment, 2007*	*Average net replacement rate at average wage, %, 2009*	*Percent of labour force participating in programmes, 2010*
Social-democratic				
Denmark	1.50	0.26	70	0.5
Finland	1.96	0.10	68	1.7
Norway	2.69	0.18	75	0.6
Sweden	1.87	0.14	60	n.a.
Average	2.01	0.17	68	0.9
Continental market				
Austria	1.93	0.12	68	0.6
Belgium	2.18	0.14	67	5.6
France	3.05	0.09	73	0.8
Germany	2.12	0.05	74	3.2
Italy	1.89	0.06	70	3.3
the Netherlands	1.95	0.23	79	0.8
Switzerland	1.14	0.14	81	1.1
Average	2.04	0.12	73	2.2
Liberal market				
Australia	1.15	0.03	50	n.a.
Canada	0.75	0.02	76	0.3
Ireland	1.11	0.11	56	1.0
Japan	1.43	0.01	61	2.7
New Zealand	1.40	0.07	51	0.2
United Kingdom	0.75	0.01	54	n.a.
United States	0.21	0.02	58	0.2
Average	0.97	0.04	58	0.9
Ex-dictatorships				
Greece	2.73	0.02	62	n.a.
Portugal	3.15	0.05	85	0.1
Spain	2.98	0.07	72	1.0
Average	2.95	0.05	73	0.6

Notes: EPL for all workers, permanent and temporary, from OECD, http://stats.oecd.org/Index.aspx, accessed 18 April 2012. ALMP from an analysis of OECD data by Schmitt (2011). UI from OECD Tax model, 39720238.xls. Work-sharing from Hijzen (2010).

social-democratic and continental market economies, and low in the liberal market economies, particularly in the United States. Expenditures per unemployed person on active labour market policies (ALMPs), which include training, job search assistance, and even subsidies for private and public sector employment, are highest in the social-democratic and continental market economies, and are much lower in the liberal market and ex-dictatorships.

The generosity of unemployment insurance benefits (as measured by the replacement rate, net of taxes, for a worker receiving the average wage) is consistently high in the social-democratic, continental market, and ex-dictatorship countries, and is generally lower in the liberal market economies. The use of work-sharing, one aspect of the unemployment insurance system that has taken on greater significance since the onset of the Great Recession, tends to be highest in the continental market economies, particularly Belgium, Germany, and Italy, and less important everywhere else (Finland and Japan are exceptions).

These data suggest that labour market institutions tend to follow broadly similar patterns within each of the four major political groupings, even if countries within each grouping occasionally choose somewhat different institutional mixes. Table 7.3, however, shows that across the social-democratic, continental, and liberal market economies, these different institutional structures produced remarkably similar inflation and GDP growth outcomes. Inflation was higher in the countries in all three regime types in the 1980s, then fell substantially in the 1990s, and remained consistently low through 2011. Per capita GDP growth was in the 2 per cent range – slightly higher in the liberal market economies, slightly lower in the continental market economies – from 1980 through to 2007. In the Great Recession, however, the continental market economies generally saw smaller declines in GDP (Italy was an exception) than occurred in the social-democratic and liberal market economies. (The ex-dictatorships, which started at a much lower level of GDP per capita, had consistently higher inflation, until the Great Recession, and only about average per-capita GDP growth over the same period.) At least with respect to inflation and growth, the range of institutional variation in place across these OECD countries appears to have had little systematic impact.

With respect to unemployment, however, the story is more complicated (see Table 7.4). In 2007, just before the onset of the Great Recession, the liberal market economies had a low average unemployment rate of 4.6 per cent, with all countries in the category clustered between 3.7 per cent (New Zealand) and 6 per cent (Canada). The average unemployment rate in the social-democratic countries was virtually the same (4.8 per cent), but the range of unemployment experiences was much wider, from a low of 2.5 per cent in Norway to 6.9 per cent in Finland. The continental market economies also had a wide dispersion of unemployment rates around a higher average unemployment rate (6 per cent). Two continental market economies, Switzerland (3.4 per cent) and the Netherlands (3.6 per cent), had unemployment rates lower than all of the liberal market economies, but four also had rates above all of the liberal market countries (Italy, 6.1 per cent; Belgium, 7.5 per cent; France, 8.4 per cent; and Germany, 8.7 per cent). Meanwhile, the ex-dictatorships had the highest average unemployment, with all falling between 8 and 9 per cent. Excluding the ex-dictatorships, the differences in the average unemployment rates across the three political types are, in economic terms, swamped by the differences in unemployment rates within countries in each of the other three political traditions. The unemployment data for earlier years follow a similar pattern (though the dispersion of unemployment rates in the liberal market economies was wider in earlier years), as do the corresponding data for the employment-to-population ratio in the second half of the same table.

To recap this review of the data so far, the four political traditions appear to capture some important and persistent differences in the employment relations regimes across the countries we analyzed, including patterns in union density, collective bargaining coverage, employment protection, and other labour market policies. But inflation rates and GDP growth do not vary much across the countries analyzed here, suggesting that the institutional arrangements are not important determinants of these two key macro-economic outcomes. Given that we see little difference in these outcomes across any of the countries, this conclusion does not hinge on accepting the political groupings we've used to organize our discussion of the data. Nor do institutional differences seem to explain substantial

Table 7.3 Macro-economic indicators: inflation and GDP growth, 1980–2011

	Inflation				*GDP Growth per capita*			
	1980–1990	*1990–2000*	*2000–2007*	*2007–2011*	*1980–1990*	*1990–2000*	*2000–2007*	*2007–2011*
Social-democratic								
Denmark	5.9	2.1	1.9	2.4	2.0	2.2	1.3	−2.3
Finland	6.6	1.9	1.4	2.2	2.6	1.7	2.9	−2.0
Norway	7.6	2.3	1.7	2.4	2.1	3.1	1.6	−1.6
Sweden	7.6	2.3	1.6	1.8	1.9	1.7	2.6	−0.8
Average	6.9	2.2	1.6	2.2	2.2	2.2	2.1	−1.7
Continental market								
Austria	3.5	2.3	2.0	2.2	2.0	2.2	1.7	−0.4
Belgium	4.5	2.1	2.0	2.5	1.9	1.9	1.4	−0.7
France	6.3	1.7	1.8	1.6	1.8	1.5	1.1	−1.0
Germany	2.6	2.4	1.6	1.6	2.2	1.6	1.4	0.0
Italy	9.6	3.8	2.3	2.1	2.4	1.6	0.7	−2.3
the Netherlands	2.4	2.4	2.2	1.8	1.7	2.5	1.6	−0.5
Switzerland	3.4	1.9	0.9	0.7	1.6	0.5	1.2	0.2
Average	4.6	2.4	1.8	1.8	1.9	1.7	1.3	−0.7
Liberal market								
Australia	8.1	2.2	3.0	3.1	1.5	2.4	2.1	0.1
Canada	5.9	2.0	2.3	1.8	1.6	1.9	1.5	−0.8
Ireland	7.7	2.5	3.8	0.2	3.3	6.0	3.0	−4.3
Japan	2.0	0.8	−0.3	−0.2	4.1	0.9	1.5	−1.2
New Zealand	10.7	1.8	2.6	3.1	1.3	1.6	2.1	−0.4
United Kingdom	6.0	2.7	1.7	3.4	2.6	2.6	2.4	−1.8
United States	4.7	2.8	2.7	2.1	2.3	2.2	1.4	−1.2
Average	6.4	2.1	2.2	1.9	2.4	2.5	2.0	−1.4
Ex-dictatorships								
Greece	19.0	9.3	3.3	3.3	0.2	1.8	3.7	−2.7
Portugal	17.1	4.9	3.1	1.7	3.1	2.7	0.6	−0.6
Spain	9.3	3.9	3.2	2.2	2.6	2.5	1.8	−1.9
Average	15.1	6.0	3.2	2.4	1.9	2.3	2.1	−1.7

Source: Based on OECD and authors' calculations.

Notes: Data for multi-year periods are annualized rates over period.

Table 7.4 Macro-economic indicators: unemployment and employment, 1980–2010

	Unemployment					*Employment to Population Ratio*				
	1980–1989	*1990–1999*	*2000–2007*	*2007*	*2010*	*1980–1989*	*1990–1999*	*2000–2007*	*2007*	*2010*
Social-democratic										
Denmark	6.5	6.9	4.6	3.8	7.6	74.4	74.4	76.2	77.1	73.4
Finland	5.4	11.9	8.6	6.9	7.8	71.9	65.3	68.5	70.5	68.3
Norway	2.8	5.1	3.7	2.5	3.3	74.5	74.2	76.4	76.9	75.4
Sweden	2.6	7.2	6.6	6.1	7.5	80.4	74.4	74.7	75.7	72.7
Average	4.3	7.8	5.8	4.8	6.6	75.3	72.1	74.0	75.1	72.4
Continental market										
Austria	3.1	3.9	4.4	4.4	4.2	n.a.	68.2	69.0	71.4	71.7
Belgium	9.3	8.5	7.7	7.5	7.2	52.9	56.4	60.6	62.0	62.0
France	8.1	10.1	8.8	8.4	9.7	62.2	59.9	63.4	64.3	64.0
Germany	3.9	7.5	9.4	8.7	6.0	62.8	65.0	66.0	69.0	71.2
Italy	7.8	10.2	8.1	6.1	8.4	52.6	52.1	56.6	58.7	56.9
the Netherlands	6.6	5.3	3.9	3.6	4.4	54.2	65.6	72.3	74.4	74.7
Switzerland	0.6	2.9	3.4	3.4	3.8	n.a.	77.2	78.2	78.6	78.6
Average	5.6	6.9	6.5	6.0	6.2	56.9	63.5	66.6	68.3	68.4
Liberal market										
Australia	7.6	8.8	5.6	4.4	5.1	64.8	66.9	70.6	72.9	72.4
Canada	9.4	9.6	7.0	6.0	7.4	66.8	68.1	72.1	73.5	71.5
Ireland	15.4	12.1	4.4	4.6	14.5	50.7	54.5	66.5	69.2	60.4
Japan	2.5	3.1	4.7	3.9	4.6	67.1	69.3	69.1	70.7	70.1
New Zealand	4.6	8.2	4.7	3.7	6.5	n.a.	68.0	73.0	75.2	72.3
United Kingdom	9.5	8.0	5.1	5.3	8.1	68.2	70.1	72.5	72.3	70.3
United States	7.3	5.8	5.0	4.6	9.0	68.8	72.4	72.1	71.8	66.7
Average	8.0	7.9	5.2	4.6	7.9	64.4	67.0	70.8	72.2	69.1
Ex-dictatorships										
Greece	5.9	9.0	10.0	8.3	17.7	55.0	54.4	58.7	61.4	59.6
Portugal	7.6	5.7	6.9	8.9	12.9	64.7	65.7	68.1	67.8	65.6
Spain	15.3	17.3	10.2	8.3	21.6	49.1	50.5	61.9	66.6	59.4
Average	9.6	10.6	9.0	8.5	17.4	56.2	56.9	62.9	65.2	61.5

Notes: Data for multi-year periods are averages over the period. Unemployment data for 1980–1989 for Denmark, Austria, Germany, Ireland, Greece, and Portugal for 1990–1999 and for Austria and Germany use national definitions of unemployment chained to the harmonized series. Employment data for 1980–1989 for Denmark, France, and Greece and for 1990–1999 for Austria and Switzerland do not cover the full ten-year period.

Source: Based on OECD and authors' calculations.

differences across countries in unemployment and employment rates. In the period before the recent world recession, the average unemployment rate in the liberal market economies was relatively low and the dispersion around the average was fairly small. But the labour market institutions associated with the social democratic and continental market economies produced unemployment rates that varied widely, with countries in both political traditions outperforming and underperforming the liberal market economies.

These broad-brush data provide some context for the more formal econometric findings in the preceding section, which pointed to the fragile nature of the early findings of a connection between institutions and macro-economic performance, especially unemployment. The data also suggest that factors other than institutions are responsible for the very varied unemployment and employment outcomes within countries with broadly similar institutions. We argue that the most important of these other factors are macro-economic institutions and macro-economic policy.

Divergent paths to full employment and GDP growth: complex interactions among institutions

As the previous sections have shown, the evidence does not support the argument that there is a straightforward relationship between labour market institutions and macro-economic outcomes. The assumption that labour market rigidities are central to the explanation of cross-country differences in employment and GDP growth does not stand up to scrutiny. Nevertheless, despite the lack of evidence that protective labour market institutions reduce growth and raise unemployment, mainstream orthodoxy still prevails today in policy discussions, especially in Europe. The policies prescribed for Greece, Spain, and Italy, for example, call for a weakening of these institutions and a reduction in the size of public sector employment – all justified on the grounds that more flexible labour markets (i.e. more like those of the USA) are required in order to achieve more rapid economic growth, more jobs and less unemployment. Macro-economic policy, meanwhile, is left out of the discussion on the grounds that there is no alternative to austerity. The hold of mainstream orthodoxy on the influential policy-makers in the 'troika' – the European Central Bank and the International Monetary Fund, and the European Commission (EC) – has not been weakened.

The weight of the evidence from studies carried out over the last decade has persuaded even the OECD to carry out a comprehensive reassessment of its 1994 Jobs Study. Acknowledging that the 1994 study and jobs strategy had been interpreted to endorse 'one right configuration for achieving employment outcomes' (OECD 2006: 190), the OECD now embraced the view that it is the interactions among the institutions and policies that make up a country's institutional constellation that matters for macro-economic outcomes. Countries can achieve equally good results, according to the OECD's review of 'an increasing body of empirical evidence about such interactions' (ibid.: 190), by following different strategies. The OECD found that good labour market performance in a number of English-speaking countries is associated with relatively light employment protection legislation, relatively low unemployment benefits, low-to-moderate active labour market programmes, and below-average union density and collective bargaining coverage. These countries also have less strict product market regulation and relatively low tax wedges.

But the OECD also found that equally good employment outcomes have been achieved by some European countries with very different institutions and policies. These countries, of which Denmark is usually seen as the leading example, have a high degree of coordination in their industrial relations systems, a high degree of collective bargaining coverage, generous unemployment benefits and a strong and comprehensive social safety net, strong active labour market policies and moderate to high levels of employment protection. Product market regulations are relatively less strict in these countries, but they have moderate to high tax wedges.

Thus, there is not a single road to good employment performance. Looking at these two groups of countries with good employment performance, the OECD observes that, on average, they exhibit 'extremely different degrees of 'interventionism' in almost every [of the above] selected policy areas' (ibid.: 192). A policy mix with high unemployment benefits and high investment in active labour market policies performs just as well as a policy mix with low unemployment benefits and low investment in active labour market policies. A policy mix with high collective bargaining coverage and high coordination of industrial relations performs as well as one in which unions are weak, collective bargaining coverage is low, and coordination is negligible.

There are a number of channels through which economies with more 'interventionist' institutions achieve good employment results. Unions may be harmful to employment when they are able to impose a high wage level on firms, but not sufficiently encompassing to take the possible detrimental macro-economic effects of their actions into account. In countries with a high degree of coordination of industrial relations, bargaining over wages between workers and employers can more easily take these effects into account. Thus, wage moderation to avoid adverse effects on inflation, employment, and the trade balance can be achieved either through decentralization of wage bargaining, as in the USA, or through coordinated wage bargaining, as in the Nordic countries. To take another example, generous unemployment benefits do not necessarily lead to higher unemployment; when they are combined with strict employment protections and high investment in active labour market policies, the effects on employment can be quite good (for a fuller discussion, see Amable 2003: 124–42).

These outcomes should not be surprising. The orthodox view that there is one best way of organizing labour markets and, more broadly, economies has been challenged over the past decade by the 'Varieties of Capitalism' literature (Hall and Soskice 2001; Amable 2003). The emphasis in this literature is on the various spheres in which firms must develop relationships to resolve coordination problems, with coordination of bargaining over wages and working conditions a key dimension. Hall and Soskice, for example, distinguish two types of economies. In liberal market economies (which, in Hall and Soskice's framing, largely overlap with the liberal market economies as we have defined them), firms coordinate their activities primarily through market mechanisms; market institutions may be an effective means of coordinating the endeavours of economic actors. In coordinated market economies (which, in Hall and Soskice's scheme, largely combine the two groups we labelled social democratic and coordinated market economies), strategic interactions among actors in the economy complement, and to some extent displace, market mechanisms; and in combination with appropriate labour market institutions these may also be effective mechanisms for coordinating the activities of firms. Finer-grained classification schemes have also been explored (Freeman 2000; Amable 2003; Huber and Stephens 2005).

The experience of the Great Recession has only reinforced the conclusion that labour-market institutions interact in complex ways. One implication is that some constellations of labour market institutions may be better suited to dealing with economic downturns than others, at least in the short run. A brief comparison of three countries – Denmark (social-democratic), Germany (continental market), and the United States (liberal market) – representing three of the four political traditions analyzed earlier provides several important insights.

From about the mid-1990s through the Great Recession, Denmark had what was arguably the most successful labour-market performance in the rich OECD countries. Unemployment rates were consistently among the lowest in the OECD, as was the level of economic inequality (Westergaard-Nielsen 2008). Denmark's strong emphasis on 'flexicurity' – labour market institutions that gave employers relative freedom to fire and hire, while providing workers with security in the form of high wages, generous unemployment benefits, and extensive opportunities for education and training – was widely seen as the key to the country's success. The Danish unemployment rate, however, almost doubled between 2007 and 2010 (from 4 to 7.8 per cent). The system's emphasis on numerical flexibility and the retraining of displaced workers worked well when aggregate demand was consistently high, as in the run-up to the Great Recession. But when aggregate demand collapsed from 2008 on, the ease with which firms could shed workers became a liability and the reliance on training and placement efforts was largely ineffective when actual vacancies were scarce.

By contrast, the German economy had been struggling from shortly after unification in the 1990s through the onset of the Great Recession (Bosch and Weinkopf 2008). In 2007, for example, the German unemployment rate was already higher – at 8.7 per cent – than it was in Denmark three years into the recession (7.8 per cent in 2010). A remarkable development, however, occurred in Germany: the unemployment rate actually fell over the course of the downturn. The most important reason for the decline in unemployment was that German labour market institutions channelled adjustment to the decrease in demand toward a reduction in hours, rather than a reduction in employment. German unions negotiated shorter work weeks; workers in firms with annual hours contracts and 'time banks' drew down their stored up hours; and a sizable share of workers participated in the short-time compensation programme known as *Kurzarbeit*. At least in the short-term, German labour market institutions appear to have succeeded where the Danish institutions had failed.[9]

Meanwhile, labour market performance in the United States – the paragon of flexibility, with a low private-sector union density and the weakest employment protection in the OECD – looked a lot more like Denmark than it did like Germany. In the United States, unemployment also roughly doubled between 2007 and 2010, with most of the adjustment to declining demand falling on employment rather than average hours. The Danish and US cases suggest that institutions that lead to low unemployment in one economic context may not work so well in another.

Macro-economic policies and employment outcomes

While labour market institutions have been at the core of the mainstream analysis of cross-country employment and unemployment outcomes, monetary and fiscal policy have largely been absent from the discussion. The inattention to macro-economic policy flows from the dominant New Classical model, which sees macro-economic policy as ineffective in moving the economy away from its equilibrium value of unemployment. In contrast to the common-sense notion that human decisions are made in the absence of full knowledge of conditions and that judgements about the future may differ, New Classical models rely on the assumption of 'rational expectations'. That is, these models assume that workers and employers are able to predict increases in prices and wages and can correctly anticipate and act on this knowledge. Under these assumptions, monetary policy cannot affect output and employment, at least in the middle and long run as firms and workers adjust their expectations, and maybe not even in the short run if expectations are assumed to adjust very quickly. Any attempt to increase demand, in this view, will lead wages and prices to adjust by the same amount, and will leave the real wage (the nominal wage, adjusted for the price level) unchanged. Since employers make hiring decisions based on the real wage, attempts to increase employment by increasing demand will fail. This broad consensus was the basis for monetary policy under the German central bank, the Bundesbank, and it continues to underlie the policies of the European Central Bank (ECB) today. The only effective use of monetary policy in New Classical models is to maintain price stability so that expectations remain stable; hence the commitment of monetary authorities to extremely low inflation targets. In this framework, the use of monetary policy to keep inflation low has no effect on unemployment.

We have already seen, however, that low unemployment is consistent with various constellations of labour market institutions, some of which are very 'interventionist' and not consistent with completely competitive labour markets. This evidence suggests that New Classical models are wrong; unemployment is not uniquely determined by labour market institutions. Indeed, there is substantial evidence that, as Keynes (1936) argued during the Great Depression, monetary policy and other determinants of aggregate demand (e.g. government spending and tax policies) do affect employment. However, Keynesian economics never enjoyed the same degree of acceptance in continental Europe that it had in the USA and other English-speaking countries in the post-war decades. The Keynesian approach guided economic policy in the USA through the 1960s, but fell out of favour in the high inflation period of the 1970s. Nevertheless, despite vociferous opposition from academic economists, it continued to exert some influence on the actual conduct of macro-economic policy in the USA. In particular, the approach of the US central bank, the Federal Reserve, was far more expansionary than its continental European counterparts.

Schettkat and Sun (2009) examined a large number of studies of the effects of monetary policy on GDP and employment. They conclude that: '[A] whole battery of recent research suggests that monetary policy is not neutral to output, employment, and unemployment, but that it leaves scars identifiable in the data even after 5 and 10 years.' As Schettkat and Sun explain:

> [A] restrictive monetary policy will reduce growth in a recovery and will not allow the economy to return to its initial growth path. This is especially true if the policy is . . . overly concerned with price stability . . . If, in addition, investment depends on expected growth as many studies have shown . . . [an over-emphasis on price stability] will also reduce investment and thus potential output.
>
> (ibid.: 97)

As they show in their empirical analysis of German monetary policy during the period from the first quarter of 1975[10] through the fourth quarter of 1998, the Bundesbank's monetary policy was 'asymmetric'. There was little expansionary monetary policy during periods of slack, but aggressive restrictive policies during periods of growth out of fear of inflation. As a result, cumulative growth rates for output (GDP) were lower following recessions in Germany compared with the USA, most notably in the early 1990s. Expansions were more sustained in the USA. The result, Schettkat and Sun argue, is that capacity was underutilized in Germany and unemployment was higher than it would have been had the Bundesbank increased the money supply when there was slack in the economy. The ECB, as is well known, has adopted the policy stance of the Bundesbank which it supplanted. Thus, differences in economic performance between the USA and the continental European economies in the Eurozone are due in no small measure to the different approaches taken by the central banks of the two areas.

Summarizing macro-economic institutions and policy across 21 countries and three decades is a daunting task. The core components of macro-economic policy-making involve complex decisions about interest rates, money supply, exchange rates (regimes and levels), fiscal deficits (in turn, the outcome of tax and expenditure policies), and public debt (gross and net). Sometimes these individual components are, indeed, policy levers (the central bank sets certain short-term interest rates, for example); at other times, they are policy outcomes (actors in the financial markets may react to central bank efforts to lower short-term rates by raising long-term rates). Given space and conceptual constraints, we will focus on only a few persistent features of macro-economic institutions and policies, which we believe have received insufficient attention among those interested in employment relations.

The first issue, which is widely acknowledged but not fully appreciated, is the role of central banks in creating or combating unemployment. 'Independent' central banks have become a central feature of modern, capitalist economies. This alleged independence typically manifests itself by insulating central bankers from accountability to elected officials. In practice, these arrangements give the financial sector a significant advantage in influencing central bank policies, since representatives of the financial sector typically have key roles in oversight and even the administration of central bank policy. Even in the most accountable of central banking systems (such as the US Federal Reserve Board), this frequently translates into policy biased in favour of low inflation and against full employment. This policy bias is exaggerated when the central bank is, as is the case with the European Central Bank (ECB), tasked only with price stability and has no explicit mandate to also seek full employment (Franzese and Hall 2000; Schettkat and Sun 2009).

The second issue, which is closely related in practice to the issue of central banks, is the role of national currencies. As Table 7.5 shows, the four political traditions established in the immediate post-war period are strong predictors of whether a country will have its own currency. All of the social-democratic countries have their own currency. None of the ex-dictatorships do (all use the euro). All but one of the liberal market economies – Ireland – has its own currency. All but one of the continental market economies – Switzerland – use the euro. A shared currency such as the euro presents serious challenges to getting national macro-economic policy right. Even if the ECB had a mandate to pursue both price stability and full employment, attempting to lower high unemployment in a context where some members of the Eurozone were near full employment and others were far from it will be inherently difficult. In the current European context, where the ECB has a legal obligation to pursue price stability without regard to the impact on employment, monetary policy is at best neutral and often pushing against any national attempt to increase employment. Separate from the issue of the correct monetary policy stance across a set of economies that are likely to not always be in sync, is the issue that a shared currency also makes it impossible for countries experiencing high unemployment to adjust through devaluation, a major constraint for Greece, Spain, Portugal, and Ireland in the period since 2008.[11]

The final issue we highlight is the role of deficit spending. Over the last three decades, the social-democratic countries have consistently had higher surpluses or lower deficits, as a share of GDP, than the average for countries in the other three political traditions (see Table 7.6). The continental market economies have generally had larger deficits, as a share of GDP, than the liberal market economies. But, notably, the United States, probably the quintessential liberal market economy, has consistently had fiscal deficits at or near the high end of all of countries in the rich OECD countries, except those in the ex-dictatorships.

Table 7.5 Currency regimes, 2012

Regime type	*Country*	*Own currency?*
Social-democratic		
	Denmark	Yes
	Finland	Yes
	Norway	Yes
	Sweden	Yes
Continental market		
	Austria	Euro
	Belgium	Euro
	France	Euro
	Germany	Euro
	Italy	Euro
	the Netherlands	Euro
	Switzerland	Yes
Liberal market		
	Australia	Yes
	Canada	Yes
	Ireland	Euro
	Japan	Yes
	New Zealand	Yes
	United Kingdom	Yes
	United States	Yes
Ex-dictatorships		
	Greece	Euro
	Portugal	Euro
	Spain	Euro

Source: Authors' analysis, May 2012.

The data on labour market and macro-economic institutions reinforce and extend the econometric studies discussed in the preceding section. Individual labour market institutions appear to have little influence on key macro-economic outcomes including inflation, unemployment, employment, and growth. In the case of inflation and growth, the rich OECD countries show remarkably small differences in performance over the last three decades. With respect to unemployment and employment, the variations in outcomes *within* countries with broadly similar institutional structures in the labour market far exceed the variations in performance between countries grouped together by broad institutional similarities. Taken together, these conclusions point to the need for incorporating additional factors into analyses of the determinants of macro-economic performance, most crucially the effects of macro-economic institutions and policies on employment and unemployment.

Economic policy and the Great Recession

The varied policy responses to the Great Recession have provided current and future economic policy-makers with an enormous amount of data to evaluate the effectiveness of different approaches to a major world recession. As we have emphasized so far, the standard view, developed in the 1980s and 1990s, was that labour-market institutions were the major determinant of national employment and unemployment rates, with little or no role for macro-economic policy. In the face of a world-wide collapse in demand, however, even

Table 7.6 Deficits and debt

	Deficit-to-GDP ratio			*Gross debt-to-GDP ratio*					*Net debt-to-GDP ratio*				
	1980–1989	*1990–1999*	*2000–2007*	*1980*	*1990*	*2000*	*2007*	*2010*	*1980*	*1990*	*2000*	*2007*	*2010*
Social-democratic													
Denmark	n.a.	n.a.	2.4	n.a.	n.a.	60.4	34.1	43.4	n.a.	n.a.	22.5	−3.8	−1.3
Finland	2.6	−2.6	4.1	10.8	13.8	43.8	35.2	48.4	−177.1	−208.3	−31.1	−72.5	−64.7
Norway	5.1	2.6	13.3	47.3	28.9	32.7	56.8	49.6	n.a.	−31.8	−67.2	−138.9	−165.3
Sweden	−1.9	−3.7	1.3	n.a.	n.a.	53.9	40.2	39.4	n.a.	n.a.	2.2	−17.5	−22.3
Average	1.9	−1.2	5.3	29.1	21.4	47.7	41.6	45.2	−177.1	−120.0	−18.4	−58.2	−63.4
Continental market													
Austria	n.a.	−3.4	−1.7	n.a.	56.2	66.2	60.2	71.8	n.a.	36.6	43.2	40.9	52.0
Belgium	−6.3	−4.5	−0.4	74.3	125.6	107.8	84.1	96.2	65.5	112.3	97.4	73.2	80.2
France	−2.3	−3.9	−2.8	20.7	35.2	57.3	64.2	82.4	n.a.	26.2	51.4	59.5	76.6
Germany	n.a.	−3.3	−2.2	n.a.	n.a.	60.2	65.2	83.2	n.a.	n.a.	41.1	50.4	56.8
Italy	n.a.	−7.4	−2.9	n.a.	94.1	108.5	103.1	118.7	n.a.	89.0	93.1	86.9	99.0
the Netherlands	n.a.	n.a.	−0.6	n.a.	n.a.	53.8	45.3	62.9	n.a.	n.a.	24.9	21.6	27.5
Switzerland	0.4	−2.0	0.2	n.a.	38.2	61.3	55.9	50.1	n.a.	4.5	21.2	11.4	4.8
Average	−2.7	−4.1	−1.5	47.5	69.9	73.6	68.3	80.7	65.5	53.7	53.2	49.1	56.7
Liberal market													
Australia	n.a.	−1.5	1.6	n.a.	16.4	19.5	9.7	20.4	n.a.	9.6	7.1	−7.3	4.4
Canada	−6.0	−4.5	1.1	45.6	75.2	82.1	66.5	85.1	14.5	43.7	46.2	22.9	30.4
Ireland	−9.0	−0.9	1.4	65.2	93.5	37.5	24.8	92.5	65.2	93.5	36.4	11.1	76.9
Japan	−2.0	−2.8	−5.5	50.6	67.0	140.1	183.0	215.3	16.8	13.2	59.6	80.5	112.8
New Zealand	n.a.	0.2	3.1	n.a.	59.0	31.8	17.4	32.3	0.4	46.6	18.2	−5.7	3.5
United Kingdom	−2.3	−3.6	−1.9	46.1	32.6	40.9	43.9	75.1	40.5	26.7	33.6	38.1	71.1
United States	−4.2	−3.1	−3.1	42.3	63.9	54.8	67.2	98.5	25.8	45.9	35.6	48.2	73.1
Average	−4.7	−2.3	−0.5	50.0	58.2	58.1	58.9	88.5	27.2	39.9	33.8	26.8	53.2
Ex-dictatorships													
Greece	−8.1	−8.5	−5.5	22.6	73.3	103.4	105.4	142.8	20.6	64.2	77.4	105.4	142.8
Portugal	n.a.	−5.4	−3.7	n.a.	57.2	48.4	68.3	93.4	n.a.	n.a.	41.9	63.7	89.2
Spain	−4.0	−4.4	0.3	16.6	42.5	59.3	36.3	61.2	n.a.	30.3	50.4	26.7	49.7
Average	−6.1	−6.1	−3.0	19.6	57.7	70.4	70.0	99.1	20.6	47.3	56.5	65.3	93.9

Source: IMF, World Economic Outlook database, accessed 18 April 2012; US data for 1980s and 1990s from CBO (2009).

fairly orthodox economic policy-makers – the Bush administration in the United States, for example – were willing to abandon the labour-market-focused policy approach, at least initially. More in line with Keynesian than New Classical economics, many countries engaged in macro-economic stimulus measures, including automatic stabilizers (such as unemployment insurance benefits, which increase with unemployment), fiscal stimulus packages, cuts in interest rates, and quantitative easing.[12] As the recession and the weak subsequent recovery dragged on, however, many governments, even some on the centre-left, began to revert to a focus based on 'institutional reform' and macro-economic austerity (Leschke and Watt 2010). At the time of writing, Europe is caught in an economic battle pitting advocates of austerity and labour-market reform against social forces, led by various national labour movements, resisting austerity and the proposed institutional reforms. The outcome of this policy debate will determine the future of the euro and the European political project.

The macro-economic policy response differed in important ways across the OECD. At first blush, the Fed, the ECB, and other central bankers appeared to respond in a similar fashion to the downturn – fairly aggressive cuts in interest rates, followed, when rate cuts seemed insufficient to the task, by unconventional monetary policy actions, including, most notably 'quantitative easing' (implemented by purchasing longer-term public, private, and agency debt). The Fed, however, was consistently more aggressive than the ECB both with respect to interest rate cuts and the volume of 'quantitative easing'. The fiscal policy response to the Great Recession also varied substantially (OECD 2009; ILO 2009; Heyes *et al.* 2012). Automatic stabilizers[13] provided important and immediate boosts to demand in many countries, especially Germany (Dolls *et al.* 2010). Several countries also enacted explicit stimulus programmes. The United States implemented two separate fiscal packages, the first in the Spring of 2008 (about 1 per cent of GDP), the second in early 2009 (about 5 per cent of GDP over roughly two years).[14] At the European level, policy-makers organized a smaller stimulus (about 1 per cent of European Union GDP), with several countries pursuing additional, generally small stimulus programmes. (One exception was Spain, where the fiscal stimulus totalled almost 4 per cent of GDP spread over three years.) Taking the automatic stabilizers and including government expenditures at all levels of government significantly alters our understanding of fiscal policy over the Great Recession. Total government expenditures on goods and services over the current downturn, for example, have increased more in Germany, which had little explicit stimulus, than they have in the United States, which had the largest federal stimulus package among rich countries, because federal stimulus was partially offset by government spending cuts at the state and local level.

In recent years, fiscal policy has shifted explicitly towards austerity, in all of the peripheral Eurozone countries (Greece, Portugal, Spain, and Ireland) and several other major OECD economies, including the United Kingdom. The argument for austerity is based on some combination of a belief that investor confidence has been undermined by high government deficits and that labour-market institutions, not a lack of aggregate demand, are the biggest barrier to restored growth. The lessons of the United States in 1937 – when, after several years of robust growth, the Roosevelt administration suddenly attempted to balance the budget, driving the economy into another deep recession – appear to have been lost on the current generation of European economic policy-makers. A major institutional constraint on the macro-economic policy response to the Great Recession has been the existence of the euro. The countries that suffered most in the downturn and have recovered most slowly or not at all – Greece, Portugal, Ireland, and Spain – were all members of the Eurozone. If these countries had their own currencies, they would have been well positioned to devalue the currencies in order to boost aggregate demand (by exporting more and importing less), as part of a broader programme to restore growth. The problems caused by the inability to devalue were exacerbated by the decision of the European Central Bank to focus monetary policy on price stability across Europe, rather than full employment in these 'peripheral' European economies. This recap of macro-economic policy since 2008 suggests that few, if any, of the major OECD countries got macro-economic policy right in the wake of the Great Recession.[15] Fiscal policy was underpowered everywhere. Monetary policy was most helpful in the United States, but largely counterproductive in the Eurozone. Meanwhile, the euro greatly hampered the ability of the smaller Eurozone economies to respond to the economic crisis.

Differences in labour-market institutions across the major OECD countries appear to have little systematic influence on key macro-economic measures, including inflation, growth, and unemployment. These institutions are likely have an important impact on measures of economic inequality – with liberal market economies generally showing higher levels of inequality than coordinated market economies, which in turn, are generally more unequal than the social democracies of northern Europe. The inability of institutional differences to explain national variations in macro-economic performance suggests that we should look elsewhere to account for both structural and cyclical differences in macro-economic performance. Macro-economic institutions – from the structure of central banks to the use of a common currency – and macro-economic policy – particularly the use of countercyclical monetary and fiscal policy – have been curiously absent from the discussion of international differences in macro-economic performance. Researchers, policy-makers, and the social partners interested in comparative employment relations ignore macro-economic institutions and policy at their peril.

Notes

1 For OECD data on unemployment and employment rates, see Table 7.4.

2 Heyes *et al.* also argue against a 'preoccupation with institutions', but emphasize the need to focus more attention on 'social agency and the dynamics of the capitalist mode of production' (2012: 222).

3 See http://en.wikipedia.org/wiki/We_are_all_Keynesians_now (accessed 26 May, 2012).

4 New Classical macro-economic theory is a term applied to macro-economic thinking based on the idea of 'rational expectations' and places a central emphasis on microeconomic foundations for macroeconomic analysis; the term is distinct from the broader 'neo-classical economics'.

5 Nickell's paper is the twelfth most-cited article in the history of the *Journal of Economic Perspectives* (Autor 2012).

6 For a review and evaluation of this debate, see Freeman (2005).

7 Another version of the deregulationist view argues that institutions do not primarily affect the level of employment or unemployment, but rather the composition across groups defined by gender, education, age, ethnicity, and other factors. Schmitt and Wadsworth (2004), however, find no connection between the flexibility of labour market institutions and relative employment and unemployment outcomes for frequently marginalized groups including youth, women, and workers with the lowest levels of formal education.

8 Our categories are based on the methodology set out by Huber and Stephens (2001a, 2001b) and used in Navarro, *et al.* (2004) and Schmitt and Mitukiewicz (2012). The four political categories are based on the political parties in power in each country for the longest period between 1946 and 1980, with the idea that the relative political power during this part of the post-war period defined many of the characteristics of each country's welfare state.

9 For a discussion of Denmark and Germany during and after the Great Recession, see Schmitt (2011).

10 According to Schettkat and Sun (2009), prior to the mid-1970s the Bretton Woods system of exchange rates and global governance moderated the behaviour of the German Bundesbank.

11 We leave aside the problems that a shared currency can create when the economy is in an upswing. The creation of the euro certainly facilitated the large capital inflows that fuelled the housing bubble in Spain or initially financed Greek sovereign debt at low interest rates, for example.

12 Quantitative easing (QE) refers to a situation in which a central bank – e.g. the US Federal Reserve Bank or the European Central Bank – buys up long-term government, agency and private bonds. This can stimulate economic activity through a variety of channels. It increases the money supply and makes it easier for banks to lend to businesses and households. It reduces the volume of long-term bonds available in the economy, leading to higher prices for these assets. Prices and interest rates of bonds are inversely related, so this reduces the interest rate and encourages businesses and households to borrow and spend. Finally, increases in the money supply can raise concerns about inflation. If businesses and households believe that prices will rise in the future, they may be more inclined to purchase goods and services now, before prices rise. QE is relatively rare and is distinct from the open market operations of central banks. Central banks routinely engage in buying and selling short-term government bonds in order to stabilize the money supply and raise or lower short-term interest rates.

13 Demand can be stabilized without discretionary policy measures, through the automatic stabilizers in the tax and transfer system. If households pay 30 per cent of their income in taxes, then 30 per cent of a decline in gross income will be absorbed by lower tax payments. Disposable income will fall by much less than gross income, thus helping to stabilize household purchasing power. Unemployed workers are eligible for payments from the unemployment insurance system. These transfers to the unemployed help stabilize income and demand. The more generous unemployment insurance systems in Europe are a key reason that automatic stabilizers play a larger role there than in the USA.

14 The United States subsequently instituted several measures such as a payroll tax cut that was generally not billed as an explicit stimulus package, but acted as such. In recent years, however, much of the stimulus enacted at the federal level has been undercut by expenditure cuts at the state and local government levels.

15 One apparent exception is Australia, which appears to have weathered the Great Recession much better than the rest of the rich OECD economies.

References

Amable, B. (2003) *The Diversity of Modern Capitalism*, Oxford: Oxford University Press.

Autor, D. (2012) 'The *Journal of Economic Perspectives* at 100 (issues)', *Journal of Economic Perspectives*, 26(2): 3–18.

Baccaro, L. and Rei, D. (2005) *Institutional Determinants of Unemployment in OECD Countries: A Time Series Cross-Section Analysis*, Geneva: International Institute for Labour Studies, IILS Discussion Paper DP/160/2005.

Baker, D., Glyn, A., Howell, D. R. and Schmitt, J. (2005) 'Labour market institutions and unemployment: a critical assessment of the cross-country evidence', in D. R. Howell (ed.) *Fighting Unemployment: The Limits of Free Market Orthodoxy*, Oxford: Oxford University Press.

Barro, R. J. (1976) 'Rational expectations and the role of monetary policy', *Journal of Monetary Economics*, 2(1): 1–32.

Bean, C. R. (1994) 'European unemployment: a survey', *Journal of Economic Literature*, 32(2): 573–619.

Belot, M. and van Ours, J. C. (2004) 'Does the recent success of some OECD countries in lowering their unemployment rates lie in the clever design of their labour market reforms?', *Oxford Economic Papers*, 56(4): 621–42.

Blanchard, O. and Wolfers, J. (2000) 'The role of shocks and institutions in the rise of European unemployment: the aggregate evidence', *The Economic Journal*, 110(462): C1–C33.

Bosch, G. and Weinkopf, C. (2008) *Low-Wage Work in Germany*, New York: Russell Sage Foundation.

CBO (2009) (Congressional Budget Office) *The Budget and Economic Outlook: Fiscal Years 2009 to 2019*, Washington, DC: Congressional Budget Office.

Dolls, M., Fuest, C. and Peichl, A. (2010) *Automatic Stabilizers and Economic Crisis: US vs. Europe*, Cambridge, MA: National Bureau of Economic Research, Working Paper No. 16275.

Elmeskov, J., Martin, J. and Scarpetta, S. (1998) 'Key lessons for labour market reforms: evidence from OECD countries' experiences', *Swedish Economic Policy Review*, 5(2): 205–52.

Fitoussi, J-P. (2003) 'Comments on Nickell, Mumziata, Ochel, and Quintini', in P. Aghion, R. Frydman, J. Stiglitz and M. Woodford. (eds) *Knowledge, Information, and Expectations in Modern Macroeconomics: In Honor of Edmund S. Phelps*, Princeton, NJ: Princeton University Press.

Franzese, R. J. Jr. and Hall, P. A. (2000) 'The institutional interaction of wage-bargaining and monetary policy', in T. Iversen, J. Pontusson and D. Soskice (eds) *Unions, Employers and Central Banks: Macroeconomic Coordination and Institutional Change in Social Market Economies*, Cambridge, MA: Cambridge University Press.

Freeman, R. B. (2000) *Single Peaked Vs. Diversified Capitalism: The Relation Between Economic Institutions and Outcomes*, Cambridge, MA: National Bureau of Economic Research, Working Paper 7556.

—— (2005) 'Labour market institutions without blinders: the debate over flexibility and labour market performance', *International Economic Journal*, 19(2): 129–45.

Hall, P. A. and Soskice, D. (2001) 'An introduction to the varieties of capitalism', in P.A. Hall and D. Soskice (eds) *Varieties of Capitalism: The Institutional Foundations of Comparative Advantage*, Oxford: Oxford University Press.

Heyes, J., Lewis, P. and Clark, I. (2012) 'Varieties of capitalism, neoliberalism and the economic crisis of 2008–?', *Industrial Relations Journal*, 43(3): 222–41.

Hizjen, A. and Venn, D. (2010) *The Role of Short-Time Work Schemes during the 2008–09 Recession*, Paris: Organization for Economic Cooperation and Development, Employment and Migration Working Paper No. 115.

Howell, D. R. (2010) *Institutions, Aggregate Demand and Cross-Country Employment Performance: Alternative Theoretical Perspectives and the Evidence*, New York: New School for Social Research, Schwartz Center for Economic Policy Analysis, Working Paper 2010–5.

——, Baker, D., Glyn, A. and Schmitt, J. (2007) 'Are protective labour market institutions at the root of unemployment? A critical review of the evidence', *Capitalism and Society*, 2(1): 1–73.

Huber, E. and Stephens, J. D. (2005) 'Welfare states and the economy', in N. J. Smelser and R. Swedberg (eds) *The Handbook of Economic Sociology*, Princeton, NJ: Princeton University Press.

—— (2001a) *Development and Crisis of the Welfare State: Parties and Policies in Global Markets*, Chicago: University of Chicago Press.

—— (2001b) 'Welfare state and production regimes in the era of retrenchment', in P. Pierson (ed.) *The New Politics of the Welfare State*, Oxford: Oxford University Press.

International Labour Organization (ILO) (2009) *The Financial and Economic Crisis: A Decent Work Response*, Geneva: International Labour Organization.

International Monetary Fund (IMF) (2003) *World Economic Outlook: Growth and Institutions*, (April). Available at: http://www.imf.org/external/pubs/ft/weo/2003/01/pdf/chapter4.pdf.

Keynes, J. M. (1936) *The General Theory of Employment, Interest and Money*, London: Macmillan.

Layard, R., Nickell, S. and Jackman, R. (2005) *Unemployment: Macroeconomic Performance and the Labour Market*, Oxford: Oxford University Press.

Leschke, J. and Watt, A. (2010) *How Do Institutions Affect the Labour Market Adjustment to the Economic Crisis in Different EU Countries?*, Brussels: European Trade Union Institute.

Lucas, R. E. Jr. (1972) 'Expectations and the neutrality of money', *Journal of Economic Theory*, 4(2): 103–24.

Navarro, V., Schmitt, J. and Astudillo, J. (2004) 'Is globalisation undermining the welfare state?', *Cambridge Journal of Economics*, 28(1): 133–52.

Nickell, S. (1997) 'Unemployment and labour market rigidities: Europe versus North America', *Journal of Economic Perspectives*, 11(3): 55–74.

—— (2003) *Labour Market Institutions and Unemployment in OECD Countries*, Munich: CESifo Group, DICE Report, 2/2003.

——, Nunziata, L. and Ochel, W. (2005) 'Unemployment in the OECD since the 1960s: what do we know?', *The Economic Journal*, 115(5): 1–27.

OECD (1994) *OECD Jobs Study*, Paris: OECD.

—— (2006) *OECD Employment Outlook*, Paris: OECD.

—— (2009) *Fiscal Packages Across OECD Countries: Overview and Country Details*, Paris: OECD.

Saint-Paul, G. (2004) 'Why are European countries diverging in their unemployment experience?', *Journal of Economic Perspectives*, 18(4): 49–68.

Sargent, T. J. (1973) 'Rational expectations, the real rate of interest, and the natural rate of unemployment', *Brookings Papers on Economic Activity*, 1973(2): 429–72.

Scarpetta, S. (1996) *Assessing the Role of Labour Market Policies and Institutional Settings on Unemployment: A Cross-Country Study*, Paris: OECD, OECD Economic Studies, 26: 43–98.

Schettkat, R. and Sun, R. (2009) 'Monetary policy and European unemployment', *Oxford Review of Economic Policy*, 25(1): 94–108.

Schmitt, J. (2011) *Labour Market Policy in the Great Recession: Some Lessons from Denmark and Germany*', Washington, DC: Center for Economic and Policy Research. Available at: http://www.cepr.net/documents/publications/labour-2011-05.pdf.

—— and Mitukiewicz, A. (2012) 'Politics matter: changes in unionisation rates in rich countries, 1960–2010', *Industrial Relations Journal*, 43(4): 260–80.

—— and Wadsworth, J. (2004) 'Is the OECD jobs strategy behind US and British employment and unemployment success in the 1990s?' in D. Howell (ed.) *Fighting Unemployment: The Limits of Free Market Orthodoxy*, Oxford: Oxford University Press.

Siebert, H. (1997) 'Labour market rigidities: at the root of unemployment in Europe', *Journal of Economic Perspectives*, 11(3): 37–54.

Visser, J. (2011) *ICTWSS Database*. Available at: http://www.uva-aias.net/208 (accessed 10 June 2012).

Westergaard-Nielsen, N. (2008) *Low-Wage Work in Denmark*, New York: Russell Sage Foundation.

8 Employment relations, welfare and politics

Anke Hassel

Introduction

The employment relationship and the welfare state are intricately linked.[1] Formal employment is the welfare state's main source of funding. The main share of income taxes derives from formal employment and in many countries the welfare state is funded by additional payroll taxes. Entitlements to social transfers as well as social insurance are tied to formal employment relationships. In particular, pension schemes and unemployment insurance schemes are generally designed for employees rather than for all citizens. In turn, the welfare state shapes the labour market by providing employees with different kinds of skills, education and protection. The level of transfer payments and their conditionality on length of employment and job seeking behaviour influence the way individuals are integrated into the labour market. If transfer payments are too high, labour market participation might be low; if they are too low, investments in skills might go down because individuals may not be able to bear the costs of training. Social policies and labour market policies are all centred around the way private business hires, trains and employs staff.

During the golden years of welfare state development, employment and welfare had reached a high level of functional and normative integration which was additionally linked by family patterns (Hassel 1999). These systems were closely tied and complemented each other, leading to a highly integrated framework. The gender division defined the link between family and employment; the employment-based funding of social protection characterized the link between employment and welfare; and population growth and birth rates were the basis on which the link between welfare and the family was defined. The social model of post-war employment was based on a family with one permanently employed breadwinner, whose employment generated income for the whole family and which also accumulated sufficient funds for social protection and welfare expenditures. Today, the relationship between welfare and employment faces fundamental challenges from changes in family and employment patterns as well as from the fiscal crisis of the state. Decreasing wage levels, combined with growing job insecurity, no longer allow for traditional one breadwinner family models. Increased female employment undermines the traditional division of labour within families. Persistent high levels of unemployment and underemployment put pressure on social security budgets and unemployment funds. Social spending, however, remains at high levels and so almost all advanced industrialized countries face a fiscal crisis.

There has long been a debate as to whether the welfare state is a precondition or a burden for the success of business. There is a clear correlation between the size of the welfare state and the wealth of a nation. While some assume the welfare state's expansion occurred as nations grew wealthier and were able to afford extensive social insurance programmes

(Alber 1980), others maintain that the modern social insurance system provided a foundation for the economic growth of the twentieth century. Both processes therefore feed each other; investing in education and social services facilitates skills, which in turn maintains innovation and competitiveness. Crucial questions are, how much social protection does a family need in order to invest in the skills needed by a modern economy? And how much social spending can a modern government afford in the light of the current fiscal crisis?

Experiences in different countries are mixed: there is no one way to organize the labour market or the welfare state. Labour market institutions, such as employment protection legislation and collective bargaining structures as well as social protection schemes of the welfare state, are subject to long-term historical and path-dependent developments under intense political contestation, and countries have therefore developed their very individual configurations of regulations, provisions and institutions. Various combinations of different labour market institutions and welfare state types have developed complementarities and interdependencies and in general have proved to be stable over time. At the same time, advanced industrialized countries all face similar challenges: globalization, the rise of the service economy, feminization and dualization (divisions within the labour market) are phenomena that can be found in the majority of countries. The relationship between employment and welfare is characterized by parallel processes of adjustment under very different local settings. During the past few decades, welfare provisions have been restructured in many countries in order to provide sufficient incentives for people to take up employment. Labour market policies have encouraged greater levels of flexibility and these policies have been accompanied by increasing divisions between labour market insiders and outsiders.

Varieties of welfare regimes and the employment relationship

Cross-country comparisons between industrialized countries have highlighted significant differences in welfare and employment regimes. In some countries, employment is flexible and fluid; there are few rules to be followed when hiring and firing; and people move between jobs frequently. In other countries, employment is far more rule-bound and rigid. One way to classify the flexibility of labour markets is the employment protection index produced by the Organization for Economic Co-operation and Development (OECD).[2] It covers three different aspects of employment protection: (1) individual dismissal of workers with regular contracts; (2) additional costs for collective dismissals; and (3) the regulation of temporary contracts. For each of these aspects several indicators are used. For example, individual dismissal of workers with regular contracts incorporates three aspects of dismissal protection: (1) procedural inconveniences that employers face when starting the dismissal process, such as notification and consultation requirements; (2) notice periods and severance pay, which typically vary by tenure of the employee; and (3) the difficulty of dismissal, as determined by the circumstances in which it is possible to dismiss workers, as well as the repercussions for the employer if a dismissal is found to be unfair (such as compensation and reinstatement). Based on these indicators an index ranging from 0–4 has been constructed. The United States has the most flexible labour market among the OECD countries whereas employment protection is strongest in Turkey.

Strong employment protection often goes hand in hand with representation of trade unions within firms. Employers need to have valid reasons to make employees redundant and must consult trade unions or the elected representatives of their employees. Protection and trade union representation require a far greater degree of negotiation but also cooperation between management and employees in order that firms can remain competitive. Union representation and employment regulation have a profound effect on work organization, innovation patterns and productivity. Comparative studies on production regimes have long established that cooperative workplace relations are related to higher degrees of functional flexibility and productivity (Maurice *et al.* 1986). The decline of British and US American manufacturing industries is in part due to hostile relations between management and employees at the plant level.

These differences between employment relationships in different countries correspond to huge differences in welfare regimes. Again, the extent and the ways in which governments protect their citizens from economic hardship vary substantially. For instance, government expenditure for social protection in 2009 ranged from 9 per cent of GDP in the United States to 25 per cent in Denmark.[3] The understanding of social risks and the responsibility of government to cover these risks can take many forms: in some countries, risks are defined in a minimalist way and in some cases not seen as risks at all. For instance, in the United States unemployment and old age risks are only minimally covered by government schemes. On the other hand, the awareness of social risks in Europe is very high and politically salient. Moreover, social risks can be insured by both the state and the individual. In the USA, the private insurance of risks is supported through tax credits, which do not take the form of direct government spending. Finally, there is also a very different understanding of the role of the state in delivering social services. In Scandinavian countries, for example, welfare provision includes extensive childcare and training services, which are not such a major part of the welfare state in other countries. Both employment relations and welfare regimes are not only characterized by national variety and difference but they are also systematically linked. For an understanding of these systematic linkages, we can draw on two main academic approaches.

Welfare capitalism

In Gosta Esping-Andersen's seminal study, *The Worlds of Welfare Capitalism*, three welfare regimes were identified (Esping-Andersen 1990).[4] Welfare regimes were classified by the level of 'decommodification', which describes the 'degree to which individuals, or families, can uphold a socially acceptable standard of living independently of market participation' (ibid.: 37). Decommodification is strongest in the social-democratic regimes where there is universal provision of a wide range of entitlements. Social-democratic welfare states were designed to secure high standards for all, not just to support those in need. Their political project was equality between the classes. Status differences between blue-collar and white-collar workers were eradicated within a universal insurance system, although benefits continued to be based on customary earnings. Exemplary cases are the Scandinavian countries of Sweden, Norway, Finland and Denmark. At the other end, a liberal welfare regime developed in the Anglo-Saxon countries and in other countries such as Switzerland. Here welfare provisions are minimal and means-tested, and the state encourages market solutions by subsidizing private welfare schemes; public schemes are universal but provisions are too low to maintain the income levels that were achieved during employment. Third, in conservative welfare states, social security is provided mainly by the state and the share of the market is minimal. Provisions and entitlements are, however, not as comprehensive as in the social-democratic welfare regime; the emphasis is not on equality but on the preservation of status differentials. Redistributive effects are therefore negligible. Conservative welfare states are primarily to be found on the European Continent. Many countries combine elements of different welfare regimes. The Danish welfare state combines both liberal and social-democratic elements. In the less wealthy countries of southern Europe, a mix of liberal and conservative elements can be found. In Italy, for instance, employment protection is strong while social benefits are low. Different combinations indicate the different relative importance of conflicting goals in social security provision: equality, the maintenance of status differentials, and market reliance.

Ultimately, however, the three worlds of welfare capitalism depict different types of welfare regimes whose relevance does not lie so much in their expenditure ranking but in the contrast of different structures of welfare provision (ibid.). The biggest difference between the social-democratic and the conservative welfare state 'lies not so much in their de-commodifying income-maintenance guarantees as in their approach to services and sponsoring women's careers' (Esping-Andersen 1999: 88). Decommodification protects the individual from market fluctuations during the business cycle; unemployment will not reduce living standards as much, and old age is less of a social risk. However, decommodification comes in different forms. The labels 'social-democratic' versus 'conservative' describe the distinction between the universal character of the Nordic welfare states versus the 'status-oriented' nature of benefit provisions in the conservative states. The distinction between social-democratic and conservative helps us to understand welfare production regimes (see below) by pointing to the administrative logic of welfare provisions in countries with specific skills. A status-oriented welfare state provides special benefits to particular groups of employees, particularly employees in the manufacturing sector with very specific sets of skills. The insurance-based nature of the benefit system ensures via its 'equivalence-principle' that benefits are tightly coupled to contributions. Social democratic welfare regimes, such as the Nordic countries provide services and insurance for coping with change. Rather than maintaining the status of individuals, they assist in changing status. While social spending might be as high or even higher in social-democratic welfare regimes, the focus is not on the protection of a particular job but on the income level of a household.

Welfare production regime

The second approach is based on the concept of the 'welfare production regime' (WPR) introduced by Estevez-Abe *et al.* (2001). Welfare production regimes aim to capture the ways in which social protection regimes, skills regimes and production regimes are interconnected. As Estevez-Abe *et al.* put it, 'welfare production regimes are the set of product market strategies, employee skill trajectories, and social, economic, and political institutions that support them' (ibid.: 146). The starting point of the welfare production regime literature is the idea of different business systems or 'varieties of capitalism' (VoC). Hall and Soskice (2001) distinguish between two opposing forms of production regimes: coordinated market economies (CMEs) and liberal market economies (LMEs). They can be distinguished based on five spheres and their respective attributes and they relate the workings of national institutions to the behaviour of firms. The first sphere is that of *industrial relations* where the working conditions as well as the wage level are coordinated by companies in cooperation with labour, labour unions, as well as other employers. Industrial relations can be either highly centralized and organized, as in many European countries, or highly decentralized as in many Anglo-American countries. *Vocational training and education* is the second sphere in which companies contribute through the production of either specific or general skills of their workers, which in turn shapes their production strategies. The *corporate governance* sphere determines the ability of firms to draw on 'patient capital', that is, capital invested for the long term rather than the short term. The fourth sphere refers to *inter-firm relations*, in which standards regarding technology and supplier relations are organized. The fifth sphere is the relationship with the *employees* and coordination with regard to the employees' commitment and work motivation within the firm (ibid.: 6). Based on these five distinguishing spheres and their respective indicators, a distinction between two types of production regimes is possible.

The VoC literature contrasts the working of coordinated market economies (CMEs) with liberal market economies (LMEs) based on the role of market mechanisms. CMEs are based on non-market mechanisms, such as organizational interaction and long-term relationships. The Nordic and Continental European countries are both classified as CMEs. In coordinated market economies, firms' product market strategies rely heavily on the availability of specific skills. Specific skills are those skills that can only be used in a particular firm or industry and cannot easily be transferred. General skills can be used in any context. In order to protect their investment in specific skills, workers demand social insurance policies that protect these skill investments, such as employment protection, job-specific unemployment insurance and earnings-related pensions. Firms then pursue product market strategies based on incremental innovation or 'diversified quality production' (Streeck 1991) because of the abundance of specific skills. According to this logic, skilled workers will join with manufacturing employers in supporting social protection and training policies that support this high skill equilibrium.

Key institutions in this perspective are those which protect the acquisition of specific skills, either through high degrees of employment protection (dismissal protection) or specific welfare provisions for groups of skilled employees. Highly specific skills are correlated with more welfare provisions aimed at protecting these skills and with less flexible labour markets. Demands by specifically skilled workers in manufacturing industries have led to specifically designed welfare programmes, as well as to relatively strong employment protection legislation. The strong focus on protecting specific skills has led to the adoption of systems, which – in contrast to the Nordic countries – did not ask skilled workers to change their skill sets, but rather promised life-long earning-related benefits in case of unemployment with no obligation or expectation to acquire new skills or move to new occupations. In countries with more general skill sets, the demand for skill-specific social protection is lower and programmes are more employment-friendly in nature. In both liberal and Nordic countries, the benefits focus much more on moving unemployed workers into new employment rather than protecting their acquired skills. This policy focus is closely related to the training system of some of the Continental European countries, in which companies invest highly in initial skill sets (Anderson and Hassel 2013).

Four models of employment and welfare regimes

The combination of the two theoretical perspectives – one based on welfare decommodification and the other on the production regime – can be used as two axes for classifying countries in the way they link welfare and employment (Figure 8.1). The liberal countries score high on the degree of labour market flexibility compared to Continental and southern Europe. The Nordic and Continental European countries score considerably higher with regard to the degree of social protection/decommodification compared to both liberal and southern European welfare states. Both country groups are similar with regard to income maintenance.

In this perspective, countries are situated on a continuum of flexibility of labour markets and the character of the benefit system.[5] In liberal countries with education systems that focus on school-based rather than vocational education, the regulation of labour markets is loose and benefits are aimed towards high employment levels. The group of coordinated market

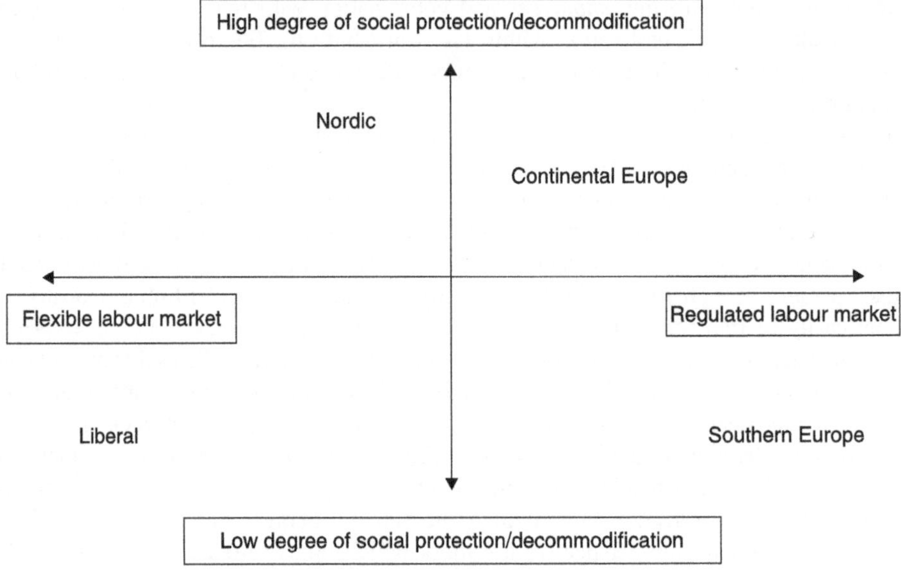

Figure 8.1 Degree of social protection by type of welfare production regime.

economies is divided into three different groups: the Nordic countries are closest to the liberal model with regard to the universality of the benefit system universality and the degree of flexibility in the labour market. In contrast, Continental European and southern European countries have more strongly regulated labour markets. Southern Europe combines a strongly regulated labour market with a meagre welfare regime. Employment protection often takes the place of social security as income maintenance is guaranteed with a permanent job.

An important implication of this approach is that it removes the traditional stark contrast between liberal and Nordic models and puts both groups of countries on the same level. Both models are similar not only regarding employment levels and the role of women in the labour market, but also in terms of education levels and the importance of general skills. The Nordic countries are closer to the Anglo-Saxon world than to their Continental European counterparts.

Critics might take issue with the notion of the Nordic countries as being more flexible in terms of labour market regulations. Standard measures of employment protection for regular employment by the OECD give most of the Nordic countries (with the exception of Denmark) a similar score compared to standard Continental European countries (see Table 8.1). Scholars of the region frequently disagree with the notion of labour market flexibility as a Nordic trait. However, practice in the Nordic countries prefers labour market activation over job preservation as high employment rates are a precondition for high taxation. Though all CMEs are characterized by high social spending, countries with strong social-democratic incumbency differentiate themselves with regards to the employment-friendly nature of their social policies (Huo *et al.* 2008). As a case in point, social-democratic welfare state regimes are characterized by high spending on active labour market policies and generous short-term unemployment replacement rates, which relate to higher employment levels (Bradley and Stephens 2007). Christian Democratic states, in contrast, demonstrate strong employment protection, high social security taxes, and generous long-term unemployment replacement

Table 8.1 Employment protection and social expenditure in four types of welfare regimes

	Employment Protection Index	*Government expenditure for social protection (per cent of GDP)*	*Average job tenure (in years)**
LME	1.12	14.52	9.93
Nordic	2.23	22.57	10.00
Continental	2.71	20.62	11.54
Southern Europe	2.88	17.9	12.56

Source: OECD Statistics, latest available year (2009/2010).

Note: LME = the UK, the USA, New Zealand, Australia, Ireland, Canada; Nordic = Sweden, Denmark, Norway, Finland; Continental = Germany, Austria, Belgium, the Netherlands, France; Southern = Portugal; Spain, Italy, Greece.

* USA, New Zealand and Australia missing; Greece data for 2001.

rates, which relate to lower employment levels (ibid.). In Sweden, the Rehn-Meidner model recognized in the 1950s that workers benefit from mobility between jobs rather than fighting for the stability of existing workplaces. Therefore, active labour market policies were combined with early investment in education, good childcare facilities, centralized wage bargaining and a large public sector. Today, Denmark excels at achieving high growth rates, high employment levels, high levels of labour turnover and high degrees of worker mobility.

Labour market flexibility in Scandinavia also becomes apparent when looking at job tenure rates. In the Nordic countries average tenure rates are considerably shorter than in Continental European countries and fall exactly between the high turnover rates of liberal market economies and the substantially lower rates of Continental Europe (Table 8.1). To depict the Nordic countries as lying in between those of Continental Europe and those of more liberal economies has important implications in judging reform movements. A movement towards the Nordic model by the Continental European countries is, at the same time, a move towards liberalization. In other words: approaching the Nordic model from a Continental European viewpoint would entail a dose of liberalization, even if policy-makers have a 'social-democratic' model in mind.

Mapping the advanced industrialized countries like this provides us with a set of important dimensions which are useful in assessing policy reforms and the trajectory of change. It also fits in neatly with the policy debate on 'flexicurity', which is currently the most sophisticated policy approach that aims to combine change, flexibility and the protection of workers. Flexicurity has been discussed within the European Union for about the last decade and since 2007 has moved high up the agenda of the European Commission.[6] The Commission described flexicurity as an optimal balance between labour market flexibility and security for employees against labour market risks.[7] Rather than protecting jobs, the notion is now to protect people. Denmark, in particular, has been used as a test case for flexicurity, but in the analysis in this chapter, all the Nordic countries combine a comparatively high degree of flexibility in the labour market with a high degree of social protection, namely high levels and generous conditions of social benefits for the unemployed.

Politics: political institutions, class structures and voting patterns

Research on the relationship between voting behaviour and redistributive welfare policies starts from the assumption that the positioning of the median voter will affect the redistributive focus of governing parties. In general, it is assumed that the lower the income of the median voter and the higher his/her exposure to risks, the more likely it is that governing parties will pursue redistributive policy programmes. However, voting results indicate that low-income workers in precarious labour market situations are less likely to vote than high-income workers in more stable positions, leading to a distorted picture of the median voter (Lijphart 1997). Political institutions play a major role when explaining differences in redistribution between countries. Iversen and Soskice (2006) claim that the electoral system has a key influence on electoral support for redistribution. Electoral systems shape the electoral success of parties which are formed along socio-economic cleavages. Majoritarian electoral systems (in which one party often wins a majority of seats without necessarily having a majority of votes) favour centre-right parties, which are against redistribution, whereas centre-left parties, generally in favour of redistribution, fare better under regimes based on proportional representation (ibid.).

Why countries have either majoritarian electoral systems or proportional representation can in turn be explained by different kinds of economic organization during key phases of democratization. Proportional representation was easier to implement in countries with locally organized skilled unions as it allowed different groups to coordinate their specific interests and build cross-class compromises. Conversely majoritarian electoral regimes evolved when labour unions and their interest representation were feared by ruling classes (ibid.: 378, 383). In consequence, government dominance was ensured through vote majorities built on the median voter, independent of group-specific interests or needs. Schneider and Soskice (2009) argue that in coordinated market economies economic institutions and consensus-based politics are complementary and were effectively a major tool for reducing inequality and reinforcing the strength and stability of a distributive welfare state. In contrast, liberal market economies characterized by competitive political systems based on majority voting, lead to welfare states based on minimal standards and higher levels of inequality.

Political systems and economic institutions are complementary and are influenced by the effects of partisanship and the nature of coalitions formed in order to take office (Iversen and Soskice 2006). The electoral system determines the strength of partisanship and the policy position of the government. Political systems characterized by proportional representation allow a variety of different groups access to the policy-making process and are hence generally biased towards centre-left governments. In political systems characterized by majoritarian voting rules, competition over middle-class votes usually leads to a bias to the centre-right (Schneider and Soskice 2009: 22). Similar to economic institutions, political systems turn out to be very stable over time. In sum, coordinated market economies are correlated to welfare regimes due to political and economic institutional factors. Business structures as well as wage bargaining are characterized by co-decision and involvement at all levels. Both capital and labour thus have a vested interest in politically contributing and deciding on the parameters of a fairly egalitarian income redistribution. In liberal market economies, the middle-class voter is the key voter. This leads to an orientation of political parties more towards general welfare provisions and minimum standards and less to protection of specific groups. Based on this classification, we can now add to the notion of welfare capitalism and varieties of capitalism the role of political institutions (Table 8.2, and see Schneider and Soskice 2009).

The issue of redistribution is highly contested and its salience differs by government partisanship and across countries. Facing the dilemma that democratic governments must respond to the needs and preferences of their citizens in order to be re-elected, the determinants of

Table 8.2 System classifications in OECD countries: varieties of capitalism, welfare states and political institutions

	Liberal (Anglo-Saxon): the US, the UK, Canada, Australia, New Zealand, Ireland	*Coordinated (Northern European): Denmark, Finland, Norway, Sweden, Austria, Belgium, Netherlands, Germany, Switzerland*
Variety of capitalism (Hall and Soskice)	Liberal market economies	Coordinated market economies
Welfare state (Esping-Andersen)	Safety net	Insurance plus redistribution
Political system (Lijphart)	Majoritarian	Consensus (PR)

Source: Schneider and Soskice (2009: 21).

individual level support for income redistribution have to be taken into consideration. There are two different motivations behind individual support for income redistribution: (1) the desire for equity (people aim at redistribution because of their own disadvantaged position); and (2) the desire for insurance (individuals seek an insurance against risks) (Rehm 2007: 48–9). The first motivation can either be based on purely egoistic grounds, or alternatively can be a form of altruism, aiming for general equity in society. The empirical evidence suggests that individuals with income above the national mean are less likely to be in favour of redistribution than individuals with income below the national mean (the difference is 7 per cent) (ibid.: 60). The second motivation is redistribution as personal insurance against the risks of income shocks (Rehm 2005: 30). With regard to skill formation, the findings suggest that the more specific the skills of individuals, the more likely they are to support income redistribution (ibid.: 63). Women are more in favour of redistribution than men and support declines as income increases, while the self-employed are less in favour of redistribution than employees. The data confirm that both logics for redistribution are at play: 'individuals are in favour of redistribution either because they are poor or because they expect to be poor in the future' (Rehm 2007: 65). These findings support the claim that countries with strong specific skill-formation institutions have stronger welfare states (Esping-Andersen 1990).

Welfare and employment reforms

The main challenge for welfare state politics is to keep pace with modernization, to adopt policies that address new pressing problems in the globalized post-industrial society. As employment structures change, social programmes are in danger of spending resources on outdated risks (Iversen 2005; Häusermann 2010). Some of the most pressing changes and challenges as defined in the literature are the transition to the service economy, the pluralization of employment forms such as increasing rates of temporary and part-time work, the increasing flexibilization of labour markets, the increase of atypical and female employment, and family instability as well as ageing. In addition, fiscal constraints on the welfare state force governments to continuously adjust welfare programmes. The transition of the employment system from male and manufacturing-based to predominantly female and service sector-based leads to a simultaneous process of declining resources and concomitant increasing financial needs. Therefore, many countries have over the past two decades have witnessed a process that aims to balance old with new social risks. The process combines a simultaneous call for welfare state retrenchment with an expansion of welfare in response to the needs of new employment groups (Pierson 2000; Häusermann 2010: 2).

The translation of economic and social changes into policy outputs is far from straightforward and is shaped by the interplay between institutions and actors' preferences and strategies. A number of factors shape this process: the level of multidimensionality of the policy issue, the degree of fragmentation of interest groups and political parties, and the potential for conflicts. More fragmentation implies more flexibility and a greater degree of coalition formation and therefore implies change (Häusermann 2010). Governments formed by proportional representation have managed to include more specific interests and to enhance welfare state politics based on cross-class compromises (Cusack *et al.* 2007). Regarding employment, two main reform patterns have emerged over the past two decades: activation and dualization.

Activation

Over the course of the post-war period, patterns of labour market participation changed radically. While the participation of women steadily increased, the employment rates of elderly workers, low-skilled workers and men all dropped. The recession following the 1970s oil shock led to a further fall in activity rates. Most governments during the 1990s pursued a policy of activation, increasing the rate of participation in the labour force (Bonoli 2010). In Anglo-Saxon liberal countries, activation strategies were based on incentivizing the unemployed into finding work by cutting welfare entitlements. In the rest of Western Europe, governments pursued mixed approaches which combined lower welfare payments, with positive incentives, but also sanctions and training and education measures. Those groups of unemployed who had dropped out of the labour market completely were the focus of activation measures. As the pressure to find employment was tightened, the distinction between insurance-based social protection and poverty relief measures was often blurred. In the past, unemployment benefit entitlements from social insurance were intended to secure a good standard of living for a certain period of time. These benefits were often seen as detrimental to incentivizing the unemployed to find work. Instead, flat rate and means-tested benefits were introduced which were tightly coupled with the obligation of the individual to look for work. Welfare restructuring for the long-term unemployed and activation strategies were pioneered by the Clinton Administration in the USA, and then followed by the British Labour government, as well as by governments in the Netherlands, Germany and Denmark (Hassel and Schiller 2010).

Similarly, existing programmes on early retirement had led to declining employment rates among the elderly. These programmes were dismantled step by step over the last two decades and employment rates for the elderly (as well as the pension age) generally increased. Moreover, the level of state pensions was generally cut (Ebbinghaus 2011a).

Dualization

Dualization denotes the process in which policies differentiate between rights, entitlements as well as services among different groups or categories of citizens. The main distinction is between labour market insiders and outsiders. Labour market insiders are in a secure employment position, while those without employment or holding insecure employment are described as labour market outsiders.[8] In the process of restructuring the welfare state, both groups are treated differently and subject to one of three different forms of dualization:

(1) an acceleration of the differential treatment of insiders and outsiders; (2) the shift of some labour market insiders to the outsider category; and, finally, (3) the development of new institutional dualisms (Emmenegger *et al.* 2012: 10).

'New' and non-traditional groups entering the labour market such as women, young employees or migrants are particularly at risk of being 'assigned' to the outsider group as their chances of entering stable and skilled standard employment relationships are smaller than for groups such as older men (Barbieri and Scherer 2009; McDowell *et al.* 2012). This phenomenon directly links to the increased visibility of dualization processes in society. Whereas until the 1970s, the precarious situation of women was not visible at the political level, as family and marriage policies provided them with protection, the past few decades have increasingly politicized this problem. The same is also true for the immigrant outsider group who are often over-represented in non-standard precarious working conditions (Kalleberg 2009; Emmenegger and Careja 2012: 128).

Increasing institutional dualization can also be explained by looking at the median voter. As employed insiders shape the preferences of the median voter, the support for insider-oriented dualization-maintaining policies also increases. If, as a consequence, insiders perceive that political parties enhance outsider-oriented welfare policies, they risk losing insider votes (Lindvall and Rueda 2012: 279). Dualization is not a completely new phenomenon and has certainly featured in labour market policies in the past. However, the number of people now affected, the composition of both groups, in particular of outsiders, as well as the visibility of the divide and the political sources of dualization are significantly different from the past (Emmenegger *et al.* 2012).

To what extent dualization is pursued as a clear political strategy is disputed. Rueda argues that centre-left governments in OECD countries in particular have tended to promote less egalitarian policies in favour of insiders (Rueda 2006: 405). Social-democratic parties are more committed to labour market insiders compared to the centre-right and have therefore been willing to sacrifice the interests of labour market outsiders. Similarly, trade unions, even more than social-democratic governments, are tempted to defend the interests of their insider members because the unemployed or people working in precarious employment relations are generally not unionized (Esping-Andersen 1999).

Future challenges posed by globalization and the service economy

In contrast to the golden years of democratic capitalism which lasted from the end of the Second World War to the early 1970s, no new economic model combining employment and welfare has yet been found. Rather, national political economies have entered a phase of ongoing restructuring in which business, employment and social policy have to be readjusted on a continuous basis. The main drivers for the process are the changing division of labour in the global economy, in which emerging economies take on parts of manufacturing production that have previously dominated the economies of the industrialized world. We can therefore identify three main processes of change: globalization, deindustrialization, and technological change.

Globalization

The global economy has now become a dominant influence on many jobs, not just in the export industries. However, to what extent globalization is undercutting terms and conditions of employment and forces governments to cut social spending, is a matter of dispute. Initially the balance of economic openness for modern economies was positive. Katzenstein (1985) long ago identified that small open economies tended to have large welfare states, because governments aimed to compensate the losers of structural change and smooth the effects of economic fluctuations. There is also little evidence that globalization has led to a race to the bottom: taxation and public spending have remained high in many countries and public investment in education and infrastructure remain important contributors to productivity. Countries have long adhered to different taxation rules and high tax countries have not suffered an exodus of investors (Garrett 1998: 823). Others, however, such as Dani Rodrik, have argued that the effects of globalization will lead to more tensions between winners and losers. International trade will undermine social norms in many countries and increase the pressure to maintain competitiveness. Governments will thus find it difficult to safeguard social protection (Rodrik 1997: 4–5). Economic openness has certainly contributed to the stagnation of average wages in many advanced economies. Offshoring might have kept some industries competitive, but has led to the loss of employment in these sectors. Unskilled workers in developed economies have experienced declining wages and job insecurity.[9]

Proponents of increased trade openness argue that a high degree of international trade integration can lead to long-term welfare benefits. First, foreign direct investors, mainly from industrialized countries, can import some of the basic labour standards from their home countries (Mosley 2006: 1). A similar argument contends that both exporting firms and foreign-owned plants have comparatively better working conditions than domestic employers (Moran 2002; Harrison and Scorse 2004). Second, globalization may even increase politicians' room to manoeuvre due to better access to capital: governments 'wishing to expand the public economy for political reasons may do so (including increasing taxes on capital to pay for new spending)' (Garrett 1998: 823). Foreign direct investment (FDI) is said to improve local living situations, thus also labour standards (Flanagan 2006: 188). However, as Sengenberger (2005: 66) emphasizes, these findings are hardly surprising, given that 'both the source and the destination of recent FDI flows were the most developed countries with comparatively high labour standards'.

This critical approach is backed by others, who claim that globalization will decrease the stability of employment relations (Rodrik 1997) or, at worst, lead to competition around the lowest common denominator (Deacon 2000). In contrast to the compensation thesis, which predicts an increase of welfare due to global trade, the competition thesis argues that global trade leads to a decrease of social spending (for an overview, see Genschel 2004). It has, however, proven difficult to find robust empirical evidence. While several authors have found a positive correlation between foreign economic penetration and government respect for civil liberties in developing countries (Meyer 1998; Richards and Gelleny 2003), other authors report mixed influences (Mosley and Uno 2007) or evidence for a negative correlation (Cingranelli and Tsai 2003). Then again, several studies find little or no evidence that variations in collective labour rights are due to differences in FDI (Busse 2003; Neumayer and de Soysa 2006). The increase of precarious working conditions is a phenomenon often attributed to the process of globalization, capital mobility and the continuous pursuit of low cost production in less developed countries (Kalleberg 2009). In the political discourse it is used as a term to symbolize the changing employment relations in Western economies. This process takes place in all countries, however, irrespective of the welfare regime.

Deindustrialization

Some authors have argued that globalization has been accompanied by an ever more drastic challenge at the national level that has led to the need for increased welfare state restructuring and expansion: deindustrialization (Iversen and Cusack 2000: 316). Deindustrialization defines the process in which the employment structure in a country moves from employment in the first (agricultural) and second (manufacturing) sectors towards the dominance of employment in the third (service) sector. The structural changes away from manufacturing and towards the service economy began in the 1960s and the reasons for this shift are manifold: the saturation of domestic demand in the wealthy industrialized economies for traditional manufactured products; shifting patterns of demand; increased female employment; technological progress; and the increasing demand for service-based activities (Iversen and Cusack 2000; Häusermann 2010).

One of the challenges of deindustrialization has been the non-transferability of skills between manufacturing and service-based occupations (Iversen and Cusack 2000: 327). Depending on the original focus and importance of skills within the national employment structure, the process of deindustrialization leads to an increased level of welfare state expansion to cope with this phenomenon. This argument contradicts the perspective outlined by Esping-Andersen that strong and egalitarian welfare states are linked to strong and participatory industrial working classes. Despite varying forms of deindustrialization across OECD countries, all governments have reacted to the problems posed by deindustrialization, underlining its importance (ibid.: 346). Moreover, Iversen and Cusack claim that in fact deindustrialization has more explanatory power in relation to welfare state expansion and reform in the last few decades than globalization or political partisanship. They argue that an increased level of welfare state expansion was necessary in order to protect workers in the first and second sectors if their employment position was threatened by technological change or if their skills or social benefits were not transferable to the service sector (ibid.: 325).

However, Manow *et al.* are critical of the consolidation of both first and second sector employment shifts as 'deindustrialization' and propose a finer distinction between 'de-agrarization' and 'deindustrialization' in order to explain the shifts in employment as well as the concomitant shifts in welfare expansion in the post-war period (Manow *et al.* 2013). They claim that in contrast to the transition from second to third sector, labour transition from agriculture to manufacturing with regard to skills was less problematic as the majority of manufacturing jobs required only a modest level of qualification in that period. On this view the deindustrialization theory of Iversen and Cusack denotes only the period since the 1980s marked by involuntary shifts from the second (industry) to the third sector (services) due to a decrease in demand for manufacturing employment because of technological innovation.

The flip side of deindustrialization is the rise of the service economy which carries both potential and risks for employment relationships (Schelkle 2011). The increase in employment possibilities for women and younger generations benefits the economy and society as it increases the overall workforce. At the same time, trade unions are barely represented in this sector. Second, trade unions have failed to adjust their image in line with the changing forms of employment. Recent studies indicate that trade union representation is perceived to be beneficial only for long-term stable employment relationships, because this is still the main interest group organized by unions. By protecting these insiders from the risks of atypical and insecure employment relations, labour market outsiders tend to be kept away from unions (Johnston *et al.* 2011). The increase of atypical employment forms therefore has a negative impact on worker interest in labour representation. The probability of individuals joining a union is on average 4.5 per cent smaller if the individual has either a part-time or a non-permanent contract (Ebbinghaus 2011b: 115–18).

Conclusion

Employment relations and the welfare state are closely related and shape each other in various ways. Changes in the welfare state have repercussions on employment relations and vice versa. The dynamic relationship between the two can be systematically assessed by comparative research since both vary considerably between countries. However, both employment relations and the welfare state have developed over the last century in tandem under very specific economic circumstances. Both are a product of the rise of mass production in advanced industrialized countries, in which the majority of the population was either directly or indirectly employed through manufacturing firms. Mass production implied stable jobs and a clear division of labour and responsibility between employers, workers and the state.

This situation has now changed. In the last quarter of the twentieth century, advanced industrialized countries have seen a rapid and deep transformation of their economies. Manufacturing employment has declined or been moved offshore, the service economy has expanded and policy-makers have moved away from protective and Keynesian policies towards supply side reforms and 'commodification'. The majority of workers in national labour markets are now women workers and atypical work – part-time, fixed-term and precarious work – is on the rise.

The new labour market requires a new welfare state. Politics and policy-makers are busy adjusting welfare provisions and institutions. Political coalitions are shifting and formerly clear and stable political alliances such as that between trade unions and centre-left parties are coming under strain. The process of adjustment and transformation has not come to a new equilibrium but is currently ongoing. It remains to be seen whether, when and how a new stable arrangement can be found.

Notes

1 I would like to thank Bettina Wagner for superb research assistance and the editors for very helpful comments. All remaining errors are mine.
2 Available at: http://www.oecd.org/employment/employmentpoliciesanddata/oecdindicatorsof-employmentprotection.htm.
3 OECD Data Set National Accounts at a Glance 2011. Data extracted on 30 May 2012 from OECD. Stat.
4 The approach has been criticized for its incompleteness regarding other basic factors for stratification such as race or gender. Other authors have proposed additional forms of welfare capitalism in order to include countries that do not fit into existing categories (Leibfried 1992; Kangas 1994).
5 This conceptualization is similar to that of Anderson and Hassel (2013), who propose a similar typology based on training regimes. It therefore moves away from the standard assumption of the VoC literature, which is organized around two poles.
6 The concept was endorsed by the European Council of Ministers in December 2007 and has informed the discussion on revitalizing the Lisbon Agenda.
7 See EU Commission (2006).
8 Definitions of insiders and outsiders vary. See Häusermann and Schwander (2012) and Rueda (2006).
9 For a good summary of the arguments, see Freeman (1995).

References

Alber, J. (1980) 'Der Wohlfahrtsstaat in der Krise? Eine Bilanz nach drei Jahrzehnten Sozialpolitik in der Bundesrepublik', *Zeitschrift für Soziologie*, 9(4): 313–42.

Anderson, K. and Hassel, A. (2013) 'Pathways of change in CMEs: training regimes in Germany and the Netherlands', in A. Wren (ed.) *The Political Economy of the Service Transition*, Oxford: Oxford University Press.

Barbieri, P. and Scherer, S. (2009) 'Labour market flexibilization and its consequences in Italy', *European Sociological Review*, 25(6): 677–92.

Bonoli, G. (2010) 'The political economy of active labor-market policy', *Politics and Society*, 38(4): 435–57.

Bradley, D. H. and Stephens, J. D. (2007) 'Employment performance in OECD countries: a test of neoliberal and institutionalist hypotheses', *Comparative Political Studies*, 40(12): 1486–510.

Busse, M. (2003) 'Do transnational corporations care about labor standards?', *The Journal of Developing Areas*, 36(Spring): 39–57.

Cingranelli, D. L. and Tsai, C-Y. (2003) 'Democracy, globalization and workers' rights: a comparative analysis', paper presented to the American Political Science Association, 2003 Annual Meeting, Philadelphia.

Cusack, T.R., Iversen, T. and Soskice, D. (2007) 'Economic interests and the origins of electoral systems', *American Political Science Review*, 101(3): 373–91.

Deacon, B. (2000) 'Eastern European welfare states: the impact of politics of globalization', *Journal of European Social Policy*, 10(2): 146–61.

Ebbinghaus, B. (ed.) (2011a) *The Varieties of Pension Governance: Pension Privatization in Europe*, Oxford: Oxford University Press.

—— (2011b) 'The role of trade unions in European pension reforms: From "old" to "new" politics?', *European Journal of Industrial Relations*, 17(4): 315–31.

Emmenegger, P. and Careja, R. (2012) 'From dilemma to dualization: social and migration policies in the "reluctant countries of immigration"', in P. Emmenegger, S. Häusermann, B. Palier and M. Seeleib-Kaiser (eds) *The Age of Dualization: The Changing Face of Inequality in Deindustrializing Societies*, New York: Oxford University Press.

Emmenegger, P., Häusermann, S., Palier, B. and Seeleib-Kaiser, M. (2012) 'How we grow unequal', in P. Emmenegger, S. Häusermann, B. Palier and M. Seeleib-Kaiser (eds) *The Age of Dualization: The Changing Face of Inequality in Deindustrializing Societies*, New York: Oxford University Press.

Esping-Andersen, G. (1990) *The Three Worlds of Welfare Capitalism*, Cambridge: Polity Press.

—— (1999) 'Politics without class? Postindustrial cleavages in Europe and America', in H. Kitschelt, P. Lange, G. Marks and J. D. Stephens (eds) *Continuity and Change in Contemporary Capitalism*, New York: Cambridge University Press.

Estevez-Abe, M., Iversen, T. and Soskice, D. (2001) 'Social protection and the formation of skills: a reinterpretation of the welfare state', in P. A. Hall and D. Soskice (eds) *Varieties of Capitalism: The Institutional Foundations of Comparative Advantage*, Oxford: Oxford University Press.

EU Commission (2006) *Employment in Europe Report 2006*, Brussels: EU Commission.

Flanagan, R. (2006) *Globalization and Labor Conditions: Working Conditions and Worker Rights in a Global Economy*, New York: Oxford University Press.

Freeman, R. B. (1995) 'The large welfare state as a system', *The American Economic Review*, 85(2): 16–21.

Garrett, G. (1998) 'Global markets and national politics: collision course or virtuous circle?', *International Organization*, 52(4): 787–824.

Genschel, P. (2004) 'Globalization and the welfare state: a retrospective', *Journal of European Public Policy*, 11(4): 613–36.

Hall, P. A. and Soskice, D. (2001) 'An introduction to varieties of capitalism', in P. A. Hall and D. Soskice (eds) *Varieties of Capitalism: The Institutional Foundations of Comparative Advantage*, Oxford: Oxford University Press.

Harrison, A. and Scorse, J. (2004) 'The impact of globalization on compliance with labor standards: a plant-level study', in S. Collins and D. Rodrik (eds) *Brookings Trade Forum*, Washington, DC: Brookings Institution Press.

Hassel, A. (1999) 'The erosion of the German system of industrial relations', *British Journal of Industrial Relations*, 37(3): 483–505.

—— and Schiller, C. (2010) *Der Fall Hartz IV. Wie es zur Agenda 2010 kam und wie es weiter geht*, Frankfurt am Main: Campus.

Häusermann, S. (2010) *The Politics of Welfare State Reform in Continental Europe: Modernization in Hard Times*, New York: Cambridge University Press.

—— and Schwander, H. (2012) 'Switzerland: building a multi-pillar pension scheme for a flexible labor market', in K. Hinrichs and M. Jessoula (eds) *Flexible Today, Secure Tomorrow? Labor Market Flexibility and Pension Systems*, London: Routledge.

Huo, J., Nelson, M. and Stephens, J.D. (2008) 'Decommodification and activation in social democratic policy: resolving the paradox', *Journal of European Social Policy*, 18(1): 5–20.

Iversen, T. (2005) *Capitalism, Democracy and Welfare*, Cambridge: Cambridge University Press.

—— and Cusack, T. R. (2000) 'The causes of welfare state expansion: deindustrialization or globalization?', *World Politics*, 52(3): 313–49.

—— and Soskice, D. (2006) 'Electoral institutions and the politics of coalitions: why some democracies redistribute more than others', *American Political Science Review*, 100(2): 165–81.

Johnston, A., Kornelakis, A. and Rodriguez d'Acri, C. (2011) 'Social partners and the welfare state: recalibration, privatization or collectivization of social risks?', *European Journal of Industrial Relations*, 17(4): 349–64.

Kalleberg, A. L. (2009) 'Precarious work, insecure workers: employment relations in transition', *American Sociological Review*, 74(1): 1–22.

Kangas, O. (1994) 'The merging of welfare state models? Past and present trends in Finnish and Swedish social policy', *Journal of European Social Policy*, 4(2): 79–94.

Katzenstein, P. (1985) *Small States in World Markets: Industrial Policy in Europe*, Ithaca, NY: Cornell University Press.

Leibfried, S. (1992) 'Towards a European welfare state? On integrating poverty regimes into the European Community', in Z. Ferge and J. E. Kolberg (eds) *Social Policy in a Changing Europe*, Frankfurt am-Main: Campus.

Lijphart, A. (1997) 'Unequal participation: democracy's unresolved dilemma', *The American Political Science Review*, 91(1): 1–14.

Lindvall, J. and Rueda, D. (2012) 'Insider-outsider politics: party strategies and political behavior in Sweden', in P. Emmenegger, S. Häusermann, B. Palier and M. Seeleib-Kaiser (eds) *The Age of Dualization: The Changing Face of Inequality in Deindustrializing Societies*, New York: Oxford University Press.

McDowell, L., Batnitzky, A. and Dyer, S. (2012) 'Global flows and local labour markets: precarious employment and migrant workers in the UK', in J. Scott, S. Dex and A. C. Plagnol (eds) *Gendered Lives: Gender Inequality in Production and Reproduction*, Cheltenham: Edward Elgar.

Manow, P., van Kersbergen, K. and Schumacher, G. (2013) 'De-industrialization and the expansion of the welfare state: a reassessment', in A. Wren (ed.) *The Political Economy of the Service Transition*, Oxford: Oxford University Press.

Maurice, M., Sellier, F. and Silvestre, J.-J. (1986) *The Social Foundations of Industrial Power: A Comparison of France and Germany*, Cambridge, MA: MIT Press.

Meyer, W. H. (1998) *Human Rights and International Political Economy in Third World Nations*, Westport, CT: Praeger.

Moran, T. H. (2002) *Beyond Sweatshops: Foreign Direct Investment and Globalization in Developing Countries*, Washington, DC: The Brookings Institution.

Mosley, L. (2006) 'Varieties of capitalists? Economic globalization and labor rights in the developing world', paper presented at the Southern Political Science Association, 2006 Annual Meeting, Atlanta, GA, USA.

—— and Uno, S. (2007) 'Racing to the bottom or climbing to the top? Economic globalization and collective labor rights', *Comparative Political Studies*, 40(8): 923–48.

Neumayer, E. and de Soysa, I. (2006) 'Globalization and the right to free association and collective bargaining: an empirical analysis', *World Development*, 34(1): 31–49.

OECD (2001) 'The characteristics and quality of service sector jobs', in OECD, *Employment Outlook 2001*, Paris: OECD, Available at: http://www.oecd.org/dataoecd/11/15/2079411.pdf.

Pierson, P. (2000) 'Three worlds of welfare state research', *Comparative Political Studies*, 33(6–7): 791–821.

Rehm, P. (2005) *Citizen Support for the Welfare State: Determinants of Preferences for Income Redistribution*, Berlin: Wissenschaftszentrum, Discussion Paper, SP II 2005 – 02.

—— (2007) 'Who supports the welfare state? Determinants of preferences concerning redistribution', in S. Mau and B. Veghte (eds) *Social Justice, Legitimacy and the Welfare State*, Aldershot: Ashgate.

Richards, D. L. and Gelleny, R. D. (2003) 'Is it a small world after all? Economic globalization and human rights in developing countries', in S. Chan and J. Scarritt (eds) *Coping with Globalization*, London: Frank Cass.

Rodrik, D. (1997) *Has Globalization Gone Too Far?*, Washington, DC: Institute for International Economics.

Rueda, D. (2006) 'Social democracy and active labour market policies: insiders, outsiders and the politics of employment promotion', *British Journal of Political Science*, 36(3): 385–406.

Schelkle, W. (2011) 'Reconfiguring welfare states in the post-industrial age: what role for trade unions?', *European Journal of Industrial Relations*, 17(4): 301–14.

Schneider, B. R. and Soskice, D. (2009) 'Inequality in developed countries and Latin America: coordinated, liberal and hierarchical systems', *Economy and Society*, 38(1): 17–52.

Sengenberger, W. (2005) *Globalization and Social Progress: The Role and Impact of International Labour Standards*, Bonn: Friedrich-Ebert-Foundation, Report.

Streeck, W. (1991) 'On the institutional conditions of diversified quality production', in E. Matzner and W. Streeck (eds) *Beyond Keynesianism: The Socio-Economics of Production and Employment*, London: Edward Elgar.

Part 3

Employment regulation in national contexts

9 The United States

Gerald Friedman

The hegemon after hegemony?

More than war made the United States the world's unchallenged economic power after World War II. American industrial supremacy dates back much earlier, to the late-nineteenth century when giant industrial enterprises were established with bureaucratized labour management systems and a high-wage system (dubbed 'Fordism' by some observers) joining mass consumption with mass production. Already by 1900, American industrial success was threatening an international trading system based on European supremacy in the production and sale of manufactured goods. American supremacy did not last a century. By the 1970s, American companies were searching for a new competitive strategy. Abandoning Fordism and building trust through long-term relationships, they found renewed profits in using markets and the threat of job loss to discipline labour. They have largely driven unions, the ultimate protector of the Fordist arrangement of high wages and high productivity, from much of American industry. Instead, the American workplace today is filled with scared workers grateful for temporary work and willing to accept low wages and bad treatment from fear of losing their jobs to China.

This chapter reviews the development of the new industrial relations system. In the next section, I discuss the Fordist system and the role of paternalist enterprises and powerful labour unions in maintaining a high-road economic programme of mass production and mass consumption. Next, I discuss the crisis of the 1970s, and the threat that rising labour militancy posed to America's high-road companies. Finally, I discuss the new industrial relations system that emerged from this crisis and the implications of the changing industrial relations system for economic performance and the opportunity for progressive economic changes.

Big business and Fordism in the New Deal era

Long before the Great Depression of the 1930s, pioneering businesses, including such giants as United States Steel, International Harvester, and the Ford Motor Company, were experimenting with high wage policies and internal labour markets (Jacoby 1985; Brody 1993). President Franklin Roosevelt's New Deal spread these initiatives by requiring companies to recognize labour unions and to pay higher wages. While associated with Keynesian economics, Roosevelt entered the White House committed to a more intrusive role for government in labour and product markets. Rather than manipulating monetary or fiscal policy levers several steps removed from the business enterprise, the New Deal sought to promote recovery by directly changing market wages and prices through government and private regulation.

New Deal economists like Rexford Tugwell were institutionalists who believed that the development of the giant business had fundamentally transformed the economy in ways that undermined competitive markets and made traditional *laissez-faire* policy irrelevant (Clark 1926; Tugwell 1971; Berle 1991). They believed that the large scale of production and heavy overhead costs effectively limited market competition, requiring new forms of public regulation to protect consumers and workers from exploitation. Large-scale modern enterprises had reduced market competition, distorting the distribution of income by favouring a few capitalists against small businesses and workers alike. Growing overhead costs, including the costs of maintaining a skilled workforce, furthermore, made businesses vulnerable to labour disruption; a threat many addressed by creating job ladders, employer-specific benefits, and careers intended to tie workers to a single employer. These businesses sought to become monopsonists, exploiting captive workers. They soon learned that their new bureaucratized labour system had also made them vulnerable to unionization (Cohen 2008; Bernstein 2010).

Instead of dysfunctional competitive markets, Roosevelt's institutionalist economists argued for a regulatory regime where prices and wages would be set through conscious planning and negotiation. Condemned by Keynes and by Keynesians since as a bizarre measure designed to inflate prices irrationally during a depression, the National Industrial Recovery Administration (NRA) was the central element of this institutionalist programme, intended to revive the economy by increasing purchasing power, raising wages and prices to levels where worker-consumers could buy products again from producers able to cover their overheads (Keynes 1933; Brinkley 1995). Higher wages and higher prices would then be self-justifying by leading to increased effective demand.

The 'corporatist' idea behind the NRA was that, in a modern economy with large-scale enterprises, competitive markets had disappeared. Wages, prices, working conditions, and production levels were controlled by a few corporate giants; instead, they should be set through negotiation, planning, and democratic participation. Such ideas may have had their greatest influence in the administration of a conservative Republican, Richard Nixon, who was advised by Arthur Burns, student of Columbia's leading institutionalist, Wesley Clair Mitchell. Persuading Nixon that the economy was dominated by powerful corporations and labour unions able to manipulate prices with little regard for economic conditions, Burns won Nixon over to a 'new economic policy' in 1971, a return to New Deal-style regulation, including a wage-price review board, composed of distinguished citizens, who would pass judgment on major wage and price increases.

Roosevelt's NRA included minimum wage and maximum hour regulations, and the first protection for the right of workers to form labour unions.[1] With this promise of government support, the NRA inspired a wave of popular protest and workplace mobilization, including most famously, a leaflet from the United Mine Workers stating baldly that 'the President wants you to join the union'. Popular unrest and the ideas of the New Deal's institutionalist economists led to other New Deal measures regulating wages and hours and protecting the right to form unions. Enacted in 1935, the National Labour Relations Act (NLRA or the 'Wagner Act' named after its chief sponsor, Senator Robert Wagner of New York) established a legal right to form independent unions to bargain collectively with their employers. While many supported the Wagner Act to promote union organization and workplace democracy, the law was explicitly intended to promote economic recovery by redistributing income and raising popular purchasing power. Wagner, himself, blamed the Depression on economic inequality due to the 'inequality of bargaining power between employees who do not possess full freedom of association or actual liberty of contract, and employers who are organized in the corporate or other forms of ownership association'. This imbalance causes 'recurrent business Depressions, by depressing wage rates and the purchasing power of wage earners in industry and by preventing the stabilization of competitive wage rates and working conditions within and between industries'.

The Wagner Act established that:

> Employees shall have the right of self-organization, to form, join, or assist labor organizations, to bargain collectively through representatives of their own choosing, and to engage in concerted activities, for the purpose of collective bargaining or other mutual aid or protection.

It forbade employers from interfering, specifying that it would be an 'unfair labor practice' for employers to 'interfere with, restrain, or coerce employees in the exercise of the rights guaranteed in section 157 of this title', to 'dominate or interfere with the formation or administration of any labor organization'; or to discharge or discriminate against workers because of their involvement in a labour organization. It established procedures for workers to select representatives to be the 'exclusive representatives of all the employees in such unit for the purposes of collective bargaining in respect to rates of pay, wages, hours of employment, or other conditions of employment'. The Act required that employers negotiate with the chosen representatives of the employees. And it established a National Labour Relations Board to oversee the entire process.

An important symbolic statement of the government's support for unions and collective bargaining, and a means of sorting out competing union claims, compared with organizing through strikes and by directly pressuring employers, the Wagner Act procedures were slow and hard to navigate. As such, the cumbersome process it established for specifying bargaining units and elections contributed little to the rapid expansion of unions in the 1930s and after. Instead, most of the union membership gains came outside of the NLRA process. Two of the most important union victories were won through direct worker action, including the recognition in early 1937 of the United Auto Workers by General Motors (GM) and of the Steel Workers Organizing Committee by United States Steel. At GM and elsewhere, sit-down strikes forced employers to recognize unions; later, the War Labour Board pushed employers to recognize unions to avoid labour unrest during World War II. The Wagner Act contributed little.

The boundaries of union organization were set largely by the limits of popular protest in the 1930s. By 1947, workers in many northern industries, including rubber, steel and metal fabrication, trucking, mining, autos, and clothing, had formed strong unions, but elsewhere, in retail trade, office work, domestic service, and in the South as a whole, unions remained marginal. Nonetheless, the New Deal union upsurge was different from earlier surges, such as the 1880s or around World War I, as unions were able to hold onto many of their gains (Figure 9.1). While the Wagner Act may have contributed to this success, the Federal government's support was too weak to push organizing much beyond the boundaries set by the upheaval of the mid-1930s. The New Deal industrial relations system was severely limited by race, gender, and region. While some industrial unions successfully organized non-white workers, women, and in the South during the 1930s and World War II, few survived long. Nor did government regulations do much for women and non-white workers. The Wagner Act, the Fair Labor Standards Act and the retirement and unemployment insurance provisions of the Social Security Act explicitly excluded agricultural workers, domestic servants, and the employees of the small establishments that employed many Southerners, women, and African-Americans (Brown 1999; Kessler-Harris 2001; Katznelson

Figure 9.1 Union density, United States, 1880–2006.

2005). Even when national legislation was extended to Southern workers, racist and reactionary state officials were able to limit its impact. Many workers in the region's booming textile industry were covered by New Deal legislation, but attempts to unionize foundered on the opposition of local and state officials (Griffith 1988; Friedman 2000). Some Southern workers were covered by unemployment insurance and Aid to Families with Dependent Children covered the South, but these programmes were administered by local authorities who limited access to their benefits.

Into the 1980s, the American labour movement remained largely within the boundaries set by the union explosion of the 1930s. Unions are strongest in the Northeast, Midwest, and along the Pacific Coast; there are relatively few members in the South. They were strongest in industries organized in the 1930s and during World War II: construction, mining, manufacturing and transportation; few union members are found elsewhere, including in industries employing large numbers of women and minorities, agriculture, personal service, or wholesale or retail trade. The only major breakthrough after the 1940s came in the late-1960s and in the 1970s with the organization of women and minority workers in the public sector, especially education (see Figure 9.2). Even while dramatically changing the gender and racial make-up of unions, the success of public sector unions did not change the geographic locus of unions; public sector unions remained weak in the South.

The limited extension of the New Deal order to the South and the continued weakness of unions among women and non-white workers challenged the labour movement's aspirations to solidarity and to promote social democracy. A movement of Northern white men had limited political and moral appeal, and, eventually, limited economic leverage as well. Labour's continued weakness in the South also limited the scope of progressive politics; any national majority depended on super-majorities in the North to overcome the continued domination of Southern politics by racists and reactionary Democrats and (later) Republicans. The persistence of a low wage region within the United States left Northern workers vulnerable to competition with low wage threats to move production south and to hire non-union workers (Lichtenstein 2002).

There was another, hidden dilemma behind the union success in the New Deal era. After the excitement of the 1930s, unions survived at least in part because they were *useful* to

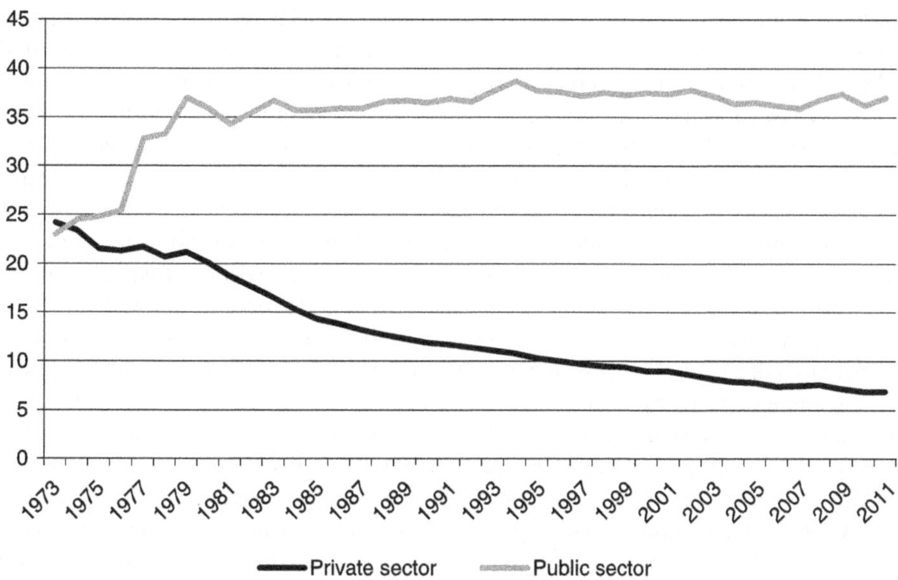

Figure 9.2 Declining union density, public and private employment, 1973–2011.

capitalist managers and government officials. This is not to say that union leaders were corrupt, although some were (Fitch 2006; Witwer 2009). In many firms, unionization ratified and entrenched changes in American capitalism and industrial relations that pre-dated the 1930s, changes made because the managers of the new giant corporation found it advantageous to isolate their workers from competitive market processes through internal labour markets. Through written contracts with specified work rules, unions promoted the bureaucratization of management, the replacement of managerial autonomy with company systems (Jacoby 1985; Berle 1991). Even without unions, businesses established systems for internal promotion and job ladders, pensions, and systems of deferred compensation to internalize labour markets and to separate the internal operations of the firm from external influences (Dunlop 1958; Chandler 1977; Doeringer 1985; Jacoby 1997). Collective bargaining reinforced the new management systems, and protected management from labour unrest among its internal workforce by restraining strikes and regimenting labour unrest. Managers in many of America's larger corporations accepted collective bargaining because it helped them to do what they were already doing (Slichter 1960).

Even within its northern and western strongholds, American unionism was a limited movement. The young unions that were established in the 1930s quickly learned that employers might concede higher wages but would fiercely resist further restrictions on what quickly came to be known as 'managerial rights'. To avoid undermining their relationship with management or antagonizing potential political allies, unions disciplined the strike, limiting it to specified times and circumstances even at the risk of alienating the most active union members and limiting the opportunities for rank-and-file activism (Moody 1988; Friedman 2007). This strike restraint function was strengthened when the unions confronted a legal system and judiciary wedded to an individualist concept of rights fundamentally at odds with the needs of a collective movement of workers (Klare 1975; Tomlins 1985).

Notwithstanding its limits, unionism in the New Deal era transformed life for many American workers. Collective bargaining transformed social relations within American workplaces, empowering workers by compelling management to explain itself to the workers. Not only did unions force employers to grant workers higher wages and shorter hours, they forced management to grant workers a measure of respect, limiting the regular abuse that has been the fate of workers in a capitalist hierarchy (Stein 1998; Metzgar 2000). Collective bargaining also changed the *mix* of compensation in ways that tied workers to their employers by enhancing their security and providing more workplace public goods. As Richard Freeman has shown, unions and collective bargaining transform the process of compensation setting from a market process responsive to the wishes of *marginal* participants, ready to opt out at any time, to a political process response to the wishes of *infra-marginal* participants committed to remain even in the face of disagreeable changes in the mix. Set through a market process, the mix of compensation will tilt towards the interests of young and mobile workers in cash compensation, minimizing pensions and health benefits important to older and settled workers with families. Collective bargaining reverses this tilt, dramatically increasing the share of compensation in the forms of pensions, health benefits, and also in workplace safety (Freeman 1976; Freeman and Medoff, 1984; Mishel and Walters 2003). Where unions raise wages by 20 per cent, they raise the proportion covered by health insurance by 35 per cent, the proportion with pensions by 65 per cent, and the number of inspections by the Occupational Safety and Health Administration in manufacturing by 45 per cent. Shifting compensation towards health care and pensions provides protection for family members and the elderly, turning unionized establishments into small welfare states.

Perhaps the most important effect of unions was on the workers themselves who were no longer at the mercy of autocratic managers and supervisors. By protecting workers from arbitrary abuse, formal grievance procedures and seniority systems allowed workers to speak up for themselves as democratic citizens. Observing the union impact on the lives of his neighbours and his own family, Jack Metzgar grants that many of the gains made by the new unions 'were nothing to brag about'. Even with Social Security, for example, the Steelworkers' pension left retirees close to poverty. Nonetheless, for the workers who had been oppressed for so long, the opportunity to voice their grievances made the union 'a social revolution – a fundamental transformation of the conditions of daily life' (Metzgar 2000: 54).

Unions and the New Deal state changed America, raising productivity and assuring workers of a fair share of productivity gains. Within enterprises, unions raised productivity (Freeman and Medoff 1984; Eisenbrey 2007). By preventing arbitrary dismissal, they improved communication between the shop floor and management and forced management to justify policies and to eliminate unproductive managerial abuse. Shifting compensation towards pensions and other benefits favoured by longer-tenured workers allowed firms to economize on hiring and training. Linking wages to productivity through regular collective bargaining gave workers an interest in productivity increases, even in those that might require greater work effort. Knowing that wages would be rising steadily, management was kept on the lookout for ways to raise productivity. At the same time, a national commitment to full employment assured companies that they could sell their increased output. Compared with the earlier period, unemployment rates were lower and per capita income grew significantly faster during the New Deal era. Because per capita income grew 1 per cent faster every year during 1947–73 than in the 50 years before the Great Depression, income was nearly a third higher in 1973, a gain of over $5000 per person. Keeping pace with accelerating

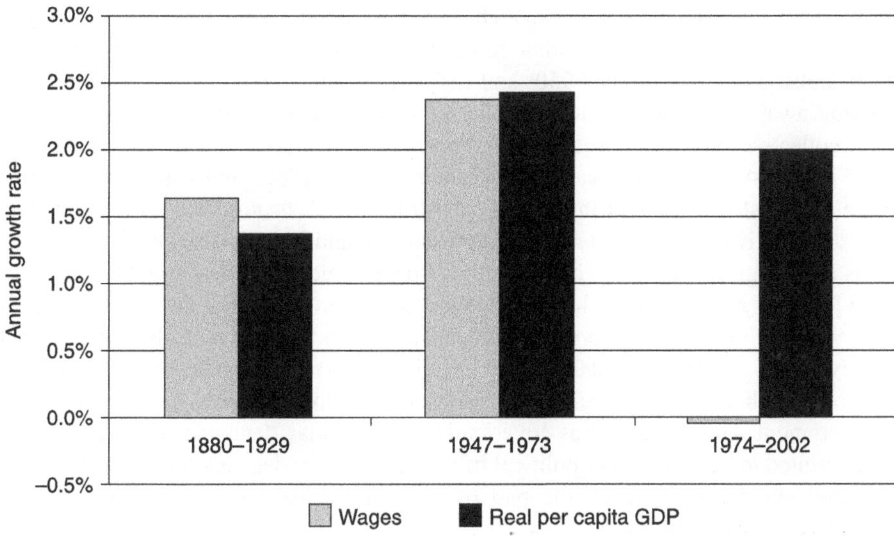

Figure 9.3 Annual growth in wages and per capita income, pre-New Deal, New Deal, and neo-liberal eras.

per capita income growth, wages also grew faster, rising 2.4 per cent per year during 1947–73 compared with 1.6 per cent per year before 1929. Wages were nearly 25 per cent higher in 1973 than they would have been had they increased at the rate of the pre-union, pre-New Deal era (see Figure 9.3).

During the New Deal era, the combination of unions and government regulation dramatically reduced inequality. Increases and extension of the federal minimum wage placed a rising floor under the labour market, raising wages for the lowest-wage workers. Unions also reduced wage variation within establishments by establishing a 'common rate' on jobs and reducing managerial favouritism (Freeman 1982). They also limited the disparity between workers' wages and executive salaries because managers knew that they would have to justify their salaries during collective bargaining. America's corporate managers were well paid in the New Deal era, earning 40 times as much as the workers under them; but managerial salaries soared after the union collapse in the 1980s.

Government policy also reduced income inequality directly. High and steeply progressive income taxes put the burden of public services on those with the 'ability to pay', dramatically narrowing post-tax income differentials (Piketty and Saez 2003). Unions' political support for expanding social welfare programmes, including investments in education and health programmes, served to redistribute income away from the rich towards the rest.

The 1970s and the crisis of the New Deal order

By the 1960s, many on the political Left had grown disenchanted with American unions complaining that they were too bureaucratized, too accommodating to management, and had joined the power structure rather than overturning it. This was never a complete statement of organized labour's status in the American polity. By their very nature, unions continued to uphold democratic values fundamentally at odds with those of a capitalist hierarchy. Even while some unions resisted the entry of women or African-American workers, others provided essential leadership and funds for the Civil Rights movement and even for the radical student movement. The greater challenge to labour came from the Right where capitalists lost interest in unions that failed to provide strike restraint and to channel popular unrest. For a time in the 1950s and early 1960s, unionization was associated with a 'withering away of the strike' (Kerr 1964). In some industries, strikes were replaced by routine collective bargaining and regular consultation between leaders of business and labour. This post-war labour peace collapsed in the late-1960s and early 1970s with an upsurge in unrest that brought the number of strikers back to immediate post-war levels. Rising strike activity was associated with broader demands for civil rights, for democratic reforms and for greater equality, demands that worried leading academics who warned of a general 'crisis of governability'. Lamenting that 'people no longer felt the same compulsion to obey those whom they had previously considered superior to themselves in age, rank, status, expertise, character, or talents', a widely cited report warned of a general 'breakdown of democracy' because of excessive demands by the lower orders for participation in self-government. Government was 'overloaded' by popular demands because too many citizens wanted to be involved in political life, whereas order depends 'on some measure of apathy and non-involvement on the part of some individuals and groups' (Crozier and Trilateral Commission 1975).

As frightening as the unrest was the clear inability of established unions to restrain or to channel protest. Insurgent rank-and-file movements challenged established union leaders when a wave of 'wildcat' strikes swept the United States in 1970–71. Led by unofficial rank-and-file committees, strikers pushed protest far beyond the limits of established unions and collective bargaining (Barkin 1983; Friedman 2007; Cowie 2010). Rejecting attempts by union leaders to channel protest, demands overflowed to issues of shop-floor management that challenged established 'management rights'. Strikers demanded safer workplaces, protested against discriminatory actions by supervisors and managers, complained of harsh working conditions, and demanded a voice in management. In the spring of 1972, workers at the Lordstown, Ohio, General Motors plant struck against the speed of the world's fastest assembly line, demanding 'a more humane work environment'. 'They just want to be treated with dignity,' explained Gary Bryner, insurgent head of the union local. 'That's not asking a hell of a lot' (Cowie 2010: 48).

The consumer activist Ralph Nader hoped that Lordstown would do for workers what Berkeley 1964 had done for students (Cowie 2010: 42–3). This was exactly the prospect that terrified capitalists and managers who feared that unions and union leaders had lost the capacity, if not the will, to enforce social peace. Lacking a better alternative, managers granted wage concessions to lure workers back to work, cutting sharply into corporate profits. Rising worker militancy and declining profits drove down investor confidence: the Dow Jones Industrial average stood at over 900 in January 1968 but its real value fell by over half in the next seven years.

In 1971, Lewis Powell, soon to be nominated to a seat on the United States Supreme Court, warned the leaders of the United States Chamber of Commerce that 'the American economic system is under broad attack' (Powell 1971). Powell and others came to join the many American businesses, which had never accepted the New Deal system and had never stopped fighting unions and collective bargaining. As a share of the labour force, union membership peaked right after World War II and again in the mid-1950s. Serious decline, however, set in only after the early 1970s. When Powell wrote his memo in 1971, union membership still comprised over 28 per cent of the labour force. From there, however, unions began to haemorrhage members (see Figure 9.1). Comparing actual membership with the membership that unions would have had at constant density rates within industries, private-sector unions lost over 5 million members during 1970–83 although rising public-sector membership kept the aggregate decline to 1.5 million.[2] After 1983, even public sector unions stopped growing and total membership fell by over 4 million between 1983 and 1994 and another 4 million between 1994 and 2006. Even before the economic crisis began in 2007, private sector unions enrolled fewer than 7 per cent of workers.

Employer opposition to unions

Declines in membership have come despite rising support for unions among American workers. Recent surveys have found that 76 per cent of American workers want *some* form of increased worker representation, including over 40 per cent who would vote for a union (Freeman 1999, 2007). Even while unions have been losing members over the past 30 years, the proportion who want a union has been rising, creating an ever growing representation gap (Freeman 2007: 6). Workers themselves blame growing employer opposition to unions for this gap. Two-thirds of workers surveyed say that employers try to stop workers from forming unions, citing tactics ranging from 'requiring employees to attend anti-union presentations on company time to firing union supporters' (Peter Hart survey, cited in Freeman 2007: 9). Even this data understates the extent and impact of employer resistance to unions. A study of over 1000 National Labour Relations Board (NLRB) certification elections during 1999–2003 found that it is 'standard practice for workers to be subjected to threats, interrogation, harassment, surveillance, and retaliation for union activity.' Employers threatened to close facilities in 57 per cent of elections, threatened to cut wages and benefits in 47 per cent, threatened workers in 54 per cent, and discharged workers in 34 per cent (Bronfenbrenner 2009: 2). Employer opposition has been growing over time; many employers regularly engage in coercive and punitive tactics that in the past were restricted to a few. American employers now spend over $200 million annually on direct payments to consultants and lawyers hired to try to stop union drives, or over $2000 per worker in an NLRB election (Kleiner 2001: 522). They get value for these expenditures from consultants. Employers defeat over a third of union organizing campaigns even before elections are held and only 15 per cent of organizing drives under the NLRB end with a contract; the share is 30 per cent lower when there are unfair labour practices (Ferguson 2008).

A former NLRB General Counsel complained of employers undermining 'the expression of employee free choice by manipulating Board procedures to create delay'.[3] Delays are only one weapon employers use against unions. Despite declining union organizing activity, the number of unfair labour practices by employers increased from barely 9,000 in 1960 to more than 24,000 in 1990; and the incidence of illegal firings increased from one per 700 union supporters in the 1950s to one for every 50 union supporters in 1990 to one for every 25 union supporters by the late 1990s (United States 1994; Kleiner 2001: 522–3). One observer finds that 'aspirations for representation are being thwarted by a coercive and punitive climate for organizing that goes unrestrained due to a fundamentally flawed regulatory regime that neither protects [workers'] rights nor provides any disincentives for employers to continue disregarding the law' (Gross 1995; Bronfenbrenner 1998, 2009: 3; Compa 2000). The comparison with public sector unionization is particularly stark. While private sector membership has plummeted, in most northern states, where public managers do not intrude in the process, the majority of workers have chosen to join unions.

Employer resistance to unionization is not new. American employers have been notorious for their opposition to unions and their readiness to resort to illegal means to resist union organization (for a small sample of this literature, see Jacoby 1997; Friedman 1998; Smith 2003; Archer 2007). Since the 1970s, rising employer resistance has been helped by a legal system that favours individual rights over the rights of individuals to engage in effective collective action, abetted by changes in the American political environment. Since the early 1970s, employers have exploited loopholes in American labour laws to subvert the intention of the Wagner Act. Their efforts have been protected by conservative politicians, including the Reagan (1980–88) and the two Bush Administrations (1988–92 and 2000–08) which appointed anti-union activists to the National Labour Relations Board and by conservative southern and western senators who successfully killed attempts to reform law by using the filibuster.

As collective movements to produce public goods, unions face a fundamental problem in mobilizing individuals to contribute to collective action because selfish individuals would do better for themselves to 'free ride', or leave others to advance the collective project while they remain aloof. While this is a problem facing organizations from the Jewish Community of Amherst to the Sierra Club, it is a particular problem when the collective action is against an opponent, an employer, with a strong interest in punishing participants and rewarding those who remain outside the collective movement. Instead of contributing to produce public goods available to all, many workers will reason logically, as did one construction worker in 1914 who said that 'If the union's movement fails, we will have risked nothing, and if it succeeds, we will share the benefits' (Joran 1914: 114). The only way to advance common interests in public goods is by compelling all to contribute. For labour, the liberty that comes through public regulation of the workplace has to be a social product and therefore requires some measure of compulsion. The labour movement is thus necessarily at odds with a legal system based on individual rights.

The courts and the government

It is here in the US legal culture, not in the popular culture or in the attitudes of workers, that we see the impact of America's liberal origins. As producers of public goods through collective action, unions necessarily require coercive instruments that clash with the individualist premise of liberal American jurisprudence. This has been the drift in labour law since the Supreme Court surprisingly upheld the Wagner Act in 1937. In the *Jones and Laughlin* decision upholding the law, the Court carved out an area of individual autonomy, stating (falsely from the Congressional record) that the Act was not intended to change relations between capital and labour. Instead, the Court concluded in terms that emphasize individual liberty while equating the situation of employees and the employers:

> The statute goes no further than to safeguard the right of employees to self-organization and to select representatives of their own choosing for collective bargaining or other mutual protection without restraint or coercion by their employer.
>
> (Supreme Court of the United States, 1937: 31–3)

Here was the limit of American political economy even at the height of the New Deal. The Court walked away from the intention of promoting labour organization as a balance against employer power. By contrast, measures used by employers against unions are all grounded in the rights of individuals as interpreted by the Supreme Court. In *Phelps Dodge v. NLRB*, for example, the Court found that employers who refused to hire a worker because of his or her union involvement were guilty of an unfair labour practice, but it assessed a penalty based only on the damage to the individual from the discharge, back pay minus earnings from alternative employments. This was typical of Court rulings that sacrificed the public interest in promoting labour organization to the formal maintenance of individual rights of employers. The 1938 decision in *NLRB v. Mackay Radio & Telegraph Co*, for example, protected the rights of striking workers in their jobs but also stated that employers were free to retain strike breakers (replacement workers) in their place after a strike. In *NLRB v. Gissel Packing Co., Inc.* the Court established 'an employer's free speech right to communicate with his employees'. Ignoring the real impact of such speech on dependent wage earners, it protected such speech under the First Amendment to the US Constitution.

Add *Gissel* to *Phelps Dodge* and *Mackay* and we have virtually abandoned the promise of the Wagner Act, the commitment by the Federal government to promote unions and collective bargaining. Instead, employers have been allowed to attack unions and union activists with virtual impunity, interfering with their employees' choice of a union, discharging union activists, threatening workers, replacing strikers, and refusing to bargain with certified unions. Since the 1970s, American employers have constructed a new non-union industrial relations system, one increasingly based on individual contracting within markets favouring capital against labour. The result has been to redistribute income from wage workers towards managers, from labour towards capital, while dramatically reducing the security enjoyed by American workers (Figure 9.4).

By itself, the withdrawal of effective Wagner Act protection need not have undermined the New Deal system of unionized industrial relations. Other conditions, however, made the withdrawal of state protection deadly for unions. Most important was the turn of employers against unions. Into the 1970s, many employers continued to accept unions not only as necessary evils but as valuable allies in the maintenance of a Fordist system of high wages

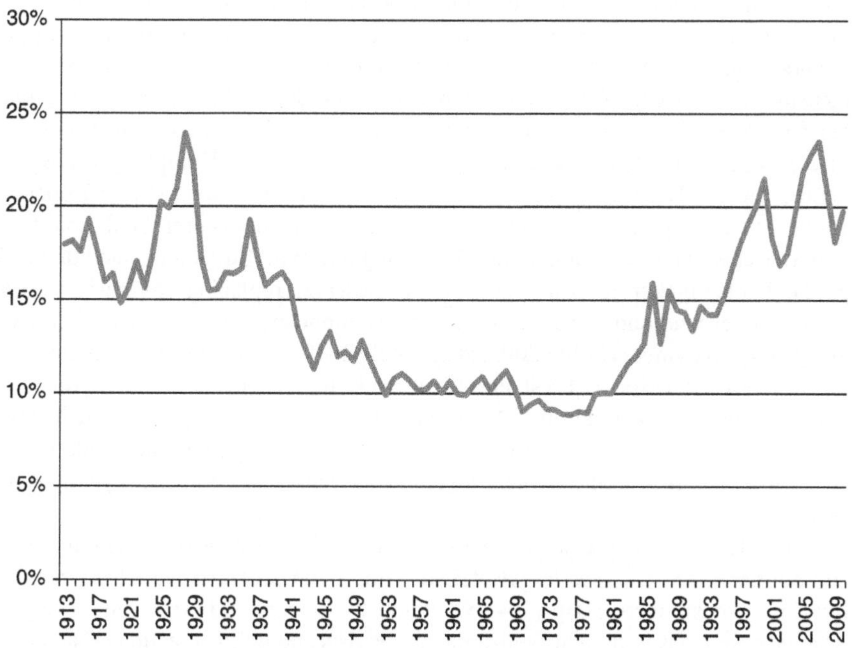

Figure 9.4 Share of national income going to richest 1 per cent of Americans, 1913–2009.

and high productivity built on the maintenance of long-term employment relations. Along with systems of deferred compensation, job ladders, and pensions, unions were barriers against the resort to the market. They protected *employers* from worker default, the reneging by workers on long-term implicit contracts where workers received training and were introduced into productive businesses in exchange for a commitment to stay with the business even if wages were less than they might attract on the outside market. It was this agreement that made it possible for companies to provide training and to establish long-lasting production teams.

For employers, however, implicit contracts and long-term relationships gave hostages to fortune: the company was accepting additional risk from fixed costs regardless of current sales for steady employment, wage and salary increases, pensions and other benefits. As such, the New Deal-era business was vulnerable to two changes in economic circumstances in the 1970s: rising short-term economic fluctuations that threatened companies' ability to cover the costs of fixed labour during business downturns even while growing competition threatened their ability to continue to support heavy legacy costs on a pay-as-you-go basis.[4] The burden of these costs, and the opportunity to dramatically increase profits by shedding them and reneging on commitments to workers and retirees, have led companies such as Continental Airlines and United Airlines to casually default on obligations, even to declare bankruptcy to cancel contracts binding them to make payments to their workers and retirees. Failure to do this makes companies easy prey for financiers, including private equity firms such as Bain Capital which profited from dumping the pension obligations of GSI steel, among other firms (Mattera 2005; Georgetown and McCrum 2012).

Long-term employment systems protect companies and their investments in their workers' training and human capital from the otherwise pernicious effects of labour market competition and full employment. Not only are these systems vulnerable in periods of economic uncertainty with declining employment, they also have less value in these times because workers have fewer alternatives. Just as industry deregulation in the 1970s and the opening of US markets to foreign competition undermined long-term employment relationships by leading to more variance in market demand for a firm's products, changes in macro-economic policies in the late 1970s gave American employers reason to be less concerned about labour market competition for their workers. By rejecting in 1978 the Humphrey-Hawkins Full Employment Act, a Democratic Congress and Democratic President (Carter) opened the door for the full use of monetary policy and high unemployment to control inflation. In 1979, President Carter walked through that door by caving into Wall Street's demand that in 1979 he appoint Paul Volcker to head the Federal Reserve, replacing his early appointee, G. William Miller who had opposed disinflationary monetary policy for fear that it would lead to high unemployment (Pollin 2005, 2012; Stein 2010). Carter and Volcker, and Ronald Reagan, Carter's successor as President, were ready to accept that unemployment was a price worth paying for price stability. By the early 1980s, the unemployment rate had passed 10 per cent, nearly triple the rate of the late 1960s; the unemployment rate would not fall to 4 per cent, the interim full employment level of the 1960s, for another 20 years, and then only briefly.

Unions resisted the policy changes that undermined the New Deal employment system, but their political *démarche* has largely failed. Those who favoured New Deal regulations and full employment were simply overwhelmed by a rising tide of business-supported conservative politicians with their well-funded lobbyists and political action (Hacker 2010). Coming out of the 1960s, unions were also handicapped by lingering conflicts with others on the political Left over foreign policy, environmental policy, and civil rights (Stein 1998,

2010; Cowie 2010). They were also handicapped intellectually by the collapse of institutional economics, the intellectual movement behind the New Deal (Yonay 1998; Frege 2007; Rutherford 2011). To fight the rising conservative tide, organized labour dramatically increased its political activity, but there too labour's best efforts were a mere rear-guard defence against a flood of corporate political spending (Pollin 2005; Francia 2006).

Flexibility, contingent work, and the new industrial relations

Like its pre-New Deal predecessor, the post-New Deal industrial relations system is built on individual contracting between workers and employers without union or other collective representation. Unlike its predecessor, however, this post-New Deal system is being constructed without internal labour markets or other measures to tie workers to large employers. Instead, more businesses are hiring workers on short-term contracts and using contingent labour to fill a growing share of their employment. Instead of the giant, centrally coordinated businesses of the twentieth century, American industry is being reshaped into 'hollow corporations' that provide brand name and coordinating functions while outsourcing their productive work to independent businesses or freelancers. Slimmed-down, hiring labour through continuous market adjustments, businesses are operating without the weight of an established workforce or internal labour markets, free to take on or to shed labour, technologies, product lines, production facilities, and to relocate production to take advantage of any cost advantage. The new weightless corporation values flexibility above all; flexible in production and in its workforce, the company is free to shed product lines and to adopt new products and technologies in response to changing opportunities. Freed of fixed costs, the company can shift the risk of changing economic conditions onto contingent workers and their communities. Freed of commitments, the new lean corporation can provide a secure basis for stable and growing profits.

Those who approve of the new flexible system talk of 'freelance' workers but the better term is 'contingent', workers hired for a particular time or task. Without employment or income security, contingent workers now comprise as much as 30 per cent of the labour force in occupations ranging from music and entertainment, to construction, factory work, landscaping, retail trade, restaurants and hotels, and even many technical occupations (including graphic arts, college teaching, accounting, and law) (Houseman 1999; Greenwald 2012; Greenwald and Katz 2012; one analyst who praises the new system is Pink 2001). They are employed in what one observer calls the 'gig economy', a freelance army without job security, pensions, or access to unemployment or health insurance linked to regular employment, often without a fixed place of employment (other than the local Starbucks with its free Wi-Fi). Working 'for themselves', they have no meaningful protection from the New Deal's labour laws including the Fair Labour Standards Act and minimum wage laws.

By undermining the security provided by unions and other New Deal regulations, the spread of the 'gig economy' has brought the position of many white men down to the level of non-whites and women. Without an active voice at work or the security of job ladders and deferred compensation programmes, even educated white men have faced dramatically rising annual variation in income. The transitory variance, the year-to-year variation, of male income increased substantially in the 1980s and has remained at this higher level since. Income fluctuations have increased for all income levels; the gig economy has spread from day labour up the job ladder to include engineers, lawyers, physicians, and academics (Hacker 2006; Hacker and Jacobs 2008; Moffitt and Gottschalk 2008).

One of America's most successful companies, General Electric (GE), illustrates the new management style with its disdain for established relationships, and for its workers. GE's long-time head, Jack Welch, famously said that 'ideally you'd have every plant you own on a barge' – ready to move if any national government tried to regulate the factories' operations, or if workers demanded better wages and working conditions. With this attitude, GE shed half its American workers after the mid-1980s, relocating its own operations to foreign countries and outsourcing a growing share of its business (Mokhiber 1999; Mokhiber and Weissman 2000).

Corporate strategies like that of GE are not the product of inexorable technology or the genius of individual businessmen. They depend on particular government policies beginning with the abandonment of the New Deal commitment to support worker collective action as part of a larger push for industrial democracy, greater equality, and to maintain purchasing power with full employment. The United States has not only abandoned the New Deal's commitment to economic democracy and labour unions, it has stepped away from the commitment to provide security to workers. Government subsidies to 401(k) retirement plans and to Individual Retirement Accounts have encouraged companies to abandon defined benefit pension plans, shifting the risk of market fluctuations onto workers even while separating workers' retirement pensions from any particular employer.

Organized labour has been slow to adapt to the changing labour system and the rise of the 'gig economy'. While continuing to look to restore good jobs and income security through stable employment, some unions have adjusted their organizing strategies to recruit contingent workers. With their Justice for Janitors (J4J) campaign in the 1990s, the Service Employees International Union demonstrated how a regionally based, social movement-style union campaign could organize contingent workers and improve working conditions even for employees of 'hollow' corporations (Fantasia 2004; Service Employees International Union 2010). As in the earlier Congress of Industrial Organization (CIO) campaigns, such bottom-up campaigns not only challenge employers but they threaten the position of established union leaders. Caught between an entrenched leadership, powerful employers, and a vulnerable workforce, there have been few successful organizing drives on the J4J model (Milkman and Voss 2004; Friedman 2007; Moody 2007).

While the new industrial relations system has been praised by business analysts, it has been associated with declining wages and slower economic growth rates than in the New Deal Era (see Figure 9.3). Thus far, it has worked well for businesses and their affluent owners who have enjoyed dramatically rising profits even during the current recession. Rising profits might be surprising because, compared with their vertically-integrated predecessors, the modern American corporation lies exposed to markets, vulnerable to a period of real full employment when it would face sharply rising wages and discontent among its contingent freelancers. To repeat the point made earlier, the hollow corporation survives only because government has maintained a reserve army of the unemployed large enough to keep fear of job loss in the hearts of workers while allowing companies access to a world-wide force of potential substitute labour. It is government policy that protects companies from the risk involved in a contingent workforce. A commitment to limit inflation even at the expense of high unemployment ensures a workforce for the hollow corporations. Free trade agreements allow the movement across national borders of finance and products, but labour remains tied to particular locations, vulnerable to all the risk and uncertainty of a modern economy (Stiglitz 2003; Lichtenstein 2006). Multinational behemoths are free to roam the world, using the cheapest labour and locations to maximize profits and to beat down wages and working conditions while workers are increasingly powerless to use markets or politics to defend themselves. This, however, is not because of any inevitable technology, but because governments allow it to be so.

Recognizing the central role of government policy in replacing the New Deal labour system with the 'gig economy' highlights the central role of government in sustaining the new system and the possibilities for political action. Not only is government macro-economic policy necessary to protect the hollow corporations from labour market competition but public services are even more essential to sustain the new industrial relations system than they were for the old system. Where the old system of long-term employment provided incentives for worker training and the maintenance of workers over time, companies now depend on a ready supply of workers, trained presumably by the public sector and sustained through public services. Even the combination of contingent employment and high levels of unemployment in the neo-liberal era emphasizes the necessary role of the public sector, needed to prevent the economy from sliding further into recession or deeper into depression.

Conclusion: neo-liberal industrial relations and the economic crisis

For a time, stagnant wages could be combined with rising productivity through the accumulation of public and private debt. Then a predictable crisis came in 2007. For some, the Great Recession that began in 2007 has raised the hope that, as in the 1930s, the crisis would lead to a renegotiation of the social contract, a new government policy that would favour working-class collective action. So far, these hopes have been disappointed. Some have blamed the great power of capital, political and ideological power accumulated since the early 1970s (Phillips-Fein 2009; Hacker 2010; Frank 2012). The situation facing unions and their allies may be even worse than this suggests. The New Deal reforms of the 1930s were built on tendencies of American capitalism, the development of the vertically integrated business with internal labour markets. Entering the twenty-first century, however, American business has moved in another direction, towards a footloose capital without commitments to place or to people. We may need a new New Deal with a renewed programme of income and worker security. But this time, it would have to be built against the drift of modern capital.

Emerging from war, the United States in the 1940s abandoned exceptionalist visions to lead the capitalist world to a new variety of capitalism, one of high wages and productivity sustained by long-term relationships and negotiation between organized labour and organized capital. While that variety of capitalism may be fading because of government commitments to free trade and flexible markets, America may yet renew its leadership by recognizing that expanded public services for education, health, and income maintenance may be as essential for the new gig economy as strong unions were for the New Deal era. From this perspective, the campaign by the Obama Administration for public schools, state-support for health care, and to protect unemployment insurance and social security may be this era's equivalent to New Deal era programmes for unions and subsidies for employment-based health insurance and private pensions.

Notes

1 Section 7 of the National Industrial Relations Act provided that:

> Employees shall have the right to organize and bargain collectively, through representatives of their own choosing, and shall be free from the interference, restraint, or coercion of employers of

labor, or their agents, in the designation of such representative or in self-organization or in other concerted activities.

2 This is the number of members they would have had in 1983 if the unionization rate had remained what it was in 1970, minus the actual number of members. Calculations for 1983–94 and 1994–2006 are done in the same way on a basis of the 1983 membership rate and the 1994 rate.

3 Testimony of Frederick L. Feinstein before the United States, Commission on the Future of Worker-Management Relations, 29 September 1994, available at: http://digitalcommons.ilr.cornell.edu/key_workplace/341.

4 In the auto industry, for example, declining market share led General Motors to shed 60 per cent of its employees in the 20 years before 2005, dropping from 811,000 to 324,000 employees. In 2008, the company had nearly three retirees for every active worker and retiree benefits, notably health care, cost nearly $20/hour per labour hour, adding $3000 to the cost of every car made, accounting for most of the difference in cost between a car made by GM and one made by a foreign transplant or in Japan or Korea.

References

Archer, R. (2007) *Why Is There No Labour Party in the United States?*, Princeton, NJ: Princeton University Press.

Barkin, S. (1983) *Worker Militancy and Its Consequences: The Changing Climate of Western Industrial Relations*, 2nd edn, New York: Praeger.

Berle, A. A. (1991) *The Modern Corporation and Private Property*, New Brunswick, NJ: Transaction Publishers.

Bernstein, I. (2010) *The Turbulent Years: A History of the American Worker, 1933–1941*, Chicago: Haymarket Books.

Brinkley, A. (1995) *The End of Reform: New Deal Liberalism in Recession and War*, New York: Alfred A. Knopf.

Brody, D. (1993) *Workers in Industrial America: Essays on the Twentieth Century Struggle*, 2nd edn, New York: Oxford University Press.

Bronfenbrenner, K. (ed.) (1998) *Organizing to Win: New Research on Union Strategies*, Ithaca, NY: ILR Press.

—— (2009) *No Holds Barred: The Intensification of Employer Opposition to Organizing*, Washington, DC: Economic Policy Institute, Briefing Paper. Available at: http://www.epi.org/page/-/pdf/bp235.pdf.

Brown, M. K. (1999) *Race, Money, and the American Welfare State*, Ithaca, NY: Cornell University Press.

Chandler, A. D. (1977) *The Visible Hand: The Managerial Revolution in American Business*, Cambridge, MA: Belknap Press.

Clark, J. M. (1926) *Social Control of Business*. Chicago: University of Chicago Press.

Cohen, L. (2008) *Making a New Deal: Industrial Workers in Chicago, 1919–1939*, 2nd edn, New York: Cambridge University Press.

Compa, L. (2000) *Unfair Advantage: Workers' Freedom of Association in the United States under International Human Rights Standards*, New York: Human Rights Watch. Available at: http://www.hrw.org/sites/default/files/reports/uslbr008.pdf.

Cowie, J. (2010) *Stayin' Alive: The 1970s and the Last Days of the Working Class*, New York: New Press.

Crozier, M., and Trilateral Commission (1975) *The Crisis of Democracy: Report on the Governability of Democracies to the Trilateral Commission*, New York: New York University Press, The Triangle Papers No. 8.

Doeringer, P. B. (1985) *Internal Labour Markets and Manpower Analysis*, Armonk, NY: M.E. Sharpe.

Dunlop, J. T. (1958) *Industrial Relations Systems*, New York: Holt.

Eisenbrey, R. (2007) *Strong Unions, Strong Productivity*, Washington, DC: Economic Policy Institute. Available at: http://www.epi.org/publication/webfeatures_snapshots_20070620/.

Fantasia, R. (2004) *Hard Work: Remaking the American Labour Movement*, Berkeley, CA: University of California Press.

Ferguson, J.-P. (2008) 'The eyes of the needles: a sequential model of union organizing drives, 1999–2004', *Industrial and Labor Relations Review*, 62(1): 3–21.

Fitch, R. (2006) *Solidarity for Sale: How Corruption Destroyed the Labour Movement and Undermined America's Promise*, New York: Public Affairs.

Francia, P. L. (2006) *The Future of Organized Labour in American Politics*, New York: Columbia University Press.

Frank, T. (2012) *Pity the Billionaire: The Hard Times Swindle and the Unlikely Comeback of the Right*, New York: Metropolitan Books/Henry Holt.

Freeman, R. B. (1976) 'Individual mobility and union voice in the labour market', *The American Economic Review*, 66(2): 361–8.

—— (1982) 'Union wage practices and wage dispersion within establishments', *Industrial and Labor Relations Review*, 36(1): 3–21.

—— (1999) *What Workers Want*, Ithaca, NY: ILR Press.

—— (2007) *Do Workers Still Want Unions? More Than Ever*, Washington, DC: Economic Policy Institute, Briefing Paper: Agenda for Shared Prosperity. Available at: http://www.sharedprosperity.org/bp182/bp182.pdfhttp://www.sharedprosperity.org/bp182/bp182.pdf.

—— and Medoff, J. L. (1984) *What Do Unions Do?*, New York: Basic Books.

Frege, C. M. (2007) *Employment Research and State Traditions: A Comparative History of Britain, Germany, and the United States*, Oxford: Oxford University Press.

Friedman, G. (1998) *State-Making and Labour Movements: France and the United States, 1876–1914*, Ithaca, NY: Cornell University Press.

—— (2000) 'The political economy of early Southern unionism: race, politics, and labour in the South, 1880–1953', *The Journal of Economic History*, 60(2): 384–413.

—— (2007) *Reigniting the Labour Movement: Restoring Means to Ends in a Democratic Labour Movement*, London: Routledge.

Georgetown, R. M. and McCrum, D. (2012) 'A tale of private equity and steel', *Financial Times*, 13 January. Available at: http://www.ft.com/cms/s/0/33356c82-3e05-11e1-ac9b-00144feabdc0.html#axzz2C1aLSeCu.

Greenwald, R. (2012) 'Contingent, transient and at risk: modern workers in a gig economy', *Huffington Post*. Available at: http://www.huffingtonpost.com/richard-greenwald/contingent-transient-and-_b_1554619.html.

—— and Katz, D. (2012) *Labour Rising: The Past and Future of Working People in America*, New York: The New Press.

Griffith, B. S. (1988) *The Crisis of American Labour: Operation Dixie and the Defeat of the CIO*. Philadelphia, PA: Temple University Press.

Gross, J. A. (1995) *Broken Promise: The Subversion of U.S. Labour Relations Policy, 1947–1994*, Philadelphia, PA: Temple University Press.

Hacker, J. S. (2006) *The Great Risk Shift: The Assault on American Jobs, Families, Health Care, and Retirement and How You Can Fight Back*, New York: Oxford University Press.

—— (2010) *Winner-Take-All Politics: How Washington Made the Rich Richer – and Turned Its Back on the Middle Class*, New York: Simon and Schuster.

—— and Jacobs, E. (2008) *The Rising Instability of American Family Incomes, 1969–2004: Evidence from the Panel Study of Income Dynamics*, Washington, DC: Economic Policy Institute, EPI Briefing Paper. Available at: http://www.epi.org/page/-/old/briefingpapers/213/bp213.pdf.

Houseman, S. (1999) *Flexible Staffing Arrangements*, Washington, DC: United States Department of Labor. Available at: http://www.dol.gov/oasam/programmes/history/herman/reports/futurework/conference/staffing/flexible.htm.

Jacoby, S. M. (1985) *Employing Bureaucracy: Managers, Unions, and the Transformation of Work in American Industry, 1900–1945*, New York: Columbia University Press.

—— (1997) *Modern Manors: Welfare Capitalism Since the New Deal*, Princeton, NJ: Princeton University Press.

Joran, R. (1914) *L'Organisation syndicale dans l'industrie du bâtiment*, Paris: A. Savaète.

Katznelson, I. (2005) *When Affirmative Action Was White: An Untold History of Racial Inequality in Twentieth-Century America*, New York: W.W. Norton.

Kerr, C. (1964) *Industrialism and Industrial Man: The Problems of Labor and Management in Economic Growth*, 2nd edn, New York: Oxford University Press.

Kessler-Harris, A. (2001) *In Pursuit of Equity: Women, Men, and the Quest for Economic Citizenship in 20th Century America*, New York: Oxford University Press.

Keynes, J. M. (1933) *An Open Letter to President Roosevelt*. Available at: http://newdeal.feri.org/misc/keynes2.htm.

Klare, K. E. (1975) 'Judicial deradicalization of the Wagner Act and the origins of modern legal consciousness, 1937–1941', *Minnesota Law Review*, 62(3): 265–339.

Kleiner, M. (2001) 'Intensity of management resistance: understanding the decline of unionization in the private sector', *Journal of Labor Research*, 22(3): 519–40.

Lichtenstein, N. (2002) *State of the Union: A Century of American Labour*, Princeton, NJ: Princeton University Press.

—— (ed.) (2006) *Wal-Mart: The Face of Twenty-First-Century Capitalism*, New York: New Press.

Mattera, P. (2005) *Broken Promises: The Business Assault on Legacy Costs*, Corporate Research E-Letter. Available at: http://www.corp-research.org/e-letter/broken-promises.

Metzgar, J. (2000) *Striking Steel: Solidarity Remembered*, Philadelphia, PA: Temple University Press.

Milkman, R. and Voss, K. (eds) (2004) *Rebuilding Labour: Organizing and Organizers in the New Union Movement*, Ithaca, NY: Cornell University Press.

Mishel, L. R. and Walters, M. (2003) *How Unions Help All Workers*, Washington, DC: Economic Policy Institute, Briefing Paper. Available at: http://www.epi.org/publication/briefingpapers_bp143/.

Moffitt, R. and Gottschalk, P. (2008) *Trends in the Transitory Variance of Male Earnings in the U.S., 1970–2004*, Boston, MA: Boston College, Department of Economics, Boston College Working Papers in Economics. Available at: http://ideas.repec.org/p/boc/bocoec/697.html.

Mokhiber, R. (1999) *Corporate Predators: The Hunt for Mega-Profits and the Attack on Democracy*, Monroe, ME: Common Courage Press.

—— and Weissman, R. (2000) 'GE: no company's record better illustrates the glories of corporate globalization for the well-off, and the misery for the many', *Common Dreams*. Available at: http://www.commondreams.org/views/051700-108.htm.

Moody, K. (1988) *An Injury to All: The Decline of American Unionism*, London: Verso.

—— (2007) *US Labour in Trouble and Transition: The Failure of Reform from Above, the Promise of Revival from Below*, London: Verso.

Phillips-Fein, K. (2009) *Invisible Hands: The Making of the Conservative Movement from the New Deal to Reagan*, New York: W.W. Norton and Company.

Piketty, T. and Saez, E. (2003) 'Income inequality in the United States, 1913–1998', *The Quarterly Journal of Economics*, 118(1): 1–39.

Pink, D. H. (2001) *Free Agent Nation: How America's New Independent Workers Are Transforming the Way We Live*, New York: Warner Books.

Pollin, R. (2005) *Contours of Descent: U.S. Economic Fractures and the Landscape of Global Austerity*, London: Verso.

—— (2012) *Back to Full Employment*, Cambridge, MA: MIT Press.

Powell, L. (1971) *The Powell Memo*, available at: http://reclaimdemocracy.org/corporate_accountability/powell_memo_lewis.html.

Rutherford, M. (2011) *The Institutionalist Movement in American Economics, 1918–1947: Science and Social Control*, New York: Cambridge University Press.

Service Employees International Union (2010) *Justice For Janitors Campaign: Rooted in the Struggle for Immigrant Rights, SEIU.org*. Available at: http://www.seiu.org/2010/06/justice-for-janitors-campaign-rooted-in-the-struggle-for-immigrant-rights.php.

Slichter, S. H. (1960) *The Impact of Collective Bargaining on Management*, Washington, DC: Brookings Institution.

Smith, R. M. (2003) *From Blackjacks to Briefcases: A History of Commercialized Strikebreaking and Unionbusting in the United States*, Athens, OH: Ohio University Press.

Stein, J. (1998) *Running Steel, Running America: Race, Economic Policy and the Decline of Liberalism*, Chapel Hill, NC: University of North Carolina Press.

—— (2010) *Pivotal Decade: How the United States Traded Factories for Finance in the Seventies*, New Haven, CT: Yale University Press.

Stiglitz, J. E. (2003) *Globalization and Its Discontents*, New York: W.W. Norton.

Supreme Court of the United States (1937) 'NLRB V. Jones & Laughlin Steel Corp. – 301 U.S. 1' (1937), *Justia US Supreme Court Center*. Available at: http://supreme.justia.com/cases/federal/us/301/1/case.html.

Tomlins, C. L. (1985) *The State and the Unions: Labour Relations, Law, and the Organized Labor Movement in America, 1880–1960*, New York: Cambridge University Press.

Tugwell, R. G. (1971) *The Trend of Economics*, Port Washington, NY: Kennikat Press.

United States (1994) *Fact Finding Report*, Washington, DC: U.S. Department of Labor and U.S. Department of Commerce.

Witwer, D. S. (2009) *Shadow of the Racketeer: Scandal in Organized Labor*, Urbana, IL: University of Illinois Press.

Yonay, Y. P. (1998) *The Struggle over the Soul of Economics: Institutionalist and Neoclassical Economists in America Between the Wars*, Princeton, NJ: Princeton University Press.

10 The United Kingdom[1]

John Kelly

Employment relations in the United Kingdom[2] underwent a dramatic transformation starting in the last quarter of the twentieth century and continuing into the first decade of the present century (see Table 10.1). The structure of the economy shifted away from manufacturing and towards services, both private and public, and the large manufacturing plants of the 1960s and 1970s gave way to far smaller plants. A growing number of companies were increasingly exposed to international product market competition while the labour market operated at historically high levels of unemployment. Many firms outsourced basic organizational functions such as catering, cleaning, security and IT services to other companies, either in Britain or increasingly overseas (a phenomenon described as 'offshoring'). Collective bargaining covered almost three-quarters of the workforce in 1979 and was then the dominant method of pay determination. By 2010, the position was transformed: unilateral regulation of pay by the employer had become the norm and collective agreements covered only a minority of the workforce. Between 1979 and 2010, the level of trade union density was halved and by the early 2000s the number of days lost to strikes was a small fraction (less than 10 per cent) of the average 1970s figure. In other words the power resources of workers had substantially declined and so had their capacity to influence terms and conditions of employment through negotiations, and collective action was severely diminished.

How can we explain these rapid and far-reaching changes? What have been their consequences for the different actors in employment relations? And what are the implications for the economy and society? The research literature in comparative employment relations contains a variety of theoretical approaches to these questions (see Chapter 2, in this volume) and we shall explore these in the final section of this chapter. The first section of the chapter

Table 10.1 Employment relations in the UK, 1979–2011

	1979	*2011*
% labour force in manufacturing	30	10
Trade union density %	53.4	26
Mainly private sector unions in TUC top ten	7	3
TUC unions with female General Secretary % (N)	0.9 (1/109)	24.1 (13/54)
Female union membership as % of total	30.2	54.7
Collective bargaining coverage %	70	31
Number of strikes	2125	92

Sources: Based on Brownlie (2012); TUC (2012): http://www.ons.gov.uk/ons (accessed 29 November 2012)

briefly describes the origins of the British system of employment relations and then describes the main actors in employment relations, the trade unions, employers and government. It also describes the main processes in employment relations, including collective bargaining, unilateral decision-making by the employer and the increasingly important role of legal regulation. The second section looks at the far-reaching changes in British employment relations from a number of theoretical perspectives and weighs up competing arguments about the roles of markets, institutions and actors and their impact on the balance of power in employment relations.

The actors and processes in employment relations

Origins of the British system of employment relations

Some of the most important attributes of British employment relations originated in the attempts by workers in the early nineteenth century to improve their terms and conditions of employment. Organizing collectively to overcome their weakness as isolated individuals, they formed trade unions and tried to negotiate with employers. By the late nineteenth century they had secured some limited legal freedoms but their leaders had also inherited a profound mistrust of the legal system and of the judiciary. Because unions lacked an effective political voice that could pass legislation to protect their organization and activity – the Labour Party was not formed until the beginning of the twentieth century – unions preferred to pursue the interests of their members through bargaining and strikes, free from legal regulation. At that time there were no legal rights to bargain or to strike and the collective agreements that emerged from this adversarial system of employment relations were not legally binding on any of the parties. Government proposals to regulate issues such as low wages, dismissals and redundancies were strongly opposed by unions until late into the twentieth century.

In the post-Second World War period this 'voluntarist' system of employment relations was reinforced by full employment which considerably enhanced workers' bargaining power. Interestingly the 'voluntarist' system was also supported for many years by most big employers. They too were content to avoid a legally regulated system in which unions enjoyed extensive rights and, like unions, they preferred to resolve disputes through the exercise of bargaining power. It was only in the 1960s that this system began to unravel. British economic performance and productivity growth after the Second World War were poor relative to its main competitors, such as the USA and the major economies of Western Europe – France, Germany and Italy – and many commentators linked these problems to the country's system of employment relations. Large-scale negotiated reforms of collective bargaining were attempted between 1968 and the late 1970s but were fairly unsuccessful because of strong resistance by still powerful trade unions, and their failure paved the way for the more radical Conservative governments of Margaret Thatcher. Between 1979 and 1997, these governments sought to effect a radical shift in the balance of power in favour of employers and against trade unions. They abandoned state support for full employment, enacted legislation to restrict strike action and presided over a dramatic decline in union membership and influence (Howell 2005).

Trade unions and collective bargaining

The state of the trade union movement cannot be assessed simply by examining trends in membership and density. For example, British trade union density in 2008 was 27 per cent, twice the Spanish level of 14.3 per cent. Yet the Spanish trade union movement has proved to be highly influential in its relations with government despite low membership density because what it lacks in numbers it makes up for in mobilizing capacity and political influence, through strikes and demonstrations (Hamann 2011). The state of the trade union movement must therefore be measured along a number of dimensions, namely membership, economic influence, political influence and institutional vitality, or the capacity to monitor its environment and develop strategies (Behrens *et al.* 2004). Trade union membership has declined in most advanced capitalist countries since the early 1980s but the scale of decline has been more severe in the UK than in most other countries. Going back a little further in time, the trajectory of union membership in the UK since 1945 can be broken down into four phases (Figure 10.1). From 1945 until the late 1960s, trade union membership rose slowly and steadily from 7.9 million to 10.2 million but only just kept pace with employment growth so that trade union density – the proportion of employees in union membership – was approximately constant over this period at around 44 per cent. From 1968, both membership and density rose dramatically, peaking at 13.3 million and 54 per cent respectively in 1979. The next two decades witnessed an equally dramatic decline in union membership, which fell to approximately 7.5 million by 1997, a figure that represented 32 per cent density. Finally, the period since 1997 has seen continued union decline but at a much slower rate than in previous decades. By 2011, union density was approximately 26 per cent and comprised 6.4 million members, less than half the peak membership total of 1979 which was 13.3 millions. The overwhelming majority of these trade unionists are organized within a single confederation, the Trades Union Congress (TUC), in contrast to many other countries where union membership is divided between different confederations reflecting political or occupational cleavages.

The composition of the British trade union movement has changed in line with employment patterns, at least to some degree. In 2011, there were just under three million people

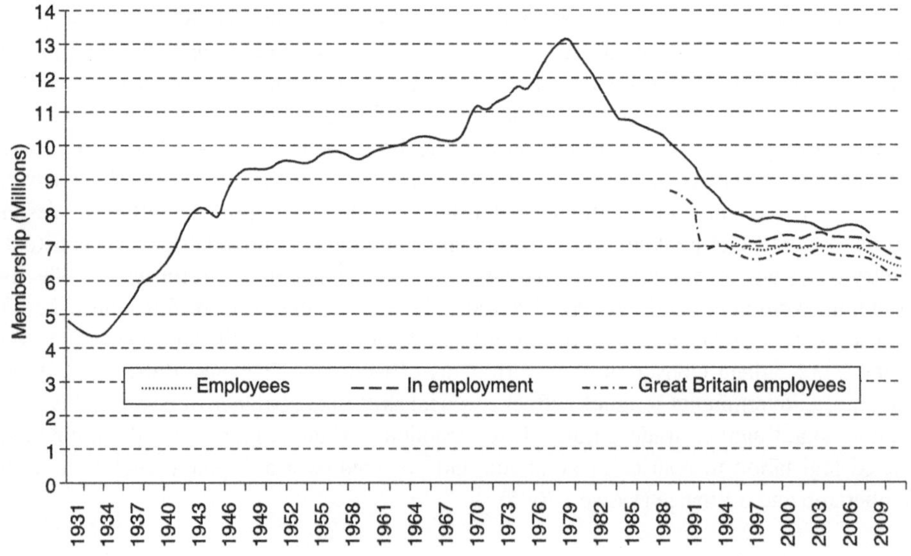

Figure 10.1 UK trade union membership, 1930–2009.

Source: Adapted from Brownlie (2012: 8).

employed in manufacturing, down from seven million in 1979 while the number of service sector employees rose over the same period from 17 to 23.5 millions. Service work itself is highly differentiated between the extremes of wages, status and skill: 'personal services' such as hairdressing comprises many low paid women while financial services is dominated by men on much higher average salaries (Korczynksi 2002: 10–12 and Table 10.2). Union density in manufacturing is now down to just 18.7 per cent and is even lower in many branches of services, such as wholesale and retail (11.9 per cent) or hotels and restaurants (3.9 per cent). Union density in the private sector as a whole is just 14.1 per cent but stands at 56.6 per cent in the public sector with a heavy concentration of membership among professional workers such as doctors, teachers and civil servants. The trade union movement in 2011 is predominantly public sector (61 per cent of membership), female (54 per cent) and professional, compared with the 1970s when the typical trade unionist was a male manual worker in manufacturing industry (Brownlie 2012). Woman have also advanced within trade union organizations: in 1979, there was just one woman General Secretary among the TUC's 109 affiliated unions but by 2011 woman led 13 (24 per cent) of the TUC's 54 unions, including all of the four big teaching unions, the Association of Teachers and Lecturers (ATL), NASUWT, the National Union of Teachers (NUT) and the University and College Union (UCU). In 2012, the TUC made an historic decision when it appointed Frances O'Grady to the post of General Secretary, the first woman ever to lead the organization in its 144-year history.

Collective bargaining coverage – the proportion of employees whose pay is determined by union–employer negotiations – has slumped in Britain, from approximately 70 per cent of the workforce in 1979 to just 31 per cent in 2010 (Brownlie 2012: 37; Hamann and Kelly 2008: 139). Pay bargaining at the level of an entire industry, common in Britain until the late 1970s, had practically disappeared by the late 1990s (Brown *et al.* 2009: 34). These trends are in marked contrast with most of Western Europe where employer and government support for collective bargaining means that bargaining coverage has remained fairly stable at around 80 per cent and industry-wide bargaining is still prevalent (Visser 2011). Collective bargaining over wages and conditions remains widespread in the public sector (where 2011 coverage was 67.8 per cent) compared with just 16.7 per cent in the private sector. Within the latter, it is in the ex-public sector organizations – in utilities and transport – that collective bargaining coverage remains high, at approximately 50 per cent (Brownlie 2012: 12).

Trade union political influence over governments has diminished since the 1970s for three main reasons: first, during the years of Conservative government – 1979 until 1997 – direct union contacts with, and influence over, ministers quickly declined and government eventually abolished the main tripartite body, the National Economic Development Council, in 1992 (Hamann and Kelly 2011: 73–4). Second, trade union membership and strike

Table 10.2 Service sector employment in the UK, 2011

Sector	*Total in millions*
Personal services e.g. residential care, hotels, restaurants	3.1
Distribution – retail, transport, communications	6.6
Producer services – banking, business, property	3.4
Social services – education, health, government	8.8

Source: http://www.ons.gov.uk/ons/ (accessed 29 November 2012).

activity, central components of trade union power, were both declining sharply in the 1980s. Third, successive Labour Party leaders – Neil Kinnock (1983–92), John Smith (1992–94) and Tony Blair (1994–2008) – radically restructured party–union relations in order to reduce the influence of trade unions in the election of the party leader, the selection of parliamentary candidates and the formation of policy at annual conference (McIlroy 1998). One limit to this process of party–union detachment is set by the dependency of the Labour Party on union financial contributions. Unlike many parties in Western Europe whose income derives mainly from the state and from party members, the British Labour Party in 2008 still obtained approximately 66 per cent of its annual income from trade unions (Koβ 2011: 83). This relationship allowed the unions to secure Labour commitment in the early 1990s to enact a statutory national minimum wage as well a legal procedure through which a union could obtain recognition for collective bargaining from an employer. Yet once those two laws were enacted – in 1998 and 1999 respectively – there is little evidence of union influence over the 1997–2010 Labour governments, despite a significant increase in union–ministerial contacts compared with previous years (Kelly 2005).

As union membership continued its seemingly relentless decline in a hostile environment, one common response by unions was to merge in order to try to realize economies of scale. The total number of trade unions affiliated to the TUC stood at 150 in 1970, 109 in 1980 and just 54 by 2011 (Ebbinghaus and Waddington 2000: 742; TUC 2012). While the British TUC still contains far more union affiliates than many West European union confederations, membership is increasingly concentrated in a handful of large, multi-occupational, multi-industry unions. In 2011, the four largest unions – Unite, UNISON, the General and Municipal Workers (GMB) and the Union of Shop, Distributive and Allied Workers (USDAW) – comprised 63 per cent of TUC membership. Another common response was to commit resources to organizing new members. Between 1995 and 2010, British trade unions ran organizing campaigns that resulted in 3625 new union recognition agreements, covering approximately 947,000 workers (Gall 2011). Yet this impressive upsurge in organizing activity has not proved sufficient to offset the tide of membership losses due to the closures and contractions of unionized workplaces and the recent retrenchment in the public sector as part of government austerity policy (see below). Moreover much of the union membership growth recorded since the late 1990s has been influenced by employment expansion in well-organized sectors such as health and education rather than by organizing greenfield sites.

Employers and employer organizations

Employers associations used to play a significant role in British industrial relations as the main agents of collective bargaining at industry level. From the early 1980s, however a growing number of firms abandoned this level of bargaining – in food retail, banking, engineering and in the utilities after privatization (Brown *et al.* 2009: 33–4). As the locus of pay determination shifted to the level of the individual firm, so the bargaining function of many of these employer associations disappeared and they have survived in much reduced form mainly as advisory bodies to individual firms (Traxler 2008). Where collective bargaining had been in place before the 1980s, it continued so long as the firm remained in existence, but new firms, both in services and manufacturing, were highly unlikely to recognize unions as bargaining agents for the workforce (Machin 2003). Even in those workplaces that continued to recognize trade unions, the scope of collective bargaining has been considerably narrowed down as employers exploited the declining power of trade unions, reasserting their right to make unilateral decisions about employment relations issues. For example, in

1980, managers in 49 per cent of unionized workplaces negotiated with trade unions on staffing levels; by 2004, that figure had slumped to just 6 per cent as employers used their power to confine the bargaining agenda to rates of pay, hours of work and some conditions of work, such as annual leave (Brown 2010: 262–3). The types of employment contracts offered by employers have also changed over the past 20 years with a decline in the proportion of the workforce on full-time contracts and an increase in the numbers of part-time employees. In 1991, 22.2 per cent of employees worked part-time but by 2011 this had increased to 26.8 per cent (Brownlie 2012: 29). The proportion of employees on fixed-term contracts has risen throughout much of Western Europe but in Britain the proportion of workers on such contracts was the same in 2009 as in 1991, at 5.7 per cent (European Commission 2003, 2010). In addition, many large firms have outsourced organizational functions such as catering, cleaning, security and building maintenance while many telephone call centres run by banks, insurance and travel firms have been 'offshored' to countries such as India (Taylor 2010). In the public sector, such outsourcing was made compulsory by legislation first enacted in 1988.

In the growing sectors of the economy, without unions and collective bargaining, employers have rarely put in place an alternative system of collective employee 'voice', such as joint consultation, that would provide workers with some influence and power. Indeed, the incidence of consultation between management and workforce has declined over this period from 34 per cent of all workplaces in 1980 to 24 per cent in 2004 (Willman *et al.* 2009: 106). In the large and growing non-union sector of the economy, employers have often preferred to implement very specific practices to regulate particular aspects of the employment relationship. For example many operate some form of performance-related pay system, often linked to a performance appraisal system. In 2004, almost 70 per cent of private service workplaces had some form of contingent pay scheme, especially in distribution and finance (Pendleton *et al.* 2009: 262, 269). There is also evidence that some employers compare their pay rates with those for similar workers in other similar firms (a process sometimes known as 'benchmarking') (Bryson and Forth 2008).

The literature on employer policies has centred around two main themes: the growth of the Human Resource Management (HRM) function in relation to the management of labour; and the extent to which the pursuit of HRM has been undercut and inhibited by business strategies centred on cost reduction rather than product and service quality (the 'low vs the high road' to competitive success respectively) (e.g. Sisson and Purcell 2010, and see Chapter 6, this volume). In the 1970s, personnel managers (as they were then known) were primarily involved in resolving disputes with unions, handling individual grievances and negotiating pay and conditions. The pay negotiation and dispute resolution functions have significantly declined because of the reduced coverage of collective bargaining and the dramatic decline in strike activity. In contrast, the main function of the HR manager, at least in theory, is to promote employee commitment to corporate objectives through mechanisms such as team briefings, team working, training, contingent pay and performance appraisal. Survey data suggests that some HRM practices have become very widespread, for example, regular management–staff meetings were found in 91 per cent of workplaces and teamworking was present in 72 per cent of workplaces in 2004. In contrast, gender and ethnic monitoring of recruitment was found in just 24 per cent of workplaces (Kersley *et al.* 2006: 248). One strand of the HRM literature suggests that HRM practices are likely to be effective only when used together, as a 'bundle' or 'cluster'. Taking a set of just three HR practices – teamworking, functional (or task) flexibility, and problem-solving groups – as an indicator of strong commitment to HR practices, the 2004 Workplace Employment Relations Survey

(WERS) found that only 14 per cent of workplaces (covering 28 per cent of employees) met this criterion, similar to the figure for 1998 (ibid.: 96).

If we turn from HR practices to their impact on employees, then the picture is very mixed. According to Green and Whitfield (2009: 228), writing about the years up to 2004:

> workers have, on the one hand, experienced higher wages, greater use of their skills and reduced insecurity and risk of accident. But, on the other hand, they have experienced the intensification of work effort and a decline in worker autonomy.

This type of evidence has been used to point up a contradiction in the UK between the logic of HRM and the rival logic of cost reduction business strategies. Put simply, the philosophy of HRM rests on the premise that labour is the firm's most valuable asset and that it is rational for a firm to pay workers well and to invest heavily in their training. A business strategy based on cost and price competition entails a very different logic, of paying low wages and benefits and deskilling work to minimize wage costs and training expenditure. In UK food retailing, Marks and Spencer epitomizes the former strategy with 2011 hourly wage rates starting from £8.00 compared with much lower rates paid by Safeway and Sainsbury's (Incomes Data Services 2011). In airlines, the low cost and low wage carriers such as EasyJet and Ryanair have exerted significant competitive pressure on the major carriers such as British Airways where pay rates and staffing levels are significantly higher (Bamber *et al.* 2009).

The evolution of the management of labour over the past 30 years is therefore marked by contradictory trends. The rhetoric, and some of the practices, of HRM have become more widespread but they have been deployed in an increasingly competitive economic environment and associated with downward pressure on wages, with work intensification and with weakened trade unions (McGovern *et al.* 2007; Thompson and McHugh 2009: 231–2).

Government

The government continues to play a number of distinct roles in employment relations: it remains the largest employer in the UK, with approximately six million employees in 2011 (around one-fifth of total employment); it has introduced an unprecedented volume of employment legislation since the 1970s, partly driven by domestic pressures and more recently in response to binding European Union Directives; it directs macro-economic policy, education and labour market policy and welfare spending; and it continues, both indirectly and indirectly, to play a role in dispute settlement through the Advisory, Conciliation and Arbitration Service (ACAS).

Government policy in the 1970s was strongly influenced by the Keynesian view that the key role of the state was to ensure full employment through policies of demand management. One of the consequences of full employment was a powerful trade union movement whose impact on wages, productivity and employment dominated governmental policy at that time. Governments appointed two committees of inquiry into industrial relations – in 1965 (the Donovan Commission) and 1975 (the Bullock Committee) – and also tried to restrain wage growth through state-imposed incomes policies limiting the permitted annual increase in wage rates.

The Conservative government, elected in 1979, was the first post-war administration explicitly to abandon the goal of full employment and to reject the conventional wisdom that government should seek to cooperate with trade union power rather than curb it. Under the leadership of Prime Minister Margaret Thatcher, it pursued a neo-liberal policy of deregulating markets, reducing taxation and cutting public spending in the belief these measures would stimulate growth and reduce unemployment. One mechanism of public spending reduction was the wholesale privatization of state industrial corporations: ports (1983), shipbuilding (1984), airlines (1987), utilities (1987–96), steel (1988), coal (1994) and railways (1996). In addition, the government passed legislation in 1988 that required public sector organizations to outsource a range of functions such as catering, cleaning, building maintenance and refuse collection. Integral to Conservative government policies was a far-reaching legal assault on trade union power. Seven major pieces of legislation between 1980 and 1993 introduced legal restrictions on solidarity strikes, on picketing and on the range of issues over which unions could lawfully engage in strike action. Lawful strikes had to be preceded by a secret ballot and the regulations governing such ballots became increasingly complex over the years. Successive Conservative governments also reduced the legal protections of individual employees faced with dismissal. They did this by raising the qualifying period of employment before an employee could file a legal claim of unfair dismissal from 6 months to 12 months (in 1979) and then in 1985 from 12 to 24 months. Both these collective and individual law reforms were framed as part of a wide-ranging programme to shift the balance of power in favour of employers or in the government's parlance, to reduce the 'burdens on business'.

The Labour governments of 1997–2010 retained most of the Conservative employment relations laws but departed from them in three ways: first, a statutory national minimum wage was introduced in 1998; second, the Employment Relations Act (1999) introduced a legal procedure whereby trade unions could secure recognition from an employer for collective bargaining. If a secret ballot of all employees in the 'bargaining unit' (normally a group of workers in a single workplace) showed a majority of those voting in favour of a union (and the turnout was at least 40 per cent), then the employer was obliged to recognize the union for collective bargaining. Third, the Labour governments reversed the Conservative 1992 opt-out from European social policy and began to implement European Directives in the field of employment relations. These measures introduced a 48-hour limit on weekly working hours, prescribed a minimum of 20 days paid annual leave, harmonized many of the employment rights of part-time and full-time workers and set a four-year limit on the duration of successive fixed-term contracts. The Labour governments also benefitted unions indirectly through the expansion of employment – by 1.1 million 1999–2010 – in the highly unionized public services, especially in health and education. However, the Labour government's macro-economic policy was generally very similar to its Conservative predecessors and influenced by similar neo-liberal ideas (Crouch 2011): control of inflation took precedence over full employment and after 1998 became the responsibility of the independent central bank (the Bank of England); privatization and outsourcing continued although in new forms as private firms were encouraged to bid for public sector work, such as running schools and prisons and taking over some National Health Service work; and access to unemployment and invalidity benefits was made harder in order to reduce the number of welfare recipients (Bach 2004; Daniels and McIlroy 2009).

Employment relations outcomes

One of the main aims of the Conservative governments' neo-liberal policies was to improve Britain's economic performance by weakening or removing what they believed to be the main obstacles to growth: trade union power, high taxation and public spending and a large public sector. Measured by membership density and strike rates, union power has certainly declined since the 1970s and early 1980s (see above). Corporation tax stood at 36 per cent in 1982 and 20 years later had been cut to 26 per cent (Glyn 2006: 165). The wage share in national income fell significantly from its 1975 peak of 71.6 per cent to 64.0 per cent by 2010, indicating a substantial redistribution of national income from labour to capital (profits, rent and interest) (European Commission 2012). However, social spending on welfare and pensions actually rose as a proportion of GDP from 17.9 per cent in 1980 to 21.8 per cent in 2001 thanks in part to higher levels of unemployment and rising pension costs (Glyn 2006: 166). Unemployment in Britain averaged around 10 per cent throughout the 1980s and then fell to around 5 per cent by the late 1990s where it remained for the next ten years before climbing once again from 2008 (Gregg and Wadsworth 2011a: 24). Real earnings growth remained modest over the period 1979–2009 at approximately 2 per cent per annum, although real earnings fell in the recessions of the early 1980s, early 1990s and late 2000s (Gregg and Wadsworth 2011b: 16–17). The average figure, however, conceals substantial variation; the real earnings of the highest paid 10 per cent of employees increased twice as fast as the bottom 10 per cent during 1980–89 and again between 2000 and 2008 (Turnbull and Wass 2011: 277). The pay of those at the very top of the earnings distribution, such as Chief Executive Officers (CEOs) of large corporations, has increased even more rapidly. In 1979, the reward packages (pay, pension contributions and shares) of the CEOs of four of the UK's largest companies – Barclays Bank, British Petroleum, GKN and Lloyds Bank – were approximately 15 times greater than the average pay of their employees. In 2010, the reward packages for these same CEOs were 65 times greater than average employee pay (High Pay Commission 2011). Significant consumption increases were made possible, however, even for low wage workers by the easy availability of credit, a policy described by Crouch (2011) as 'privatized Keynesianism'. Total house loans (mortgages) reached 129 per cent of total disposable income in 2006 compared with just 71 per cent in Germany and 39 per cent in Italy (Crouch 2010: 45).

If we turn to employment relations processes, one of the major changes in the regulation of employment relations has been the growth of individual legal claims against employers. In 2000–01, for example, there were almost 140,000 claims of legal rights violations made by employees to the Employment Tribunals (ETs); in 2010–11, the number of claims had climbed to 218,000 (Ministry of Justice 2011). The growth of individual litigation has at least two main causes. The first is the expansion of employment law since the late 1990s, providing rights in new areas (such as working time) and for categories of employees not previously covered by separate legislation (such as fixed-term contract workers). The second cause is the decline of trade unionism and the absence in many workplaces of any collective mechanism for resolving grievances. This means that approximately 75 per cent of ET claims emerge from non-union workplaces (Colling 2010). Whether the decline of collective systems of employee representation has also generated a more profound and pervasive individualistic approach by employees to problem solving at work is a question that has generated some research but which still remains open (see, for example, Pollert 2008).

Theoretical perspectives

In Chapter 2 (this volume), we set out a number of broad theoretical approaches that emphasized market forces, institutions and actors' choices respectively and their implications for the balance of power. The impact of labour and product market competition on wage bargaining outcomes and on levels of union membership are familiar themes in employment relations research, and the globalization of competition appears to have lent added force to the analytical power of the economic 'lens' (cf. Brown 2008). Other things being equal, intensified and global product market competition coupled with heightened unemployment will tend to shift the balance of bargaining power in favour of employers and away from workers and trade unions. Yet one of the staple propositions of recent comparative political economy is that 'institutions matter'. For despite the immense economic pressures brought to bear on European welfare states, wage bargaining systems and labour markets in recent years, it is clear they continue to display substantial cross-national variations (see, for instance, Katz and Darbishire 2000; Hall and Soskice 2001; Swank 2002). If the properties of economic and other institutions provide one alternative approach to that of market economics, a third approach lays more emphasis on actors' policies. In mainstream employment relations, the role of government policies has been deployed by Chris Howell (2005) in his seminal historical analysis of the transformations of British industrial relations since the late 1880s.

Market forces and the transformation of British industrial relations

The opening-up of the British economy (and other economies) to increased international competition from the early 1980s onwards has exposed less efficient firms to tremendous cost pressures and led to a dramatic 50 per cent contraction in the volume of manufacturing employment between 1981 and 2006 (Exell 2008: 322). Some firms simply went out of business; others raised productivity through automation and labour intensification and shed jobs; others again relocated some or all of their production overseas to cheap labour locations, in particular China and India (Dicken 2011: 42–3). All of these processes reduced union membership and bargaining power and led to a fall in the numbers covered by collective agreements. Similar outcomes appeared in industries that were privatized, unless they were able to form private monopolies and to some degree insulate themselves and their employees from market forces (Brown 2008, 2010). The structure of collective bargaining in Britain became highly decentralized as firms sought to extricate themselves from industry-wide agreements in order to adjust their wages and conditions more precisely to competitive conditions and to exploit the declining power of trade unions. Since unions were finding it increasingly difficult to redistribute income from profits to wages in the more globalized economy, they found their appeal to workers was significantly diminished and their membership quickly went into sharp decline. The labour market impact on bargaining power has also played a role in moderating wage settlements: unemployment averaged approximately 3 per cent in the 1970s but climbed to 10 per cent in the early 1980s and it was almost 20 years before it fell back below 5 per cent (Brown and Edwards 2009: 11; Gregg and Wadsworth 2011a: 24).

This market account undoubtedly captures part of the story about the transformation of employment relations in the UK since the early 1980s (see, for instance, Hauptmeier 2011). Yet even in its own terms, the market account is problematic: unemployment has not fallen as much as some analysts had expected following the decline in trade union membership and strike activity and since 1980 has remained at historically very high levels. In any case it is too simplistic to say that global market forces are the whole or even the main part of the explanation for the transformation of British employment relations. First, the reduction in union power and membership witnessed in the UK did not occur on anything like the same scale in other parts of Western Europe. In the small Scandinavian economies, even more exposed to global competition than the UK because of their export-oriented industries, union density only began to fall in the late 2000s. In Germany, union density was very stable until the late 1990s, despite the fact the country was governed by a conservative Christian Democratic administration from 1982 until 1998 (Hamann and Kelly 2008).

Second, if institutions that maintain wages, such as industry-wide collective bargaining and national minimum wages, are incompatible with global market forces, then why have they persisted throughout much of Western Europe? According to Hall and Soskice (2001), there are different ways in which economies can be organized in order to compete successfully in global markets. The low wage, weak trade union, flexible labour market approach of the UK – the liberal market economy (LME) – is one variety of capitalism, but the high wage, strong trade union, high employment protection approach more common throughout Western Europe is another. In the LMEs, many firms pursue a 'low road' to competitive success competing primarily on price whereas, in the coordinated market economies (CMEs), firms are more likely to compete on quality. The former strategy places a premium on low and flexible wages unhindered by collective bargaining; the latter strategy requires wages to be taken out of competition so that high wage firms are not driven out of business by wage competition. Industry-wide bargaining therefore acts as a 'beneficial constraint' on firms, making it difficult for them to compete in global markets on price and labour cost but raising the incentives for them to compete on quality and service. In other words, the employment relations outcomes of market forces depend on the interaction between employment relations institutions and company business strategies.

Third, while many researchers would agree that changes in product and labour markets have played a significant role in reducing the level of strike action, especially in those parts of the private sector exposed to international competition, does this mean that trade union power and influence in society as a whole have declined? Recent research on general strikes in Western Europe has found this type of collective action, directed against government rather than employers, has increased significantly in frequency since 1980 (although not in the UK). Moreover, analysis of the results of such strikes, on issues such as welfare, pension and labour market reform, has found that just over one-third of them have elicited significant concessions from government (Hamann *et al.* 2013). There have been no general strikes in Britain where they are unlawful but their existence and effectiveness elsewhere in Western Europe demonstrate why it is important not to generalize about unions and union power from the experience of just one country.

Institutions

We have already noted that one of the truisms of comparative employment relations research is that 'institutions matter'. In other words, you cannot read off the impact of market forces without paying attention to other variables, such as institutions. Take the case of the statutory national minimum wage (SNMW), introduced in the UK in 1998. The neo-classical claim was that, by raising the price of labour, the SNMW would depress labour demand and significantly increase unemployment among low-skilled, low-paid workers. In fact, the available evidence suggests there was no discernible impact on unemployment (Metcalf 2009). What 'varieties of capitalism' theorists call the 'beneficial constraint' of the minimum wage appears to have forced many employers to find ways of recouping higher labour costs without laying off workers, such as raising productivity, putting up prices or reducing worker hours. In other words, employers adapted to an' institutional constraint', and this type of evidence shows the potentially powerful role of institutions in weakening the downward pressure of market forces on wage levels.

One implication of the 'varieties of capitalism' approach (see Chapter 2) is that institutions possess a remarkable degree of resilience even in the face of powerful market pressures, and that institutional changes that do occur are likely to be incremental, revealing a strong degree of 'path dependency'. The approach helps us understand why collective bargaining coverage has remained extremely high throughout most of Western Europe since 1980 despite calls from some employers for more local bargaining and wage flexibility (Hamann and Kelly 2008). Yet if institutions are so resilient, then why did collective bargaining coverage fall so precipitately in Britain from levels in the 1970s that were comparable to those elsewhere in Western Europe? One explanation, remaining within the ambit of institutional theory, digs beneath the surface of institutions and emphasizes their degree of 'embeddedness' or rootedness within society. Collective bargaining agreements and structures arguably had rather shallow roots in Britain because they were not anchored in legal or constitutional foundations as in many other parts of Western Europe. Collective agreements were not (and are still not) legally binding; there are no extension mechanisms to ensure that agreements apply to all workers in a sector; there is no obligation on employers to negotiate with unions unless a majority of workers has voted for union recognition in a secret ballot; employers organizations are not involved in collective bargaining; and there are hardly any tripartite structures that embody the views and interests of the social partners, unions and employers. For all these reasons, British employment relations institutions were far weaker than their equivalents elsewhere in Western Europe and were therefore more susceptible to the shifting balance of power consequent on mass unemployment, increased product market competition and the anti-union legislation of the Conservatives.

What also remains unclear from an institutional perspective is exactly how much institutions matter compared with other factors such as markets. After all, union density as well as bargaining and works council coverage in Germany, the textbook example of a coordinated market economy built on stable institutions, has been challenged by a number of employers since the early 1990s (Hassel 2007). This finding could suggest that institutions can delay the impact of market forces, on trade unionism, for example, but sooner or later the corrosive effects of market competition will triumph. The examples of rapid institutional change in the UK and the increased exposure of firms and their workers to product and labour market competition bring us to a third theoretical perspective that helps explain employment relations change, namely, strategic choice.

Actors' policies

Chris Howell's (2005) important study of the evolution of British industrial relations in the twentieth century links to the role of choices made by successive governments. He argues that at a few key historical periods, marked by economic restructuring and heightened industrial conflict, it became possible for the government to initiate a radical overhaul of the existing industrial relations institutions. Howell's study belongs to a growing body of comparative research that has argued markets and institutions generate constraints and opportunities for the different industrial relations actors, but there always remains some degree of latitude within which the actors can make significant policy choices under the influence of particular sets of ideas or ideologies (see also Boxall 2008). For example, it is clear that the incidence of human resource management practices varies significantly even among firms in the same sector of the British economy and that these differences reflect choices made by employers (Wood and Bryson 2009).

Three types of evidence can be adduced to support the importance of actor choices in shaping industrial relations structures, processes and outcomes in the UK. First, the speed of industrial relations change in certain economies, such as Britain in the 1980s, suggests that institutional analysis is unlikely to shed much light on these developments because institutional change is normally very slow. The second type of evidence draws on comparative research and uses similar national cases to control for economic, institutional and other variables, arguing that residual differences in industrial relations and economic outcomes must therefore reflect actors' choices. For example, both Irish and British governments in the 1970s responded to union militancy and rising inflation by trying to secure union support for incomes policy. These corporatist experiments enjoyed only short-lived success at best. From the 1980s, however, government policy in the two countries radically diverged: in Ireland, successive governments opted for tripartite social pacts negotiated with trade unions and employers. In contrast, British Conservative governments chose to pursue a policy of union exclusion from policy formation and steadily abolished a number of tripartite institutions at the same time as they sought to reduce trade union power (Hamann and Kelly 2011). The third type of evidence in favour of actor policies consists of studies showing substantial intra-organization debate around different policies. Insofar as the outcomes of such debates are hard to predict, then the existence of debate is consistent with the claim that government, employer or trade union policies are not simply constrained by external forces but are open to some degree of choice. For example, the British Conservative Party in the 1970s was divided between a union-exclusionist neo-liberal wing (led by Margaret Thatcher) and a union-inclusionist corporatist wing (led by James Prior). The British Labour Party in the late 1980s was divided between a centre-left group committed to union inclusion (led by Michael Meacher and others) and a centre-right group (led by party leader Neil Kinnock) willing to distance the party from trade unions in order to secure electoral success (Howell 2005; Hamann and Kelly 2011). The victories for the union exclusionists in the respective parties were not inevitable since all of the intra-party groupings could, and did, mobilize substantial levels of support for their respective platforms. In principle, these debates could have yielded different outcomes and led the respective governments and parties to make different choices.

As Bacon (2008) has argued, however, it remains unclear how much choice and over what issues is available to employers and governments in different institutional and market environments. Moreover, some of this evidence is sufficiently ambiguous that it does not decisively confirm the value of emphasizing actor policy choices because, although institutions may not change rapidly, markets do. Between 1979, when the Conservatives were elected to office, and 1983 (when they were first re-elected), unemployment in Britain rose from 1.3 to 3.1 million, suggesting that product and labour market pressures and the consequent shifts in the balance of power are surely a major part of the explanation for the precipitate decline of British trade unionism in the early 1980s. It is also possible to provide an institutional account of some of the actor choices we have already described. For example, the type of decisive legislative action pursued by the Thatcher government in the 1980s was made possible by key features of the British institutional environment: a majoritarian electoral system that often yields single party majority governments, a weak upper chamber, a strong executive and an unwritten Constitution. Consequently governing parties in the British system have weak incentives to negotiate reforms and have clear opportunities to enact radical reforms. In Germany, by contrast, the Christian Democrat governments of Helmut Kohl (1982–98) would have found it much harder to pursue a 'Thatcherite' programme because of the country's closer approximation to the 'consensus', as opposed to the

'Westminster', model of democracy. In consensus models, proportional representation often results in coalition administrations in which government action is more constrained by a strong upper chamber and a written Constitution. This set of institutions creates strong incentives for governing parties to negotiate reforms with each other and with the major economic interest groups, employers and trade unions (Lijphart 1999:10–21). In relation to trade union strategies, Kelly and Frege (2004: 183–5) have argued that the late 1990s decisions by a number of British unions to commit substantial resources to union organizing, compared with unions in Germany, Spain and Italy, was in part a reflection of the different institutional opportunities and constraints prevailing in the respective countries. In particular, the low levels of bargaining coverage and the weak legal supports for centralized collective bargaining in the UK increased the incentives to focus on union organizing and membership recruitment in order to try to stem the erosion of union density.

Conclusion

This chapter has described the main features of British employment relations as they have evolved over the past 30 years or so. Prior to 1980, many of the contentious issues in employment relations, such as wage rises, dismissals and redundancies, were settled through negotiations between unions and employers while government was frequently involved as a third party in dispute resolution. This system of employment relations reflected a balance of power between employers and unions that was underpinned by full employment and was reflected in a particular set of union and collective bargaining institutions. Since then the balance of power in employment relations has shifted dramatically under the impact of government policy, increased product market competition and slacker labour markets. Comparing 2011 with 1979, union membership has halved, strike activity has declined dramatically and less than one-third of employees are covered by collective bargaining. Contentious issues in employment relations are now determined either through unilateral action by the employer or by employee recourse to Employment Tribunals in pursuit of individual legal rights. A unionized sector remains, but is now much smaller than in the past.

The second part of the chapter turned to the important question of how best to explain these far-reaching changes, focusing on markets, institutions and actor choices. It would be easy to say that all of these causal factors have played a role but that would be a rather obvious and un-illuminating conclusion. It does not tell us how much leeway is open to governments, union or employers in responding to market pressures. Nor does it throw light on how institutions can be reshaped and moulded to suit the preferences of different actors. One interpretation of recent developments is that the relatively 'weak institutions' of British employment relations were more vulnerable to market pressures than the more deeply embedded institutions more common throughout Western Europe. That combination of market forces and institutions does not, in and of itself, lead to the type of radical change we have witnessed in recent years. Such change also requires actors with the willingness and the power to push through change. In Britain, the main strategic actor was arguably the Conservative government which enjoyed the tacit support of employers and which benefited from large parliamentary majorities and declining trade union power. Yet the transformation of British employment relations was also the result of the Labour Party's acceptance of much of the Conservative government's anti-trade union legislation and the decision by the 1997–2010 Labour governments to leave most of it in place.

What of the prospects for the future? At the time of writing (November 2012), the UK is in the midst of a deep economic recession, marked by high unemployment and high inflation (over 3 per cent). The shakeout of jobs in both private and public sectors is further eroding trade union membership and collective bargaining coverage but whether the upsurge of public sector strikes since late 2010 will stimulate membership growth remains to be seen.

Notes

1 Some of the material in this chapter first appeared in Kelly (2011).
2 Great Britain consists of England, Scotland and Wales. The United Kingdom comprises Great Britain plus Northern Ireland.

References

Bach, S. (2004) *Employment Relations and the Health Service: The Management of Reforms*, London: Routledge.

Bacon, N. (2008) 'Management strategy and industrial relations', in P. Blyton, N. Bacon, J. Fiorito and E. Heery (eds) *The Sage Handbook of Industrial Relations*, London: Sage.

Bamber, G., Gittell, J. H., Kochan, T. A. and von Nordenflycht, A. (2009) *Up in the Air: How the Airlines Can Improve Performance by Engaging their Employees*, Ithaca, NY: Cornell University Press.

Behrens, M., Hamann, K. and Hurd, R. (2004) 'Conceptualizing labour union revitalization', in C. M. Frege and J. Kelly (eds) *Varieties of Unionism: Strategies for Union Revitalization in a Globalizing Economy*, Oxford: Oxford University Press.

Boxall, P. (2008) 'Trade union strategy', in P. Blyton, N. Bacon, J. Fiorito and E. Heery (eds) *The Sage Handbook of Industrial Relations*, London: Sage.

Brown, W. (2008) 'The influence of product markets on industrial relations', in P. Blyton, N. Bacon, J. Fiorito and E. Heery (eds) *The Sage Handbook of Industrial Relations*, London: Sage.

—— (2010) 'Negotiation and collective bargaining', in T. Colling and M. Terry (eds) *Industrial Relations: Theory and Practice*, 3rd edn, Chichester: Wiley.

—— and Edwards, P. (2009) 'Researching the changing workplace', in W. Brown, A. Bryson, J. Forth and K. Whitfield (eds) *The Evolution of the Modern Workplace*, Cambridge: Cambridge University Press.

——, Bryson, A. and Forth, J. (2009) 'Competition and the retreat from collective bargaining', in W. Brown, A. Bryson, J. Forth and K. Whitfield (eds) *The Evolution of the Modern Workplace*, Cambridge: Cambridge University Press.

Brownlie, N. (2012) *Trade Union Membership 2011*, London: Department for Business Innovation and Skills.

Bryson, A. and Forth, J. (2008) 'The theory and practice of pay setting', in P. Blyton, N. Bacon, J. Fiorito and E. Heery (eds) *The Sage Handbook of Industrial Relations*, London: Sage.

Colling, T. (2010) 'Legal institutions and the regulation of workplaces', in T. Colling and M. Terry (eds) *Industrial Relations: Theory and Practice*, 3rd edn, Chichester: Wiley.

Crouch, C. (2010) 'British industrial relations: between security and flexibility', in T. Colling and M. Terry (eds) *Industrial Relations: Theory and Practice*, 3rd edn, Chichester: Wiley.

—— (2011) *The Strange Non-Death of Neoliberalism*, Cambridge: Polity.

Daniels, G. and McIlroy, J. (eds) (2009) *Trade Unions in a Neoliberal World: British Trade Unions under New Labour*, London: Routledge.

Dicken, P. (2011) *Global Shift: Mapping the Changing Contours of the World Economy*, 6th edn, London: Sage.

Ebbinghaus, B. and Waddington, J. (2000) 'United Kingdom/Great Britain', in B. Ebbinghaus and J. Visser (eds) *Trade Unions in Western Europe Since 1945*, Basingstoke: Macmillan.

European Commission (2003) *Employment in Europe 2003*, Luxembourg: Office for Official Publications of the European Communities.

—— (2010) *Employment in Europe 2010*, Luxembourg: Office for Official Publications of the European Communities.

—— (2012) *Annual Macro-Economic Database*. Available at: http://ec.europa.eu/economy_finance/db_indicators/ameco/index_en.htm (accessed 25 August 2012).

Exell, R. (2008) 'Wage bargaining in the UK', in M. Keune and B. Galgóczi (eds) *Wages and Wage Bargaining in Europe: Developments since the Mid-1990s*, Brussels: European Trade Union Institute.

Gall, G. (2011) 'Union recognition in Britain: the end of legally-induced voluntarism?' paper presented at British Universities Industrial Relations Association Conference, London, July.

Glyn, A. (2006) *Capitalism Unleashed: Finance, Globalization, and Welfare*, Oxford: Oxford University Press.

Green, F. and Whitfield, K. (2009) 'Employees' experience of work', in W. Brown, A. Bryson, J. Forth and K. Whitfield (eds) *The Evolution of the Modern Workplace*, Cambridge: Cambridge University Press.

Gregg, P. and Wadsworth, J. (2011a) 'The labour market in winter: the 2008–2009 recession', in P. Gregg and J. Wadsworth (eds) *The Labour Market in Winter: The State of Working Britain*, Oxford: Oxford University Press.

—— (2011b) 'Unemployment and inactivity', in P. Gregg and J. Wadsworth (eds) *The Labour Market in Winter: The State of Working Britain*, Oxford: Oxford University Press.

Hall, P. A. and Soskice, D. (2001) 'An introduction to varieties of capitalism', in P. A. Hall and D. Soskice (eds) *Varieties of Capitalism: The Institutional Foundations of Comparative Advantage*, Oxford: Oxford University Press.

Hamann, K. (2011) *The Politics of Industrial Relations: Labor Unions in Spain*, New York: Routledge.

—— and Kelly, J. (2008) 'Varieties of capitalism and industrial relations', in P. Blyton, N. Bacon, J. Fiorito and E. Heery (eds) *The Sage Handbook of Industrial Relations*, London: Sage.

—— (2011) *Parties, Elections, and Policy Reforms in Western Europe: Voting for Social Pacts*, London: Routledge.

——, Johnston, A. and Kelly, J. (2013) 'Striking concessions from governments: the outcomes of general strikes in Western Europe 1980–2009', *Comparative Politics*, in press.

Hassel, A. (2007) 'What does business want? Labour market reforms in CMEs and its problems', in B. Hancké, M. Rhodes and M. Thatcher (eds) *Beyond Varieties of Capitalism: Conflict, Contradictions, and Complementarities in the European Economy*, Oxford: Oxford University Press.

Hauptmeier, M. (2011) 'Reassessing markets and employment relations', in P. Blyton, E. Heery and P. Turnbull (eds) *Reassessing the Employment Relationship*, Basingstoke: Palgrave Macmillan.

High Pay Commission (2011) *Cheques with Balances: Why Tackling High Pay Is in the National Interest*, London: High Pay Commission.

Howell, C. (2005) *Trade Unions and the State: The Construction of Industrial Relations Institutions in Britain, 1890–2000*, Princeton, NJ: Princeton University Press.

Incomes Data Services (2011) *Pay Report*, various issues.

Katz, H. C. and Darbishire, O. (2000) *Converging Divergences: Worldwide Changes in Employment Systems*, Ithaca, NY: ILR Press.

Kelly, J. (2005) 'Social movement theory and union revitalization in Britain', in S. Fernie and D. Metcalf (eds) *Trade Unions: Resurgence or Demise?*, London: Routledge.

—— (2011) 'The political economy of comparative employment relations', in M. Barry and A. Wilkinson (eds) *Research Handbook of Comparative Employment Relations*, Cheltenham: Edward Elgar.

—— and Frege, C. M. (2004) 'Conclusions: varieties of unionism', in C. M. Frege and J. Kelly (eds) *Varieties of Unionism: Strategies for Union Revitalization in a Globalizing Economy*, Oxford: Oxford University Press.

Kersley, B., Alpin, C., Forth, J., Bryson, A., Bewley, H., Dix, G. and Oxenbridge, S. (2006) *Inside the Workplace: Findings from the 2004 Workplace Employment Relations Survey*, London: Routledge.

Korczysnki, M. (2002) *Human Resource Management in Service Work*, Basingstoke: Palgrave.

Koβ, M. (2011) *The Politics of Party Funding: State Funding to Political Parties and Party Competition in Western Europe*. Oxford: Oxford University Press.

Lijphart, A. (1999) *Patterns of Democracy: Government Forms and Performance in Thirty-Six Countries*, New Haven, CT: Yale University Press.

McGovern, P., Hill, S., Mills, C. and White, M. (2007) *Market, Class and Employment*, Oxford: Oxford University Press.

Machin, S. (2003) 'Trade union decline, new workplaces and new workers', in H. Gospel and S. Wood (eds) *Representing Workers: Union Recognition and Membership in Britain*, London: Routledge.

McIlroy, J. (1998) 'The enduring alliance? Trade unions and the making of "New Labour 1994–97"', *British Journal of Industrial Relations*, 41(4): 727–49.

Metcalf, D. (2009) 'Why has the British national minimum wage had little or no impact on employment?', *Journal of Industrial Relations*, 50(3): 489–512.

Ministry of Justice (2011) *Employment Tribunals and Employment Appeal Tribunal Statistics 2010–11*, London: Ministry of Justice.

Pendleton, A., Whitfield, K. and Bryson, A. (2009) 'The changing use of contingent pay at the modern workplace', in W. Brown, A. Bryson, J. Forth and K. Whitfield (eds) *The Evolution of the Modern Workplace*, Cambridge: Cambridge University Press.

Pollert, A. (2008) 'The unorganized worker: the decline in collectivism and new hurdles to individual employment rights', in S. Bolton and M. Houlihan (eds) *Work Matters: Critical Reflections on Contemporary Work*, Basingstoke: Palgrave Macmillan.

Sisson, K. and Purcell, J. (2010) 'Management: caught between competing views of the organization', in T. Colling and M. Terry (eds) *Industrial Relations: Theory and Practice*, 3rd edn, Chichester: Wiley.

Swank, D. (2002) *Global Capital, Political Institutions, and Policy Change in Developed Welfare States*, New York: Cambridge University Press.

Taylor, P. (2010) 'The globalization of service work: analysing the transnational call centre value chain', in P. Thompson and C. Smith (eds), *Working Life; Renewing Labour Process Analysis*, Basingstoke: Palgrave Macmillan.

Thompson, P. and McHugh, D. (2009) *Work Organisations: A Critical Approach*, 4th edn, Basingstoke: Palgrave Macmillan.

Traxler, F. (2008) 'Employer organizations', in P. Blyton, N. Bacon, J. Fiorito and E. Heery (eds) *The Sage Handbook of Industrial Relations*, London: Sage.

TUC (2012) *TUC Directory 2012*, London: Trades Union Congress.

Turnbull, P. and Wass, V. (2011) 'Earnings inequality and employment', in P. Blyton, E. Heery and P. Turnbull (eds) *Reassessing the Employment Relationship*, Basingstoke: Palgrave Macmillan.

Visser, J. (2011) *ICTWSS: Database on Institutional Characteristics of Trade Unions, Wage Setting, State Intervention and Social Pacts in 34 Countries between1960 and 2007*, Amsterdam: Institute for Advanced Labour Studies. Available at: http://www.uva-aias.net/208 (accessed 29 November 2012).

Willman, P., Gomez, R. and Bryson, A. (2009) 'Voice at the workplace: where do we find it, why is it there and where is it going?', in W. Brown, A. Bryson, J. Forth and K. Whitfield (eds) *The Evolution of the Modern Workplace*, Cambridge: Cambridge University Press.

Wood, S. and Bryson, A. (2009) 'High involvement management', in W. Brown, A. Bryson, J. Forth and K. Whitfield (eds) *The Evolution of the Modern Workplace*, Cambridge: Cambridge University Press.

11 France

Nick Parsons

Introduction

France has traditionally been seen as the archetypal *dirigiste* state. The period since the end of the great post-war economic boom of the 'thirty glorious years' has been one of considerable change in this respect, as France has attempted to adapt to and accommodate the competitive pressures unleashed by economic globalization. Such adaptation has led to profound change in the conduct of French industrial relations as the state has attempted to withdraw from the regulation of employment relations. However, this change has been problematic, not only for the state, but also, particularly, for organized labour. This is not just a case of unions being weakened by structural economic change. Shifts in ideological paradigms have left the labour movement bereft, not only of material resources due to economic change, but also of ideological resources as trade union histories and identities have impacted upon current reactions to globalization and crisis. Understanding the recent trajectory of French employment relations, and particularly the exceptional weakness of organized labour in a comparative context, therefore requires not only an examination of the structural foundations of the interactions between industrial relations actors, but also an actor-centred and institutional analysis that incorporates the role that histories, identities and ideas play in shaping employment relations. It is to such a task that we now turn, beginning with an overview of the French political economy, before examining the main actors and institutions in French employment relations. Recent developments in French employment relations will then be outlined before the salience of different theoretical approaches to the study of employment relations is considered in the light of evidence from France.

Actors and processes in French political economy

In contrast to the pluralist polities of Anglo-Saxon countries, in France, the political culture of Jacobinism[1] has been hostile to intermediary bodies between the State and the people. Following the 1789 French Revolution and the triumph of Rousseau's (1762) notion of the 'general will', organized interest groups have traditionally been seen as undesirable as they deform the 'general will' through the representation of narrow sectionalist interests. Hence, unions were outlawed by the Le Chapelier Law of 1791 and only legalized in 1884. In a largely agrarian economy, workers were difficult to organize and weak unions faced severe repression from both employers and the state, in the name of *laissez-faire* economics and the property rights of owners, until well into the twentieth century. The corollary of such weakness and repression was a radical anti-capitalist trade union movement with a strong current of anarcho-syndicalism (Magraw 1992). Union weakness and ideological polarization meant that conflict predominated over collective bargaining.

Following the Second World War, *laissez-faire* capitalism was seen to have failed France in the 1930s, resulting in weak industrial and military power and the humiliation of defeat and occupation in 1940. Liberation therefore saw a tripartite government of Communists, Socialists and Christian Democrats implement an ambitious reform programme involving the nationalization of key sectors of the economy – particularly energy, transport and finance – and the establishment of a generalized welfare state. This, coupled with the introduction of an extensive planning policy under the aegis of a National Planning Commissariat, resulted in the most statist economy among the advanced liberal democracies. In the workplace, although works committees were legislated for in 1945, these were merely consultative non-trade union bodies, and unions had no legal right to a presence in the workplace. At national level, although the social partners were given the responsibility for the bipartite management of social security funds when the welfare state was established in 1946, the general picture was one of a strong state faced with weak interest organizations, and particularly trade unions, divided along ideological, strategic and religious lines.

Under the Fifth Republic, established in 1958, President de Gaulle rejected any claims of interest groups to determine policy, claiming that even the most representative lacked authority and political responsibility, as opposed to the state which, alone, could incarnate and serve the national interest. On the other hand, he accepted that they should be consulted over policy in exchange for material and immaterial benefits (Knapp and Wright 2006: 312–13). These included the financial resources and political legitimacy associated with participating in state-sponsored consultative fora. At the national level, the Economic and Social Council was created in 1958 for the consultation of interest groups over economic and social policy, while the planning commissions also provided this opportunity. However, such consultation was largely a sham with both bodies used to test opposition to government policies (Milner 2002; Parsons 2002). As a consequence, achieving consensus was impossible, and the state was able to dominate interest organizations by a selective choice of interlocutor, playing organizations off against one another or ignoring them completely. Protest was therefore seen as the main way to put pressure on the government, and this was often used as part of an overall strategy to include institutionalized bargaining and consultation (Knapp and Wright 2006: 321). However, the general picture was one of highly centralized state-dominated policy-making.

In addition to a Jacobin political culture, this dominance of the state can be explained institutionally, especially after 1958, by the presence of a strong executive, supported by cohesive parties in a weak parliament. This resulted in the relative isolation of ministers from interest group activities, and the predominance of a technocratic approach to decision-making overseen by a strong self-assured bureaucracy produced in the system of elite *grandes écoles*. From the 1980s, however, this system began to be dismantled as the Jacobin state came under pressure, externally from globalization and Europeanization and internally from state policies of decentralization, deregulation and privatization.

The post-war period was the golden age of French industry. The industrial working class was at its height, representing some 39 per cent of the working population in 1975 (Gildea 1996: 103), and factories increasingly employed Taylorist production techniques in large-scale units. The productivity gains afforded by economies of scale, the use of more modern production methods and broadly Keynesian economic policies of demand management fed into higher wages, full employment and improved welfare provision while company profitability could be maintained and improved. Under state guidance, the French economy appeared to be firmly locked into a virtuous circle of 'Fordist growth' (Boyer 1988: 16–17). However, growing international interdependence posed an increasing threat to this model, based as it was on the circulation of money within the national economy. Even before the crises of the 1970s, the 1960s saw a highly interventionist industrial policy aimed at creating 'national champions' able to compete on international markets as French trade increasingly switched from protected colonial markets, which were being lost in the wave of decolonization, to the European markets which were to become increasingly important in the wake of the 1957 Treaty of Rome establishing the European Economic Community.

However, it was the oil crises of 1973 and 1979 that fully and brutally revealed France's exposure to international economic interdependencies. Higher energy prices fuelled a downward spiral in growth, balance of payments deficits and an upwards surge of inflation and unemployment (Parsons 2005: 14–19). After experimenting with Keynesian policies in 1981–82, the Socialist government of President François Mitterrand operated a major policy U-turn as reflation in a deflationary global context only served to suck in imports, increasing budgetary imbalances and inflation without promoting growth or employment. As increasing reference was made to the 'external constraint' of international economic interdependence, a policy of competitive disinflation was sketched out and followed by all succeeding governments, whether of the Left or Right. This had four main elements. In order to stimulate export-led growth, the strength of the franc was defended by anchoring it to the deutschmark, ruling out any competitive devaluation. The public sector was used as the spearhead of a policy of wage moderation and attempts were made to control public spending in order to contain and reduce inflation. Finally, economic liberalization became a cornerstone of economic policy, with privatization programmes raising money and reducing government spending (Hocblat 2007: 178–9). Ultimately, the policy was successful in enabling France to meet the Maastricht criteria for entry into the Eurozone in 1999, but a heavy price was paid in terms of persistently high unemployment due to the compression of internal demand. Indeed, French unemployment rates have consistently been above EU15 averages from the mid-1990s onwards, more often than not by more than a full percentage point (INSEE 2011a).

The effects of developments in the political economy since the 1980s have been several. First, France has opened up to the global economy. Imports and exports now account for over half of GDP, compared with one quarter in the 1950s. Investment has also internationalized, with increased inflow and outflow of foreign direct investment (FDI) (Parsons 2005: 14–19). Second, the major victims of this internationalization have been the traditional heavy industries upon which unions relied for recruitment, with coal mining, iron and steel, and shipbuilding particularly hard hit. As a result, industry now accounts for just 22.5 per cent of employment in France, with services accounting for 74.6 per cent of the active population (INSEE 2011b). The expansion of the service sector, however, has not fully compensated for the loss of manufacturing jobs, with the result that France has had one of the most persistently high unemployment rates in Europe since the early 1980s, with the young, unskilled and unqualified particularly hard hit. After dipping below 7.5 per cent of the active population for the first time in 25 years in 2008, unemployment in France rose to 9.4 per cent in 2010 under the impact of the global crisis originating in the US sub-prime mortgage market (INSEE 2011c). For those in employment, work has become increasingly insecure and flexible. In 2008, part-time employment affected 16 per cent of those in work, double the figure for 1975, while 8.3 per cent were on temporary contracts, four times the figure for 1982 (Parsons 2005: 107–8; Chevalier and Mansuy 2009). These changes have not been without consequence for the industrial relations actors.

Trade unions

The French labour movement has been characterized by radicalization and a consequent fragmentation and weakness. In a mutually reinforcing relationship, weakness has often fed further radicalization. The earliest divisions centred on religion, with the *Confédération Française des Travailleurs Chrétiens* (CFTC) being established in 1919 as a Catholic alternative to the Marxist-leaning *Confédération Générale du Travail* (CGT), which was created in 1895. The next major development occurred in 1948, when *Force Ouvrière* (FO) was established following a split within the CGT in reaction to the increasing influence of the French Communist Party (PCF) over the confederation, which was cemented in the Second World War Resistance movement. In addition, the *Confédération Française Démocratique du Travail* was created in 1964 when the majority of the CFTC decided to de-confessionalize and pursue a 'third way' between the reformist FO and CFTC, on the one hand, and the bureaucratic state socialism of the CGT-PCF tandem on the other. The result has been that French unions have wasted much time, energy and resources fighting one another, reducing their capacity to defend their members' interests in the face of often authoritarian employers.

The CGT emerged from the Second World War as the largest French union confederation, greatly influenced by the PCF, for whom it acted as a 'transmission belt' throughout the 1950s and 1960s. From the 1970s onwards, however, it has been in constant decline, and in the 1990s was overtaken by the CFDT in terms of membership numbers, although not in shares of votes in professional elections (Parsons 2005: 50–1 and see Table 11.1). To combat this trend, it has, since the 1980s, attempted to distance itself from the declining PCF. Nevertheless, while all unions have faced decline, the CGT has been worst hit due to the erosion of its ideological resources – the collapse of Soviet Russia and the general discrediting of left-wing ideologies during a period of neo-liberal ideological hegemony – and its membership base, as the traditional heavy industries that formed its backbone went into

Table 11.1 Trade union density in France, 1949–2008 (% of labour force)

Year	*Density*
1949	30.1
1950	26.7
1955	20.6
1960	17.7
1965	17.3
1970	19.7
1975	19.9
1980	16.6
1985	12.6
1990	9.8
1996	8.2
2000	8.6
2005	7.6
2006	7.6
2007	7.6
2008	7.6

Source: 1949–2005 Ministère de l'Emploi, de la Formation Professionnel et du Dialogue. Sociale; 2006–2008 OECD.

decline. Under the impact of economic crisis in the 1970s and globalization in the late twentieth century, the CFDT was followed by the CGT in moving – albeit hesitatingly – towards the social-democratic middle ground in an attempt to negotiate solutions to crisis. This opened up space on the left for the so-called 'autonomous' unions, unattached to any confederation, to grow. Thus, movements such as *Solidaires, Unitaires, Démocratiques* (SUD) and the *Fédération des Syndicats Autonomes* (FSA) have been at the forefront of many radical strike actions in the past 20 years. In addition, the social-democratic UNSA has also grown to strengthen the 'reformist pole' of unions. The overall result, however, is further union fragmentation (Parsons 2005: 59–62). Indeed, these new unions are now challenging the supremacy of the established unions in their one remaining area of relative strength – the public sector. In workplace elections in October 2011, the FSA emerged as the largest union in the education sector with 40.6 per cent of votes cast, while UNSA was the largest in the health sector with 34.2 per cent, and SUD won the lion's share of the vote – 24 per cent – in France Télécom. As a result, trade union representation on the *Conseil Supérieur de la Fonction Publique de l'Etat* – a government and civil servant advisory body – is split between seven unions (Fonction Publique 2011).

For the union movement, this is all the more worrying when one considers that, taken as a whole, in terms of membership, French unions are the weakest in the industrialized world. Although an early emphasis on direct militant action resulted in a lack of concern for building up large memberships for collective bargaining purposes, decline since the 1970s has been staggering, with unions losing two-thirds of their membership since the mid-1970s (Andolfatto 2007: 233). Since the mid-1990s unionization has stabilized at around 8 per cent with most union members now concentrated in the public sector, and private sector presence largely confined to larger companies (Wolff 2008). Unions, however, argue that their strength should not be judged on membership figures. Other observable measures, such as workplace election results and levels of conflict, however, show the same decline over the long term (Parsons 2005: 50–2; and see Table 11.2).

Table 11.2 Works committee election results, France, % of votes cast

*Cycle**	*CGT*	*CFDT*	*FO*	*CFTC*	*CFE–CGE*	*Other union*	*Non-union*
1968–1969	45.0	19.0	7.5	3.0	5.0	5.0	15.0
1977–1978	38.5	20.5	10.0	2.5	6.0	5.5	17.5
1980–1981	34.6	21.8	10.6	3.0	6.1	4.7	19.3
1982–1983	31.7	22.6	11.3	3.6	6.5	5.1	19.2
1984–1985	28.6	21.1	13.3	4.4	6.7	5.4	20.6
1986–1987	27.0	21.3	12.7	4.3	6.7	5.5	22.5
1988–1989	25.9	20.9	12.4	4.2	6.1	5.6	24.9
1990–1991	22.7	20.2	12.2	4.0	6.5	5.6	28.7
1992–1993	22.2	20.5	11.9	4.5	6.2	6.5	28.2
1994–1995	22.0	20.7	12.2	4.7	6.0	6.5	27.9
1996–1997	22.1	21.2	12.1	4.8	6.1	6.7	27.1
1998–1999	23.0	22.3	12.1	5.3	6.0	6.3	14.9
2000–2001	23.6	22.9	12.7	5.7	5.9	6.8	22.4
2002–2003	23.3	22.4	12.6	6.1	6.1	7.2	22.4
2004–2005	23.6	20.3	12.5	6.4	6.3	7.9	22.9

Source: 1968–1969 and 1977–1978 Parsons (2005: 51); all other years DARES.

Note: *Elections take place every two years in a particular workplace, but not all workplaces have elections in the same year. Figures are given by two-year electoral cycle.

With only 8 per cent of the working population in France unionized, fragmentation is a source of weakness, with unions in competition with one another for members and resources. Indeed, ideological division and rivalry have made it difficult for unions to join together in unified action. This does, however, occur on occasion, such as in the 2010 protests against pension reform. On such 'days of action', unions can give the appearance of impressive displays of strength, aimed at pressuring the government for reform. In the *trente glorieuses*, when the state played a central role in economic management, this was a viable strategy and met with some success. However, since the 1970s, the withdrawal of the state from economic management, as well other factors such as the decentralization of industrial relations, and labour market, industrial, political and social change, have all conspired to leave French unions in a weak position. As Chris Howell (2009: 230) has put it:

> There is a marked disparity between the level of appearances and the level of reality as widespread social mobilization has served to delay but not turn back the tide of reform; protesters have largely won small victories while losing the war.

Employers

French employers traditionally argued for a mixture of protection from foreign competition and free market liberalism at home, looking, like unions, to the state to safeguard their interests. After the Second World War, the main employers organization, the *Conseil National du Patronat Français* (CNPF) was opposed to both trade unions and European integration. Growing state economic and social intervention, the internationalization of the economy and industrial modernization have all reinforced the neo-liberal outlook of the major employers' organization, with flexibility, decentralization and individualization being the clarion calls from the late 1970s on. Although the 1982 Auroux Laws (see below) were opposed as a state-sponsored initiative, employers soon realized that they had much to gain from their decentralizing tendencies and have successfully pushed for further reform in this direction. Thus, following the announcement in 1997 by Lionel Jospin, the socialist Prime Minister, of legislation for a 35-hour week, the CNPF elected a new president, changed its name to the *Mouvement des Entreprises de France* (MEDEF) in 1998, and reformed its structures to give greater influence to grass-roots employers and entrepreneurs rather than trade associations or officials of the organization. This reinforced the organization's neo-liberal leanings, and in 1999 it called for a 'new social constitution' (*refondation sociale*) involving a complete overhaul of employment relations and social protection systems with the aim of sidelining the state. Although the MEDEF has found it difficult to achieve its aims, particularly in the area of social protection, it has been successful in arguing for a decentralization of collective bargaining. It still campaigns vociferously for labour market and welfare reform, arguing that labour market rigidities and high social charges are responsible for poor economic performance and high unemployment in France.

In the field of company management, the influence of small companies in the French economy fostered highly paternalistic and authoritarian attitudes. In the nineteenth and early twentieth centuries, the owner-manager was considered to be the *pater familias*, and the company his private fiefdom. In larger companies disciplinarian management and ferocious anti-unionism were combined with the provision of housing, medical care, schooling for workers' children and social amenities for workers. In reality, this paternalism reinforced authoritarianism as it enabled social control to be exercised over all aspects of the workers' lives (Magraw 1992). After the Second World War, although the growing size and complexity of companies, particularly in ownership terms, and the development of the welfare state, rendered this control more difficult to exercise, industrial modernization had little impact on managerial attitudes. Indeed, the more widespread implementation of Taylorist production processes reinforced the traditional tight hierarchical control and strict discipline on the shopfloor (Parsons 2005: 93–4).

Such control strategies were to be undermined by several developments. First, the May 1968 strike wave gave rise to a rejection of Taylorism and demands for a 'humanization of work'. Second, industrial modernization and the increased levels of skills needed to operate technologically more sophisticated machinery rendered such strategies problematic, based as they were on task control. Although quality circles became a widespread tool aimed at increasing employee involvement in the 1980s, these strategies, and other participative and human resource (HR) management strategies, were used as a means of individualizing relations and bypassing trade unions in the workplace. In the low trust environment of the French workplace, the main thrust of employer strategies was to switch from control of the task to control of performance and to enhance flexibility in the deployment of labour through a variety of mechanisms: target-setting – particularly in the financial sphere; the individualization of pay and attempts to relate it to performance; regular employee appraisals that emphasized subjective qualities such as 'goodwill'; and the use of ISO 9000 norms for the certification of quality, which allow faults to be traced back to the individual employee.[2] In addition, greater flexibility has been sought through outsourcing and the increased use of fixed-term and part-time contracts (ibid.: 96–112).

The state and employment relations

Politically, France has traditionally been seen as a polarized country with a strong Communist Party mustering a large share of the working-class vote until the 1980s. In consequence, the state has played an essential mediating role between capital and labour in the French system of employment relations. This was due in part to its own interventionism in economic policy-making and in part to the ideological hostility between capital and labour that rendered collective bargaining problematic and under-developed. As both parties turned to the state for reform in their favour, the result was a system of industrial relations in which conflict and state intervention acted as a substitute for collective bargaining (van Ruysseveldt and Visser 1996).

The state had several major weapons in its armoury to influence the regulation of labour in the post-war period. First, it introduced the national minimum wage in 1950, and has been able to use this, not only as a redistributive tool, but also to end social conflict, such as in 1968, when it was raised by 35 per cent as part of the Grenelle Agreement that formed the basis of a negotiated end to the May 1968 strike wave. Second, it could use its position as a major employer to influence wage levels and employment conditions. Further, it could use the 'extension procedure' contained in the 1950 Collective Bargaining Act whereby any collective agreement deemed socially or economically beneficial could be extended economy-wide by the Minister of Labour after consultation with the tripartite National Commission for Collective Bargaining. A combination of the latter two methods was seen in 1955 when a deal in the state-owned Renault company gave workers a pay rise in line with productivity, company pensions and a third week's paid holiday. The latter two provisions were then extended economy-wide.

In the post-war period such interventionism was necessary. Inter-union competition meant that weak unions which could exercise little control over their base confronted anti-union employers, rendering both voluntarist and corporatist approaches to bargaining impossible. Furthermore, collective bargaining was problematic due to the dominance of the anti-capitalist CGT among trade unions and the consequent anti-union tendencies of French employers. The solution was an attempt to dilute the influence of the CGT by allowing smaller reformist unions to play a role over and above that which their membership figures would permit, and for the state to use its position as legislator and dominant employer to influence employment conditions and wage formation. There were several ways in which smaller union confederations were encouraged. First, trade unions acquired certain rights if they were deemed to be 'nationally representative'. This representativeness was based upon criteria such as supposed political independence, resources and membership numbers, but was ultimately a function of trade union attitudes during the Second World War: any union that had resisted the Nazi occupier was deemed to have acted patriotically and was therefore entitled to represent the French working class. These unions were accorded certain privileges, such as the right to put forward candidates in the first round of workplace elections for works committees and employee representatives, and to sit on welfare fund and national consultative bodies. Under the 1950 Collective Bargaining Act, they could also sign collective agreements, and under this law the national industry level was the main level at which bargaining took place. As only one union needed to sign a deal for it to be valid, small reformist unions could sign national agreements regulating the laws of a trade, thereby sidelining the CGT. The latter was free to either accept or, more usually, denounce as class collaboration, any deals signed in this manner. Trade union fragmentation as a block to bargaining was, theoretically, overcome, although it resulted in weak agreements with little legitimacy and a consequently underdeveloped and conflictual collective bargaining system.

Following the May 1968 strike wave, unions were, for the first time, given the legal right to establish workplace branches by a law of December of that year. A 1971 reform of the 1950 Collective Bargaining Act also gave greater scope for company-level bargaining, although this had little impact as unions confronted economic crisis in a position of weakness. Furthermore, the architecture of collective bargaining made local deals unlikely. In effect, the 1950 Act had created a framework which worked according to an improvement principle: lower-level deals could only improve upon higher-levels deals, and/or legislation. This gave employers little incentive to engage in a process that could only improve upon the terms and conditions of employment set out in national industry-level deals. Although not originally conceived as a response to globalization, state-sponsored reforms in the 1980s began a trend towards more flexible decentralized bargaining before it was reinforced by the pressures of greater international competition.

Decentralization of collective bargaining

The 1982 Auroux Laws obliged employers, for the first time, to bargain annually, at company level, with unions, where they were present, over wages and working time. To reinforce the legitimacy of agreements, unions gaining over half the votes cast in workplace elections could veto any agreements signed at this level. To reinforce the role of unions in the collective bargaining process, they were given greater rights to company information, and the right to bring in expert help to decipher that information. The Auroux Laws aimed to strengthen the position of unions within the company, thereby allowing the state to withdraw from the regulation of employment relations, and for that reason were opposed by employers. However, subsequent developments suggest that they have been more favourable to employers seeking greater flexibility than they have been to unions or workers (Howell 1992, 2009; Parsons 2005).

First, a decree of January 1982 introduced the possibility of dispensation from the law through local agreement in the area of working time – a specific area for local negotiation in the Auroux Laws. The 1993 Five Year Employment Law made this possible in companies without a union presence, through consultation with elected representatives before the law of 12 November 1996 implemented the provisions of the multi-industry collective agreement of 30 October 1995. As well as permitting elected representatives to sign agreements, the law introduced the notion of 'mandated' employees. In the absence of unions, these were either elected by the whole workforce or 'mandated' by an external union organization to negotiate single issue agreements on behalf of the workforce, including dispensatory agreements. These provisions were further promoted in the 1998 and 2000 Aubry Laws to stimulate the decentralized negotiation of the 35-hour week. Given the complexity of the negotiation of the reduction of the working week, the second Aubry Law of 2000 introduced the notion of 'majority consent'. This required agreements to be signed by unions, or in their absence, by elected representatives, representing the majority of employees in the workplace, as measured by election results. Failing this, agreements could be signed by 'mandated' employees and ratified by a referendum of the whole workforce. Thus, the thrust of legislation in the last two decades of the twentieth century was to decentralize bargaining and, given the weakness of union representation in anything other than large private sector companies, to achieve and legitimize the process through non-union bargaining and majority consent where unions were not present.

In the 2000s, this decentralized regulation of the employment relationship has been pushed further. First, a 'common position' signed in 2001 by the MEDEF and all the major confederations, bar the CGT, reiterated the above trends, stipulating that local agreements would be valid if signed or not opposed by unions gaining 50 per cent of the votes in workplace elections. Non-union agreements required approval by the majority of employees in a workplace referendum. This agreement was transposed into law in 2004 by the Fillon Law, named after the Prime Minister. This also allowed for dispensatory agreements (departing from the terms agreed at national level) to be signed in any area, bar four: minimum wages, job grading, complementary regimes of social protection (pensions, etc. and the funding of vocational training).

In an attempt to rationalize decentralized bargaining in a context of union fragmentation, a 2008 reform has pushed the logic of union representativeness and majority consent further by stipulating that from 2013 only unions gaining 10 per cent of the votes in workplace elections can engage in collective bargaining, and that collective agreements require the signature of unions representing at least 30 per cent of the workforce in order to be valid. Again, unions representing half or more of the workforce can veto such agreements. A law passed on 15 October 2010 also aims to reinforce trade union representativeness and the legitimacy of agreements at national and industry levels by organizing elections in workplaces employing fewer than 11 people from the end of 2012. The results of these elections will be combined with elections in larger workplaces to determine trade union representativeness for bargaining and consultation purposes (Ministère du Travail de l'Emploi et de la Santé 2011: 141–7). From 2013, at national and industry levels, unions must gain 8 per cent of the votes to be considered representative, and national agreements need to be signed by unions gaining 30 per cent of the votes but can be opposed by any union or unions gaining 50 per cent.

Thus, since the 1980s, the thrust of state intervention has been to decentralize collective bargaining and to make it more flexible by allowing for dispensatory agreements to be signed at company level. Not only has this voluntarily reduced the state's capacity to regulate employment relations in France by turning the legal and collective bargaining framework, with its improvement principle, on its head, but it has also called into question the unions' claims to act as representative organizations. When lower-level agreements could only improve upon higher-level ones or the law, it was not problematic that they were signed by minority trade unions. Once lower-level agreements could downgrade the dispositions of higher-level agreements or the law in the name of local productive efficiency, they required a greater legitimacy than the fact that they were signed by organizations deemed to be 'nationally representative', irrespective of their local, or indeed national, membership strength. Whether the reforms of union representativeness will push unions into amalgamation for greater bargaining efficiency, as the state hopes, remains to be seen.

Working time and employment contracts

The other major area in which the French state has attempted to promote greater decentralization and flexibility is in the area of employment contracts and working time. As far as working time is concerned, greater flexibility was afforded by the Auroux Laws which permitted derogation from higher-level agreements through local bargaining. The 1996 Robien Law gave employers a financial incentive to reduce working time to save jobs by reducing social security charges for employers signing such deals. Essentially the Aubry Laws of 1998 and 2000 made what was voluntary under the Robien Law obligatory, but the second Aubry Law introduced greater flexibility by allowing the 35-hour week to be calculated on an average basis, by annualizing hours. Although the right-wing government under Sarkozy did not repeal the 35-hour week legislation, it made it 'all but voluntary' by suspending its application to small firms, introducing greater flexibility through permitting an extended use of overtime and exempting managerial staff from much of the legislation (Howell 2009).

In addition to flexibility in working time, numerical flexibility has also been encouraged by the state since the mid-1980s with a view to encouraging job creation and improving company profitability by lowering labour costs. Under the premiership of Jacques Chirac, the need for administrative authorization for collective redundancies – first introduced in 1975 by the same Chirac to forestall the wave of redundancies occurring in the wake of crisis – was replaced in 1986 by the need to accompany such redundancies with a 'social plan' covering redundancy payments and redeployment and/or retraining as alternatives to lay-offs. The Five Year Employment Plan of 1993 made recourse to short-time working easier and reduced employer social charges on part-time labour. While the 1997–2002 socialist government promoted a reduction in working time to combat unemployment, succeeding Gaullist governments returned to an emphasis on numerical flexibility through successive reforms of work contracts. In 2004, the *Contrat d'Activité* was introduced, providing work and training for two years in return for 75 per cent of the minimum wage and was followed in 2005 by the *Contrat Nouvelle Embauche* (New Employment Contract), which allowed employers to dismiss an employee within two years of hiring without needing to give a justification and without the usual compensation. However, when a *Contrat Première Embauche* was proposed, paying those under 26 less than the minimum wage and allowing employers to fire at will, it was greeted by mass street protests and was withdrawn by the government. Next, in 2008, a 'unique' work contract (*Contrat Unique*) was proposed and introduced the same year and this phases in employment protection according to length of service.

Such actions have been taken in response to long-standing complaints from employers that the competitiveness of French companies and creation of employment are hampered by labour market rigidities that make it impossible for them to react to changing product markets through labour-cost adjustment. The other major complaint of employers – that social charges are a brake on competitiveness and employment – have been tackled over the last 30 years through numerous schemes that also aim to stimulate job creation by reducing social charges on low-paid employment. As the unskilled still suffer disproportionately from unemployment, such schemes have been criticized as providing a windfall to employers who in some cases would have taken such workers on anyway, without addressing underlying problems of skills and productivity (Dassault 2007).

Although the main thrust of state intervention in employment relations over the past three decades has been in the direction of decentralization, national-level developments also merit some mention. Here, one can detect a certain 'Europeanization' of French industrial relations through the aim of promoting social dialogue. Thus, in January 2007, the government adopted a 'Law on Modernizing Social Dialogue' obliging the government to consult with the social partners before proposing any reforms to labour law. Reflecting arrangements that first appeared in the Social Protocol of the 1992 Maastricht Treaty, this could result in a cross-sector collective agreement which could be taken into account when legislation is drafted. Whether this has made any difference in practice, however, is open to question. First, tax policies and social protection, including pensions, are exempt from the law. Second, union leaders have always had access to ministers to discuss reform and legislation on a formal and informal basis, and unions have long had formal consultation rights through various bodies. They have generally viewed such consultation as a sham, arguing that a technocratic view of policy-making is imposed, wherein state elites merely inform organizations as to their plans rather than engage in meaningful consultation (Milner 2002). Indeed, such accusations were heard in 2010 over pension reform, despite the fact that unions managed to act with a rare unity and mobilize impressive numbers of demonstrators to take to the streets in opposition to the Sarkozy government's plans to raise the retirement age from 60 to 62. Ultimately, the government was able to push through its reforms despite widespread opposition.

Industrial relations outcomes

The period since the 1970s has seen considerable change in the conduct of French industrial relations, with some apparently paradoxical results. The institutional position of French trade unions has never been stronger. They have more bargaining rights and more access to representative institutions than ever before, and collective bargaining coverage is the highest of any European Union (EU) country at 95 per cent (Venn 2009). However, changes in the external environment have generally been detrimental to French trade unions. Politically, the decline of the French Left, and particularly the Communist Left, has robbed the CGT, especially, of ideological resources; economically, labour market change – feminization, the shift to services and growing employment insecurity and high unemployment levels – has undermined membership resources; and social change – the growth of consumerism and individualism, along with the decline of class identification – has undermined their sociological appeal as class-based organizations, while unions have failed to develop individual services to members.

However, the nature of French trade unions may be changing. The extension of workplace institutions for employee representation (see Parsons 2005: Chapter 7) means that trade unions, suffering a loss of membership and activists, are often overloaded at workplace level. The greater number of positions to be filled, particularly in larger companies, means that trade union activists accumulate time off to the point where they effectively become full-time trade union officials within the company. The result is an institutionalization of trade union representatives, who are no longer lay officials working alongside those they represent, but increasingly trade union bureaucrats engaged in full-time representation, negotiation and policing agreements. For some, in spite of their continued capacity to mobilize on specific issues such as pensions, this increasing 'professionalization' of trade union activity risks changing the nature of trade unions: from social movements relying on their mobilization capacity, to para-public regulatory agencies with an electoralist relationship to their base and dependent upon the public purse to the extent that electoral representativeness gives access to funds and resources at both local and national levels. The 2008 reform of trade union representativeness may well exacerbate such trends (Béroud *et al.* 2011: 48–50).

The decentralization of collective bargaining – the major trend in French industrial relations since the 1970s – is part and parcel of this institutionalization. However, it is still problematic in many respects. Certainly, collective bargaining has been decentralized. From 1960 to 1967, only 356 plant-level agreements per year were signed (Goetschy and Rozenblatt 1992). By the end of the 1980s, following the passing of the Auroux Laws, the number of company-level agreements had risen to 6,000 per year (Parsons 2005: 122). In 2010, the Ministry of Labour (Ministère du Travail, de l'Emploi et de la Santé 2011: 499–546) recorded 66,959 company-level agreements. Of these, however, 28 per cent were unilateral decisions by the employer and 21 per cent were ratified by workplace referendum. Only 36 per cent were signed by trade union delegates or employees mandated by unions, and 14 per cent were signed by elected workplace representatives. Although unilateral employer decisions and referenda were mainly used for employee savings schemes – essentially share ownership – which do not require trade union agreement, only a little over a third of company level agreements were signed with the involvement of trade unions. This reflects the absence of union representatives, particularly in smaller workplaces in France. Thus, in 2005, 38 per cent of workplaces employing more than 20 people had a trade union delegate, but this number varied between 23 per cent of those employing less than 50 and 97 per cent of those employing more than 500 (Pignoni and Tenret 2007).

Furthermore, despite the growth in company-level collective bargaining over the last 30 years, the *Activité et Conditions d'Emploi de la Main d'œuvre* (Acemo) survey of 2007 found that only 15 per cent of private sector non-agricultural companies employing more than 10 people engaged in collective bargaining, with this percentage rising with company size and trade union presence (Carlier and Naboulet 2009). High levels of collective bargaining coverage can therefore be explained by the extension procedure and the applicability of branch level agreements to all companies in a given sector. These procedures, however, only set out basic terms and conditions, particularly wages, with further negotiation and/or adaptation often needed for application at company level. Where trade union delegates are lacking and employees have little access to external expertise, doubts can be cast on the quality of such application at local level.

The Acemo survey also found that, in eight out of ten companies where a strike had taken place during the year, collective bargaining had also taken place, with the proportion of companies declaring that they had known a strike in the year rising with the intensity of collective bargaining, as measured by the number of themes addressed (ibid.). Thus, collective bargaining is itself associated with conflict, while it is far from certain that the decentralization of bargaining has been advantageous to wage-earners (Parsons 2005).

Although there were widespread union demonstrations against President Sarkozy's handling of economic crisis and pension reform towards the end of the first decade of the twenty-first century, there is little evidence of such mobilization being translated into membership growth. Rather, continuing militant action suggests that the enduring weaknesses of the French industrial relations system – weak unions and a weak collective bargaining system – are still pertinent. In 2000, for example, textile workers threatened with redundancy at the Cellatex plant in Givet occupied the factory with 56,000 litres of sulphuric acid and 46 tons of carbon sulphide stored on the site. Having threatened to blow the factory up, they eventually poured thousands of litres of acid onto the streets (Larose *et al.* 2001). In 2004, electricity workers engaged in 'Robin Hood' actions, going into working-class estates and reconnecting supplies at the cheapest rates in order to protect the right to energy, particularly for the poorest households, during power strikes against plans to privatize French gas and electricity provision (Béroud 2005). In 2009, workers threatened with redundancy at New Fabris in Châtellerault placed gas canisters around the site and threatened to blow up their factory unless they were given redundancy payments of €30,000 (*Nouvel Observateur* 2009). In 2009–10, workers in many companies took to illegal action when faced with redundancy as a result of the financial and economic crisis that started in the US sub-prime mortgage market. Having little confidence in the traditional route of collective bargaining, they sequestrated managers in what became known as 'bossnappings' in an effort either to renegotiate the extent of redundancies or to secure higher compensation payments for losing their jobs (Parsons 2012).

Theoretical considerations

Understanding change and continuity in French industrial relations requires more than an examination of institutions. Certainly, employing Dunlop's (1958) systems approach can shed light on how new legislation has changed the 'web of rules' and forced a decentralization of collective bargaining in the context of economic and technological change associated with globalization. However, a focus on rule-making and consensus can tell us little about why conflict has endured despite the greater institutionalization of employment relations and what many saw as the 'domestication' of previously radical trade unions in the 1980s and 1990s (Goetschy and Rozenblatt 1992; van Ruysseveldt and Visser 1996). Likewise, Kerr *et al.*'s (1960) convergence theory can inform us about general trends towards decentralization and greater flexibility that are occurring in all advanced (post-) industrial societies as a result of technological change and greater international economic interdependency, but says nothing of why such a process has entailed such a pivotal role for the state, or why it has been, and remains, a conflictual one in France.

Certainly, strategic choices on the part of all the main actors are important. Thus, the 1981–84 socialist government enacted the Auroux Laws as a means of improving industrial democracy and shoring up the position of trade unions, while employers opposed them as unwarranted state intervention. Employers soon changed their tune, however, seeing decentralization as a means to increase flexibility and boost competitiveness, and pushed for further reform in the following decades. The state responded by trying to exchange greater flexibility for social progress in the workplace, for example, through the decentralized implementation of a reduction in working time at the turn of the century. Unions, on the other hand, found it difficult to adapt due to their previous neglect of workplace issues, their concentration on national political change and consequent weakness at workplace level (Parsons 2005). In common with other countries, the result has undoubtedly been a shift in the balance of power to employers.

Part of the explanation for this shift has to be that, in the terms of the 'varieties of capitalism' (VoC) literature, privatization, deregulation, European integration – particularly competition policy – and institutional reform all mean that the French coordinated market economy is less coordinated than it was at the end of the 1970s. This is not to say that it has moved into the liberal market economy camp; the French state still has a major influence over the conduct of industrial relations in France, and not only through legislative reform. It wields great influence in wage setting through control of the minimum wage and of wages in the public sector, in which, despite the privatization programmes of the 1980s and 1990s, 26.2 per cent of employees still worked at the end of 2008 (Brenot-Ouldali 2010). Economic strategies have protected some public utilities, such as gas and electricity, from privatization, while legislative reform can be seen to be attempting to reinforce the legitimacy of trade unions, and extending the link between them and employees in small enterprises where they have no presence. In effect, state intervention is still needed to compensate for weak union structures and bargaining power.

This shift towards less state coordination can also be explained by regulation theory (Boyer 1988; Howell 1992). Like VoC theory, the core of regulation theory centres on institutional arrangements, but the focus is on the implications of these for labour regulation. Thus, a particular pattern, or regime, of capital accumulation corresponds to a set of institutions – a mode of regulation – necessary for that accumulation to take place. In France, as in other systems since the Second World War, there has been a shift from Fordist to post-Fordist modes of regulation. Under Fordism, workers exchanged any claim to control of the workplace and accepted industrial modernization, essentially in the form of Taylorism, for the higher wages and greater social protection afforded by productivity gains. This 'Fordist compromise' depended upon an 'intensive' regime of accumulation, or the deepening of domestic markets for national production. As the national workforce was the primary consumer of national production, the maintenance of domestic demand through Keynesian economic management was the focus of government macro-economic policy. Union militancy could be bought off through wage and non-wage gains for labour. While this system was already under strain from the late 1960s due to inflation and the unwillingness of the workforce to put up with managerial authoritarianism combined with the monotony of assembly-line production – as witnessed in the 1968 strike wave – the growing international openness of the economy from the 1970s onwards tore it asunder.

As a result of greater international economic interdependency and competition, the link between domestic wages and company profitability was broken. In effect, wages were no longer seen as a source of future profit, but measured in terms of cost. As President Mitterrand found in 1981–2, domestic reflationary strategies now sucked in imports rather than stimulating domestic profits and growth. In response, the macro-economic policy of governments of all hues focused on international competitiveness rather than domestic demand to stimulate growth and create jobs. In regulation theory terms, export-oriented growth meant a shift in the regime of accumulation away from intensive towards extensive accumulation, that is, the expansion of French capitalism into new areas of the globe. The mode of regulation therefore underwent change in the direction of 'micro-corporatism' whereby workers are organized into a 'firm-wide collectivity' and corporatist-style bargaining occurs within the firm, resulting in a 'decapitation' of firm-level structures from the wider regulatory environment. The result is a 'structural bias towards cooperation' which is 'centred around the needs of the firm' as workers are integrated into it. This is achieved not only through HR policies, but also through decentralization and the extension of non-union forms of bargaining as well as greater employment flexibility (Howell 1992: 24, 2009).

While the micro-corporatism thesis undoubtedly describes the general trend in French employment relations, it does not tell the whole story. First, the external legal environment, and therefore the state, cannot be sidelined as easily as the micro-corporatist argument implies. The state has had to legislate for decentralized bargaining to take place, and laws on representativeness give the state a major role in conferring legitimacy on industrial relations actors at the local, as well as national, level. Although streamlined compared with its predecessors, the revamped French Labour Code that came into force in May 2008 still contains some 10,000 articles covering all aspects of the employment relationship (EIRO 2008). Moreover, as the collective strength of labour has diminished, workers have increasingly turned to industrial tribunals to seek satisfaction of their grievances, often with the backing of unions. In 1995, industrial tribunals dealt with more than 155,000 new cases, with only 2,000 of these brought by employers. With tribunals seemingly overburdened due to the rise in cases over the previous decade, the government sought other means of resolving disputes, legislating for 'legal mediation' in 1995 (EIRO 2004). Nevertheless, the number of new cases before the tribunals continued to rise, reaching a peak of 225,000 in 2002, and 202,000 in 2008 (Ministère de la Justice et des Libertés 2006: 37; 2010: 41). Finally, national political reforms to social security and pension systems will also impact upon labour markets and the regulation of labour and, therefore, local employment conditions. Thus, employment relations remain embedded in a wider political and institutional environment.

Furthermore, micro-corporatist theory assumes a bias towards cooperation and therefore cannot explain the enduring association of conflict with bargaining or the propensity to protest witnessed in France. Although strike levels are historically low, their number has been underestimated in official statistics (Carlier 2008), while radical action still occurs sporadically and is seen as legitimate. In effect, what is needed is an approach that takes account not only of the institutional and political framework within which employment relations are conducted, but also its ideational environment. Such an approach is offered by historical institutionalism, which argues that 'understanding change lies in the intersection of ideas and institutions and the tension between ideological traditions and institutional capacities' (Lieberman 2002: 709).

In France, then, early repression of the labour movement on the part of employers and the state combined with the structural weakness of a minority working class to result in a radical politicized trade union movement that drew on a revolutionary tradition going back to 1789 to present a revolutionary, if necessary violent, overthrow of capitalism as the only means of achieving the emancipation of the working class. This state and employer strategy of 'labour exclusion' (Ross 1982) persisted after the Second World War in a mutually reinforcing relationship with radicalism as the CGT emerged as the most powerful union confederation and the state adopted a technocratic approach to economic and industrial policymaking. With a pro-Communist confederation dominant in a divided, fragmented and generally weak union movement, corporatism was never an option for the state, which acted as a substitute for collective bargaining in its self-proclaimed role of guardian of the general interest. Faced with a dominant union that denied the legitimacy of capitalist relations of production, employers refused dialogue. As a result, the state became the focal point of a highly centralized, politicized and conflictual industrial relations system. Thus, labour, employer and state traditions, ideologies and strategies interacted to produce a weak institutional architecture for the conduct of industrial relations, with outcomes more dependent upon '"raw" power relations' (Ferner and Hyman 1992: xxxiv) than any search for consensus in the name of productive efficiency. Indeed, according to Borrel (1996), the non-market reforms associated with the construction of the French welfare state were the result of worker protest rather than of any search for consensus.

This mode of development has created certain path dependencies. Thus, the state, in its guise as incarnation of the general will and guardian of the French 'social model' – involving high levels of state economic intervention and public spending to correct market dysfunctions – cannot subscribe wholeheartedly to MEDEF's demands for a neo-liberal accommodation to globalization. Instead it hesitates between decentralized labour regulation and social interventionism, while arguing for 'managed' globalization. State strategies here are also informed by the wider intellectual debate in France about, and scepticism over, globalization, which has been more intense than elsewhere, sparked more protest and entered the political mainstream (Hay and Rosamond 2002; Waters 2010). This also means that the state still has to attempt to shore up a weak labour movement, presently through legislation aimed at improving the representativeness and legitimacy of unions, in order that flexibility in the workplace is achieved through negotiation and social compromise rather than unilaterally imposed by employers.

Unions remain weak, however, not only due to wider structural changes, but also because the legacy of politicization, and current divisions, represent a brake on recruitment despite a generally favourable public impression of them. In one survey, 58 per cent of respondents had confidence in unions and 70 per cent found them effective, but 61 per cent felt they were 'too ideological' and 76 per cent 'too divided' (MonSondage 2008). The free-rider problem and division are certainly part of the explanation here, but so too is a historical dependency upon committed activists, who join out of ideological affinity. The result is that unions are slow to change – or at least are seen to be so – while negotiated reform is difficult due to the structural imbalance in power in the bargaining relationship and owing to union, especially CGT, concerns not to cede that which has been gained through struggle. In consequence, collective bargaining is still associated with conflict, despite the greater institutionalization of employment relations in France since the early 1980s (Carlier and Naboulet 2009; Parsons 2012). Likewise the effectiveness of street protest and 'days of action' are also increasingly called into question as unions appear unable to prevent reforms of the social protection system in the face of economic globalization and crisis. As a result, at times of crisis, workers engage in radical action outside of their union structures, legitimizing their action through appeals to long-standing traditions of militancy and notions such as fairness and equality of treatment in the face of crisis. During the spate of 'bossnappings' that occurred in 2009–10, the state was unable to act for two reasons that amply demonstrate the importance of ideas in industrial relations actions and outcomes. First, President Sarkozy portrayed the crisis as one caused by an 'Anglo-Saxon' form of deregulated capitalism operating at a global scale, and of which the protesting workers were the victims. Second, this framing of the crisis as a result of 'Anglo-Saxon' globalization, together with pre-existing fears over the consequences of globalization, legitimized the militant action in the eyes of a majority of the population (Parsons 2012).

Conclusion

French employment relations have undergone significant decentralization and flexibilization since the early 1980s. Paradoxically, as part of this movement, the institutional position of unions has improved, but they have become structurally weaker. Furthermore, collective bargaining still appears to be associated with conflict, suggesting that consensual bargaining is weakly embedded in France, while traditions of radicalism live on among French workers, with the development of new radical trade unions and sporadic outbursts of highly militant action. This apparent paradox of greater institutionalization and continued conflict cannot be easily understood without an analysis, not only of the regulatory institutions of collective bargaining and employee representation, but also of the traditions, ideologies and strategies of unions, employers and the state. Indeed, the tension between the social movement vocation of unions that stems from the historical conditions of their formation and their consequent traditions of action, on the one hand, and their increasingly institutionalized, regulatory role, on the other, is crucial for understanding the development and current predicament of trade unions and industrial relations in France. This notion of unions as incarnations and purveyors of ideas must also be applied to the state and the employers to understand the often conflictual interactions of the actors in, and difficult institutionalization of, the French employment relations system. This is not to underestimate the role of external factors such as globalization, which have shifted power more firmly to capital. These factors are undoubtedly important, but the integration of such factors into an historical institutionalist approach, where strategies and ideologies are part of the analysis, provides greater explanatory power to any attempt to explain the trajectory and current state of employment relations in France.

Notes

1 The term 'Jacobin' emerged in the 1789 French Revolution to denote a member of the Jacobin Club, a revolutionary far-Left movement named after the St Jacques convent in Paris where it first met. In modern France, Jacobin refers to the concept of a highly centralized republic with power concentrated in the hands of the national government.

2 ISO is the International Organization for Standardisation whose national branches issue certificates to firms that comply with its quality management processes.

References

Andolfatto, D. (2007) 'Syndicalisation', in *L'Etat de la France 2007–2008*, Paris: Editions La Découverte et Syros.

Béroud, S. (2005) *Les Robins des bois de l'energie*. Paris: Le Cherche Midi.

——, Yon, K., Dressen, M., Gantois, M., Guillaume, C. and Kesselman, D. (2011) *La Loi du 20 Août 2008 et ses implications sur les pratiques syndicales en entreprise: Sociologie des appropriations pratiques d'un nouveau dispositif juridique*, Paris: DARES, Rapport de Recherche, halshs-00609506.

Borrel, M. (1996) *Conflits du travail, changement social et politique en France depuis 1950*, Paris: L'Harmattan.

Boyer, R. (1988) 'Wage/labour relations, growth and crisis: a hidden dialectic', in R. Boyer (ed.) *The Search for Labour Market Flexibility: The European Economies in Transition*, Oxford: Clarendon Press.

Brenot-Ouldali, A. (2010) 'L'emploi public dans l'emploi total', in Ministère du Budget, des Comptes Publics, de la Fonction Publique et de la Réforme de l'Etat, *Rapport annuel sur l'état de la fonction publique*, vol. 1: *Faits et chiffres*, Paris: La Documentation Française.

Carlier, A. (2008) *Mesurer les grèves dans les entreprises: des données administratives aux données d'enquêtes*, Paris: DARES, Documents d'Etudes No. 139.

—— and Naboulet, A. (2009) 'Négociations collectives et grèves dans les entreprises du secteur marchand en 2007', *Premières Synthèses*, 18(2), Paris: DARES.

Chevalier, F. and Mansuy, A. (2009) 'Une photographie du marché du travail en 2008. Résultats de l'enquête emploi', *INSEE Première*, No. 1272. Paris: INSEE.

Dassault, S. (2007) *Quelle efficacité des contrats aidés de la politique de l'emploi?*, Paris: République Française, Rapport d'information de M. Serge DASSAULT, fait au nom de la Commission des Finances no. 255 (2006–2007), 21 February.

Dunlop, J. (1958) *Industrial Relations Systems*, New York: Henry Holt.

EIRO (European Industrial Relations Observatory) (2004) *Thematic Feature: Individual Labour/Employment Disputes and the Courts*. Available at: http://www.eurofound.europa.eu/eiro/2004/03/tfeature/fr0403107t.htm (accessed 18 January 2012).

—— (2008) *New User-Friendly Labour Code Comes into Force*. Available at: http://www.eurofound.europa.eu/eiro/2008/06/articles/fr0806019i.htm (accessed 18 January 2012).

Ferner, A. and Hyman, R. (1992) 'Introduction: industrial relations in the new Europe', in R. Hyman and A. Ferner (eds) *Industrial Relations in the New Europe*, Oxford: Blackwell.

Fonction Publique (2011) *François Sauvadet annonce les résultats définitifs des élections professionnelles dans la Fonction Publique de l'Etat et la composition du prochain conseil supérieur de la Fonction Publique de l'Etat*. Available at: http://www.fonction-publique.gouv.fr/ministre/presse/communiques-355 (accessed 22 May 2012).

Gildea, R. (1996) *France Since 1945*, Oxford: Oxford University Press.

Goetschy, J. and Rozenblatt, P. (1992) 'France: the industrial relations system at a turning point?', in A. Ferner and R. Hyman (eds) *Industrial Relations in the New Europe*, Oxford: Blackwell.

Hay, C. and Rosamond, B. (2002) 'Globalisation, European integration and the discursive construction of economic imperatives', *Journal of European Public Policy*, 9(2): 147–67.

Hocblat, N. (2007) 'Politique macroéconomique. Une mise en perspective', in *L'Etat de la France 2007–2008*, Paris: Editions La Découverte et Syros.

Howell, C. (1992) *Regulating Labor: The State and Industrial Relations Reform in Postwar France*, Princeton, NJ: Princeton University Press.

—— (2009) 'The transformation of French industrial relations: labor representation and the state in a post-dirigiste era', *Politics and Society*, 37(2): 229–56.

INSEE (National Institute of Statistics and Economic Studies) (201la) *Taux de chômage*. Available at: http://www.insee.fr/fr/themes/tableau.asp?reg_ id=98&ref id=CMPDD004 (accessed 22 May 2012).

—— (2011b) *Emploi total par grand secteur dans l'Union Européenne*. Available at: http://www.insee.fr/fr/themes/tableau.asp?reg_id=98&ref_id=CMPTEF03136 (accessed 23 January 2012).

—— (2011c) *Taux de chômage depuis 1975*. Available at: http://www.insee.fr/fr/themes/tableau.asp?reg_id=0&ref_id–ATnon03337 (accessed 14 February 2012).

Kerr, C., Dunlop J. T., Harbison F. H. and Myers, C. A. (1960) *Industrialism and Industrial Man*, Cambridge, MA: Harvard University Press.

Knapp, A. and Wright, V. (2006) *The Government and Politics of France*, 5th edn, New York: Routledge.

Larose, C., Béroud, S., Mouriaux, R. and Rabhi, M. (2001) *Cellatex: Quand l'acide a coulé*, Paris: Editions Syllepse/Editions VO.

Lieberman, R. C. (2002) 'Ideas, institutions and political order: explaining political change', *American Political Science Review*, 96(4): 697–712.

Magraw, R. (1992) *A History of the French Working Class*, vol. 2: *Workers and the Bourgeois Republic*, Oxford: Blackwell.

Milner, S. (2002) 'France in historical perspective: the impossibility of partnership', in S. Berger and H. Compston (eds) *Policy Concertation and Social Partnership in Western Europe: Lessons for the 21st Century*, New York: Berghahn Books.

Ministère de la Justice et des Libertés (2006) *Annuaire Statistique de la Justice 2006*, Paris: La documentation Française.

—— (2010) *Annuaire Statistique de la Justice 2009–2010*, Paris: La documentation Française.

Ministère du Travail, de l'Emploi et de la Santé (2011) *La négociation collective en 2010*, Paris: Ministère du Travail, de l'Emploi et de la Santé.

MonSondage (2008) '61% des salariés reprochent aux syndicats d'être trop idéologiques'. Available at: http://www.mon-sondage.com/Sondage/445/61-des-salaries-reprochent-aux-syndicats-d-etre-trop-ideologiques.html (accessed 25 January 2012).

Nouvel Observateur (2009) 'Les salariés de new fabris décideront vendredi', *Nouvel Observateur*, 30 July 2009. Available at: http://tempsreel.nouvelobs.com/actualites/20090730.OBS5900/?xtmc=newfabris&xtcr=3 (accessed 24 November 2009).

OECD (Organization for Economic Cooperation and Development). Available at: http://stats.oecd.org/Index.aspx?Queryld=20167 (accessed 21 May 2012).

Parsons, N. (2002) 'France in the 1990s: still struggling with the weight of history', in S. Berger and H. Compston (eds) *Policy Concertation and Social Partnership in Western Europe: Lessons for the 21st Century*, New York: Berghahn Books.

—— (2005) *French Industrial Relations in the New World Economy*, London: Routledge.

—— (2012) 'Worker reactions to crisis: explaining "bossnappings"', *French Politics, Culture and Society*, 30(1): 111–30.

Pignoni, M-T. and Tenret, E. (2007) 'Présence syndicale: des implantations en croissance, une confiance des salariés qui ne débouche pas sur des adhésions', *Premières Synthèses*, No. 14(2), Paris: DARES.

Ross, G. (1982) 'The perils of politics: French unions and the crisis of the 1970s', in P. Lange, G. Ross and M. Vannicelli (eds) *Unions, Change and Crisis: French and Italian Unions and the Political Economy 1945–1980*, London: Allen and Unwin.

Rousseau, J-J. (1762) *Du Contrat social*, Paris: Garnier Flammarion (1966 edition).

van Ruysseveldt, J. and Visser, J. (1996) 'Contestation and state intervention forever? Industrial relations in France', in J. van Ruysseveldt and J. Visser (eds) *Industrial Relations in Europe: Traditions and Transitions*, London: Sage.

Venn, D. (2009) *Legislation, Collective Bargaining and Enforcement: Updating the OECD Employment Protection Indicators*, Paris: OECD, OECD Social, Employment and Migration Working Paper.

Waters, S. (2010) 'Globalization, the Confédération Paysanne and symbolic power', *French Culture, Politics and Society*, 82(2): 96–117.

Wolff, L. (2008) 'Le paradoxe du syndicalisme français: un faible nombre d'adhérants, mais des syndicats bien implantés', *Premières synthèses*, 16(1), Paris: DARES.

12 Germany

Martin Behrens

Introduction

For decades, employment relations in Germany have served as something of a role model for stability and orderliness. As Katzenstein put it in his seminal work, *Policy and Politics in West Germany*, this stability was the result of several factors:

> The reformist ideology and practices of unions that are centralized and leave little scope for rank-and-file militants; a well-institutionalized system of works councils which involves workers at the plant level; and laws that constrain what unions and business can do.
>
> (Katzenstein 1987: 126)

To understand where this system comes from and probably also where it is heading, it is important to take a brief look at German history. Many of the core features of German employment relations have their roots in the time of the Weimar Republic and even earlier, and most obviously this is true for multi-employer collective bargaining and works councils, the latter being based on the Works Council Law of 1920 (Müller-Jentsch 1995). It should be noted, however, that the shape and inner logic of the German industrial relations system were not established until the reconstruction of the country after the Second World War.[1] Core features not established until at least 1950 were the unified union movement and also the 'tamed' role of the German state. These new elements represent key lessons that important parts of German society (of course, critically informed by the occupying forces) had learned from the breakdown of the first German democracy – the Weimar Republic – and the resulting horrors of Nazi dictatorship and the Second World War.

Thus, the so-called autonomy of collective bargaining (*Tarifautonomie*) could be understood as a response to a close involvement of the state with collective bargaining, which during the years of the Weimar Republic seemed to have paralyzed the ability of unions and employers to bargain and to take responsibility for the results of bargaining. At that time, provisions which had entitled the state to issue binding arbitration verdicts (*Zwangsschlichtung*) had effectively reduced the ability of unions and employers to agree on terms and conditions of employment (Artus 2001: 55). The lesson drawn from this experience was embodied in Section 9 III of the 1949 Constitution of the Federal Republic of Germany which guaranteed the right to build associations for collective bargaining free from state interference. In addition, Section 4 I of the Collective Bargaining Act states that collective agreements have the direct and enforceable power to regulate the subjects covered by them.

Another lesson from the pre-war years concerns the structure of the German union movement, or to be more precise, the union movements. Up to the point when Hitler and his followers had effectively banned free unions and had collapsed all existing organizations into the 'Deutsche Arbeitsfront', the German labour movement had been split into three wings: a socialist/Communist, a liberal and a Christian union movement (Schneider 2000). Because these wings were often in conflict with each other (most dramatically after the break-up of the first and strongest wing into social-democratic and Communist organizations), they failed to build up effective resistance to the Nazi dictatorship. A more unified union movement, representing workers' interest within one but not three peak confederations, would – according to this perspective – have made it easier to give organized labour a powerful voice even in times of authoritarian rule. Consequently, when the occupying forces in the west and the east allowed unions to be reconstructed after the war, some of the key leaders of the Weimar unions, on their return from either prison or exile, created a unified union movement with the Federation of German Trade Unions, the Deutscher Gewerkschaftsbund (DGB), as its main key confederation (Jacoby 2000: Chapter 3).

In this sense, German industrial relations can be considered a 'late developer' in two different ways: first, because in Germany industrialization occurred comparatively late (1830–73), decades after the Industrial Revolution had shaken the United Kingdom, and, second, because major key elements of the German model of employment relations did not come into being before the mid-1950s, at the time when reconstruction of the country was well underway.

Core features of the post-war model

As we saw in the previous section, a unified union movement was one of the core features of German employment relations after its reconstruction. Until the late 1980s, the DGB had 16 affiliates, organizing workers in both the public and the private sectors. The most important function of these unions was, and probably still is, industry-wide collective bargaining with one of the approximately 700 employers associations, most of them directly or indirectly affiliated to the Confederation of German Employers (BDA) (Behrens 2011). Collective agreements were mostly negotiated for an entire industry within a certain region (in most cases this is one of the 16 German states (*Länder*)) but a few national-level agreements can be identified, for example, in banking but also in the public sector. The German Collective Bargaining Act (*Tarifvertragsgesetz*), however, also allows for company-level agreements to be negotiated between a union and a company's management. Today, when as a result of several mergers, the number of unions within the DGB has been reduced to eight, 36 per cent of establishments in west Germany and 20 per cent in east Germany are covered by a collective agreement (both types: industry- and plant-level) (Ellguth and Kohaut 2011: 243).[2] Because the likelihood of coverage increases along with company size, this leads to 63 per cent of all employees in west Germany and 50 per cent in east Germany being covered by a collective agreement. While, in general, multi-employer agreements are the most common form of collective agreement, single employer agreements also determine the wages, hours and working conditions of a significant number of employees. Such company-level (single employer) agreements, however, are more popular in east Germany than in the western parts of the country. In the east, 13 per cent of all employees are covered by a company agreement while for the west this share is just 7 per cent (ibid.: 243).

A second feature of the post-war model, which together with multi-employer collective bargaining constitutes the so-called 'dual system' of employment relations, is establishment-level interest representation through works councils (Frege 2002; Müller-Jentsch 2003). According to the Works Constitution Act, workers in establishments with more than five employees have the right to elect a works council. Once elected, works councils are entitled to a variety of codetermination rights, which include the right to information and consultation, but in some cases also more far-reaching participation rights. According to 2010 survey data, 10 per cent of all establishments (only those with more than five employees) had set up a works council. Because the overwhelming majority of the large establishments with 500 and more employees do have formal interest representation, 44 per cent of all workers are employed in an establishment with a works council (ibid.: 246).

Over a long period of time this dual system, with industry-level collective bargaining, on the one hand, and establishment-level codetermination, on the other, has structured German employment relations in a way that has separated different spheres of conflict. Conflicts over bread-and-butter issues such as wages, hours and working conditions, have been assigned to unions and employer associations, mostly operating at the industry-level, and generally occur in the form of strikes and lockouts. Because works councils are neither allowed to pursue collective bargaining nor to call a strike, they are able to enter rather peaceful negotiations with the individual establishment-level management. This does not mean, however, that there is no conflict to be found at the establishment level (Kotthoff 1981: 11). Indeed, there are still disputes over a variety of issues but they are 'constrained' in the sense that conflict is over different issues and there are different mechanisms through which they are dealt with and resolved. As works councils are not allowed to call a strike, they apply pressure on their particular employer by, for example, refusing to permit overtime work. In certain areas the Works Constitution Act assigns arbitration panels (*Einigungsstellen*) that have the task of resolving conflict with the help of a neutral chairperson assigned to wield the tie-breaking vote on such bi-partite panels (Behrens 2007).

The federal state, in turn, protects this system by enabling key actors to pursue their duties. The German Constitution and its interpretation by the Federal Constitutional Court (*Bundesverfassungsgericht*) as well as the Federal Labour Court (*Bundesarbeitsgericht*) support collective bargaining autonomy through major rulings. The state assists collective bargaining by way of providing statutory minimum standards for workers such as minimum vacation time but also by way of some welfare state regulation – most prominently the pay-as-you-go pension system, the unemployment insurance system and a mandatory health insurance system. While some of these benefits have been reduced since 2000 – a process which triggered protest from the trade unions – in most areas, the German welfare state still frees unions and employers from regulating welfare state issues through collective bargaining. For example, in contrast to their counterparts in the USA, German unions do not have to negotiate provisions for providing workers with elementary health insurance (although several German unions, however, have included provisions on supplementary private pensions in their collective agreements). While the state has an important role to play when it comes to regulating the welfare state, regulation in other areas is less comprehensive. Currently, there is no universal statutory minimum wage in Germany and, to the regret of most unions, there are only limited opportunities to extend collectively agreed wages to industries and workers which are not directly covered (*erga omnes extension*). This is in stark contrast to most other West European countries which do provide for the extension of collective agreements as well as minimum wages.

Key actors within the German system of employment relations

Trade unions

As shown in Figure 12.1, trade union membership within the major peak confederation has been in decline since the aftermath of German unification. It reached its peak in 1991, after west German unions extended their jurisdiction to the new east German states and organized 11.8 million members. This number had declined to 6.2 million by the end of the year 2011, almost cutting total DGB membership in half in just two decades.

This membership development also finds its expression in the figures on union density. While union density was approximately 35 per cent in the early 1980s, even under the conservative Christian Democrat Chancellor Helmut Kohl, elected in 1982, this changed only slightly. Density peaked at 36 per cent in 1991, the year after German unification, but the following two decades were marked by continuous decline.

A large part of the decline in the first half of the 1990s was the result of high union density in the eastern states (close to 100 per cent) falling to reach west German levels. For the years following this meltdown, however, scholars have identified several other reasons to account for unions' continuing membership loss. Among the most important factors that have been identified are the fading appeal of unions within the public debate (Pyhel 2006), the increased mobility of capital and workers as well as more flexible work organization (Fitzenberger *et al.* 2011: 160), the low level of perceived effectiveness of the unions and their reduced capacity for mass mobilization of workers (Dribbusch 2011: 232). In addition, changes in the average size of establishments and the growth of the private service sector (a sector with predominantly low union density) have also been associated with membership decline. In contrast, however, some authors have argued that some of the usual suspects, that is changes in the composition of workforce characteristics (full-time/part-time work, age, skill), have contributed little to explaining the fading membership strength of the unions (Figure 12.2) (Schnabel and Wagner 2007; Fitzenberger *et al.* 2011).

Among the DGB's eight affiliates, the metalworkers' union, IG Metall, and Ver.di, the United Services Union, are by far the largest unions, representing more than two-thirds of total DGB membership. As a product of several union mergers, starting with the creation of

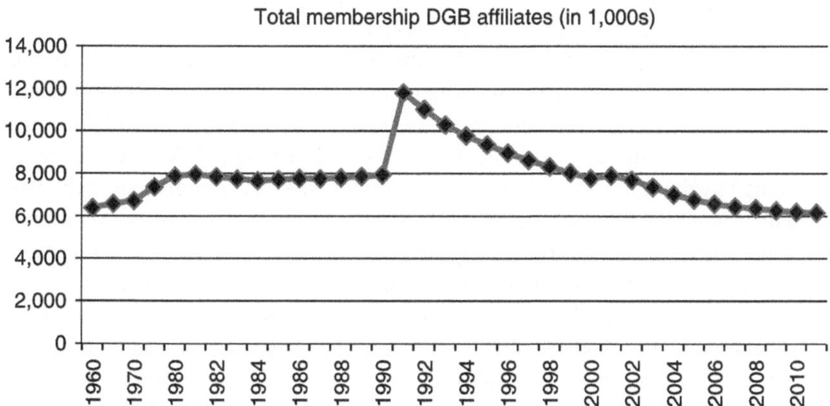

Figure 12.1 Total DGB membership, 1960–2010.

Source: Based on DGB data.

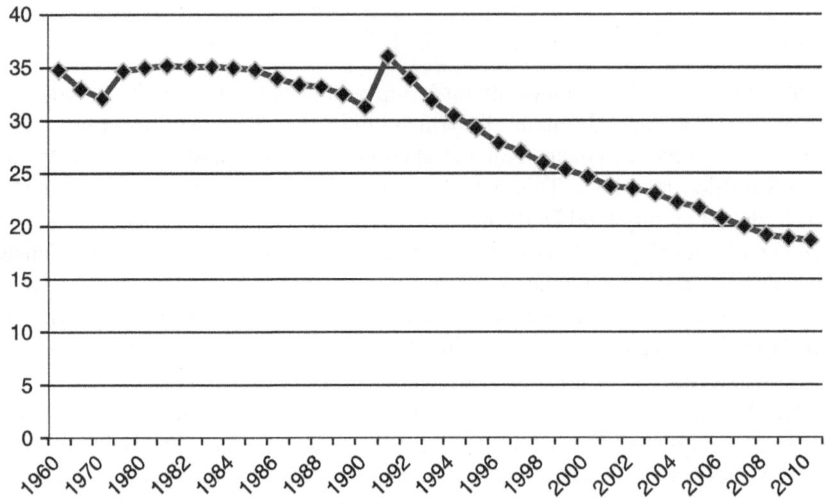

Figure 12.2 Net union density, 1960–2010, all unions (%)

Source: Based on ICTWSS database (Vissier 2011).

the media and print shop workers' union, IG Medien, in 1989 and including the creation of Ver.di (an amalgamation of five former independent unions) in 2001, union membership in Germany is now fairly concentrated in a small number of organizations (Waddington and Hoffmann 2005; Keller 2005). During a rather short period of just 12 years the number of independent affiliates of the DGB was halved, from 16 to 8. While the motivations of individual unions to engage in merger activity are quite diverse, ongoing membership decline during the 1990s and the financial hardship arising from this fact, have served as powerful facilitators to drive union mergers (Streeck and Visser 1997).

The system of a universal union movement, however, always did and still does have its exceptions. Even immediately after the reconstruction of German labour relations in the late 1940s, there were a number of independent labour organizations not affiliated to the main peak confederation, the DGB. The most prominent example was the German Federation of Career Public Servants (Deutscher Beamtenbund, dbb), with its 39 affiliates representing 1.25 million members. Most of these members are life-long public servants but there are also about 360,000 public sector employees with regular employment contracts (Dribbusch 2010: 25). While employment conditions for those regular employees are subject to collective bargaining, the wages, hours and working conditions for life-long public servants are unilaterally determined by the state.[3] While the bulk of former Christian Unionists from the Weimar years ended up joining the ranks of the DGB's affiliates, there also remained a smaller (rival) Christian Trade Union Confederation of Germany (CGB) with 17 affiliates and total membership of about 283,000 (in 2009). Finally, there are also about a dozen independent unions, which are not affiliated to any peak confederation. Only the Marburger Bund, the Hospital Doctors Trade Union, has membership higher than100,000, but despite most of these unions being very small, they have played an increasingly prominent role in recent collective bargaining campaigns (Schroeder *et al.* 2011). Small specialist unions such as the German union of air traffic controllers, GdF, the pilots' union, Cockpit, or the train conductors union, GDL (an affiliate of the dbb), although small in size, are very effective in achieving wage increases for employees within their small jurisdiction – in some cases, by far exceeding those increases negotiated by the DGB's affiliates (Keller 2009). The bargaining strategy applied by some independent occupational unions has recently been subject to some criticism. From a union perspective, a number of observers have argued that some of these contracts negotiated by small independent unions achieve benefits for a small group of privileged workers only, which are perceived to be at the expense of wage increases for other, less exclusive groups of workers within the broader jurisdiction. Because competing unions with overlapping collective bargaining jurisdictions have created more frequent strike activity in industries such as hospitals, air and rail transportation, representatives of the government and employers (for some time even supported by the DGB and some of its affiliates) have proposed new legislation to rule out unions competing for the same jurisdiction within collective bargaining units. At the time of writing (September 2012), the new 'Unity of Collective Bargaining' Bill (*Tarifeinheitsgesetz*) has been frozen after Ver.di, the DGB's second largest affiliate, decided to withdraw its support.

Employers

Traditionally, employers have played a very prominent role within the German system of employment relations. Due to the special system of industry-wide collective bargaining, employers' capacity to organize has been crucial in bringing collectively-agreed standards to a majority of German employees. Despite a union density of less than 20 per cent, it is still the case that more than 60 per cent of all workers are covered by a collective agreement. In Germany, business interests are covered by two different systems of representation. First, there are product-market-related interests of business which are represented by business organizations, with the BDI, the Confederation of German Industry, being the national-level peak organization of those interests. Second, there is a system of representation for labour-market-related interests. About 700 employers associations and their national peak confederation, the BDA, are in charge of multi-employer collective bargaining. In some industries, there are also associations which represent both labour and product-market interests of companies within one organization. However, in most areas the separation into two separate systems of representation – at least up to now – remains in place (Schroeder and Weßels 2010).

Employers associations have something in common – they pursue a collective bargaining function vis-à-vis the unions but according to a variety of issues. Within the structure of the BDA we find small associations side by side with some heavyweights such as Gesamtmetall and its state-level affiliates, which represent employers in the automobile, metal, machine-tool and electronics industries, or the BAVC, representing employers in the chemical engineering industry. While the larger associations are usually equipped with sufficient resources and thus are able to provide their members with a broad spectrum of membership services, many of the smaller associations find it difficult to mobilize sufficient resources to hire staff to provide membership services beyond collective bargaining. Larger and more resourceful associations can support their members in a variety of ways. They not only negotiate collective agreements, they also provide the expertise to apply those agreements. For example, a number of affiliates of Gesamtmetall have hired engineers who assist companies in applying a new wage scale to their workforces and to assign new wage classifications to individual employees. Other services include advice in the area of labour and employment law (even representing companies' interests in the courtroom), assistance in public relations and the training of employees.

The most prominent task to be pursued by those associations, however, is still collective bargaining. This has slightly changed since the beginning of the 1990s when many associations started to introduce a so-called 'OT' membership status (Völkl 2002; Haipeter and Schilling 2006; Behrens 2011). 'OT' is the short form for 'without collective bargaining coverage' (*ohne Tarifbindung*) and means that those associations offer an opt-out clause to their membership. Individual companies are allowed to maintain membership of the association but are exempt from applying the terms and conditions of the industry-wide collective agreement to their workforce. As members, companies can still benefit from all the other services provided by that association but are free to either determine standards for wages, hours and working conditions with workers individually or to negotiate a separate company-level collective agreement. Based on survey data, it is estimated that between a third and half of all German employers associations offer their members such an opt-out (Behrens and Helfen 2010; Behrens 2011). As Table 12.1 shows, at least in the case of Gesamtmetall, one of the BDA's largest and most powerful affiliates, the use of bargaining-free (OT) membership status is becoming increasingly popular among member companies. After its introduction in the mid-2000s, OT membership status expanded within Gesamtmetall and in fact accounts for the association's entire membership growth in the second half of the decade. In 2010, the last year for which data are available, more than 42 per cent of all member companies have the 'bargaining-free' status. When looking at the right side of Table 12.1 (the final three columns) it also becomes apparent that OT-membership status is an issue for small and medium-sized firms rather than for large companies: in 2010, while representing 42.3 per cent of all member companies, OT firms only accounted for 16.5 per cent of all employees employed by Gesamtmetall's member firms.

Government

The government's role in employment relations is restricted in the sense that the state's ability to interfere with issues of collective bargaining is limited by the German Constitution and the famous concept of 'bargaining autonomy' (*Tarifautonomie*). As Katzenstein (1987) has described it, along with federalism and coalition government, this strong role of autonomous 'para-public' institutions constitutes what he calls a 'semi-sovereign' state. This limit on government power does not mean, however, that German employment relations are free of state influence. Indeed, the state plays a dominant role in shaping what is known as the German 'Bismarckian' welfare state, with its four pillars: the unemployment insurance system, the old-age pension system, the health insurance, and the social care insurance, the latter system being the most recent addition to the welfare state (created in 1995) and which pays for the care of patients in need. While the four pillars are administered by tripartite bodies (operating under public law and public control) rather than by the state itself, state law is crucial in deciding the contributions individual employees and employers pay into that system as well as the benefits received by employees who are covered by the system. Also, through changes in the Works Constitution Act (first enacted in 1952), the state has massively affected works councils' ability to represent workers' interest at the establishment level on several occasions in post-war history. Major reforms occurred in the years 1972 and 2001, in both cases initiated by a government under social-democratic leadership.

After the Second World War, the German unions were reconstructed as a uniform movement (*Einheitsgewerkschaft*) without separate peak confederations for different political orientations. The DGB and its affiliates therefore include in their ranks workers with different party affiliations. While we find a large number of union members who belong to either the

Table 12.1 Membership development of Gesamtmetall, 2000–2010

	Total membership (firms)	*Firms (with CB coverage)*	*Firms (without CB coverage)*	*Share OT/total membership (firms) (%)*	*Total number of employees*	*Number of employees (with CB coverage)*	*Number of employees (without CB coverage)*	*Share OT/total membership (employees) (%)*
2000	6,252	6,252	0	0	2,122,472	2,122,472	0	0
2001	6,093	6,093	0	0	2,103,799	2,103,799	0	0
2002	5,704	5,704	0	0	2,061,622	2,061,622	0	0
2003	5,109	5,109	0	0	1,922,167	1,922,167	0	0
2004	4,774	4,774	0	0	1,859,026	1,859,026	0	0
2005	5,861	4,429	1,432	24.4	1,986,792	1,822,441	164,351	8.3
2006	6,113	4,214	1,899	31.1	2,003,115	1,779,145	223,970	11.2
2007	6,321	4,017	2,304	36.4	2,065,812	1,775,620	290,192	14.0
2008	6,366	3,897	2,469	38.8	2,101,471	1,772,173	329,298	15.7
2009	6,334	3,789	2,545	40.2	2,016,986	1,698,738	318,248	15.8
2010	6,437	3,712	2,725	42.3	2,025,127	1,690,310	334,817	16.5

Source: Gesamtmetall, own calculations.

Social Democratic Party (SPD), the Christian Democratic Party (CDU), the Greens (Bündnis 90/Die Grünen, founded 1980) or the new Left Party (Die Linke, founded 2007), there traditionally existed something which was called a 'privileged partnership' between the unions and the SPD (Schroeder 2005, 2008), a close relationship which has even led some observers to claim that both are 'Siamese twins' (Ebbinghaus 1995). The share of union members within the SPD is particularly high. According to a recent (2009) survey among members of German parties, 42 per cent of SPD members held a union card, while this share was only 13 per cent for CDU members. Union members represented 26 per cent of Green Party membership and 32 per cent of Die Linke membership (Klein 2011: 53). This data on cross-membership between the SPD and the unions might explain why, despite holding on to the concept of *Einheitsgewerkschaft*, labour's hopes for worker and union-friendly policies have always been particularly high at times when the SPD has been in government. Indeed, we find major pro-labour reforms of the Works Constitution Act at times when the Chancellor came from the SPD (1969–82, the Brandt and Schmidt governments, and the Schröder government, 1998–2005).

During the Schröder administration, the party–union relationship came under severe strain. With a series of labour market reforms, known as the Hartz laws (named after Peter Hartz, at that time Volkswagen's leading HR executive and chairman of a commission on labour market reforms), the Social Democrats aimed to make the German labour market more flexible (Bothfeld *et al.* 2009). Among other elements, the reforms included an easing of the rules surrounding agency work, cuts in unemployment benefits for some recipients, and increasing demands on the unemployed to seek new employment, the latter being famously framed as a strategy of 'encouraging and challenging' ('*fördern und fordern*'). In the case of agency work, the new law now enables employment agencies to hire agency workers on a fixed-term basis, to match the duration of the agency workers' work contracts with the time they are hired out to other employers and finally to relax restriction on the maximum duration of employment with those employers (previously two years). For the majority of workers, unemployment benefits which are a fixed percentage of employees' earlier income are paid for the duration of one year maximum. After this year, unemployed persons are transferred to a secondary scheme which is commonly known as 'Hartz IV'. These recipients receive housing subsidies plus a fixed sum to cover the costs of living (currently €374 per month for an adult recipient) but are also subject to stiff fines if they do not collaborate with the employment agency or refuse to accept a job offer. Along with other measures, such as raising the retirement age from 65 to 67 and introducing an additional (private) pension scheme, these Schröder and post-Schröder years (the first grand-coalition of CDU and SPD under Chancellor Merkel) have marked a watershed in the privileged partnership between the SPD and the unions, with some member unions within the DGB emphasizing their autonomy vis-à-vis partisan politics.

It should be noted, however, that this alienation between the unions and the SPD was far from being complete. Three reasons may account for this: first, when the Social Democrats were voted out of office in 2009, they were eager to reach out again to the unions. Second, because a significant share of SPD activists maintains a dual membership as a party and a union member, this relationship – even when it came under strain during the Schröder years – found strong institutional support. Finally, the federal structure of the German state had always provided unions with multiple opportunities of collaboration so that multiple patterns of union–party relations could be maintained. While the lion's share of policies which are significant for unions is located at the federal level, some issues can also be regulated by the state (*Länder*) governments. Among other issues, this is true for public procurement laws and the extension of collective agreements but also to some degree for policies aiming at the structural development of particular industries.

Despite this privileged partnership with the SPD, German unions have sought to maintain collaborative relations with governments at several levels, even at times when the SPD was part of the opposition camp. During the recent world financial crisis, for example, with a centre-right coalition government led by Chancellor Merkel in office, unions have been engaged in talks with the government to try to facilitate increased use of state-subsidized short-term work as well to help set up a government programme to subsidize the purchase of smaller, more fuel-efficient cars. Most scholars seem to agree that short-term work and also more flexible work-time regimes negotiated between works councils and plant management have significantly enabled the creation of what is known as the 'German job miracle' (remarkable employment stability at times of the most severe recession in Germany's post-war history) (Zapf and Herzog-Stein 2011). Yet there is still dispute as to whether the labour market flexibilization brought on by the Hartz reforms has contributed significantly to the good performance of the German labour market during the crisis that began in 2008–09 (Herzog-Stein *et al.* 2010).

Employment relations processes and outcomes: general trends and developments

During the past two decades and even beyond, German employment relations have been subject to several processes of change through decentralization, growing inequality and Europeanization and all three phenomena have been at the centre of academic debate.

Decentralization

Issues of decentralization mostly occur within the dual system, which is at the heart of German employment relations. When scholars talk about decentralization, they usually mean a process through which competences are transferred from the industry or national level to the company or establishment level, with de-unionization being the most extreme form of bargaining structure decentralization (Katz 1993: 12). Observations of decentralization mostly refer to the area of collective bargaining where it is assumed that powers to determine wages, hours and working conditions by establishment-level actors such as works councils, workers and management, have been increased at the expense of industry-level actors such as unions and employers associations. Decentralization has different aspects, but it also takes different forms. Focusing on the ways in which decentralization emerges, scholars differentiate between 'organized' and 'disorganized' decentralization (Traxler 1995) or 'controlled' and 'wildcat' decentralization respectively (Bispinck and Schulten 1999). Organized decentralization involves the deliberate delegation of bargaining tasks to the lower level, whereas disorganized decentralization has frequently involved either outright labour market deregulation or the withdrawal of key collective actors, such as employers, from older, more centralized system (Traxler 1995: 6–7).

Organized decentralization first originated in the mid-1980s, when IG Metall introduced new terms into its famous collective agreement on the introduction of the 35-hour working week. The agreement included a clause which allowed company-level actors to more flexibly adjust working time regimes to the needs of the company (Schmidt and Trinczek 1986; Thelen 1991). Following this first 'opening clause', all German unions have subsequently included such clauses into their industry-wide agreements: allowing for more flexibility in adjusting collectively agreed standards to the specific conditions at the establishment level and thus in many cases empowering works councils to take on bargaining responsibilities. Most frequently, such opening clauses allow for the adjustment of collectively agreed standards for working time and the annual bonus but in some cases wages have also been included (Bispinck and Schulten 2011). Also, to safeguard jobs in times of crisis, unions and employers have frequently negotiated agreements in the context of company-level 'Pacts for employment and competitiveness'. Such agreements (in many cases based on opening clauses or even separate company-level collective agreements) included concessions from unions and works councils in exchange for job guarantees (Seifert and Massa-Wirth 2005; Rehder 2006).

Disorganized decentralization occurred in the context of the declining ability of employers associations to organize a stable share of their constituency. As shown in Figure 12.3, the share of the German workforce which is covered by an industry-wide collective agreement has been declining since 1995 (the first year for which data are available) although in west Germany the decline seem to have halted during the last four years.

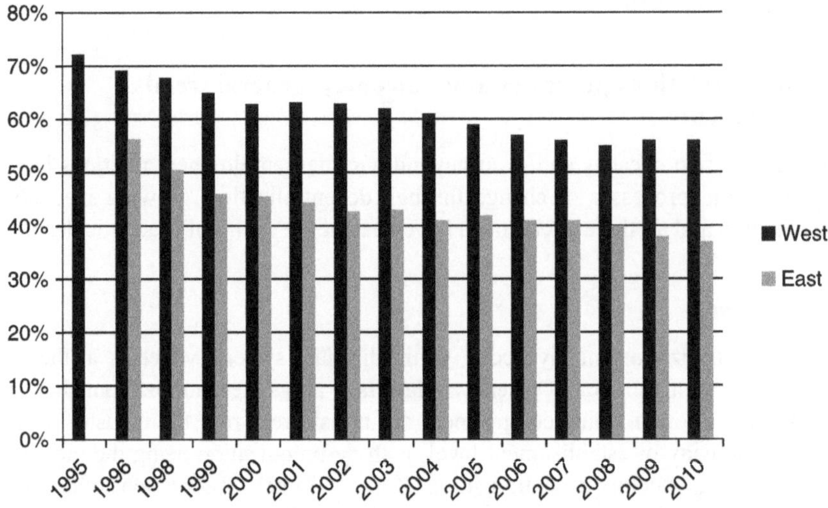

Figure 12.3 Collective bargaining coverage, 1995–2010 (employees covered by industry-level agreements in East and West Germany).

Source: IAB Establishment Panel, various years (Ellguth 2011).

There are various reasons for this type of disorganized decentralization. During the years following German unification, many companies left employers associations because they were dissatisfied with the results of collective bargaining, but later decline was due more to the declining ability of associations to recruit new companies into the organization. When in the mid-1990s the first associations started to offer companies a so-called 'bargaining-free' (OT) membership status, this policy also contributed to the decline of bargaining coverage.

Growing inequality

Until the mid-1990s, wages in Germany were quite compressed, with a relatively small gap between earnings at the upper and lower ends of the income distribution. One common measure to express wage inequality is the D9/D1 ratio (sometimes called the 90:10 ratio) which measures how many times the incomes of employees at the 9th decile of the distribution exceeds the income of workers at the 1st decile. According to this measure, wage inequality rises along with an increasing D9/D1 ratio. In 1989, German wages at the 9th decile were 2.84 times those at the 1st decile, but by 1999 the ratio had increased to 3.12; by 2005 it had risen still further to 3.44, matching inequality levels in the UK (Schettkat 2007: 338–9). Other calculations – using the Gini coefficient – also show increasing income inequality, which grew substantially between 1991 and 2005 before entering a period of stability between 2005 and 2009 (Sachverständigenrat zur Begutachtung der Gesamtwirtschaftlichen Entwicklung 2011: 338). Closer analysis reveals that the growth of inequality in Germany is mostly due to the growing low-wage sector (Kalina and Weinkopf 2012). According to data for 2010, 23.1 per cent of all employees earn less than two-thirds of the national median wage (which is the common definition of a 'low wage') – more than a 5 per cent increase when compared with data for the year 1995 (ibid.). In addition, 12 per cent earn less than 50 per cent of the median wage (the 'poverty wage') (George 2011: 551). Even when we focus on employees working full-time, the proportion of employees earning a low wage is substantial: 15.3 per cent for German men and 21 per cent for women (ibid.: 554).

While there are many reasons that account for low-wage income and resulting from this, increasing inequality of income, two root causes deserve particular attention. First, as pointed out in the previous section, declining collective bargaining coverage (in west Germany alone a decline of 16 percentage points during the past 15 years) along with declining union power has muted the ability of unions to raise collectively agreed wages above the low-wage level. Second, a series of labour market reforms known as the Hartz laws has improved the ability of employers to take advantage of atypical employment, which is associated with low-wage income (Brehmer and Seifert 2008; Wingerter 2009). For example, there has been a massive increase of so-called mini-jobs which, in 2009, numbered close to seven million (Keller and Seifert 2011: 14). This new type of job, with a monthly income of below €450 and for which no social security contributions have to be paid, had been introduced in 2003 with the aim of making the German labour market more flexible (Voss and Weinkopf 2012). Other labour market reforms (all data for 2009) eased the use of agency work (0.6 million jobs), part-time work (9.1 million jobs), fixed-term work (3 million jobs) and individual self-employment (2.4 million jobs) (Keller and Seifert 2011: 14). Compared with the year 2003, the most dramatic increase was in the case of agency work (+ 86.5 per cent) followed by part-time work (+ 26.6 per cent) and self-employment (+ 20.2 per cent). During the same time period (2003–09) total employment increased by only 6.7 per cent (ibid.).

Europeanization

As Marginson and Sisson (2006:1) claim, the term 'European social model' has acquired widespread currency throughout Europe. In this sense the 'European social model' is understood to be a combination of fundamental principles within the policy domains of the following rights: to work, to social protection and to civilized standards in the workplace. While the focus of much European-level legislation was on implementing basic social standards in areas such as working time, health and safety and gender equality, a second focus was on providing new institutions to accompany the ongoing transnationalization of businesses.

The most important of these institutions are European Works Councils (EWCs) and worker representation on company boards as provided for by the European Company

Directive (SE). Currently there are 938 EWCs in Europe, about 160 of which operate in companies which have their headquarters in Germany (data for the year 2009, according to the European Works Council Database). Thus, close to a third of German multinational companies, which would be eligible to create an EWC actually do have one (Waddington 2011: 61). Compared with German national works councils, EWCs lack a number of more far-reaching participation rights, yet they still contribute a great deal to giving labour a voice within multinational corporations. In terms of their ability effectively to represent employees' interests, there is substantial variation ranging from what Kotthoff (2006) calls 'the toothless tiger', a deficient EWC type, to 'the actively participating committee' as a more effective type of employee representation. Within the latter group – as recent research has confirmed – there are some impressive examples of participation which far exceed the legal rights provided by the European Works Council Directive (Hauser-Ditz *et al.* 2010; Hertwig *et al.* 2010). For example, the activities of the Ford European Works Council exceed mere information and consultation rights by entering negotiations with the management side. The most important agreement resulting from those negotiations was the 'Agreement Governing the Separation of the Ford Visteon Organization' which was concluded in January 2000 and among other issues provides that workers transferred to Visteon enjoy the same basic standards in terms of wages, hours and working conditions as their fellow employees at Ford (Hauser-Ditz *et al.* 2010: 324–9).

While in the case of EWCs, institution building has aided transnational coordination of labour (Greer and Hauptmeier 2008), Europeanization also manifests itself in the context of voluntary coordination, most prominently on the issue of European collective bargaining (Schulten 2004, 2009). Such efforts at coordination have been pursued since the late 1990s (along with the introduction of the European Monetary Union) and are based on, first, an exchange of information on collective bargaining at the European level and, second, joint targets or even 'rules' to be followed in national collective bargaining (Erne 2008). Coordination is mostly pursued by the European Union confederations, such as the European Metalworkers' Federation (EMF) or the European Mine, Chemical and Energy Workers Federation (EMCEF)[4] , but there are, however, no powerful instruments to enforce compliance by the national unions to those rules.

The institution-building face of Europeanization and increased coordination of bargaining help organized labour to maintain relations with multinational companies as the 'key proponents of economic integration' (Marginson and Sisson 2006: 216). There is, however a second face of Europeanization, which is closely associated with the four key principles (or 'four freedoms') of the European Union, namely the free movement of goods, capital, services and people. For example, Höpner and Schäfer (2008: 14) have argued that we are witnessing a substantial shift in the balance of power between key actors within the European Union (EU), leading to increasing emphasis on liberalization. Indeed, recent developments reinforce the view that within the EU there has been a shift in the balance of power, strengthening the advocates of a free-market perspective. First, a series of decisions by the European Court of Justice (ECJ) have interfered with national-level union rights and labour market regulation. In the famous cases of *Viking* and *Laval*, the ECJ decided that strike activity by Finnish and Swedish unions violated European law (see Chapter 22 for a discussion). Although these decisions did not directly affect German unions, they did, however, spark a vibrant debate on the role of the ECJ, leading some commentators to argue for civil disobedience vis-à-vis the court. According to this view, EU member states should simply refuse to obey the ECJ's decisions (Scharpf 2008). Another prominent case, that of Rüffert, directly affected labour standards in Germany. In that case the court decided that the public procurement law in the state of Lower Saxony violated the principle of free exchange of services within the EU (Brunn *et al.* 2010; Bücker and Warneck 2010). As a consequence of the Rüffert decision, most German states which had public procurement laws have abandoned them or simply refused to apply them (Schulten and Pawicki 2008) and it has taken many years before those state legislatures have passed revised laws in line with the ECJ decision.

In essence, these developments prove that the impact of Europeanization on national employment relations is both ambivalent and heavily contested. On the one hand, Europe provides labour with an opportunity to build new transnational representative structures; on the other, the European Commission (and the European Council) are promoting the liberalization of national-level employment relations systems.

Theoretical perspectives

For some time, Germany has served as a paradigmatic case within the literature on 'Varieties of Capitalism' (VoC) and has been used as a proxy for a group of countries labelled 'coordinated market economies' (CMEs) (see Hall and Soskice 2001; Crouch 2005; Hall and Gingerich 2009). According to this approach, it has also been assumed that because of 'institutional complementarities' such models of national political economies are somewhat resistant to institutional change. As Turner (2009: 307) has argued:

> as global liberalization proceeds and competition intensifies, reforms become necessary and adjustments are made. But a central message of the literature [on 'varieties of capitalism'] is that 'the more things change, the more they stay the same'.

As was shown in the previous section, there are indeed important signs of change in terms of employment relations institutions and structures as well as outcomes. While the major institutions of multi-employer collective bargaining are still in place, we have seen a remarkable decentralization of selected responsibilities to the company- or establishment-level. We have also seen the birth of new European-level institutions which help labour to expand the range of activity to the transnational level. At the same time, however, we can also observe strong forces at the EU-level which challenge certain national institutions and are pushing towards liberalization. In the area of employment relations outcomes, we observe the erosion of important parts of the German 'high road' model (Turner 1991, 1998) sometimes described as a model of 'diversified quality production' (Streeck 1991) with its elements of (comparatively) high skills, high product quality, good pay and a high level of social equality. Studies reveal increasing levels of income inequality which are, to a large extent, caused by a growing low-wage sector.

But how can we understand change in German employment relations? As Doellgast and Greer (2007; and Greer 2008) have suggested, beyond the 'complementarities view' put forward by proponents of the VoC approach, there are two other popular perspectives on the German case. First, there is the 'disorganization perspective', as put forward by Lash and Urry (1987), who predict that, as a consequence of growing world markets, institutional structures and national wage coordination will collapse throughout the capitalist world. Second, there is a 're-embedding view' (Greer 2008: 182) which states that liberalization is always accompanied by counter-measures taken by society to balance the effects of free markets (Streeck and Thelen 2005: 4). When we confront the empirical evidence and the observations on changing employment relations in Germany presented in the previous section with the theoretically grounded predictions of the complementarities/stability, disorganization and re-embedding approaches, it is impossible to pick a winner. Decentralization of collective bargaining, significant increases in income inequality and liberalization approaches pursued by key European-level actors support neither the complementarities/stability view nor a blunt disorganization view which would assume that core industrial relations institutions would be disappearing. While this evidence might support the re-embedding view, it would still be open for debate whether proponents of re-embedding (for example, large companies) would be strong enough to diffuse stabilizing measures throughout the national political economy.

To further evaluate the chances of re-stabilization, we turn to the theoretical approaches put forward in Chapter 2 of this volume. Employment relations were essentially conceptualized as the product of a balance of power and it has been argued that three areas deserve particular attention when investigating employment relations: market forces, institutions, and actors' choices. From a disorganization perspective, one would assume that market forces gain importance at the expense of institutions, while, from a re-embedding perspective, one would expect to find institutional forces counter-balancing markets, and thus remaining in place or even gaining in importance. Whether institutions are downgraded vis-à-vis market forces or even gain importance, and which strategies key actors pursue within these developments, is a question to which we now turn.

Market forces

The German economy is strongly exposed to international competition and has been so for a long time. Germany has a strong competitive position in international product markets in manufacturing industries such as automobiles, machine tools and chemical products. Even at the start of the recent world financial crisis in 2008–09, companies such as VW, BASF and Mercedes were doing particularly well. It is remarkable that exactly those industries which are most heavily integrated into the global economy and which are most dependent on international markets are those with the strongest unions and also the strongest employment relations institutions. Union density in the chemical, automotive and machine tool industries is among the highest in the whole of Germany, in some cases only surpassed by some parts of public services and energy production. In addition, industry-wide collective agreements, works councils and even supervisory-board level codetermination are widespread within this part of the economy. In contrast, employment relations institutions and actors are weakest in private services, a sector which is mostly sheltered from international competition and dominated by small and medium-sized firms. Rapidly growing industries such as security and fitness studios are almost entirely without collective representation. Even in traditional industries such as hotels, restaurants and retail but also in formerly state-owned or regulated industries such as telecommunications, postal services and air transportation, unions, works councils and the institutions of collective bargaining are very weak and in some cases hardly exist at all. It seems to be counter-intuitive that employment relations are strongest in industries where international competition is most intense and weakest where domestic competitors dominate the market, and one explanation for this paradox might lie in the institutions of employment relations.

Institutions

Proponents of the complementarities/stability view have argued that certain combinations of institutions have the potential to support the competitive position of companies. Thus, in contrast to firms in the liberal market economies, German capital is 'patient' and oriented to longer-term returns on investment because of the supportive systems of employment relations, training and education, corporate governance and inter-firm relations and their associated competitive advantages (Hall and Soskice 2001: 22). Indeed, even without subscribing to a fully-fledged complementarities view, recent research on the German call centre industry reveals a positive association between the institutions of collective bargaining and establishment-level interest representation through works councils, on the one hand, and the adoption of high-involvement management practices, on the other (Doellgast 2008). These findings, however, do not explain why union density has been almost halved in just two decades and why collective bargaining coverage is in continuing decline, a process Anke Hassel (1999) has called the 'erosion' of German industrial relations. One root cause for this erosion might be structural changes within the German economy. Through ongoing restructuring, which in some cases might even lead to 'vertical disintegration' (Doellgast and Greer 2007), the average company size is in decline. Given that union density, collective bargaining coverage, and the existence of a works council are all positively associated with company size, it can hardly be surprising that restructuring is hurting the key institutions of German employment relations. This effect is not exclusively caused by management strategies of outsourcing units from large companies into independent small units; it is also the result of a process of rapid employment growth in the service sector, dominated as it is by small firms. While the growth of the private service sector is market-driven, the shrinking average firm size due to restructuring is surely management-driven and thus reflects actors' choices.

Actors' choices

From a theoretical perspective, actors in employment relations can be conceptualized in two different ways (see Chapter 2). The strategic choice perspective, as put forward by Kochan *et al.* (1986) has most prominently focused on management strategies and explained the transformation of US industrial relations, mostly with reference to the re-orientation of US top management, as seen in the relocation of production to the southern states in the USA or the introduction of sophisticated human resource management practices.

A second theoretical perspective is strongly informed by social movement theory and conceptualizes actors' choices in the context of their capacity for mobilization (Kelly 1998; Ganz 2000) and focuses on the ability of unions to mobilize workers for strikes or other forms of labour unrest. While both aspects are important in order to understand recent developments in German employment relations, it appears that in terms of the major changes such as collective bargaining decentralization but also labour market restructuring, it is business (single companies and employers associations) and the federal government which have taken the initiative: companies have decided to restructure their businesses (in some cases along a new production chain); employers' associations have introduced bargaining-free 'OT' membership; and the federal government has eased employers' opportunities to take advantage of atypical work such as agency work or 'mini-jobs'. While there are clear signs that businesses are making strategic choices, the mobilization by labour, the second aspect of the actor choice perspective is in most cases rather reactive and patchy.

Conclusion

As this brief account of the impact of markets, institutions and actors' choices indicates, there is little evidence that it is either pure market forces, unleashed by increasing global competition, which is driving the development of German employment relations, or complementary and strong institutions which are reproducing the inner logic and identity of what is known as the German model. Rather, the findings indicate a significant impact of actors' choices on both the development of industrial relations institutions and their outcomes. More precisely, government choices and employer strategies have contributed substantially to changing the face of German employment relations.

Today, German employment relations look very different from the system depicted in academic accounts up to the early 1990s. As shown in the previous sections, they are more European than they used to be (for better or for worse), they are more decentralized and they have lost some of their power to provide social equity. This is not to say that we are witnessing a process of convergence to the liberal market model, whereby the German employment relations become similar to those in the USA or the UK (see Katz and Darbishire 2000). Although German levels of income inequality have recently matched British levels, and there are growing sections of the German economy where key institutions such as multi-employer collective bargaining hardly exist at all, there is still a stable core of institutions within the system. The irony of these developments is that they provide support for both the re-embedding and disorganizations hypotheses but at the same time raise doubts as to which captures the main developments in the German employment relations system. New and still growing sectors of the economy, many in private services, seem to follow the pattern predicted by the disorganization hypothesis: key institutions of employment relations such as multi-employer collective bargaining or establishment-level interest representation through works councils, are weak or non-existent; wages are comparatively low; and atypical employment is widespread. At the same time we find sectors such as automobiles and chemical engineering where key institutions are still comparatively strong and, despite the growing importance of agency work and other forms of atypical employment, wages are comparatively high. As experience during the world financial crisis has shown, institutions within this core are comparatively stable and capable of withstanding very severe shocks. With the help of state-funded short-time work programmes and the ability of unions and works councils to negotiate pacts for employment and competitiveness, it has been possible to stabilize employment levels even during the most severe crisis in post-war history. In this sense, German employment relations in 2012 increasingly resemble Richard Locke's (1995) description of the Italian political economy of the 1980s and 1990s. In his perspective, what at first glance appears to be evidence of disorganization or even chaos turns out to be a 'heterogeneous composite of diverse subnational patterns that coexist within the same national territory' (ibid.: 20).

Notes

1 As Jacoby (2000) has shown, continuity is much more pronounced in education, at least when compared to industrial relations. In her analysis of the development of the German system of education and training, Thelen (2004) comes to similar conclusions.

2 It is striking that, even 20 years after German unification has extended the reach of West German industrial relations laws and institutions to the territory of the former German Democratic Republic (GDR), differences in major practices such as bargaining coverage but also establishment-level interest representation through works councils still remain substantial between the two former Germanies.

3 While the state ordinarily applies the collectively agreed standards negotiated between the public sector unions and state representatives at the municipal, *Länder* and federal level, it does so on a voluntary basis, and it can deviate (and in recent years sometimes has) from those 'patterns' established in collective bargaining. A second difference is that lifetime civil servants are not allowed to strike (although this rule is contested under European law) but in exchange enjoy lifetime job security.

4 In 2012 both confederations merged to create Industri All.

References

Artus, I. (2001) *Krise des Deutschen Tarifsystems. Die Erosion des Flächentarifvertrags in Ost und West*, Wiesbaden: Westdeutscher Verlag.

Behrens, M. (2007) 'Conflict, arbitration, and dispute resolution in the German workplace', *International Journal of Conflict Management*, 18(2): 175–92.

—— (2011) *Das Paradox der Arbeitgeberverbände. Von der Schwierigkeit, durchsetzungsstarke unternehmensinteressen Kollektiv zu vertreten*, Berlin: Edition Sigma.

—— and Helfen, M. (2010) 'Employers' exit from multi-employer bargaining. organizational change in German employers' associations', in *Proceedings of the 9th IIRA European Congress, 29 June–1 July 2010, Copenhagen*, Geneva: International Industrial Relations Association.

Bispinck, R. and Schulten, T. (1999) 'Flächentarifvertrag und betriebliche Interessenvertretung', in W. Müller-Jentsch (ed.) *Konfliktpartnerschaft. Akteure und Institutionen der industriellen Beziehungen*, 3rd edn, Munich and Mehring: Rainer Hampp Verlag.

—— (2011) *Sector-Level Bargaining and Possibilities for Deviations at Company Level: Germany*, Dublin: European Foundation for the Improvement of Living and Working Conditions.

Bothfeld, S., Sesselmeier, W. and Bogedan, C. (2009) *Arbeitsmarktpolitik in der Sozialen Marktwirtschaft. Vom Arbeitsförderungsgesetz zum Sozialgesetzbuch II und III*, Wiesbaden: VS Verlag.

Brehmer, W. and Seifert, H. (2008) 'Sind atypische Arbeitsverhältnisse prekär? Eine empirische Analyse sozialer Risiken', *Zeitschrift für Arbeitsmarktforschung*, 41: 501–31.

Bruun, N., Jacobs, A. and Schmidt, M. (2010) 'ILO Convention No. 94 in the aftermath of the Rüffert case', *Transfer*, 16(4): 473–88.

Bücker, A. and Warneck, W. (2010) *Viking – Laval – Rüffert: Consequences and Policy Perspectives*, Brussels: European Trade Union Institute.

Crouch, C. (2005) *Capitalist Diversity and Change: Recombinant Governance and Institutional Entrepreneurs*, Oxford: Oxford University Press.

Doellgast, V. (2008) 'Collective bargaining and high-involvement management in comparative perspective: evidence from U.S. and German call centers', *Industrial Relations*, 47(2): 284–319.

—— and Greer, I. (2007) 'Vertical disintegration and the disorganization of German industrial relations', *British Journal of Industrial Relations*, 45(1): 55–76.

Dribbusch, H. (2010) *Tarifkonkurrenz als gewerkschaftspolitische Herausforderung: Ein Beitrag zur Debatte um die Tarifeinheit*, Düsseldorf: WSI-Diskussionspapier No. 172, August.

—— (2011) 'Organisieren am Konflikt: Zum Verhältnis von Streik und Mitgliederentwicklung', in T. Haipeter and K. Dörre (eds) *Gewerkschaftliche Modernisierung*, Wiesbaden: VS Verlag.

Ebbinghaus, B. (1995) 'The Siamese twins: citizenship rights, cleavage formation, and party-union relations in Western Europe', *International Review of Social History*, 40, Supplement 3: 51–89.

Ellguth, P. and Kohaut, S. (2011) 'Tarifbindung und betriebliche Interessenvertretung. Aktuelle Ergebnisse aus dem IAB-Betriebspanel 2010', *WSI-Mitteilungen*, 64: 242–7.

Erne, R. (2008) *European Unions: Labor's Quest for a Transnational Democracy*, Ithaca, NY: ILR Press.

Fitzenberger, B., Kohn, K. and Wang, Q. (2011) 'The erosion of union membership in Germany: determinants, densities, decompositions', *Journal of Population Economics*, 24(1): 141–65.

Frege, C. M. (2002) 'A critical assessment of the theoretical and empirical research on German works councils', *British Journal of Industrial Relations*, 40(2): 221–48.

Ganz, M. (2000) 'Resources and resourcefulness: strategic capacity in the unionization of Californian agriculture, 1959–1966', *American Journal of Sociology*, 105(4): 1003–62.

George, R. (2011) 'Niedriglohn und Geschlecht im europäischen Vergleich', *WSI-Mittelungen* 64: 548–55.

Greer, I. (2008) 'Organized industrial relations in the information economy: the German automotive sector as a test case', *New Technology, Work and Employment*, 23(3): 181–96.

—— and Hauptmeier, M. (2008) 'Political entrepreneurs and co-managers: labour transnationalism at four multinational auto companies', *British Journal of Industrial Relations* 46(1): 76–97.

Haipeter, T. and Schilling, G. (2006) *Arbeitgeberverbände in der Metall- und Elektroindustrie. Tarifbindung: Organisationsentwicklung und Strategiebildung*, Hamburg: VSA.

Hall, P. and Gingerich, D.W. (2009) 'Varieties of capitalism and institutional complementarities in the political economy: an empirical analysis', in B. Hancké (ed.) *Debating Varieties of Capitalism: A Reader*, Oxford: Oxford University Press.

Hall, P. A. and Soskice, D. (2001) 'An introduction to varieties of capitalism', in P. A. Hall and D. Soskice (eds) *Varieties of Capitalism: The Institutional Foundations of Comparative Advantage*, Oxford: Oxford University Press.

Hassel, A. (1999) 'The erosion of the German system of industrial relations', *British Journal of Industrial Relations*, 37(3): 483–505.

Hauser-Ditz, A., Hertwig, M., Pries, L. and Rampeltshammer, L. (2010) *Transnationale Mitbestimmung? Zur Praxis Europäischer Betriebsräte in der Automobilindustrie*, Frankfurt: Campus.

Hertwig, M., Pries, L. and Rampeltshammer, L. (2010) *European Works Councils in Complementing Perspectives*, Brussels: European Trade Union Institute.

Herzog-Stein, A., Lindner, F., Sturn, S. and van Treeck, T. (2010) *From a Source of Weakness to a Tower of Strength? The Changing German Labour Market*, Dusseldorf: Hans Böckler Stiftung, IMK-Report No. 56, November.

Höpner, M. and Schäfer, A. (2008) 'Grundzüge einer politökonomischen Perspektive auf die Europäische Integration', in M. Höpner and A. Schäfer (eds) *Die politische Ökonomie der Europäischen Integration*, Frankfurt: Campus.

Jacoby, W. (2000) *Imitation and Politics: Redesigning Modern Germany*, Ithaca, NY: Cornell University Press.

Kalina, T. and Weinkopf, C. (2012) *Niedriglohnbeschäftigung 2010: Fast Jede/r Vierte arbeitet für Niedriglohn*, Duisburg: IAQ-Report 01/2012.

Katz, H. (1993) 'The decentralization of collective bargaining: a literature review and comparative analysis', *Industrial and Labor Relations Review*, 47(1): 3–22.

—— and Darbishire, O. (2000) *Converging Divergences: Worldwide Changes in Employment Systems*, Ithaca, NY: ILR Press.

Katzenstein, P. (1987) *Policy and Politics in West Germany: The Growth of a Semi-Sovereign State*, Philadelphia, PA: Temple University Press.

Keller, B. (2005) 'Union formation through merger: the case of Ver.di in Germany', *British Journal of Industrial Relations*, 43(2): 209–32.

—— (2009) 'Berufs- und Spartengewerkschaften. Konsequenzen und Optionen', *Sozialer Fortschritt*, 59: 118–28.

—— and Seifert, H. (2011) *Atypische Beschäftigung und soziale Risiken. Entwicklung, Strukturen, Regulierung*, Bonn: Friedrich-Ebert-Stiftung, WISO-Diskurs, October.

Kelly, J. (1998) *Rethinking Industrial Relations: Mobilization, Collectivism and Long Waves*, London: Routledge.

Klein, M. (2011) 'Wie sind die parteien gesellschaftlich verwurzelt?', in T. Spier, M. Klein, U von Alemann, H. Hoffmann, A. Laux, A. Nonnenmacher and K. Rohrbach (eds) *Parteimitglieder in Deutschland*, Wiesbaden: Verlag für Sozialwissenschaften.

Kochan, T. A., Katz, H. and McKersie, R. (1986) *The Transformation of American Industrial Relations*, New York: Basic Books.

Kotthoff, H. (1981) *Betriebsräte und betriebliche Herrschaft: eine Typologie von Partizipationsmustern im Industriebetrieb*, Frankfurt: Campus.

—— (2006) *Lehrjahre des Europäischen Betriebsrats. Zehn Jahre transnationale Arbeitnehmervertretung*, Berlin: Edition Sigma.

Lash, S. and Urry, J. (1987) *The End of Organized Capitalism*, Oxford: Polity Press.

Locke, R. M. (1995) *Remaking the Italian Economy*, Ithaca, NY: Cornell University Press.

Marginson, P. and Sisson, K. (2006) *European Integration and Industrial Relations: Multi-level Governance in the Making*, Basingstoke: Palgrave Macmillan.

Müller-Jentsch, W. (1995) 'Germany: from collective voice to co-management', in J. Rogers and W. Streeck (eds) *Works Councils: Consultation, Representation, and Cooperation in Industrial Relations*, Chicago: The University of Chicago Press.

—— (2003) 'Re-assessing co-determination', in W. Müller-Jentsch and H. Weitbrecht (eds) *The Changing Contours of German Industrial Relations*, Munich/Mehring: Rainer Hampp Verlag.

Pyhel, J. (2006) 'Warum ist man Gewerkschaftsmitglied? Determinanten der Mitgliedschaftsneigung', *WSI-Mitteilungen*, 59: 341–6.

Rehder, B. (2006) 'Legitimitätsdefizite des Co-managements: betriebliche Bündnisse für Arbeit als Konfliktfeld zwischen Arbeitnehmern und betrieblicher Interessenvertretung', *Zeitschrift für Soziologie*, 35(3): 227–42.

Sachverständigenrat Zur Begutachtung der Gesamtwirtschaftlichen Entwicklung (2011) *Verantwortung für Europa Warnehmon. Jahresgutachten 2011/12*, Wiesbaden: Statistisches Bundesamt.

Scharpf, F. (2008) 'Der einzige Weg ist, dem EuGH nicht zu folgen. Interview', *Die Mitbestimmung*, 7+8: 18–23.

Schettkat, R. (2007) 'Sind 3 Euro schon zu viel? Aufklärendes zu Lohnspreisung und Beschäftigung', *WSI-Mitteilungen*, 60: 335–43.

Schmidt, R. and Trinczek, R. (1986) 'Erfahrungen und Perspektiven gewerkschaftlicher Arbeitszeitpolitik', *Prokla*, 64: 85–108.

Schnabel, C. and Wagner, J. (2007) 'The persistent decline in unionization in Western and Eastern Germany, 1980–2004: what can we learn from a decomposition analysis?', *Industrielle Beziehungen*, 14(2): 118–32.

Schneider, M. (2000) *Kleine Geschichte der Gewerkschaften. Ihre Entwicklung in Deutschland von den Anfängen bis heute*, Bonn: Dietz Nachfolger.

Schroeder, W. (2005) 'Sozialdemokratie und Gewerkschaften', *Berliner Debatte Initial*, 16: 12–21.

—— (2008) 'SPD und Gewerkschaften: vom Wandel einer privilegierten Partnerschaft', *WSI Mitteilungen*, 61: 231–7.

—— and Weßels, B. (2010) 'Die Deutsche Unternehmerverbändelandschaft: vom Zeitalter der Verbände zum Zeitalter der Mitglieder', in W. Schroeder and B. Wessels (eds) *Handbuch Arbeitgeber- und Wirtschaftsverbände in Deutschland*, Wiesbaden: VS Verlag.

——, Kalass, V. and Greef, S. (2011) *Berufsgewerkschaften in der Offensive: vom Wandel des Deutschen Gewerkschaftsmodells*, Wiesbaden: VS Verlag.

Schulten, T. (2004) *Solidarische Lohnpolitik in Europa: zur politischen Ökonomie der Gewerkschaften*, Hamburg: VSA.

—— (2009) 'Zehn Jahre europäische Koordinierung der Tarifpolitik – eine Zwischenbilanz', in H. Schlatermund and M. Flore (eds) *Zukunft von Arbeitsbeziehungen und Arbeit in Europa (ZAUBER)*, Osnabrück, 103–18.

—— and Pawicki, M. (2008) 'Tariftreueregelungen in Deutschland – ein aktueller Uberblick', *WSI-Mitteilungen*, 61: 184–90.

Seifert, H. and Massa-Wirth, H. (2005) 'Pacts for employment and competitiveness in Germany', *Industrial Relations Journal*, 36(3): 217–40.

Streeck, W. (1991) 'On the institutional conditions of diversified quality production', in E. Matzner and W. Streeck (eds) *Beyond Keynesianism: The Socio-Economics of Production and Employment*, London: Edward Elgar.

—— and Thelen, K. (2005) *Beyond Continuity: Institutional Change in Advanced Political Economies*, Oxford: Oxford University Press.

—— and Visser, J. (1997) 'The rise of the conglomerate union', *European Journal of Industrial Relations*, 3(3): 305–32.

Thelen, K. (1991) *Union of Parts: Labor Politics in Postwar Germany*, Ithaca, NY: Cornell University Press.

—— (2004) *How Institutions Evolve: The Political Economy of Skills in Germany, Britain, the United States, and Japan*, Cambridge: Cambridge University Press.

Traxler, F. (1995) 'Farewell to labour market associations? Organized versus disorganized decentralization as a map for industrial relations', in C. Crouch and F. Traxler (eds) *Organized Industrial Relations in Europe: What Future?*, Aldershot: Avebury.

Turner, L. (1991) *Democracy at Work: Changing World Markets and the Future of Labor Unions*, Ithaca, NY: Cornell University Press.

—— (1998) *Fighting for Partnership: Labor and Politics in Unified Germany*, Ithaca, NY: Cornell University Press.

—— (2009) 'Institutions and activism: crisis and opportunity for a German labor movement in decline', *Industrial and Labor Relations Review*, 62(3): 294–312.

Völkl, M. (2002) *Der Mittelstand und die Tarifautonomie:Arbeitgeberverbände zwischen Sozialpartnerschaft und Dienstleistung*, Munich/Mehring: Rainer Hampp Verlag.

Voss, D. and Weinkopf, C. (2012) 'Niedriglohnfalle Minijob', *WSI-Mitteilungen*, 65: 5–12.

Waddington, J. (2011) *European Works Councils: A Transnational Industrial Relations Institution in the Making*, London: Routledge.

—— and Hoffmann, J. (2005) 'Germany: towards a new form of German trade unionism?', in J. Waddington (ed.) *Restructuring Representation: The Merger Process and Trade Union Structural Development in Ten Countries*, Brussels: P.I.E.-Peter Lang.

Wingerter, C. (2009) 'Der Wandel der Erwerbsformen und seine Bedeutung für die Einkommenssituation Erwerbstätiger', *Wirtschaft und Statistik*, 11: 1080–98.

Zapf, I. and Herzog-Stein, A. (2011) 'Betriebliche Einsatzmuster von Arbeitszeitkonten während der großen Rezession', *WSI-Mitteilungen*, 64: 60–8.

13 Sweden

Torsten Svensson

Introduction

In a narrow Swedish perspective, industrial relations underwent dramatic changes during the last decades of the twentieth century. Some of the characteristics of what was once called the Swedish Model were said to have changed or even vanished (Hermansson *et al.* 1999; Swenson and Pontusson 2000; Rothstein 2001). According to some researchers and in a comparative perspective, this had important and extensive effects on the labour market regime (Fulcher 1991; Visser 1996: 179; Iversen 1998; Swenson and Pontusson 2000; Wallerstein and Golden 2000; Elvander 2002a). First and foremost, a central part of the Swedish model, the centralized bargaining system, was gradually replaced with more decentralized forms. Peak organizations lost ground to national unions and the details in national agreements were often settled at local level (Kjellberg 1998). At the same time unionization has continuously declined. Within the political sphere the strong bonds between unions and the Social Democratic Party have loosened. Industrial organizations have partly withdrawn and partly been excluded from administrative agency boards involved in labour market regulation. This has resulted in less influence over the agencies responsible for regulating and implementing government policies in all policy areas, most importantly less influence over welfare and labour market policies. Supporting labour laws and welfare policies based on a high-tax system have been put under pressure. Privatization, deregulation and tax reforms imply less generous contributions and less support for union demands.

Although recognizing these changes, one can still argue that, compared with changes in other countries, these developments should not be exaggerated (Thelen 2001; Elvander 2002a; Svensson and Öberg 2002, 2005). However, in the wake of the economic crisis, marked by wage inflation and rising unemployment, Sweden witnessed a new development in collective bargaining at the end of the 1990s, namely, the Industrial Agreement (Elvander 2002a). In a comparative perspective, unionization is still extraordinarily high and the welfare state still represents a distinct Scandinavian Model. The cross-class alliance between organized labour and capital, agreed upon back in the 1930s and formerly characterized as social corporatism (Katzenstein 1985), organized capitalism (Magnusson 2006) or as negotiated solidarism (Swenson 2002), seems to have cast off its old shell and emerged in a new modernized version typical of the coordinated market economy (Hall and Soskice 2001; Wood 2002).

The actors and processes in employment relations

Origins of the Swedish system of employment relations

From the 1930s, industrial relations in Sweden can be characterized as a tripartite corporatist system based on collective bargaining, with the state staying in the background but ready 'for action' and active within an institutionalized dialogue between the three parties on basic conditions and main goals.

This regime had its roots in the strikes at the beginning at the century leading to the so-called 'December compromise' in 1906. The Swedish Confederation of Trade Unions (LO) was established in 1898 by leading Social Democrats and as a response the Swedish Employers Confederation (SAF) was established in 1902. After some years of turmoil on the labour market, the newly established peak organizations reached a weak but basic agreement signifying mutual recognition of unions, the workers' right to organize and employers' prerogatives (Fleming 1967; Swenson 1991a; Kjellberg 1998, 2000). In parallel a first corporatist-like arrangement emerged in the form of local public employment agencies. Later on, these agencies developed into the Central Labour Market Administration, a cornerstone in post-war labour market policies (Rothstein 1996).

The real breakthrough for the corporatist model came in the late 1930s in a 'historic compromise' between labour and capital. This implied both a political compromise and a new industrial relations regime. Politically, a coalition between the Social Democrats and the Farmers Party paved the way for intervention in the labour market and in the economy. In the context of the mass unemployment of the late 1920s and the exceptionally high rate of industrial conflict, new potent economic theories were developed in Sweden that promoted and made sense of state intervention and active measures against unemployment (King and Rothstein 1993; Blyth 2002). The crucial ingredient in the compromise was a cross-class alliance between the unions and the employers organizations. Interestingly, this process was initiated by the employers, particularly those in metal and engineering industries exposed to international competition. They had strong interests in keeping wages down both in their own and in other sectors of the economy and so pushed strongly for centralization of collective bargaining (Swenson 1991a: 519 et ff.). They also received help from the Social Democratic government. Confronted with high unemployment as well as large strikes and lockouts in high-wage sectors of the economy, the government made clear that it would actively intervene if the partners failed to reach an agreement on their own. Faced with the prospect of a fundamental threat to their power and independence, the unions and employers concluded the Basic Agreement of 1938, also called the Saltsjöbaden Agreement (Swenson 1991a; Kjellberg 1998, 2000). Employer prerogative and labour peace were exchanged for social reforms and full employment. This meant centralized collective agreements at the peak level built upon a strong centralization of unions and employers organizations (Kjellberg 2000: 609 et ff.). A mandatory but union-run unemployment insurance scheme, a Ghent system, had been introduced in 1934. After the Second World War, an active labour market policy was introduced, aiming for full employment and economic growth. It implied supply side measures in the form of employment assistance, labour market training and employment subsidies as well as direct job creation in addition to the Keynesian tools of demand management (Lindvall and Sebring 2005; Bonoli 2010). In the 1950s, these policies were combined into the so-called 'Rehn–Meidner solidaristic wage policy', proposed by two economists within the main union confederation, the LO. Wage bargaining had to follow productivity in sectors exposed to the world market and unions kept to the rule of 'equal pay for the same kind of work'. At a time of constant growth and inflationary pressure, the government would apply a strict fiscal and economic policy: 'by raising taxes and allowing less private demand the government would hold back inflation, create islands of unemployment, and allow less productive firms to close down' (Magnusson 2006: 7). Consequently, the state and their partners actually agreed on a policy that stimulated technical change, closures of unproductive plants and worker mobility. Active labour market policy worked as a measure to facilitate the transition for those who suffered from these policies while welfare policies compensated for restrained wage demands (Meidner 1986; Magnusson 2006).

Thus, a tripartite corporatist model of industrial relations was set in place between the 1930s and the 1970s, where the state played an important role together with the main organizations representing labour and capital. Sweden occupied a more or less extreme position in respect of almost all the important components of an industrial relations system and, in particular, labour market power was concentrated in the peak organizations in dialogue with the state (Elvander 1988: 32; Fulcher 1991: 76–81). The Swedish model involved regular, institutionalized talks and cooperation between the state and the leaders of the peak organizations on the whole policy-making process. Unions and employers organizations took part in government commissions of inquiries leading to law-making as well as implementation of policies by the boards of different administrative agencies, the most important of which was the National Labour Market Board (Svensson and Öberg 2005; Lindvall and Rothstein 2006).

In short, the corporatist system can be described as an exchange system: 'The purpose was to make organizations capable of moderating members' demands and securing industrial peace. In exchange, unions obtained comprehensive welfare policies, protective measures and the right to collective bargaining and to strike' (Öberg *et al.* 2011: 370). As Katzenstein points out, this was a particular strategy among small export-oriented states where conflicting interests found common ground in their response to a hostile world market (1985: 35). However, these corporatist exchanges presuppose that both parties can deliver what they promise. In the wake of the oil crises in 1973 and 1979 and a weakened world market, declining growth, rising inflation and unemployment as well as globalization undermined the state's ability to distribute wealth and uphold full employment. Step-by-step de-industrialization changed the configuration of the labour force leading to a heterogeneous cluster of labour unions. White-collar unions grew stronger and union centralization weakened. At the same time individualization grew and the electorate, not least within the unions, experienced a political radicalization. Some of the resulting protests were directed against union leaders, responsible for the effects of the structural transformation of society they had agreed upon; moderation in employment relations became hard to achieve (cf. Öberg *et al.* 2011).

From declining growth in the 1970s to the economic crisis of the 1990s

The downturn of the economy in the 1970s with low growth as well as rising unemployment, as well as political radicalization within the labour movement, made the unions change course. As the possibility of bargaining for higher wages became restricted, unions turned to the Social Democratic government for political reforms and the government delivered. Several laws on employment protection such as rules for codetermination, employment security and improved work environment and safety were introduced. In the employers' view, some of these measures were attacks on the management prerogative and a clear break with the historical compromise from the 1930s. In particular, the politically controversial proposal for wage-earner funds agitated the employers, and was looked upon as a fierce and hostile socialist attack on the core of capitalism. The original idea implied a form of automatic collectivization of profits in the private industry, gradually transferring the power over capital and investments to union- or state-led funds. The employers managed to mobilize a strong political counter-attack, uniting the non-socialist parties and even went out in the streets in large demonstrations against the funds. When the final watered-down version was decided in 1982, the relations between the labour market parties had turned from cooperative to hostile (Elvander 2002b: 128). The employers reacted with demands for deregulation of the labour market, a unilateral withdrawal from corporatist arrangements, and demands for a decentralized wage-bargaining system (Kjellberg 2000: 610; Elvander 2002b: 128).

After the '*trente glorieuses*' between 1945 and 1975, the Swedish economy slowed down. A period of extraordinary growth and rising nominal incomes in the late 1980s, partly spurred by a big devaluation of the Swedish krona, dramatically ended at the beginning of the 1990s (for details of these processes, see Svensson, T. 2002; Svensson *et al.* 2006). Sweden experienced an economic downturn and crisis comparable to the Depression in the 1930s. The figures displayed in Table 13.1 all point consistently in the same direction.

Economic growth came to a halt in 1990 and the first half of the decade showed zero growth and, in some years, even negative growth figures. Unemployment rose dramatically, increasing fourfold in ten years, while at same time employment declined rapidly. Sweden was stuck with high unemployment and low employment figures when growth began to rise again. The economic crisis was also associated with increasing inequality (by almost 10 per cent in 15 years) and very low productivity growth during the acute phase of the crisis (and even negative figures during the last five-year period). The crisis partly coincided with, and partly opened up, changes in the labour market. The consequences of the crisis were severe and constituted an important source for institutional and structural changes in the labour market. Consequently, the crisis of the 1990s therefore opened 'a golden window of opportunity for those wanting to liberalize the corporatist capitalist models' which implied 'welfare cuts and extensive deregulation of product and labor markets' (Lindgren 2011: 49).

Trade unions

Sweden experienced a late and astonishingly rapid industrialization and urbanization between 1880 and 1920. As a result, unions were established as class organizations (where

Table 13.1 Economic outcomes in Sweden, 1970–2010

	1970–1974	*1975–1979*	*1980–1984*	*1985–1989*	*1990–1994*	*1995–1999*	*2000–2004*	*2005–2010*
Growth	3.4	1.5	1.8	2.7	0.1	3.1	2.6	1.1
Unemployment	2.2	1.9	3.0	2.2	5.8	8.6	5.5	6.7*
Employment	73.6	77.8	78.8	80.0	75.7	70.5	72.9	67.4
Inequality	–	21.1	20.3	21.2	24.5	26.4	28.6	31.5
Productivity	–	–	–	0.5	0.4	1.4	2.1	−0.9

Sources: Armingeon *et al.* (2008); Lindgren (2011) and in addition: Growth: Annual growth rate of real GDP in per cent (OECD data); Unemployment: Standardized unemployment rates (OECD data, from 2005, Statistics Sweden); Employment: Civilian employment as percentage of the population aged 15–64 (OECD data) and from 2000 population aged 15–74 (Stastistics Sweden); Inequality: The Gini coefficient of disposable income (Statistics Sweden);Productivity: Annual multi–factor productivity growth in per cent (OECD data).

all workers were organized locally by the dominating union at a workplace) rather than being built around craft, and in close cooperation with the emerging Social Democratic Party. The Swedish Confederation of Trade Unions (LO), established in 1898 by leading Social Democrats, became a strong union in a small economy strongly exposed to global competition and heavily dependent on export industry.

In order to understand the development of industrial relations and the strength of the labour movement in Sweden, one has to recognize the strong relations and close cooperation between the unions (LO) and the Social Democratic Party (SAP) and how these developed and reinforced each other. Within the labour movement, they considered themselves, and were looked upon, as two branches of the same tree. Union and political struggle, collective bargaining, on the one hand, and labour and welfare legislation, on the other, became two different but still complementary means for safeguarding workers' interests (Åmark 1988; Svensson 1994; Kjellberg 2000). During the first decade after the unions' confederation was established, tensions were strong between party activists, who first and foremost wanted unions to act in the interest of the party, and trade unionists, who focused on union development and workers' immediate and local needs. The use of the unions as a political vehicle came to a halt after the failure of the massive strike in 1908 in which union membership almost halved. However, the conditions for union growth and union independence improved as party and unions' central organizations reached a compromise agreement regarding union affiliation to the party. The solution, of voluntary rather than compulsory local collective affiliation to the party, coupled with the possibility for individual exit, preserved strong and equal relations between the two organizations. Mutual dependence worked as an important vehicle for massive unionization as well as for a strong social democratic party. The principle of collective affiliation lasted until as 1987 as one important element of Swedish corporatism (Svensson 1994: 51 et ff.; Kjellberg 2000: 607 et ff.).

The agreement in the 1930s paved the way for a distinctive feature of the Swedish unions: the combination of centralization and decentralization, with strong local presence and organization. These particular characteristics, together with strong relations to the Social Democratic Party, especially as the party turned into a hegemonic political force, had a great impact on unionization figures. In a comparative perspective, Swedish unions stand out with remarkably high union density (Åmark 1988; Svensson 1994; Kjellberg 1998, 2000). Another unique feature contributes to this development, namely the pronounced divide between unions representing employees of different kinds. This divide is clearer in Sweden than anywhere else. There are separate confederations for blue-collar (LO), white-collar (TCO) and academics (SACO), including unions organizing within both the private and public sectors, and all have a high degree of union density. In fact, the unionization rate within the high status occupational groups is, and has been, remarkably high for many years. The high unionization rate also implies that density figures have remained quite resistant to structural changes. As unionization became widespread among all groups, recent developments within the labour force following de-industrialization and a growing service sector do not seem to have had the huge negative influence on union membership that is reported in other countries (Kjellberg 1998, 2000).

The introduction of the public unemployment insurance scheme in the 1930s was crucial for the development of union strength and several researchers believe it is the most important factor. In the light of massive unemployment in the 1930s and the low coverage of the unions' own poor insurance systems, the Social Democratic government fought for public unemployment insurance. In 1934, the SAP Minister of Social Affairs, Gustaf Möller, struck a deal with the liberals and succeeded in introducing the 'Ghent system'. It was a voluntary unemployment insurance system insofar as it was ‘owned’, administered and run by the unions, yet it was financially supported and controlled by the state. The unions obtained ‘the power to decide what kind of work an unemployed person would be obliged to take on pain of losing allowances, and no one would be forced to take jobs at workplaces affected by legitimate industrial disputes’ (Rothstein 1990: 330). Informally, it was understood that an insured union member should not to have to accept a job on a salary below wage levels set in collective agreements. Informally as well, union membership was perceived as a condition for being insured. In practice, together with other selective incentives for being a member of a union, it became a powerful system for ‘recruiting and keeping members’ supported by the state (ibid.: 329; cf. Oskarsson 1997; Holmlund and Lundborg 1999; Scruggs 2002; Kjellberg 2011).

The historical figures on unionization that followed these developments are impressive. Apart from a short drop at the second half of the 1980s, union membership grew more or less steadily from the end of the Second World War until the middle of the 1990s. Union density was around 60 per cent in 1945 and reached its peak, fully 88 per cent, during the economic crisis in 1994. Table 13.2 shows how the figures have developed on average for five-year periods between 1970 and 2010. On the one hand, there is a clear decline from the middle of the 1990s onwards. The drop seems consistent and quite significant, from 85 per cent during 1990–94 to less than 73 per cent in the most recent period. On the other hand, the present figures are still higher than at the beginning of the 1970s and way above average in an international comparison.

However, during the past decade, most interest has been focused on the decline, and for good reasons. Unions have experienced a gradual decline during the past 15 years, followed by a sharp drop from 2007 and onwards as a result of changes in workforce composition, linked to de-industrialization as well as political decisions aimed at a reduced public sector through tax cuts, privatization and outsourcing. The transfer of workers from the public to the private sector has simultaneously implied a transfer from industry to the service sector. As Kjellberg puts it: ‘[J]obs are transferred from the sector with the highest unionization to that with the lowest’ (2011: 71). These changes have interacted with the marked decline in unionization among young people and foreign-born workers, the newcomers to the labour market. Young people show the most critical attitudes towards unions, at the same time as they constitute a large proportion of temporary workers and are weakly linked to the labour market. Most of the decline in union membership is linked to the younger cohorts (Kjellberg 2011: 68 et ff.; Medlingsinstitutet 2012: 34 et ff.). The weak unionization among young people is considered to be one of the most urgent problems for the unions (LO-Rapport 2007). The latest dramatic fall in unionization from 2007 onwards has a more short-term and political cause. In order to put pressure on the unions to restrain wage demands, the Liberal-Conservative government changed the rules of the unemployment insurance system,

Table 13.2 Union density and employer density in Sweden, 1970–2010 (%)

	1970–1974	*1975–1979*	*1980–1984*	*1985–1989*	*1990–1994*	*1995–1999*	*2000–2004*	*2005–2010*
Union density	71.0	75.7	79.1	83.3	84.8	83.5	78.3	72.6
Employer density	–	–	–	–	–	86	83	83

Sources: Union density: Net union density in percentages. Visser (2011), Medlingsinstitutet (2012); Employer density: Kjellberg (2011), based on Statistics Sweden; – data not available.

simultaneously raising membership fees considerably and abolishing tax reductions for membership dues in what Kjellberg (2011: 87) described as 'a kind of penalty tax on wage increases'. The effect on union membership followed immediately, but there was less effect on wage demands (ibid.).

These political reforms also reflect changing political conditions for the unions due to developments in the political arena as well as value changes among the electorate. The Social Democrats slowly lost their hegemonic position between the late 1970s and the 1990s. At the end of the twentieth century the party no longer stood out as the natural party of government. In order to secure access to power, the unions had to reconsider their strong links to the Social Democrats and be open for talks also with other parties. Discontent also grew within the party. As the working-class share of the electorate decreased, the open and strong links between the party and the blue-collar unions and LO, the union confederation, were increasingly criticized. This was perceived as an obstacle to the party's chances of regaining political power and implementing liberal reforms and renovating the public sector in order to appeal to new groups of voters. These developments coincided with a growing urge for individual freedom among important parts of the electorate and discontent with the 'Strong Society', marked by bureaucracy and statist policies. In addition, there was strong opposition from industry to socialist reforms initiated by the unions. A mutual need for a looser party–union relationship emerged in the 1980s (Gidlund 1988; Swenson 1991b: 385 et ff.; Taylor 1993; Allern *et al.* 2007). One clear sign of this trend was the decision at the SAP Congress in 1987 to abolish the collective affiliation of union members. The leader of the Swedish Metal Workers Union described collective affiliation as 'a millstone around the labour movement's neck' (Gidlund 1988: 299). However, the party–union relationship remained close at the top level and in relation to electoral platforms.

Another concern for the unions during recent decades has been the implications of the Swedish EU membership in 1994 and especially of EU legislation. The Services Directive (known as the Bolkestein Directive) implying the removal of national market obstacles as well as legislation on minimum wages threatened to interfere in domestic labour legislation and make collective agreements obsolete. It is not far-fetched to draw a comparison to the situation in 1938 when the state threatened to interfere in the negotiations between unions and employers:

> There is a fear that the spread of individual legal rights may eventually undermine the systems of national collective agreements, threaten the existing autonomy of the trade unions (and their counterparts, the employers' associations), and consequently weaken the power base of both parties.
>
> (Andersen 2006: 35)

However, this time the government is not as union-friendly as in the 1930s. (For a description of the *Laval* case that triggered the debate, see Woolfson and Sommers 2006, and Chapter 22 in this volume.)

Unions have experienced weakened power resources during the past few decades owing to several factors: decreasing union density, less public support, a weaker link to the Social Democratic Party, a weaker peak organization and a European labour market based on individual legal rights rather than on national collective agreements. Formal talks with the Liberal-Conservative government as well as cooperation among unions on the Nordic or European level seem to be feeble imitations of former times and cannot really compensate for lost power resources.

Employers and employers organizations

Most employers, covering well over 80 per cent of the workforce, are members of nationwide employers organizations, organized according to their line of business and coordinated by the Confederation of Swedish Enterprise. From a market-liberal perspective, the existence of employers organizations may be looked upon as self-contradictory. However, historically Swedish employers organized early and, at least partly, as a consequence of the development of strong and widespread trade unions. The export-oriented and internationally exposed Swedish industry had to find ways to curb unions' wage demands and strike activity (Swenson 1991a). The class compromise in the 1930s implied a sort of equilibrium between two strong actors, both strongly dependent on the export industry, and political institutions that supported the compromise as well as the interests of both actors. According to Katzenstein (1985), a social-democratic corporatist system emerged where strongly organized employers, dominated by the export-oriented industry, and strong unions found common ground with the government to adjust to the global market. Firms became embedded in a web of relations and a political and institutional system supporting such relations, including a financial system, welfare policies, educational institutions and systems for vocational training and a wage bargaining and industrial relations system. In the words of later theories focused on 'production regimes', Sweden developed into one of the coordinated market economies in which national-level bargaining institutions have been 'shored up' by employers who have oriented their competitive strategies around 'high value-added production that depends on a high degree of stability and cooperation with labour' (Thelen 2001: 73; and see also Hall 1999; Hall and Soskice 2001).

The labour reforms introduced in the 1970s and 1980s – laws on employment protection and codetermination and the introduction of wage-earner funds in 1982 (see above) – were perceived as attacks on the management prerogative in the eyes of the employers and a clear break with the historic compromise from the 1930s. This view was in line with the interpretation by one of the main architects of the wage-earner funds, Rudolf Meidner, who saw the reform as an abandonment of the free market philosophy of the 1960s and a step towards a planned economy and economic democracy (Meidner 1986). The employers reacted with demands for deregulation of the labour market and a decentralized wage bargaining system (Kjellberg 2000: 610; Elvander 2002b: 128). One important step by the employers was their decision in 1985 unilaterally to withdraw from several corporatist arrangements. The main target was the Labour Market Board, one of the pillars of corporatist labour market policymaking, where the peak organization had participated in a tripartite arrangement together with representatives from the union confederations and the state (Rothstein and Bergström 1999; Johansson 2003). During the same phase of reinterpretation of the 'Swedish Model' of centralized bargaining, the employers association for the metalworking industry (now Verkstadsindustrier, VI) broke with earlier settlements and bargaining traditions. It turned to a radical new strategy and struck a deal at the industry level with the metalworkers union in 1983. This was an attack on solidaristic wage setting as well as on the whole system of centralized bargaining. Among some parts of the 'employers' family' it was seen as a first step to decentralization of bargaining down to the level of the firm (Thelen 2001: 86 et ff.).

The transformation of the employers' own peak organization in 2001, merging the Swedish Employers Confederation (SAF) with the Federation of Swedish Industries into the Confederation of Swedish Enterprise (SN), formed an essential part of the changed strategy and implied a development from a negotiating organization to a lobbying organization. In future, the central organization would not take part in negotiations and make decisions in the name of Swedish business. Collective bargaining had already been decentralized and now the employers' organization seemed to close the door on any re-centralization. Furthermore, political participation should be organized through open public debate and around public opinion, rather than within state agencies and board meetings (Rothstein and Bergström 1999; Svensson and Öberg 2002). Changes in employers' policies were more often than not expressed in ideological terms. However, the change in strategy was based on an analysis of whether or not existing solutions served their interests. Employer participation within state agency boards entailed the tendency for their representatives to become victims of bureaucratic 'capture' as they seemed to walk hand-in-hand with their union and government counterparts, instead of serving the interests of industry. Centralized collective bargaining implied low pay differentials and allegedly worked against the interests of export-oriented industry (Lewin 1994; Rothstein and Bergström 1999; Johansson 2003).

However, the idea of fully decentralized wage bargaining failed in the mid-1990s. As employers met with strong national and local unions in their industries, the strategy became controversial within their own membership (Thelen 2001). Likewise, participation within state agencies and governmental committees also continued, although in other forms and with more focus on certain areas; corporatism declined but it did not vanish (Svensson and Öberg 2002). At the same time as employer organizations participate less in corporatist arrangements, they have developed their public relations and political contacts in a much more profound and professional way than their union counterparts. Between 1999 and 2005 employers associations almost doubled their frequency of direct political contacts and their use of professional consultants, outperforming the unions in both areas (Öberg *et al.* 2011; Öberg and Svensson 2012). Employers organizations are now highly integrated into the political system and put a lot of effort into their participation in the political process.

The ambition among employers to fight labour laws and wage-earner funds and to dismantle the classical corporatist model as well as central bargaining did not imply that they also dismantled their own organizations. At the same time as union density has declined, employers remain highly organized. As Table 13.2 reveals, the decline in union density has been accompanied by consistently high employer density. Employers organization density has been stable since the 1990s and is well above 80 per cent, measured as a proportion of employees in employment (cf. Kjellberg 2011: 85–6). In sum, employers and employers organizations seem to have strengthened their relative positions vis-à-vis the unions. Political developments have also worked in favour of business interests, opening the door to reformed industrial relations.

Government and political intervention

Historically, it has been left to the unions and the employers to settle industrial relations among themselves. The historic compromise in the 1930s implied that the state kept its distance, and bargaining and disputes on wages, employment and work conditions were left to the main organizations in the labour market. The Social Democrats' part of the compromise was to actively stimulate growth, support economic transformation by means of active labour market policies and to redistribute the economic surplus. Industrial peace and employer prerogatives on employment were exchanged for social reforms. Through the corporatist system and with close cooperation with the peak organizations in the labour market, including the leaders of the large firms, the Social Democrats focused on welfare policies and social security rather than on socialism in a classical sense. High taxes on labour and consumption were the building blocks for the Swedish welfare state, the 'Strong State', encompassing all citizens in welfare policies, combining universal coverage with generous benefits. So long as Sweden experienced economic growth, this system functioned well.

However, as economic growth failed in the 1970s and unemployment increased, unions changed course. Bargaining for wage rises became increasingly difficult so unions turned to the Social Democrats for political reforms instead. Beside the demands for the politically controversial wage-earner funds, several laws on employment protection and codetermination were introduced. At the same time, the possibility of raising taxes to finance the welfare state as well as afford new reforms came to a halt. This problem coincided with growing discontent within important parts of the electorate over high taxes, excessive bureaucracy, lack of individual freedom and self-determination and non-responsive public arrangements and welfare solutions (Petersson 1991). New sentiments, especially among important swing voters, were closely connected to the political opposition parties and to mobilization from the employers organizations against the wage-earner funds, the co°determination laws, centralized bargaining and corporatism (Pontusson 1993).

For the first time in 45 years, non-socialist governments replaced the Social Democrats during the second half of the 1970s. However, stalled growth and oil crises in 1973 and 1979 as well as lingering social-democratic hegemony and a weak parliamentary position restrained the non-socialist parties from pursuing radical policy changes. Back in power in 1982, the new Social Democratic government boosted the economy with a substantial devaluation. During the late 1980s, the Social Democrats introduced several welfare state reforms in order to meet the challenges from global economic pressures, the interests of swing voters and technological change. In order to keep the political initiative, several proposals for de-regulation and privatization were pursued. The first reform, the de-regulation of the credit market, was crucial for the labour market as well as for the financial reforms that followed it. In 1985, all ceilings on loans from banks and finance companies as well as governmental regulation of the bank boards were abolished. Some years later this was followed by the abolition of foreign exchange controls. There were no longer any restrictions on the flow of different types of securities, bonds and shares. Marketization in the form of far-reaching de-regulation and privatization within financial product markets and infrastructure soon followed (Svensson 2002). After almost ten years in government, the Social Democrats were replaced by a centre-right government in 1991. Like the earlier non-socialist governments, the new centre-right period in office coincided with a huge economic crisis. Great plans for tax cuts and a 'revolution of choice' were more or less replaced by crisis agreements with the Social Democrats. Once again, Social Democrats came to power and stayed there between 1994 and 2006 and were then replaced by a new centre-right Conservative-led government. In short, liberal reforms started with the Social Democrats in the 1980s, and the following centre-right governments have continued and reinforced these reforms in the same direction.

As Table 13.3 shows, product market deregulation in Sweden has been extensive, although most countries have experienced the same trend. However, Sweden is today among the most liberal countries in this respect. The credit market reform was followed by a tax reform in 1990, known as 'the tax reform of the century', based on an agreement between the government and parts of the political opposition. The reform implied lower marginal tax rates, uniform indirect taxes combined with a sharp increase in real after-tax borrowing rates. Further plans for tax cuts from the new centre-right government in 1991 were put on ice due to the economic depression (Lindgren 2011). However, as Table 13.3 shows, the reform still had some effects: marginal taxes have continued to decrease during the whole period reinforced by several tax cuts.

Table 13.3 Welfare benefits, taxes, labour and product market regulations in Sweden, 1970–2004

	1970–1974	*1975–1979*	*1980–1984*	*1985–1989*	*1990–1994*	*1995–1999*	*2000–2004*	*2005–2010*
Unemployment benefits	7.5	9.1	9.9	11.0	11.8	10.9	10.4	
Sickness	14.7	15.4	15.4	15.5	15.0	14.1	13.7	
Pensions	13.0	15.6	18.5	18.1	16.0	14.8	11.8	
Tax wedge	–	50.7	50.7	51.7	46.7	50.3	48.3	45.3
Employment Protection Legislation*	1.9	3.4	3.5	3.5	3.1	2.3	2.2	2.1
Product market regulations**	–	4.5	4.5	4.5	3.6	2.5	2.0	1.8

Sources: Detailed variable description in Lindgren (2011). Unemployment benefits: Index of overall generosity of unemployment benefits. Sickness: Index of overall generosity of sickness benefits. Pensions: Index of the overall generosity of the pension system. Data on these three variables from Scruggs (2005) and Scruggs and Allan (2006). Tax wedge: OECD data. Employment Protection Legislation: Strictness of employment protection legislation. Scale ranging from 1 to 5 in 1970–2003 and 1 to 6 in 1985–2008 from Allard (2005) and Venn (2009). Product market regulations: Regulations in seven non–manufacturing industries. Scale 0–6 from least to most restrictive, OECD.Stat. The time–series for UB, Sickness and Pensions ends in 2002. For these variables the figures in the last column refers to 2000–2002. * Last period covers 2005–2008. ** Last period data includes 2005–2007.

The wave of reforms that started in the 1980s also included the labour market, social insurance and pensions, as well as different social services and educational systems. Table 13.3 also shows some of these changes in the core programmes with importance for the labour market. The developments with regard to generosity in sickness and pension benefits as well as employment protection are similar. Generosity increased up to 1990 after which it has declined, and with regard to pensions generosity has even fallen below the figures for 1970–74. There have in both these systems been a number of changes in addition to the level of compensation. For instance, a period of qualifying time has been reintroduced into health insurance; the level of individual contribution to the pension scheme has been increased; and the number of qualifying years has been increased. These changes increase the dependence of individuals on the market, making it more costly to remain outside the workforce for even a short time. The strictness of employment protection legislation shows the same pattern of liberalization: for instance, some restrictions on vacancies and time-limited jobs have been repealed and some exceptions have been made in the rules of priority in cases of redundancy.

The figures on unemployment benefits seem to be untouched during the period and differ from the other parts of the social insurance system. However, the figures do not tell the whole story as they do not include the most recent events. Traditionally the unemployment funds were in the hands of the unions and were substantially subsidized by the government. In 2007, the government decided to radically change the financing system for these funds by raising the membership fees dramatically and at the same time abolishing the tax exemption for the fees as well as for the costs of union membership (for more details, see above).

A new majority coalition government was formed after the 2006 election and was re-elected as a minority administration in 2010. Yet in order to get elected and to stay in power the government had changed strategy dramatically. The Conservative Party, the strong and dominant partner within the Alliance in both instances, did not explicitly preach a market orientation and radical liberal reforms. It rather presented itself as the new labour party, focusing on job creation and fighting unemployment. The right-wing parties tried and succeeded in beating the Social Democrats on traditional labour issues. Earlier messages promising sweeping liberal reforms in the labour market, decentralization of the bargaining system and abolition of labour laws were replaced with more pragmatic and labour-friendly attitudes. The government invited the labour market organizations to discussions in order to find common ground and they retained the existing labour laws, including the hotly debated dismissal rules, as well as the collective bargaining system. Furthermore, it has left the unemployment insurance system intact and thus still in the hands of the unions. The parties reached an agreement on shorter working hours and are aiming for formal tripartite talks and settlements in the future regarding several crucial issues affecting the labour market (*LO-tidningen*). The recent (2012) talks also produced a policy package on reducing youth unemployment. It is worth mentioning that the employers peak organization seems to have returned from its abdication as a representative of the employers' interests.

Paradoxically, the crucial decisions that brought about radical changes seem to have been the decentralization and liberal reforms initiated by the Social Democratic governments in the 1980s. Some of these measures were introduced to make the welfare state bureaucracy more responsive to citizens' needs; other steps were first and foremost a way to handle the ever growing costs. These initiatives, however, paved the way for the more radical reforms introduced by the non-socialist government in the early 1990s, focused on deregulation and fostering freedom of choice within the welfare system. Despite deregulation, the welfare system remains a public, compulsory and general system, including all citizens in the same way, contributing to at least basic security. In many cases, it is still a generous system offering income security. The welfare state is still strongly supported by the public and the impact of the 'revolution of choice' was not as radical as its proponents and its principles initially suggested.

Employment relations outcomes

In the 1930s, employers first initiated and then strongly adhered to centralized wage bargaining in order to make the export sector set the benchmark for wages and therefore keep wages down within the sheltered sector of the economy. However, an unintended consequence was a 'solidaristic wage policy' that narrowed wage differentials between skilled and unskilled workers. This in turn resulted in growing problems of recruitment of skilled workers in manufacturing industry and especially in the export-oriented industries. In the course of time, representatives from export industries, especially the metals industry, in alliance with the metal workers union, reconsidered their position and in 1983 they openly defected from central agreements (Traxler *et al.* 2008; Hall and Thelen 2009: 15). Wage settlements varied between centralized and industry level during the following years in the 1980s. The ultimate break with centralized bargaining came in 1990 when the employers main organization, the Swedish Employers Confederation (SAF), settled the matter by turning the organization into a lobbying group and conclusively abdicated its role as a negotiating partner (Kjellberg 2011: 85 et ff.; Lindgren 2011; Öberg *et al.* 2011). The decision signalled a clear movement towards decentralized wage bargaining. The movement was temporarily delayed and moderated by the economic crisis and an agreement was reached under the guidance of a mediation commission initiated by the government (the Rehnberg-kommisionen), after a spectacular governmental intervention proposing a wage and strike freeze. The following bargaining round, in 1993, was more decentralized and carried out in a pattern-bargaining mode. However, it was accomplished in the same spirit as the preceding round and under the guidance of a mediation group. In the following round in 1995–96, the metal industry employers once again took the initiative and the resultant wage bargaining was the most uncoordinated and decentralized since the end of the Second World War (Elvander 2002a, 2002b; Lindgren 2011). The bargaining round in 1995–96 provoked great tensions in the labour market, resulting in a lack of wage moderation combining uncoordinated wage demands and wage drift. In the words of one researcher, '[it] was the most conflict ridden in Sweden since that of the "great conflict" in 1980, caused great discord within the employer collective and increased awareness of the risks associated with uncoordinated wage bargaining' (Lindgren 2011: 55; see also Elvander 2002b).

Thus, wage bargaining was decentralized in the 1980s and 1990s and the peak organizations of unions and employers lost some influence. These changes signified a development from the three-tier to a two-tier bargaining system where the collective agreements at the national level between national unions and the employer representatives in different lines of business were mostly were about basic terms and conditions. The detailed and concrete parts of the agreements were transferred to the workplace between the employer and local unions (Kjellberg 1998). Statistics clearly show this downward trend in wage coordination from the 1970s to the end of the 1990s. However, in a comparative perspective, coordination remained quite high and, due to strong national unions and high union density, bargaining never became fragmented or placed entirely on the firm level (Kenworthy 2001; Lindgren 2011; Visser 2011).

The newly elected 1996 Social Democratic government threatened to intervene in the wage bargaining process, unless the social partners did not begin to cooperate, and their action resulted in two important outcomes: the Industrial Agreement of 1997 and the creation of a new mediation institute, the 'Medlingsinstitutet', introduced by parliament in 2000. The 1997 agreement was initiated by unions within the industrial sector, led by the metal workers, and covered almost the whole competitive sector and included both blue-collar and white-collar unions. The first round of negotiations based on this agreement was carried out in 1998 under the guidance of private mediators appointed by a joint committee, and with a successful outcome, establishing a wage norm following the European Union (EU) average and without any industrial disputes. The settlement set the pattern for other sectors which quickly concluded agreements without any threats or actions (Elvander 2002a, 2002b). The first Industrial Agreement has been followed by several bargaining rounds and the pattern set by the manufacturing sector has been more or less respected by other sectors since then, in spite of growing discontent from the non-manufacturing unions (Lindgren 2011). A new Industrial Agreement was concluded in 2011 and the subsequent figures for working time lost to industrial conflicts are almost zero. Central bargaining has not been re-established but Sweden has witnessed the revival of coordinated capitalism.

The decentralization of bargaining and the movement towards an uncoordinated labour market in the 1990s became an interregnum between two different means for wage coordination. There has been a transition from centralized wage bargaining to coordination through pattern-bargaining. Collective bargaining coverage – the proportion of employees covered by collective agreements – has remained very high. It has declined by about 5 per cent since the mid-1990s but is still as high as 90 per cent across the whole labour market (Kjellberg 2011: 86; Medlingsinstitutet 2012).

Conclusion

After a remarkable period of economic growth following the Second World War, the Swedish economy slowed down during the 1970s and 1980s. The slowdown and the subsequent economic crisis seemed to pave the way for market liberal ideas, huge public deficits, unstable and shifting political alliances and radical changes in the labour market.

What happened to the actors during this period? The unions had already experienced less public support and weakened links to the Social Democratic Party. In comparative perspective the figures for union density are still very high with a unionization rate reaching over 70 per cent of the workforce. However, since the 1990s, unionization figures have declined; the main union organizations have lost their former position; and the development of a European labour market based on individual legal rights rather than on national collective agreements reflects to some extent the weakened union power resources. At the same time, employers remain highly organized and their peak organization has been transformed into a political lobbying body. In combination with their enhanced political influence, due to professionalized political lobbying as well as the existence of non-socialist governments and the end of centralized wage-bargaining, employers and employers organizations seem to have strengthened their relative positions vis-à-vis the unions. Regarding governmental action and policies, there is a clear tendency for liberalization during these years: slightly less generous social insurance and pension systems, less strict employment protection, somewhat lower taxes and strongly deregulated product markets. In all, the welfare state seems less decommodified than before although the reforms still represent marginal adjustments to a public, compulsory and universal system. Industrial relations changed as well during the period and the centralized system of wage bargaining was significantly undermined in 1990 when the employers peak-level organization openly abandoned centralization and actively aimed for decentralized wage bargaining. Nevertheless there was a return to more bargaining coordination after the Industrial Agreement in 1997.

In one respect, market forces and exogenous events had obvious effects on the actors, on industrial relations and on political decisions. Declining international competitiveness due to rising costs and solidaristic wage policies related to centralized wage bargaining led export-oriented employers to defect from the predominant order. Economic stagnation in the 1970s also led the unions to propose legislation that was perceived to threaten the old class compromise and employers' prerogative. Declining union density seems to be, at least partly, related to de-industrialization as well as to value changes among new generations of citizens. European legislation on minimal wages and on individual rights is discordant with the Swedish model of collective bargaining and seems to be a serious threat to the core values of the system.

However, the reactions to exogenous shocks and events among the main actors on the labour market differ depending on the institutional and political context. The actual industrial structure and the configuration of formal institutions and organizations vary between different states. Actors calculate their gains and losses differently and therefore act differently depending on their relative power and on supporting institutions. The drive for liberalization has meant quite different things in Sweden compared to Britain:

> Liberalization in Britain was associated with the decline of unions and employers associations, effectively dismantling some kinds of coordinating capacities. In Sweden, in contrast, liberalization involved a movement away from national-level wage coordination, accompanied by cross-class realignment that brought much closer coordination between blue and white collar bargaining within the export sector.
>
> (Hall and Thelen 2009: 23)

Market forces (as well as ideological swings or similar general events) of course make a difference, but have varied outcomes in the relevant 'systems'. Globalization has an impact but the direction and size of the impact are determined by the interplay between actions and institutions, creating divergent trajectories in different types of institutional set-up (Svensson 2002; Oskarsson 2003; Hall and Thelen 2009).

Considering the political situation with radical liberals in the driving seat and an employers organization aiming for far-reaching decentralization, the most interesting question regarding the Swedish trajectory from the 1990s and onwards seems to be the continuity rather than change. As wages increased way above acceptable levels and conflicts intensified, it became apparent that the liberal experiment was simply not compatible with strong trade unions. The proponents of liberal reforms had to put their first-order preferences aside. As Lindgren puts it:

> In a context . . . characterized by high union density, few restrictions on the use of industrial action, and generous welfare benefits that increased the bargaining position of the unions by decreasing competition from 'outsiders', decentralized wage bargaining has entailed substantial risk for employers.
>
> (2011: 56)

Welfare retrenchment was motivated and realized only as a way to handle budget deficits (Swank and Martin 2001). The support for the universalistic and generous welfare state remained strong among the public even during economic crisis, and arguments for sweeping liberal reforms met strong opposition from the trade unions. The idea of 'institutional complementarities' and the associated constraints on interests and decision-making seems to go well with what happened in Sweden. The constraints on radical reform also explain why the Conservative Party a decade later presented itself as the 'New Workers' Party' and embraced collective agreements and existing labour laws.

The cross-class alliance between organized labour and capital, agreed upon back in the 1930s and generally characterized as social corporatism, seems to have adapted to new economic and political pressures and emerged in a new modernized version in which Sweden still represents a typical coordinated market economy. The industrial agreement can be seen as a new cross-class coalition between the partners within the manufacturing sector and has implied the revival of coordination through new pattern-setting mechanisms of wage bargaining. Although the current industrial relations system has not been free of challenges, it seems so far to have survived threats from declining unionization, the growth of the service sector and a shrinking unionized industrial working-class as well as competition from an open European labour market.

References

Allard, G. J. (2005) *Measuring Job Security Over Time: In Search of a Historical Indicator for EPL (Employment Protection Legislation)*, Madrid: Instituto de Empresa, Working Paper No. 17.

Allern, E. H, Aylott, N. and Christiansen, H. J. (2007) 'Social Democrats and trade unions in Scandinavia', *European Journal of Political Research*, 46(5): 607–35.

Åmark, K. (1988) 'Sammanhållning och intressepolitik', in K. Misgeld, K. Molin and K. Åmark (eds) *Socialdemokratins Samhälle. SAP och Sverige under 100 år*, Stockholm: Tiden.

Andersen, S. K. (2006) 'Nordic metal trade unions on the move: responses to globalization and Europeanization', *European Journal of Industrial Relations*, 12(1): 29–47.

Armingeon, K., Gerber, M., Leimgruber, P., and Beyler, M. (2008) *Comparative Political Data Set 1960–2006*, Bern: Institute of Political Science, University of Bern.

Blyth, M. (2002) *Great Transformations: Economic Ideas and Institutional Change in the Twentieth Century*, Cambridge: Cambridge University Press.

Bonoli, G. (2010) 'The political economy of active labor-market policy', *Politics and Society*, 38(4): 435–57.

Elvander, N. (1988) *Den Svenska Modellen: löneförhandlingar och inkomstpolitik, 1982–1986*, Stockholm: Allmänna Förlaget.

—— (2002a) 'The new Swedish regime for collective bargaining and conflict resolution', *European Journal of Industrial Relations*, 8(2): 197–216.

—— (2002b) 'The labour market regimes in the Nordic countries', *Scandinavian Political Studies*, 25(2): 117–37.

Fleming, R. W. (1967) 'The Labor Court idea', *Michigan Law Review*, 65(8): 1551–68.

Fulcher, J. (1991) *Labour Movements, Employers, and the State: Conflict and Co-operation in Britain and Sweden*, Oxford: Clarendon Press.

Gidlund, G. (1988) 'Folkrörelsepartiet och den politiska styrelsen. SAP: organisationsutveckling', in K. Misgeld, K. Molin and K. Åmark (eds), *Socialdemokratins Samhälle. SAP och Sverige under 100 år*, Stockholm: Tidens Förlag.

Hall, P. A. (1999) 'The political economy of Europe in an era of interdependence', in H. P. Kitchelt, G. Lange, D. Marks and J. D. Stephens (eds) *Continuity and Change in Contemporary Capitalism*, New York: Cambridge University Press.

—— and Soskice, D. (2001) 'An introduction to varieties of capitalism', in P.A. Hall and D. Soskice (eds) *Varieties of Capitalism: The Institutional Foundations of Comparative Advantage*, Oxford: Oxford University Press.

—— and Thelen, K. (2009) 'Institutional change in varieties of capitalism', *Socio-Economic Review*, 7(1): 7–34.

Hermansson, J., Lund, A., Svensson, T. and Öberg, P. O. (1999) *Avkorporativisering och Lobbyism*, Demokratiutredningens Forskarvolym XIII, Stockholm: SOU (Swedish Government Report), 1999:121.

Holmlund, B. and Lundborg, P. (1999) 'Wage bargaining, union membership, and the organization of unemployment insurance', *Labour Economics*, 6(3): 397–415.

Iversen, T. (1998) 'Wage bargaining, hard money and economic performance: theory and evidence for organized market economies', *British Journal of Political Science*, 28(1): 31–61.

Johansson, J. (2003) 'Mid-level officials as policy makers: anti-corporatist policy change in the Swedish Employers' Confederation, 1982–1985', *Scandinavian Political Studies*, 26(4): 307–25.

Katzenstein, P. (1985) *Small States in World Markets: Industrial Policy in Europe*, Ithaca, NY: Cornell University Press.

Kenworthy, L. (2001) *Wage-Setting Coordination Scores*, Tucson: University of Arizona, Department of Sociology Dataset. Available at: http://www.u.arizona.edu/~lkenwor/WageCoorScores.pdf.

King, D. and Rothstein, B. (1993) 'Institutional choices and labor market policy', *Comparative Political Studies*, 26(2): 147–77.

Kjellberg, A. (1998) 'Sweden: restoring the model?', in A. Ferner, and R. Hyman (eds) *Changing Industrial Relations in Europe*, Oxford: Blackwell.

—— (2000) 'Sweden', in B. Ebbinghaus and J. Visser (eds) *Trade Unions in Western Europe Since 1945*, London: Macmillan.

—— (2011) 'The decline in Swedish union density since 2007', *Nordic Journal of Working Life Studies*, 1(1): 67–93.

Lewin, L. (1994) 'The rise and decline of corporatism: the case of Sweden', *European Journal of Political Research*, 26(1): 59–79.

Lindgren, K. O. (2011) 'The variety of capitalism in Sweden and Finland', in U. Becker (ed.) *The Changing Political Economies of Small West European Countries*, Amsterdam: Amsterdam University Press.

Lindvall, J. and Rothstein, B. (2006) 'Sweden: the fall of the strong state', *Scandinavian Political Studies*, 29(1): 47–63.

—— and Sebring, J. (2005) 'Policy reform and the decline of corporatism in Sweden', *West European Politics*, 28(5): 1057–74.

LO-rapport (2007) *Röster Om Facket och Jobbet: ungdomar och facket*, Stockholm: Landsorganisationen i Sverige.

LO-tidningen (2012), weekly paper of the LO, No. 6.

Magnusson, L. (2006) 'The Swedish model in historical context', *Kobe University Economic Review*, 52: 1–8.

Medlingsinstitutet (2012) *Avtalsrörelsen och Lönebildningen 2011*, Stockholm: Medlingsinstitutet (Swedish National Mediation Office).

Meidner, R. (1986) 'Swedish union strategies towards structural change', *Economic and Industrial Democracy*, 7(1): 85–97.

Öberg, P. O and Svensson, T. (2012) 'Civil society and deliberative democracy: have voluntary organizations faded from national public politics?', *Scandinavian Political Studies*, 35(3): 246–71.

Öberg, P. O, Svensson, T., Munk Christiansen, P., Sonne Nørgaard, A., Rommetvedt, H. and Thesen, G. (2011) 'Disrupted exchange and declining corporatism', *Government and Opposition*, 46(3): 365–91.

OECD (Organisation for Economic Cooperation and Development). Available at: http://stats.oecd.org (accessed 8 June 2012).

Oskarsson, S. (1997) *Påverka och Påverkas. 1994 års reformering av arbetslöshetsförsäkringen*, Uppsala: Uppsala Universitet, PISA-Projektets Rapporter.

—— (2003) *The Fate of Organized Labor*, Uppsala: Acta Upsaliensis Universitatis.

Petersson, O. (1991) 'Democracy and power in Sweden', *Scandinavian Political Studies*, 14(2): 173–91.

Pontusson, J. (1993) 'The comparative politics of labor-initiated reforms: Swedish cases of success and failure', *Comparative Political Studies*, 25(4): 548–78.

Rothstein, B. (1987) 'Corporatism and reformism: the social democratic institutionalization of class conflict', *Acta Sociologica*, 30(3/4): 295–311.

—— (1990) 'Marxism, institutional analysis, and working class power: the Swedish case', *Politics and Society*, 18(3): 317–45.

—— (1996) *The Social Democratic State: The Swedish Model and the Bureaucratic Problem of Social Reforms*, Pittsburgh, PA: University of Pittsburgh Press.

—— (2001) 'Social capital in the social democratic welfare state', *Politics and Society*, 29(2): 207–41.

—— and Bergström, J. (1999) *Korporatismens Fall och den Svenska Modellens Kris*, Stockholm: SNS Förlag.

Scruggs, L. (2002) 'The Ghent System and union membership in Europe', *Political Research Quarterly*, 55(2): 275–97.

Scruggs, L. and Allan, J. P. (2006) 'The material consequences of welfare states: benefit generosity and absolute poverty in 16 OECD countries', *Comparative Political Studies*, 39(7): 880–904.

Statistics Sweden. Available at: http://www.scb.se/Pages/SSD/SSD_TreeView_340506.aspx (accessed 8 June 2012).

Svensson, T. (1994) *Socialdemokratins Dominans*, Uppsala: Acta Universitatis Upsaliensis.

—— (2002) 'Globalization, marketization and power: the Swedish case of institutional change', *Scandinavian Political Studies*, 25(3): 197–229.

——, Mabuchi, M and Kamikawa, R. (2006) 'Managing the bank-system crisis in coordinated market economies', *Governance*, 19(1): 43–74.

—— and Öberg, P.O. (2002) 'Labour market organizations' participation in Swedish public policy-making', *Scandinavian Political Studies*, 25(4): 295–315.

—— and Öberg, P.O. (2005) 'How are coordinated market economies coordinated?', *West European Politics*, 28(5): 1075–100.

Swank, D. and Martin, C. J. (2001) 'Employers and the welfare state: the political economic organization of firms and social policy in contemporary capitalist democracies', *Comparative Political Studies*, 34(8): 889–923.

Swenson, P. (1991a) 'Bringing capital back in, or social democracy reconsidered', *World Politics*, 43(4): 513–44.

—— (1991b) 'Labor and the limits of the welfare state: the politics of intra-class conflict and cross-class alliances in Sweden and West Germany', *Comparative Politics*, 23(4): 379–99.

—— (2002) *Capitalists against Markets*, Oxford: Oxford University Press.

—— and Pontusson, J. (2000) 'The Swedish employer offensive against centralized wage bargaining', in T. Iversen, J. Pontusson and D. Soskice (eds) *Unions, Employers, and Central Banks*, New York: Cambridge University Press.

Taylor, A. J. (1993) 'Trade unions and the politics of social democratic renewal', *West European Politics*, 16(1): 133–55.

Thelen, K. (2001) 'Varieties of labor politics in the developed democracies', in P. A. Hall and D. Soskice (eds) *Varieties of Capitalism: The Institutional Foundations of Comparative Advantage*, Oxford: Oxford University Press.

Traxler, F., Brandl, B. and Glassner, V. (2008) 'Pattern bargaining: an investigation into its agency, context and evidence', *British Journal of Industrial Relations*, 46(1): 33–58.

Venn, D. (2009) *Legislation, Collective Bargaining and Enforcement: Updating the OECD Employment Protection Indicators*, Paris: OECD Social, Employment and Migration Working Papers.

Visser, J. (1996) 'Corporatism beyond repair? Industrial relations in Sweden', in J. Van Ruysseveldt and J. Visser (eds) *Industrial Relations in Europe*, London: Sage.

—— (2011) *ICTWSS: Database on Institutional Characteristics of Trade Unions, Wage Setting, State Intervention and Social Pacts in 34 countries between 1960 and 2007, Version 3*, Amsterdam: University of Amsterdam Institute for Advanced Labour Studies. Available at: http://www.uva-aias.net/208.

Wallerstein, M. and Golden, M. (2000) 'Postwar wage setting in the Nordic countries', in T. Iversen, J. Pontusson and D. Soskice (eds) *Unions, Employers and Central Banks*, New York: Cambridge University Press.

Wood, S. (2002) 'Labour market regimes under threat?', in P. Pierson (ed.) *The New Politics of the Welfare State*, Oxford: Oxford University Press.

Woolfson, C. and Sommers, J. (2006) 'Labour mobility in construction: European implications of the Laval un Partneri dispute with Swedish labour', *European Journal of Industrial Relations*, 12(1): 49–68.

14 Japan

D. Hugh Whittaker

Introduction

Once the subject of great admiration – and fear – Japanese employment relations have come under intense pressure for change over the past fifteen years.[1] Pressure stems from changes in the competitive environment, legal and regulatory change, the prolonged domestic recession and economic turbulence, and the ageing workforces, among other factors. Empirical studies have shown a *partial* shift away from Japan's 'classic model', with greater prominence given to market forces, and increased diversity in employment practices. Institutionalist perspectives have mainly been deployed to explain the nuances of change and continuity, often within a 'varieties of capitalism' framework. Political or political economy perspectives (see Chapter 2 in this volume) have received less attention. This chapter stresses the need to understand actors, *and agency*, and specifically how changing competitive conditions and challenges have been perceived, debated and responded to, in terms of employment and employment relations. Significantly, this applies to continuity as much as change. The chapter begins with the evolution of employment relations in Japan, and the main actors under the 'classic model' or 'Japanese-style' employment. This creates threads for the subsequent discussion of pressures for change and responses by the key actors. Theoretical interpretations of the resulting mixture of change and continuity are then discussed.

Evolution of employment relations in Japan

The Meiji period (1868–1912) saw a momentous transformation in Japan, as the feudal order was consciously dismantled and a new industrial order was constructed under the banner 'Japanese spirit, Western technology'. The relationship between 'Japanese spirit' and 'Western technology' was hotly contested, but also encouraged considerable experimentation and improvization. In the area of employment regulation, for instance, proponents (largely bureaucrats and academics) argued for legislation to preserve social stability and peace, while opponents (largely industrialists) claimed it would destroy Japan's 'beautiful customs' through the interjection of 'cold' Western legal practices. Both groups, however, agreed that factories should be a moral community, and industrialists were under pressure to demonstrate this to legitimize capitalism in the new order. After almost three decades, the Factory Law was finally enacted in 1911 (Dore and Whittaker 2001: Chapter 9).

Industrialization accelerated in the 1910s, boosted by the need for import substitution, as the First World War interrupted the importation of many industrial supplies, and provided opportunities for exporting to Asia. Manufacturing output increased by 75 per cent between 1914 and 1919, spurring rapid urbanization. By 1918, an urban labour movement had begun to emerge, which, when set alongside riots over rising rice prices, and the visible example of revolution in Russia, gave rise to new concerns about social stability. These concerns led to the formation of the semi-bureaucratic Kyochokai (Cooperation and Harmony Association) in 1919, which:

> took the lead in creating and articulating the new industrial ideology, the new tradition that its members hoped would redefine economic relationships. The organization and its spokesmen emphasized the 'primacy of moral community and the need for industrial harmony and cooperation'.
>
> (Kinzley 1991: xiv)

Significantly, the organization stressed the subordination of both capital and labour interests to national objectives of economic growth and social stability. Employers were already grappling with stability in their workforces. In shipyards in the 1910s, turnover was commonly in excess of 100 per cent. Skilled craftsmen were particularly mobile, and *oyakata* – foremen or gangers – could quit and take their whole gang with them.[2] In order to incorporate or control the *oyakata*, as well as to train workers and then retain them, and to contain the growing labour movement, managers began to experiment with mechanisms to foster loyalty, such as wage increases and bonuses based on length of service.

These developments coincided with the growing professionalization of managers in the 1910s, which conversely led to friction with capitalists who 'buy up stock for speculative reasons, control the future course of the company, make imprudent plans to increase stock . . . [and] keep the employees in a miserable state and endanger the basis of the existence of the company'.[3] The balance of power swung towards the managers, especially in the new science-based industries which were emerging in the 1920s; champions such as Masatoshi Okochi, director of Riken, strongly advocated 'science-based industry' as opposed to 'capitalistic industry' (Cusumano 1989).

The late 1910s and 1920s, then, saw the budding of 'Japanese-style employment,' as well as a distinctive producer-oriented capitalism whose legitimacy depended on its contribution to larger national goals. With growing militarization and colonial expansion in the 1930s, state intervention increased in all areas of the economy, including employment relations. As Japan plunged into war in China in 1936, and the Pacific in 1941, worker mobility was suppressed, wage systems were regulated based on cost of living calculations, and the remnants of independent unions were squeezed into bureaucrat-dominated 'Patriotic Industrial Associations' (*Sanpo*).

Gordon (1985) argues that Japanese employment relations are the result of pre-war management initiatives, wartime bureaucratic decree, and early post-war worker pressure, subsequently reshaped by management. During the post-war Allied Occupation independent unions were legalized, and by the late 1940s over half of the workforce belonged to a union. These were particularly concerned with employment security, securing basic living wages, and the removal of large status differences which relegated blue-collar workers to second-class status. The Occupation authorities eventually became alarmed at the growing militancy of the labour movement, and changed their emphasis from democratization to economic rehabilitation; Japan was to become an ally in US geo-politics. Employers regrouped, and eventually emerged victorious in a number of key disputes in the late 1940s and 1950s. In the process, they confronted the labour movement, suppressed trans-corporate activities and encouraged enterprise unions, and within these, favoured 'moderate' as opposed to confrontational factions (cf. Kawanishi 1992). They worked hard to reassert managerial control over the shop-floor. Critically, however, they did not negate key post-war demands of workers, noted above, but worked to reshape them.[4]

As the economy picked up in the 1950s, initially stimulated by Korean War procurements, attention turned to improving quality and productivity, which lagged far behind the USA. The tripartite (management, labour and academic) Japan Productivity Centre was formed in 1955, based on three key principles – employment security; joint consultation; and a 'fair distribution' of the fruits of productivity increases between management, labour and the consumer (shareholders were not mentioned). The diffusion of these concepts, as well as organizational innovations such as the incorporation of 'new foremen' into the management hierarchy in order to promote technological innovation, created a basis for the establishment of cooperative industrial relations aligned with corporate growth objectives for which Japan subsequently became famous. A second crucial development in 1955 was the formalization of *Shunto*, the Spring wage offensive. Under *Shunto*, powerful unions became 'pattern setters', attempting to create a wage increase which would become normative, even in smaller businesses, where the receding tide of union organization was reducing the bargaining power of workers. *Shunto* became the unofficial wealth distribution mechanism of the government's income doubling campaign of the 1960s.

As the economy boomed into the 1960s, companies were forced to provide training for 'golden egg' middle school leavers, which included setting up their own schools for technical education. They also had to provide housing in the form of company dormitories built in and around the industrial cities. These measures evolved into comprehensive packages described vividly by Dore (1973) as 'welfare corporatism'. This differed from pre-war paternalism in that post-war welfare provision was an institutionalized employee right, derived from collective bargaining and joint consultation (cf. also Hazama 1979).

As we shall see, Japanese employment relations have continued to evolve, but the basic shape of the 'classic model' had been laid down by the 1960s, and was consolidated in the economic turbulence of the 1970s. The model is commonly depicted in terms of 'three pillars' of lifetime (or long-term) employment, *nenko* (seniority plus merit) wages and promotion, and enterprise unions. These employment relations, moreover, were strongly supported by government policies and legal rulings, which upheld employment security, and at the same time facilitated the movement of workers from declining industries to emerging ones through retraining programmes (Sugeno 1996).

There were fierce debates about the extent to which Japan's model was exceptional. Despite the evolutionary changes noted above, some scholars emphasized underlying continuity with Japan's pre-industrial past, whether in the form of village-like (*mura*) relations, or family or household (*ie*) relations. Many believed that Japan's distinctive features would disappear as the country modernized. Hence: 'For modern companies lifetime employment makes it difficult to adjust workforces with technological innovation. Henceforth the demerits of maintaining managerial welfarism will come to outweigh the merits' (Hazama 1960: 123).[5] Dore (1973), on the other hand, thought that as a 'late developer' Japan had skipped a stage of development – competitive individualistic capitalism – and plunged directly into a stage of organized capitalism more suited to modern industrial production. Rather than Japan changing to become more like the UK, he predicted the reverse would happen. This prediction was borne out to some extent in the 1980s (cf. Oliver and Wilkinson 1992).

Actors

Let us now delve deeper into the 'classic model' or 'Japanese-style' employment relations in their heyday from the 1960s to the end of the 1980s by looking at the actors, starting with labour unions.

Labour unions

Attempts to organize unions in the Meiji period were unsuccessful, but three days after the Meiji Emperor's death, the Yuaikai (Friendly Society) was launched, taking the name of earlier counterparts in the UK. The driving figure, Bunji Suzuki, pressed on to form a Japanese version of the American Federation of Labor, which was finally launched in 1919 as Sodomei. The organization was plagued by ideological schisms, and by the mid-1920s, under employer pressure, enterprise unions had become the predominant form of worker organization. Employers had decided that if unions could not be suppressed, then they would negotiate with people who shared common interests with them.[6] This legacy, plus the wartime *Sanpo* associations, and the early post-war 'workplace struggles', laid the foundations for the resurrection of enterprise unions in the post-war period. Other types of unions did exist, however, and some of these have become more prominent in recent years, as we shall see.

Enterprise unions are not 'company unions'. First, early post-war union leaders were well aware of the dangers of 'enterprise egoism', and they attempted to balance within-enterprise 'workplace struggles' with 'political struggle' (typically opposing ruling conservative Liberal Democratic Party policies) outside enterprises. The tide of labour militancy was eventually rolled back in both spheres in the 1950s, culminating respectively with defeat in the miners Miike Dispute – similar in many ways to the 1984–85 miners strike in the UK – and the signing of the US-Japan Security Treaty, both in 1960. While industrial relations became more cooperative, however, strike activity was not notably low by international standards. Second, 'enterprise union' does not necessarily mean that an enterprise only has one union. Originally many factories had separate unions, which over time were amalgamated into an enterprise union. Conversely, however, sometimes there were splits, often around ideology and willingness to cooperate with management. Even in the late 1980s some 15 per cent of enterprises with one union also had a second union.

Third, most unions were affiliated with industry-level federations and ultimately a national centre or confederation. The balance between these levels differed. Industrial affiliates of the more left-wing national centre Sohyo were more likely to comprise enterprise- (or factory-) level branch organizations, while affiliates of the more right-wing national centre Domei (formed in 1964) were more likely to be federations of enterprise-level unions. That said, the predominant form of organization which emerged in the 1950s–1960s was the enterprise union, which organized both blue-collar and white-collar regular workers up to junior management level. In most cases a closed shop arrangement operated, with automatic check-off of union dues. Authority to negotiate wages and to call strikes ultimately resided at the enterprise level. Not surprisingly, such unions were easier to sustain in large companies, and after the tide of union organization began to recede in the 1950s, workers in smaller companies were often left high and dry.[7]

Wage negotiations, however, did not take place in a vacuum. As noted above, from the mid-1950s *Shunto* became a strong and normative influence on enterprise-level bargaining. After its formation in 1964, the Japanese Chapter of the International Metalworkers Federation (IMF-JC) gradually became the pattern setter, and ultimately a force for wage restraint to maintain competitiveness and jobs (Sako 1997). This was particularly important in curbing wage (and price) inflation in the 1970s. As the scope for bargaining wage increases shrank, however, and as attention turned from nominal wage increases to real wage increases, unions sought 'voice' on other issues, such as working hours and welfare conditions. Aspects of these issues could not be bargained over in single enterprises, or by a fragmented labour movement, so IMF-JC leaders pushed for unification of national centres, and greater participation in national policy formation (*seisaku sanka*). These efforts culminated with the dissolution of Sohyo and Domei and the formation of Rengo (the Japanese Trade Union Confederation) in 1989. Although Japan never developed the neo-corporatist institutions of, for example, Sweden or even Germany, it could no longer be dismissed as a country of 'corporatism without labour'.[8] Just months after Rengo was formed, however, Japan's asset bubble burst, and the country entered a new era, along with a new Emperor.

Employers

The counterpart to labour unions in shaping employment relations is employers. Before we pass over this apparently banal statement, we should first pause to consider who the 'employers' are. The term was once used almost interchangeably with 'capital', and in Japan was preferred by those who rejected class struggle. But in fact the interests of the legal owners of the firm, the shareholders, are not necessarily the same as those who make the decisions about employment matters, who are typically managers. As we have seen, the interests and influence of the former were curbed in pre-war and wartime Japan. And as we have also seen, shareholders did not feature as worthy recipients of the fruits of productivity increases in the founding principles of the Japan Productivity Centre.

The ownership structure of Japanese firms underwent an enormous shift after the Second World War as the holding companies of the *zaibatsu* – the financial or business groups – were dismantled and their shares were dispersed. Some enterprise groups subsequently re-formed (minus holding companies), often around a core bank. Shares came to be held by other companies in the same group, or by companies which had trading, banking, insurance or other links with each other. These 'stable' shareholders by and large accepted a fixed return on their shares. In the absence of gross misconduct or prolonged poor performance, executives were essentially free to carry on with managing growth, and managing employment relations for this growth.

In the immediate post-war period employers (executives) were faced with re-establishing production, and regaining control over the production process in workplace struggles. Nikkeiren (the Japan Federation of Employers' Associations) was formed in 1948 to coordinate employers' responses and to combat militant trade unionism. It was comprised of a combination of regional and industry employers organizations.[9] Within companies, and on shop-floors, employers gradually regained the 'right to manage', and as they did so, they implemented new personnel policies, including appraisal, which were eventually applied to all regular employees and opened up ladders for promotion from the shop-floor. New joint consultation mechanisms were introduced to reduce workplace friction. Over time the threat of militancy was replaced by a new fear of 'apathy', which managers sought to combat through further personnel reforms, including the introduction of quality control circles. Some of these innovations bear a strong resemblance to Human Resource Management (HRM) which *later* emerged in the USA and other Western countries.

It is worth noting, too, that the overwhelming majority (roughly three-quarters) of directors of large companies were themselves internally promoted employees. From the 1960s onwards, this meant that they were likely to have been members of the enterprise union themselves before promotion. It was not uncommon, in fact, for them to have been in senior positions of the union in the past. When they sat down at the bargaining table, they bargained with juniors, who in turn might be in their seat in the future. They were able to appeal to overlapping interests, and the fact that short-term gains by workers could be at the expense of their long-term interests.

Thus, the 'three pillars' of lifetime (or long-term) employment, *nenko* (seniority and merit) wages and promotion and enterprise unions were not just features of employment relations, but in fact helped to shape employment relations, and wider aspects of company management and governance, notably the company-as-community system (Dore 1973; Inagami and Whittaker 2005). They did not appear suddenly as the result of culture or labour markets, but were a product of tense labour–management relations in the volatile post-war milieu, as well as management determination to reshape employment relations to build competitive products and businesses. This point is worth emphasizing as it points to the need to encompass the institutions for economic growth with political and market coordination perspectives. Agency was important for the evolution of the 'classic model', and as we shall see, it remains important today, albeit in less dramatic fashion.

Government

The main features of the classic model as described above 'are simply practices or customs; they are not mandated by law' (Araki 2009: 224). Araki contrasts Japan's 'practice-dependent' model with Germany's 'legally sanctioned' model. Indeed, many of the key features of Japanese employment relations are practice-dependent, but this does not mean that law or government have not had an important role in shaping them, a role which has become more visible in recent years.

Government regulation had a direct and increasing influence on employment and industrial relations during the lead-up to, and passage of, the Second World War. With Japan's defeat, the legal framework for employment relations was recast, in a mould bearing both domestic and foreign – especially US New Deal – influences.[10] Article 28 of the post-war (1946) Constitution guaranteed workers the right to organize, bargain and act collectively. Rights and protections were extended in a number of laws, the most important being the Trade Union Law (1945, revised 1949), which covered the rights to organize, bargain collectively and strike, the Labour Relations Adjustment Law (1946), which covered dispute settlement, and the Labour Standards Law (1947), which concerned working conditions.[11]

Whereas the Labour Standards Law gave employers the freedom to terminate employment at will after 30 days notice, the courts developed a more stringent line, negating dismissals without just cause, and creating a high bar for establishing just cause. This derived from an interpretation of the Civil Code proscribing 'abuse of rights'. According to Sugeno (1986: 110):

> The establishment of the doctrine of just cause has had a far-reaching impact upon Japanese labour law. Once the most essential management prerogative, i.e. the right of dismissal, was strictly regulated, it became easy and natural for the courts to introduce similar regulation in other aspects of personnel management. Thus, personnel practices such as disciplinary measures, transfers, termination of temporary or probationary employment and suspension of employment have been subject to scrutiny by the courts asking whether the measure violates an explicit or implicit term of the employment contract or whether it constitutes an abusive exercise of employer rights. In this way, it appears as though the Japanese courts are assuming a role similar to that of the labour arbitrator in the United States for all Japanese employees, union or non-union.

Tripartite (labour, management and academic) Labour Relations Commissions were set up, but many of the cases they dealt with concerned minority unions in large firms, or labour and employment relations in small firms. Sugeno (1996) has also argued that government policies more broadly, including economic and industrial policies, were pro-employment creation and maintenance, and greatly contributed to employment stability in Japan. Thus, while Japan may have developed a 'practice-dependent' model of employment relations, law and policy were also crucial. Efforts by unions to participate in policy formation, while also practice-dependent, attest to the importance of policy frameworks. Conversely, however, some groups, notably many female workers, found themselves not covered by such policies and practices.[12]

Employment relations processes

To see how the actors interacted to shape employment relations and the employment experiences of workers in Japan, let us look at large companies, whose processes and practices were held up as exemplary, but were imperfectly mimicked in small firms with fewer resources and stronger influence of owner-managers. We will draw illustratively on Hitachi Ltd, Japan's largest general electric company and group.[13] The point of departure in Hitachi's case is a traumatic three-month strike in 1950, which left both managers and many union leaders determined to avoid a similar occurrence in future. The union was defeated, and management regained the 'right to manage' and union policies became more oriented towards cooperation over output and productivity increases, with collective bargaining – and where necessary short, sharp strikes – securing a share of the gain. Indeed, the labour share of gross value added increased steadily from the late 1950s.

These dynamics resulted in a complex set of processes and bodies, ranging from formal collective bargaining between management and the union, through matters over which there was formal consultation but not bargaining, through less formal consultation to notification (Figure 14.1). Which matters fell into which category were spelled out in some detail, but the details acted largely as a fall-back or reference position. In practice, consultation was widespread and substantial, blurring some of these categories. The union, in effect, could appeal that aggressive managerial action threatened to undermine fairness and motivation, while management could appeal to competitiveness and long-term job security if the union pushed too far.

Enterprise unions and industrial relations interlocked with the other two pillars of lifetime or long-term employment and *nenko* wages and promotion. If employees could not be laid off easily, it made sense to select them with care, and, once selected, to ensure that their skills were developed, and that they were motivated to contribute to the company's growth and prosperity. University graduate hires at Hitachi, as at other companies, began with several months of 'front line' experience, followed by a two-year trainee period of on-job-training, off-job seminars, plant visits, language training and social events. Initial orientation and training for blue-collar workers were also extensive. These processes produced skilled and motivated workers, with a commitment to production and productivity increases.[14] The tradeoff for job security was flexibility. While the courts often backed Japanese workers against unfair dismissal, they often backed the company's right to assign workers to different workplaces.

Lifetime/long-term employment made it possible to construct a wage and promotion system which rewarded contributions over time. Broadly speaking, the *nenko* system did this, functioning as long as wage rises were matched by skill and contribution increases (and initially benefiting from the demographic dividend of a youthful workforce). It was overlaid, moreover, on the concept of a livelihood (breadwinner) wage, which rose along with family expenses. Employers frequently expressed an antipathy towards *nenko*, and supplemented it with job-based components and ability-based components. This sometimes resulted in an extraordinarily

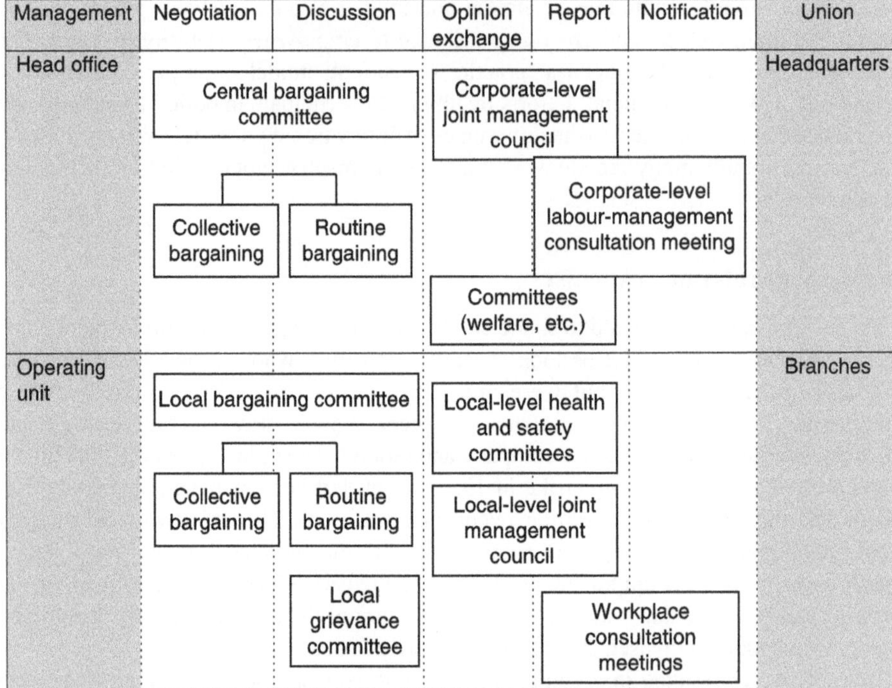

Figure 14.1 Bargaining, consultation and notification at Hitachi Ltd.

Source: Based on Hitachi Workers' Union, *Hitachi Workers' Union*, undated, p. 17.

complex wage systems, but nonetheless a predictable wage curve which sloped upwards with age; more for those seen as doing more difficult jobs and/or contributing more, but within relatively tight limits. Promotion, too, took place within relatively predictable age bands. Over time, the wage gap between blue-collar and white-collar workers narrowed substantially. The monthly wage was supplemented by a twice-yearly 'bonus', which came to about five months wages, and was also the subject of collective bargaining. Finally, there were a number of indirect welfare-related costs, which in Hitachi's case amounted to 30 per cent of direct wage costs, roughly split between statutory costs, non-statutory costs, and retirement and pension provision. Indeed, these were very elaborate as well – for 'lifetime employment' there was 'lifetime welfare' – and they reinforced the sense of company-as-community. A retiring employee could be expected to finish paying off their mortgage with the retirement lump sum, and thereafter live on a combination of company and public pension.

Needless to say, the 'three pillars' were most fully realized in large, private sector firms. From there a spectrum unfolded, with medium-sized businesses partially realizing them, perhaps substituting the mechanisms shown in Figure 14.1 with formal consultation, through less systematic practices with informal employee voice mechanisms to unilateral management discretion, along with decreasing firm size. Core regular workers were clearly the beneficiaries, while 'non-regular' workers were not, again to varying extents. Some of the latter were effectively buffers, to enhance the stability of the system for regular workers. Thus unions were not keen to organize non-regular workers.

Pressures for change and actors' reactions

Japanese employment relations seemed ideally suited for twentieth-century industrial capitalism. Contrary to many predictions, they came through the turbulent 1970s strengthened, and enjoyed their heyday of international admiration in the 1980s. The bursting of Japan's asset bubble in 1989–90, however, marked a new phase in Japan's economic development, with prolonged recession followed by woes in the financial sector, and eventually, in the wake of the Asian Financial Crisis of 1997, woes in the manufacturing heartland itself.

Financial institutions, which had been riding high with the yen's rise in the late 1980s, began to struggle with bad debts and deflated assets after 1990, and were forced to radically restructure after the Asian Financial Crisis of 1997–98. This restructuring had consequences for manufacturing. The practice of stable – often reciprocal – holding of shares began to unravel, and shares were increasingly bought by investors interested in returns rather than a business relationship *per se*. The patience of capital could no longer be taken for granted, increasing pressure on managers to adopt strategies to improve bottom-line performance. The 'new IR' – investor relations, not industrial relations – represented a new axis of tension for managers. Manufacturers faced increasing challenges in product markets as well. Emerging East Asian competitors had learned a lot about Japanese manufacturing techniques, and new modular production systems combined with global outsourcing from the USA produced a squeeze from both, especially in the ICT industries. Nowhere was this more apparent than in the semiconductor industry, which Japanese integrated electronics companies wrested control of in the 1980s, only to lose by the late 1990s. In the same way that UK and US manufacturing giants had been forced to restructure in the late 1970s and 1980s, as a result of Japanese competitive pressure, now the shoe was on the other foot. Japanese manufacturers, hugely expanded from their recent competitive successes, struggled to adapt nimbly to the changing environment. Many succumbed to 'large firm malaise'.

Mergers and acquisitions began to rise with corporate restructuring, initially within enterprise groups but increasingly beyond them. Aggressive investors began to test the waters of hostile takeovers. Most dramatic, perhaps, was the attempted takeover of Nippon Broadcasting System (NBS) by IT upstart Livedoor in February 2005, and the subsequent Tokyo District Court ruling which prevented NBS from diluting Livedoor's 30 per cent shareholding. Although Livedoor was ultimately defeated, and its president thrown in jail, tensions in (the new) IR continued (see, for instance, Whittaker and Deakin 2009).

Government

Significantly, the government also became an agent for change by chipping away at legislation and regulations which had underpinned Japan's corporate structures and employment security. From 1997 changes to the Anti-Monopoly Law and Commercial Code made it possible (or easier), for example, to establish holding companies, to restructure and to transfer undertakings. The 2002 changes to the Commercial Code made it possible for large companies to change their corporate governance structures by adopting a (US-inspired) 'company with committees system'. Accounting regulations were changed at the same time, with the overall effect of removing some of the distinctive features of Japanese regulation, and nudging Japanese companies towards US or 'global' standards.

Employment legislation was not excluded. 1980s legislation promoted opportunities for women and other groups as well as flexibility, such as the Equal Employment Opportunity Law (1985, revised 1997), the Worker Dispatching Law (1985, revised 1999), the Older

Persons Employment Stabilization Law (1986, 1994), a revision of the Disabled Persons' Employment Protection Law (1987), the Immigration Law (1990), the Childcare and Family Care Leave Law (1991, 1996) and the Part-Time Work Law (1991). The Labour Standards Law was overhauled in 1987 and 1998. Such legislation had the overall effect of shifting labour law from promoting long-term employment to a more neutral stance (Araki 2002; Inagami and Whittaker 2005: 32).

Araki (2009: 228) notes that: 'From 1995 onward, the government explicitly identified a number of labour market regulations, in particular regulations on fee-charging placement services and worker dispatching agencies (or temporary employment agencies), as urgent targets for deregulation.' This involved changes to the Employment Security Law and the Worker Dispatching Law, which essentially became permissive rather than proscriptive. Araki argues, however, that this did not in itself result in an erosion of employment security; indeed, some measures sought to enhance security in the face of corporate restructuring. To counteract the possible effects of the Transfer of Undertakings Law and changes to the Commercial Code, for example, a Labour Contract Succession Law was introduced in 2000, which stipulated that under certain conditions employment contracts would be automatically transferred to the new entity. And in the 2003 revision of the Labour Standards Law, an explicit provision on abusive dismissals was introduced as a result of a tripartite compromise.

Reflecting the growing individualization of employment relations in Japan, as well as the growing number of disputes in the face of restructuring, a new Labour Tribunal system was set up in 2006 for individual dispute resolution. And, finally, a series of legislative measures in 2007, including changes to the Part-Time Law, offered further protection for workers. These, Araki (2009: 238) concludes, have attenuated the effects of increased deregulation and corporate restructuring.

Employers

Competitive pressures on employers in the late 1990s were not new: in industries such as textiles, shipbuilding and steel they had been faced since the early 1970s. The reactions of employers in these industries offer a hint at subsequent employer restructuring measures, and industrial relations stances.

Toray Industries, a major synthetic fibre and materials producer, came under considerable pressure to reduce its workforce from the mid-1970s. Internal redeployment could not cope. A joint labour–management committee met frequently between 1975 and 1977, and one outcome was a rapid rise in the number of employees seconded to other companies in the Toray Group. By the late 1980s, over a third of the workforce was on secondment. Similarly, at Nippon Steel, the number of employees on secondment began to rise from the late 1970s, and spiked as the yen soared in the mid-1980s. When employment could no longer be maintained within such core companies, the 'lifetime employment zone' was effectively extended to the enterprise group, creating 'quasi internal labour markets'. Peripheral group companies often paid lower wages than the core company, but the latter typically made up the difference, at least for several years, to preserve 'lifetime earnings'. Secondment increasingly turned into permanent transfer, however, and the process became more strategic (Inagami and Whittaker 2005).

By the late 1990s, many more industries faced intensified competitive pressures, and the number of workers on 'loan' to group and related companies increased. By this time, however, there was more ambivalence about the virtues of the classic model. The effects of the Asian Financial Crisis were still being felt, while the US economy was riding high. And the global tide of corporate governance reform had reached Japan. Nikkeiren and Keizai Doyukai crystallized their thoughts on corporate governance in 1998.[15] Nikkeiren advocated the need to make companies attractive to both capital and labour. Others spoke more bluntly in favour of shareholder interests, including the massive Pension Fund Association. Whether or not they agreed, company executives were now having to spend more time thinking about 'investor relations' as the proportion of non-Japanese shareholders rose, and as the domestic business press joined in the chorus for bold reforms to create better returns for shareholders.

Indeed, employers began to cast an envious eye at the speed with which US competitors in particular could restructure, and new legislation in Japan presented them with new possibilities for restructuring of their own. The pressures, however, were not all external. Baby Boomers, who had provided a competitive advantage in their youth with low wages in the 1960s, were now in their fifties, and much more expensive in terms of wage costs. This was not the only demographic bulge. Many companies had been on a hiring spree in the late 1980s and early 1990s, amid fears of a shrinking youth population. This bulge of recruits, seen as less diligent than earlier generations, was surging towards management tracks. And finally, while the majority of recruits in manufacturing in the 1960s were production workers, by the late 1990s most were white-collar workers, and most were university graduates. Japanese production methods had created extremely efficient factories; productivity in offices was less tangible and more difficult to manage.

In this context, employers began to introduce performance management. At Hitachi, for example, a new HRM system introduced in 1998 de-emphasized seniority for promotion and wage increases, and clarified criteria for advancement through 15 job-type descriptions. The wage system placed greater emphasis on performance, and a new work system incorporated flexi-time, and sought to encourage individual creativity and responsibility. The welfare system was amended to allow greater individual choice from a menu of options, and to encourage greater independence on the part of employees. Pension entitlements were adjusted to place less emphasis on long service and loyalty. The first round of reforms targeted the pre-management employee bulge. The second round in 2000 targeted managers, by linking their appraisals and advancement directly with qualities and behaviour deemed important for achieving the medium-term strategic plan. High performers would gain accelerated promotion, while demotion became a possibility. These two rounds were systematized and applied to all non-management workers in 2004. The new system would reward actual performance, and de-emphasize 'uniform considerations like age, service and education'.

Such reforms were widespread. It is possible to see such them as fundamentally changing the nature of employment relations, finally heralding the demise of lifetime employment and *nenko* wages and promotion. Ishida and Sato (2011: 71) see them as part of 'a larger paradigm shift from thinking of personnel in organizational terms to thinking of personnel in market-based terms'. Furthermore: 'It is no exaggeration to say that the reforms that led to today's pay-for-performance ideas represented as thorough a dismantling as was possible of the seniority-based pay regime' (ibid.: 72). Others, however, point out that performance pay was introduced cautiously, especially after it was seen as contributing to a decline in performance at the ICT giant Fujitsu. Japanese companies may have moved in a market-oriented direction, but within limits.

Related to the partial shift is the limited appeal of shareholder-capitalism to Japanese executives, even in companies which changed their corporate governance systems. This in turn is linked to underlying continuity in senior managers' career structures: the overwhelming majority are still 'insiders'. Reforms may have been implemented to shore up the community firm rather than to dismantle it. Thus, according to Inagami (2009: 181–2):

> Ironically, it might be argued that in order to save the community firm, of which shareholders and non-regular employees are not full members – shareholders were emphasized and employees de-emphasized. Without a viable business, there is no community firm. In order to protect the firm, it can be argued that executives as well as (regular) employees and union leaders acted in concert to address the challenges they faced, the latter, for example accepting voluntary redundancies, pay freezes and other measures. Rather than destroying community firm consciousness, it may have been strengthened.

Unions

Unions were placed on the back foot by changing competitive conditions, the emergence of performance management and more individualized employment relations. *Shunto*, which had already become a vehicle for wage moderation, was threatened with complete demise as deflation and economic turbulence undermined grounds for wage increases. Indeed, in some cases, unions were forced to accept pay cuts. The focus of the offensive shifted to maintaining employee support for unions and nurturing union consciousness, as well as non wage-related issues such as extending the mandatory retirement age and employment of older workers (which was the theme in 2012).

It should be noted that unions did not face an outright assault as they did in countries such as the UK. They could point to the fact that they had fully cooperated with management, and hence competitiveness problems could not be placed at their door. As such, the burdens of restructuring should not fall disproportionately on workers. Whether union members/ employees themselves feel that their interests were protected by this logic, however, is a moot point. Nakata and Miyazaki (2011) show from their large-scale survey of electronic industry union members that working hours and working conditions deteriorated, impacting on motivation and workplace relationships, to the extent of impacting on productivity, as well as deterring young people from becoming engineers. And nominal wages in Japan fell by 11 per cent between 1995 and 2010 (Kotake 2012), while the unionization rate fell below 20 per cent overall, and was even lower in the private sector (Figure 14.2).

'Non-regular' workers and their significance

Falling wages and union membership should also be seen in the context of (post-industrial) changes in the economy, particularly tertiarization, and changes in types of employment. The two are interconnected. Out of the spotlight, employers in service industries have developed different employment strategies to meet their competitive conditions, with fewer industrial relations constraints from the early post-war years. These employment strategies, moreover, have increasingly permeated the manufacturing sector.

The most common category of non-regular workers is the part-time worker. Only a decade after Japan effectively reached full employment in the 1960s, the turbulent 1970s cautioned employers against taking on too many regular workers, and instead they opted for a combination of overtime and part-timers to help them buffer against business fluctuations. Many of the part-timers were women who came back into the labour force to supplement family income which was being stretched by inflation. Family responsibilities and tax incentives encouraged them to do this on a part-time basis.[16] Thereafter, the proportion of non-regular employees continued to grow, with a notable surge at the turn of the century (Figure 14.3). In 1988, more than 80 per cent of the workforce were regular workers, while the balance was

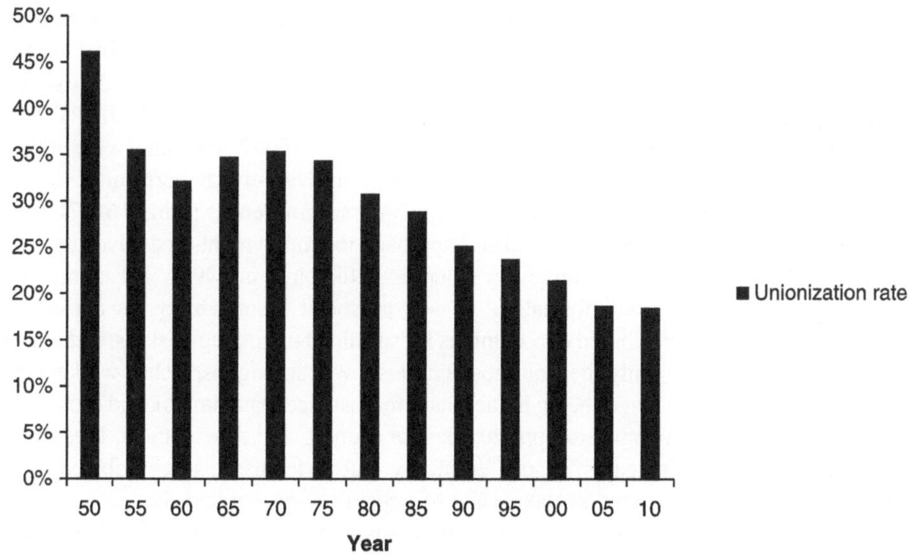

Figure 14.2 Unionization rate in Japan, 1955–2010.

Source: Ministry of Health, Labour and Welfare, *Basic Survey on Labour Unions*, cited in JILPT (various years).

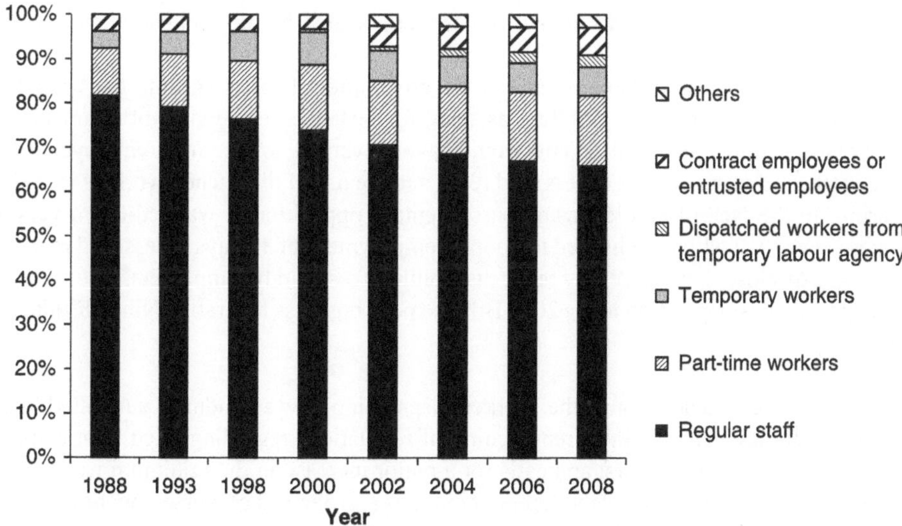

Figure 14.3 Proportion of employees by type of employment.

Source: Adapted from JILPT (2009: 23).

made up of part-timers, temporary and contract staff. Twenty years later, less than two-thirds were regular employees, and more than 35 per cent were non-regular. In industries such as hospitality and food services, as well as merchandise retail, the proportion of non-regular employees exceeded two-thirds (Asao 2011).

While employment of part-timers and temporary workers surged in the 1990s, in the 2000s other categories such as contract and 'dispatched' (often agency) workers grew, reflecting deregulation of the labour market. From just 360,000 in 2000, dispatched workers climbed to 1.4 million in 2008, before the double blow of the global financial crisis and currency appreciation saw their numbers slashed to just 900,000 in mid-2010 (JILPT 2011: 15, 21). While almost 90 per cent of part-timers were female in 2007, and many were middle-aged, some 38 per cent of dispatched workers were male, and two-thirds were under 40 years old. A much higher proportion worked in bigger businesses, moreover (ibid.: 16–17).

This suggests the emergence of a 'portfolio' approach to employment, first advocated (in a somewhat different form) by the employers federation Nikkeiren in 1995.[17] It has important implications for long-term skill formation as well as social sustainability, as non-regular employment typically offers limited opportunities for sustained upgrading of skills, and inferior conditions for supporting family life. Job satisfaction is lower among dispatched workers than other types (despite hourly wages being higher than, for instance, part-timers), and satisfaction is markedly lower when it comes to opportunities for training and development. Pressure on regular employees from increases in such employee categories has also contributed to the discontent of engineers registered in Nakata and Miyajima's survey, noted above.

The fierce cuts of dispatched workers in 2009 intensified a debate about whether Japan's youth have borne the sacrifices linked to struggling economic performance in recent years, in the form of unemployment and underemployment – and indeed over-employment. The suicide of a 26-year-old female employee of a major food service company in 2008 highlighted the extreme working hours and conditions in some parts of the service sector. In this case, her overtime hours exceeded 140 per month. After a four-year struggle by her family, in February 2012, the death was recognized as work-related by the accident compensation insurance examiner.

These debates appear to have prompted the government to start shifting the weight of regulation once more towards stability, as seen, for instance, in the attempt to amend the Worker Dispatching Law in 2010. This would have prevented, for example, employers from hiring workers for two months or less, and restricted the use of dispatched workers in manufacturing. In the face of employer and parliamentary opposition, a watered-down version was passed in 2012 which prohibited temporary employment of 30 days or less, and required agencies to disclose their share of worker dispatching fees paid by employers.

In expressing its opposition to the 2010 Bill, the peak business federation Nihon Keidanren argued:

> In recent years, in addition to the Worker Dispatching Law amendment submitted to the Diet, there are calls for the strengthening of regulations regarding fixed term contract workers and older workers, and calls for a major increase in the minimum wage. Such excessive strengthening of labour regulation runs a strong risk of worsening the domestic business environment and reducing employment.[18]

It further warned that this would impede human capital formation and called for employment creation through economic growth. Unions, on the other hand, saw such regulation as necessary for both human capital formation and economic growth, and furthermore argued that returning more profit to workers would stimulate consumption and help to overcome deflation (Rengo-RIALS 2009).

The rise of non-regular employment has had important implications for industrial relations. For the unions, it has posed serious challenges, but also new opportunities. From a high of 55.8 per cent in 1949, union density declined to the low 30 per cent range from the late 1950s–1970s, and from the mid-1970s it further declined until it reached just 18.1 per cent in 2008. This did not reflect a direct employer assault on unions, but it certainly did reflect the changing composition of workforces, because enterprise unions and their federations displayed little enthusiasm for organizing non-regular workers. Things began to change from the late 1990s, however. From just 2.6 per cent in 2000, the proportion of part-timers in unions had more than doubled to 5.6 per cent by 2010, nudging the overall unionization rate up to 18.5 per cent in 2009 and 2010. The proportion of union members who were part-time workers rose from just 2.3 per cent in 2000 to 7 per cent in 2009 (Fujimura 2012).

While enterprise unions have long displayed little enthusiasm for organizing part-timers, general unions, and increasingly community unions were more active, to the extent that the national centres began to strengthen their regional organizations from the late 1990s. Consequently, argues Oh (2012: 69), they 'have experienced an upward trend both in the number of unions and the number of union members. The general unions can truly be said to be in their heyday.' Even enterprise unions have started to become more positive about recruiting non-regular employees, typically because of growing communication problems between regular and non-regular employees, fears for employee morale and even fears for competitiveness on the part of both unions and company managers (cf. Hashimoto 2012). It is still too early to tell, however, whether these developments, in conjunction with a growing appetite to curb the demands of capital providers in the aftermath of the global financial crisis, and government's (cautious) willingness to re-regulate labour markets to curb growing social divisions, will significantly slow or even turn the tide of union decline.

Change, inertia and institutions

Almost all observers would agree that market forces have been allowed to permeate Japanese employment relations to a degree that few would have predicted, even in the mid-1990s. The tightening of the link between remuneration and advancement on the one hand, and (shorter-term) performance for regular employees on the other; and the increase in non-regular or contingent workers, and differentiation within this category, are manifestations of this permeation. Most observers see Japanese employment relations as now situated somewhere between the organizational pole of the 'classic model' and the 'market pole' of, for example, the USA. Indeed, this middle ground has attracted interest in recent years from researchers interested in incremental institutional change, particularly change from coordinated market economy (CME) institutional configurations towards liberal market economy (LME) configurations. The combination of tight institutional interlock and motivational congruence of the 'classic model' noted by Dore (2000: 45–8) has loosened, resulting in an increase in institutional diversity (Sako 2007; Lechavalier, 2007).[19] The diversity is heightened in companies that have experienced merger or acquisition by a non-Japanese company, which in some cases have seen a rejection of the holistic 'package' of employment practices, rapid 'de-institutionalization' of some of them, and the introduction of new practices from the acquiring firm (Olcott 2009).

Using Streeck and Thelen's (2005) typology of institutional displacement, layering, drift, conversion and exhaustion, Sako highlights the conversion of old institutions to new ends using the example of *Shunto*, and layering (of new on top of old) with the increasing employment of non-regular employees. Vogel (2005) also points to conversion and layering. He argues that:

> [Japan] cannot maintain its existing economic system due to forces for change, and it cannot converge on the liberal market model due to the logic of its own existing institutions. But these constraints are themselves major drivers of institutional innovation.
>
> (ibid.: 147)

This is an astute observation, to which we will return. Vogel argues that we can account for institutional resilience (limited change) equally well by reference to (economic) rationality or (sociological) legitimacy – interests or norms:

> If we want to understand why a Japanese firm might be reluctant to lay off workers, for example, we might suggest that the firm is calculating the cost savings against the potential damage to its cooperative relationship with the remaining workers. Or we might conclude that it is simply adhering to prevailing norms of acceptable firm behavior.
>
> (ibid.: 150)

With these two lenses, he argues that Japanese firms have responded to increased pressure to cut costs in 'remarkably predictable ways' (ibid.: 153).

Hindsight certainly produces clarity; few actually predicted the responses before they unfolded, which brings us to agency. Actors, as analytically *non*-substitutable agents, are largely absent in both rational choice and sociological variants of institutionalism, although for different reasons. Constructivist institutionalists, on the other hand, argue that actors' behaviour is not a direct reflection of material interests, or of unambiguous social norms, but of *perceptions* of them, which in times of crisis become blurred or problematized (Hay 2006). The role of understandings and especially ideas in institutional change is stressed (Blyth 2002). This applies particularly to *path-shaping* institutional change.

But do individual understanding and ideas matter when we are largely talking about *path-dependent* institutional change? Arguably they do. What is path-shaping and what is path-dependent may be difficult to distinguish, and may indeed be deliberately obscured – or conversely over-hyped – by those promoting change. Returning to Vogel's observation, tensions between existing institutions and values and external models, presented as dichotomies, have often been used to frame and enlarge options for change in Japan. At the national level this was famously captured by the catchphrase 'Japanese spirit, Western technology' in the Meiji period, as well as in the democratization and economic catch-up period following the Second World War. The same can be said to apply to more recent times, as was evident, for example, in the debates about the 'company with committees' system of corporate governance. At the firm level, a number of companies (though not many) adopted the US-inspired system, as well as stock options for executives, to encourage perceptual and behavioural changes of managers and employees. Indeed, some firms have hired non-Japanese CEOs to promote change, not all of them successful. Actual change is negotiated in the space between the status quo and the polarized 'foreign' alternative.

Relatedly, the scope for change is constrained by a broad social acceptance that economic vitality and social stability or cohesion are both important. Market liberalism as theory or ideology has historically had few adherents in Japan (Morris-Suzuki 1991), and has typically been treated as the foreign 'other' which stretches the boundaries of conceivable change, but within limits. In a sense, Polanyi's (1944) 'double movement' of liberalist disembedding of markets followed by re-embedding has taken place within a tighter space, both ideologically and temporally.[20] Also related to this, as in the 1920s, Japanese political and business leaders have generally been resistant to the promotion of finance capitalism, and have sought in recent years to reinvigorate industrial or producer-oriented capitalism. Thus, in Japan's case, it might be argued that ideas do matter, although paradoxically for path-dependent institutional change.

Two additional comments are warranted. First, rational choice models with too little emphasis on social norms and over-socialized models of behaviour that place too much emphasis on norms leave insufficient space to recognize the dilemmas faced by industrial relations actors: union leaders and employees in the 1950s who wrestled with whether to collaborate with managers and risk a split in the union, or conversely whether to fight them and risk their careers;[21] or more recently company leaders deciding whether their predecessors would approve or disapprove of a plan to sell a problematic but historically important business unit to a rival; or a government official weighing up whether non-regular workers really do deserve equal treatment with regular workers for the same work, and whether this is measurable. Too often the neglect of such nuances has led to portrayals of Japanese workers as culturally stamped robots, and more recently of managers as obstinate mules.

Second, there is another reason to dig under the surface of stability or path-dependent change. The textile industries were crucial for the early industrial development of both the UK and Japan. Many of Japan's textile- (and apparel-) makers, including its old cotton-spinning companies, not only survive, but have reinvented themselves in recent years as manufacturers of functional fibres and high tech films. In the face of severe hardship in the late 1990s and early 2000s they relied on the strengths of their employment relations – such as the reciprocal commitments of employers and employees – to achieve their transformation. Somehow the term 'conversion' diminishes the agency required to achieve this type of change. In contrast, almost all UK textile-makers (and most apparel makers as well) have disappeared.[22]

A final comment, however, should go to the growing number of young people in Japan, and the older Japanese outside the relatively secure career tracks of regular employees in large companies, for whom continuity is of little benefit. There may be a blurring of lines between regular and non-regular employment – a spectrum of employment types – but the benefits of 'regular' employment continue to elude them.[23] Japanese employment will undergo further evolution in the coming years. Whether they can be reshaped to address current and emerging socio-economic needs as successfully as in the past hundred years remains to be seen.

Notes

1 Support from MEXT's Ministry of Education, Culture, Sports, Science and Technology Program for the Strategic Research Foundation for Private Universities (ITEC/Doshisha University) is gratefully acknowledged. I would also like to thank Junpe Higuchi for help and useful comments in preparing this chapter.
2 Gordon (1985) gives a compelling account of the turbulence in this period, as well as the evolution of labour relations in Japan between 1853 and 1955.
3 Spinning company manager, cited in Morikawa (1989: 42).
4 Kumazawa (1996) argues that Japanese unions gained 'citizens' rights' at the expense of 'villager autonomy'.
5 This quote from 1960 points to the dangers of heralding the end of Japanese-style employment. The 'end' has been predicted for as long as the model has been identified; see Whittaker (1990).
6 The fact that large employers emerged relatively early in Japan's industrialization probably also played a part; see Palmer (1983) who noted large employers' preferences for enterprise unions generally.
7 In 2009, 46.2 per cent of private sector workers in firms with 1000+ employees were organized, as against 14.2 per cent in firms with 100–999 employees and just 1.1 per cent in firms with less than

100 employees. In the last two categories, percentages had almost halved since the late 1980s (JILPT 2011: 71). For critical views of how enterprise unions emerged, and the consequences, see Kawanishi (1992) and Gordon (1998).

8 See Pempel and Tsunekawa (1979). With almost eight million members, Rengo did not quite achieve the unification objective; in 1989, two competing organizations – Zenroren and Zenrokyo – were also formed, with almost a million members between them. For a positive view of the achievements of labour unions in post-war Japan, see Kume (1998).

9 For a critical view of Nikkeiren's history, see Crump (2003).

10 See Gould (1984). As Sugeno (1986) points out, there were earlier British and German influences as well as American ones.

11 Controversially, the right to bargain and to strike was removed from public sector workers in 1948 after prohibition of a planned general strike and the subsequent shift in Occupation policies and national politics.

12 When compounded with 'bureaucratic informalism', access and redress were made even more difficult, see Upham (1987).

13 For more details, see Dore (1973) and Inagami and Whittaker (2005). Many 'excellent company' books were written (in Japanese) about Hitachi in the 1970s and 1980s.

14 Such workers were sometimes disparagingly referred to as 'company men'. See Rohlen's (1979) classic account of white-collar employees at a regional bank.

15 Keizai Doyukai – the Japan Committee for Economic Development – is an organization of 'progressive' executives advocating 'reformed capitalism' (a kind of stakeholder capitalism) since 1946.

16 In this way the second 'hump' of the M-curve began to rise, and as marriage and childbirth patterns changed, the dip in the middle became shallower. See, for example, Lam (1992).

17 Nikkeiren (1995) advocated a 'portfolio' consisting of 'long-term, accumulation type' employees, 'highly specialized skilled' mobile employees and 'flexible-type' employees. Whereas many part-timers choose their job to work at a convenient time or to earn extra income, many dispatched workers do so because they have no choice (JILPT 2011: 24). There are at least two categories of dispatched workers, one quasi-regular, and one on fixed-term contracts.

18 Nihon Keidanren (2011: 18). Nikkeiren and Keidanren merged in 2002.

19 The institutional interlock features of the classic model have been highlighted by other researchers as well to account for limited institutional change; see Witt (2006) and Vogel (2005).

20 Cf. Jacoby's (2005) 'embedded corporation'. Polanyi argued that the emergence of market society, or the strengthening of market forces, always generates a reaction in favour of some form of social protection, a process he referred to a a 'double movement'. After the neo-liberal dis-embedding phase of a second Polanyian 'double movement', we may be about to enter a re-embedding phase. In Japan, however, this is likely to be influenced by the continued quest for economic vitality.

21 See, for example, Kumazawa's (1996) classic account of the Marxist bank employee Kawabe who worked meticulously in capitalism's citadel, while facing increasing discrimination and isolation.

22 Hitachi, too, celebrated its 100th anniversary in 2010. English Electric, with which Dore (1973) compared the company, disappeared long ago, as did its successor GEC, and eventually much of the UK electronics industry.

23 See, for example, some of the blogs cited in Meyer-Ohle (2009).

References

Araki, T. (2002) *Labour and Employment Law in Japan*, Tokyo: Japan Institute of Labour.

—— (2009) 'Changes in Japan's practice-dependent stakeholder model and employee-centred corporate governance', in D. H. Whittaker and S. Deakin (eds) *Corporate Governance and Managerial Reform in Japan*, Oxford: Oxford University Press.

Asao, Y. (2011) 'Overview of non-regular employment in Japan', in JILPT *Non-regular Employment: Issues and Challenges Common to the Major Developed Countries*, Tokyo: JILPT, Report No. 10.

Blyth, M. (2002) *Great Transformations: Economic Ideas and Institutional Change in the Twentieth Century*, Cambridge: Cambridge University Press.

Crump, J. (2003) *Nikkeiren and Japanese Capitalism*, London: Taylor & Francis.

Cusumano, M. (1989) ' "Scientific industry": strategy, technology and entrepreneurship in prewar Japan', in W. Wray (ed.) *Managing Industrial Enterprise: Cases from Japan's Prewar Experience*, Cambridge, MA: Harvard University Press.

Dore, R. (1973) *British Factory – Japanese Factory: The Origins of National Diversity in Industrial Relations*, London: Allen and Unwin.

—— (2000) *Stock Market Capitalism, Welfare Capitalism: Japan and Germany versus the Anglo-Saxons*, Oxford: Oxford University Press.

—— and Whittaker, D.H. (2001) *Social Evolution, Economic Development and Culture: What It Means to Take Japan Seriously*, Cheltenham: Edward Elgar.

Fujimura, H. (2012) 'Japan's labour unions: past, present, future', *Japan Labour Review*, 9(1): 6–24.

Gordon, A. (1985) *The Evolution of Labour Relations in Japan: Heavy Industry, 1853–1955*, Cambridge, MA: Harvard University Press.

—— (1998) *Wages of Affluence: Labour and Management in Postwar Japan*, Cambridge, MA: Harvard University Press.

Gould, W. (1984) *Japan's Reshaping of American Labor Law*, Cambridge, MA: MIT Press.

Hashimoto, S. (2012) 'Unionization of non-regular workers by enterprise unions', *Japan Labour Review*, 9(1): 25–43.

Hay, C. (2006) 'Constructivist institutionalism', in R. Rhodes, S. Binder and B. Rockman (eds) *The Oxford Handbook of Political Institutions*, Oxford: Oxford University Press.

Hazama, H. (1960) 'Keiei kazoku-shugi no ronri to sono keisei katei' [Logic and emergence of managerial paternalism], *Shakaigaku Hyoron*, 11(1): 2–18.

—— (1979) *Keiei Fukushi-Shugi No Susume* [Recommendations for welfare managerialism], Tokyo: Toyo Keizai Shinposha.

Inagami, T. (2009) 'Managers and corporate governance reform in Japan: restoring self-confidence or shareholder revolution?', in D.H. Whittaker and S. Deakin (eds) *Corporate Governance and Managerial Reform in Japan*, Oxford: Oxford University Press.

—— and Whittaker, D.H. (2005) *The New Community Firm: Employment, Governance and Managerial Reform in Japan*, Cambridge: Cambridge University Press.

Ishida, M. and Sato, H. (2011) 'The evolution of Japan's human resource management', in H. Miyoshi and Y. Nakata (eds) *Have Japanese Firms Changed?*, Basingstoke: Palgrave Macmillan.

Jacoby, S. (2005) *The Embedded Corporation: Corporate Governance and Employment Relations in Japan and the United States*, Princeton, NJ: Princeton University Press.

JILPT (Japan Institute for Labour Policy and Training) (2009) *Labour Situation in Japan and Analysis: General Overview 2009/2010*, Tokyo: JILPT.

—— (2011) *Labour Situation in Japan and Analysis: Detailed Exposition 2011/2012*, Tokyo: JILPT.

—— (various years), *Japanese Working Life Profile*, Tokyo: JILPT.

Kawanishi, H. (1992) *Enterprise Unionism in Japan*, London: Kegan Paul International.

Keizai Doyukai (1998) *Dai 13 Kai Kigyo Hakusho: shihon koritsu jushi keiei* [The 13th Corporate White Paper: Capital Efficiency-Oriented Management], Tokyo: Keizai Doyukai.

Kinzley, D. (1991) *Industrial Harmony in Modern Japan: The Invention of a Tradition*, London: Routledge.

Kotake, H. (2012) 'Opinion: solving deflation issue requires broad vision', *Nikkei Shinbun*, evening edition, 14 March.

Kumazawa, M. (1996) *Portraits of the Japanese Workplace: Labor Movements, Workers and Managers*, Boulder, CO: Westview Press.

Kume, I. (1998) *Disparaged Success: Labor Politics in Postwar Japan*, Ithaca, NY: Cornell University Press.

Lam, A. (1992) *Women in Japanese Management: Discrimination and Reform*, London: Routledge.

Lechevalier, S. (2007) 'The diversity of capitalism and heterogeneity of firms - a case study of Japan during the lost decade', *Evolutionary and Institutional Economic Review*, 4(1): 113–142.

Meyer-Ohle, H. (2009) *Japanese Workplaces in Transition: Employee Perceptions*, Basingstoke: Palgrave Macmillan.

Morikawa, H. (1989) 'The increasing power of salaried managers in Japan's large corporations', in W. Wray (ed.) *Managing Industrial Enterprise: Cases from Japan's Prewar Experience*, Cambridge, MA: Harvard University Press.

Morris-Suzuki, T. (1991) *A History of Japanese Economic Thought*, London: Routledge.

Nakata, Y. and Miyazaki, S. (2011) 'Have Japanese engineers changed?', in H. Miyoshi and Y. Nakata (eds) *Have Japanese Firms Changed? The Lost Decade*, Basingstoke: Palgrave Macmillan.

Nihon Keidanren (2011) *Keidanren Seicho Senryaku 2011: minkan katsuryoku no hakki ni yoru seicho kasoku ni mukete* [Keidanren Growth Strategy 2011: Towards growth acceleration through private sector vitality], Tokyo: Keidanren.

Nikkeiren (1995) *Shinjidai No Nihonteki Keiei* [Japanese-style management for a new era), Tokyo: Nikkeiren.

Oh, H-S. (2012) 'The current status and significance of general unions: concerning the resolution of individual labour disputes', *Japan Labour Review*, 9(1): 63–85.

Olcott, G. (2009) *Conflict and Change: Foreign Ownership and the Japanese Firm*, Cambridge: Cambridge University Press.

Oliver, N. and Wilkinson, B. (1992) *The Japanization of British Industry*, Oxford: Basil Blackwell.

Palmer, G. (1983) *British Industrial Relations*, London: Taylor and Francis.

Pempel, T. and Tsunekawa, K. (1979) 'Corporatism without labour? The Japanese anomaly', in P. Schmitter and G. Lehmbruch (eds) *Trends Towards Corporatism Intermediation*, London: Sage.

Polanyi, K. (1944) *The Great Transformation: The Political and Economic Origin of Our Time*, Boston, MA: Beacon Books.

Rengo-RIALS (2009) *FY2009-10 Economic Situation Report: Creation of a New Foundation for Employment and Livelihoods*, Tokyo: Rengo-RIALS.

Rohlen, T. (1979) *For Harmony and Strength: Japanese White-Collar Organization in Anthropological Perspective*, Berkeley, CA: University of California Press.

Sako, M. (1997) 'Shunto: the role of employer and union coordination', in M. Sako and H. Sato (eds) *Japanese Labour and Management in Transition*, London: Routledge.

—— (2007) 'Organizational diversity and institutional change: evidence from financial and labour markets in Japan', in M. Aoki, G. Jackson and H. Miyajima (eds) *Corporate Governance in Japan: Institutional Change and Organizational Diversity*, Oxford: Oxford University Press.

Streeck, W. and Thelen, K. (2005) 'Introduction: institutional change in advanced political economies', in W. Streeck and K. Thelen (eds) *Beyond Continuity: Institutional Change in Advanced Political Economies*, Oxford: Oxford University Press.

Sugeno, K. (1986) 'Book Review: Gould, W., Japan's Reshaping of American Labour Law', *Comparative Labour Law and Policy Journal*, 8(Fall): 107–13.

—— (1996) *Koyo Shakai No Ho* [Laws of employment society], Tokyo: Yuhikaku.

Upham, F. (1987) *Law and Social Change in Postwar Japan*, Cambridge, MA: Harvard University Press.

Vogel, S. (2005) 'Routine adjustment and bounded innovation: the changing political economy of Japan', in W. Streeck and K. Thelen (eds) *Beyond Continuity: Institutional Change in Advanced Political Economies*, Oxford: Oxford University Press.

Whittaker, D.H. (1990) 'The end of Japanese-style employment?', *Work, Employment and Society*, 4(3): 321–47.

—— and Deakin, S. (eds) (2009) *Corporate Governance and Managerial Reform in Japan*, Oxford: Oxford University Press.

Witt, M. (2006) *Changing Japanese Capitalism: Societal Coordination and Institutional Adjustment*, Cambridge: Cambridge University Press.

15 Brazil

Mark S. Anner and João Paulo Cândia Veiga

Introduction

Employment relations practices in Brazil have suffered from a lack of attention in the field of comparative employment relations. This is unfortunate, because Brazil does not fit neatly into existing models of employment relations; it is a unique system that deserves deeper exploration. Brazil is the fifth most populous country in the world and, measured in terms of nominal GDP, it is the seventh largest economy in the world. Brazil is an important and prominent member of the BRIC countries (Brazil, Russia, India and China). Understanding Brazil's unique employment relations system requires an historical analysis. Employment relations in Brazil have slowly and unevenly transformed over a tumultuous history that spans oligarchic rule (1889–1930), authoritarian corporatism (1930–45), populism (1945–64), military dictatorship (1964–85), neo-liberal reforms (1990–2002), and, most recently, the eight-year presidency of ex-trade union leader, Luiz Inácio 'Lula' da Silva (2003–10).

Trade unions in Brazil have maintained their numbers over the last decades, and also have enjoyed increased political influence as the Workers' Party (PT) entered into its third term in office in 2011 with President Dilma Rousseff. Yet, behind these general trends, the neo-liberal reforms that began in the 1990s, notably privatization and economic openness, have transformed the Brazilian labour movement with adverse consequences for some segments of the workforce. The overall rate of unionization has held steady at around 18–21 per cent of the workforce. Approximately twice this number of workers is covered by collective bargaining agreements. Yet, while overall the unionization rate has remained steady, the rate of unionization in the manufacturing sector has been in decline. In contrast, public sector unionism has risen since the enactment of the 1988 Constitution, which granted public employees unionization rights. At the same time, there has been a growth of national trade union centres and a proliferation of small unions and unions that remain outside the purview of the country's main labour confederations, contributing to a fragmentation of the labour movement.

Brazil fits neither the liberal market economy (LME) nor the coordinated market economy (CME) models. Rather, it is better understood as what Latin America scholars have labelled a hierarchical market economy built on strong foreign direct investment and domestic capital and atomistic labour relations. It is also a system that has been profoundly influenced by labour and social movement dynamics. In the sections that follow, we will explore the Brazilian system by outlining the evolution of Brazil's model of employment relations, looking at its history, actors, labour market trends, and outcomes.

The actors and processes in employment relations

Origins of the Brazilian system of employment relations

The modern Brazilian system of employment relations begins with the Iberian conquest and colonization. Portuguese control had two lasting impacts on the Brazilian system: first, it established a system of civil law (also known as Roman law) that dictates the logic of the labour law system. Unlike the common law system in Britain and ex-British colonies, under civil law, core principles are codified in a collection of written laws that shape labour relations dynamics. Second, the Portuguese conquest influenced Brazil's insertion into the global economy. Under colonial rule, one of Brazil's first major agro-export crops was sugar, and the large sugar cane plantation owners of the northeast demanded slave labour. Brazil received more slaves than any other country in the Americas, including the United States. And Brazil, in 1888, was the last country in the western hemisphere to legally abolish slavery.

It is also notable that, unlike other Latin American states, Brazil's independence was achieved without war, but rather as a proclamation of separation by the regent prince. Consequently, the Brazilian state emerged as an independent monarchy. What resulted was a highly aristocratic two-party system in which the emperor was placed above the parties and parliament (Lamounier 1999). When the sugar plantation economy declined, production shifted south and, since coffee production depended on wage labour not slavery, Brazilian elites began to promote European and Japanese immigration. A strong oligarchic class emerged, which was divided between São Paulo, Minas Gerais, and Rio Grande, as coffee and dairy production expanded during the era known as *café com leite* (coffee with milk). Organizing rights and welfare provisions were limited partly due to the large labour surplus in the country, which weakened labour's ability to organize and demand state protection (Skidmore and Smith 2001). Yet, European emigrant workers brought with them more than their labour power; they brought the radical ideologies of communism, anarchism, and anarcho-syndicalism which influenced the labour movement. Anarcho-syndicalism particularly appealed to workers during the period of early industrialization as harsh factory conditions and political disenfranchisement engendered more radical world-views. Indeed, workers' enthusiasm for electoral democracy was understandably subdued given that legal requirements often curtailed the ability of most Brazilians to vote. The Brazilian Constitution of 1891 abolished minimum income requirements to vote, allowing men over 21 years old to participate in elections. Women and indigents were forbidden to vote until 1934.

In 1930s, in the context of the Great Depression and in response to a stolen election, Getúlio Vargas came to power via a military *coup d'état*, and centralized political power, replacing the old *café com leite* political divisions. The Depression legitimized greater government intervention in the economy, and the desire to move beyond the then obsolete political pact between the states of São Paulo and Minas Gerais motivated Vargas to increase central authority (Lamounier 1999). As the Depression deepened and radical labour ideologies grew, Vargas sought to control labour by incorporating trade unions into officially-sanctioned social organizations. Vargas, who had for a time pursued a military career, was particularly influenced by Mussolini's *Carta Lavoro* (Workers' Charter), which he drew on to establish the foundation of Brazil's corporatist system. He is noted for instilling a form of state (as opposed to societal) corporatism in Brazil in which the state held the privileged position of power in the tripartite relations among state, employers and labour (Schmitter

1974). Vargas wanted a strong state to balance regional rivalries in the geographically large and economically complex country. As social organizations were too weak to balance state power, Brazil's subordinate classes were incorporated into the political process directly through the state as opposed to incorporation through a strong official political party (Collier and Collier 1991). Unlike Argentina, Brazil lacked the equivalent of a powerful Peronist party, that is, a labour-based political party built around a charismatic populist leader such as Juan Perón (Cardoso and Gindin 2009).

Vargas established the Ministry of Labour, and, in 1931, enacted the 'Law of Unionization' (*Lei de Sindicalização*), which gave the state extensive powers over union formation and activity. The law prohibited unions from participating in political activity; denied them the right to affiliate to international organizations; and prevented them from using union income for strike activity. Indeed, the law explicitly defined unions as 'organs of collaboration with the State' (Antunes [1980] 1999: 46–7). Thus, official unionism displaced the anarchist and communist unions that had dominated the movement until that time. The state, with labour union collaboration, was to take care of Brazilian workers, and Brazilian workers were expected to be loyal to the state in return. In 1940, a minimum wage was established, and a labour code was first introduced in 1943 (Barbosa and Moretto 2011). The union structure established under this system denied unions both the ability to have national peak associations and shop-floor representation. The law also established that there could be only one union per economic category in a given geographical territory no less than the municipal level (a practice known as *unicidade*). Thus, under Brazilian corporatism, a decentralized form of unionism emerged that facilitated state control. Once a union was formed, all workers in that region and category had to pay a union tax (*imposto sindical*) equivalent to one day's salary per year, thus guaranteeing the financial stability of the union system (Almeida 1997). The union tax system also meant that unions could have a limited relationship with the workforce without the risk of losing their economic support.

In 1937, the Vargas regime became more dictatorial. Strikes were declared illegal and independent unions were banned. In the years that followed, a comprehensive system of labour legislation was consolidated into the *Consolidação das Leis do Trabalho* (CLT) with the goal of establishing social harmony with state control (Humphrey 1982). In the words of Vargas, 'The State does not want and does not recognize class struggle. The labour laws are laws of social harmony' (cited in ibid.: 14). This period marked the beginning of the 'New State' (*Estado Novo*). Unions transformed from independent defenders of workers' interests to 'financially secure, bureaucratic welfare agencies' (ibid.: 15), which were constricted in their activities by a 'statist straitjacket' (French 1992).[1] Union interests were subordinated to state control and surveillance, and Vargas's dictatorship developed strict instruments to monitor union leaders. Workers' interests were thus to be ensured not through independent strike activity, but rather through loyalty to the state and the benevolence of the ruler and the new worker welfare agencies that the unions helped to administer.

The Vargas era of authoritarian rule (1930–45) was superseded by a democratic era in which Vargas returned to power as an elected president until his suicide in 1954. The democratic period of 1945 to 1964 witnessed a new era of labour activism, which culminated with the administration of the Left-oriented presidency of João Goulart (1961–64). Elite fear of a Cuban-style regime consolidating power (notably unfounded) and economic crisis created conditions for a military coup in 1964 (Skidmore 1973). During the era of authoritarian rule (1964–85), the military renewed the state's controls over unions, declared all strikes illegal, and placed many unions under the control of the Ministry of Labour. Notably, neither the democratic governments nor the military governments fundamentally altered the corporatist labour laws from the Vargas era. The military regime found that it was able to use the existing laws to effectively control labour.

Under military rule, as economic conditions deteriorated following the global oil crises of the 1970s and the concentration of industrial workers in São Paulo's industrial metropolitan area increased, workers regained their voice and formed what became known as 'new unionism', which organized the strikes of late 1970s in the industrial belt around São Paulo. These unionists were influenced by progressive segments of the Church, and socialist and Communist parties, and represented an oppositional or class-based ideology. A few years later, with 'democratic openness', these new actors organized the Central Única dos Trabalhadores (Central Workers Union, CUT) in 1983, whose leaders included Luiz Inácio 'Lula' da Silva (Humphrey 1982; Keck 1989). The CUT's bye-laws offer this definition of its goals and mission:

> The *Central Única dos Trabalhadores* is a labor union organization of the masses of the maximum level that is classist, autonomous and democratic. Its main goals include a commitment to the defense of the immediate and historic interests of the working class, the struggle for better living and working conditions, and the engagement in the process of transformation of the Brazilian society toward democracy and socialism.
>
> (CUT Bye-laws, Title II, Chapter I, Article 2, cited in Anner 2011)

Through the massive strikes of metalworkers and bank employees (among others) in the late 1970s and early 1980s, CUT unionists demanded not only wage increases above the effective (as opposed to official) inflation rate, but also an end to military rule and the corporatist system of labour control. Indeed, during this era, due to the weakness of Brazil's party system, trade unions played an increasingly political role in society (Rodrigues 1999). As the protests escalated and the economic crisis deepened, the military embarked on a process of liberalization and then democratization (O'Donnell *et al.* 1986). In 1985, the civilian, Jose Sarney, assumed the presidency, and the era of authoritarian rule was considered to have ended.

Contemporary employment relations practices in Brazil

The end of the military dictatorship and the enactment of the1988 Constitution ushered in the contemporary era in Brazilian employment relations. The state no longer significantly intervened in unions' internal affairs. Public sector workers could organize and, with certain limitations, strike. Labour reforms gave job security to union leaders, reduced the maximum work week from 48 to 44 hours a week, increased overtime pay from 20 to 50 per cent, and added profit-sharing provisions. For the first time in Brazilian history, rural workers achieved the right to pensions and a minimum wage, which had been one of the more important demands of the rural workers' movement since the early 1980s. As stipulated in Article 11 of Brazil's new Constitution, firms with more than 200 workers were allowed to elect a representative to bargain with management (Cook 2002). In the early 1980s, almost all auto manufacturers had a base-level plant commission with rules and norms for elections and bargaining. Metalworkers from Ford set up the first commission in 1982, then workers from Scania and Volkswagen soon followed suit, with considerable support from the Volkswagen works council and trade unionists in Germany (Anner 2011).

Following the constitutional reforms, there was a growth in the number of union members, most of whom were civil servants who had previously been prohibited from forming unions. This growth in membership was also accompanied by dramatic growth in the number of unions, reflecting a growing fragmentation of the union movement (Almeida 1997). At the same time, core aspects of the corporatist system remained unchanged. This included the *unicidade sindical* system, which limited union formation to one union per economic activity per territorial unit, and the *imposto sindical* (union tax) where all workers in the unionized economic or sectoral category (e.g. metalworkers, chemical workers) paid a union tax regardless of their membership status. A portion of this union tax is also paid to federations and confederations, which contributed to an institutionalized system of labour representation disconnected from the labour movement at the local level, unless unions took extraordinary steps to guard against this possibility. Some unions in the CUT, for example, refused to accept the income from the union tax, preferring instead to rely exclusively on voluntary union membership dues.

In response to economic stagnation caused by the economic plan of Fernando Affonso Collor de Mello (1990–92), the government established a set of tripartite negotiations known as sectoral chambers (*câmaras setoriais*) which spread to different industries outside the official structures of traditional state labour institutions (Martin 1997). This mechanism helped to maintain jobs and economic recovery in the early 1990s, but most of the tripartite rules broke down in 1995 with the Mexican economic crisis that erupted in December of 1994, and resulted in a return to a more liberal system of interest representation (Comin 1998). The presidency of Fernando Henrique Cardoso (1995–2002) is most noted for deepening Brazil's neo-liberal reforms and promoting macro-economic stabilization. Privatization, trade liberalization, and labour market flexibility became priorities of the government. This resulted in the lack of significant legal or contractual obstacles to the highly flexible use of labour. It became extremely easy for employers to fire workers, to suspend production, or to force employees to work overtime (Bresciani 1997: 66). The precarious Brazilian economy maintained its course until the Asian crisis in 1997 when the financial doors were opened for the future devaluation of the *Real* currency and the end of the 'managed' exchange rate system. After being elected for a second term, Cardoso signed a new agreement with the International Monetary Fund and the associated macro-economic conditions narrowed the government's options in dealing with demands from workers for wage rises to match increased inflation rates.

When Lula became president in 2003, he did not re-establish the sectoral chambers, but attempted labour law reform through a national tripartite forum. Through this national bargaining arena created in his first term, over six hundred leaders from unions, government, and employers associations participated and discussed controversial topics, such as the ratification of the International Labour Organization (ILO) Convention 87 (on freedom of association and the right to organize), union representation at the workplace, the legal status of trade union confederations such as CUT, and the end of the union tax (Zylberstajn 2006; Hall 2009). Divisions emerged not only between employers and labour, but also within the labour movement. For example, labour unions were divided on whether to reform the 'union exclusivity' rule under which there is only one union allowed per sector and per territory. Some unions had gained representation rights several decades ago and, as their membership levels declined, they saw any change to the law as being detrimental to their interests since they stood to lose representation rights. For them, it was better to remain with the old system. In contrast, new and growing unions correctly perceived such changes to the law as their only opportunity to represent workers.

Despite these differences, in 2005, the Forum reached a draft proposal. Yet by then the government was caught up in a major corruption scandal and the legislature was preoccupied with establishing anti-corruption commissions and could not concern itself with labour law reform. The following year was a re-election year, and again labour reforms did not make it on to the legislative agenda. Additionally, Lula's Workers' Party (PT) fell far short of a simple majority in Congress needed to pass the reforms alone, and the major opposition parties were against the reforms, especially after the Lula government resolved several impasses by siding with the workers' position (Anner 2011).

Trade unions

Following the return to democracy, the new Constitution of Brazil and the labour code granted private and public sector workers the right to form trade unions (with the exception of the military, uniformed police, fire-fighters, and some other state employees). In this context, between 1991 and 2000, workers formed 1,964 new unions, the largest number in a one-decade period in the history of Brazil. Yet, the growth of union membership did not keep pace with increases in the size of the workforce, and the unionization rate faced a minor decline over the 1990s and early 2000s, from 24.88 per cent to 23.58 per cent (IBGE 2002). More importantly, the legalization of unions in the public sector and their subsequent growth hid an important decline of unionization in the industrial sector in this period. Indeed, over the course of the 1990s, labour unions in Brazil lost more than 500,000 members in the manufacturing sector and the rate of unionization in manufacturing declined by 10 per cent (Cardoso 2001). Today we find that 72.56 per cent of unions represent private sector workers, whereas 14.57 per cent represent public sector workers (see Table 15.1).

In Brazil, union formation is unevenly distributed across the regions of the country, with the highest levels of unionization in the northeast (19.5 per cent) and the south (21.2 per cent). In contrast, the north has the lowest level of unionization (13.3 per cent). In 2007, the national unionization rate stood at 17.7 per cent of the workforce (see Table 15.2).

Table 15.1 Union members by category

	Number (thousands)	*%*
Private Sector Workers	7.17	72.56%
Public Sector Workers	1.44	14.57%
Others	1.27	12.87%

Source: Cadastro Nacional de Entidades Sindicais, Ministério do Trabalho e Emprego, http://portal.mte.gov.br [accessed 30 April 2012]

Table 15.2 Unionized and non-unionized workers by region, 2007

	Unionized		*Non-unionized*		
Region	*Number*	*%*	*Number*	*%*	*Total*
North	897,404	13.30%	5,837,162	86.70%	6,734,566
Northeast	4,617,384	19.50%	19,029,396	80.50%	23,646,780
Southeast	6,439,568	16.50%	32,477,262	83.50%	38,916,830
South	3,138,405	21.20%	11,653,715	78.80%	14,792,120
Centre-west	94,612	14.10%	5,749,603	85.90%	6,695,723
Brazil	16,038,881	17.70%	74,747,138	82.30%	90,786,019

Source: IBGE and DIEESE 2007.

Barbosa and Abdal (2010), two leading experts in labour markets, provide indicators for the recent expansion of employment rates in Brazil. As Table 15.3 shows, the growth rate of the number of workers employed (in both formal and informal sectors) is 11.34 per cent, which is higher than the growth rate of the Working Age Population (WAP) and the Economically Active Population (EAP). The unemployment rate has fallen, reaching 7.2 per cent in 2008 (Barbosa and Abdal 2010).

In terms of distribution of workers and sectors, only in the agriculture, hunting, and forestry sector do we see a significant decline in employment. In contrast, employment in construction and manufacturing grew at 31 per cent and 20 per cent respectively. The service sector remains the largest source of employment in the country, creating more than eight million jobs in this period and representing over 60 per cent of total employment. Growth was particularly strong in real estate and other personal services. The wholesale and retail trade sector is the largest single source of employment in the country, providing 18 per cent of jobs in Brazil (Barbosa and Abdal 2010; and see Table 15.4).

Table 15.3 WAP, EAP, and employment growth in Brazil, 2003–2008

	2003	*2008*	*Growth rate*
WAP	144,340,657	157,933,643	9.42%
EAP	88,587,236	97,800,478	10.40%
Employed	79,950,114	89,018,784	11.34%
Unemployed	8,637,122	8,003,549	−7.34%

Source: Authors' calculations based on Barbosa and Abdal (2010).

Table 15.4 Workers by sector, Brazil, 2003–2008

	2003	*2008*	*Growth rate*	*% Total employment*
Primary Sector	16,714,405	15,483,552	−7.36%	17.07%
Agriculture, hunting, and forestry	16,059,146	14,759,193	−8.09%	16.27%
Fishing	342,964	348,845	1.71%	0.38%
Mining and quarrying	312,295	368,603	18.03%	0.41%
Industry	16,418,713	20,239,789	23.27%	22.31%
Construction	5,216,448	6,821,512	30.77%	7.52%
Electricity, gas, and water supply	332,223	373,134	12.31%	0.41%
Manufacturing	10,870,042	13,045,143	20.01%	14.38%
Services	46,816,996	55,006,705	17.49%	60.63%
Wholesale and retail trade	14,207,311	15,980,815	12.48%	17.61%
Hotels and Restaurants	2,890,884	3,556,867	23.04%	3.92%
Transport, storage, and communications	3,722,703	4,563,101	22.57%	5.03%
Financial intermediation	1,025,218	1,152,697	12.43%	1.27%
Real estate, renting, and business services	4,492,644	5,957,178	32.60%	6.57%
Public administration and defence	3,985,728	4,498,422	12.86%	4.96%
Education	4,345,204	5,050,574	16.23%	5.57%
Health care and social work	2,816,488	3,417,204	21.33%	3.77%
Personal and other services	2,980,909	4,063,862	36.33%	4.48%
Activities of private households	6,147,531	6,568,765	6.85%	7.24%
Extra-territorial organizations and bodies	202,376	197,220	−2.55%	0.22%
Total	79,950,114	90,730,046	13.48%	100.00%

Source: Authors' calculations based on Barbosa and Abdal (2010).

Over the course of the 1990s and early 2000s, the number of unions in Brazil increased dramatically, reaching a total of 9,883 by 2012, with 72 per cent in urban areas and 28 per cent in rural areas. A substantial number of these unions are registered but not active and many are very small: some 71 per cent of Brazilian unions have fewer than 1,000 members. In addition, 62 per cent of unions have chosen to remain unaffiliated to any of the established national trade union centres (IBGE 2002). Further fragmenting the labour movement is Brazil's system of occupational unionism, whereby unions are organized not according to the industry in which workers are employed, but rather according to their job category. A manufacturing plant, for example, might have over a dozen unions, with one representing one type of production worker, another representing administrative staff, a third representing workers in the cafeteria, and so on.

The reason union-friendly collective labour reforms did not provide for a stronger union movement in the industrial sector can be found in the nature of industrial restructuring. The changes brought on by market liberalization and industrial restructuring dramatically affected the geography of industrial production in Brazil. Many major new plants built in the 1990s and early 2000s were situated outside the core industrial district of greater São Paulo, in regions where unions were weaker and wages were lower (Arbix 2001). For example, auto corporations moved from the São Paulo industrial belt to the South (General Motors) and the Northeast (Ford). This fragmentation of the workforce was particularly detrimental to unions in Brazil because labour reform did not alter the emphasis on union formation and collective bargaining at the sub-national level. That is, workers in isolated regions with new manufacturing plants did not benefit from the support of national industrial unionism since this was precluded by law. Rather, these workers had to form or join a relatively weak local union.

While Brazil has a long history of national trade union centres, it was not until November 2007 that trade union centres achieved legal recognition as such and were allowed to represent workers in court, public councils and other bodies. To do so, they must meet the following criteria: (1) affiliation of at least 100 unions across five regions; (2) affiliation of unions in at least five sectors; and (3) affiliation of at least 5 per cent of all union members nationally in the first year of operation and at least 7 per cent in the two subsequent years. The three largest and most representative trade union centres in Brazil are the Central Única dos Trabalhadores (CUT), the Força Sindical (FS), and the União Geral dos Trabalhadores (UGT) (see Table 15.5). Of these, the CUT is the largest with an estimated seven million members. It was founded with a strong socialist orientation, although over time it has come

Table 15.5 Main trade union centres

Main trade union centres	*# of unions*	*Members (millions)*
CUT (Central Única dos Trabalhadores)	2191	7
FS (Força Sindical)	1710	2,1
UGT (União Geral dos Trabalhadores)	1027	1,35
NCST (Nova Central Sindical de Trabalhadores)	972	na
CTB (Central dos Trabalhadores e Trabalhadoras do Brasil)	584	na
CGTB (Central Greral dos Trabalhadores do Brasil)	283	na
CBDT (Central do Brasil Democratica de Trabalhadores)	118	na
Conlutas (Central Sindical e Popular)	84	na

Source: Brazil, Ministry of Labour and Employment, Loken and Barbosa (2008).

to moderate its orientation, joining the International Confederation of Free Trade Unions (ICFTU, now renamed the International Trade Union Confederation, ITUC) and maintaining a close relationship with the governing Workers' Party. Força Sindical and the UGT have had a more conservative orientation than the CUT. Força Sindical was a former ally of the Collor presidency in the early 1990s and later supported many of Cardoso's labour market flexibility initiatives. It emerged out of remnants of several prominent corporatist unions – most notably the metalworkers' union of São Paulo. Critical of the CUT's more confrontational and class-based approach, these unions refer to themselves as 'modernizing' and 'results-based' (Nogueira 1997; Força Sindical 2000). Força Sindical argued that labour market 'flexibility is essential for the country' (Força Sindical 2000). The UGT, which was founded in 1989, was once led by Antonio Rogerio Magri, who served as the Minister of Labour in the Collor government. Both these union centres, with their conservative orientations, were created with the support of the Collor presidency to balance CUT's influence in the labour movement.

Collective bargaining and collective action in Brazil

All unions legally registered with the Ministry of Labour have the right to bargain collectively with employers. Some 72 per cent of registered unions exercise this right. Reflecting Brazil's trade union structure, collective bargaining occurs largely at the municipal or territorial levels, comprised of several neighbouring municipalities. Agreements at this level set minimum standards that may then be improved upon by negotiations between an enterprise and the municipal union. Confederations and federations have a limited role in collective bargaining (Cardoso and Gindin 2009).

Brazilian labour law makes a distinction between collective *agreements* and collective *conventions*. The former is the result of direct bargaining between a union and a firm; the latter results from bargaining between the union and all firms in the jurisdiction of the union. The terms and conditions of a collective bargaining agreement may be extended to non-union workers in the jurisdiction of the union and the occupational category of workers covered by the union. To do this, the union must bargain a collective convention with an employers association and/or a group of employers. Once a collective convention is established, its provisions are mandatory for the entire category of workers in a given jurisdiction (ibid.). Historically, the right of public sector workers in Brazil to bargain collectively has been curtailed. Under the Lula administration, the Board of Public Service was established, and Lula agreed to pursue ratification of ILO Convention 151, the Public Services Convention.

While from 1978 to 1985, nominal wage increases were only marginally influenced by collective bargaining, from 1986 onwards collective bargaining had a strong impact on wages (Horn 2009). Traditionally, bargaining has focused predominately on wage negotiations, yet there has been a trend to bargain increasingly over job stability issues such as job losses (DIEESE 2001). One study on collective bargaining agreements in the state of Rio Grande do Sul found that not only had the number of provisions in collective bargaining agreements increased over time, but so had the scope of these provisions. While employment relations practices such as recruitment, for example, were not included in any agreement in 1978, by 1995 there were on average 4.5 provisions for recruitment per collective bargaining agreement, suggesting collective bargaining had 'strengthened its role vis-à-vis traditional statutory regulations and unilateral regulations by management' (Horn 2009: 121).

Success in collective bargaining often depends on the mobilization capacity of unions, and unions in Brazil achieved some of the most significant gains during periods of intense

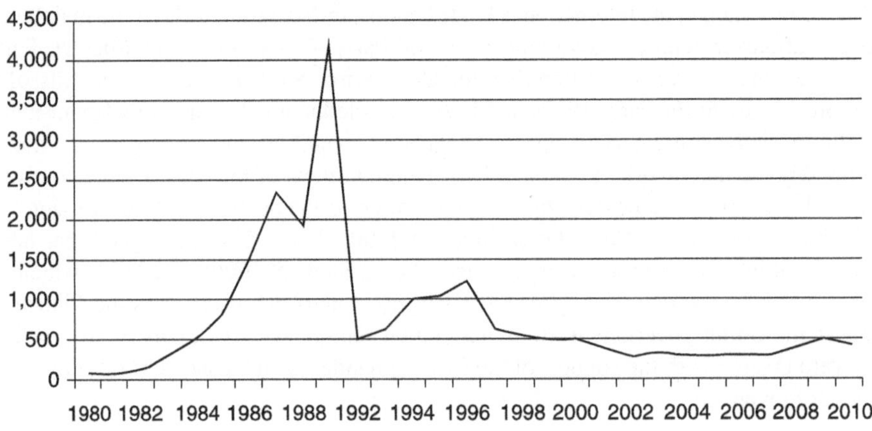

Figure 15.1 Number of strikes in Brazil, 1980–2010.

Sources: ILO, DIEESE.

strike activity (DIEESE 2001; Cardoso and Gindin 2009). Strikes have been considered a feature of contemporary employment relations in Brazil most notably since the metalworkers in the São Paulo region organized massive protests against military rule in the late 1970s and early 1980s. And strikes escalated in the context of political liberalization and democratization in the mid-1980s. In general, strikes have declined dramatically in number since the late 1980s. However, strike activity did increase in 2009 by 26 per cent relative to the previous year, largely in response to pressures created by the global economic recession (see Figure 15.1).

In 2010, there were more strikes in the public sector than in the private sector, and strikes by public sector employees – particularly at the federal level – contributed the most to total worker strike hours (DIEESE 2012a). It is also worth noting that in 2010, 43.9 per cent of strikes in the public sector and 47.7 per cent of strikes in the private sector had 'defensive' demands – striking to defend current working conditions or to secure employer compliance with previously agreed provisions (ibid.).

Employers and employer organizations

Employers associations in Brazil are regulated by the labour code, and they have the same legal status as trade unions. As part of the corporatist legacy, employer organizations have been large, encompassing associations that organize nearly all businesses in the country. Yet, they are often weak and marginalized within the political system (Schneider 2004). The largest employers association, the Confederação Nacional de Indústria (CNI), was founded in 1938 and represents 27 state-level federations, which encompass over a thousand associated employers' organizations and almost 100,000 industrial establishments. State-level federations are given one vote each in the governance structure of the CNI, which gives small rural states the same voting power as Brazil's industrial centre, São Paulo. São Paulo's industrialists have thus felt under-represented by CNI and have increasingly turned to their state-level association, the Federação das Indústrias do Estado de São Paulo (FIESP), which

Table 15.6 Employers organizations

Employers' organizations	*Sector*
CNI (Confederação Nacional da Indústria)	Industry
CNC (Confederação Nacional do Comércio)	Commercial
CNA (Confederação da Agricultura e Pecuária do Brasil)	Agriculture
CNF (Confederação Nacional das Instituições Financeiras)	Financial Insitutions
CNT (Confederação Nacional do Transporte)	Transportation
CACB (Confederação das Associações Comerciais e Empresariais do Brasil)	General

Source: Løken and Barbosa (2008).

has played an increasingly vocal role in speaking for industry (Schneider 2004). Other employers associations include the Confederación Nacional de Transporte (CNT), which was founded in 1954. It covers 29 associations, 2 unions, and 16 affiliated associations in the Brazilian area of transportation. Its structure includes 60,000 transport companies and 700,000 self-employed carriers. Also of importance are the Confederación Nacional de Agricultura (CNA) and the Confederación Nacional de Comercio, Bienes, Servicios y Turismo (CNC) which represent over 5 million businesses in Brazil (see Table 15.6).

Government and political parties

The party system in Brazil, despite numerous transitions over the decades, has always been weakly institutionalized (Mainwaring 1999). Indeed, the first Vargas-era was seen as 'partyless authoritarianism' (Lamounier 1999), with labour's incorporation into the system pursued directly through the state and not through a strong labour party. Parties established themselves in the democratic era (1945–64), but were rendered insignificant again with military rule. While some old parties re-emerged with political liberalization in the late 1970s and early 1980s, most of the main political parties are less than 45 years old. Today the Brazilian party system is characterized as 'fragmented multi-party presidentialism with a highly permissive proportional electoral system' (ibid.). Indeed, not only is the party system one of the most fragmented in the world, but parties are loosely disciplined, and voting by elected representatives against the party leadership (and changing parties) is frequent. The one significant exception among the larger parties is the Workers' Party, where members are expected to show more discipline in voting, and where strong ties exist between the party and the main trade union confederation, the CUT. Parties represent the full range of political ideologies, from communist to right-wing parties. Ideological polarization, however, has diminished since 1992 (Mainwaring 1999), and labour centres such as FS have called for greater separation between unions and parties, although their leaders often are politically active (Anner 2011).

While presidents in Brazil have had moderate partisan power due to the weakness of the party system, they do enjoy relatively strong constitutional power, which includes the abilities to enact decrees in almost any policy area (Smith 2005). What is noticeable about the role of the government in Brazil from the period of Vargas to the present is how slowly the system has evolved from its earliest corporatist foundations. Gone are the days of government intervention and control over labour unions, but the state still plays an important role in employment relations practices, from determining how trade unions can be formed, setting pension policies, and establishing minimum wage rates.

Perhaps one of the biggest challenges in the Brazilian system is labour law enforcement. The 2005 ILO Committee of Experts report noted, 'local inspection offices . . . are ill-equipped and inadequate and often lack computers, telephones, and even the most basic furniture (tables, chairs) needed by inspectors to carry out their duties' (CEACR 2005: 310). Scholars have found:

> In Brazil, the distance of firms from the local office of the Ministry of Labour (where workplace inspectors are based) directly influences the likelihood of a firm being inspected. An increase of one hour in the distance from a firm to the local labour office reduces the likelihood of inspection by around 10 per cent.
>
> (Almeida and Carneiro 2006, cited in Venn 2009)

In the era of neo-liberal reforms and the philosophy of reduced state intervention in employment relations, resources dedicated to enforcement declined considerably. For example, during the era of Cardoso, the number of workplaces inspected by the state and the number of workers covered by those inspections experienced an overall decline. However, during the Lula era, and continuing on to the era of his successor, Dilma Rousseff, the number of workplaces covered by workplace inspections has increased steadily over time (see Figure 15.2).

The labour market

The development of labour markets in Brazil can be categorized into three periods (Barbosa 2003). In colonial times, slavery was the dominant pattern in the production of sugar cane, domestic services, mining and craft production. During the period of the first Republic (1889–1930), workers were fragmented into regional labour markets where wage earners were incorporated into the production process through personal ties, often without labour contracts. Most workers were linked to either subsistence or export agriculture (Barbosa and Moretto 2011). In the decades after the rise of power of Vargas in 1930, a national labour

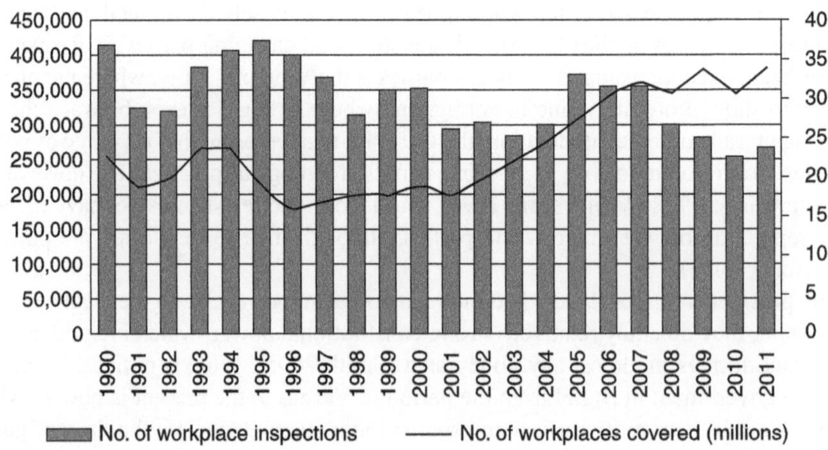

Figure 15.2 Labour enforcement in Brazil.

Source: Ministry of Labour.

market emerged. The number of registered wage-earners grew more rapidly than the Economically Active Population (EAP) and industrialization of the country created a working class and protective labour legislation. However, the labour regulatory framework only covered a segment of the workforce. A salaried middle class emerged during this period in response to rising demand for technical expertise and professional services.

Brazil was one of the fastest-growing economies in the world from 1930 to 1980, with an average annual expansion of approximately 6 per cent. In spite of booming economic and social modernization (or perhaps because of it), the traditional Brazilian pattern of inequality increased, and there was a high percentage of unregistered wage-earners. Indeed, a large percentage of the labour force remained outside the formal sector in both rural and urban areas and did not enjoy the benefits of a universal system of social protection (Barbosa and Moretto 2011). Over the decades, these inequalities and disparities have remained as economic growth peaked.

The process of economic expansion was interrupted in the early 1980s with the foreign debt crisis. Following the Mexican default in 1982, Brazil announced the suspension of its payments on its foreign debt in 1983, and the government was forced to sign agreements with the International Monetary Fund to raise domestic interest rates and to generate trade surpluses in order to pay back its public and private bank loans. Up to the mid-1990s, inflation soared, investment stagnated, and the domestic market slowed in what became known as the *lost decade*. The government then pursued a deep privatization programme to generate a budget surplus and foster foreign capital inflow. This period saw increased unemployment and the casualization of employment. In 1999, open unemployment neared 10 per cent at the national level and informality (measured by lack of access to social security) exceeded 50 per cent of all those employed. During the Lula era, foreign debt was reduced and exports more than tripled between 2003 and 2008, and international capital proved more accessible. The ratio of external debt to exports, which had reached 4.5 in the late 1990s, came down to less than 1 in 2008 (Barbosa and Moretto 2011).

In his first term, Lula maintained a conservative approach to monetary and fiscal policies, and foreign direct investments returned to the country, now in the form of *greenfield* investments. Agribusiness exports soared and a new wave of optimism emerged. Brazil received US$45 billion in foreign direct investment in 2008, three times more than in 2003. As Barbosa and Moretto (2011) point out: 'A combination of growth in exports and an expanding domestic market, coupled with an increase in public and private investment, boosted job creation.' From 1999 to 2006, not only did employment expansion outpace the growth of the workforce, but also formal employment grew at an even faster pace than informal employment (see Table 15.7). The open unemployment rate peaked to its highest level in Brazilian history in 2003, after which it fell almost continuously, reaching 6.7 per cent in 2010 (Barbosa and Moretto 2011).

Yet, most job growth was in low wage sectors of the economy. As a result, despite the growth levels of formal employment, traditional inequality remained in terms of a high concentration of jobs in poorly paid occupations. Over 90 per cent of total formal sector jobs paid no more than three times the minimum wage (ibid.). Others segments of employment – such as the self-employed, domestic workers, unpaid workers (mostly in family enterprises) and subsistence workers – made up a third of the Brazilian labour force. Only 47 per cent of the employed population is registered with Brazil's social security system (Løken and Barbosa 2008).

In general, for lower-income workers, the Lula era was a period of rising employment, substantial wage and income gains, and social mobility. What is more, this was one of the

Table 15.7 Employment by job status, 2003–2008

	2003	*2008*	*% of total (2008)*	*Rate of change since 2003*
Registered wage-earners	29,264,358	38,069,128	38.93%	30.09%
Non-registered wage-earners	14,268,559	15,607,386	15.96%	9.38%
Self-employed workers	17,863,720	18,183,833	18.59%	1.79%
Domestic workers	6,147,143	6,568,765	6.72%	6.86%
Unpaid workers	5,642,387	4,258,549	4.35%	−24.53%
Workers in subsistence economy	3,400,905	3,946,310	4.04%	16.04%
Employers	3,359,867	4,096,075	4.19%	21.91%
Unemployed	8,637,122	7,070,432	7.23%	−18.14%
Total	88,584,061	97,800,478	100.00%	10.40%

Source: Authors' calculations based on Barbosa and Moretto 2011.

few periods in Brazil's history when the economy grew and income distribution improved, even if the overall development pattern did not change substantially.

Employment relations outcomes

There are several notable employment relations outcomes resulting from the political, social, and economic dynamics explained above. The history of state corporatism and import substitution industrialization based on privileging high end sectors was conducive to rapid economic growth with significant social exclusion, making Brazil one of the most unequal countries in the world. Yet, policies under the recent Workers' Party administrations have favoured re-distribution policies while also encouraging collective bargaining. The result has been a decline not only in inequality but also informality, which is not the trend elsewhere in Latin America.

Unions and collective bargaining have become increasingly fragmented and decentralized. Yet, despite this trend, labour has been able to use the bargaining process not only to increase wages, but to ensure salary adjustments above the inflation rate. Notably, in 2003, when Lula became president, only 18.8 per cent of collective bargaining agreements stipulated a wage increase above the inflation rate. In 2011, at the end of his term, negotiated wage increases were above the inflation rate in 86.8 per cent of collective agreements (DIEESE 2012b, and see Figure 15.3).

As noted above, the strike rate in general has declined noticeably since the tumultuous 1980s and early 1990s as employment relations institutions consolidated and labour increased its access to the formal political process. At the same time, there has been an increasing 'judicialization of class relations' as more labour disputes end up in court and not on the streets. For example, from 1988 to 1997, the mean growth of judicial demands in the first layer of the labour judicial system was more than 112,000 cases per year, compared with a growth rate of 34,000 cases per year during the preceding two decades (Cardoso 2002). At the same time, poverty, which declined in the mid-1990s and then stabilized, has been in steady decline since the early 2000s. This is perhaps the most noteworthy legacy of recent state policies, most especially since poverty and inequality had come to characterize Brazil for so many decades (see Figure 15.4).

In addition to programmes such as 'Zero Hunger' which provide state subsidies to low-income families, one of the most important mechanisms for addressing poverty is through

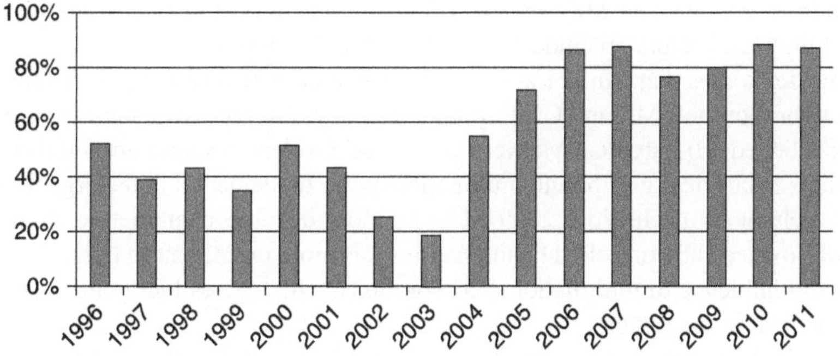

Figure 15.3 Collective bargaining outcomes.

Source: DIEESE, 2012b.

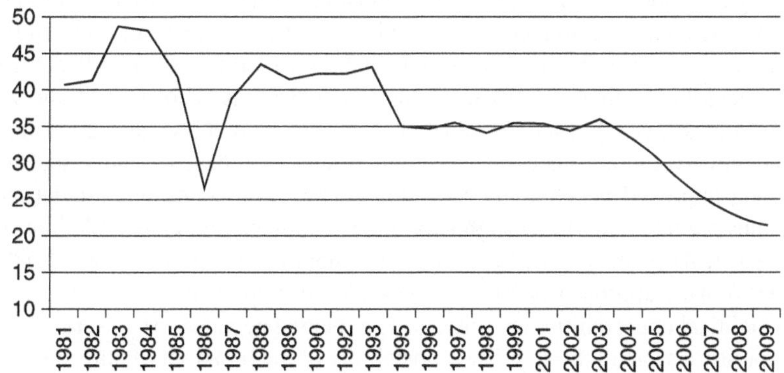

Figure 15.4 Proportion of the population living in poverty.

Source: World Development Indicators.

minimum wage levels since so many workers either receive the minimum wage or have their wage set as a multiple of the minimum wage. Lula's presidency represented a positive era for poorer workers. Poverty in Brazil is often measured according the 'basic basket' of food and a few other needs. In the Cardoso years, the minimum wage covered around one 'basket'. By the end of Lula's era, the figure had doubled to over two 'baskets', the highest ratio since 1979 (DIEESE 2010).

Theoretical perspectives

How does our exploration of Brazilian employment relations inform our discussion of theory? More specifically, what have been the roles of markets, institutions and actors in shaping the patterns through which labour, employers, and the state have interacted and influenced employment relations outcomes? Brazil provides an important case because it does not fit neatly into the 'Varieties of Capitalism' literature in that it is neither a clear case of a liberal market economy (LME) nor of a coordinated market economy (CME). State intervention, at least since the 1930s, has been too pervasive to consider it a pluralist system with limited government intervention (the LME topology). Yet, the role of market forces and the relative weakness of the social actors preclude a CME conceptualization.

Ben Schneider argues that, while Latin American countries like Brazil to a certain degree represent a hybrid of the LME and CME topologies, they also represent something distinct, what he has labelled 'Hierarchical Market Economies' (HMEs) because non-market hierarchical relations in business groups and multinationals are fundamental in the organization of capital and technology (Schneider 2009). Unlike more developed market economies, the role of family-owned and controlled business groups is more prominent in Latin America as is the powerful influence of multinational corporations, which gives hierarchical characteristics to capitalism in the region.

In the Marxist labour movement tradition, Beverly Silver argues that, as manufacturing jobs move from the Global North to the Global South, the next great labour upsurge will follow this geographic shifts in manufacturing (Silver 2003). Brazil is used as an important test case of her argument. Yet, while it is certainly true in a general sense that labour mobilization did escalate as the industrial workforce grew, what we also find is that the peak in strike activity does not coincide with a peak in manufacturing employment, but rather occurs at a very specific political conjuncture as Brazil moved from a period of political liberalization to democratization. What this suggests is that the Brazilian case highlights the importance of politics in shaping movement dynamics. Indeed, as scholars of Latin American labour movements have observed, given labour's limited market leverage, trade unions have often found they have more success in targeting the state as opposed to individual employers when seeking improved benefits and rules guiding working conditions. Social movement dynamics thus provide important insights for understanding employment relations dynamics in Brazil, particularly those associated with the political process approach (Tilly 1978; Tarrow 1998). This approach is based on the idea that movement dynamics are shaped largely by political opportunities and threats. The relative openness or closure of the institutionalized political system, the stability or instability of the broad set of elite alignments, the presence or absence of elite allies, and the state's capacity and propensity for repression have all been shown to shape when and how movements emerge (McAdam 1996).

Brazil in the 1980s was in the process of relative openness following the most repressive era of authoritarian rule. Delegitimization and thus instability among governing elites were on the rise, as was a decline in the state willingness to impose severe repression. The mass mobilization of workers and the strike wave of the 1980s were as much about these shifts in the political context as about the growth of the industrial working class. As Ching Kwan Lee observes in her study of labour protests in China, what is missing from Silver (as well as Polanyi) is a deeper analysis of the state and how state structures and policies shape specific forms of labour protests (Lee 2007: 10). Increased strike activity during the period of political liberalization illustrates the important of political process – and not just economic structures – in shaping movement dynamics in Brazil, as does the decline in strike activity following democratic consolidation and employment relations institutionalization, despite increased employment in strategic manufacturing sectors such as autos. Within the democratic era, there were more strikes during the Cardoso presidency in the 1990s than during the Lula presidency in the 2000s, suggesting that when labour has a strong ally in power, it is more likely to pursue its goals through channels of political access rather than through labour mobilization in the streets.

As suggested by Silver, a large industrial labour force in strategic sectors may provide labour movements' necessary conditions for mobilization, but they are far from sufficient.

In addition to shifting political structures, actor strategies and broader ideological and cultural influences also matter. In other words, just as Howell (2005) argues that there always remains some degree of space within which policy-makers can make significant choices, so too is there a large degree of space within which labour can choose its strategies. And as Lee indicates, there is a need for complex understandings of the agency of workers, because 'worker subjectivity cannot be reduced to material interests. Equally important are workers' sense of dignity, justice, and their need for recognition' (Lee 2007: 15–16).

It is notable that one of the factors that significantly contributed to worker protests in Brazil was their *perception* of an injustice following an independent report that the government had fixed the inflation rate in order to keep down wage increases which were indexed to the inflation rate. Thus, as Kelly (1998) suggests, perceived injustice at the workplace contributes to waves of social movement protest, in this case, a wave of protest so powerful that it contributed to the ultimate demise of authoritarian rule in Brazil. Worker subjectivities also can explain variations in union responses. For example, research on union responses to economic restructuring in the Brazilian auto industry shows that unionists facing similar competitive pressures might pursue transnational labour alliances with unionists working for the same company elsewhere or they might shun transnationalism in favour of collaboration with management in a form of micro-corporatism. The difference lies not in market structure, but the political orientations of trade unionism, which are deeply embedded in world-views and historical experiences (Anner 2011). For example, Left-oriented auto unionists in the CUT were likely to combine plant-level worker mobilization with transnational labour ties with German and Canadian unions in response to the pressures created by economic restructuring. In contrast, the more nationalist world-view of the moderate auto unionists in Força Sindical led them to respond to the pressures of restructuring by seeking pacts with employers at the plant level in a form of micro-corporatism while shunning international labour solidarity (ibid.).

If one element of the Brazilian case is clear, it is that developments have been far from linear. This is not a story of constantly evolving market liberalization and declining unionization rates with declining union power. During the era of greater market liberalization – the 1990s under the administration of Cardoso – precarious work increased and strong industrial unions lost many members and some of their influence. But trade unions held their overall numbers and largely maintained the capacity for political mobilization. This is partly because institutions are resilient, as are Brazil's strong culture of workplace mobilization and activism. Much of this culture was born in the fight against the dictatorship, and some forms of resistance can be traced back to the influence of liberation theology and Christian Base Communities that were very active in Brazil (Keck 1992).

In the 2000s, we find improvement in many employment relations outcomes. Unions broadened some of their organizational rights, increased their political leverage, and saw an expansive role of regulatory mechanisms such as workplace inspections. At the same time, the effectiveness of collective bargaining as a mechanism for regulating the employment relations practices increased. Not only have trade unions been able to achieve more substantial wage increases as a result of collective bargaining – as opposed to reliance on government wage setting through minimum wage regulation – but they also have been able to regulate other aspects of the employment relationship. This is not merely the result of evolving market mechanisms or the stickiness of employment relations institutions, but also of actor strategies and the complex social movement interactions between a dynamic labour movement, employers, and state actors.

Conclusion

Brazil provides an importance illustration of employment relations practices in a large middle-income country with a tumultuous political history. The foundation of today's system rests with the corporatist model developed during the Vargas era in the 1930s–1950s. The system encompasses a form of decentralized occupational unionism and relatively weak employers associations that have allowed for a strong role of the state. What is noticeable about the history of employment relations is how little certain elements of the system have changed, despite military rule, democratization, neo-liberal reforms, and a progressive government led by an ex-trade union leader.

In many ways, Brazil has developed its own path toward economic development and employment relations. The recent global economic crisis (2008–10) had a less dramatic effect on Brazil than many European countries. At a time when many countries have seen an increase in informalization and a decline in unionization, in Brazil, formal sector employment has increased in recent years and trade unions have maintained their membership levels.

Brazil's unique history and employment relations practices make it difficult to explain with any one dominant theory of employment relations. Labour market structures – particularly the growth of an industrial working class in the São Paolo region – help explain the rise of workers' protests in the 1970s and 1980s, but the political dynamics of a broad societal push for democratization certainly contributed to the timing of those protest events. The stickiness of employment relations institutions helps to explain the continuation of many cumbersome practices, but institutions fail to explain the changes that did take place under the governments of Cardoso and Lula. Nor does Brazil fit neatly into the liberal market or coordinated market categories of the 'varieties of capitalism' approach. Rather, what we find is that Brazil remains a hybrid employment relations system influenced by social movement dynamics that is likely to continue to defy expectations for years to come.

Note

1 Although French (1992) also notes that, despite the 'statist straitjacket', there was a considerable degree of (previously ignored) bottom-up activism during this period.

References

Almeida, M.H. T. de (1997) 'Unions in times of reform', in M. D'A. G. Kinzo (ed.) *Reforming the State: Business, Unions and Regions in Brazil*, London: Institute of Latin American Studies.

Anner, M. (2011) *Solidarity Transformed: Labor's Responses to Globalization and Crisis in Latin America*, Ithaca, NY: ILR Press.

Antunes, R. C. (1999) *O Que É Sindicalismo?*, São Paulo: Editora Brasiliense, first published 1980.

Arbix, G. (2001) 'Fiscal wars in the Brazilian automobile industry: the unbalanced alliance between governments and multinational enterprises', unpublished MS.

Barbosa, A. de Freitas (2003) 'A formação do mercado de trabalho no brasil: da escravidão ao assalariamento', Master's thesis, Instituto de Economia, São Paulo, Universidade Estadual de Campinas.

—— and Abdal, A. (2010) *Employment and Labour Situation in Brazil*, Enclosure No. 2. Prepared for the Overseas Vocational Training Association of the Government of Japan. Available at: http://www.ovta.or.jp/info/southamerica/brazil/pdffiles/06labor.pdf.

—— and Moretto, A. (2011) 'Development pattern, labour market and social protection in Brazil: what has (and what has not) changed under the Lula government?', in G. Rodgers (ed.) *The Challenge of Aligning Economic and Social Goals in Emerging Economies*, New Delhi: Institute for Human Development.

Bresciani, L. P. (1997) 'Os desejos e o limite: reestruturação industrial e ação sindical no complexo automotivo Brasileiro', in M. de P. Leite (ed.) *O Trabalho em Movimento: reestruturação produtiva e sindicatos no Brasil*, São Paulo: Papirus Editora.

Cardoso, A. M. (2001) 'Problemas de representação do sindicalismo Brasileiro: o que aconteceu com a filiação sindical?', in E. De La Garza (ed.) *Los Sindicatos Frente a los Procesos de Transición Política*, Buenos Aires: CLASCO.

—— (2002) 'Neoliberalism, unions, and socio-economic insecurity in Brazil', *Labour, Capital and Society*, 35(2): 282–316.

—— and Gindin, J. (2009) *Industrial Relations and Collective Bargaining: Argentina, Brazil and Mexico Compared*, Geneva: International Labour Office, Industrial and Employment Relations Department, DIALOGUE Working Paper No. 5.

CEACR (Committee of Experts on the Application of Conventions and Recommendations (2005) *Report of the Committee of Experts on the Application of Conventions and Recommendations*, Geneva: ILO. Available at: www.ilo.org/public/english/standards/relm/ilc (accessed 30 November 2005).

Collier, R. B. and Collier, D. (1991) *Shaping the Political Arena: Critical Junctures, the Labor Movement, and Regime Dynamics in Latin America*, Princeton, NJ: Princeton University Press.

Comin, A. (1998) *De Volta para o Futuro – Política e Reestruturação Industrial do Complexo Automobilístico nos Anos 1990*, São Paulo, Brasil: Annablume Editoria.

Cook, M. L. (2002) 'Labor reform and dual transitions in Brazil and the Southern Cone', *Latin American Politics and Society*, 44(1): 1–34.

DIEESE (Departamento Intersindical de Estatística e Estudos Sócio-Econômicos) (2001) *A Situação do Trabalho no Brasil*. São Paulo: Departamento Intersindical de Estatística e Estudos Sócio-Econômicos.

—— (2010) *Custo da Cesta Básica Tem Redução em 2009*, São Paulo, Brazil: Departamento Intersindical de Estatística e Estudos Socioeconômicos. Available at http://trovatore.dieese.org.br/analisecestabasica/2010/201001cestabasica.pdf (accessed 5 May 2012).

—— (2012a) *Balanço das Greves em 2009 e 2010*. São Paulo: Departamento Intersindical de Estatística e Estudos Sócio-Econômicos.

—— (2012b) *Balanço das Negociações dos Reajustes Salariais em 2011*. São Paulo: Departamento Intersindical de Estatística e Estudos Sócio-Econômicos.

Força Sindical (2000) 'A modernidade no mundo do trabalho', *Força Sindical*, 14–15 March.

French, J. D. (1992) *The Brazilian Workers' ABC: Class Conflict and Alliances in Modern São Paulo*, Chapel Hill, NC: The University of North Carolina Press.

Hall, M. M. (2009) 'The labor policies of the Lula government', in J. L. Love and W. Baer (eds) *Brazil under Lula: Economy, Politics, and Society under the Worker-President*, New York: Palgrave Macmillan.

Horn, C. H. (2009) *Collective Bargaining in Brazil: A Study on Joint Regulation of the Employment Relationship in Manufacturing*, Saarbrücken: VDM Verlag.

Howell, C. (2005) *Trade Unions and the State: The Construction of Industrial Relations Institutions in Britain, 1890–2000*, Princeton, NJ: Princeton University Press.

Humphrey, J. (1982) *Capitalist Control and Workers' Struggle in the Brazilian Auto Industry*, Princeton, NJ: Princeton University Press.

IBGE (Instituto Brasileiro de Geografiae Estatística) (2002) *Sindicatos: indicadores sociais 2001 (primeiros resultados)*, Rio de Janeiro: Instituto Brasileiro de Geografia e Estatística.

Keck, M. E. (1989) 'The new unionism in the Brazilian transition', in A. Stepan (ed.) *Democratizing Brazil: Problems of Transition and Consolidation*, New York: Oxford University Press.

—— (1992) *The Workers' Party and Democratization in Brazil*, New Haven, CT: Yale University Press.

Kelly, J. (1998) *Rethinking Industrial Relations: Mobilization, Collectivism and Long Waves*, London: Routledge.

Lamounier, B. (1999) 'Brazil: inequality against democracy', in L. Diamond, J. Hartlyn, J. J. Linz and S. M. Lipset (eds) *Democracy in Developing Countries: Latin America*, 2nd edn, Boulder, CO: Lynne Rienner Publishers.

Lee, C. K. (2007) *Against the Law: Labor Protests in China's Rustbelt and Sunbelt*, Berkeley, CA: University of California Press.

Løken, E. and Barbosa, A. de F. (2008) *Industrial Balacao? Industrial Relations in Norway and Brazil and within Norwegian Companies in Brazil*, Oslo: Institute for Labour and Social Research (FAFO).

McAdam, D. (1996) 'Conceptual origins, current problems, future directions', in D. McAdam, J. D. McCarthy and M. N. Zald (eds) *Comparative Perspectives on Social Movements: Political Opportunities, Mobilizing Structures, and Cultural Framing*, New York: Cambridge University Press.

Mainwaring, S. (1999) *Rethinking Party Systems in the Third Wave of Democratization: The Case of Brazil*, Stanford, CA: Stanford University Press.

Martin, S. B. (1997) 'Beyond corporatism: new patterns of representation in the Brazilian auto industry', in D. A. Chalmers, C. M. Vilas, K. Hite, S. B. Martin, K. Piester and M. Segarra (eds) *The New Politics of Inequality in Latin America: Rethinking Participation and Representation*, New York: Oxford University Press.

Nogueira, A. J. F. Mi. (1997) *A Modernização Conservadora do Sindicalismo Brasileiro: A experiência do sindicato dos metalúrgicos de São Paulo*, São Paulo: EDUC/FAPESP.

O'Donnell, G. A., Schmitter, P.C. and Whitehead, L. (1986) *Transitions from Authoritarian Rule*, Baltimore, MD: Johns Hopkins University Press.

Rodrigues, I. J. R. (1999) 'A trajetória de novo sindicalismo', in I. J. Rodrigues (ed.) *O Novo Sindicalismo Vinte Anos Depois*, São Paulo: Editora Vozes Ltda., EDUC, UNITRABALHO.

Schmitter, P. C. (1974) 'Still the century of corporatism?', *Review of Politics*, 36(1): 85–121.

Schneider, B. R. (2004) *Business Politics and the State in Twentieth-Century Latin America*, New York: Cambridge University Press.

—— (2009) 'Hierarchical market economies and varieties of capitalism in Latin America', *Journal of Latin American Studies*, 41(3): 55–75.

Silver, B. J. (2003) *Forces of Labor: Workers' Movements and Globalization since 1870*, New York: Cambridge University Press.

Skidmore, T. E. (1973) 'Politics and economic policy marking in authoritarian Brazil, 1937–71', in A. Stepan (ed.) *Authoritarian Brazil: Origins, Policies, and Future*, New Haven, CT: Yale University Press.

—— and Smith, P. H. (2001) *Modern Latin America*, 5th edn, New York: Oxford University Press.

Smith, P. H. (2005) *Democracy in Latin America: Political Change in Comparative Perspective*, New York: Oxford University Press.

Tarrow, S. G. (1998) *Power in Movement: Social Movements and Contentious Politics*, 2nd edn, New York: Cambridge University Press.

Tilly, C. (1978) *From Mobilization to Revolution*, Reading, MA: Addison-Wesley.

Venn, D. (2009) *Legislation, Collective Bargaining and Enforcement: Updating the OECD Employment Protection Indicators*, Paris: OECD, Directorate for Employment, Labour and Social Affairs, Social, Employment and Migration Working Papers. Available at: www.oecd.org/els/workingpapers.

Zylberstajn, H. (2006) 'President Lula's union reform', *Korean Journal of Industrial Relations*, 16: 1–27.

16 Russia

Sarah Ashwin and Irina Kozina

Russia has undergone a historic transformation since the collapse of the Soviet Union in 1991. Employment relations are central to understanding the outcomes of this change. On the eve of reform, the trade unions inherited from the Soviet past were the sole organizations of civil society with the potential to impose social constraint on Russia's new ruling elite. The Federation of Independent Trade Unions of Russia (FNPR) – the successor organization to the Soviet trade unions – entered the transition with a union density of nearly 99 per cent, but also with a history of subordination to management and the political authorities. As will be seen, the unions proved unable to escape their dependence, and therefore failed to provide effective representation of workers' interests during economic reform. This gave the economic reformers a free hand, with disastrous consequences.

The Russian case shows that the ability of actors to exercise strategic choice varies greatly according to context. Russian unions were strongly constrained in their response to reform – 'over-determined' is the word that comes to mind in relation to their apparently pusillanimous conduct. The Russian state was ostensibly far less confined in its decision-making, but it still found it hard to escape the 'sticky' institutions of the past. It was not the formal institutions of Soviet power which proved most resilient, but the inherited pattern of clientelist relations and politicized resource allocation, which subverted the economic and political 'transition'.

Actors and processes

The origins of the Russian employment relations system

Russia's neo-liberal reform programme, launched after Yeltsin came to power in 1991, was a political and economic project intended 'to dissolve the past by the fastest means possible' (Burawoy and Verdery 1999: 5). Disregarding institutions and the rule of law, the reformers relied on the creative destruction of the market, which they believed would 'make all things new'. This vision failed. In the face of economic meltdown, Soviet practices and informal institutions showed a good deal of resilience. This is certainly the case in employment relations, which in many respects retain a distinctly Soviet form. The traumatic transformation of the 1990s left its mark, but, as will be seen, the Soviet institutional legacy remains a dominant influence on employment relations. This section considers this inheritance.

According to the ruling Communist Party, Soviet employment relations were 'non-antagonistic', because both managers and workers were employees of a state led by the Communist Party which ruled on behalf of the working class. The state was the sole property owner, and directed economic activity in the interests of the proletariat, Marx's 'universal class'. Trade unions were therefore not needed to represent workers' interests. Instead, Lenin conceded that they could act as 'mediators' in cases where tension arose from 'bureaucratic distortions' in the state administration (Lenin [1922] 1947: 761–2). They were also to facilitate links between workers and the Party, by becoming, in Lenin's famous phrase, 'transmission belts from the Communist Party to the masses' (ibid.: 766). The other main role ascribed to trade unions was improving productivity and labour discipline – in which capacity they were serving what was claimed to be the 'objective' interests of workers in the rapid economic development of the USSR. Meanwhile, during the Stalin era the unions were also charged with administering the social services provided by enterprises. Acting as the social and welfare departments of enterprises over time became their most important role.

Given the way their role was defined, trade unions were unable to act as workers' representatives. At the enterprise level they were subordinate to both management and the Party. There was no input from below; the unions were strictly hierarchical and all policy was made at the highest level. Moreover, workers did not trust the unions – they were well aware that they were not independent organizations. At a central level, the trade unions were organized into large branch and territorial organizations uniting all the employees (including managers) in an industry. These in turn belonged to the All-Union Central Council of Trade Unions (VTsSPS). These organizations could provide information and advice to government and state planners. However, in doing so they were acting as an agency of the state rather than as representatives of their members. Any power they possessed was not derived from their membership, but was dependent upon their relationship with the Party.

Managers were similarly dependent. Managers of state enterprises were subject to political control through the presence of Communist Party cells in enterprises. In addition, the majority of them were Party members. Their main task was to meet the production targets set by state planners. They did not have to make a profit or maximize efficiency. Indeed, their interest lay in minimizing plan targets by concealing the productive capacity of the enterprise, while trying to maximize centrally-allocated inputs. A whole series of tasks carried out by managers of capitalist firms, such as marketing and accounting, were not required in the Soviet system. Formally, managers also had no scope to develop independent personnel policies, since terms and conditions were centrally defined. Instead, they needed to be skilled managers of informal relations – with relevant state officials, suppliers and workers. The deficiencies of the planning system meant that informal incentives were required in order to ensure the smooth running of enterprises. For example, dealing with shortages of inputs required creativity and flexibility on the part of workers. The discretionary allocation of monetary and non-monetary rewards was an important tool in securing this (see Ashwin 2003, for more details).

The state was the linchpin of this system and it had to maintain a delicate balance. On the one hand, through the Five-Year Plans, the state aimed to increase production by what Lenin called 'enormous dimensions' (Lenin [1922] 1947: 763). On the other hand, it needed to secure political quiescence. Worker protest had the potential to undermine the legitimacy of a regime that claimed to rule on behalf of the proletariat. Managers were therefore required to deliver the plan – but not at the cost of provoking open resistance. One of the roles of the Party in the enterprise was to ensure that this equilibrium was maintained. A key way in which it did this was by providing channels through which *individual* workers could address their grievances. A disgruntled worker could approach the Party, the enterprise legal advisor, the trade union or line management. The Party was the only organization capable of constraining managerial discretion, and often did so in the interests of social order. The Party and the KGB (the security police) intervened quickly in cases of strikes or protests, often granting concessions and sacking the managers or local bureaucrats deemed to be responsible for the problem (Connor 1991: 222). Meanwhile, workers could also seek legal redress, either through the enterprise legal advisor, or the trade union. The enterprise legal advisor was able to negotiate private agreements with individual workers, and help resolve disputes over issues such as overtime pay, vacation entitlement and dismissal (Shelley 1981). This meant workers could 'often receive rapid and fair resolution of their problems' (Shelley 1984). Workers could also seek help from the union in cases of dismissal, which required union consent. Mary McAuley found that, during the period of her study (1957–65), enterprise unions in Leningrad refused approximately half such requests (1969: 123). In all these cases, the social cohesion of the enterprise was a key consideration in the granting of concessions. Finally, workers could also make individual approaches to enterprise directors, or to line managers, who performed an informal representative function within enterprises (Ashwin 1997). The state insistence on meeting plan targets while maintaining social peace defined the parameters within which managers responded to worker complaints.

The collapse of the Soviet Union threw this system into flux. The (ostensible) aim of the state shifted from building Communism to creating a market economy, with dramatic consequences for employment relations. Managers and trade unions were forced to adapt as the political and economic certainties of the Soviet system were destroyed. And yet, as will be seen, the responses of the employment relations actors were shaped by the logic of past institutions as much as by the reformers' teleological vision.

The state

For the purposes of contextualization, our consideration of the Russian employment relations system has to begin with the initiator of Russia's transformation: the state. After the collapse of the Soviet Union in 1991, the then President of the Russian Federation, Boris Yeltsin, was quick to seize the initiative, launching simultaneous economic and political reform. At this stage the presumed destination was a market-oriented democracy.

The reformers' chosen route to the market was the standard structural adjustment model proposed by the International Monetary Fund (IMF), which was applied with rigid inattention to the specificities of the local environment. The package entailed market liberalization (of prices, trade and capital flows), stabilization and privatization. Most prices were freed overnight in January 1992, plunging Russia into hyperinflation, and wiping out savings. Inflation was then controlled by high interest rates and strict control of the money supply – so-called 'stabilization'. This was also intended to drive out inefficient producers as state support for industry dried up, but instead it deprived enterprises of capital and pushed up the exchange rate, reducing the competiveness of domestic producers suddenly exposed to foreign competition. The lack of liquidity led enterprises to develop non-monetary survival strategies: they reverted to barter, left their employees unpaid, and ceased investment, leaving plant and equipment to deteriorate (Woodruff 1999; Clarke 2007). Price liberalization and stabilization set the stage for a very corrupt privatization process. Voucher privatization formally allowed workers whose savings had been destroyed by inflation to gain a share in their enterprises, but the privations of 'stabilization' quickly induced workers to sell their (usually much depreciated) shares back to management. The consolidation of ownership was completed by the 1995 loans-for-shares scandal, in which the government acquired loans to finance Yeltsin's re-election campaign from private banks, many of them owned by friends of the government. Shares in state enterprises were put up as collateral, creating instant billionaires when the government defaulted on the loans. In effect, enterprises ended up in the hands either of their managers, or of political insiders with close relationships with the government.

'Shock therapy' failed to bring any of the gains anticipated by the reformers, instead leading to unprecedented economic decline. In the period 1990–99 GDP fell by 54 per cent and industrial production by almost 60 per cent (Stiglitz 2002: 143). This led to a devastating decline in living standards for the majority of the population. In mid-1998 statistical real wages were a little over half their 1985 level. Moreover, this decline was accompanied by a huge growth in inequality,[1] implying the position of the poorest had declined even further (Clarke 1999: 120). Unemployment was not as high as was expected, reaching 9.7 per cent in 1996, and rising to a peak of 13.2 per cent in 1998 (Goskomstat 2003: 130). Comparatively low unemployment was little cause for celebration, however, since it merely reflected the fact that labour was so cheap and flexible that enterprises had little reason to shed staff. Enterprises routinely resorted to late payment of wages, short time and enforced leave during the 1990s, and encountered little protest from workers who continued to work without pay for months at a time (Ashwin 1999).

Amid this economic turmoil, the government facilitated the development of a comprehensive system of social partnership, with the enthusiastic support of the trade unions. In November 1991, Presidential Decree No. 212 'On Social Partnership and the Resolution of Labour Disputes (Conflicts)' provided for the establishment of the Russian Tripartite Commission for the Regulation of Social-Labour Relations (RTK), and similar commissions at branch (industry) and regional levels. The RTK was established in 1992 and stands at the apex of a system of branch, regional and sub-regional tripartite (or sometimes bipartite) agreements, with enterprise collective agreements at the base. This system of social partnership was given a secure legal foundation with the Federal Law 'On the Russian Tripartite Commission for the Regulation of Social-Labour Relations' of 1 May 1999.

The state's promotion of this elaborate system of dialogue was at odds with its toleration and perpetration of mass violations of the Labour Code in the 1990s (most notably through non-payment of wages). But this apparent contradiction caused the government little problem because the unions were in no position to call it to account. Instead, as will be seen, the unions used the system of social partnership as a lifeline, gratefully accepting the status of interlocutor, but unable to use it to defend workers' interests. Thus, national and regional agreements were characterized by general unenforceable provisions, a tendency to defer rather than initiate action, and repetition of existing law (Ashwin and Clarke 2003: 138–68). Enterprise collective agreements and branch tariff (industry) agreements were little better, with the former in particular frequently illegal, including worse terms than prescribed by law (ibid.: 228–34). Meanwhile, the violation of agreements carried no consequences, as no sanctions were mandated in the case of non-fulfilment. Only enterprise collective agreements were in principle enforceable, since the unions had the right to initiate a collective labour dispute when their terms were violated, but in practice this very seldom occurred for reasons related to their dependence on management, explained below.

Social partnership was thus a superficial façade, beneath which the government approached employment relations with impunity. Its attitude to protest can be defined as 'unresponsive toleration'. Unlike the Soviet regime it was not scared of open dissent, which did not challenge its legitimacy. Indeed, resisting the claims of those derided as 'rent-seekers' was a badge of honour for a neo-liberal reformer. Yeltsin's government generally opted to ignore worker protest and offered only limited concessions at politically sensitive moments such as election periods, or when a strike was sufficiently disruptive (Borisov and Clarke 1996; Ashwin 1999). Most strikes concerned wage delays, and when it was forced into action, the typical government response was to send emergency funds to some of the strikers, promising full repayment later. This usually succeeded in demobilizing workers, who rarely secured anything beyond the initial payout. For example, a miners' strike against wage delays in December 1996 crumbled after Prime Minister Victor Chernomyrdin announced an emergency transfer of funds (Borisov and Clarke 1996). In doing so, he acknowledged that huge sums promised in the past had often not materialized (Associated Press, 5 December 1996). Such concessions never altered the overall direction of economic policy – the stabilization policy which was the root cause of the non-payment crisis remained in place until the collapse of the rouble in August 1998.

In the Putin era, the position of the state has shifted. Key to Vladimir Putin's success was his ability to present himself as a force for order, stability and the reassertion of state power (Sakwa 2008), after what most Russians perceived to be the chaos of the Yeltsin era. In policy terms, Putin did not abandon economic liberalism, though over time he did soften it through schemes such as the 'national projects' of government investment in socially important policy areas (Lukin 2009: 76). Despite the continuity in economic policy, Putin appeared to offer greater protection to society – so much so, that one respected academic commentator has characterized Putin's leadership as a Polanyian counter-movement against the ravages of the free market (Sakwa 2008: 880–1).[2] In policy terms it is hard to see it as such, but it may well have been experienced in this way by Russians after the economic catastrophe of the 1990s.

Putin's approach is well illustrated by the introduction of the new Labour Code. In line with the government's liberal leanings, its initial draft of the code proposed a radical deregulation of the labour market. This was vigorously opposed by the unions, which supported the 'deputies' variant' of the code put forward by a working group of eight deputies from various parties. The FNPR unions used their nationwide network of organizations to mount an impressive mass lobbying campaign. According to the FNPR, in the week before the planned Duma hearing, its member organizations convened more than 100,000 meetings to discuss the draft Labour Code, 'mass actions' took place in 63 regions, and 90,000 letters and appeals were sent, signed by eight million people, with an average of 200 letters being sent to each Duma deputy (for more details, see Ashwin and Clarke 2003: 65–6). In the face of such concerted opposition, at the last minute the government shied away from confrontation. The Duma[3] hearing of the government draft was postponed to allow a conciliation commission to come up with a new draft. This led to the development of a compromise proposal, which was signed into law on 30 December 2001. The compromise Code represented a significant improvement on the government draft, retaining many of the protective and regulatory features of its Soviet predecessor, and actually advancing the position of workers in some respects (for example, prescribing the payment of interest on unpaid wages, and allowing workers to stop work, without pay, after a wage delay of over 15 days). Crucially, from the perspective of the FNPR, its regulation of strikes and collective bargaining weakened the alternative unions, by stipulating conditions only likely to be fulfilled by FNPR-affiliates (for more details, see Bronstein 2005).

The struggle over the Labour Code reveals that Putin's concern for social order trumps economic liberalism. It also shows that, despite the unions' limited capacity for mobilization, the government is wary of outright confrontation. As for the FNPR, it was forced into action because the initial liberal version of the Code would have seriously undermined its institutional position. But even on this issue it was cautious, putting more effort into letter-writing and lobbying than organizing demonstrations, for fear that these would fall flat (Ashwin and Clarke 2003: 66). Faced with mass violations of workers' rights, it has been even more risk-averse.

A key difference in the state's approach to employment relations after 2000 lies in its attitude to industrial conflict. The Putin regime is less able to ignore protest than was the Yeltsin government. This is partly due to the strength of the security services within the government, whose members, Putin included, have a deeply ingrained aversion to open dissent. But the government is also constrained by public opinion. The restoration of order is seen as a key Putinite achievement, while Putin's 'strength' has been a valued attribute. The regime has therefore edged back towards Soviet methods of containing industrial conflict. Low-level repression is routinely used: it is difficult to get permission to protest; legal strikes are virtually impossible to organize; organizations capable of mobilizing protest are subject to police harassment and intimidation; protestors are liable to arrest and other forms of punishment. Meanwhile, as in the Soviet era, managers and regional leaders are keenly aware that allowing open conflict to develop on their watch will incur official displeasure. They therefore act to pre-empt protest wherever possible. When significant labour protest does occur, the regime can be forced into concessions, as was dramatically demonstrated during the Pikalevo dispute of May 2009, when the town's laid-off, unpaid workers blocked the Federal highway and demanded Putin's intervention, after domestic hot water supplies were cut off. Putin flew to the troubled town, denouncing enterprise bosses (one of whom was Oleg Deripaska, a Russian billionaire industrialist) as 'cockroaches' in a nationally televised meeting and forcing them into a settlement.

Unions could have made use of the President's conflict-aversion, had not it also prompted an intensification of the pressure on unions to demonstrate their 'loyalty'. Early on in his period in office Putin indicated that he had the ability to undermine the unions when, in the run-up to the 2001 FNPR Congress, the presidential administration sponsored initiatives to undermine the FNPR and remove Mikhail Shmakov, its leader since 1993 (for details, see Ashwin and Clarke 2003: 68–71). Since then, the unions have been regularly reminded of their dependence on the government, with any perceived slight quickly reprimanded.

Trade unions and collective bargaining

The unions responded with alacrity to the changes of the Gorbachev era. The Soviet trade union centre, the VTsSPS, asserted its independence from the Party as early as 1987, and was later replaced by a new General Confederation of Trade Unions (VKP) in October 1990, in which the organizations of what were still the republics of the Soviet Union, and the branch trade unions, had a greater degree of autonomy. From the spring of 1990, branch unions – organized on an industry basis, with all the workers (and managers) in a particular industry belonging to the same union – began to establish republican organizations. At this time the Russian confederation, the FNPR, was established, again asserting its independence of the Party and state, but also fighting for greater independence from the VKP. The Russian branch trade unions initiated similar name changes and declarations of reform. The FNPR remains the main union confederation in Russia, and in institutional terms has negotiated the choppy waters of reform very effectively. It has kept most of its assets, many of its institutional privileges, and a significant proportion of its membership.

As in all countries of the former Soviet bloc, independent trade unions opposed to the former Soviet trade unions emerged during the early reform era. In Russia, this movement was led by the miners, with the establishment of an Independent Miners' Union (NPG) in

1990. However, the 1991 miners' strike, which looked like a promising beginning, instead turned out to be the high point in the influence of the independent workers' movement. Independent trade unions found it very difficult to expand beyond their small base in mining and transport. Independent trade unions have had some notable local successes, and are generally far less equivocal in their defence of workers than their FNPR-affiliated counterparts. Nevertheless, their membership remains scattered and small; by 2000, new independent trade unions represented at the very most 5 per cent of union members (ibid.: 1).

Before analyzing the formal position of the unions with regard to indicators such as density and collective bargaining coverage, a note of caution is required. It is well known that such indicators do not adequately capture union strength (see Frege and Kelly, Chapter 2 in this volume). This is certainly the case in Russia, where relatively 'strong' indicators by international standards do not convey the weakness of the union movement. The key reason for this is the unions' inability to escape their Soviet-era dependence on the state and management. As will be discussed in the theoretical section on actor-based theories, the unions' freedom of action was tightly circumscribed by inherited structural constraints (Ashwin 1999). Even the most determined attempt to develop an independent position based on the ability to mobilize union members would have faced doubtful prospects. In the event, however, the FNPR eschewed such risky strategies. Instead, at every level, the unions generally confined themselves to their accustomed soviet role as mediators rather than as workers' representatives (Ashwin and Clarke 2003). This secured their institutional survival, but did little to develop their effectiveness as defenders of their members' rights.

On the eve of reform, the FNPR organized approximately 99 per cent of the Russian labour force. Since then, their membership has fallen steadily, and this decline shows little sign of halting. While at the end of the 1990s, trade union density still looked high by international standards at 54 per cent (ibid.: 86), continued decline during the 2000s means that the FNPR now represents only approximately a quarter of the employed population (see Table 16.1). In relation to these figures, one specificity of Russian trade union membership should be noted. FNPR unions have substantial membership among students in professional and vocational institutions and among pensioners who either do not pay dues or pay at a reduced rate. In 2010, for example, such members made up over 22 per cent of FNPR membership. We have therefore calculated density using the figures for employed members only.

Table 16.1 Russian trade union membership, 2002–2010

	2002	*2003*	*2004*	*2005*	*2006*	*2007*	*2008*	*2009*	*2010*
Employed population (thousands)	66,266	67,152	67,134	68,603	69,157	70,813	70,965	69,258	69,803
Trade union membership including students and pensioners (thousands)	36,200	31,800	30,500	28,600	27,800	27,100	25,800	24,700	24,200
Trade union membership employees (thousands)	28,960	25,440	25,071	22,800	21,900	21,700	20,600	19,500	18,800
Density (%)	43.7	37.8	37.3	33.2	31.6	30.6	29.0	28.1	26.9

Sources: Authors' own calculations, using FNPR figures on union membership and Rosstat employment data. Rosstat data, table available at: http://www.gks.ru/bgd/regl/b11_36/IssWWW.exe/Stg/d1/03-10.htm.

In formal terms, collective bargaining coverage is quite high, with many workers covered by more than one agreement. In 2011, there were 60 branch tariff agreements in operation, covering more than 46 million workers, approximately 62 per cent of the employed population. Meanwhile, 27.9 million employees were covered by enterprise collective agreements, just under 40 per cent of the employed population (although the Ministry of Health and Social Development, into which the Ministry of Labour is now subsumed, cites this as 63 per cent of employees 'in real sectors of the economy', which appears to exclude trade and services).[4] However, this respectable level of coverage has only a marginal impact on wages and conditions. Simon Clarke found that neither trade union membership, nor the presence of the trade union at an enterprise, nor a collective agreement had a statistically significant influence on wage variation in Russia (2002: 641–2). Given the character of the agreements discussed above, this is not surprising.

While union weakness is related to the specificities of the Soviet heritage, the reasons for the decline in membership are similar to those in other industrialized countries. Trade union membership is known to fall during periods of economic contraction – and Russia has endured nearly a decade of precipitous decline. Compositional changes have also worked against the unions. As in many other countries, employment in traditional union heartlands has declined, while new areas of employment have generally proved less conducive to union organizing. Thus, the proportion of Russian workers in industrial employment has almost halved during the post-Soviet era. Between 1992 and 1999, employment in what the state statistical agency then referred to as 'industry' declined from 29.6 per cent of the employed population to 22.2 per cent (Goskomstat 2000: 79). This trend continued between 2000 and 2009, with employment in what is now referred to as 'manufacturing' declining from 19.1 per cent to 15.4 per cent of the employed population.[5] Meanwhile, the area that enjoyed the largest rise in its share of employment was the new category of 'wholesale and retail trade, repair of motor vehicles, motorcycles, household goods and personal items' which increased from 13.7 per cent of total employment in 2000 to 17.8 per cent in 2009, overtaking manufacturing to become the largest category of employment.[6] Employment in this grouping is typically in small and medium-sized enterprises, where the FNPR acknowledges its organizing campaigns have made little headway (FNPR 2010: 4). This is not surprising, since even the most effective union movements have difficulty organizing in such environments. The FNPR attributes the recent decline to the impact of the 2008 economic crisis, as well as the ongoing enterprise restructuring and the spread of atypical forms of employment (ibid.: 4). In the light of international experience this seems a plausible explanation.

The FNPR's institutional embeddedness in enterprises established during the Soviet era has helped it retain members (Kozina 2009a: 25–6). At the same time, its links to the past may be an inhibiting factor in organizing new establishments. Opinion polls generally find very low levels of trust in trade unions. Only 4 per cent of respondents in a 2011 Gallup poll expressed their trust in trade unions, up from 3 per cent in 2004. However, it should be stressed that most public institutions, such as the media, local authorities and political parties received similar results, with only the President securing respectable trust levels (20 per cent in 2011, down from 59 per cent in 2004).[7] The dilemmas faced by the FNPR in preserving its influence and institutional position are discussed in the section on actor-related theories.

As it declines, trade union membership is feminizing: women comprised 59.8 per cent of total union membership in 2010, up from 59.2 per cent in 2009. Meanwhile, women dominate in leadership positions near the bottom of the union hierarchy, with 76.8 per cent of primary trade union organizations led by women. This proportion steeply declines further up the union hierarchy, however, with only 6.8 per cent of national or inter-regional unions led by women (FNPR 2010: 4–5). Unfortunately, women's strong representation as leaders of primary organizations has rather negative connotations. Analysis of the processes through which jobs are gendered in Russia (Kozina and Zhidkova 2006) suggests that it probably reflects the low status of the unions, as well as the conception of the trade union officer as a form of 'social worker' rather than a negotiator or representative.

Employers and employers associations

In the Soviet era, the state was the only employer. Privatization created a class of private employers, who united to form employers associations relatively quickly. However, developing 'governability' (Traxler 1995) – the ability to represent members and ensure their compliance with agreements – has proved to be more difficult.

Given the complex multi-level system of social partnership, employers organizations have been required to negotiate at various levels. Initially, the government and trade unions filled in for the missing employers organizations. Thus, the employer representatives in the first Tripartite Commission (RTK) were primarily representatives of ministries and quasi-ministerial bodies, using their position to press their branch interests on the government, and a number of self-styled employer representatives, mostly claiming to represent entrepreneurs and small businesses, who were selected by government patronage (Ashwin and Clarke 2003: 145). Likewise, during the 1990s, the vast majority of tariff agreements were bipartite, involving the government and the trade union, with only about one-fifth being signed by private employers' representatives in 2001 (ibid.: 148–9). At regional level, there was a patchwork of representation, with the regional administration and trade unions playing an important role in pushing employers to organize (ibid.: 154–7).

Since then employers' organizations have continued to consolidate. At national level employers are represented by the Russian Union of Industrialists and Entrepreneurs (RSPP), which unites 356 organizations, including over 100 regional and inter-branch organizations. The organization represents all the key sectors of the economy, with the enterprises included in the organization producing over 60 per cent of Russian GDP.[8] All the members of the employers' side on the RTK are drawn from this organization. RSPP was originally established in 1991 as a producers' rather than an employers' organization. Indeed, it initially allied itself with the unions against the government's reform programme. The (then) president of the FNPR, Igor Klochkov, explained this arrangement in terms of the need to preserve Russian industry, noting in an interview with a French newspaper:

> I admit that it is a bit strange to see the unions and the employers forming a common front . . . Today what is primary is the survival of our production. We have therefore concluded a pact with the employers.
>
> (*Le Figaro*, 27 January 1993)

In the 1995 Duma election, the FNPR joined with RSPP to establish the social-political organization Trade Unions and Industrialists of Russia – Union of Labour. The organization made little headway, gaining only 1.59 per cent of the party list vote, well below the threshold to gain Duma representation (Ashwin and Clarke 2003: 49). Nevertheless, its very existence is indicative of the political orientation of employers in the early reform period.

This alliance between trade unions and employers extended to the enterprise level (Ilyin 1996a: 68–9). The Soviet ideal of the enterprise as a united 'labour collective' led by a paternalist director persisted into the 1990s (Ashwin 1999). This was not entirely fictitious. The survival of enterprises in this era depended not on the efficient use of labour to produce a profit, but rather on the external connections of senior managers to government officials and other enterprises, which were the key to providing access to materials, markets and financial support (King 2002; Clarke 2007: 55). Thus, workers and managers shared an interest in securing the survival of enterprises, which was notoriously expressed in 'directors' strikes', in which management supported strikes aimed at securing funds from the political authorities. This does not mean that Russian employment relations were a picture of harmony. As has been noted, non-payment of wages reached mass proportions during the 1990s. This was mainly due to the liquidity crisis which starved enterprises of cash, but there is no doubt that endemic non-payment also allowed opportunism to flourish. Some employers did not pay their workers simply because they could get away with not doing so (Earle and Sabrianova 2002). Nevertheless, the main line of conflict remained between 'producers' and the government.

How far do these arguments apply to the 2000s? After the 1998 crash, the Russian economy did begin to grow as a result of devaluation of the currency, and the increase in world fuel and metal prices. The weakening of the banks after the crisis also led to a reorientation of domestic investment into production. Holding companies began to acquire industrial enterprises on a large scale, and for the first time began to invest in the hope of securing a profit from production (Clarke 2007: 62–3). However, before the 2008 financial crisis, the process of transforming enterprises into productive capital was still in its early stages. While senior management had been transformed, personnel and production management largely continued along Soviet lines (ibid.). In most large privatized enterprises inherited from the Soviet era, line management continue to see their role as delivering the production plan laid down by senior management, rather than optimizing efficiency, and they have retained the autonomy to organize work as they see fit. As in the Soviet era, they have continued to represent workers within the management hierarchy, arguing that adequate remuneration and working conditions are required for workers to meet their targets. But this approach to line management is coming under pressure (see ibid.: 189–226). In the minority of enterprises where line management has been fully subordinated to senior management, it has led to more conflictual employment relations, the paradigmatic example of which is the Ford plant in Leningrad Oblast, where a radical trade union has emerged, fighting for improved terms and conditions (Ilyin 2006).

The state–business relationship has changed in the 2000s, with employers' freedom of action being sharply curtailed (Hanson and Teague 2005). The importance of business 'loyalty' to government was underlined by the arrest of former Yukos oil company director, Mikhail Khodorkovsky, in 2003 after he signalled his intention of entering politics. Khodorkovsky's incarceration sent a clear message that political activity on the part of business would not be tolerated. Meanwhile, the Kremlin has been exerting increased control over what it sees as strategic industries by appointing trusted state officials to positions of authority on their boards (Hanson and Teague 2007). Employers still have the autonomy to direct their own personnel policies, with the proviso in the case of large employers that their action should not provoke worker protest. More generally, the regime's concern for order means that large employers are somewhat more cautious regarding violations of labour law such as non-payment than in the 1990s.

At central and regional levels, the employers have continued to participate in tripartite dialogue. The RSPP website includes a statement of support for social partnership, the development of which is listed as one of the organization's goals.[9] Nevertheless, the development of employers' representation is still incomplete, with many branch tariff agreements still concluded with the government rather than with the employers. This reflects the fact that employer involvement in social partnership is motivated by political conformity, rather than by the need to form a common negotiating position against a powerful union movement.

Employment relations outcomes and processes

Russia's structural adjustment programme was socially catastrophic. The social impact of reform was most visible in mortality rates – particularly among working-age men. One estimate places the number of premature deaths caused by the shock therapy of 1990–98 as high as 3.4 million (Rosefielde 2001). Male life expectancy plummeted in the reform era, declining from 64.2 years in 1989 (Goskomstat 2002: 105), to a low of 57.5 years in 1994. It then recovered to 61.3 in 1998, only to fall back to 58.4 in 2002 (Goskomstat 2003: 117). In contrast, female life expectancy showed less variability, declining from 74.4 in 1989 (Goskomstat 2002: 105) to a nadir of 71.1 in 1994, followed by a stabilization at over 72 between 1996–2002 (Goskomstat 2003: 117). Researchers searching for the causes of this catastrophe have cited the 'state of confusion, uncertainty and calamity' experienced by Russians in the face of 'dramatic changes in the labor market' – in short, severe social stress (Shkolnikov *et al.* 1998: 2008–9). A recent study in *The Lancet*, arguing that rapid mass privatization programmes in the former Eastern bloc were associated with a short-term increase in mortality rates of working-age men, also showed that social capital (as measured by the proportion of the population who belonged to at least one social organization) significantly reduced this association (Stuckler *et al.* 2009). In Russia, neither economic policy nor its impact was ameliorated by 'social capital'. The lack of collective agency is well captured by the words of one cabinet minister of the early Yeltsin era, who remarked that Russians reacted to reform by 'going into their homes and dying' (Standing 1996: 250).[10]

Correspondingly, underneath the civilized veneer of social partnership, employment relations in the 1990s were chaotic. Workers developed survival strategies on the basis of their networks, both within enterprises where they sought the protection of managerial patrons, and outside, where they developed diverse means of securing a livelihood. Only in extreme desperation – typically after wage delays of several months – were workers pushed into collective action. Such action was generally not supported by the FNPR unions, and was dealt with on an ad hoc basis by government. It thus left little organizational legacy, and did not prevent the problems recurring.

In the 2000s, non-payment of wages – the source of most conflict in the 1990s – has become far less widespread, both as a result of economic growth, and the government's emphasis on restoring social order. When violations of workers' rights occur, the FNPR unions' approach to dealing with them is similar to the 1990s, and indeed to the Soviet era. They continue to eschew collective conflict, preferring to defend workers through the courts. Amid the mass non-payment of wages in the 1990s, this method proved wholly inadequate, and served only to drag out disputes, sometimes over several years. Moreover, success in court by no means guaranteed the payment of wage debts (Ashwin 2004). In the 2000s, this approach is more successful and the unions win over 95 per cent of cases regarding wage delays. Rather than reflecting more effective union representation, this is related to the more manageable proportions of wage delays, combined with a shift in the position of the courts, which in the late 1990s became more receptive to hearing labour-related cases, with fewer delays and more favourable judgments (Ashwin and Clarke 2003: 192).

The unions' Soviet approach to employment relations was utterly inappropriate to the conditions of the 1990s, and did nothing to challenge the routine violation of labour law, and the stabilization programme which necessitated this. In the era of 'managed democracy', the FNPR tradition of defending workers through bureaucratic methods such as legal representation has been more successful. Just as in the Soviet era, the unions help retain some equilibrium in employment relations by providing a politically safe outlet for workers' grievances. Likewise, unions continue to represent workers through the formal channels of social partnership, in a way that recalls their role as a bureaucratic sponsor of workers within Soviet government bodies. But there are now whole swathes of the economy where the FNPR has no membership, so their stabilizing function is less potent than in the past. A similar issue can be seen in China, which has led the government there to support union-organizing campaigns (see Chapter 17). The FNPR has more autonomy than the All China Federation of Trade Unions (ACFTU), but it still remains dependent on the state, and on employers. Whatever the FNPR unions' successes in defending workers using conciliatory methods, such as appeal to the courts, the missing ingredient remains the ability to mobilize members. Without this, unions remain essentially supplicants, and are unlikely to attract new members

Theoretical perspectives

It is difficult to disentangle the influence of the forces which are the focus for the theories laid out in Chapter 2. The 'strategic' action of the state in attempting to create a market economy had a huge influence on Russian development. But at the same time, institutions 'bit back' – it proved much more difficult to slough off the past than the reformers had first envisaged. Meanwhile, the actions of unions and employers were shaped by the economic and institutional environment in which they found themselves.

To paraphrase Karl Marx:

> [Employment relations actors] make their own history, but they do not make it just as they please; they do not make it under circumstances chosen by themselves, but under circumstances directly encountered, given and transmitted from the past. The tradition of all dead generations weighs like a nightmare on the brain of the living.
>
> ([1852] 1963: 1)

Pierre Bourdieu says something similar when he argues that action is always structured by what he calls the 'two states of the social' – 'history objectified in the form of structures and mechanisms' and 'history in bodies' (Bourdieu 2000: 150–1). Embodied history takes the form of dispositions 'schemes of perception, thought and action' (1990: 54), which are 'durable' and 'can outlive the economic and social conditions in which they were produced' (ibid.: 62). Having said this, the degree of constraint experienced by either individuals or collective actors is not equal. More powerful subjects typically have more latitude. Thus, in the Russian case, the state had a greater capacity for strategic action than did the unions. It was able to launch a historic economic and political transformation in 1991. But at the same time, its choice of reform strategy was certainly structured by particular historical circumstances: the collapse of the Soviet Union occurred at a time when neo-liberal ideology was dominant, and promoted by all the international financial institutions from which the Russian state sought to borrow money. Meanwhile, its reforms did not necessarily have the intended effects, as existing structures proved more resilient than anticipated.

Market forces and the transformation of Russian employment relations

It would be misleading to see Russia's economic transformation as linked to exogenous market forces. Rather, market-making was a conscious political project launched by the governing elite, as was the strategy of rapid integration into the world economy by the removal of trade barriers. The Chinese case shows that a different path was theoretically possible, but, as already noted, the international political pressures on the Russian elite to choose a neo-liberal strategy were considerable.

In one sense, marketization had predictable consequences for the unions. As already noted, the reduction in industrial employment and growth of small business made union organizing more difficult, and fragmented labour as a collective subject. But the development of capitalism does not only have negative connotations in the Russian context. As discussed above, the fact that capitalism has still not fully penetrated the 'hidden abode' of production in post-Soviet enterprises, serves to preserve the paternalist relations of the past and inhibits independent workers' organization. In enterprises where the transition to capitalist production is more advanced, particularly those owned by multinational corporations, what Vladimir Ilyin (1996b) calls the 'leading social contradiction' shifts from that between the labour collective and external environment, to the 'internal' antagonism between workers and managers. Such workplaces provide the social basis for a new form of employment relations, and a different political orientation.

The outcome of this can be seen in the wave of industrial action which occurred between 2006–08 in the most prosperous sectors such as fuel and energy and companies with foreign owners (Chetvernina 2009: 426; Germanov 2009: 112–13). In contrast to the disputes of the 1990s, which overwhelmingly concerned non-payment of wages, these strikes were 'pro-cyclical', the result of rising expectations in a growing economy (Greene and Robertson 2010). Workers' demands were typically for higher wages and improved conditions (Kozina 2009b: 28–30). Their rhetoric also shifted away from the traditional emphasis on the common interests of the labour collective towards a class-based framework. As the leader of the influential Ford trade union put it: 'It's naked Marxism, capital against the workers, that's all' (Kozina 2009b: 30). The disputes sometimes led to the establishment of alternative trade unions (Chetvernina 2009: 427), suggesting that capitalist development could create the conditions for the emergence of a transformed union movement (Ashwin 1999: 182; Greene and Robertson 2010).

A similar development has occurred in Poland in the 2000s with the 'budding emergence' of what David Ost, following Beverly Silver, calls a 'Marx-type labor movement' – that is, 'a forward-looking labor movement trying to make gains, instead of simply resist decline' (2009: 27). In neither Russia nor Poland is this a dominant tendency, but it nonetheless reveals the paradoxical potential of marketization to reinvigorate labour movements in post-socialist environments. As the principle of profit-making enters the sphere of production, the social basis of enterprise paternalism is destroyed. This creates at least the possibility of a new class identity, a renewed labour movement and interest-based politics.

Institutions

It is hard to place Russia within a classic 'Varieties of Capitalism' framework (Hanson and Teague 2007; King 2007). Russia's emergent capitalist system has spawned a variety of definitions including 'merchant capitalism' (Burawoy and Krotov 1992), 'patrimonial post-communist capitalism' (King 2007), and 'Weberian political capitalism' (Hanson and

Teague 2007), terms that are discussed below. While Russia's attempted transition to capitalism highlights the limits of the traditional 'varieties of capitalism' approach in relation to emergent economies, it nevertheless strongly reinforces the case that 'institutions matter'.

The Russian state has attempted radical transformation on several occasions, but it has proved hard to escape the dead hand of the past. Lenin with his notorious 'revolutionary impatience' launched a revolution in a peasant country with a tiny proletariat, determined to transform the country by sheer force of will. This, as is well known, led to a police state rather than a communist utopia. Likewise, neo-liberal reformers attempted to transfigure the country at breakneck speed. While Lenin put his faith in the wisdom of the vanguard Party, the neo-liberals trusted to the omnipotence of the market. Both were frustrated by the resilience of existing institutions and practices.

In the 1990s, the reformers' haste meant that the task of building alternatives to the (informal) institutions of the past was not taken seriously. They failed to establish the basic institutional prerequisites of a functioning market economy (Stiglitz 2002: 139). 'Shock therapy' began in the absence of an appropriate social safety net, banking laws and anti-monopoly regulation, to name some of the most glaring omissions. Most importantly, although Russia was supposedly a democracy, little emphasis was placed on the establishment of the rule of law, with the implementation of economic reform encouraging rather than inhibiting lawlessness.[11] Quite apart from the social consequences, this arguably established the preconditions for the end of the democratic experiment of the 1990s, as Russians opted for authoritarian government in preference to the Hobbesian 'war of all against all' which began to take hold in the Yeltsin era.

The content of the reform programme likewise undermined its supposed purpose. The stabilization programme meant that industry was deprived of the funds needed for restructuring. Instead, managers used personal ties in the quest for survival, seeking resources from government, and barter relations with other firms. Meanwhile, the descent into barter deprived the government of tax revenue, leading to a dramatic erosion of state capacity (King 2007: 321). The state became 'riddled' with patron–client ties between government and business and 'market success came to depend on arbitrary political decisions and the exercise of private force' (ibid.: 321). Even the 'winners' in this system do not have secure property rights and are vulnerable to expropriation if their patron loses power. Thus, the most basic elements of a functioning market economy – the right to private property and market rather than administrative allocation of resources – have not been secured by Russia's radical economic reform. Instead, the politicized resource allocation of the past prevails, with many of the networks through which resources flow inherited from the Soviet era. Thus, the prospects for continued capitalist development discussed in the previous section remain uncertain.

It is thus evident why researchers have turned to Weber's concept of 'political capitalism' to conceptualize Russia's variety of capitalism. Hanson and Teague's understanding draws on one aspect of Weber's characterization of political capitalism: the salience of 'predatory profits from persons connected with politics' (Weber 1978: 164). Correspondingly, Hanson and Teague place particular emphasis on the state's determination to control the 'commanding heights' of the Russian economy through the appointment of trusted state officials to their boards. King also uses a Weberian framework, but understands 'patrimonial post-communist capitalism' as a product of the 'decomposition of the bureaucratic (in the Weberian sense of the term) nature of the state' (2007: 307). In this respect he is close to Ganev, who again contends that Russia exhibits Weberian 'political capitalism'. Ganev argues that this entails not simply state predation on the private sphere *à la* Hanson and Teague, but 'a massive hemorrhage [*sic*] of institutional capacity' (Ganev 2009: 658) as civil servants abandon themselves to private gain: 'an important trait of political capitalism is that the civil service behaves as an uncoordinated multitude of self-interested agents pursuing immediate financial gratification' (ibid.: 656). These competing definitions capture an important paradox in relation to the Russian state. On the evidence provided in Hanson and Teague's contribution, the state appears strong, overweening, predatory – able to expropriate property and imprison opponents at will. But on the other hand, the fragile unity of the elite is only sustained by allowing its members opportunities for vast private gain, which comes at the cost of gradual evisceration of the state services and businesses from which the money is stolen. This is the degeneration of the bureaucratic state emphasized by King and Ganev.

The Russian case highlights the limits of the traditional varieties of capitalism approach in relation to emergent economies. But it also strongly reinforces the case that 'institutions matter'. The destruction of the formal institutions of the Soviet state was not accompanied by a concerted attempt to develop the institutional prerequisites of a market-oriented democracy, such as the rule of law. The magic of the market was supposed to sweep away the remnants of the past. Instead, the stabilization and privatization programmes created the conditions in which the clientelist networks and politicized allocation mechanisms of the past were re-vivified. This has taken Russia down what increasingly looks like a developmental cul-de-sac.

Actors' strategic choices

As has been seen, the state had a seemingly huge capacity for agency, but was unable to remodel Russia in the way it intended. Meanwhile, business leaders can be seen as co-creators of political or patrimonial capitalism, from which they benefit, but also suffer. This section, however, focuses on the unions. The FNPR unions proved unable to escape their accustomed dependence, and under Putin are increasingly subordinate. Was it possible for the unions to avoid this, or were the structural constraints too strong? This question is important, because, according to King (2002), the weakness of the labour movement is one of the factors which allowed the development of patrimonial capitalism. He argues that the relaxation in the stabilization programme secured by labour in Poland played a significant role in allowing the country to escape the patrimonial trap. Weak labour in Russia was unable to offer this 'beneficial constraint'. Within a different analytical framework, Stiglitz (2002) has made a similar point, arguing that structural adjustment has been an economic failure in most places it has been introduced precisely because of the lack of popular control and input into the reform plans.

The unions' inherited dependence on management and the political authorities defined the limits within which they made policy. At enterprise level, lacking the support of members in the immediate post-Soviet era, unions relied on management to tolerate their existence. They therefore continued to play a non-conflictual, and non-representational, role as mediators, and administrators of the social sphere (Ashwin and Clarke 2003; Ashwin 2004). Attempts to secure members' trust through active defence of their interests risked undermining unions' status and presence within enterprises, for uncertain gain. Unions' equivocal position was mirrored by workers, who tended to perceive the labour collective as having shared interests. But even when management was clearly not acting in the interests of the 'collective', and workers themselves had initiated a collective labour dispute with management, FNPR enterprise unions often refused to side with their members against management, much less lead them (Ashwin 2004). Disputes with management tended only to occur when there was conflict within the management team, and the union supported the opposition faction (Ashwin and Clarke 2003: 256).

At a central level, the FNPR was similarly constrained. Lacking an independent base which could be mobilized around its campaigns, the union had little bargaining power in relation to the state or regional authorities. Its strength lay in the inherited institutional infrastructure and resources from the past, but the government was quick to indicate that these could be removed from the unions at a stroke of the presidential pen. That this was no idle threat was demonstrated on the only occasion that the union openly sided with the opposition against the government. This was during Yeltsin's confrontation with the Congress of People's Deputies in autumn 1993, when the union called on workers to use all available means, including strikes, to protest against Yeltsin's anti-constitutional actions (ibid.: 41). The government responded to the unions' 'disloyalty' by freezing the FNPR bank accounts, cutting off their telephones, banning the check-off of union dues, and depriving them of their control of the state social insurance fund, and responsibility for the health and safety inspection (ibid.: 41–2). This underlined the dangers of an oppositional stance – whatever the potential long-term gains, the short-term risk was institutional annihilation.

The union learned this lesson well, and from 1993 adhered to the policy of 'social partnership',[12] which entailed collaboration with managerial and government interlocutors at all levels. In effect, the unions secured a defined institutional position and role, and in return were expected to act as guarantors of social peace. They could not stop spontaneous strikes or protests occurring, but they could refrain from leading and coordinating these – a role which after 1993 they performed consistently. Thus, sporadic protest was not amplified or built upon by the FNPR, and rarely posed a significant political challenge. The unions' caution has only been strengthened in the Putin era. In this context, 'framing' workers' grievances in ways that served to generalize them, or direct them against government policy, would be very risky. The unions have adapted to this environment, and are careful to ensure that their opposition to specific measures stays within the bounds of 'loyalty'.

Given the apparent weakness of the unions, the state's willingness to sponsor social partnership may appear to constitute 'over-payment' for the unions' forbearance. But the context needs to be taken into account. The reform programme of the 1990s made no concessions to social stress, and did, as we have seen, provoke sporadic spontaneous protests. The only bodies with the requisite membership and institutional capacity to 'frame' and generalize such action were the trade unions – and the government was not prepared to take the risk of leaving them a free hand to do so (Bytchkova 2011). Meanwhile, in the Putin era, the dominance of the security services increased the caution of the government. Former KGB officers have a tendency to regard dissent as an inadmissible failure of government control rather than as a normal attribute of democratic politics. A good example is the authorities' overreaction to the 'punk prayer' performed by the feminist collective Pussy Riot in Moscow's Cathedral of Christ the Saviour in February 2012, in protest against the Russian Orthodox Church's support for Putin's re-election. The Russian government's allergy to protest is almost certainly counterproductive, but it is deeply ingrained, and has to be taken seriously by social organizations.

It is unclear whether the FNPR unions could have charted a more independent course. As noted above, to do so would certainly have entailed significant risks. And the dispositions of trade union officers did not incline them to take such chances. The vast majority had been schooled in the art of bureaucratic politics; mobilization and conflict were alien concepts. Interviews with trade union officers have repeatedly shown that industrial harmony was perceived as the norm, while deviations from this were blamed on the failings of individual managers (Ashwin 1999; Ashwin and Clarke 2003). For many, a conflictual campaigning stance would have been literally 'unthinkable'. This is not to say that union movements are always so constrained. Unions' freedom of action depends on the institutional and market environment in which they find themselves. Some situations offer more room for creativity than others. The Russian environment was particularly non-conducive to the development of an effective union movement.

Future prospects

In the majority of large privatized enterprises, employment relations still retain many features of the Soviet past such as representation by line management, and individualized resolution of grievances using the law. However, where capitalist relations have reached the shop-floor, this has begun to change. In some cases, this has led to the emergence of a new breed of trade unions fighting for improved terms and conditions. Of course, the establishment of unions does not follow automatically from the spread of capitalist relations, but these do at least provide the structural basis for the emergence of a new form of unionism.

The continued restructuring of enterprises will depend in part on the action of the state. As has been noted, the state has moved to increase its control over the 'commanding heights' of industry. Meanwhile, we have argued that Putin's commitment to economic liberalism is balanced by a concern for social order. This may encourage the preservation of paternalist features in the industries where the state has an interest, which would in turn inhibit the emergence of new unionism. Whatever happens in large enterprises, they are likely to be surrounded by a sea of non-union labour in small and medium-sized enterprises, especially those established since 1991. There is little prospect of the unions remedying this in the near future.

If we compare Russia's attempted transition from state socialism with the authoritarian state-led programme in China, on the one hand, and the 'democratic' Polish experience, on the other, it is difficult to escape the conclusion that the Russian approach combined the worst of all worlds. As noted in Chapter 18, for all its faults, China's model of state-controlled marketization has secured 10 per cent average annual GDP growth for more than 30 years, and has lifted millions out of poverty. While China's economic reform programme was far from democratic, it was what Stiglitz has called a 'homegrown' programme, sensitive to local conditions (2002: 186). The Chinese Communist Party was forced to take some account of the social impact of its policies, because it still derived its legitimacy from its claim to represent the masses. At the same time, the institutions of the past, in particular the Party bureaucracy, were retained and adapted to new conditions. As Stiglitz put it: 'China built the foundation of a new economy on existing institutions, maintaining and enhancing its social capital, while in Russia it eroded' (ibid.: 185). Thus, the Chinese authorities have preserved a modified version of the state socialist approach to employment relations entailing: state-sponsored trade unions, with some autonomy to press workers' concerns in their capacity as a facet of the state; an individualized labour dispute resolution system; state responsiveness to collective protests, combined with occasional repression, and some duty on managers of state-owned enterprises to balance economic objectives with the need to preserve industrial peace.

Such a model of employment relations would suit the increasingly authoritarian Putin regime, and indeed elements of it are in place. For example, we have noted that union complaints against employers in the courts have a high success rate, while the state is more fearful of, and hence more responsive to, labour protest than was the case in the 1990s. What is missing is the administrative coherence necessary to promote sustainable economic development. For example, foreign investment is hampered by the lack of secure property rights and the rule of law, while the growth of small business is inhibited by predatory state officials. This is where the fruits of Russia's democratic deficit are evident. As has been noted, King argues forcefully that in countries such as Poland and Hungary where economic reformers were forced to modify the content of structural adjustment by democratic pressure, the patrimonial path was avoided, paving the way for a more benign pattern of development (2002, 2007). By contrast, unmodified structural adjustment in Russia preserved clientelist networks and destroyed state capacity, leading to the bureaucratic degeneration entailed in 'patrimonial' or 'political' capitalism.

In the 1990s, Russia's ruling elite was constrained neither by a concern for social order and state legitimacy (as in China), nor by civil society (as in Poland). It was therefore free to inflict another utopian experiment on Russian society, with the unhappy consequences outlined above. In the civic desert inherited from the Soviet era, the trade unions were the one body capable of organizing resistance to the economic reform programme, and they proved unable to do so. Contemplation of Russia's current predicament provides a salutary reminder of the crucial role that organized labour can play in democratization and embedding 'civilized' models of capitalism.

Notes

1 The Gini coefficient increased from 0.26 in 1991 to 0.5 in 1993 (Clarke 1999: 120).
2 Polanyi's argument is that the 'disembedding' of the market from society that has occurred during periods in which free market ideology has dominated is socially unsustainable. In his view, 're-embedding' eventually occurs to prevent social implosion. Polanyi is, however, tantalizingly vague regarding the social forces which bring about the taming of the market (Polanyi [1944] 2001).
3 The Duma is the Russian legislature.
4 Figures from Ministry of Health and Social Development website. Available at: http://www.minzdravsoc.ru/labour/relationship/76.
5 Rosstat data, table. Available at: http://www.gks.ru/bgd/regl/b11_36/IssWWW.exe/Stg/d1/03-10.htm.
6 Ibid.
7 Romir Gallup International poll. Available at: http://www.romir.ru/studies/259_1318276800/.
8 RSPP website, available at: http://xn--o1aabe.xn--p1ai/about.
9 RSPP website, available at: http://xn--o1aabe.xn--p1ai/about.
10 Guy Standing does not name the minister, who made the comment during a discussion they had in 1993.
11 The most dramatic examples of this tendency were Yeltsin's military assault on the Russian parliament in 1993 because of its resistance to reform, and the routine use of non-payment of wages and pensions as a form of economic management. Both practices were accepted by the international financial institutions as necessary evils of the reform era.
12 For an account of this policy, see Ashwin and Clarke (2003: Chapter 6).

References

Ashwin, S. (1997) 'Shop floor trade unionism in Russia: the prospects of reform from below', *Work, Employment and Society*, 11(1): 115–31.

—— (1999) *Russian Workers: The Anatomy of Patience*, Manchester: Manchester University Press.

—— (2003) 'The regulation of the employment relationship in Russia: the Soviet legacy', in D. Galligan and M. Kurkchiyan (eds) *Law and Informal Practices: The Postcommunist Experience*, Oxford: Clarendon Press.

—— (2004) 'Social partnership or "a complete sellout"? Russian trade unions' responses to conflict', *British Journal of Industrial Relations*, 42(1): 23–46.

—— and Clarke, S. (2003) *Russian Trade Unions and Industrial Relations in Transition*, Basingstoke: Palgrave.

Borisov, V. and Clarke, S. (1996) 'The Russian miners' strike of February 1996', *Capital and Class*, 59: 23–30.

Bourdieu, P. (1990) *The Logic of Practice*, Cambridge: Polity Press.

—— (2000) *Pascalian Meditations*, Cambridge: Polity Press.

Bronstein, A. (2005) 'The new labour law of the Russian Federation', *International Labour Review*, 144(3): 291–318.

Burawoy, M. and Krotov, P. (1992) 'The Soviet transition from socialism to capitalism: worker control and economic bargaining in the wood industry', *American Sociological Review*, 57(1): 16–38.

Burawoy, M. and Verdery, K. (1999) 'Introduction', in M. Burawoy and K. Verdery (eds) *Uncertain Transition: Ethnographies of Change in the Post-Socialist World*, Lanham, MD: Rowman and Littlefield.

Bytchkova, M. (2011) 'The role of social partnership in Russia: experience of Samara and Ul'yanovsk regions', PhD thesis, London School of Economics.

Chetvernina, T. (2009) 'Trade unions in transitional Russia: peculiarities, current status and new challenges', *South East Europe Review for Labour and Social Affairs*, 12(3): 407–32.

Clarke, S. (1999) *New Forms of Employment and Household Survival Strategies in Russia*, Coventry: Centre for Comparative Labour and Studies, and Moscow: ISITO.

—— (2002) 'Market and institutional determinants of wage differentials in Russia', *Industrial and Labor Relations Review*, 55(4): 628–48.

—— (2007) *The Development of Capitalism in Russia*, New York: Routledge.

Connor, W. D. (1991) *The Accidental Proletariat: Workers, Politics, and Crisis in Gorbachev's Russia*, Princeton, NJ: Princeton University Press.

Earle, J. S. and Sabrianova, K. Z. (2002) 'How late to pay? Understanding wage arrears in Russia', *Journal of Labor Economics*, 20(3): 661–707.

FNPR (2010) *O Svodnoi Statistcheskoi Otchetnosti no Profsoyuznomu Chlenstvu I Profsoyuznym Organam Za 2010 God*'. Available at: http://www.fnpr.ru/print/2/15/187/6378.html.

Ganev, V. I. (2009) 'Postcommunist political capitalism: a Weberian interpretation', *Comparative Studies in Society and History*, 51(3): 648–74.

Germanov, I. A. (2009) 'Samoorganizatsii rabotnikov i protestnaya aktivnost', in I. Kozina (ed.) *Profsoyuzy na Predpriyatiyak Sovremennoi Rossii: Vozmozhnosti Rebrendinga*, Moscow: ISITO.

Goskomstat (2000) *Rossiya v Tsifrakh*, Moscow: Goskomstat Rossii.

—— (2002) *Demograficheskii Ezhegodnik Rossii 2002*, Moscow: Goskomstat Rossii.

—— (2003) *Rossiiskii Statisticheskii Ezhegodnik 2003*, Moscow: Goskomstat Rossii.

Greene, S.A and Robertson, G.B. (2010) 'Politics, justice and the new Russian strike', *Communist and Post-Communist Studies*, 43: 73–95.

Hanson, P. and Teague, E. (2005) 'Big business and the state in Russia', *Europe-Asia Studies*, 57(5): 657–80.

—— (2007) 'Russian political capitalism and its environment', in D. Lane and M. Myant (eds) *Varieties of Capitalism in Post-Communist Countries*, Basingstoke: Palgrave Macmillan.

Ilyin, V. (1996a) 'Russian trade unions and the management apparatus in the transition period', in S. Clarke (ed.) *Conflict and Change in the Russian Industrial Enterprise*, Aldershot: Edward Elgar.

—— (1996b) 'Social contradictions and conflicts in state enterprises in the transition period', in S. Clarke (ed.) *Conflict and Change in the Russian Industrial Enterprise*, Aldershot: Edward Elgar.

—— (2006) *Pervichnaya Profsoyuznaya Organizatsiya Zavoda "Ford Motor Kompani" vo Vsevolozhske (Leningradskaya Oblast')*. Available at: http://go.warwick.ac.uk/russia/intas.

King, L. (2002) 'Postcommunist divergence: a comparative analysis of the transition to capitalism in Poland and Russia', *Studies in Comparative International Development*, 37(3): 3–34.

—— (2007) 'Central European capitalism in comparative perspective', in B. Hancké, M. Rhodes and M. Thatcher (eds) *Beyond Varieties of Capitalism: Conflict, Contradiction, and Complementarities in the European Economy*, Oxford: Oxford University Press.
Kozina, I. (2009a) 'Sotsial'no-ekonomicheskaya transformatsiya i novye vyzovy profsoyuznomu dvizheniyu', in I. Kozina (ed.) *Profsoyuzy na Predpriyatiyak Sovremennoi Rossii: vozmozhnosti rebrendinga*, Moscow: ISITO.
—— (2009b) 'Industrial'nye konflikty v sovremennoi Rossii', *Ekonomicheskaya Sotsiologiya*, 10(3): 16–33.
—— and Zhidkova, E. (2006) 'Sex segregation and discrimination in the new Russian labour market', in S. Ashwin (ed.) *Adapting to Russia's New Labour Market: Gender and Employment Behaviour*, London: Routledge.
Lenin, V. I. ([1922] 1947) 'The role and functions of trade unions under the New Economic Policy', in *The Essentials of Lenin*, vol. 2, London: Lawrence & Wishart.
Lukin, A. (2009) 'Russia's new authoritarianism and the post-Soviet political ideal', *Post Soviet Affairs*, 25(1): 66–92.
Marx, K. ([1852] 1963) *The Eighteenth Brumaire of Louis Bonaparte*, New York: International Publishers.
McAuley, M. (1969) *Labour Disputes in Soviet Russia, 1957–65*, Oxford: Clarendon Press.
Ost, D. (2009) 'The consequences of postcommunism: trade unions in Eastern Europe's future', *East European Politics and Societies*, 23(1): 13–33.
Polanyi, K. ([1944] 2001) *The Great Transformation: The Political and Economic Origins of Our Time*, Boston, MA: Beacon Press.
Rosefielde, S. (2001) 'Premature deaths: Russia's radical economic transition in Soviet perspective', *Europe-Asia Studies*, 35(8): 1159–176.
Sakwa, R. (2008) 'Putin's leadership: character and consequences', *Europe-Asia Studies*, 60(6): 879–97.
Shelley, L. (1981) 'Law in the soviet workplace: the lawyer's perspective', *Law and Society Review*, 16(3): 429–54.
—— (1984) *Lawyers in Soviet Work Life*, New Brunswick, NJ: Rutgers University Press.
Shkolnikov, V., Cornia, G., Leon, D. and Meslė, F. (1998) 'Causes of the Russian mortality: evidence and interpretations', *World Development*, 26(11): 1995–2011.
Standing, G. (1996) 'Social protection in Central and Eastern Europe: a tale of slipping anchors and torn safety nets', in G. Esping-Andersen (ed.) *Welfare States in Transition: National Adaptations in Global Economies*, London: Sage.
Stiglitz, J. (2002) *Globalization and Its Discontents*, London: Allen Lane.
Stuckler, D., King, L. and McKee, M. (2009) 'Mass privatisation and the post-communist mortality crisis: a cross-national analysis', *The Lancet*, 373: 399–407.
Traxler, F. (1995) 'Two logics of collective action in industrial relations?', in C. Crouch and F. Traxler (eds) *Organised Industrial Relations in Europe: What Future?*, Aldershot: Avebury.
Weber, M. (1978) *Economy and Society*, vol. 1, Berkeley, CA: University of California Press.
Woodruff, D. (1999) 'Barter of the bankrupt: the politics of demonetization in Russia's federal state', in M. Burawoy and K. Verdery (eds) *Uncertain Transition: Ethnographies of Change in the Post-Socialist World*, Lanham, MD: Rowman and Littlefield.

17 India

Vidu Badigannavar

Introduction

The growing interest in Indian employment relations has been primarily sparked by the economic reform programmes pursued by the Indian government since 1991 (Agarwala *et al.* 2004; D'Costa 2005; Papola *et al.* 2007; Ahsan and Pages 2009; Hill 2009; Budhwar and Bhatnagar 2009). These economic policies of liberalization, privatization and globalization marked a new beginning in the trajectory of the Indian economy which hitherto was typified as an inward-looking socialist-style economy, based on an import substitution strategy. Following the balance of payment crisis in 1991, the government of India embarked upon economic reforms which shifted the focus from import substitution to an export orientation (D'Costa 2005). This shift in economic policies has increased the country's GDP growth from a low 2–3 per cent per annum until the 1980s to an average of 8 per cent per year for a decade and half starting from the early 1990s (Panagariya 2008). It is argued that this change in economic policies has impacted employment relations, with trade unions in India now finding themselves increasingly excluded from the political process, affecting employment relations at both national and state levels (Kuruvilla and Erickson 2002). In this chapter, we shall first examine the historical evolution of employment relations in India, followed by the role of key stakeholders, namely, the state, trade unions and the employers. We then look at the salient employment relations outcomes in India and, finally, we shall attempt to explain the developments in Indian employment relations from various theoretical perspectives.

The historical evolution of Indian employment relations

The employment relations framework in India evolved under British colonial rule (1858–1947). In 1859, the colonial government enacted the Workmen's Breach of Contract Act and in 1860 there followed the Employers and Workmen (Disputes) Act and the Indian Penal Code. The primary aim of these statutes was to curtail any uprising by agricultural workers and peasants and to criminalize any such attempts by workers. During this period the labour movement was gaining momentum and had become part of the Indian independence movement spearheaded by the Congress nationalists. The colonial rulers were equally concerned about the growing intervention of Communists in the labour movement and the politicization of industrial conflicts which also hindered the cheap supply of goods and raw materials that kept factories in Britain running (Myers 1958; Karnik 1967 and Murphy 1981, both cited in Shyam Sundar 2009a).

In 1926, the British rulers in India passed the Trade Union Act which aimed at legitimizing unions and offering them some immunity against civil and criminal liabilities. The government also enacted the Trade Disputes Act in 1929 which created machinery for the adjudication and conciliation of labour disputes. It also outlawed political strikes and required 14 days notice of strikes in public utility services. In an attempt to quell the threat from Communist unions in the 1940s and to help break strikes, the British government supported its own favoured union called the Indian Federation of Labour (ibid.: 34). This was the beginning of the political patronage of unions which has since then flourished in post-Independence India. In 1946, the British government passed some very important labour laws which have shaped the architecture of labour market regulation in India since Independence in August 1947. The first of these laws was the Bombay Industrial Relations (BIR) Act of 1946. This statute provided for the recognition of an 'approved union' which enjoyed some rights, such as membership recruitment and dues collection at the workplace, communicating with workers at the employer's premises and having some say in working practices. However, it imposed several restrictions on the union: the acceptance of compulsory arbitration imposed by the state, a prohibition on wildcat strikes, and strikes to be used as a last resort and only on the endorsement of a majority of the workforce (ibid.: 35). The other significant statutes introduced at this time were the Industrial Disputes Act (1947) and the Industrial Employment (Standing Orders) Act of 1946. Around this time the Congress Party, which was spearheading the independence movement, formed its own trade union called the Indian National Trade Union Congress (INTUC).

India secured its independence on 15 August 1947 and the Congress government which took over the reins of the country decided to continue with the legal framework of employment relations created by the British colonial government. This continuance is largely attributed to the economic model of centralized planning and import substitution adopted by the Indian government. The emphasis was on maintaining industrial peace and harmony to ensure high industrial growth and national development. Import substitution was to protect domestic industry from foreign competition and to promote its growth. Equally, it was to protect the limited foreign exchange reserves that the country had at the time. During this time of nation-building, the emphasis was on curtailing conflict but at the same time promoting democratic rights and social partnership between the state, employers and trade unions. In the post-Independence period and particularly in the post-economic reforms period, employer associations in India such as the Confederation of Indian Industry (CII 2006) have consistently argued that the labour regulatory framework in the country confers disproportionate powers on workers and trade unions at the expense of employers. Hence they have argued the labour laws in India need radical reforms to restore a balance of power between capital and labour and make India an attractive destination for private domestic and foreign investments. Some analysts have suggested that this pro-labour regulatory framework derives from the close alliance between political parties and trade unions during the Independence movement and later in the post-Independence period when trade unions offered a captive vote bank for parties to win elections (Ramaswamy 1983, 1997).

It has been suggested that the pro-labour regulatory framework has been inimical to India's economic growth and has resulted in higher levels of labour inflexibility, low industrial productivity, high unemployment and poverty (Fallon and Lucas 1993; Beasley and Burgess 2004; Ahsan and Pages 2009). Thus the employment relations debate in India has largely centred on the regulation of labour markets. It is rooted in the institutional approach to employment relations which argues that the globalization of product and capital markets has intensified competition among firms worldwide, especially those firms which hitherto operated in protected markets with high entry barriers. However, following the formation of the World Trade Organization (WTO), its member states are required to lower, or in some cases dismantle, entry barriers and open their domestic markets to international competition. The intensified competition in turn provides a greater impetus and opportunity for capital to move across national boundaries in search of cheaper labour and infrastructure (Bhagwati 2004). As a result of globalization and increased capital mobility, it is suggested that unions can no longer afford to engage in conflictual and adversarial industrial relations, nor can workers take improvements in their wages and conditions for granted. Union survival is now increasingly dependent on their ability to engage in cooperative employment relations with employers and to link collective bargaining more closely to the business goals of the enterprise (Haynes and Allen 2001). To what extent such labour–management cooperation has materialized in the Indian context is an empirical question which is yet to be fully explored. However, some recent evidence (Badigannavar 2012) suggests that the current labour regulatory framework in India is not conducive to promoting such cooperation. Venkata Ratnam (2003) reports a growing employer dominance and union weakness in collective bargaining agreements and Shyam Sundar (2010) reports a rise in employer hostility towards unions in the post-economic reforms period.

Actors in Indian employment relations

The state in employment relations

Since the independence of India from British colonial rule in 1947, the state has by and large continued with the regulatory framework constituted by the British. Consequently, some of the most repressive measures codified by the colonial rulers in the Indian Penal Code (1860) and the Criminal Procedure Code have been retained by the state. For instance, Section 144 of the Criminal Procedure Code of India prohibits an assembly of five or more persons and can be imposed by a magistrate to prevent any form of assembly. This section has reportedly been widely used to thwart even lawful protests and agitations by workers and trade unions. The police are in charge of enforcing the magistrate's order under this section and any violations by members of the public can lead to criminal prosecution under Section 188 of the Indian Penal Code which can lead to imprisonment ranging from one to six months and/or a fine (www.legalservicesindia.com/articles/crpc.htm).

State intervention in Indian employment relations was at its most extreme during the national emergency imposed by the Congress government led by the charismatic leader Mrs Indira Gandhi from 1975–77 (Shyam Sundar 2009a: 43–4). The imposition of emergency rule followed a spate of industrial disputes and rising strike activity in the preceding year. The Congress government during this period arrested political and union leaders of rival parties and trade unions and imposed its own affiliated union federation, the INTUC, on workers both in the public and private sectors. Strikes and any forms of agitation were banned. The government froze wages and living allowances of workers and even cut bonus payments on the grounds that inflation needed to be kept under control. Anti-labour collective agreements were imposed on workers with the help of state-friendly unions resulting in lay-offs, retrenchments and firm closures. Official estimates at the time suggest that half a million workers lost their jobs during the second half of 1975 (Sharma 1982; Sen 1997, cited in Shyam Sundar 2009a).

During this period, however, the Congress government in 1976 amended the employment protection provisions in the Industrial Disputes Act, requiring any employer with 300 or more workers in their establishments to seek prior permission from the state before laying off or retrenching any workers or closing down their firm. This limit was further lowered to

100 or more workers in 1984. The post-emergency period did not witness any dilution of the repressive provisions in the criminal procedure codes. Recently, in July 2012, the district magistrate of Gurgaon near New Delhi imposed a prohibition order against an assembly of five or more people in an industrial township following worker agitation in a Japanese joint venture automobile company (*Hindustan Times*, 24 July 2012).

The interventionist nature of the state is codified in the key employment relations law in India, namely the Industrial Disputes Act (IDA) of 1947. Under this law the state can prohibit even a legal strike and refer any industrial dispute for compulsory arbitration or adjudication without the consent of the employers or unions. It is argued that such interventionist policies have thwarted the development of voluntary collective bargaining between employers and unions (Jain 2007). In total there are 60 federal laws and 200 state laws governing labour relations in India (Saini 2011: 24). The IDA has been the most contentious piece of central legislation in India, primarily due to its employment protection provisions. The IDA technically applies only to enterprises in manufacturing, mining and plantations. However, over the years, federal and state governments have included many other industries in the purview of this legislation (Jain 2007). According to the provisions of the IDA, a firm employing 100 or more workers has to secure prior permission from the appropriate government before laying-off or retrenching even a single worker or closing down the firm. Some analysts suggest that governments are reluctant to grant such permission due to political expediency (Bhattacherjee and Ackers 2010). There have been suggestions from employer lobbies to increase this threshold from 100 workers to 300 or perhaps 1000 workers (Saini 2010). Another provision of the IDA requires employers to give 21 days' notice to workers and their unions if the employer intends to make any changes to their service conditions. According to some analysts (ibid.: 41–2), this allows unions to raise an industrial dispute resulting in prolonged negotiations and, in turn, a missed opportunity for employers to restructure their internal labour markets and stay competitive. The Trade Unions Act 1926 allows registration of trade unions by any seven employees (including managers) in an establishment or a minimum of 10 per cent of workers employed in an industry or 100 workers, whichever is less. Even where a union is formed, there is no legal obligation on the employer to recognize the union for collective bargaining. There are some states in India, such as Maharashtra and Madhya Pradesh, where unions can seek an enforcement order from state bodies or the courts which requires an employer to recognize a union. Once registered as a trade union, its office bearers and members secure immunities from some civil and criminal acts which, if pursued in an industrial dispute (e.g. cessation of work) might otherwise constitute a conspiracy (Saini 2010: 31–2).

Another important piece of labour legislation which has been much debated in the post-economic reforms era is the Contract Labour (Regulation and Abolition) Act 1970. This is primarily due to the significant rise in the number of contract or casual workers, even in enterprises in the formal or 'registered' sector of the economy and in the wider labour market (Bhaumik 2003; Saini 2010). This law stipulates the tasks for which an employer can hire workers on short-term contracts and prohibits employment of contract labour in core activities of the firm which are carried out on a long-term and continuous basis. It also provides for the fair payment of wages to contract workers and stipulates supervision of wage payment by the principal employer. Furthermore, it requires the contractor/agent, or in some instances the principal employer, to provide for the health and safety of the contract workers employed in the enterprise. There is some cross-referral to the Industrial Disputes Act 1947 (IDA). Section 25-B of the IDA states that if a worker has continuous service of 240 days (which includes contract workers), then that worker can claim permanency of employment which in turn confers upon him/her the statutory protections under various labour laws.

The Maharastra Recognition of Trade Unions and Prevention of Unfair Labour Practices Act 1971 (MRTU & PULP) is an Act applicable to establishments operating in the state of Maharashtra. This is a bespoke union recognition law rarely found in other states of the country. The Act came into force on 8 September 1975 and covers all industries covered by the IDA 1947 and the BIR Act 1946. The primary purpose of the statute is to set out the procedure for trade union recognition and describes what constitutes unfair labour practices on the part of employers and unions. It also sets out the enforcement machinery and the penalties for engaging in such unfair labour practices. A union with 30 per cent membership in an undertaking for a continuous period of six months can apply to the Industrial Court for recognition. Once granted recognition, the employer is obliged to engage in collective bargaining with the recognized union and failure to do so constitutes an unfair labour practice.

Other unfair labour practices stipulated under the MRTU & PULP law include dissuading employees from joining a union through the use of threats or favouritism, organizing a non-recognized union, victimizing employees for union activities, dismissal of employees for engaging in legal strikes, attempting to break a strike through outsourcing work to subcontractors and employing casual or temporary workers for years without giving them permanency of employment (Thakker 2009: 17–19).

Thus, overall, the statutory provisions of some of the key federal and state labour laws in India summarized above suggest a fairly protective legislative environment for workers and trade unions in the formal sector of the economy. According to Deakin and Sarkar (2011: 8): 'India has a system of labour regulation that is pro-worker by reference to international comparisons, the effect is largely due to its laws on termination of employment.' It is worth noting, however, that only about 15 per cent of the total workforce of about 400 million workers is covered by the provisions of various labour and welfare laws. The remaining 85 per cent are effectively excluded (Papola *et al.* 2007).

In the post-economic reforms period since 1991, there has been a growing disenchantment among workers and trade unions in India based on the belief that the state favours private capital to the extent of violating the fundamental labour rights enshrined in the Indian Constitution. Even in the pro-worker communist-ruled state of West Bengal, the Chief Minister in 2008 publicly stated that he did not support worker agitations, labelling them as 'illegal' and 'immoral' (Shyam Sundar 2010: 213). More disturbingly, state police are frequently deployed at the behest of employers to oppress workers and curtail attempts at unionization. Sharma (2008) reports that the government in the north Indian state of Uttar Pradesh set up a special Police Cell headed by senior police officials which holds regular meetings with employers to resolve labour-related disputes. This practice erodes the legitimacy of the state's Labour Department and sends an unequivocal message to employers that they can access state-sponsored violence for the smooth running of their enterprises.

The state of Maharashtra, which ostensibly has a pro-worker labour regulatory framework (Beasley and Burgess 2004; Deakin and Sarkar 2011), has been at the forefront of introducing export-oriented Special Economic Zones (SEZs). Establishments operating in these zones are exempt from the provisions of all major employment relations laws such as Section 9A of the Industrial Disputes Act 1947 which regulates changes in work practices and work reorganization. Likewise, other crucial trade union laws do not apply to firms operating in the SEZs: i.e., the Trade Unions Act 1926, the MRTU & PULP 1971, and the

BIR 1946 which offers representative status to trade unions and requires employers to engage with unions on matters of changes to work practices and terms and conditions. Furthermore, private enterprises operating in SEZs across India are classified as 'public utility services' which allows the state to impose the much dreaded 'Essential Services Maintenance Act' and intervene to thwart any industrial dispute in these units under the guise of protecting the national interest. The Labour Commissioner or labour officers of the state have no jurisdiction over enterprises operating in SEZs and cannot intervene to resolve worker grievances (Shyam Sundar 2008; Desai 2009).

One could argue that it is imperative for the state as an employer in public sector undertakings to honour its commitments under various labour laws and thereby set an example as a 'model employer' for the private sector to follow. However, studies on agricultural labour have revealed that, in some states, the government has set minimum wages for agricultural workers at a level below the official poverty line, thereby violating their constitutional right to a decent standard of life (Badigannavar 1998). There have been instances reported by trade unions where contract workers employed in public sector enterprises were being paid wages below the official minimum wage. Even permanent workers employed in the State Road Transport Corporation in the state of Bihar are in some instances being paid less than the minimum wage despite court rulings directing the management to pay full wages with back arrears.[1] Non-payment of minimum wages under the Bonded Labour Abolition Act 1976 is deemed to be slavery. This indeed is an ironical situation where, on the one hand, the state abolishes the practice of bonded labour and, on the other hand, fails to check such exploitative practices in its own enterprises.

Trade unions

The trade union movement in India is highly fragmented. Until the 1980s, most trade unions in India were affiliated to a political party through a national federation (also known as central trade union organizations). For instance, the Indian National Trade Union Congress (INTUC) is affiliated to the Congress Party; the All India Trade Union Congress (AITUC) is affiliated to the Communist Party of India; the Centre of Indian Trade Unions (CITU) is affiliated to the Communist Party of India (Marxist); the Bhartiya Mazdoor Sangh (BMS) is affiliated to the nationalist Bhartiya Janata Party; and the Hind Mazdoor Sabha (HMS) is the socialist labour wing. Shyam Sundar (2010: 59–60) reports verified (by state agencies) membership of ten national trade union federations which are politically affiliated. According to his figures, as of 31 December 2002, the ten major politically affiliated trade unions in India had a total membership of about 22.7 million workers, of which around 1.6 million workers were from the formal or organized sector and the rest from the informal or unorganized sector of the economy. Calculating trade union density in India is highly complex. This is because of the difficulty of precisely defining and categorizing enterprises and workers employed in them as belonging to the formal/regulated or 'organized' sector or to the informal/unregulated or 'unorganized' sector of the economy. Second, only a small minority of registered trade unions submits annual membership returns to the state agencies (Shyam Sundar 2009b). Frenkel and Kuruvilla (2002) estimated union density at about 18.9 per cent in 1993. Some recent estimates suggest that about 34 per cent of regular non-agricultural workers in India are trade union members although this figure varies significantly across states. For instance, about 74 per cent of formal workers in the state of Tripura are union members compared with only 19 per cent in Delhi (Pal 2008). Overall, trade union density in India is fairly low.

Since the mid-1980s onwards, there has been a rise in the number of politically non-affiliated trade unions which are largely enterprise-based unions. In some of the highly industrialized states like Maharashtra, nearly 72 per cent of all trade union members belong to politically non-affiliated unions (Shyam Sundar 2009c). This rise in politically non-affiliated unions is largely attributed to worker disenchantment with politically affiliated unions which are perceived to be subservient to the agenda of their political parties (which tends to be pro-employer) and hence are unable to protect the best interests of workers at the enterprise level. Besides, these unions are perceived as electoral machines designed to help the party win elections and secure power and they are seen to be less interested in workplace level bargaining. The result is that workers have been leaving politically affiliated unions and forming their own independent enterprise level unions.

A second reason which might explain the rise of such politically non-affiliated unions is the large (and growing) number of workers employed in the informal or unregulated sector of the economy. There are about 400 million workers in the Indian labour market. Of these, only about 7 per cent are employed in the formal or regulated sector enterprises. The remaining 93 per cent are employed either in agriculture or in small and medium-sized enterprises in the unregulated or informal sector of the economy. Historically, politically affiliated unions have shown little or no interest in organizing workers in the informal sector and have concentrated their resources on organizing and representing workers in the formal sector establishments in the public and private sectors. Thus workers in the informal sector or those employed as casual and contract workers in the formal sector have formed their own politically independent unions sometimes with the help of non-governmental organizations (NGOs). For instance, the Confederation of Free Trade Unions of India (CFTUI) is a politically non-affiliated national union federation with about 110 union affiliates and represents nearly 600,000 workers across seven states. Nearly 70 per cent of their members are employed in the informal sector of the economy. According to some of the leaders of these politically independent unions, in the automobile sector of Maharashtra there is an element of hypocrisy among the politically affiliated unions when representing interests of workers.[2] On the one hand, they protest against the employment of workers on short-term contracts and as casual labour while, on the other hand, several of these union leaders, from all political hues, were reportedly themselves agents or suppliers of contract labour to automobile companies. They are therefore benefitting financially from the exploitation of contract labourers. Such behaviour has further frustrated both permanent and contract workers in those automobile companies who have resigned from the politically affiliated unions and formed their own politically independent unions.

Political patronage of unions has been a state policy to curtail conflict and to marginalize rival unions. This policy in many cases has chimed favourably with employers (Shyam Sundar 2009a). The INTUC which is the second largest trade union federation in India, with nearly eight million members, has reportedly secured favourable union recognition deals with employers due to its affiliation to the ruling Congress Party both in the federal and state governments. In the 1980s, one of the INTUC-affiliated unions in the textile industry in Mumbai secured recognition as a 'representative union' for the entire textile industry in the state under legally questionable circumstances (ibid.). The union has since retained this status despite attempts by rival unions to have it derecognized. It is alleged that in the major textile mills strike of the early 1980s, this union helped employers to break the strike, imposed inferior pay deals on workers and even helped employers arrange firm closures to release land for property development[3] (see Van Wersch 1992). Likewise, Ramaswamy (1997) reports that employers in West Bengal favoured having a communist union in their enterprise because the state was ruled by the Communist Party of India (Marxist) for nearly three decades. Employers found it relatively easy to curtail any form of union militancy by seeking the intervention of the Communist Party leaders who would admonish their unions for making 'unreasonable' demands on management. A senior union leader of the HMS (a socialist trade union) reported that in a large port trust authority in the state of Maharashtra, management actively encouraged workers to quit HMS, which had a majority membership, and join a rival right-wing union which was affiliated to a regional political party in the state. This is because the party leadership had promised no strikes and favourable pay agreements to management.[4]

This fragmentation of trade unions has inevitably resulted in the weakening of the labour movement in India which some argue has resulted in a demise of class consciousness and political articulation of grievances (Roy Choudhary 2008). The politically affiliated trade union federations now find themselves on a losing streak even with their political parties. A senior union official of the INTUC reported that this is because of falling membership levels in the formal sector (especially manufacturing) and the unions' inability to organize workers in the informal sector. Consequently, political parties no longer see some of their affiliated union federations as electoral assets.[5]

Employers and employers organizations

There are four major national employers associations in India which lobby government on economic and labour policies. None of these national federations directly engages in collective bargaining with union federations at national or industry levels. However, they do provide professional support to their members in the form of training and consultancy on HRM and employment relations issues. The Confederation of Indian Industry (CII) was founded over 117 years ago and represents nearly 90,000 companies from various industrial sectors in India. The CII is the most vociferous of all the employers associations in the country which has consistently argued for the deregulation of labour markets and the weakening of labour laws for competitive advantage (CII 2006). The CII's theme for 2012–13 is 'Reviving Economic Growth: Reforms and Governance', whereby it lobbies government and state institutions for structural reforms to attract foreign direct investment in the country. The adverse impact of such structural reforms on labour markets has been well documented (e.g. Papola 2004). The CII also offers consultancy services to their members on HR issues such as change management, teamworking, leadership and motivation to enhance firm competitiveness.

The Federation of Indian Chambers of Commerce and Industry (FICCI) was founded in 1927 and claims to represent nearly 250,000 member companies in India. The Associated Chambers of Commerce and Industry of India (ASSOCHAM) was formed in 1920 and represents about 400,000 member firms in the country. Finally, the Employers Federation of India (EFI), established in 1933, currently represents 250 regional employer associations and chambers of commerce in the country. These regional associations together cover several million employees in India although the exact figures were not available at the time of writing. The EFI is a specialized organization representing employers' views to the state on issues of employment relations and labour policies. It also provides training and consultancy services to both employers and trade unions on matters of labour laws and reward policies.

The employers associations in India, particularly the CII, have argued that, although the country has deregulated its product and capital markets, the labour market regulations are archaic and in dire need of reform to attract private investment. According to the CII, the current labour law framework in India is too favourable to workers and unions in the organized sector enterprises and consequently this leads to labour inflexibilities, industrial conflict, low productivity and joblessness. The second National Commission on Labour (NCL 2002) appointed by the government of India, endorsed this view in its submission to the government. The NCL recommended significant reforms to union certification laws and to the provisions for recognition as a bargaining agent. While the NCL's recommendations are yet to be implemented, they reflect the neo-liberal orthodoxy that has prevailed in state policy on labour since the early 1990s (Chakrabarti and Dasgupta 2007). The employers' position on labour reforms is influenced by the work of the Organization for Economic Co-operation and Development (OECD), especially its *Jobs Strategy* (OECD 1996, 2006) and the World Bank's *Doing Business Reports*, which call for deregulation of labour markets to improve economic performance. The veracity of these claims has been widely debated and scrutinized and hence do not require further elaboration here (see Casey 2004; Lee *et al.* 2008; Bakvis 2009).

Recent studies on union experiences of workplace employment regulations in India have revealed that, even in an ostensibly favourable regulatory environment, the labour laws offer little or no protection to workers and unions against employer excesses. Furthermore, there was very little evidence of union militancy but, on the contrary, there was evidence of rising employer hostility against workers and unions in the post-economic reforms period. The proportion of employer imposed lock-outs on workers was nearly five times as high as worker strikes in the post-reforms decade. Likewise, the number of workers affected and the proportion of worker-days lost due to employer lock-outs were substantially higher compared with the corresponding figures for worker strikes (Shyam Sundar 2010; Badigannavar 2012; Badigannavar and Kelly 2012). This rise in employer lock-outs can be largely attributed to two reasons. Employers in India use lock-outs as a proxy or precursor to firm closures. During lock-outs, employers are not required to pay wages to their workers whereas if the employer were to lay off or retrench workers, then they would be required to give severance pay or wages during the lay-off period (Mathur 1991, 1992; Sen Gupta and Sett 2000). Second, employers use lock-outs to impose inferior pay and conditions on workers and to demobilize unions.

To some extent, this employer militancy has been supported by the state during periods of economic reform. According to senior officials of the state Labour Commissions, the number of employer lock-outs seems to increase just before the state or national elections are due whereas the number of strikes during this period seems to fall. This is because political parties persuade or coerce their affiliated unions to refrain from any form of agitation that would accrue bad media publicity. At the same time they withhold state intervention in disputes involving employer lock-outs in exchange for political donations. The employers consequently enjoy a free rein to impose inferior pay deals or voluntary retirement schemes on workers who find their unions unable to protect them.[6] Finally, the law on strikes and lock-outs seems to be much more benevolent to employers as compared to workers. An employer who imposes an illegal lock-out on workers without giving prior notice of his actions can reverse the illegality of the lock-out by giving notice during the course of the lock-out, but a union cannot do the same if it were to engage in a strike without notice. Such a strike would be deemed illegal and may lead to the arrest of workers and union leaders and de-certification of the union (Badigannavar 2012).

Although the labour law framework in India is ostensibly pro-worker, employers for decades have managed to circumvent the provisions of these laws without being held accountable by the state or the judiciary (Singh 2008; Saini 2010). Mathur (1991, 1992) and

Sen Gupta and Sett (2000) have reported how employers deprive workers of permanent employment and the statutory protections that come along with it. Contract and casual workers are not allowed to complete 240 days of continuous service in the firm. They are given artificial breaks in service of a few days or weeks just before they complete the minimum statutory period of 240 days that would qualify them for employment security. Workers are terminated and then rehired on new employment contracts or they are moved between sister companies of the same employer, and on each occasion hired on new contracts to prevent them accruing 240 days of continuous service. Employers also redesignate workers' job titles and thus take them out of the purview of the employment protection legislation. For example, a telephone operator is redesignated as a 'communications officer' and an accounts clerk is called a 'payroll executive'.

One of the common unfair labour practices reported in several studies is the victimization of union activists by management during negotiations (see Shyam Sundar 2010; Badigannavar 2012). Employers often cite 'worker indiscipline' as a cause of industrial disputes leading to suspensions, terminations and lock-outs. Shyam Sunder (2010: 82) cites an interesting report from the West Bengal Labour Bureau dating back to the early 1990s which documents the 'real causes' of employer lock-outs when the stated cause was 'worker indiscipline'. The real causes documented by the state officials investigating these disputes were as follows: management's intention to reduce the business and impose job cuts, high prices of raw materials, poor financial management ('uneconomic running') and financial difficulties faced by management. Thus the stated cause of 'indiscipline' was merely a management ploy to restructure or close the business or camouflage financial mismanagement. Shrouti and Nandkumar (1995) have reported that management creates artificial problems by defaulting on repaying their bank loans or utility bills and then referring the firm to the Board of Industrial and Financial Reconstruction (BIFR) for liquidation. In the liquidation process, the BIFR accords very few rights to workers and unions as stakeholders in the firm and prioritizes payments of loans to creditors over payment of workers' wages. Many such 'sick firms' have successfully relocated to areas with lower taxation and cheaper labour elsewhere in India. It is reported that such 'sickness and relocation' strategies have been used by firms to demobilize unions.

Some examples of industrial disputes in the post-economic reforms period are quite illustrative of employer hostility towards unions. Multinational corporations operating in India, and particularly those in the automobile manufacturing sector (which is one of the fastest-growing industrial sectors in the country), are allegedly flouting trade union and workers rights with impunity. For instance, Shyam Sundar (2010: 95–9) reports strong anti-unionism on the part of management in the German MNC Bosch operating in Pune, in the state of Maharashtra. The Bosch group has had four companies operating in India since 1953 and currently employs about 18,000 workers. One of its operations in Pune manufactures brake systems for automobiles. Since 2005, the Bosch management has successfully thwarted three attempts at unionization by workers at the Pune plant. Workers involved in the unionization campaign were selectively dismissed and victimized, thus violating statutory provisions on unfair labour practices. Eventually, and with great difficulty, the workers formed an enterprise-level union but management refused to negotiate with it and began to recruit large numbers of contract/casual workers on inferior terms and conditions. It also refused to implement pay agreements dating back to 2007. The union objected to this exploitation of contract workers and non-implementation of wage agreements and finally went on strike in July 2009. The Bosch management suspended the union secretary and dismissed 540 contract workers who are still fighting a court battle to secure their employment rights.

It is interesting to note that a German multinational which ostensibly has its roots in a mature tripartite system of social dialogue in its 'home' country should engage in such anti-union activities in a developing country like India. The company has shown little or no compliance with the labour law regime of the 'host' country and attempts to exploit workers through rather 'low road' employment relations practices.

Similarly, Hyundai Motors India Ltd (HMIL), a Korean automobile company operating in India, has aggressively resisted unionization of its employees and has refused to recognize an independent employees union. Instead it has tried to foist upon its employees a management-sponsored workers committee which has no legal mandate. When workers and the union protested against such anti-union practices, the management dismissed 65 workers, suspended another 34 and imposed a pay cut on 840 workers. The union president and secretary were transferred to plants in other parts of the country (Shyam Sundar 2010: 107–8).

Employment relations outcomes

In this section we discuss some of the key employment relations outcomes over the past decade or so with respect to collective bargaining, wages and productivity and work organization. According to Venkata Ratnam (2003), of the total labour force of around 400 million in India, only about 28 million are employed in the formal or regulated sector of the Indian economy. Of these, nearly 14 million workers are employed in public services and are thus covered by various pay commissions that decide on their wage levels. The commissions are government-appointed and hear representations from employer associations and trade unions. Since independence, India has had six pay commissions to decide on the salaries of employees in the civil service, judiciary and defence forces. Thus collective bargaining over wages in the public services takes place within the remit of the pay awards sanctioned by the pay commissions.

The average tenure of collective agreements in public services now stands at around ten years. In the private sector, however, collective agreements usually are of two to three years' duration. In some sectors of the economy, collective bargaining over wages and conditions of service takes place at the industry or sector levels. For example, banking and insurance, ports and docks, and coal mining, all have industry-level collective bargaining. The Indian Banks' Association, for instance, which has members from both the public and private sectors, negotiates with the All Indian Federation of Bank Employees on wages and conditions. Since the 1990s there has been a growing trend towards establishment-level bargaining in the private sector and in many cases this has replaced industry bargaining (Venkata Ratnam 2003: 21).

Venkata Ratnam (2003) analyzed about 200 collective bargaining agreements over a ten-year period following the launch of economic reforms. He found increasing employer assertiveness in the drafting of these agreements with wages being closely linked to productivity. For example, he cites the agreement in Asian Paints Ltd., in the then communist-ruled state of Kerala, where the collective agreement states that wages are agreed for a standard labour output and any shortfall in this output will result in proportionate deductions in wages. In another automobile components company in the state of Maharashtra, the collective agreement provides for deduction in wages if a worker repeatedly produces defective materials. Goldar and Banga (2005) analyzed the wage–productivity relationship in the formal sector of manufacturing industry in India. They analyzed data over a 20-year period (ten years prior to the economic reforms and 10 years post-economic reforms). At the national level they found the growth rate in labour productivity was 6.6 per cent per annum, whereas the growth rate in real wages over the same time period lagged behind by 3.3 per cent. Thus in terms of the wage–productivity bargain, the employers benefitted most at the expense of workers. Venkata Ratnam (2003) also reports a growing trend among employers to transfer jobs from the bargainable to non-bargainable categories by either redesignating workers without any material change to their wages or conditions or simply subcontracting or outsourcing work to smaller units. While unions have resisted such changes, in several cases they have had to concede these changes in order to protect the jobs of their members. Goldar and Banga (2005) attribute the increasing gap in real wages and labour output to a number of factors including the diminishing influence of trade unions in the manufacturing industry. Sen and Dasgupta (2009) analyzed whether wage–profit ratios differ between high-growth and low-growth manufacturing firms. They found that, even in high-growth firms, wage shares were significantly smaller compared to profit shares. They conclude that improvements in labour productivity have not resulted in improvements in wages in the post-economic reforms period. As one HMS trade union official put it: 'When wage shares across industries have been consistently falling for decades, the whole argument of a labour aristocracy in India is a cruel joke.'[7]

A significant change in work organization in the formal sector enterprises in India has been the increased use of workers on short-term casual contracts in place of regular, permanent workers. Deshpande *et al.* (2004) report that larger firms employing 1000 or more workers are much more likely to employ casual and contract workers on low wages than smaller or medium-sized firms. Furthermore, these large firms are less likely to invest in training their permanent workers, thereby showing a clear preference for numerical flexibility over functional flexibility through skill upgrading. Saini (2010) estimates that in the formal manufacturing sector about 26 per cent of workers are employed as contract or casual workers with little or no statutory protection. Venkata Ratnam (2003) reports the use of 'parallel production' systems and a two-tier workforce whereby employers increasingly subcontract their operations to third parties and employ workers through labour contractors or agents. These workers are paid significantly lower wages and are employed on precarious terms and conditions.

There have been some positive employment relations outcomes for workers employed in the informal or unregulated sector of the economy. About 372 million workers are employed in the informal sector of the economy and until 2008 there was very little statutory protection for these workers. Some state governments had passed individual pieces of legislation to protect these informal sector workers, e.g. laws to protect workers employed as 'head loaders' in wholesale and retail markets or laws to protect those employed as 'security staff' in private security agencies. In 2008, the federal government passed the Unorganised Workers Social Security Act which makes welfare provisions for millions of workers employed in the informal or unregulated sector of the economy. The legislation has had a mixed response with some leading NGOs such as the Self-Employed Women's Association (SEWA) welcoming its provisions of health service and old age pension provisions for unorganized workers, while other groups, such as the Lawyers Collective, finding it inadequate because of its inability to regulate wages and working conditions (Sankaran 2009).

Theoretical perspectives

The preceding sections have outlined the historical evolution of employment relations in India and the role of the state, the trade unions and employers. This section attempts to explain the observations made so far from various theoretical perspectives. While Dunlop's systems approach would explain the nature of institutions and the web of rules that govern the actors within those institutions, it would stop short at explaining the relative imbalances in power between the actors and the articulation of their interests. From an institutional perspective, what would explain the relative imbalance of power between capital and labour in India? Recent work on this issue has focused on the role of the judiciary and the state in regulating employment relations (Babu and Shetty 2007; Roy Choudhary 2008; Singh 2008). According to Weiss (2003), the conventional argument that states are now constrained in their ability to protect labour's interest due to economic globalization is untrue. She argues that national governments and institutions do have a choice in the extent to which they expose their labour, capital and product markets to global competition and the terms on which they compete globally. However, the argument of market forces offers a cloak of legitimacy to introduce reforms which serve the interests of capital at the expense of labour (Rodrik 1997; Roy Choudhary 2008). This is evident in the Indian context, for instance, with respect to state policies on special economic zones.

The judiciary in India has also come into the spotlight. It is argued that, in line with the neo-liberal agenda of the state, the judiciary has in recent years passed judgments that tilt the balance of power squarely in favour of employers. For instance, in 2006, the Supreme Court of India in a case involving a public sector enterprise (*Secretary, State of Karnataka & Others versus Uma Devi and Others*) ruled that casual and temporary workers, even after a continuous period of service spanning several years, have no right to claim permanency in their employment as they were not hired through due process and were instead recruited through the 'back door'. This informal system of hiring deprives other potential candidates from securing that job (Shyam Sundar 2010). What the Supreme Court seems to have ignored in its ruling is that this supposed 'back door' entry was for the convenience of the management and their labour contractors and not workers. Hence to penalize workers for management's failings and to deny them employment security is unjustified. In 2001, the Supreme Court passed a similar anti-labour judgment in the case of contract workers in another public sector enterprise – the Steel Authority of India Limited (Cox 2008). The repercussions of these anti-labour judgments by the courts are now felt by workers across the country, resulting in a loss of employment security for millions of contract and casual workers (Ray 2008).

Peters (2011: 45) discusses the role of individuals within institutions and their actions which have become a focus of research in comparative politics. Babu and Shetty (2007) suggest that the judiciary in India largely comprises upper-class affluent men who also tend to belong to the upper castes in the social hierarchy. These individuals tend to be unsympathetic to the grievances of the working classes and hence are more likely to interpret laws in favour of employers. The pro-employer bias in the Indian judiciary is well documented (Singh 2008). So although the laws may have originally been drafted in a pro-labour direction, their interpretation by judges whose interests increasingly correspond with those of employers has tilted the balance of power in favour of capital at the expense of labour. This perhaps explains why employers in India tend to be more militant in their use of lock-outs and more litigious compared to unions.

Peters (2011) conceptualizes *actors' interests* as an important variable in analyzing political processes. Along these lines, Burgess (2004) examines the intricate relationship between political parties and trade unions as actors in employment relations. She suggests that party–union relationships are more likely to be tested in times of economic instability or when political parties introduce major institutional reforms which hurt the interests of union members. In times such as these, union leaders have to decide whether to side with the political party they are affiliated to and risk antagonizing their membership or to confront the party and stand by the interests of their members. In her view, union leaders base their judgements on which of the two constituencies (party versus union members) are likely to offer better incentives to the union leadership, and equally, which of them are likely to punish them the most. Party incentives could include the opportunity to contest elections, senior posts within the party's executive, political intervention to secure union recognition with employers or securing favourable collective bargaining arrangements. It is likely that a political party is in a better position to offer such incentives to union leaders when they enjoy an absolute majority in the government. The party's ability to offer such incentives is likely to be constrained when it is part of a coalition government. Union members are more likely to stay with the union if they believe the leadership can deliver the desired outcomes either through the union's bargaining power or through the leadership's ability to secure better deals from employers via political interventions.

In the Indian context, the federal government has consisted of a coalition of nearly a dozen regional and national parties for nearly 15 years. Likewise, industrially developed states such as Maharashtra have been governed by coalition governments for nearly a decade. It is quite likely that ruling parties such as the Congress are now unable to offer the same level of political patronage to its affiliate INTUC unions in securing union recognition with employers or favourable collective bargaining outcomes. This might also explain why politically affiliated unions such as the INTUC federation have witnessed a fall in their membership levels. Ramaswamy (1983) suggests that union membership in India is largely driven by narrow materialistic considerations on the part of workers rather than an ideological commitment towards their union. This, according to him, explains to some extent the rise of enterprise-level 'economic unions' as opposed to 'political unions'.

It would be difficult to make direct comparisons of the Indian employment relations system with that of Britain. Nevertheless given the historical legacy which has left a lasting footprint on the labour regulatory framework of India, some cross-references might be analytically useful in the current debate on employment relations. Kelly (in Chapter 10 in this volume) suggests that one of the reasons why collective bargaining in Britain remained weak compared with other European countries is the 'Westminster model' of government, coupled with the absence of a written constitution and a historical distrust of unions in the judiciary and legislative framework and their preference for voluntarism. He argues that such 'institutions' by their very presence in some of the European countries have provided a favourable degree of stability and credibility to employment relations institutions and, in particular, collective bargaining even in the face of globalization and market forces. If these parameters were to be applied to the Indian employment relations system, then it reveals a completely different picture. India has a written Constitution which proclaims the nation as a 'socialist state'. The Constitution guarantees the fundamental rights to its citizens including freedom of association (Article 19.3) and equality before law and equal protection by the law (Article 14). 'Labour' is a constitutional subject and appears on the concurrent list of the Indian Constitution, which means the federal as well as state governments can take appropriate measures to legislate on matters of labour rights and labour welfare.

Furthermore, the country probably has one of the highest numbers of labour laws in the world (over 200 pieces of legislation) and the trade unions and workers had trust in the judiciary and the legislative provisions to protect their interests, at least until the mid-1990s (Singh 2008). In the post-Independence period, the state created a large regulatory machinery which provides for conciliation, arbitration and special adjudication through labour courts and tribunals. And despite all these features, that should in theory promote a favourable environment for workers and unions, we find that they are, and have been for decades, victims of employer oppression and state subjugation. One can ask whether workers and unions were simply victims of misjudged optimism for all these years, to have trusted a socialist state and an independent judiciary operating within it to protect their interests. Clearly the logic of institutions does not apply neatly to a developing country like India which is in a transition phase from a largely state-controlled command economy to a liberal market economy.

Mobilization theory provides a better framework to explain the employment relations dynamics in India. It is particularly relevant in explaining the role of trade unions and the state as actors in employment relations. According to mobilization theory (Tilly 1978; Kelly 1998), workers are more likely to unionize and engage in collective actions if the following conditions are met. First, there has to be a deeply and widely shared sense of injustice. Union meetings or community meetings for instance, foster social cohesion which gives workers the opportunity to discuss and share their grievances and overcome feelings of isolation. Second, workers have to attribute their grievances to a target agency such as their employer or the government, or believe that their grievances can be remedied by these agencies. Such attribution provides a target for collective actions. Workers are more likely to join a union and participate in collective actions if they perceive the union to be effective in redressing their grievances. Workers also engage in cost-benefit calculations whereby they assess the potential gains and available power resources. The attitude and actions of the state and the labour regulatory framework play a significant role in these calculations. Moreover, the role of union and political leaderships is pivotal in shaping worker perceptions and eliciting collective participation.

In the Indian context, political parties such as the Congress, the socialists and Communists and their affiliated unions historically engaged in mass mobilization of workers and communities against the British colonial rule during the struggle for independence. In the post-Independence period the state has followed the policy of political patronage and incorporation of trade unions in order to achieve industrial harmony and economic growth. These objectives were by and large achieved until the late 1970s when there was a spate of strikes in key infrastructure sectors followed by the imposition of a national emergency and suspension of the rule of law by the then Congress government. Since the late 1980s, successive governments have pursued the policy of deregulation of markets under the rubric of global competition and economic exigencies. The liberalization, privatization and globalization agenda has strained the relationship between trade unions and political parties. Trade unions which had formerly relied on political patronage are now engaged in mass mobilization of workers and union members against government policies which are hurting the working classes. For instance, on 28 February 2012, eleven national trade union federations organized a national strike against the government's economic liberalization policies and its failure to control inflation and prevent violation of labour laws by employers. There has been a series of such national strikes in the past three years, however, their impact on state policy has been minimal.

Unions have also mobilized workers at enterprise levels to secure recognition for collective bargaining or pursue claims on wage settlements and job security with employers. Some recent strikes in the airline industry (e.g. Kingfisher Airlines in May and August 2012) have attracted heavy media attention and have resulted in some favourable outcomes for pilots and employees who had not been paid wages for months. High profile strikes and worker agitation in automobile companies such as Maruti-Suzuki, Bosch and Honda (see Shyam Sundar 2010) reflect to some extent the growing mobilization capacity of workers and unions against the exploitative practices of employers. However, state policies have tilted the balance of power squarely in favour of employers. For instance, the state policy on special economic zones (SEZ) exempts firms operating in these areas from key provisions of various labour laws. These policies have made unionization of workers employed in the SEZs very difficult. This in turn is likely to erode worker perceptions of union effectiveness, hindering attempts to organize them and potentially dissuading them from engaging in collective actions. How, and to what extent, union leaders are able and willing to alter these collective perceptions is yet to be seen.

Conclusion

The economic reform policies followed by successive governments in India from 1991 onwards have brought debate about employment relations onto centre stage. This debate is largely centred on the regulation of labour markets and reforms to labour laws. Employer organizations such as the CII have vehemently argued in favour of weakening labour laws to make India an attractive destination for foreign direct investment. Historically, the state has maintained a dominant position in employment relations and continues to do so in terms of dispute resolution, for example. Increasingly, however, the state is gradually withdrawing from the regulation of labour markets without making fundamental changes to the labour law framework. Any such changes would be politically sensitive, especially with large national trade union federations affiliated to political parties. Thus, effectively, the state is attempting to reform the labour markets by stealth by allowing employers to circumvent statutory provisions and easing the burden of inspections on them (Shyam Sundar 2008, 2010). The role of the judiciary in India is increasingly being questioned with respect to their pro-employer bias in the interpretation of labour laws. The union movement in India remains weak and fragmented. Although there is a growing alliance between union federations of various political and apolitical persuasions, their influence on state policy and employer practices seems limited. The continuance of economic reforms is likely to increase pressure on the state to give in to employer demands for labour market deregulation.

Notes

1 This information comes from interviews with HMS, AITUC and CFTUI union officials in August and September 2010.
2 Data from interviews with local union leaders at Options Positive Pune, September 2012.
3 Interview with Kamgar Aghadi union official, December 2010.
4 Data from interview, December 2010.
5 Interview with RMMS official, September 2012.
6 Interviews with Labour Commission officials in UP, Karnataka and Maharashtra, October–November 2010.
7 Interviewed by the author, September 2010.

References

Agarwala, R., Kumar, N. and Ribound, M. (2004) *Reforms, Labour Markets and Social Security in India*, New Delhi: Oxford University Press.

Ahsan, A. and Pages, C. (2009) 'Are all labour regulations equal? Evidence from Indian manufacturing', *Journal of Comparative Economics*, 37(1): 62–75.

Babu, S. I. and Shetty, R. (2007) *Social Justice and Labour Jurisprudence: Justice V.R. Krishna Iyer's Contributions*, New Delhi: Sage.

Badigannavar, V. (1998) 'Organising the agricultural labour: perceived challenges and possible responses', *Perspectives in Social Work*, 13(2): 20–3.

—— (2012) 'Labour market regulations and the prospects of social partnership in India', *Journal of Social and Economic Development*, 14(2): 129–54.

—— and Kelly, J. (2013) 'Do labour laws protect workers in India? Case study of INTUC in Maharashtra, India', *Industrial Law Journal*, 49(4): 439–70.

Bakvis, P. (2009) 'The World Bank's *Doing Business Report*: A last fling for the Washington consensus?', *Transfer: European Review of Labour and Research*, 15(3–4): 419–38.

Beasley, T. and Burgess, R. (2004) 'Can labor regulation hinder economic performance? Evidence from India', *The Quarterly Journal of Economics*, 119(1): 91–134.

Bhagwati, J. (2004) *In Defence of Globalization*, Oxford: Oxford University Press.

Bhattacherjee, D. and Ackers, P. (2010) 'Introduction: employment relations in India – old narratives and new perspectives', *Industrial Relations Journal*, 41(2): 104–21.

Bhaumik, S. (2003) 'Casualisation of the workforce in India, 1983–2002', *The Indian Journal of Labour Economics*, 46(4): 907–26.

Budhwar, P. S. and Bhatnagar, J. (eds) (2009) *The Changing Face of People Management in India*, London: Routledge.

Burgess, K. (2004) *Parties and Unions in the New Global Economy*, Pittsburgh, PA; University of Pittsburgh Press.

Casey, B. H. (2004) 'The OECD Jobs Strategy and the European Employment Strategy: two views of the labour market and the welfare state', *European Journal of Industrial Relations*, 10(3): 329–52.

Chakrabarti, A. and Dasgupta, B. (2007) 'Disinterring the Report of the National Commission on labour: a Marxist perspective', *Economic and Political Weekly*, 26 May, 1958–65.

Confederation of Indian Industry (CII) (2006) *Summary of Recommendations on Union Budget 2006–07*, New Delhi: CII, available at: www.ciionline.org.

Cox, J. (2008) 'Judiciary leaves contract labour in the cold', *Combat Law*, (Nov.–Dec.): 68–70.

D'Costa, P.A. (2005) *The Long March to Capitalism: Embourgeoisement, Internationalization, and Industrial Transformation in India*, Basingstoke: Palgrave Macmillan,

Deakin, S. and Sarkar, P. (2011) *Indian Labour Law and Its Impact on Unemployment 1970–2006: A Leximetric Study*, Cambridge: University of Cambridge, Centre for Business Research, Working Paper No. 428.

Desai, S.R. (2009) *Special Economic Zones: Myth and Reality*, Mumbai: Mill Mazdoor Welfare Trust.

Deshpande, L. K., Sharma, A. N., Karan, A. K. and Sarkar, S. (2004) *Liberalisation and Labour: Labour Flexibility in Indian Manufacturing*, New Delhi: Institute for Human Development.

Fallon, P. R. and Lucas, R. E. B. (1993) 'Job security regulations and the dynamic demand for industrial labor in India and Zimbabwe', *Journal of Development Economics*, 40(2): 241–75.

Frenkel, S. and Kuruvilla, S. (2002) 'Logics of action, globalization, and the changing employment relations in China, India, Malaysia, and the Philippines', *Industrial and Labor Relations Review*, 55(3): 387–412.

Goldar, B. and Banga, R. (2005) 'Wage-productivity relationship in organized manufacturing in India: state-wide analysis', paper presented to International Conference on Wages and Income in India, Indira Gandhi Institute of Development Research, Mumbai, India. Available at: http://hdl.handle.net/2275/140 (accessed 11 November 2012).

Haynes, P. and Allen, M. (2001) 'Partnership as union strategy: a preliminary evaluation', *Employee Relations*, 23(2): 164–87.

Hill, E. (2009) 'The Indian industrial relations system: struggling to address the dynamics of a globalizing economy', *Journal of Industrial Relations*, 51(3): 395–410.

Jain, D. C. (2007) *Commentaries on Industrial Disputes Act 1947*, 3rd edn, Mumbai: Labour Law Agency.

Kelly, J. (1998) *Rethinking Industrial Relations: Mobilization, Collectivism and Long Waves*, London: Routledge.

Kuruvilla, S. and Erickson, C.L. (2002) 'Change and transformation in Asian industrial relations', *Industrial Relations*, 42(2): 171–227.

Lee, S., McCann, D. and Torm, N. (2008) 'The World Bank's employing workers index: findings and critiques: a review of recent evidence', *International Labour Review*, 147(4): 416–32.

Mathur, A. N. (1991) *Industrial Restructuring and Union Power*, New Delhi: ILO-ARTEP.

—— (1992) 'Employment security and industrial restructuring in India', paper presented at the National Seminar on Restructuring the Indian Economy, Calcutta, 17–18 January.

National Commission on Labour (2002) Ministry of Labour, Government of India, available at: www.labour.nic.in/lcomm2/nlc_report.html.

OCED (1996) *The 1994 OECD Jobs Strategy*, Paris: OECD. Available at: www.oecd.org/dataoecd/57/7/1868601.pdf.

—— (2006) *Boosting Jobs and Incomes: Policy Lessons from Reassessing the OECD Jobs Strategy*, Paris: OECD. Available at: http://www.oecd.org/els/emp/boostingjobsandincomestheoecdjobsstrategy.htm.

Pal, R. (2008) 'Estimating the probability of trade union membership in India: impact of communist parties, personal attributes and industrial characteristics', Mumbai, India: Indira Gandhi Institute of Development Research, Working Paper 015. Available at: http://www.igidr.ac.in/pdf/publications/WP-2008-015.pdf (accessed 25 April 2012).

Panagariya, A. (2008) *India: The Emerging Giant*, Oxford: Oxford University Press.

Papola, T. S. (2004) 'Globalisation, employment and social protection: emerging perspectives for the Indian workers', *The Indian Journal of Labour Economics*, 47(3): 541–50.

——, Pais, J. and, Sahu, P.P. (2007) *Labour Regulation in Indian Industry: Towards a Rational and Equitable Framework*, New Delhi: Institute for Studies in Industrial Development.

Peters, G. B. (2011) 'Approaches in comparative politics', in D. Caramani (ed.) *Comparative Politics*, 2nd edn, New York: Oxford University Press.

Ramaswamy, E. A. (1983) 'The Indian management dilemma: economic vs political unions', *Asian Survey*, 23(8): 976–90.

—— (1997) *A Question of Balance: Labour, Management and Society*, Oxford: Oxford University Press.

Ray, A.S. (2008) 'Axing regularisation', *Combat Law*, (Nov.–Dec.): 96–7.

Reserve Bank of India website. Available at: www.rbi.org.in.

Rodrik, D. (1997) *Has Globalization Gone Too Far?*, Washington, DC: Institute for International Economics.

Roy Choudhary, S. (2008) 'Class in industrial disputes: case studies from Bangalore', *Economic and Political Weekly*, 31 May, 28–36.

Saini, D. S. (2010) 'The Contract Labour Act 1970: issues and concerns', *The Indian Journal of Industrial Relations*, 46(1): 32–44.

—— (2011) 'Employment law framework: structure and potential hurdles', in P. S. Budhwar and A. Varma (eds) *Doing Business in India: Building Research-Based Practice*, London: Routledge.

Sankaran, T. S. (2009) 'A critique of India's Unorganised Worker's Social Security Act 2008', *Lawyers Magazine*. Available at: www.sacw.net/article658.html (accessed 2 May 2012).

Sen, S. and Dasgupta, B. (2009) *Unfreedom and Waged Work: Labour in India's Manufacturing Industry*, New Delhi: Sage.

Sen Gupta, A. K. and Sett, P. K. (2000) 'Industrial relations law, employment security and collective bargaining in India: myths, realities and hopes', *Industrial Relations Journal*, 31(2): 144–53.

Sharma, N. (2008) 'Honda, Garaziano – symbols of two extremes: mismanagement can turn SEZs into hot spots', *Trade Union Record*, 21 September–5 October.

Shrouti, A. and Nandkumar, G. (1995) *New Economic Policy and Changing Management Strategies: Impact on Workers and Unions*, New Delhi: Friedrich Ebert Stiftung/Maniben Kara Institute.

Shyam Sundar, K. R. (2008) 'Trade unions in India: from politics of fragmentation to politics of expansion and integration?', in J. Benson and Y. Zhu (eds) *Trade Unions in Asia*, London: Routledge.

—— (2009a) *Labour Institutions and Labour Reforms in Contemporary India: The State and the Labour Reforms Debate*, vol. 2, Hyderabad: The ICFAI University Press.

—— (2009b) *Labour Institutions and Labour Reforms in Contemporary India: Trade Unions and Industrial Conflict*, vol. 1, Hyderabad: The ICFAI University Press.

—— (2009c) *Current State and Evolution of Industrial Relations in Maharashtra*, Geneva: International Labour Organization.

—— (2010) *Industrial Conflict in India: Is The Sleeping Giant Waking Up?*, New Delhi: Bookwell.

Singh, G. (2008) 'Judiciary jettisons working class', *Combat Law: The Human Rights and Law Bimonthly*, 7(6): 24–33.

Thakker, A. R. (2009) *Labour Law: Highlights of Major Labour Enactments in India*, Mumbai: Mill Mazdoor Welfare Trust.

Tilly, C. (1978) *From Mobilization to Revolution*, New York: McGraw-Hill.

Van Wersch, H. (1992) *The Bombay Textile Strike, 1982–83*, Bombay: Oxford University Press.

Venkata Ratnam, C. S. (2003) *Negotiated Change: Collective Bargaining, Liberalization and Restructuring in India*, New Delhi: Sage.

Weiss, L. (ed.) (2003) *States in the Global Economy: Bringing Domestic Institutions Back In*, New York: Cambridge University Press.

World Bank (2009) *Doing Business 2009 Report*: Basingstoke: Palgrave Macmillan and the World Bank.

18 China

Mingwei Liu

Introduction

China's economic reform, now in its fourth decade, has gradually transformed the country from a planned economy to a mixed economy with elements of both market mechanisms and central planning. While market mechanisms have become increasingly important in resource allocation, the state still plays a critical role in economic coordination and its role has even been strengthened since the 2008–2009 global financial crisis. Moreover, the authoritarian political structure remains. The so-called 'socialist market economy' is thus characterized by dualism of coordination (involving the coexistence of bureaucratic and market forms of coordination). Nonetheless, this variety of capitalism has led to 10 per cent average annual GDP growth for more than 30 years; has lifted millions out of poverty; and has developed a burgeoning middle class, which is already larger than the entire population of the USA (Wang 2011).

The market-oriented reform has significantly changed China's employment structure. In contrast to the dramatic decline of agricultural employment, employment in the industry and service sectors has sharply increased (see Table 18.1). Moreover, state sector employment has dropped from 60.4 per cent of total formal employment in 1978 to 14.5 per cent in 2010, whereas that in the private sector, including private-owned enterprises (POEs), foreign-invested enterprises (FIEs), and township and village enterprises (TVEs), has rapidly increased. Finally, employment in China has become increasingly informalized, as suggested by an urban undocumented employment rate of 32.8 per cent (one of the measurements of informal employment in China) in 2010.

Along with the change of employment structure has come the transformation of employment relations. Under the planned economy, the Chinese employment relations system was extremely rigid and centralized. In general, workers in state-owned enterprises (SOEs) and collective-owned enterprises (COEs) enjoyed lifetime employment; standard, stable, and egalitarian wages; and 'cradle-to-grave' welfare including free housing, medical benefits, pensions, and various social and entertainment needs. Within three decades, however, the so-called 'iron rice bowl' has gradually been smashed. First, the gradually instituted labour contract system has changed employment from lifetime to contract-based, granting management autonomy in terms of hiring and firing, though legal procedures have to be followed and there are still significant restrictions on SOEs in terms of large-scale dismissals. Second, the state-administered reward system has been moving toward full autonomy of management over wages. Although the state still intends to influence wage levels, structures, and growth at the macro level and in SOEs, particularly through the non-mandatory wage guideline system, such influence has been continuously declining. Third, contributory social insurance schemes including pensions, medical, unemployment, work injury, and maternity insurance, as well as housing funds, have

Table 18.1 China's changing employment structure, 1978–2010

	Total employment (10,000)	*Agriculture (%)*	*Industry (%)*	*Service (%)*	*Total formal employment (10,000)*	*State-owned units (%)*	*Collective-owned units (%)*	*Mixed ownership units (%)*	*Private-owned enterprises (%)*	*Foreign invested enterprises (%)*	*Township and village enterprises (%)*	*Individual-owned business (%)*	*Urban informal employment (%)*
1978	40152	70.5	17.3	12.2	12341	60.38	16.60				22.91	0.12	0
1985	49873	62.4	20.8	16.8	19787	45.43	16.80	0.19		0.03	35.27	2.27	0
1990	64749	60.1	21.4	18.5	25597	40.42	13.86	0.38	0.66	0.26	36.20	8.22	13.57
1995	68065	52.2	23.0	24.8	33723	33.39	9.33	1.10	2.83	1.52	38.14	13.68	8.95
2000	72085	50.0	22.5	27.5	31881	25.41	4.70	4.21	7.55	2.01	40.21	15.90	35.26
2005	74647	44.8	23.8	31.4	36222	17.91	2.24	7.40	16.08	3.44	39.40	13.53	38.49
2010	76105	36.7	28.7	34.6	45083	14.45	1.32	8.50	20.89	4.05	35.25	15.54	32.81

Source: *China Statistics Yearbooks*, various years.

Notes: Mixed ownership units include cooperative units, joint ownership units, limited liability, and share-holding corporations.
Foreign invested enterprises include investments from Hong Kong, Taiwan, and Macao.
Urban informal employment is calculated as % of 'missing urban employment' in the official statistics of total urban employment.

been introduced to replace the 'cradle-to-grave' welfare system. However, these schemes have been enforced to different degrees, and a huge number of workers – especially migrant workers – are still excluded. Finally, the 1994 Labour Law, the 2007 Labour Contract Law, and the 2010 Social Insurance Law have further codified these changes, indicating the establishment of the new employment relations system characterized by contractual regulation.

The sections below provide closer examination of the transformation of Chinese employment relations, followed by a review of major theoretical perspectives in understanding this transformation. The chapter concludes by discussing possible future developments of Chinese employment relations.

The actors in employment relations

While in most countries trade unions, employers and their associations, and government are the three major employment relations actors, in China it is important to add workers as the fourth, separate actor, as government-sponsored trade unions are not a genuine representative of labour, and independent union organizing is still banned. In addition, as an emerging actor, labour non-governmental organizations (NGOs) have started to play a role in Chinese employment relations. Since the economic reform in 1978, not only have the four major actors themselves experienced significant changes, but their relationships have been reshaped. The changes in the power relationships between these actors are shown in Figure 18.1 and elaborated below.

Government

It is impossible to understand Chinese employment relations without a deep understanding of the Chinese government, or more accurately, the Party-state. Under the planned economy, the state was the single employer which set up detailed plans from the national level down to individual workplaces on production, allocation of resources and workers, and even

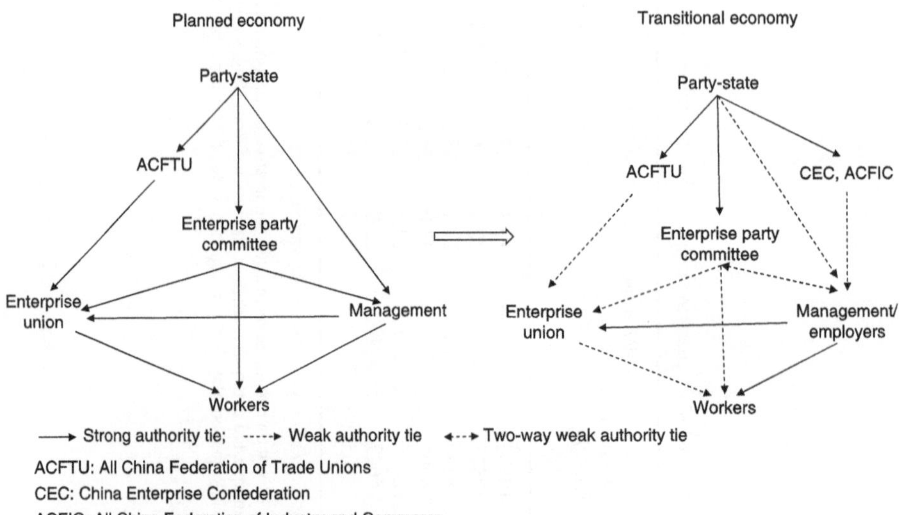

Figure 18.1 The changing power relationships of employment relations actors.

wage and welfare levels. Given the importance of political control, Party secretaries were the primary figures in enterprises, in charge of organizing the political power of the Party as well as economic and social activities (Walder 1986). Managers, under the leadership of enterprise Party committees, were simply agents of the state, lacking autonomy in production and employment issues. Moreover, as the Party-state claimed to represent the interests of the working class, the representative role of trade unions was redundant. Thus, labour–management relations appeared as vertical administrative relationships between workers and the state (Taylor *et al.* 2003).

Since the economic reform, the state has gradually withdrawn from micromanagement of workplaces. This is particularly true for the private sector in which employers have full autonomy in business operations and employment, albeit within legal frameworks. In SOEs and COEs, management no longer needs to fulfil political functions for the state, and Party committees are made either separate from, or subservient to, management in daily business operation. Nonetheless, the state still maintains considerable influence in SOEs, particularly through its appointment of top managers. Yet, this influence often tends to strengthen rather than weaken managerial despotism in the workplace, as the state and management have the common goal of improving economic efficiency (Gallagher 2005).

Despite the development of markets, heavy and frequent state intervention is still a key feature of the Chinese economy. Through the use of monetary and fiscal policies, legal regulations, centralized economic planning, industrial policies, and even direct administrative intervention including direct government investments, administrative approval of projects and the use of land, credit control through state-owned banks, and administrative control of market prices, the state aims to promote economic growth and employment, stabilize prices, and maintain an equilibrium balance of payments. The high degree of state regulation of, and intervention in, the economy may contribute to China's economic stability and strong growth during the global financial crisis, though unpredictable state economic intervention itself may also cause uncertainties in product markets (Liu 2009).

In addition to its roles as employer and macro-economic manager, the state acts as regulator, arbitrator and mediator, inspector, and welfare provider in employment relations. First, the state has established an individual labour rights-based legal framework to regulate the emerging labour market, at the centre of which is the labour contract system. Second, when conflicts arise between labour and management, the state may act as arbitrator or mediator, either formally when labour dispute cases are filed to various government agencies or informally when workers go on spontaneous strikes or protests against their employers. Third, to ensure the enforcement of various labour laws and regulations, the state takes the responsibility of inspecting the workplace, though the effect of such inspection has been very limited due to the intervention of pro-capital local governments and inadequate quantity and quality of labour inspectors (Cooney 2007; Liu 2009; Taylor *et al.* 2003). Finally, to pacify the workers affected by the economic reform and to promote employment, the state provides re-employment training, job search assistance, basic medical insurance, and minimum livelihood guarantees to urban laid-off workers and free skills training to migrant workers. Though these government welfare projects have various drawbacks, they do provide certain basic social security and help to the most disadvantaged workers in China.

Employers and employers organizations

Under the planned economy, managers had the status of cadres who were workplace agents of the Party-state in charge of production, distribution of goods and services, and upholding the interest of the Party. The economic reform, however, has diversified the forms and nature of employers and led to the emergence and rapid growth of professional managers.

Employment relations in enterprises with different ownership status tend to vary, as these enterprises operate in different historical, political, economic, and legal contexts (though all types of enterprises have to comply with the same labour laws). In SOEs, managers still hold the status of Party-state cadres and can be transferred to Party or government posts at any time. In addition, SOEs still have to act within the interests of the Party-state. In the field of employment relations, this often means that SOEs have to balance economic objectives with political concerns such as industrial peace. Therefore, while various capitalist labour practices have spread in SOEs, employment security and welfare are still relatively high in most of them, especially those holding monopolistic or strategic positions in the Chinese market. In SOEs that have experienced severe financial loss or corruption, however, both employment security and welfare have been eroded and there can be tensions between labour and management.

In FIEs, especially in those wholly owned by foreign investors, management has full autonomy in its business operation and has pioneered various capitalist labour practices (Gallagher 2005). In large Western-invested enterprises, commitment-oriented human resource practices have helped attract high-flying technical and managerial employees and maintain largely stable employment relations. Yet in some Asian-invested enterprises, sweatshop or inhumane working conditions prevail and there have been waves of strikes as well as astounding levels of employee turnover, more than 100 per cent annually in many manufacturing enterprises in Southern China (Liu and Sun 2012).

There are two major types of POEs in China: one is restructured from SOEs, COEs or TVEs, mainly through management buy-outs, and the other is founded by private entrepreneurs, most of whom started from family businesses. Most POEs are small or medium-sized and there are a large number of owner-managers who usually adopt a paternalistic management style. Working conditions in most POEs are similar to, if not worse than, those in Asian-invested enterprises and employment relations are volatile. In addition, there are many 'invisible' POEs or so-called 'black factories', where the most brutal labour practices such as child labour and slave labour are common.

Employer organizations did not exist under the planned economy. In 1979, the state created the China Enterprise Confederation (CEC) to link cadres in SOEs with government, and later consolidated it into the China Enterprise Directors' Association. The CEC was granted a monopoly by the Party-state to represent all types of employers in 1999 and became a formal employer representative when the national tripartite consultation committee was established in 2001. Although the CEC is still the sole employer representative of China in the International Labour Organization's tripartite structures, within China its monopoly has been broken due to its institutional weaknesses such as non-independence from government, lack of influence in the private sector, and absence at the county level and below (Lee *et al.* 2011). Another major employer association is the All China Federation of Industry and Commerce (ACFIC), a top-down organization representing domestic private employers. Although the ACFIC is highly dependent on the Party-state for its governance and functioning, it is often able to speak for employer interests due to its high political status, which is equivalent to that of the eight 'democratic parties'.[1] The ACFIC added the industrial relations function in 2008 to meet the representation needs of private employers and was included in the national tripartite consultation in 2010. At the local level, more and more ACFIC branches and affiliates have participated in local tripartite consultation, with or without the presence of CEC. In addition, there are employer associations based on sector, territory, and types of enterprises. While many of them have close ties with government, an increasing number are local-level voluntary associations of private entrepreneurs and foreign employers which have a range of functions including coordination of employment-related issues.

Trade unions

The All China Federation of Trade Unions (ACFTU) is the single official union in China, which adopts a pyramidal top-down structure of organization consisting of three tiers: the national, regional, and primary levels. At the bottom level, primary unions are organized according to the principle of enterprise unionism, while regional level unions are set up both along industrial lines and within geographical boundaries, with a parallel structure to that of the government administration. Trade unions at all levels are under the leadership of the Party, and this structure has largely remained unchanged since the 1950s. Still a Leninist union, the ACFTU plays a dual-function role, representing the interest of both the state and labour. At the workplace, unions traditionally perform two functions: promoting production and dealing with social welfare issues (Ng and Warner 1998).

To meet the challenge of market transition, two new functions have been added: collective consultation and labour disputes mediation. In addition, the reinstatement of Staff and Workers' Representative Congresses (SWRCs), which legally have the rights of consultation and codetermination on a wide range of business and employment issues and the power to appoint and dismiss enterprise directors and managers, provides unions with more authority in workplace decision-making, at least in principle, since enterprise unions are executive bodies of SWRCs and are responsible for organizing the election of SWRC delegates. However, these new functions and authority have failed to empower the ACFTU, due to its unchanged nature and structure. As a 'mass organization' of the Party, the power of the ACFTU comes from its status in the Party-state structure rather than from its role with organized labour (Chen 2009). Consequently, while the ACFTU at the national and regional levels, thanks to its quasi-government status, may be able to confront employers in certain circumstances, at the enterprise level, unions are often powerless and subordinated to management. Moreover, ACFTU's income comes primarily from enterprises through a 2 per cent deduction on total payroll. Although union members are also required to turn in 0.5 per cent of their wages as union dues, this policy is not widely implemented. The sources of union finance further increase the subordination of enterprise unions to employers, as does the indifference of workers to unions.

The extremely weak workplace influence of the ACFTU has led to several severe crises. As Table 18.2 indicates, the ACFTU's membership declined significantly in the 1990s, due to the large-scale restructuring of SOEs and the difficulty of setting up unions in the private sector. In addition, the ACFTU had met increasing difficulty in collecting union fees from enterprises; it faced extreme shortages of staff; and it experienced declining social relevance (Liu 2010a).

For its own survival and with the support of the Party that wants the unions to play a role in maintaining industrial peace, the ACFTU at all levels has made efforts to strengthen its representative role within the Party-state's political framework. At the national level, the ACFTU has been very active in inserting pro-labour articles into various labour regulations. In particular, it played a critical role in the enactment of the highly controversial Labour Contract Law, ensuring the passage of many articles that were favourable to workers. At the regional level, in addition to actively participating in local labour policy-making, regional union federations have initiated some new organizing methods, forms, and bargaining

Table 18.2 Development of Chinese trade unions, 1993–2010

Year	Union members (000)	Unionized grassroots units (000)	Union density (per cent)	Collectiv contract coverage (per cent)	Wage agreement coverage (per cent)	Per cent of grassroots units with SWRC system	Per cent of unionized grassroots units convening SWRC	Per cent of unionized grassroots units with LDMC	Per cent of unionized grassroots units with LPMIC
1993	101761	627	37.19			57.23	47.85	23.6	21.4
1994	102025	583	35.62			54.60	48.84	21.2	18.2
1995	103996	593	34.66			50.08	43.77	21.5	24.5
1996	102189	587	32.52	12.09		54.39	47.82	26.3	22.4
1997	91310	510	28.42	14.00		56.10	49.71	24.9	25.4
1998	89134	504	27.56	20.59		67.92	64.01	37.1	30.3
1999	86899	509	26.77	14.12		61.75	58.21		
2000	103134	859	30.81	17.91		33.53	29.74	25.9	22.4
2001	121523	1538	35.78	20.54		18.93			
2002	133978	1713	39.10	17.88	8.00	19.33	16.89	9.63	7.84
2003	123405	1574	35.08	18.87	10.1	22.29	17.48	9.73	9.59
2004	136949	1935	36.93	18.36	9.59	19.05	15.80	10.1	9.42
2005	150294	2331	38.79	25.91	9.59	18.52	14.70	9.89	9.58
2006	169942	2753	42.02	27.29	9.19	32.71	27.60	9.35	9.58
2007	193290	3193	46.19	29.96	9.48	34.02	28.28	9.74	10.2
2008	212171	3682	49.66	34.06	11.9	42.58	35.59	10.5	11.6
2009	226344	3959	51.75	37.03	14.1	46.45	39.78	10.7	12.0
2010	239965	4318	53.66	41.29	16.9	52.11	43.26	11.9	12.7

SWRC: Staff and Workers' Representative Congress; LDMC: Labor Dispute Mediation Committee; LPMIC: Labor Protection Monitoring Inspecting Committee.

Union densities are calculated as ratios of union members to total non-agriculture employment (i.e. total employment-agriculture labour-self-employed individuals); collective contract coverages and wage agreement coverages are calculated as ratios of workers covered by contract and wage agreements to total non-agriculture employment respectively.

Sources: China Statistics Yearbook (various years); China Trade Union Statistics Yearbook (various years); the Statistical Report on the Development of Trade Union Organization and Work (2009–2010); and the author's calculation.

approaches. These include the grassroots mobilization and organizing method adopted in the unionization of the first batch of Wal-Mart stores in China, the various forms of union associations for workers in small POEs and the informal sector, and sectoral wage negotiation (Liu *et al.* 2011). At the workplace level, the ACFTU has tried to empower its enterprise branches through introducing or strengthening various union functions and activities such as collective consultation, SWRCs, and labour dispute mediation committees. Moreover, several provinces have experimented with direct elections of enterprise union leaders by workers.

While the various pro-labour regulations may provide a favourable institutional environment for labour in the long run, most of the ACFTU's recent efforts have failed to improve working conditions (ibid.). In particular, the subordination of enterprise unions to management has made all the workplace union institutions and activities aiming to strengthen union power and protect workers' interests become largely formalities. As a result, the significant increases in union membership, collective contract and wage agreement coverage, and the number of union governance institutions in recent years (see Table 18.2), to a large extent, may mean nothing for workers. For instance, in its 'organizing' campaigns, the ACFTU assigns quotas to its regional branches, which usually set up grassroots unions by gaining the approval of employers rather than mobilizing workers. Although the law stipulates that enterprises with 25 or more employees should establish a grassroots union, it is still not easy for regional unions to influence private or foreign employers. In addition to asking the Party-state to impose pressures on employers, 'regional unions often have to sacrifice many union rights by guaranteeing no collective action, allowing employers to appoint union leaders and determine union functions, and reducing union fees in exchange for the establishment of grassroots unions' (Liu 2010a). Even so, unionization statistics may be fabricated by lower-level unions to achieve organizing quotas (ibid.). Workers, however, are often signed up by their employers with or without their knowledge or join unions voluntarily, since by doing so they have nothing to lose. Although this pattern of 'organizing' has rapidly increased union membership, the resultant unions tend to be toothless or merely exist on paper (Liu 2010a; Liu and Li 2012).

Workers and labour NGOs

Under the planned economy, urban workers in SOEs and COEs were the main body of the working class, who enjoyed not only high political and social status but also economic privileges attached with their employment. Consequently, workers developed an all-encompassing dependency on their enterprises which included political, social, economic, and personal aspects (Walder 1986).

The economic reform has transformed workers, the former 'masters of the country', to commodities in the labour market and fragmented the formerly homogenous working class. First, the smashing of the 'iron rice bowl' in SOEs and COEs has deprived urban workers of privileges and resulted in lay-offs of 70.66 million between 1996 and 2005, according to China's official labour statistics. While those who remain employed in SOEs or COEs are now working with labour contracts, flexible wages, and contributory social insurance, a large number of laid-off workers are struggling to make ends meet. Most of the laid-off workers are in their forties or fifties, and find it difficult to gain re-employment in the private sector due to their age or low or outdated skills. They are often dependent on government subsidies, and highly immobile for fear of losing the residual welfare provided by either their former enterprises or local governments (Tomba 2011). These laid-off workers have become the biggest 'losers' in China's market transition.

An even more salient change is that millions of rural peasants, thanks to the loosening state control of labour mobility, have flooded the cities and work mostly in manufacturing plants, construction sites and low-end service industries. According to the National Bureau of Statistics, the total number of rural peasant workers was 242.23 million in 2010, of which 153.35 million were migrant workers who left the countryside to work in the city. Some 58.4 per cent of these migrant workers were born after 1980, the so-called second generation of peasant workers. Compared with urban workers, migrant workers are less educated and skilled, but more mobile and flexible and less demanding. Due to China's migration regime and household registration system, most migrant workers are not able to become urban citizens, especially in large cities, and therefore have to apply for temporary residence permits to work and live in cities. They are often abused in the workplace, discriminated against by urban residents, and excluded from the education and social security systems.

In contrast to laid-off workers and migrant workers who have been deeply affected by China's market reform, civil servants (about 7 million) and quasi-civil servants (about 50 million) in the government sector and employees in large, profitable SOEs still enjoy stable employment, relatively high wages, and even more generous welfare and higher social and economic status than under the planned economy (Cui and Ma 2007; Wangyi Finance 2012). In addition, China has seen a rapidly growing number of young professionals who are well educated, have different values from the older generation of workers, and are highly sought after by large POEs and FIEs (Powell 2012).

In the workplace, the non-presence or marginalization of enterprise Party committees and unions leaves workers directly under managerial tyranny. The high dependency of workers on enterprises has to a large extent been transformed into 'disorganized despotism', though in a few SOEs workers may still exert some influence on their welfare (Lee 1999; Chan and Unger 2009).

Labour NGOs have emerged in China since the early 1990s, most of which are run by former worker plaintiffs, lawyers, and academics, registered as a business or not registered at all due to the government control of the registration of social organizations, and financially sponsored, more or less, by international foundations or organizations (Chan 2012). While large labour NGOs often have close connections with government agencies or institutions, small and medium ones have been frequently harassed or repressed by the government (Friedman and Lee 2010). The major activities of labour NGOs include providing workers with various legal services and labour education, helping workers get back unpaid wages, and participating in the corporate social responsibility movement (Lee and Shen 2011; Chan 2012). Through these activities, labour NGOs have played an important role in raising workers' awareness of labour laws, building up informal networks that can provide workers with mutual support and help, and protecting workers' legal rights and interests (Chan 2012). However, many limitations remain due to the government control of social organizations' operational space and the labour NGOs' lack of resources (ibid.). Moreover, as argued by Lee and Shen (2011), the focus of the labour NGOs' activities on the state-defined individual labour rights may lead to an anti-solidarity tendency rather than cultivating workers' collective power.

The processes of employment relations

Collective consultation

The equal consultation and collective contract system was formally introduced in China in 1994, and gives the ACFTU a formal role in negotiating wages, benefits, and other working conditions as workers' representative. However, this system differs from Western-style collective bargaining in that it emphasizes the non-adversarial and non-confrontational nature of the consultation process (Warner and Ng 1999). Recently the collective contract system has expanded from the enterprise to regional and sectoral levels and significantly increased its coverage (see Tables 18.2 and 18.3). However, at the enterprise level unions are too weak to take the workers' side: the process of collective consultation is usually formalistic without worker involvement and collective contracts are largely reproductions of obligations already stipulated in the existing labour regulations (Clarke *et al.* 2004; Liu *et al.* 2011). There are a few exceptions, though. In some profitable SOEs and international joint ventures, enterprise unions, with the support of Party branches or even local governments, are able to speak for workers to a certain extent in the collective consultation process and conclude some meaningful collective contracts. For example, in the Sino-Japanese joint venture studied by Liu and Li (2012), the union, with the strong support of the Chinese management side, gained substantial wage increases as well as resolving workers' grievances through collective consultation.

The two new forms of collective contracts–regional collective contracts and local sectoral collective contracts –are institutionalized by the Labour Contract Law. While regional collective consultation tends to share the same formalistic process as its counterpart at the enterprise level, a few local sectoral collective negotiations are approaching Western-style collective bargaining and may contribute to increasing real wages and improving working conditions (Liu 2010a; Pringle 2011). The short-term development of local sectoral collective consultation may be very limited, however, because it requires favourable preconditions such as a high concentration of small and medium-sized POEs in the local industry, a tight local labour market, capable union leaders, and strong government support (Liu 2010a).

While the collective contract system has largely failed to bring real gains to workers, embryonic but genuine collective bargaining, initiated by workers through spontaneous industrial action, has emerged in China and led to significant improvements in pay and working conditions. In the highly publicized strike at the Honda auto parts factory in Guangdong, the workers, with the help of academics and the intervention of the provincial union federation, re-elected an enterprise union to bargain with management, resulting in significant wage increases in both 2010 and 2011. Although this form of worker-initiated collective bargaining is often informal and unsustainable and the success rate is still low, it has the potential to develop a genuine labour movement that can pose a real challenge to the power of capital.

Table 18.3 Collective contracts in China, 2010

	Total	*Regional collective contracts*	*Sectoral collective contracts*	*Wage agreements*	*Collective contracts on safety*	*Collective contracts on women workers*	*Other collective contracts*
Number (000)	1,407	181	130	608	178	592	22
Enterprises Covered (000)	2,438	1,108	393	1,116	243	978	40
Workers Covered (000)	184,651	45,377	22,764	75,657	23,449	49,439	2,698

Source: the ACFTU.

Labour dispute resolution

The Chinese labour dispute resolution system is characterized by 'mediation, arbitration, and two trials'. When a labour dispute arises, the parties may bring the case before the enterprise labour dispute mediation committee. As Table 18.4 shows, enterprise labour dispute mediation committees handled about seven times as many cases as labour dispute arbitration committees (LDACs) in 1994, but this ratio sharply decreased to 0.45 in 2010. The decline may be caused by a number of factors: the declining density of labour dispute mediation committees in unionized units (see Table 18.2); the rapidly decreasing settlement rate of enterprise mediation (see Table 18.4); and workers' increasing distrust of those committees, given their subordination to management. The parties in dispute may also bring the case to a local People's Mediation Committee or other mediation organizations. However, because mediation is optional and mediation awards are non-binding, this stage is often bypassed by workers.

The second stage is arbitration which is mandatory before filing the case to a court. LDACs usually attempt to conciliate a dispute before accepting or adjudicating the case. If either party is dissatisfied with the arbitral award, he or she may enter the third stage of litigation unless the case falls into certain categories (e.g. claims for small amount of unpaid wages) for which the arbitral awards are final and binding. If dissatisfied with the court verdict, either party may appeal to a higher court whose verdict is final.

The formal labour dispute resolution system was highly ineffective in resolving labour disputes and protecting workers' interests due to various flaws and shortcomings such as the high costs, the short window of time for filing applications, its narrow scope, lengthy process, biased arbitrators, collusion between government and employers, and difficulty of enforcement (Cooney 2007; Liu 2009). The 2007 Labour Dispute Mediation and Arbitration Law made some improvements such as free arbitration, an extended arbitration application period, and an increased range of issues that can be arbitrated, but did not significantly change the system. Nonetheless, the number of labour dispute cases filed to LDACs sharply increased after the 2008 labour law reform (see Table 18.4). Against the backdrop of the global financial crisis, the dramatic increase in labour dispute cases has made LDACs take a tougher position toward labour which can be seen from the significant decline of cases won by labour after 2008 (Table 18.4). Moreover, voluntary mediation has been emphasized as the preferred method of resolving labour disputes by the government. More mediation organizations have been established, especially at the community level, and the mediation function of regional union federations has been significantly strengthened. The 2011 Regulations on Enterprise Labour Dispute Negotiation and Mediation require large and medium-sized enterprises to set up labour dispute mediation committees with the hope of most labour disputes being settled at the workplace. In addition, employees filing cases to LDACs are often forced to take the mediation step first and, after 2008, the cases accepted by LDACs are more likely to be settled through mediation (Table 18.4). Yet, although labour disputes may be resolved quickly through mediation, workers are often forced to settle for less than their legally defined entitlements.

Far more labour disputes are actually settled informally. When labour disputes arise, workers first tend to negotiate settlements with management either directly or indirectly through their *guanxi* (connections) or social network (Taylor *et al.* 2003). For most workers, going through the legal procedure is their last resort and they rarely do so until they have either lost or decided to quit their jobs (Liu 2009). In addition, more and more workers choose to engage in spontaneous strikes or protests to collectively resolve their labour

Table 18.4 Labour disputes resolution in China, 1994–2010

Year	*Enterprise labour dispute mediation committees*		*Labour dispute arbitration committees*									
	Cases accepted	*Settlement rate (%)*	*Cases mediated before accepted*	*Cases accepted*	*Employees involved*	*Case settled*	*Through mediation (%)*	*Through arbitration (%)*	*Through others (%)*	*Won by employers (%)*	*Won by employees (%)*	*Partially won by both parties (%)*
1994	133,522	68.67		19,098	77,794	17,962	52.12	19.29	28.59	20.00	47.80	32.21
1995	93,578	75.57		33,030	122,512	31,415	57.27	23.14	19.60	19.70	51.80	28.50
1996	86,045	81.52		48,121	189,120	46,543	52.04	27.48	20.48	20.31	50.91	28.78
1997	72,594	65.47		71,524	221,115	70,792	46.32	21.27	32.40	16.23	56.59	27.18
1998	152,071	74.08		93,469	358,531	92,288	34.11	27.51	38.09	12.93	52.72	29.65
1999	113,381	71.65		120,191	473,957	121,289	32.61	28.62	38.77	12.92	51.97	30.88
2000	135,003	59.71		135,206	422,617	130,688	32.04	41.43	26.55	10.48	53.98	28.50
2001			63,939	154,621	467,150	150,279	28.57	48.08	23.35	20.99	47.74	31.27
2002	253,813	22.81	77,342	184,116	608,396	178,744	28.49	43.27	28.24	15.11	47.24	37.65
2003	192,692	26.87	58,451	226,391	801,042	223,503	30.32	42.85	26.82	15.33	49.02	35.56
2004	192,119	28.39	70,840	260,471	764,981	258,678	32.24	42.80	24.95	13.79	47.65	36.35
2005	193,286	21.75	93,561	313,773	744,195	306,027	34.08	43.05	22.87	12.88	47.50	39.63
2006	340,193	18.52	130,321	317,162	679,312	310,780	33.60	45.52	20.88	12.63	46.99	40.38
2007	318,609	18.57	151,902	350,182	653,472	340,030	35.13	43.82	21.05	14.47	46.16	39.37
2008	322,955	20.61	237,283	693,465	1,214,328	622,719	35.54	44.09	20.39	12.92	44.45	42.63
2009	276,000	24.64	185,598	684,379	1,016,922	689,714	36.46	42.19	21.35	13.84	36.99	49.17
2010	270,000	27.78	163,997	600,865	815,121	634,041	39.45	42.03	18.52	13.41	36.19	50.40

Sources: China Statistics Yearbook (various years); China Trade Union Statistics Yearbook (various years); the Statistical Report on the Development of Trade Union Organization and Work (2009–2010).

disputes (Lee 2007). Finally, workers in SOEs and COEs in particular may choose to use the administrative procedures to petition Party organs, superior agencies, or the government's letters and visits office, which is free and simpler than going through the legal procedure. However, it may not result in any settlements and may put petitioning workers at risk of being detained or beaten (Halegua 2008).

Tripartite consultation

China formally introduced the tripartite consultation system between representatives of government, employers and employees at the national level in 2001. By 2009, this system had been extended to 95.5 per cent of the prefectural level cities and 76.8 per cent of the counties/districts (Liu *et al.* 2011). However, there are no regulations on the structure, functions, and procedures of tripartite consultation. At the national level, the representatives of government, employers and employees are the Ministry of Human Resources and Social Security (MHRSS), the CEC and the ACFIC, and the ACFTU. At the local level, the representatives of government and employers are more diverse which may also include other government agencies in charge of the administration of enterprises, other forms of employer organizations, and even a few large enterprises. While the ACFTU is the most active party in pushing forward the tripartite consultation system at all levels, it is the MHRSS and its local offices that dominate the system. The goal of the tripartite system is to promote stable employment relations through strengthening communication and coordination among the three parties and its functions are centred on providing policy advice and recommendations and seeking solutions to practical issues of employment relations.

A recent study by Shao *et al.* (2011) suggests that this embryonic tripartite system has some achievements to its credit, including setting up a regular and systematic tripartite mechanism at both national and local levels; playing an influential role in local legislation and policy-making; and effectively reducing labour disputes. However, the impact of tripartism has been greatly restrained by several factors: the disproportionately large influence of the government representatives, the non-independence of the three parties, the unions' ineffective representation of workers, the lack of representation of employers, and the low status and poor capacity of employer organizations (Qiao and Appelbaum 2011). Although both the unions and employer representatives have become more autonomous in the tripartite consultation process, these 'social organizations' are still under the control of the Party-state. Their relative autonomy and their slightly different agendas are still tied up with the interests of the Party-state. Without industrial pluralism, tripartite consultation in China is far from being genuine social dialogue as seen in the West but is a functional coordination mechanism between government and quasi-government agencies (Chen, F. 2010; Qiao and Appelbaum 2011).

Employment relations outcomes

The major goal of China's economic reform is to boost economic growth, which has certainly been achieved, given the rapid and sustained GDP growth in the past few decades. In addition, workers' income, even in terms of real wages, has significantly increased over the same period (see Figure 18.2). In particular, minimum wages across China have rapidly increased in recent years, due to rising inflation and the shortage of factory workers in coastal areas. However, as Figure 18.2 shows, the share of wages in GDP has steadily declined from 17 per cent in 1980 to 11.8 per cent in 2010 and the share of labour remuneration in GDP also

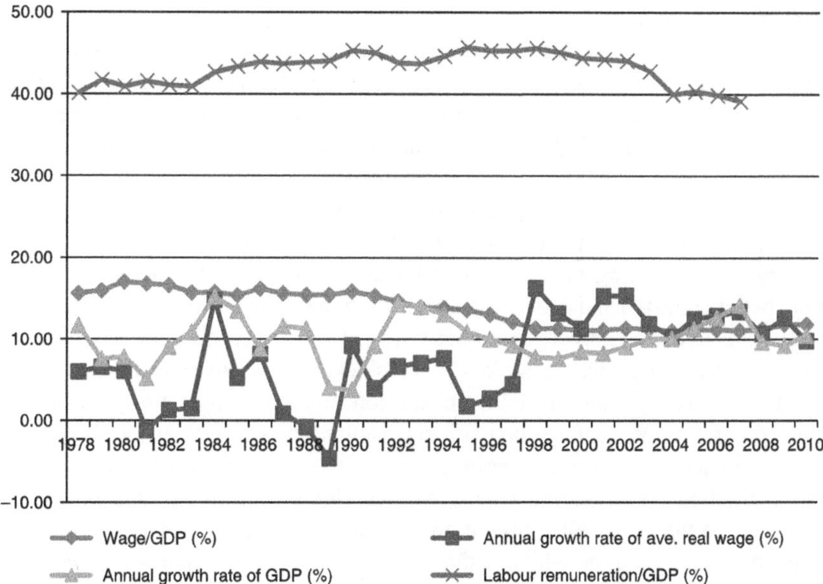

Figure 18.2 Wage, labour remuneration, and GDP, 1978–2010.

Source: *China Statistics Yearbooks* (various years); Zhang and Zhang (2010).

Note: China's official wage data may significantly overestimate wage levels of Chinese workers. According to the National Bureau of Statistics, the wage data did not cover the private sector until 2009, and even in 2009, 58 per cent of workers were excluded from the wage statistics. The real wage data also tend to be overestimated, as China's official CPI data may be significantly underestimated.

declined after the mid-1990s, which suggests that workers' income gains lagged behind economic growth. Recent wage increases, though significant, have barely kept up with sharply rising inflation, especially in basic consumption goods such as food, clothes, and housing, and Chinese wages are still very low. Another serious problem is the growth of income inequality, with the Gini coefficient reaching 0.47 in 2010 (Chen, J. 2010).

Moreover, Chinese workers' rights are frequently violated. In addition to the missing collective labour right of freedom of association, the most common individual labour right violations include no labour contracts, long working hours, non-payment of overtime and mandatory social insurance, wage arrears, unsafe or unhealthy work environments, illegal firings, and excessive fines for common workplace errors. Even in profitable SOEs, extremely long working hours and use of contingent labour are common (Liu 2009; Zhang 2010).

Given the unacceptable working conditions, many Chinese workers have 'voted with their feet' by quitting their jobs, which has contributed to the recent widespread labour shortages. In addition, labour conflicts have skyrocketed. As indicated in Table 18.4, the number of labour dispute cases accepted by LDACs increased from 19,098 in 1994 to 600,865 in 2010 and the number of employees involved increased from 77,794 to 815,121 in the same period. The major causes of labour disputes, according to official statistics, are related to pay, social insurance and welfare, alternation or termination of labour contracts, and work injuries. Yet these disputes are just the tip of the iceberg of labour conflicts. As stated earlier, the majority of labour conflicts are settled informally and there have been waves of spontaneous strikes and protests since the 1990s. According to Ministry of Public Security data, mass incidents (i.e. strikes, protests, and riots involving more than three people) increased from 8,700 in 1993 to 87,000 in 2005, and it was estimated that the number reached 127,000 in 2008 and that about one-third of these mass incidents were labour protests (Jiang 2007; *China Labour Bulletin* 2009). While labour protests occurred throughout China, most have been concentrated in the inland traditional industrial bases and export processing zones in coastal areas. Facing lay-offs, reduced or stagnant wages and benefits, and subsistence crisis, state workers in the traditional industrial bases have protested at the workplace, on the streets, and in front of local government buildings to defend their suddenly reduced livelihoods (Lee 2007).

In the new manufacturing centres in coastal areas, the second generation of migrant workers are better educated and better off materially, more attached to the pursuit of personal development and freedom, and are more prone to collective action. They have engaged in various industrial actions such as strikes, road blockages, sit-ins, and threats of suicide (Lee 2007; Chan 2010; Pun and Lu 2010). In addition, an increasing number of workers who are employed informally, such as taxi drivers, sanitation workers, and citizen-managed teachers, have joined the waves of labour protests. Strikes of migrant workers are mainly rights-based, focused on defending legally defined rights such as full and on-time wage payment, yet since the mid-2000s, the number of interest-based, offensive labour protests has significantly increased in which workers have demanded wage increases or other improvements above and beyond the law. More importantly, workers are winning, with many strikes ending in substantial gains for workers (Elfstrom and Kuruvilla 2012). In a few cases workers have even asked for more voice in workplace decision-making, such as the demand for a workers' elected union in the Honda strike mentioned earlier. Another case involved coordinated strikes by Pepsico workers in 2011, protesting at the lack of consultation on the takeover of Pepsico's bottling plants by a Taiwanese company. However, there is still little evidence that workers are demanding a political voice. Even the Honda workers did not intend to organize a union independent from the ACFTU.

Theoretical perspectives

How best can we understand the transformation of Chinese employment relations? Do market forces affect Chinese employment relations in the same way as they do in the Western market economies? How do institutions shape the unique features of Chinese employment relations? What are the roles of the state, employers, and labour in the process of employment relations transformation? In answering these questions, the growing field of China labour studies has developed several major theoretical perspectives including globalization, convergence, state corporatism, labour process, and strategic choices, which fall into the two broad categories of market-driven theories and the political economy of employment relations discussed in Chapter 2 in this volume. Though distinct from each other, these theoretical perspectives centre on the roles of the market, institutions, government, employers, unions, and workers, as well as their power relationships and interactions with each other.

Markets

Perhaps the impact of market forces on employment relations is more evident in China than in most of the other countries in this volume, as markets generally did not exist before China's economic reform. Given the unchanged political system, it may be intuitive to attribute the transformation of Chinese employment relations to the introduction of the market mechanism. Indeed, as shown in many studies, market forces have fundamentally changed the landscape of Chinese employment relations leading to their convergence toward variously defined Western models (Chan 1995a; Gallagher 2005; Liu 2009). First, the market-oriented reform has brought in the two historical processes of commodification and casualization of Chinese labour, leading to a dramatic alteration of the power relationships between workers and management (Friedman and Lee 2010). While management has gained full autonomy in business and employment, workers are often subject to the despotism of employers (Lee 1999). In addition, neo-liberal economic policies have broken the former social contract between workers and the Party-state leading to deregulation, mass lay-offs, the erosion of social welfare, and the removal of workers' entitlements (Lee 2007). The gradual integration of China into the world economy exposes both Chinese enterprises and workers to unfettered global capital. In particular, foreign direct investment has played a critical role in spreading capitalist labour practices across all types of Chinese enterprises (Gallagher 2005). Facing ever-increasing competition in both domestic and international markets, both SOEs and POEs have become 'lean and mean', adapting their employment practices to the flexibility model of the West (Liu 2009). Those Asian-invested labour-intensive enterprises, given their position in the international division of labour, however, tend to adopt highly exploitative employment practices leading to a 'race to the bottom' in labour standards (Chan 2001). Chinese workers, therefore, have become one of the most vulnerable groups in the regime of global capitalism. Nonetheless, workers have not accepted the tyranny of the market passively. As described earlier, marketization of employment relations has resulted in high levels of worker grievances and waves of spontaneous labour protests and strikes.

Therefore, to a large extent, the transformation of Chinese employment relations in the past three decades can be viewed as a story of markets, in which many protective institutions have been completely removed, significantly altered, or gradually marginalized, and the regulatory role of the state has been greatly weakened.

Institutions

Despite its strong explanatory power, the transformation of Chinese employment relations seems to be more complicated than suggested by the market account. As Lee (2007) notes, China's economic reform mixes both market-oriented and redistribution-based institutions. Such a hybrid system makes theories of either market or state insufficient to explain the changing political economy of employment relations. In particular, despite various claims of market-driven convergence, some aspects of Chinese employment relations remain unique. First, the social contract of lifetime employment, stable wages, and comprehensive welfare between employees in the public sector and the state is still intact and there are still great differences between the personnel system for government employees and the labour contract system for employees of enterprises. Second, there are significant variations in employment relations across ownership types, industries, and regions (Chan 1995b; Liu and Li 2012). In particular, in many SOEs, especially those that are profitable, employment security and welfare for the formal or core employees are still relatively high and workers still have some influence in the workplace (Chan and Unger 2009; Zhang 2010). Third, China's household registration system, an institution that imposes great restraints on labour mobility, still plays a key role in excluding migrant workers from the formal employment system, resulting in dualist employment relations in the workplace (Zhang 2010).

Fourth, the ACFTU, a key employment relations actor in China, remains an instrument of the Party-state in maintaining social stability. While trade unions in most countries have experienced significant membership loss, union density in China has dramatically increased in recent years. However, the membership of the ACFTU may be irrelevant to Chinese workers as it is not their genuine representative. Finally, the effects of markets on employment flexibility seem to be mitigated by the recent labour law reform that attempts to roll back declining employment security through new regulations on labour contracts, the use of dispatched labour (workers who are hired by employment agencies and then sent to work in their clients' work sites), labour dispute resolution, and social insurance. Therefore, China's unique institutions and circumstances may suggest that, instead of converging toward any Western model, China may be developing a model of employment relations with Chinese characteristics, a mix of elements of both capitalist and socialist employment relations. Indeed, as argued by White *et al.* (1996), without political change, convergence caused simply by economic reform is not likely.

A central claim of recent studies of comparative political economy is that 'institutions matter', which is certainly not untrue in the Chinese context. The 'varieties of capitalism' approach with its emphasis on the resilience of institutions does provide invaluable insights for our understanding of Chinese employment relations. But, in contrast to the stability or incremental path-dependent changes of institutions in advanced economies, China has experienced rapid and fundamental institutional changes in the past few decades, particularly in the area of employment relations. For a few institutions that have not significantly changed, such as those discussed above, change may be just a matter of time. In fact, the reform of the personnel system in the public sector, privatization of the remaining SOEs, and reform of the household registration system have all been on the political agenda. Moreover, while in advanced economies institutional change, if it occurs, is often caused by market pressures, in China it is the state that has ushered in new institutions (or maintained old institutions), with or without the presence of markets. The question then is, to what extent or how much do institutions matter in the transformation of Chinese employment relations compared with the role of the state?

The role of the state

In a Communist authoritarian regime like China, the state is the most powerful actor in employment relations. While the transformation of Chinese employment relations has been mainly driven by market forces, the state has facilitated, shaped, and managed the process in important ways. After all, it is the state that initiates economic reforms, introduces markets, establishes new institutions and maintains existing ones, and fundamentally defines the relationship between labour and capital. Moreover, since the mid-2000s, the most salient force driving changes in Chinese employment relations has started to shift from markets to the state (Gallagher *et al.* 2011; Deyo 2012).

Before examining the role of the state, however, it is important to note that the nature of the Party-state has significantly changed in the reform era. Although on paper it is still committed to Marxist ideology, the Party has departed from being the vanguard of the working class to representing advanced social productive forces (including capitalists and managers), the progressive development of China's culture, and the fundamental interests of the majority of the Chinese people (i.e. the 'Three Represents'). Correspondingly, the legitimacy of the Party has shifted from Marxism to economic growth and social stability (Lin 2011), which have become the operational objectives of the state. To achieve these objectives, the state has adopted the strategy of decentralized legal authoritarianism which consists of two components. The first is decentralized accumulation which, by allowing retention of fiscal revenue at local levels, induces competition across localities to liberalize local economies. The second component is legalistic legitimation of authoritarian rule, which attempts to rule the country by law without losing political monopoly (Lee 2007). However, the two objectives may have contradictory implications for economic, social, and labour policies. While economic growth necessitates market-oriented reform, the concern of social stability calls for state intervention and regulation. Consequently, there is an inherent contradiction between the twin strategies of economic decentralization and legal authoritarianism (Lee 2007). Moreover, the two objectives are weighted differently by the local and central states. In contrast to the central state's overwhelming concern with the stability of the Party's political monopoly, the local state is obsessed with economic growth, due to the incentives provided by economic decentralization. As a result, while the central state has enacted various laws aimed at providing basic labour and social protection to workers, the top priority of the local state has been given to market liberalization and attracting capital at the price of extremely weak enforcement of labour laws. The contradiction between economic growth and social stability, between the interests of the local and central state, has therefore resulted in widespread labour rights violations (Lee 2007).

To resolve the rising labour conflicts, the first response of the state, consistent with the strategy of legal authoritarianism, is to strengthen the legal system through promulgating more protective labour laws and making the labour dispute resolution system more accessible and effective. However, the inherent contradiction between economic decentralization and legal authoritarianism has not been resolved and the enforcement of individual labour rights remains very weak and uneven (Liu 2010b). Moreover, due to the incompatibility between collective labour rights or industrial democracy and political monopoly, the labour legal system is based on merely individual labour rights. The growing numbers of interest-based labour conflicts which are outside the legal framework therefore have to be resolved through a non-judicial process such as collective bargaining or mediation. Without genuine worker representation, collective consultation can hardly resolve interest disputes and neither can enterprise mediation dominated by employers or external mediation sponsored by pro-capital local states. Whether such weak, uneven, and individual labour rights-based reregulation can effectively reduce labour conflicts is therefore in serious doubt (Chen 2012).

Given the significant limitation of legal authoritarianism, the second response of the state has emerged and that is to strengthen the corporatist structures. It should be noted that while corporatism in Western capitalist democracies entails a voluntary arrangement of state, labour and capital (see Chapter 2), it takes a different form in China, i.e. state corporatism, a form of institutional arrangement wherein employers and workers are organized into corporate entities that serve as organs of the state (Schmitter 1979). The ACFTU, the CEC, and the ACFIC are all corporatist institutions that are utilized by the state to serve its interest in social control. Employment relations have faced increasing challenges since the economic reform due particularly to the exclusion of large numbers of private sector employers and workers from corporatist institutions (Unger and Chan 1995). However, because of rising labour conflicts, strengthening state corporatism, which has the potential to contain plural interests while maintaining political monopoly, becomes an attractive option for the state. Since 2000, the state has, on the one hand, maintained its tight control of the ACFTU and, on the other, strongly supported the ACFTU's efforts in organizing and representing workers, with the hope that a more inclusive and functioning official union can counter the development of independent labour movements. At the national level, the state has encouraged the

ACFTU to more actively speak up for workers in the process of labour policy-making and to more aggressively set up branches in the private sector. At the industry level, the state has played an important role in developing, coordinating, and diffusing sectoral collective bargaining, by establishing local industry associations and pressuring employers to participate in bargaining and make concessions (Liu 2010a; Pringle 2011). At the workplace level, the state has proactively intervened in collective labour conflicts and facilitated their 'voluntary' settlement via a process of quadripartite interaction between employers, workers, unions, and the state (Chen, F. 2010).

In addition, there are signs that the state may further empower enterprise unions and support their collective bargaining activities. For example, Yang Wang, the top Party leader in Guangdong Province, publicly praised the direct election of enterprise union leaders in a Japanese enterprise and called on its diffusion in 2012; and progressive regulations on collective bargaining are being promulgated in Shenzhen. Another major effort of the state in strengthening corporatist employment relations is the establishment of the tripartite consultation system from national down to local levels, which aims to facilitate participation of employers and unions in labour policy-making and settlement of collective labour conflicts. Such efforts were particularly evident during the 2008–09 global financial crisis, in which the state promoted the tripartite deal: the state helps enterprises survive through various forms of intervention; employers promise to keep workers' jobs; and workers accept lower labour standards.

Although still evolving, current state corporatism has several new features compared with the old version from the pre-reform era. First, it operates in a more pluralist context in which the interests of the state, employers, and workers differ significantly. Second, both employer organizations and the ACFTU have gained more operational autonomy. Third, as a large number of workers and employers are not covered or well represented by corporatist organizations, the state often has to engage directly with workers and employers aligning their interests with those of its own. Finally, new institutions or practices have been invented at macro, meso, and micro levels to revive state corporatism, including the tripartite consultation system, sectoral collective bargaining, enterprise collective bargaining, and quadripartite conflict resolution. Whether the emerging multi-level state corporatism can effectively reduce labour conflicts in the long run is still uncertain and may depend substantially on the extent to which the corporatist institutions can represent the interests of their constituents.

Clearly focusing on the strategies of the state significantly contributes to our understanding of change and continuity in Chinese employment relations. However, the state-centric analytical approach is not able to account for the great variations of employment relations in the workplace. Why do working conditions and employment practices vary in different enterprises? Why is there positive trade union change in some regions but not others? Despite the superior power of the state, employers, unions, and workers are still able to shape employment relations in their own ways.

Strategies of employers, unions, and workers

Transition to the market has diversified Chinese enterprises and shifted their focus from fulfilling state commands to maximizing economic efficiency. Moreover, as management has gained more autonomy in business operations, their strategies have played an important role in shaping workplace employment relations. Market forces, institutional imperatives, and state policies are either reflected by or implemented through employer strategies. First, under the pressures of market competition, employers have adopted various labour control and flexibility strategies to cut labour costs and fragment the collective interests of workers: the dormitory labour regime (where working and living are combined by using employer-controlled accommodation), lay-offs, informal employment, and hierarchical reward systems (Gallagher 2005; Pun and Smith 2007; Liu 2009; Zhang 2010). Second, though there are legal regulations regarding the establishment and functions of unions in China, employers have developed different strategies toward union organizing and functioning which play a key role in shaping unionization outcomes at the enterprise level (Liu 2010a; Liu and Li 2012). Finally, despite state regulations on working conditions and labour practices, employers are able to ignore, evade, or reduce their implementation, leading to uneven enforcement of labour regulations in the workplace (Liu 2010b).

Because state corporatism remains the fundamental institutional framework for its development, the ACFTU's identity, structure, and functions have not significantly changed since the economic reform. Then, the question is, can a Party-led non-democratic trade union effectively represent its members? Based on their analysis of the development of trade unions in three post-Communist transitional economies – China, Vietnam, and Russia – Clarke and Pringle (2009) argue that the major barriers for functioning collective representation are 'the inertia of the trade union apparatus and the dependence of primary union organizations on management', while the impact of the Party's control of unions is secondary and mainly limited to the political sphere. However, at least in China, both the inertia of the unions and the primary unions' dependence on management are rooted in the structural deficiencies of the ACFTU, which the ACFTU itself cannot change without the Party's permission. Moreover, given the close relationship between the Party-state and capital, the subordination of unions to the Party often makes them unable to effectively confront employers. Thus, although union dependence on the Party may grant unions certain political power, this may fundamentally affect their representative role in the long run (Liu 2010a). Nonetheless, it should be noted that the ACFTU is no longer a monolithic institution. Its regional branches have differed significantly with respect to their degree, focus, and method of implementing its polices and some have even taken a few locally initiated strategies such as new organizing methods and new forms of collective negotiation (Liu 2010a; Liu *et al.* 2011; Pringle 2011). Therefore, to understand the growing variation within the ACFTU, it is important to focus on the strategies and actions of lower-level unions.

The analytical approaches of markets, institutions, and state tend to overlook the role of workers in the process of employment relations transformation. Yet Chinese workers are not simply passive victims of market forces, repressive labour institutions, and state neo-liberal policies. Although lacking the support of formal institutions, workers' spontaneous industrial actions have put great pressure on employers, the ACFTU, and the state. It is workers' strikes and bargaining that are forcing many employers to increase wages and improve working conditions (Chan 2010). In addition, workers' industrial actions are the fundamental driving force in the reform of the ACFTU (Liu 2010a; Pringle 2011). Even the enactment of progressive labour regulation is essentially due to the state's concern with social stability. Therefore, it is difficult to understand Chinese employment relations without a proper understanding of the strategies and actions of Chinese workers.

The analysis above suggests the merits of different theoretical perspectives in understanding Chinese employment relations, but the example below shows that multiple perspectives often need to be integrated to gain comprehensive understanding of an employment relations phenomenon. A puzzle in the recent development of Chinese employment relations is why there have been widespread labour protests in a still stable authoritarian state which is supposed to be hostile to collective action. From the perspective of markets, it is because market reform has generated huge grievances of state workers who have benefited from socialism but are being abandoned by the state and also of the newly emerging working classes who are suffering from capitalist exploitation in production. However, rampant labour unrest has not been seen in Central and East Europe where market transition takes a more radical form. The powerful argument of Silver (2003: 41) that 'where capital goes, conflict goes' may provide an explanation: because China has become the centre of relocation of global capital, the new Chinese working classes, compared with their counterparts in Central and Eastern Europe, may be subject to more capitalist exploitation, on the one hand, and gain more marketplace and workplace power, on the other. Yet, this cannot explain why China has also seen a much larger number of protests by the old working classes (state workers and retirees) against the state's violation of the social contract. Moreover, even if workers have grievances and economic opportunities, their political concerns resulting from the lack of the right to strike may prevent them acting.

From the perspective of the state, its declining capacity to monitor the economy, the reduced appeal of the ruling party, and the contradiction between the local state's imperative for accumulation and the central state's concern with legitimation have created workers' grievances (Pei 2006; Lee 2007). In addition, the non-monolithic state, particularly the different interests of the central and local state, provides political space for workers' collective actions. Moreover, the tension between power centralization and consultation with the masses, both of which are required by the Party-state's mass line principle, has created various contradictions and ambiguities that have provided incentives and political opportunities for workers' collective action (Chen, X., 2012).

However, although both market and the state have created workers' grievances and provided opportunities, collective protests seldom happen without mobilization. From the perspective of institutions, the dormitory regime and the migrant worker communities, both of which result from the household registration system, have facilitated communication, mobilization, and the aggregation of workers' interests and demands (Lee 2007; Chan 2010). In addition, the emerging civil society in China, though still embryonic, has significantly increased workers' awareness of their rights (Elfstrom and Kuruvilla 2012). From the perspective of workers, without the leadership, mobilization, and coordination of activists, skilled workers, and even local gangs, spontaneous workers' collective actions would be rare (Lee 2007; Chan 2010).

Conclusion

This chapter presents an overview of the transformation of Chinese employment relations, with a focus on the changing power relationships between the major employment relations actors: the Party-state, the employers, the ACFTU, and the workers. Under the planned economy, Chinese employment relations were characterized by the 'iron rice bowl', which provided lifetime employment, stable wages, and comprehensive welfare to urban workers. At the workplace, workers developed high dependence on their enterprises, and labour–management relations appeared as vertical administrative relationships between workers and the Party-state. The economic reform since 1978 has smashed the 'iron rice bowl' and fundamentally changed the relationship between labour and management. Lifetime employment has been replaced with contract labour; wages have become highly variable and contingent; contributory social insurance schemes have replaced 'cradle-to-grave' welfare; and workplace relations have changed from organized dependence to disorganized despotism (Lee 1999).

This chapter has reviewed the major theoretical perspectives that have been used to explain the changing Chinese employment relations, with a focus on the role of markets, institutions, and actors' strategies. Until recently markets have played a major role in transforming Chinese employment relations. Yet institutions also matter, because some aspects of Chinese employment relations remain unchanged and Chinese employment relations still have distinct features. The state, though always important, has started to become the most salient factor driving changes in Chinese employment relations. Nonetheless, mere focus on the strategies of the state may overlook the roles of other actors, namely, the employers, the ACFTU, and the workers, who are critical for our understanding of variations within the Chinese system of employment relations.

Chinese employment relations are still evolving. Looking ahead, several trends or possibilities are noteworthy. First, the unitary employment relations may become increasingly pluralist. All of the employment relations actors are more likely to articulate their distinctive interests and the emerging new actors, including labour NGOs, multinational companies, and global civil society, are having more and more influence at the workplace. A recent example is the Apple supplier Foxconn's pledge to improve working conditions after Fair Labour Association factory audits. Second, due to increasing market competition, labour flexibility and informal employment may continue to grow. Yet, social insurance coverage may also grow, given the Party-state's concern with social stability. Third, Chinese trade unions, especially those at the regional level, may continue to change and become more representative, albeit slowly and within the framework of state corporatism. Finally, workers' spontaneous industrial actions may continue increasing in the coming years and become even more rampant if economic growth slows down. This is because economic recession may lead to more enterprise closures and restructuring which often results in labour unrest in the Chinese context. Ever-growing workers' activism may have the potential to finally change the institutional framework of state corporatism and push forward the development of genuine trade unions and collective bargaining.

Note

1 The eight 'democratic parties' are: the Revolutionary Committee of the Kuomintang, the China Democratic League, the China Democratic National Construction Association, the China Association for Promoting Democracy, the Chinese Peasants' and Workers' Democratic Party, the China Zhi Gong Party, the Jiusan Society, and the Taiwan Democratic Self-Government League.

References

Chan, A. (1995a) 'Chinese enterprise reforms: convergence with the Japanese model?', *Industrial and Corporate Change*, 4(2): 449–70.

—— (1995b) 'The emerging patterns of industrial relations in China and the rise of two new labour movements', *China Information*, 9(5): 36–59.

—— (2001) *China's Workers under Assault: The Exploitation of Labour in a Globalizing Economy*, Armonk, NY: M.E. Sharpe.

—— and Unger, J. (2009) 'A Chinese state enterprise under the reforms: what model of capitalism?', *The China Journal*, 62 (July): 1–26.

Chan, C. K-C. (2010) *The Challenge of Labour in China: Strikes and the Changing Labour Regime in Global Factories*, London: Routledge.

—— (2012) 'Community-based organizations for migrant workers' rights: the emergence of labour NGOs in China', *Community Development Journal*, Advance Access 14 March, 1–17.

Chen, F. (2009) 'Union power in China: source, operation, and constraints', *Modern China*, 35(6): 662–89.

—— (2010) 'Trade unions and the quadripartite interactions in strike settlement in China', *The China Quarterly*, 201 (March): 104–24.

Chen, J. (2010) 'Country's wealth divide past warning level', *China Daily*, 12 May.

Chen, X. (2012) *Social Protest and Contentious Authoritarianism in China*, New York: Cambridge University Press.

China Labour Bulletin (2009) *Going it Alone: The Workers' Movement in China (2007–2008)*, Hong Kong: China Labour Bulletin.

Clarke, S. and Pringle, T. (2009) 'Can party-led trade unions represent their members?', *Post-Communist Economies*, 21(1): 85–101.

Clarke, S., Lee, C. H. and Li, Q. (2004) 'Collective consultation and industrial relations in China', *British Journal of Industrial Relations*, 42(2): 235–54.

Cooney, S. (2007) 'China's labour law, compliance and flaws in implementing institutions', *Journal of Industrial Relations*, 49(5): 673–86.

Cui, G. and Ma, X. (2007) 'Causes and problems of the popularity of civil servants', *Journal of Yunnan Administrative College*, 7: 113–16.

Deyo, F. (2012) *Reforming Asian Labour Systems: Economic Transitions and Worker Dissent*, Ithaca, NY: Cornell University Press.

Elfstrom, M. and Kuruvilla, S. (2012) 'The changing nature of labour unrest in China', paper presented to the International Labour and Employment Relations Association Congress, Philadelphia, PA, July.

Friedman, E. and Lee, C. K. (2010) 'Remaking the world of Chinese labour: a 30-year retrospective', *British Journal of Industrial Relations*, 48(3): 507–33.

Gallagher, M. (2005) *Contagious Capitalism: Globalization and the Politics of Labour in China*, Princeton, NJ: Princeton University Press.

——, Lee, C. K. and Kuruvilla, S. (2011) 'Introduction and argument' in S. Kuruvilla, C. K. Lee and M. Gallagher (eds) *From Iron Rice Bowl to Informalization: Markets, Workers, and the State in a Changing China*, Ithaca, NY: Cornell University Press.

Halegua, A. (2008) 'Getting paid: processing the labour disputes of China's migrant workers', *Berkeley Journal of International Law*, 26(1): 254–322.

Jiang, S. (2007) 'Mass incidents caused by labour conflicts: a public opinion perspective', *Theory Horizon*, 3: 94–5.

Lee, C.-H., Sheldon, P., and Li, Y. (2011) 'Employer coordination and employer associations', in P. Shelton, P., Kim, S.,Li, Y. and M. Warner (eds) *China's Changing Workplace*, London: Routledge.

Lee, C. K. (1999) 'From organized dependence to disorganized despotism: changing labour regimes in Chinese factories', *The China Quarterly*, 157 (March): 44–71.

—— (2007) *Against the Law: Labour Protests in China's Rustbelt and Sunbelt*, Berkeley, CA: University of California Press.

—— and Shen, Y. (2011) 'The anti-solidarity machine? Labour nongovernmental organizations in China', in S. Kuruvilla, C. K. Lee and M. Gallagher (eds) *From Iron Rice Bowl to Informalization: Markets, Workers, and the State in a Changing China*, Ithaca, NY: Cornell University Press.

Lin, N. (2011) 'Capitalism in China: a centrally managed capitalism and its future', *Management and Organization Review*, 7(1): 63–96.

Liu, M. (2009) 'Toward labour flexibility with Chinese characteristics? The case of the Chinese construction machinery industry', Working Paper 82, Industry Studies Association, Pittsburgh, PA.

—— (2010a) 'Union organizing in China: still a monolithic labour movement?', *Industrial and Labor Relations Review*, 64(1): 30–52.

—— (2010b) 'The enforcement of the Labour Law and Trade Union Law in China', paper presented to the Chinese Trade Union Law and Labour Law: Review and Prospect Conference, Beijing Normal University, 18–19 August.

—— and Li, C. (2012) 'Environment pressures, managerial industrial relations ideologies, and unionization in Chinese enterprises', *British Journal of Industrial Relations*, online version at doi: 10.1111/j.1467–8543.2012.00908.x.

—— and Sun, Z. (2012) 'Explaining high turnover of Chinese migrant workers', Working Paper, Rutgers University, New Jersey.

——, Li, C. and Kim, S. (2011) 'Chinese trade unions in transition: a three-level analysis', in P. Shelton, S. Kim, Y. Li and M. Warner (eds) *China's Changing Workplace*, London: Routledge.

Ng, S. H. and Warner, M. (1998) *China's Trade Unions and Management*, New York: St. Martin's Press.

Pei, M. (2006) *China's Trapped Transition: The Limits of Developmental Autocracy*, Cambridge, MA: Harvard University Press.

Powell, B. (2012) 'China's talent war', *Time*, 28 May.

Pringle, T. (2011) *Trade Unions in China: The Challenge of Labour Unrest*, London: Routledge.

Pun, N. and Lu, H. (2010) 'Unfinished proletarianization: self, anger, and class action among the second generation of peasant-workers in present-day China', *Modern China*, 36(5): 493–519.

Pun, N. and Smith, C. (2007) 'Putting transnational labour process in its place: the dormitory labour regime in post-socialist China,' *Work, Employment and Society*, 21(1): 27–45.

Qiao, J. and Appelbaum, L. (2011) *Tripartite Consultation in China*, California: UCLA, Institute for Research on Labor and Employment, Research and Policy Brief No. 9.

Schmitter, P. (1979) 'Still the century of corporatism?', in P. C. Schmitter and G. Lehmbruch (eds) *Trends Towards Corporatism Intermediation*, London: Sage.

Shao, S., Nyland, C. and Zhu, C. J. (2011) 'Tripartite consultation: an emergent form of governance shaping employment relations in China', *Industrial Relations Journal*, 42(4): 358–74.

Silver, B. (2003) *Forces of Labor: Workers' Movements and Globalization Since 1870*, New York: Cambridge University Press.

Taylor, B., Chang, K. and Li, Q. (2003) *Industrial Relations in China*, Cheltenham: Edward Elgar.

Tomba, L. (2011) 'Remaking China's working class', in P. Shelton, S. Kim, Y. Li and M. Warner (eds) *China's Changing Workplace*, London: Routledge.

Unger, J. and Chan, A. (1995) 'China, corporatism, and the East Asian model', *The Australian Journal of Chinese Affairs*, 33(January): 29–53.

Walder, A. (1986) *Communist Neo-Traditionalism*, Berkeley. CA: University of California Press.

Wang, H. (2011) 'The biggest story of our time: the rise of China's middle class', *Forbes*, 21 December.

Wangyi Finance (2012) *Report on Wages in Chinese Central Government-Controlled Enterprises, 2011*. Available at: http://file.ws.126.net/money/finance/081117Stock/20110811.pdf.

Warner, M. and Ng, S.H. (1999) 'Collective contracts in Chinese enterprises: a new brand of collective bargaining under "market socialism"?', *British Journal of Industrial Relations*, 37(2): 295–314.

White, G., Howell, J., and Shang, X. (1996) *In Search of Civil Society: Market Reform and Social Change in Contemporary China*, Oxford: Clarendon Press.

Zhang, C. and Zhang, S. (2010) 'Changes in primary income distribution and resulting problems: a view of labour share in GDP', *China Population Science*, 5: 24–35.

Zhang, L. (2010) 'From Detroit to Shanghai? Globalization, market reform, and dynamics of labor unrest in the Chinese automobile industry, 1980 to the present', PhD thesis, Baltimore, MD: Johns Hopkins University.

19 South Africa

Roger Southall

The official narrative of the post-apartheid state of South Africa insists that, against a background of industrial relations in the pre-democratic era characterized by racial discrimination, conflict, cheap labour policies and authoritarian management, 'South Africa's labour legislation is among the most progressive in the world, providing for institutions to settle disputes and ensure fairness in the workplace' (South Africa Info, undated). Key parliamentary Acts passed since the inauguration of democracy in 1994 and the establishment of a battery of socially incorporationist institutions (notably the National Economic, Development and Labour Council [NEDLAC], the Commission for Conciliation, Mediation and Arbitration [CCMA] and the Commission for Employment Equity) have provided for the nurturing of 'sound, co-operative industrial relations' (ibid.). Certainly, the early years following the transition to democracy saw a marked decline in the level of strike action, albeit with a spike in the late 1990s. However, a decade later, South Africa was experiencing a surge of strikes and labour unrest (Table 19.1), with more working days being lost in 2010 as a result of strike action than in any other year on record:

Yet worse was to come, for in August 2012, South Africa was plunged into the international spotlight by a brutal industrial conflict at the Lonmin company's Marikana platinum mines in North West province, in which some 34 workers died and more than 70 were injured as a result of shootings by police after they had been called in to confront an unofficial strike. The tragedy recalled the worst days of state violence against workers under apartheid. Furthermore, whereas the post-apartheid industrial relations architecture had been intended to curb the high level of violence which had accompanied strike action during the late 1980s (Webster and Simpson 1990), the Marikana events highlighted a drift back to the use of violence by workers becoming a regular accompaniment of industrial action.[1] Consequently, for all the confusion that surrounded post-Marikana, with blame for the disaster falling variously upon the police, the government, employers and a trade union cast as having lost touch with its members, the events called into question the hopes that political democracy would usher in an era of industrial harmony.

In an early review, Webster (1998) argued that neo-liberalism undermined attempts to consolidate new democracies, threatening a return to authoritarianism, or in the worst case, social disintegration, descending into 'decentralized collective violence'. In contrast, if political democratization were to be accompanied by social policies that minimized social costs; if economic policies were designed to foster growth; and if industrial relations policies could be shaped by corporatist-style negotiation between state, unions, employers and other interest groups, the outcome would be improved policy outcomes, greater support for continuing reforms, and the further consolidation of democracy. Consequently, the South African case raised the issue whether it was possible for an industrial relations system to

Table 19.1 Working days lost as a result of strikes, 1979–2011

Year	*Number*	*Year*	*Number*
1979	100,000	1996	1,700,000
1980	250,000	1997	650,000
1981	500,000	1998	2,300,000
1982	150,000	1999	3,100,000
1983	250,000	2000	500,000
1984	950,000	2001	1,250,000
1985	1,250,000	2002	945,000
1986	1,350,000	2003	700,000
1987	9,000,000	2004	1,100,000
1988	1,500,000	2005	2,300,000
1989	3,090,000	2006	2,900,000
1990	4,000,000	2007	12,900,000+
1991	3,800,000	2008	990,000
1992	4,200,000	2009	290,000
1993	3,600,000	2010	14,600,000+
1994	3,900,000	2011	6,200,000
1995	1,600,000		

Source: SAIRR 2010–11: 417 for 1979–2010; Standard Bank (2012) for 2011. Both sources draw from data provided by Andrew Levy Employment Publications, which over decades has been regarded as a reliable and consistent source of information regarding industrial relations activity. Note, however, that the Andrew Levy figures differ considerably from those provided by the Department of Labour's annual industrial action reports which, using different methodologies, tend to offer higher estimates of the number of strikes and days lost.

Note: + Figures largely accounted for by major public sector strikes.

move in the direction of social corporatism (or 'concertation') at a time when the neo-liberal world economic order was demanding deregulation and a diminished role for the state (Webster 1998: 58).

Trade union challenge to racial exclusion under apartheid

Since the discovery of diamonds and gold in the late nineteenth century and the emergence of South Africa as a major global source of minerals, successive governments have pursued aggressive strategies of selective promotion and protection of industry. With mining heavily dominated initially by imperial and metropolitan capital, but the post-1910 state significantly shaped by Afrikaner nationalist impulses, the inter-war period was characterized by the significant growth of an Afrikaner capitalist class whose interests increasingly extended beyond agriculture into manufacturing, finance and commerce. Economic growth was premised upon the extensive use of 'extra-economic coercion' to ensure the 'cheapness' of black labour, while the white worker minority was incorporated into the development pattern, first, through the vote, which guaranteed their importance as a political constituency, and, second, through their representation within a formalized system of industrial relations. Together, the interests of Afrikaner capital and significant elements of the white working class provided for the victory of the National Party (NP) in 1948. The new government was opposed to its predecessor's policy of shifting away from reliance upon migrant African labour on short-term contracts from tribal reserves and neighbouring territories towards acceptance of the inevitability of African urbanization and 'labour stabilization' (a strategy favoured by the mining companies).

Notwithstanding official strategies to contain African urbanization, industrialization had been accompanied by the steady increase in the size of African 'township' populations. These townships provided the principal base for the growth of an African nationalist challenge linked to wider demands for racial inclusion and democracy, yet they were met by NP measures designed to tighten political control over the black majority. In time, the NP government sought to deflect African demands for political citizenship by the creation of discrete ethnic states which were granted degrees of 'self-rule', increasing to formal political 'independence', although they were devoid of economic viability.

Militant political challenges from below were met by the banning of the African National Congress (ANC) and its rival Pan-Africanist Congress (PAC). The ANC's trade union ally, the South African Congress of Trade Unions (SACTU), although not formally banned, was suppressed, and forced into exile. Foreign investment, which had collapsed after the notorious Sharpeville massacre in 1960, poured back in; and during the latter years of the decade, South Africa enjoyed globally high levels of growth based upon black political quiescence, the low cost of black labour, the privileged position of white workers and their unions, and associated foreign investor confidence. Yet in retrospect, this was merely the calm before the storm. This broke in 1973 with an unexpected surge of labour protest across the country, dubbed 'the Durban strike wave' reflecting its geographic origins. Worker struggle henceforth was to reflect the economy's mounting difficulties resulting from the oil shocks of the early 1970s, investment slow-downs, declining growth rates and increasing external pressures upon the apartheid regime.

From 1948, the rights of black labour, already highly restricted, had been subject to further erosion, notably via the Native Labour (Settlement of Disputes) Act of 1953 which reaffirmed the exclusion of African workers from the formal mechanisms of industrial relations; prohibited strikes by African workers; and, in order to render unions redundant, provided for factory 'works committees' which were to be elected by African workers but supervised by white Native Labour Officers. In 1956, an amendment to the Industrial Conciliation Act of 1924 (which had laid the foundations of the existing system of industrial relations) introduced a ban on Africans belonging to registered unions (which primarily served the interests of white workers); encouraged existing registered 'mixed' unions to split into separate White and Coloured unions; and insisted upon racially separated branches for unions remaining mixed. SACTU, founded in 1953, had challenged the imposition of racial divisions in the trade union movement by espousing not merely 'non-racialism' but 'political unionism', which argued for the indissoluble connection between the struggles for political and workplace democracy. Its defeat in the early 1960s correspondingly confirmed the symbiotic relationship between apartheid's racially structured political authoritarianism and despotism for black workers in the workplace.

The labour struggles which took place from the early 1970s emerged from within the political vacuum created by the suppression of black political organizations, the jailing of many of their leaders, and the difficulties they experienced re-establishing themselves in exile. The Durban strike wave was essentially spontaneous (albeit primed by worker education and 'wage commissions' conducted by small groups of committed university and student activists). It gave rise to the rapid formation of various African trade unions, which, although they could not be 'registered', struggled for 'recognition' by employers in individual workplaces. Critically, worker militancy found its base in the manufacturing, commerce, construction, transport and communication sectors. In contrast to the mining industry which corralled migrant labour into residential compounds, these sectors were the most feasible to organize because the rising cost of White labour meant they were increasingly dependent upon the employment of Africans. On the whole, the manufacturing and service industries constituted the highest paid sectors in the economy, reflecting the developing power and strategic location of black semi-skilled labour. Meanwhile, because Coloured and Indian working-class minorities were incorporated into the industrial relations system (albeit as racial subordinates), the newly emerging democratic trade unions premised their initial growth upon the organization of African labour.

Although the new unions faced severe repression, and were always challenged by the availability to employers of a mass of surplus labour, given an endemically high level of unemployment among black workers, they managed to survive, grow, formalize, make wage gains and erode the foundations of workplace despotism. In response, the government, now led by Prime Minister (later President) P. W. Botha, embarked upon strategies to stabilize white rule by restructuring apartheid from above. Notably, he introduced major changes in 1979 (the Wiehahn reforms) which now admitted African trade unions into the formal system of labour relations, so long as they agreed to register with the relevant authorities (and, by implication, to be subject to various controls). After harrowing internal debates, the majority of the emergent trade unions registered and used the new rights accorded them to expand the boundaries of industrial struggle. By the mid-1980s they had emerged as major players in the broader fight for political democracy, culminating in the formation of the Congress of South African Trade Unions (COSATU) in 1985, which brought together the large body of the democratic unions. In turn, again after extensive debates, COSATU also aligned itself with the United Democratic Front, which from the early 1980s had harnessed a rising tide of popular struggle and channelled it into the non-racial, 'Congress' tradition of the exiled ANC. Subsequently, COSATU was to place critical worker organization behind the ANC. Botha's successor, President F. W. De Klerk, had sought to resolve the acute crisis (plummeting growth, internal divisions, international pressure and inability to restore control over a rebellious black population) which confronted the minority regime by removing the ban from the exiled liberation movements, and inaugurating the (highly contested) process of negotiation which culminated in the transition to democracy in 1994.[2]

The post-apartheid labour relations framework

Trade unions and employers

By 1994, the democratic trade union movement had established itself as a major force within the system of industrial relations. According to the Department of Manpower, there were some 201 registered unions, with a membership of 2.89 million, and 50 unregistered unions, with a membership of 528,000 workers, at the end of 1993, bringing the total union membership to 3.2 million, or 27 per cent of the economically active population. COSATU was by far the largest body among the unions, with some 15 affiliates and 1,317,496 members (compared to some 400,000 at its inception in 1985). The second largest union federation was the National African Congress of Trade Unions (NACTU), with some 327,000 members in 18 affiliates, which was aligned with the PAC, whose internal struggles during the exile years had reduced it to a shadow of its former self, but which continued to counter the 'non-racialism' of the ANC with its own brand of 'Africanism'. Three other federations (the Federation of Salaried Staff Associations, the Federation of Independent Trade Unions, and the South African Confederation of Labour), represented a mix of white-collar unions, white unions and old-established craft unions and accounted for the large body of the remainder of trade union membership. The exception was the 30,000 or so who belonged to the United Workers' Union of South Africa, which was the creature of the Zulu-ethnic Inkatha Freedom Party (SAIRR 1994–95: 456–7).

Major contestation had taken place within and between the trade unions which had merged into COSATU in 1985, between 'workerists', who argued the necessity of building working-class power independent of political parties, and 'populists' or 'Charterists', who in the tradition of SACTU, urged the simultaneity of workplace and political struggle, and the importance of linking up with the ANC as the party of national liberation. According to Webster (1998: 45–6), the formation of COSATU in 1985 represented a 'strategic compromise' between the two streams whereby the integrity of the 'shop-floor tradition' was acknowledged while, simultaneously, the new federation committed itself to participation in the 'national democratic' struggle. Subsequently, COSATU's prominence was to be assured by its alignment with the ANC and its long-time partner, the South African Communist Party (SACP), which was to be formalized with the establishment of the 'Tripartite Alliance' in 1990 (a process which saw the absorption of SACTU into COSATU). Notionally, COSATU entered the Alliance as an equal partner, yet the ANC swiftly established its *de facto* hegemony through the leading role it took in negotiating the transition to democracy. Indeed, the power of the ANC was to be confirmed in December 1991 when COSATU's application to participate in its own right in the forum to negotiate the new constitution, the Convention for a Democratic South Africa (Codesa), was blocked by the NP and, apparently, sacrificed by the ANC. Overall, Codesa was comprised of delegates from political parties, the national government, and the governments of four juridically independent 'homelands', while excluding direct representation from popular civic organizations, business and labour. Thereafter, while COSATU played a key role in supporting the ANC's position in Codesa by flexing its muscles in the workplace and on the streets, it simultaneously began to engage in a parallel process of negotiation on the economy (ibid.: 46–8).

During the late 1980s, COSATU feared that a democratic transition would do little to transform the fundamental structures of South Africa's 'racial capitalism', especially at a time when the then government was embracing the nostrums of neo-liberalism emanating from major Western governments and global economic institutions. One response was to demand (and secure) the formation of a National Economic Forum (NEF) in which the unions could join with civil society formations and business to extend the political negotiation process to include economic restructuring. Another was to explore economic alternatives which it hoped would propel the country in a progressive direction. This culminated in COSATU playing the leading role in the drawing up of the Reconstruction and Development Programme (RDP), a broadly collectivist document which purported to offer 'an integrated, coherent socio-economic policy framework' designed for 'the eradication of apartheid and the building of a democratic, non-racial and non-sexist future' (ANC 1994: 1). The RDP was hugely popular with the majority of the newly enfranchised electorate, to whom it promised fundamental transformation. However, while it was presented as constructed around 'growth and redistribution', it was vague on policy measures and lacked any explanation of how it was to be financed, although significantly, prior to its acceptance by the ANC, it had been reworked to commit to 'ensuring a macro-economic policy environment that is stable' and which would be acceptable to domestic and international capital (ibid.: 137–8, 142–6).

Government and legislation

Organized labour secured significant gains during the early period of ANC rule. Within a few months of the new government taking office, the NEF was merged with the National

Manpower Commission (a government body created in 1956) to form the National Economic Development and Labour Council (NEDLAC), whose objectives were to seek consensus on issues of social and economic policy among business, labour, government and civil society before they were discussed in parliament. The government was represented on NEDLAC by the Department of Labour and other Departments (notably Finance) when required; labour was principally represented by COSATU and NACTU; and civil society by a raft of bodies such as the South African National Civics Organization and the National Cooperatives Association of South Africa. For their part, employers were represented by Business South Africa (BSA), formed in 1993, which had some 20 member organizations including the Chamber of Mines, the Afrikaanse Handelinstituut (the representative of Afrikaner capital), the South African Chamber of Business, and sectoral bodies (covering, for example, agriculture, automobile manufacturing, steel and engineering). Crucially, too, in the spirit of democratization, BSA combined this representation of white capital with that of the National African Federated Chambers of Commerce and Industry (NAFCOC). Alongside smaller bodies, NAFCOC voiced the interests of black business interests which, despite heavy restrictions imposed under apartheid, had emerged to serve black communities and which, after 1994, were to be joined by aspirant black entrepreneurs.

The principal achievement of NEDLAC was the passage of key Acts which restructured the framework of industrial relations. Pride of place was enjoyed by the Labour Relations Act of 1995 (LRA) which sought to replace the hitherto existing adversarial culture which characterized industrial relations by 'codetermination' between employers and employees. It had five key features (Webster 1998: 53–4; SAIRR 1995–96: 284–99). First, it brought all employees within a single system of industrial relations which provided for collective bargaining to take place in Bargaining Councils. These were to replace Industrial Councils, which had been established in 1924 to serve as forums for bargaining at industrial sector level, but which in granting access only to registered unions, had barred the right of African labour to participate. However, following the Wiehahn reforms in 1979 and the extension of the right of registration to African unions, the industrial council system had changed from a 'club representing the interests of employers and minority of skilled racially privileged workers, to an area of contestation between broadly based industrial unions and employers' (Wood 1998: 47). Critically, such participation enabled the new unions to have a say in formulating wage and service conditions across an entire industry, even covering employers with whom no formal recognition agreement had been concluded and/or in factories where a union had little presence. Importantly, the LRA now extended the right to participate in Bargaining Councils to farm, domestic and public service sectors (except the security services), whose workers had previously been excluded from the Industrial Council system. It also provided for trade unions or employer organizations which represented or employed 30 per cent of employees in a sector or area to register a Statutory Council where there was failure to secure agreement to appoint a Bargaining Council. Statutory Councils' writ included many of the powers and functions of Bargaining Councils (dispute resolution, administration of pension schemes, etc.), but excluded those of collective bargaining unless by agreement between constituent employers and unions. Nonetheless, a Statutory Council was empowered to make recommendations about wage levels to the Minister of Labour for general application, although equally, the latter was empowered to refer these to an independent body appointed for the purpose to grant exemptions.

Second, the LRA promoted collective bargaining by guaranteeing organizational rights to unions in the workplace, providing them with access to employer premises, granting them meeting rights and union subscription facilities, and allowing them to conclude closed shops (compulsory union membership agreements) under certain conditions. It also compelled employers to disclose information relevant to collective bargaining to unions which represented the majority of workers in the workplace. Further, it protected the right of employees to strike, to picket and to engage in sympathy strikes, although introducing compulsory procedures and timetables for dispute resolution, breach of which could allow a newly established Labour Court to issue interdicts to restrain workers from taking part in strikes (or employers from declaring a lock-out). Third, the Act overhauled dispute resolution procedures through the establishment of a Commission for Conciliation, Mediation and Arbitration (CCMA) which, state-funded and independent of either employers or unions, would seek to resolve disputes, initially through conciliation, with the right to impose compulsory arbitration in the case of disputes and unfair dismissals in 'essential services', or to arbitrate if a dispute was referred to it by the affected parties. Through such interventions, it was hoped the CCMA would 'reduce the frequency of strikes' (Webster 1998: 54).

Fourth, the LRA established clear rules on dismissal. Previously, these had fallen under the aegis of an Industrial Court which had wide discretion to determine unfair labour practices, and was not bound by the doctrine of precedent. Now the LRA envisaged that most cases regarding alleged unfair dismissal, severance pay issues and organizational rights would be decided by arbitration. However, where these failed, they could be referred to a new Labour Court which would have powers equal to those of the Supreme Court, and would have jurisdiction over a wide range of issues. Finally, a major innovation was the proposed introduction of workplace forums, which could only be established in workplaces with more than 100 employees and upon application by a representative trade union to the CCMA. The CCMA would proceed to draw up, by agreement with an employer and trade unions, a collective agreement between the parties, or to impose one where the parties proved unable to reach agreement. Such agreements would provide for the employer to provide employees with information regarding the financial situation of a company; for employees to be consulted regarding operational issues (such as work restructuring or company mergers); and for joint decision-making regarding disciplinary codes and protection against 'unfair discrimination'. In short, the purpose of workplace forums was to extend the potential for codetermination.

Subsequently, the LRA was supplemented by three other Acts. First, the Basic Conditions of Employment Act of 1997 aimed to regulate the right to fair labour practices conferred upon citizens by the country's new constitution. The primary objectives of the Act were to ensure that working conditions of unorganized and vulnerable workers complied with minimum standards (as defined, *inter alia*, by the International Labour Organization) while promoting flexibility in the regulation of minimum conditions of employment. The Act thus prescribed a 45-hour working week, rights to (unpaid) maternity leave and overtime rates while prohibiting employment of children under 15 (SAIRR 1996–97: 228). Second, the Employment Equity Act of 1998 sought to promote equal opportunities in the workplace by eliminating unfair discrimination in employment practice or policy. In so doing, it required employers with more than 50 employees, or annual turnovers above designated thresholds, to implement plans for affirmative action (to achieve equity along lines of race and gender), and to reduce disproportionate income differentials between different categories of staff. From 1999, the implementation of the Act was to be overseen by a Commission for Employment Equity, with employers being required to submit reports on the composition of their workforces by race and gender to the Department of Labour (SAIRR 1997–98: 228). Third, the Skills Development Act of 1998 aimed to improve the skills of the workforce by improving investment in training and development. It established a national skills authority which would advise the Minister of Education on policy and training; it also established sector and education training authorities (Setas) to monitor education and training; learnerships (incorporating traditional apprenticeships) to lead to registered qualifications; and labour centres to provide employment services for workers and work-seekers. The Act was later complemented by the Skills Development Levies Act of 1998 which rendered it compulsory for companies to pay 1 per cent of their payroll as a levy to fund skills training via the Setas (SAIRR 1999–2000: 141–2).

The LRA and the accompanying Acts constituted an attempt by the ANC to pay its debts to COSATU. However, it was doing so at a time when policy-makers were encountering neo-liberal influences and employers were beginning to argue in favour of 'labour market flexibility' and deregulation, policies that were by now taking root in many industrialized countries.

The post-apartheid restructuring of the labour market

Within two years of assuming power, the ANC-led government adopted the Growth, Employment and Redistribution (GEAR) policy. Supposedly, this was designed to implement the RDP, but it reality it replaced it with a macro-economic framework largely borrowed from the globally prominent emphases upon fiscal conservatism and debt repayment. Presaging a reduction in apartheid-era protectionist tariffs, the easing of foreign exchange transfers and the establishment of good relations with the World Trade Organization, and designed to appeal to foreign investors, it opened the way to a major restructuring of the labour market.

During the latter years of apartheid, large-scale capital had undergone a major process of consolidation into huge conglomerates as international companies disinvested in response to political turbulence and sold their assets to local buyers. In contrast, the 1990s inaugurated a reversal of trends towards concentration. From the early 1980s, South African large-scale capital had increasingly come to appreciate that only a democratic settlement could provide the opportunity for kick-starting an economy whose steadily worsening performance had its roots in the enormous costs of maintaining a repressive political apparatus based upon white minority rule. Further, by the late 1980s, it was recognized that, apart from locking capital within the country, the protectionist regime which apartheid had fostered had rendered South African companies inefficient and uncompetitive. Consequently, when democratization came, it offered not only the challenges presented by the opening-up of the economy to international competition, but also major opportunities. Large-scale capital underwent a major restructuring. Major conglomerates such as the Anglo-American Corporation, Sanlam and Old Mutual, 'unbundled', choosing to focus upon their 'core' businesses; and a number of major South African corporations (Billiton, South African Breweries, Anglo-American, Old Mutual and Liberty Life) were allowed by the government to migrate to the London Stock Exchange and to become truly multinational. Furthermore, as foreign investment increased, the economy became increasingly internationalized and financialized, developments which were matched by the growth of the service sector and changes in the composition of manufacturing. In particular, key employment sectors within manufacturing, such as clothing and textiles, were to find themselves placed under major threat by imports from low-wage competitors based in countries such as China while, in contrast, the mining sector – albeit shifting away from gold to minerals such as platinum – was to be boosted by the rising global demand for commodities (Mohamed 2010).

These structural changes were accompanied by an increase in capital intensity in some major industries, notably mining, associated industries and agriculture, thus exacerbating a trend towards the casualization and informalization of employment. Commonly, South Africa is depicted as constructed around division into 'formal' and 'informal' employment sectors. However, in a survey of the state of labour which challenged his earlier hopes for 'social concertation', Webster (2006: 23) has portrayed the structure of the labour market as divided into four segments rather than two layers, as shown in Figure 19.1.

Calculating the proportion of employees in each quadrant is problematic, given the complexity of labour force statistics. For 2011, for instance, Statistics South Africa calculated that 70.3 per cent of the working age population (aged 15–64) were in formal non-agricultural employment and 16.6 per cent in informal non-agricultural employment, but these figures are calculated on the broad definition of employment of those employed for a minimum of one hour per week (SAIRR 2010–11: 226). At the same time, these figures co-exist with South Africa's perpetually high rate of unemployment, which according to the narrow definition of those *not* working for one hour a week, even within the informal sector, has hovered around the 25 per cent mark since the year 2000. This figure increases to rates of between 30 and 40 per cent if an expanded definition of unemployment is used, that is, those without a job who want to work and make themselves available to do so. Overall, Webster proposed that the increase in the numbers of workers in casual and lower-paid jobs (Quadrant 2) or in the number that are retrenched and attempt to become self-employed (Quadrants 3 and 4) threatened those that worked in standard employment relationships (Quadrant 1).

Webster's portrayal suggests that the labour market restructuring facilitated by government and corporate strategies has had the effect of undermining the framework of the industrial relations system established during the early years of democracy. In short, he argues that the latter now caters for a declining proportion of the workforce, that element which is in 'standard employment relationships', represented directly by trade unions and/or covered by formally bargained wage agreements. In contrast, trade union rights and organizational forms do not exist for the new working poor, who are largely unprotected in the workplace, for the deregulation of the labour market means that minimum wages and working conditions officially prescribed by the government are widely ignored. The thrust of his argument is elaborated in institutional terms below.

	Informal	Formal
Employed	**Quadrant 2** Non-standard employment relationships	**Quadrant 1** Standard employment relationships
Self-employed	**Quadrant 3** Hawkers (unregulated, informal sector traders) and homeworkers	**Quadrant 4** Small, medium and microenterprises

Figure 19.1 The structure of the South African labour market.

Compromise and contestation in post-apartheid labour relations

Post-apartheid labour reforms were designed to inaugurate an industrial relations system which was more rights-based, inclusive and disposed to dispute resolution than to industrial conflict. Above all, the LRA provided for a very significant extension of industrial democracy by granting the right to belong to trade unions to workers who had previously been denied that right (public sector workers) or obstructed in exercising their rights (notably agricultural workers), even though, as can be seen from Table 19.2, trade unions still represent only a minority of workers:

As Table 19.2 also demonstrates, the LRA led to a surge in trade union registration, and that, in turn, subsequently led on to a considerable process of union mergers and consolidation within the different union federations. COSATU has remained by far the largest federation, increasing its membership from 1,317,500 in 1994 to 2,191,000 in 2012 (having overcome a decline in the early 2000s) (Buhlungu 2010: 90; COSATU 2012: 10). The other principal union bodies are the Federation of Unions of South Africa (FEDUSA, a consolidation of largely older white-dominated and/or white-collar unions, with a membership of 500,000), and NACTU, with a membership of 400,000. Although significant differences between the major trade union federations remain, notably about the virtues of alignment

Table 19.2 Number of trade unions and trade union membership, 1994–2010

Year	*Number of registered unions*	*Total trade union membership (registered unions)*	*Registered trade union membership as proportion of total employment*	*Registered union membership as a percentage of the economically active population*
1994	213	(2470481) 2980 481	31.0	24.8
1995	248	(2690727) 2950727	33.3	27.7
1996	334	(3016933) 3216933+	39.7	31.4
1997	417	3412645	45.2	34.9
1998	463	3801388	40.5	30.3
1999	499	3359497	32.4	24.8
2000	464	3552113	29.0	21.7
2001	485	3939075	35.2	24.9
2002	504	4069000	36.0	25.0
2003	369	3277685	28.7	20.7
2004	341	3134865	26.9	19.9
2005	N/a	3112000	25.3	18.5
2006	N/a	2969000	23.2	17.8
2007	253	3434000	25.8	20.0
2008	216	3298559	23.8	18.6
2009	205	3238519	25.0	18.9
2010	200	3057772	23.3	17.1

Source: SAIRR (2010–11: 412).

Note: + From 1997 onwards, the Department of Labour was no longer obliged under the LRA to keep records of unregistered unions.

with the ANC, there have been some moves towards cooperation around matters of common interest.

Likewise, the new labour dispensation made considerable strides in establishing minimum labour standards and furthering dispute resolution. These included sectoral determinations issued by the Minister of Labour prescribing minimum working conditions and wages for workers not covered by collective agreements emanating from Bargaining Councils. Notably, sectoral determinations prescribing conditions for domestic workers and farm workers (two of the most exploited categories under apartheid) came into effect in 2002, with an Unemployment Insurance Act also becoming operational in that year. Meanwhile, there was to be a steady increase in the number of disputes (collective and individual) which were to be referred to the CCMA, from 67,319 in 1997–98 (the first full year of operation), to 128,018 in 2005–06. The bulk of these pertained to cases of claimed unfair dismissal, although it was common for around a third of these to be declared 'out of jurisdiction', that is, they should have been referred to another body such as a Bargaining Council (Benjamin and Gruen 2006: 5). In 2010–11, fully 154,279 disputes were referred to the CCMA, excluding disputes handled by Bargaining Councils and private agencies (Tokiso 2012). In turn, the Labour Court has provided for the elaboration of an extensive body of labour law and precedent. Meanwhile, some 25 or more Setas have been established to facilitate worker training.

Nonetheless, developments have been uneven. For a start, trade unions have largely eschewed workplace forums, fearing that they would imitate the works committees permitted under the LRA of 1956 for African workers which employers sought to substitute for unions. Meanwhile, employers have complained bitterly about growing bureaucratization and red tape (Small Business Project 2004; Business Unity South Africa 2012). In 2005, Judge Dhihya Pillay of the Labour Court lamented that whereas the CCMA and Labour Courts were conceived of as providing a quick and efficient dispute resolution service, the CCMA in particular was being bogged down by procedures that negated those intentions (Benjamin and Gruen 2006: 40). Meanwhile, Setas have established a somewhat unfortunate reputation, not least for their relative lack of impact (e.g. Development Bank of Southern Africa 2010). The government has been the butt of considerable criticism for its poor management of further education and training colleges, for the poor quality of the college and for the limited output of trainees (SAIRR 2010–11: 495–500). Yet what is most notable about the post-LRA dispensation is the way that the bargaining system has moved in unanticipated directions.

As indicated, the LRA had sought to promote centralized bargaining and a coherent system of Bargaining Councils. Key to these goals was the extension of collective agreements to an entire sector of industry, for otherwise they could be undermined by non-participating employers. Accordingly, the Minister of Labour was bound by the Act to extend an agreement at the request of a council if an agreement met certain requirements, notably that the concerned parties covered a majority of employers and employees. Yet the Act left queries about how to arrive at such measures, not least in the context in which unregistered businesses are common, although it also provided the Minister with the discretion to extend an agreement if it was deemed 'sufficiently representative'. Nonetheless, the Act also laid down that a Bargaining Council must allow a procedure and criteria for exemption from council agreements (often pertaining to the small size of businesses and whether they are new), and provide for appeals against inclusion to be heard by a body independent of the council itself. Otherwise, Bargaining Councils were to be granted greater powers to enforce compliance by an amendment to the LRA in 2002, with provisions being made for them to acquire accreditation from the CCMA to arbitrate disputes (thus lightening the workload upon the latter body) (Godfrey *et al.* 2010: 87–99). In sum, by placing Bargaining Councils at its centre, the LRA sought to significantly extend the scope of labour market regulation.

This was not the message that established business wanted to hear as it sought to meet the challenge posed by South Africa opening up to international competition. Thus employer groups became increasingly vocal in favour of 'labour flexibility' following the passage of the LRA. A key affiliate of BUSA, the South Africa Foundation (later, Business Leadership South Africa, representative of the largest corporations), attacked the extension of Bargaining Council agreements as pricing the unemployed out of the labour market. The labour caucus in NEDLAC responded by urging greater efforts in favour of the establishment of Bargaining Councils. The government, caught between the two (and increasingly responsive to pressures by small business) dithered, declaring under its GEAR strategy that collective agreements should be sensitive to varying capital intensity, skills, regional circumstances and size and should only be extended to non-parties when it could reasonably be assured that they would not lead to job losses. Ultimately, however, although there is evidence of growing support even within the ANC for labour dualism (a policy that rights accorded to workers in formal employment should not necessarily extend to those working in the informal sector), no significant changes have been made to the LRA in favour of flexibility, not least because COSATU has used its political weight to oppose any moves that might undermine collective bargaining (ibid.: 109–14).

Nonetheless, despite the strong thrust of the LRA in favour of centralized bargaining, the number of Bargaining Councils has steadily diminished, from 77 in 1996 to 47 in 2010 (SAIRR 2010–11: 413). This is in spite of the establishment of five councils within the public sector (previously outside the system) and of a small number of new councils within the private sector. The decrease is, in part, the result of the merger of regional and sub-sectoral councils to form bigger national councils (e.g. the merger of the Clothing and Textile councils), but it also reflects councils ceasing to exist or deregistering. Thus, a survey conducted in 2004 recorded that some 48 Bargaining Councils covered some 2,358,012 registered employees and 335,420 employees at non-party firms, yet of these, fully 1,075,969 registered employees (46 per cent of the total) were accounted for by the five new public sector councils (ibid.: 116–17). In short, the number of private sector workers covered by the Bargaining Council system was relatively modest, while overall Bargaining Councils covered just 20.3 per cent of the labour force (ibid.: 114).

Two major factors seem to be at play. First, as noted by Wood (1998: 54), there is a globalized trend for management increasingly to favour decentralized bargaining. Second, the swing towards growing informalization within the labour market, encouraged by 'outsourcing', is likewise undermining various councils, especially at regional level. The drift would seem to be towards a handful of councils covering only certain sectors, 'with the vast bulk of the labour market covered by the Basic Conditions of Employment Act or sectoral determinations or plant-level bargaining (with only the latter two setting wages)' (Godfrey *et al.* 2010: 153). The problem, of course, is that, ultimately, centralized bargaining as envisaged by the LRA is underpinned by a philosophy of voluntary participation, which the Department of Labour seems to have interpreted as adopting a hands-off approach rather than pursuing proactive measures to encourage the functioning of councils (ibid.: 125–6). This is despite the fact that the proliferation of different levels of bargaining places heavy demands on trade union resources, a major reason why they tend to favour centralized bargaining (Wood 1998: 53).

The surprising fact is that, while there is a tendency for employer representatives on Bargaining Councils in the private sector to be drawn from larger employers within employer organizations, 'the bargaining council system is by and large a regulator of small firms' (Godfrey *et al.* 2010: 120). Reasons why this is so seem to range from small businesses wanting to render Bargaining Councils responsive to pleas for exemption through to their lack of experience of, or wish to avoid, involvement in the often acrimonious process of bargaining with employees. Large corporations, in contrast, have tended to opt out of the Bargaining Council system. To some extent, this has historical origins in the exclusion from the industrial council system of the emergent black unions in the 1970s, and their necessary preference for plant-level negotiation and recognition agreements.

Notionally, the LRA was meant to address the fragmentation involved, yet in practice major sectors have largely remained outside the ambit of Bargaining Councils. Hence, for instance a regional council for the contract cleaning industry in KwaZulu-Natal would seem to have attracted the support of employers because of the huge potential for wage competition or undercutting between firms, and the fact that wages of cleaners agreed in terms of the council's agreement are lower than those bargained outside it (ibid.: 193). In retail, now the largest sector for employment, historically bargaining has been within individual firms. This has remained the case, with unions bargaining at either national company level or regional or store level, with remaining firms covered by sectoral determination. Overall, collective bargaining covers only a small proportion of the sector, largely because the huge number of small retail outlets makes the sector a very difficult one to organize. Within the clothing industry, disagreement around minimum wage rates between employers and COSATU's South African Textile Workers' Union (SACTWU) within the industry bargaining council in early 2012 saw an employers' body, Apparel Manufacturers of South Africa (AMSA), approaching the Labour Court in Durban to implement its proposed wage model (which would introduce lower wages for new workers). Whereas SACTWU feared that the wage model would lower wages within the industry generally, AMSA argued the need for its enforcement by the court because its member companies' competitiveness (already stressed by the import of cheap textiles from China) was severely threatened by as many as 450 non-compliant companies which already paid lower wages.[3]

Within the automobile manufacturing industry, bitter struggles by emergent unions (culminating in the formation of COSATU's National Union of Metalworkers of South Africa, NUMSA) resulted in employers agreeing to the formation of a National Bargaining Forum (NBF) in 1990. Subsequently, the NBF concluded the first of a series of three-year agreements which cover a wide range of issues, such as skills training and reskilling of employees who are retrenched, as well as wages and conditions. At the same time, there are many variations (e.g. around incentive schemes) at company and plant level which continue to cause tensions, given the extreme exposure of the industry to global conditions. Although NUMSA would like to establish a Bargaining Council for the automobile manufacturing sector as a whole (so as to include the components industry), employers continue to exhibit a preference for more decentralized bargaining.

The mining industry had centralized bargaining dating back to 1915, when the Chamber of Mines was mandated by its members to negotiate with trade unions (predominantly representative of white workers). Subsequently, the major change to the established system occurred with the recognition of the (black) National Union of Mineworkers in 1983, yet the sector's centralized bargaining forum continues to exist outside the institutionalized system. Bargaining in the diamond and platinum subsectors (the latter, the fastest-growing subsector within the industry) also takes place outside the forum, usually at plant level. This was the case at Lonmin, where the breakdown of established industrial relations processes resulted in the tragic outcome at Marikana in August 2012, while large corporations, such as BHP Billiton and Sasol, have chosen to remain outside centrally negotiated agreements (such as that for coal).

The standard argument made by employers is that the 'inflexible labour system', as embodied in the LRA, is the major force behind the persistently high level of unemployment and the *de facto* shift to labour deregulation and informalization. The costs (pension and unemployment insurance, etc., as well as wages) of employing workers in full-time employment are argued to be artificially high, propelling employers to turn towards non-standard employment relationships and to 'outsource' work, with a consequent deterioration in wages and conditions of the staff concerned. Also symptomatic of this trend is the major growth of the labour broking industry, which supplies increasing quantities of labour to employers on a casual and temporary basis, accounting for nearly a million workers out of nearly 4 million workers said to be in 'atypical' employment by July 2011 (Sharp 2011).

A final point of contention within industrial relations is the allegedly low level of productivity of the larger section of the workforce. This is presented as a product of a 'skills crisis' brought on by failures in the public education system, the decline of the apprenticeship system, and the poor performance of the Setas. In turn, the crisis is said to be compounded by wage increases that have outstripped gains in productivity (CDE 2011). However, the debate about productivity is highly contested. Employer bodies tend to use figures emanating from the Treasury, which indicate either a very low level of productivity gain from the year 2000, or an actual decline in labour productivity. However, as Forslund (2013) has pointed out, there is rampant confusion within official data. Thus Statistics South Africa has issued revised figures for the period 1990–2006, and these show a very different picture: that, in the words of the Organization for Economic Cooperation and Development, 'South Africa has relatively strong average labour productivity' compared to other middle income countries (OECD 2008). Despite this report, the Treasury persists in lamenting low levels of productivity, probably to strengthen its argument for the imposition of tight limits on wage increases. Meanwhile, the wage share of GDP has fallen, from 55.9 per cent in 1994 to 50.6 per cent in 2010, while profits have increased (SARB 2011: S-150).

The implications for the trade union movement have been severe and extensive. Buhlungu has demonstrated how the pursuit of neo-liberal policies since the introduction of GEAR has shifted the focus of much union activity to that of macro-economic policy. He argues that, from the late 1990s, many unions have shifted resources into building their capacity for engagement at the national level of policy-making away from the workplace, thus having the effect of demobilizing union leaderships at lower levels, particularly at the workplace and within branches, leaving them ill-equipped to challenge management-imposed workplace restructuring. Furthermore, a growing distance between the shop-floor and union officials is indicative of the increasing extent to which positions within unions are being utilized as a channel of upward social mobility. Meanwhile, unions organizing within manufacturing have been hit hard by declining memberships as workers have been retrenched (Buhlungu 2010: 88–96). Thus although COSATU's membership has continued to grow, this masks a major change in its composition: first, towards a higher proportion of white-collar workers; and second, towards a far higher proportion of public sector workers, with unions primarily representative of such workers having increased from around 17 per cent of the total membership to some 41 per cent in 2011 (ibid.: 90; COSATU 2011: 195). Increasingly, therefore, there is a growing internal divide within COSATU between trade unions within the private sector which are operating within an official industrial relations system being undermined by employer pressures for greater labour flexibility; and unions within the public sector, where the industrial relations system is being maintained. The decreasing strength of COSATU within private industry and its increasing weight within the public sector add up to an increasing focus of the federation as a whole upon the importance of its alliance with the ANC.[4]

Marikana

Diverse aspects of these trends were demonstrated by events at Marikana in which police opened fire on striking miners, killing 34 and wounding 70. The unofficial strike at the Lonmin mine involved some 3000 workers. Before the final denouement, it had lasted some four weeks, as workers demanded a pay increase of up to 50 per cent. The wage demand was well in excess of an existing agreement already in place between COSATU's National Union of Mineworkers (NUM) and Lonmin, and was reflective of a far more generalized sense of worker discontent with wages and working conditions which had wide application across the entire platinum mining belt. Crucially, it appears that the NUM had lost the confidence of the workers, who had repudiated the pleas of union representatives sent to negotiate with them to return to work. Into their place stepped the leadership of the Association of Mineworkers and Construction Union (AMCU), a breakaway union from the NUM which was not recognized by the employer and which now pushed its way forward as the workers' representative. The volatility of the situation, compounded by striker violence against those who wanted to work and against NUM officials, was ratcheted up by the initial refusal of the employer, the NUM and the government to talk to AMCU, arguing its lack of formal status. Ultimately, however, in the aftermath of the shooting, prevarication in the face of continuing worker intransigence gave way to concession, and eventually – some six weeks after it had begun – the strike was brought to a close when Lonmin conceded a hefty 22 per cent pay increase after negotiations which involved AMCU as well as the NUM. Nonetheless, this failed to prevent labour unrest spreading rapidly, with employers, unions and the government alike scrambling to douse fires across the entire mining sector.

Marikana appears to represent a major challenge to the industrial relations system established since 1994. First, it indicated the development of a yawning gap between miners and the leadership of the NUM (its officials were accused of living comfortably while having failed to service the union's membership). Second, it exposed an increasing gap between workers and the ANC in government, the latter's leaders accused of siding with management and being careless of their core constituency. Third, it raised major questions about the role of the police, widely accused of reverting to apartheid-style reliance upon brute violence on behalf of the state; and, fourth, it posed serious problems for employers, who were ambivalent about the strike's consequences. On the one hand, there were suggestions that the outcome of Marikana would de-stabilize industrial relations to the inconvenience and disadvantage of larger employers who preferred to deal with unions (with membership of 50 per cent or more) deemed representative under the LRA of an entire workforce (Paton 2012). On the other, there were siren voices using Marikana to call for the overhaul of the LRA, and for the right of employers to negotiate with minority unions alongside majority ones (Sharp 2012), a demand which COSATU saw as a move for dividing workers and weakening trade unions.

South Africa's employment relations in a global context

The industrial relations system envisaged by the LRA was one which was borrowed from the late capitalist order of industrial Europe, premised upon democratic political forms and near or full employment. It sought to build upon the political citizenship extended to black South Africans in 1994 by widening the access to industrial citizenship promised to those hitherto excluded on racial grounds. The problem, however, was that the foundations for such a system were not in place. Whereas European-style capitalist democracy rested upon pluralist politics reflecting class balance and compromise, the South African transition was constructed on a significant divorce between economic and political power, with the newly elected government having only very limited capacity to control and regulate the conglomerates which dominated the economy. On the one hand, the government sought to extend controls over large-scale capital through such devices as the LRA and the introduction of demands for black empowerment. On the other, it conceded the necessity of embracing neo-liberal prescriptions for re-engaging with the global economy, thus enabling the conglomerates to unbundle, restructure and internationalize, and thereby reduce their exposure to governmental regulation. As a result, many of the progressive advances initially signified by the implementation of the LRA have been undermined by an extensive haemorrhaging of jobs in previously protected industries to lower-cost producing countries elsewhere. Consequently, as throughout much of Sub-Saharan Africa, institutionalized industrial relations are increasingly under threat as union capacity and density are corroded by mass unemployment alongside a growing informalization and casualization of labour (Kocer and Hayter 2011). Its power base within the economy eroding, COSATU now increasingly relies upon its direct relationship with the state.

Throughout much of post-colonial Sub-Saharan Africa, trade union movements have been either integrated into (or subordinated) to ruling parties, or have moved into explicit opposition. COSATU, however, has pursued a middle course whereby, although in formal alliance with the ANC, it has reserved the right to engage in extensive critique of its policies and performance. Its involvement in the alliance enabled it to play a key role in unseating Thabo Mbeki in 2007, and subsequently replacing him with Jacob Zuma, whose ascension to the Presidency was heralded as inaugurating a shift away from liberal market economics to the adoption of a 'developmental state' (Southall and Webster 2010). However, while the Zuma period has offered much rhetoric about a greater role for the state, the reality is that the infrastructure-led growth path which this envisages will be heavily dependent upon major increases in foreign investment. This could come from either major multinational corporations, who will demand appropriately attractive market conditions; and/or from state-linked corporations from 'emerging economies', such as China and Russia, who are hungry for mineral resources and new markets, which will themselves impose their own demands. In a context of continuing massive employment reserves, neither of these scenarios offers much prospect for the realization of the hopes for industrial democracy envisaged under the LRA.

Acknowledgements

I am grateful to my colleagues David Dickinson and Eddie Webster, as well as to the editors, for their comments upon a first draft of this chapter.

Notes

1 A survey of its members' attitudes conducted by the National Labour Development Institute for the Congress of South African Trade Unions, which was published in 2012, recorded that half of those interviewed viewed violence as necessary to achieve the aims of a strike (*Business Day*, 14 September 2012).

2 There are numerous accounts of the emergence of the black trade union movement during this period. See, *inter alia*, Friedman (1987), Baskin (1991) and the more recent Buhlungu (2010).
3 At the time of writing, the issue remains unresolved, SACTWU uncomfortably aware that extension of the bargaining council's minimum wages to non-compliant companies would lead to non-compliant company closures and the lay-off of as many as 21,000 workers.
4 Space limitations prevent the elaboration of a more nuanced analysis of trends within COSATU and the wider trade union movement, for which see Buhlungu (2010).

References

ANC (1994) *The Reconstruction and Development Programme*, Johannesburg: African National Congress.

Baskin, J. (1991) *Striking Back: A History of COSATU*, Johannesburg: Ravan Press.

Benjamin L. and Gruen C. (2006) *The Regulatory Efficiency of the CCMA: A Statistical Analysis of the CCMA's CMS Database*, Cape Town: University of Cape Town, Development Policy Research Unit, Working Paper 06/110.

Buhlungu, S. (2010) *A Paradox of Victory: COSATU and the Democratic Transformation of South Africa*, Scottsville: University of Kwazulu-Natal Press.

Business Unity South Africa (2012) 'The regulatory tape business wants', *Parliamentary News Watch* (BUSA), 1: 5.

Centre for Development Enterprise (CDE) (2011) *Jobs for Young People: Is a Wage Subsidy a Good Idea*? Johannesburg: CDE, Roundtable, August.

COSATU (2011) *Secretariat Report to the 5th COSATU Central Committee*, Johannesburg: COSATU.

—— (2012) *Political Report to the COSATU 11th National Congress, 2012*, Johannesburg: COSATU.

Development Bank of Southern Africa (2010) *Thinking 'Out of the Box' by Thinking 'In the Box': Considering Skills Development: Challenges and Recommendations*, Johannesburg: Midrand: DBSA.

Forslund, D. (2013) 'Labour productivity in South Africa', in J. Daniel, P. Naidoo, D. Pillay and R. Southall (eds) *New South African Review 3: The Second Phaze – Tragedy or Farce?*, Johannesburg: Wits University Press.

Friedman S. (1987) *Building Tomorrow Today: African Workers in Trade Unions 1970–1984*, Johannesburg: Ravan Press.

Godfrey, S., Maree, J., Du Toit, D. and Theron, J. (2010) *Collective Bargaining in South Africa: Past, Present And Future?*, Claremont: Juta.

Kocer, R. and Hayter, S. (2011) 'Comparative study of labour relations in African countries', Working Paper 116, Institute for Advanced Labour Studies, Amsterdam, December.

Mohamed, S. (2010) 'The state of the South African economy', in J. Daniel, P. Naidoo, D. Pillay and R. Southall (eds) *New South African Review 1: Development Or Decline?*, Johannesburg: Wits University Press.

OECD (2008) *South Africa, Policy Note*, Paris: OECD, July.

Paton, C. (2012) 'The radical new face of labour relations in South Africa', *Business Day Investors Monthly*, 26 September–30 October: 34–6.

SAIRR (South African Institute of Race Relations) (various years) *South Africa Surveys 1994–95, 1995–96, 1996–97, 1997–98, 1999–2000, 2010–2011*, Johannesburg: South African Institute of Race Relations.

Sharp, L. (2011) 'Labour unrest at its highest ever level', *Adcorp Employment Index*, July. Available at: http://www.politicsweb.co.za/politicsweb/view/politicsweb/en/page71619?oid=250162&s.

—— (2012) 'SA labour relations system fundamentally undemocratic', *Business Day*, 27 August.

Small Business Project (2004) *Counting the Cost of Red Tape for Business in South Africa*, Johannesburg: SBP.

SouthAfrica.info: The official gateway (Undated) *Regulating Labour Relations – South Africa.info*. Available at: http://www.southafrica.info/pls/procs/iac.oage?p_tl=2780&p_t2=2780&p_t3=104327p_t

South African Reserve Bank (SARB) (2011) *Quarterly Bulletins and Monetary Policy Reports*, March.

Southall, R. and Webster, E. (2010) 'Unions and parties in South Africa: COSATU and the ANC in the wake of Polokwane', in B. Beckman, S. Buhlungu and L. Sachikonye (eds) *Trade Unions and Party Politics: Labour Movements in Africa*, Cape Town: HSRC Press.

Standard Bank (2012) 'Economic strategy – South Africa', *Labour Viewpoint*, 7 June.

Tokiso (2012) *Dispute Resolution Digest*. Available at: http://www.tokiso.com.

Webster, E. (1998) 'Trade unions and democratization in South Africa', *Journal of Contemporary African Studies*, 16(1): 39–64.

—— (2006) 'Trade unions and the challenge of the informalisation of work', in S. Buhlungu (ed.) *Trade Unions and Democracy: COSATU Workers' Political Attitudes in South Africa*, Cape Town: HSRC Press.

—— and Simpson, G. (1990) 'Crossing the picket line: violence in industrial conflict', *Industrial Relations Journal of South Africa*, 11(4): 15–32.

Wood, G. (1998) *Trade Union Recognition: Cornerstone of the New South African Employment Relations*, Halfway House: International Thomson Publishing (Southern Africa).

Part 4

Transnational regulation

20 Globalization

Sarosh Kuruvilla and Tashlin Lakhani

Introduction

Although the term 'globalization' has been used in a variety of ways to refer to a variety of different phenomena, underlying most definitions is the growing distribution and integration of economic activities across national (and increasingly, firm) boundaries which have resulted, at least in part, from reductions in barriers to trade and investment and advances in technology.[1] Figures 20.1 and 20.2 show significant gross trade flows between major regions in 1995 and 2005 and illustrate the increasing fragmentation of production and integration of countries brought about through globalization. The size of the arrows in each diagram reflects the relative size of exports and each is shaded according to their domestic value-added content. From 1995 to 2005, we see a considerable increase in gross trade flows, the most notable being between China and all other major regions, as well as a decline in the domestic content of export flows.

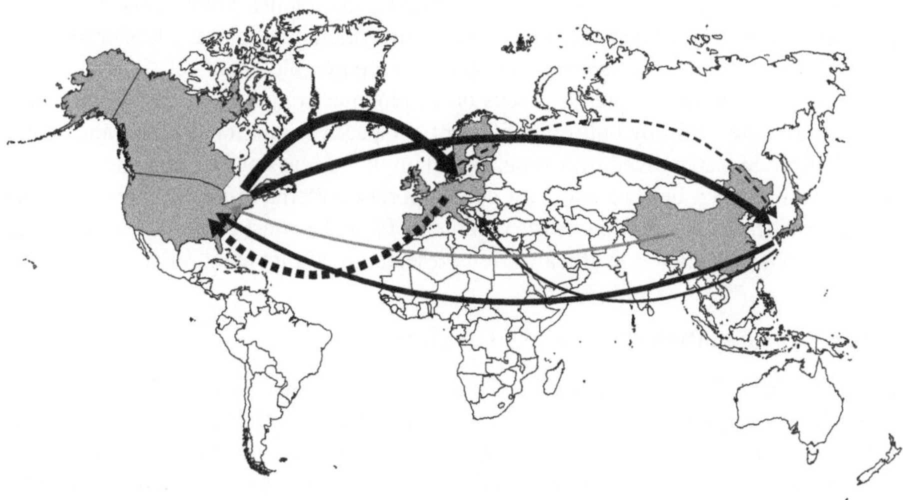

Figure 20.1 Trade flows between major regions, 1995.
Source: OECD-WTO (2012).

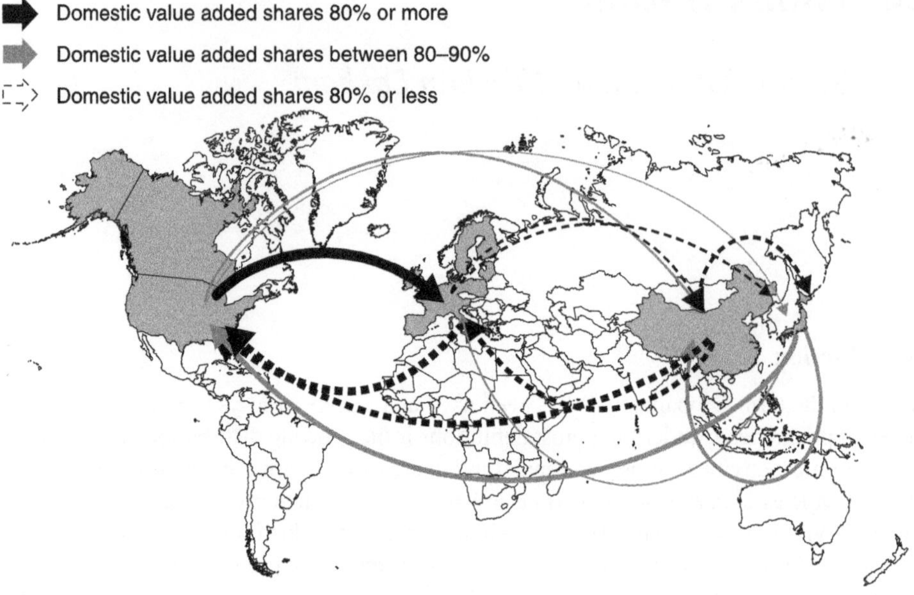

Figure 20.2 Trade flows between major regions, 2005.

Source: OECD-WTO (2012).

These diagrams demonstrate the increasingly interconnected and interdependent nature of the global economy. Globalization has increased the volume and variety of international production, trade and investment. Today, goods and services are no longer primarily produced within individual firms and countries but rather through complex global networks that integrate firms from developed and developing economies alike. This, in turn, has implications for both the theory and practice of employment relations and labour regulation.

While the chapters in the previous section examined employment relations in different national contexts, in this chapter we focus on employment relations in the international or *global* context. We begin by outlining different perspectives on globalization and examine how globalization has evolved over time. Based on this discussion, we provide a definition of globalization which best accounts for contemporary patterns of global interdependence. We then provide a brief overview of the arguments for and against globalization and discuss the implications that economic globalization presents for employment relations.

Perspectives on globalization and its evolution

In the book *Global Transformations*, Held and colleagues (2004) identify three perspectives on globalization: (1) the hyperglobalist perspective; (2) the sceptical perspective; and (3) the transformationalist perspective. According to the hyperglobalist perspective, globalization reflects a new era, characterized by the declining relevance and authority of nation states and the emergence of a 'borderless world' (ibid.). Globalization is seen as leading to a new world order – one that involves institutions of supranational (regional and global) governance and cultural diffusion. Hyperglobalists are found at both ends of the political spectrum. To the right are neo-liberals (or 'pro-globalizers'), who embrace free markets and argue that in the long run, the benefits of globalization far outweigh the costs. To the left are neo-Marxists (or 'anti-globalizers'), who argue that the new international division of labour will only create and reinforce existing inequalities within and between countries (for a summary of these positions, see Dicken 2011). Nevertheless, hyperglobalists on both sides share the belief that globalization is resulting in an increasingly integrated and boundaryless global economy.

In contrast, those falling under the sceptical perspective reject the notion of a unified global market and question what is new about contemporary levels of global economic interdependence (e.g. Hirst and Thompson 1999). Using empirical evidence on historical international trade and investment flows, sceptics argue that the world economy is less integrated today than in the past. Moreover, sceptics argue that hyperglobalists underestimate the power of national governments and their role in facilitating internationalization. Sceptics view globalization and global corporations as myths, arguing that international economic activity is concentrated in Organization for Economic Co-operation and Development (OECD) states and that multinational firms continue to be firmly rooted in their home countries and regions. They further reject notions of global culture and global governance and, with regards to the latter in particular, argue that continuing patterns of global inequality provide evidence that any such structures serve to benefit the neo-liberal strategies of the most powerful states.

The transformationalist perspective presents what might be viewed as a middle ground between the hyperglobalists and the sceptics. In this perspective, globalization is seen as a long-term historical process that has resulted in significant social, political and economic changes (Held *et al.* 2004). Transformationalists note that that, while the impacts of globalization have spread unevenly and the future trajectory is unknown, it is clear that contemporary patterns of global integration are considerably different than those of years past. Specifically, transformationalists argue that economic activity is increasingly *global* in nature, integrating communities all over the world. At the same time, contemporary globalization is reconfiguring the roles of national governments. While acknowledging the continuing importance of nation states, particularly with regards to development, transformationalists argue that national governments are no longer the only forms of governance in the world economy, as globalization has also brought forth supra-territorial forms of economic and political organization including transnational corporations, social movements and international agencies.

Consistent with the transformationalist perspective, and in response to challenges by sceptics on quantitative grounds, Dicken (2011) argues that processes of globalization in the last half of the twentieth century have been *qualitatively* different than in the past, reflecting changes in the structure of global economic integration. He argues that earlier forms of global integration were 'shallow' and took place primarily through arm's length international trade and investment. In contrast, contemporary global integration is 'deep' and occurs mainly via intra- and inter-firm global production and service networks. In support of this analysis, empirical evidence indicates that there has been substantial growth in foreign direct investment (FDI) and in fact, the growth of FDI has, for the most part, outpaced the fast growth of international trade in the last few decades (Jensen 2006, and see Figure 20.3). Dicken (2011) argues that these trends reflect the changing nature of interconnectedness in the world economy, with a shift from trade (the heart of historical global integration) to FDI. Moreover, Jensen (2006) notes that FDI may be a key factor driving the growth of world trade as trade increasingly takes place through transnational corporations (TNCs) in the form of intra-firm trade (e.g. from one part of the firm to another, typically across borders). Some have estimated that intra-firm trade accounts for 30 per cent of world trade (Markusen 1995). In the United States, intra-firm trade accounted for 48 per cent of US goods imports and

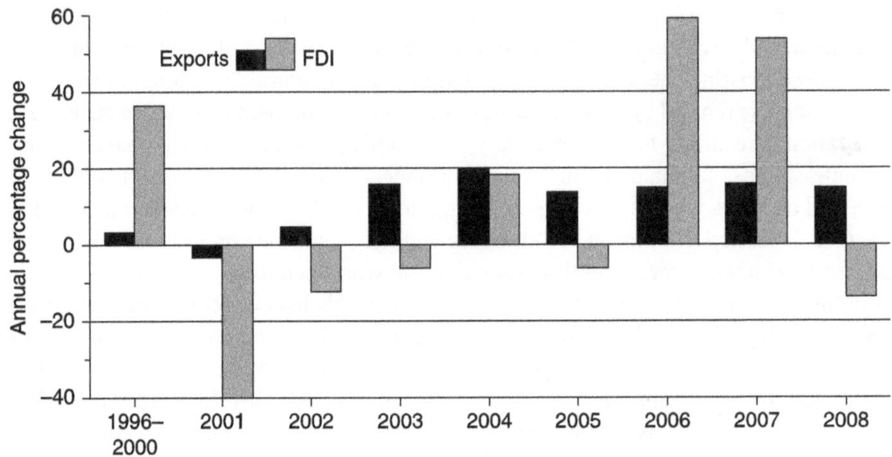

Figure 20.3 Growth of foreign direct investments and exports, 1996–2008.

Source: Calculated from UNCTAD *World Investment Report*, various issues; adapted from Dicken (2011).

30 per cent of US goods exports in 2009 and 22 per cent of US private services imports and 26 per cent of US private services exports in 2008, with evidence that the share of intra-firm trade in services has been increasing over time (Lanz and Miroudot 2011). Concurrently, there is also ample anecdotal and case study evidence which shows that the number and types of inter-firm connections between TNCs and foreign ('supplier') firms are growing as supplier firms all over the world are incorporated into global value chains (Gereffi *et al.* 2005). Accordingly, it is clear that the most recent phase of globalization involves not only the increasing volume and spread of economic activities across borders but also, and perhaps more importantly, significant changes to the nature of economic activities and relationships across geographic space (Dicken 2011). Today, countries and firms are interconnected in fundamentally different ways than ever before.

Given the importance of the processes of globalization that generate a variety of outcomes, and the differences between prior and contemporary forms of globalization, we adopt Held *et al.*'s (2004: 16) definition of globalization for the purposes of this chapter:

> Globalization can be thought of as a process (or set of processes) which embodies a transformation in the spatial organization of social relations and transactions – assessed in terms of their extensity, intensity, velocity and impact – generating transcontinental or interregional flows and networks of activity, interaction, and the exercise of power.

Consequently, contemporary globalization entails the widening, intensifying, increasing speed and growing impact of global interconnectedness which, in turn, results in a more, though not necessarily fully, integrated world economy that brings and binds together nations and regions and the actors within them. Further, globalization should not be conceived as an end-state but rather as a set of complex, continuing, non-linear processes which can be compared over time. Held *et al.*'s definition of globalization is also notable for its explicit inclusion of power as it aptly acknowledges that the interconnections and interdependencies resulting from globalization are not always equal. This conceptualization of globalization will serve as the basis for our examination of the implications that globalization in its current form holds for employment relations practice and theory. But first, we briefly examine the debates surrounding the causes and consequences of globalization, which arise, at least in part, from the different perspectives outlined above.

Causes and consequences of globalization

There is significant debate about the causes and consequences of economic globalization, and these debates have fundamental implications for state, management and labour stances and strategies. First, scholars have debated whether globalization is the result of a single cause or multiple causes (Held *et al.* 2004). Proponents of monocausal accounts of globalization have typically pointed to capitalism or technology as the primary factors driving increasing global integration. Others reject monocausal explanations and argue that globalization results from the complex interaction of political, cultural, technological and economic factors. Nevertheless, even those who favour multicausal explanations of globalization admit that certain factors, such as advances in information and communication technology, have had a significant effect on globalization (e.g. Giddens and Griffiths 2006). Some have also noted that the causes of globalization may differ based on the specific aspect of economic integration under examination. For example, changes in technology which have lowered the costs of moving goods and information are likely to play a much stronger role in international finance and multinational production than for international trade which is much more likely to be the result of traditional political factors (Garrett 2000).

The consequences of globalization are more intensely debated than its causes. Proponents of globalization argue that it has positive effects for all involved. Drawing on our earlier discussion, pro-globalizers argue that free markets and international exchange based on comparative advantage will create a 'rising tide . . . [that] lifts all boats' (Dicken 2011: 5). Globalization, it is proposed, will not only make rich nations rich but poor nations less poor. It helps developing nations through employment creation and exposure to the technology and knowledge of developed countries (Brune and Garrett 2005). In support of this argument, proponents often quote the following statement by the World Bank (2007: 160): 'Rapid growth and poverty reduction in China, India, and other countries that were poor 20 years ago, have been a positive aspect of globalization.' Proponents also point to the economic success and development of the Asian Tigers as an example of the potential that globalization holds for developing countries. Globalization is viewed as having positive economic benefits for consumers as well by increasing access to goods, lowering prices through global competition and increasing the food supply in some countries (Osland 2003).

In contrast, opponents of globalization have argued that globalization and free markets create and intensify inequalities within and between countries. They argue that globalization has placed downward pressure on the wages of the unskilled and uneducated, and point to the widening gap between the rich and the poor as evidence of the negative effects of globalization (Osland 2003). Opponents also see globalization leading to a 'race to the bottom' as developing countries compete with one another to attract investment. Investors, typically transnational corporations (TNCs), seek to set up operations in those nations, or export processing zones (EPZs) within nations, with the lowest environmental, financial and labour standards and costs. Globalization also makes the use of coercive comparisons between domestic and foreign operations more effective and results in downward pressure on pay and working conditions in developed home countries as well (Longworth 1999). In line with the hyperglobalist perspective, critics also assert that the denationalization of economies brought about through globalization threatens national sovereignty and is leading to the 'demise of social democracy and the modern welfare state' (Held *et al.* 2004: 13). Governments increasingly face pressures from powerful TNCs to deregulate and reduce tax rates and, as a result, lower social benefits (given lower tax revenue), which is particularly problematic given the pressing need for governments to assist those who have been displaced or otherwise negatively affected by globalization. Economic globalization, it is argued, also promotes cultural homogenization and threatens distinctive cultural identities and traditions, particularly as TNCs grow and impose Western ideals on countries around the world (Osland 2003). Finally, opponents of globalization warn that the increasing financial integration associated with globalization exposes countries, and especially developing countries, to financial crises and processes of contagion (Schmukler *et al.* 2004).

The difficulty in resolving these debates lies, in part, in the measurement of globalization, which itself is fraught with difficulty and contention. It is difficult to draw inferences regarding cause and effect between globalization and a wide range of variables that tend to move together (Brune and Garrett 2005), especially then there is evidence that partially supports both pro-globalization and critical arguments. We do not attempt to settle these debates here. Instead, our objective is to illustrate some of the potential issues and implications, both positive and negative, associated with globalization. It is important to note that multiple stakeholders pursue actions and strategies depending on which side of the debate they are on. Thus, for example, the debate with regards to whether globalization will lead to a competitive 'race to the bottom' decline in labour standards has galvanized action from multiple stakeholders in the employment relations arena–governments, trade unions, international organizations, employers, and civil society organizations–to focus on the regulation of labour standards globally. We review this development below.

Global regulation of labour standards

The 'Battle in Seattle' in 1999 (which brought together a coalition of labour, environment and student groups demonstrating against the World Trade Organization (WTO)) is emblematic of the debate regarding globalization's consequences and its implications for action. The central idea in this battle was that economic globalization requires new forms of international regulation to counter the negative consequences outlined earlier, especially in terms of environmental and labour standards (Charnovitz 1992). This demand for new regulation is also interspersed with calls for new models of 'global governance' that permit civil society groups to also have their voices heard in discussions about global regulation (Scholte 2004). And as the discussion below indicates, stakeholders, including globalization's proponents such as corporations, have responded to this issue in a multiplicity of ways (see Kuruvilla and Verma 2006, for more detail).

Much of the emerging regulation on international labour standards can be characterized as 'soft' regulation as opposed to 'hard' regulation. An example of hard regulation or hard law is an existing piece of legislation in any country. The legislation is characterized by a clear definition, specifies some standards and articulates consequences for failure to comply. Thus, hard regulation is always 'compulsory' and binding on the populations covered by it. Soft regulation, on the other hand, is more varied. Sisson and Marginson (2001) identify some of the key distinguishing features of soft regulation. In particular, while hard regulation deals with standard and specific rights and obligations, soft regulation typically deals with general principles and minimum provisions. Soft regulation often takes the form of recommendations, opinions or statements; is subject to interpretation and negotiation; and is best characterized as 'permissive' rather than compulsory. Soft regulation is also enforced differently, relying on a wide variety of enforcement mechanisms such as moral persuasion, monitoring and feedback, transparency, peer group audits, benchmarking, joint studies and joint papers. Notably, soft regulation tends to appear more commonly in areas that have cross-border implications. These soft regulation approaches are reviewed next.

Linking labour standards with trade

A key mechanism with considerable promise has been linking labour standards with trade. The argument is that such a linkage would force countries, and particularly those countries that are not enforcing their labour laws, to improve labour standards in order to participate in the global trading system. This effort, heavily sponsored by the USA, was not successful in the WTO Ministerial Conference in Singapore in 1996, where developing countries successfully argued that this policy would undermine the comparative advantage of lower wage trading partners. Moreover, proposals to bring labour standards into multilateral trade negotiations have been viewed as a smokescreen for protectionism – protecting industries in the 'North' that would otherwise move to the 'South'.

Although the efforts to formally link labour standards with trade at the WTO level ended with the Singapore round, incorporating labour standards into trade continues to be seen by many as the best way to improve labour conditions internationally. Indeed, the USA has embarked on a bilateral approach that links labour standards with trade. This can be seen most recently in the series of bilateral free trade agreements (FTAs) that the USA has signed with a variety of countries, including South Korea, Peru, Panama and Colombia (for a list of recently signed US free trade agreements and specific labour provisions, see ILO 2009 and www.ustr.gov). Critics have argued that the linkage of labour standards with trade in these bilateral deals does not provide sufficient 'teeth' to really improve standards, although the more recent free trade agreements negotiated by the Obama administration do reflect marked improvements over earlier agreements. For example, under the recently signed agreements noted above, labour provisions including the four basic ILO core labour standards (enumerated later) are enforceable through the same dispute resolution procedures used for other provisions, such as commercial interests (Bolle 2012).

Regionalization and labour standards

A second method to regulate labour standards across countries can be found in a variety of regionalization initiatives. Regionalization has significant implications for the transnational regulation of labour standards, given that the most developed regionalization initiatives, namely the European Union (EU) and the North American Free Trade Act (NAFTA, embracing the USA, Canada and Mexico), deal with labour issues (see Chapter 22). But, they follow vastly different approaches. Briefly, the EU follows a hard law approach, having adopted the principle of harmonization of labour regulations throughout the community (with the exception of freedom of association, collective bargaining and the right to strike). In addition, Directives with regards to labour issues proposed by the European Commission and adopted by the Council of Ministers are converted into national legislation of each EU country. It is also possible for agreements reached by labour and management representatives in different sectors to result in Directives. Thus, apart from laws, sectoral and cross-industry agreements have the potential to raise labour standards throughout the community. The European case is interesting because labour standards are based on

Europe-wide legislation in countries that have historically had high labour standards and a strong tradition of collective bargaining with high levels of union density and bargaining coverage. None of these conditions, however, are present elsewhere in the world and hence the possibility of the EU model being replicated is slim.

NAFTA's approach is to condition each member country to respect each other's labour laws and to force countries to enforce their own labour laws. While the EU's approach clearly has the capacity to create uniform labour conditions in the region, NAFTA's approach does not. Rather, the NAFTA model is a process that encourages countries to implement their current labour laws while simultaneously increasing understanding of the differences in labour laws and conditions across countries. Critics of NAFTA point to its narrow scope and limited powers to argue that this approach, while useful in educating the parties and publicizing violations, is unlikely to make an appreciable impact on a large scale (Compa 1999). In addition, there is no recourse if the labour laws in any country go against the core labour principles espoused by NAFTA.[2] Other recently emerging regionalization initiatives, such as MERCOSUR (which involves Argentina, Brazil, Paraguay and Uruguay) and AFTA, the ASEAN Free Trade Area (which involves Singapore, Malaysia, Philippines, Thailand, Vietnam, Laos, Cambodia and Brunei), have not yet developed detailed agreements on labour issues, although MERCOSUR has taken some initial steps and appears to be following the EU model of harmonizing labour standards. Nonetheless, while regional efforts such as those of the EU show considerable promise of lifting labour standards, efforts such as NAFTA seem to indicate that regionalization trade models have, at present, limited potential to be the vehicles by which core labour standards are protected. But this is an area that is ripe for more sustained research.

Multilateral model: the ILO

The ILO (International Labour Organization) offers an avenue for the multilateral regulation of labour standards. The ILO works through a series of conventions and recommendations that set forth 'International Labour Standards' aimed at ensuring basic worker rights (ILO 2012). Conventions and recommendations are drawn up by the ILO's members (representatives of governments, employers and workers of each member state) and adopted at the ILO's annual International Labour Conference. Conventions are legally binding international treaties while recommendations serve as non-binding guidelines. In many cases, recommendations serve as detailed guidelines for the effective implementation of conventions. Countries that ratify a convention are expected to incorporate the convention into national law and practice. The ILO's Declaration on Fundamental Principles and Rights (1998) identifies four core labour standards that are applicable to all countries and covered in eight 'fundamental' conventions. These are: (1) freedom of association and collective bargaining (Conventions 87 and 98); (2) the elimination of forced and compulsory labour (Conventions 29 and 105); (3) the abolition of child labour (Conventions 138 and 182); and (4) the elimination of discrimination in respect of employment and occupation (Conventions 100 and 111).

In this way, the ILO has set a process in motion that could potentially lead to better labour standards globally. Failure to implement can result in a complaint to the ILO. However, the ILO does not have any punitive power and must rely on moral persuasion. History is replete with examples of countries adopting ILO Conventions and not implementing or enforcing labour laws. For example, there are a total of 189 Conventions on a range of issues. Out of 185 members, 175 have ratified the forced labour Convention, 170 have ratified the Convention on discrimination and 151 have ratified the Convention on freedom of association. The USA, a big proponent of improving core labour rights, has only ratified 14 Conventions and has not ratified the freedom of association and collective bargaining Conventions.[3] Of greater concern, however, is the fact that there are widespread violations of labour standards even in the countries that have ratified the Conventions (Compa 2003).

Accordingly, the key issue for the ILO is enforcement. Since the ILO depends on moral persuasion and cajoling countries to improve their labour standards, many have criticized the ILO's procedures as not having enough 'teeth'. The ultimate step – that of expelling a country from the ILO – is never taken because that would negate any influence the ILO has over that country in the future. While the ILO has taken steps to curb violations, for example via transparent reporting, it is clear that at the global level, the ILO does not have the resources to monitor and enforce standards. Despite this principal weakness, the ILO is the only multilateral organization that we currently have that focuses on improving labour standards globally and providing technical assistance to poorer countries in order to do so (for details of how the ILO works in a variety of areas and the ILO's enforcement tools, see Chapter 23 in this volume). Thus, the ILO is a vitally necessary, though imperfect, mechanism for (soft) regulation in the global economy.

Voluntary methods

A range of voluntary methods has emerged in recent years as global corporations have engaged in pre-emptive moves to prevent new and unforeseen forms of hard regulation from being thrust upon them. In many cases, the adoption of such voluntary approaches has also been precipitated by the highly publicized, globally coordinated campaigns of NGOs, consumer organizations and organized labour aimed at bringing attention to exploitative working conditions in developing countries. Most common among these approaches are corporate codes of conduct that draw their inspiration from the Sullivan principles used during the fight against apartheid.[4] Generally, the scope of typical corporate codes is quite similar, focusing on the core labour standards but also including safety, health, working hours and working conditions (an example can be found at www.nikebiz.com).

Corporate codes have made some progress within the niche of internationally traded consumer goods. Codes were first established in consumer goods sectors such as toys, clothing, shoes and rugs. The growth of corporate codes is premised on a robust consumer preference in high-income countries for 'ethically-made' goods. Such codes will succeed as long as consumers are willing to pay a premium to ensure that the goods they buy are not made in sweatshops (Blank and Freeman 1994; Freeman 1994, 1998) and/or where consumers are unwilling to buy brands whose production does not follow basic labour standards. Of late, corporate codes of conduct have also grown as part of corporate 'social responsibility' initiatives. In general, corporate codes of conduct have made some progress in improving labour standards and the number of industries affected by codes has increased over time. From their original introduction in the garment and athletic shoe sectors, codes of conduct that include labour standards have now spread to electronics, accessories and jewellery, food processing, aquaculture, furniture, glue, entertainment, toys, office supplies, and pharmaceuticals, among others. However, corporate codes of conduct diffuse much more slowly in sectors whose goods are not sold directly to the consuming public and as a result, these efforts are likely to benefit only a small segment of the global workforce (Scherrer and Greven 2001). Moreover, there are also a host of problems with monitoring for compliance with corporate codes and this is true for both internal audits as well as external audits by

NGOs and private monitoring firms. A large number of monitoring companies have emerged, although it is not yet clear that monitoring has become an exact science. For example, many have recently called into question the objectivity and effectiveness of the Fair Labour Association (FLA), a non-profit multi-stakeholder initiative created to improve and monitor working conditions around the world. The FLA became the centre of controversy in the early part of 2012 after the president and CEO, Auret van Heerden, praised labour conditions at Foxconn, a key Apple subcontractor in China, shortly after Apple became a dues paying member and only weeks after the publication of a *New York Times* article documenting widespread violations of worker rights and worker suicide attempts[5] (Greenhouse 2012). Critics of the FLA have also questioned whether the FLA's monitoring efforts are effective in actually producing change.

The ability of voluntary approaches such as corporate codes of conduct to significantly improve labour standards for the majority of workers in developing countries is thus debatable. Although there is some impact, progress remains slow. A recent evaluation of Nike's efforts by Locke *et al.* (2007) provides a sobering reminder that forcing Third World factories to follow labour standards in the codes of their First World clients without a higher payment for incorporating those standards is not a fully effective method. Nevertheless, global corporations in a variety of industries are adopting codes of conduct and searching for ways to make the implementation of such codes more transparent and effective. This is a currently popular area of research, and as more corporations strive to improve labour standards in their global supply chains, there will be more and better data for students to evaluate.

Certification and reporting approaches

Another voluntary approach is certification schemes, which are quite common in a number of areas other than labour standards and have achieved considerable success (e.g. the US Department of Agriculture certifying that a particular food is 100 per cent organic). The central idea of certification is that a reliable external monitoring agency conducts inspections and certifies that labour standards are not being violated in the supply chain producing these goods. The success of RUGMARK, which certifies that carpets produced from some regions are made without child labour, has resulted in a number of additional certification schemes in the labour standards realm, such as SA8000, AA1000 and ISO14001.[6] The success of these efforts depends largely on the reputation of the monitoring agency and the effectiveness of the monitoring that they do.

Reporting systems, on the other hand, depend largely on transparency. The essential element of a reporting system is that it requires those corporations who agree to participate in the system to report on the enforcement of such standards in their own firms. The best examples of these are the Global Reporting Initiative (GRI) and the UN Global Compact. The GRI commenced in 1997 and was convened by the Coalition for Environmentally Responsible Economies and the United Nations Environment Programme. GRI's basic mission is the development of globally applicable guidelines for reporting on economic, social and environmental performance for businesses, governments and NGOs. Called the 'triple bottom line' for its simultaneous focus on environmental, social and financial reporting, the idea is to elevate sustainability reporting to the same level as financial reporting. GRI requires its participating companies to report in highly specific ways, through the creation of Sustainability Reporting Guidelines in 2000. According to GRI, a total of 1,859 organizations reported in 2010 using GRI guidelines (GRI 2012). The UN Global Compact is similar in that it requires members to take specific actions: to support and respect protection of international human rights; to make sure their corporations are not complicit in human rights abuse; to uphold freedom of association and collective bargaining; to uphold elimination of forced labour; to uphold the elimination of child labour; to uphold the elimination of discrimination; to support a precautionary approach to environmental challenges; to undertake to promote greater environmental responsibility; to encourage development and diffusion of environmentally friendly technologies; and to work against corruption in all forms. Participating organizations must sign a letter of intent to participate and then report on their performance on the above ten principles in their annual report. As of February 2012, there were more than 7,000 corporate signatories in 140 countries participating in the UN Global Compact (UN Global Compact 2012).

The key problems with this approach are as follows. First, it is a voluntary approach. Not all multinational corporations participate and many that initially agree to participate never follow through. In fact, the UN Global Compact has expelled more than 3,000 companies since 2005 for failure to communicate progress on their efforts to implement the Compact's ten sustainability principles (UN Global Compact 2012; for a full list of expelled companies, see http://unglobalcompact.org/COP/analyzing_progress/expelled_participants.html). Second, there is no monitoring; no one is going to inspect to see if corporations are following the standards. The hope is that the transparency inherent in participation in reporting systems (and the danger that someone might actually check if the corporation is following core labour standards) will be sufficient to ensure that labour rights are upheld all over the world. The limited participation works against this principle, however.

In sum, a variety of multilateral and voluntary methods have been introduced to improve labour standards globally and counter the 'race to the bottom' implication of globalization. They are diverse, not necessarily integrated with each other, and each approach has both advantages and limitations. Taken together, however, these approaches bring us closer to improving labour standards around the world. The effectiveness of these approaches and the reasons for the relatively slow progress are another area ripe for research.

Globalization and employment relations

Globalization has also spawned a variety of new research in employment relations. It is impossible to review this vast body of research in this chapter (much of the comparative industrial relations research published in the last 15 years makes reference to globalization). However, it is useful to highlight certain persistent themes. One enduring question, for example, is the continuing debate over whether, and in what ways, increasing globalization and the internationalization of markets will cause employment systems around the world to converge (Hyman 1999; Gordon and Turner 2000). While early convergence predictions regarding the effects of industrialization and advances in technology proved untrue (e.g. Kerr *et al.* 1960), the debate continues, given recent findings of increasing similarity of patterns of employment relations around the world (Katz and Darbishire 2000). However, a growing body of research (e.g. the 'varieties of capitalism' literature) has focused on the reasons why industrial relations systems continue to differ across countries. The issue of whether and how globalization is contributing to increasing similarity or differences across countries will continue to be a central theme in comparative employment relations research for the next decade.

Another enduring theme has been the effects of globalization on the strategies, roles and fortunes of traditional industrial relations actors: labour, employers and governments. Globalization's impact on labour movements is a popular topic. Almost without exception, the key findings indicate both a decline in union density and a decline in trade union power (Gordon and Turner 2000; Turner *et al.* 2001). In many countries, the decline in union density has been accompanied by a decline in bargaining coverage as well, resulting in an overall drop in employment standards (e.g. Doellgast 2012). However, bargaining coverage continues to be high in European countries that do have bargaining extension mechanisms (Traxler and Brandl 2010). More recently, there has also been a spurt in research on labour's response to globalization, for example, focusing on resources for (re)building union power (e.g. Turner and Cornfield 2007), international collaboration efforts and strategies (Bair and Ramsay 2003), and the newer development of labour's efforts to conclude International Framework Agreements, which aim to secure fundamental labour rights across the global supply chains of large multinational corporations (Riisgaard and Hammer 2011). This is a 'hot' research area at the moment and will continue to be so as the effects of globalization unfold.

Research on the strategies of employers has also endured. In contrast to findings that industrial relations systems continue to be diverse, a plethora of research on employers and multinational corporations suggests that the employment relations strategies of firms seem remarkably similar across countries with differing institutional environments (Katz and Darbishire 2000). In addition, there is increasing evidence that employers, in both developed and developing countries, are increasing their resistance to union organizing (Bronfenbrenner 2008). A more general implication is that 'low-road' employment strategies are gaining ground in developing countries such as India and China while high-road employment strategies are retreating in developed countries. Apart from firm strategy with regards to labour, globalization has also spawned research that has examined human resource management within multinationals. For example, scholars have questioned whether, and under what circumstances, employment relations should be centralized, coordinated or decentralized in global corporations (Edwards and Kuruvilla 2005). Scholars are also examining a range of other questions with regard to global human resource strategies and there is much exciting work that remains to be done in this area. The similar yet distinct literatures on global value chains and global production networks (discussed in the next section) are also germane to this research stream.

Arguably, the employment relations actor that has received the bulk of research attention has been the government. On the one hand, there is research that suggests that under globalization, governments have become more 'employer-friendly', and most commonly this has been highlighted in research on Indian employment relations after liberalization policies (Kohli 2006), and of course on Chinese employment relations during the 1990s and early 2000s (Gallagher 2004) but is also true of several other countries. A disturbing trend for employment relations is the deepening interaction between government strategies for economic development and employer strategies for employee relations. As briefly discussed with regards to the consequences of globalization, this plays out in the development of free trade zones and export processing zones introduced by governments to attract foreign investment, often with labour standards below national standards that are exploited by employers. Another stream of research has focused on government strategies and how governments should protect workers from globalization's impact. Of particular import here is the efforts of governments to enact new regulation (e.g. the new labour laws in China) to contain the trend towards informality and temporary employment that appears to be growing in Asia, North America and Europe as well as other parts of the world (e.g. Friedman and Lee 2010; Keller 2011). There is at least one comparative project on atypical employment and temporary work in the EU already (Keller 2011). Related to this issue, an under-studied, though growing, arena of research is about enforcement strategies, that is, how governments are able to better enforce their own labour regulations (Amengual 2010). Although we have only described a few illustrative themes above, research on the impact of globalization on the three actors – government, labour, and employers – is extensive.

There is also research on how globalization has affected entire employment relations systems. One illustrative framework here is provided by Frenkel and Kuruvilla (2002), who argue that employment relations patterns in any country can be explained by the dominant logic underlying employment relations policy. They identify the logic of industrial peace, that is, the need to have a system of regulation in order to contain and resolve inevitable conflict between labour and management, as being the decisive force behind the design of industrial relations systems from their inception until the 1980s. However, they argue that, since the mid-1980s, the dominant logic has been the logic of competition, driven by economic globalization, and as a result, industrial relations institutions and practices were reformed in most countries in accordance with this logic. The decentralization of bargaining and the redesign of many systems between the 1985 to 2010 period are evidence of the transformation of industrial relations based on a shift from the logic of industrial peace to the logic of competition. They argue further that a new logic, a logic of employment and income protection, may be appearing as evidenced by the recent protective labour legislation in China. While the framework is potentially useful in understanding how entire systems transform, there is still work to be done to explain why certain logics are strongest in any given period and across countries. What we need is more research and perhaps more frameworks that will allow scholars to explain and predict the future trajectory of employment relations in a globalized world.

Globalization and employment relations scholarship

Given the effects of contemporary globalization on employment relations research and practice, we must ask ourselves how appropriate traditional employment relations theories are. Can they account for the growing interconnectedness of firms and countries? And more importantly, do they identify and allow us to understand the employment relations implications of the variety of intra- and inter-firm linkages arising in the global economy?

The dominant employment relations frameworks in use today focus on the ways in which firm-level employment relations are shaped by key actors and the external environment (Dunlop's System Approach and Kochan *et al.*'s Strategic Choice Framework) and how national institutional configurations affect firm level employment relations strategies (Whitley's National Business Systems approach and the 'varieties of capitalism' perspective by Hall and Soskice). Dunlop's System Approach (1958), for example, emphasizes the centrality of key environmental contexts, namely, markets, technology and power relations, for structuring the employment relationship. While also acknowledging the importance of the firm's external environment, Kochan *et al.* (1986) focus on the strategic choices of key actors – management, labour and the government – in understanding employment relations processes and outcomes at multiple levels (e.g. the strategic level, functional level and workplace level). These frameworks have been particularly useful for the analysis of employment relations in vertically integrated firms operating in a single national institutional environment. They are much less useful, however, for understanding how employment relations systems are affected by operating across national and firm boundaries.

This is partly where comparative institutional approaches, such as those of Whitley (1999) and Hall and Soskice (2001) come in. Whitley's National Business Systems framework emphasizes the role of institutional contexts which give rise to distinctive national business systems that, in turn, structure the nature of firms and the ways in which they organize and control work. Similarly, Hall and Soskice's 'varieties of capitalism' framework focuses on the ways in which different national institutional configurations shape the competitive, and in turn employment relations, strategies and practices of firms operating in different national contexts. Hall and Soskice focus in particular on two broad 'ideal types' of political economies: liberal market economies, such as the USA, in which firms find institutional support for coordinating activities via arm's-length market relations, and coordinated market economies, such as Germany, in which firms find institutional support for coordinating activities through collaborative non-market relationships. The comparative institutional approaches of Whitley and Hall and Soskice have been especially useful for comparing the employment relations systems of firms operating in different national contexts. In addition, they provide a starting point for understanding how employment relations are structured in TNCs that operate across national boundaries (e.g. 'home' vs. 'host' country effects). However, these approaches, like Dunlop and Kochan *et al.*'s frameworks, fall short in their ability to explain the employment relations implications of inter-firm connections. That is, while they do allow us to understand how employment relations systems are likely to be affected by the increasing connectedness *within* firms across national boundaries, they do not allow us to analyze how employment relations systems will be affected by the increasing connectedness *between* firms across national boundaries.[7] Accordingly, while traditional employment relations theories go a long way in helping us to understand and analyze firm strategies and employment relations, we are in need of new theoretical lenses which are able to capture and explain the diverse employment systems that are likely to arise from the variety of interconnections in today's increasingly global economy (Batt and Hermans 2012).

Network-based approaches provide such a lens by explicitly recognizing the changing nature of economic organization in the global context. These approaches focus on how companies, typically large TNCs, organize and control global production through complex networks that cross both national and firm boundaries. Two such approaches are global value chain (GVC) theory and the Global Production Network (GPN) framework. Since both approaches explicitly take into account the interconnections of economic actors across geographical space in a way that prior theories do not, they are promising schemas for employment relations scholars.

Global value chain theory is a multidisciplinary theory that examines the ways in which global production and service networks are integrated. GVC theory begins with the notion of a 'value chain', which can be used to describe the range of activities involved in bringing a product or service from conception to the buyer and beyond (Porter 1985). The activities in a given value chain can be performed by a single, vertically integrated firm, or can be performed by multiple firms across countries. The goal of GVC theory is to understand how activities are coordinated in value chains, both within and across firms, and in particular, the governance structures put in place to manage the diverse intra- and inter-firm relationships in such chains.

In line with this approach, Gereffi *et al.* (2005) identify five main types of value chain configurations with different modes of governance: market, modular, relational, captive and hierarchy. These value chain configurations vary in their degree of explicit coordination and power asymmetry, with low levels of explicit coordination and power asymmetry in market-based configurations, high levels in vertically integrated hierarchical configurations and moderate to high levels of explicit coordination and power asymmetry in network configurations (modular, relational and captive). Three key variables determine the mode of governance or the choice of value chain configuration: (1) the complexity of task requirements; (2) the codifiability of those requirements; and (3) the capabilities of actual and potential suppliers in relation to the requirements. The higher the complexity of task requirements, the lower the codifiability of said requirements and the lower the capabilities of suppliers, the more likely that lead firms will choose value chain configurations that ensure high levels of explicit coordination and power asymmetry.

The five types of value chain configurations outlined by Gereffi *et al.* account for most types of intra- and inter-firm relationships we see today. Market value chain configurations are those in which customers or lead firms and suppliers buy and sell standard products to one another with little interaction beyond exchanging goods and services for money. Examples of this can be found in the bicycle industry where national bicycle brands purchase basic components from suppliers around the world (Galvin and Morkel 2001). Modular value chain configurations are characterized by 'turnkey' suppliers who make products or provide services according to detailed customer specifications and can be found, for example, in the electronic and apparel industries where supplier firms provide full package solutions and modules to lead firms (Bair and Gereffi 2001; Sturgeon 2003). Relational value chain configurations are characterized by complex relationships between firms and typically involve the exchange of tacit knowledge and a high degree of mutual dependence. Examples of relational value chain configurations can be found in the offshoring of knowledge work, such as software development, where lead firms work closely with suppliers and often exchange proprietary information (Piore 2004). Captive value chain configurations, in contrast, are characterized by transactionally dependent suppliers and, given low supplier capabilities, are limited to a narrow range of tasks and subject to a high degree of monitoring and control by lead firms. Firms in a variety of industries such as law and accounting often have business process units or back offices which are examples of this kind of configuration. Lastly, hierarchical value chain configurations typically refer to intra-firm relationships in which affiliates perform highly complex tasks that are key to the lead firm's competitive advantage. Examples of hierarchical value chain configurations can be found in the relationships between large MNCs in a variety of industries, such as IT, and their subsidiaries involved in strategic functions such as core R&D (Quan and Chesbrough 2010).

Similar to GVC theory, the global production network framework advanced by economic geography researchers aims to capture the dynamic relationships and processes through which goods and services are produced in the global economy (Henderson *et al.* 2002). However, the GPN framework takes a much broader perspective by not only examining the range of activities and functions involved in creating a specific product or service but also and perhaps most notably, examining the range of actors, such as national governments, multinational corporations, labour unions and consumers, within global networks and the social and institutional contexts within which those networks are embedded. Accordingly, three conceptual elements form the basis of the GPN framework: (1) value, with a focus on where and how value is created, enhanced and captured in the network; (2) power, including the different sources of power in the network (e.g. corporate, institutional and collective) and how power is used in the capturing of value; and (3) embeddedness, focusing on the territorial and network embeddedness of firms.

Recognizing the utility of these network-based approaches for the study of labour and employment in the global economy, scholars have begun to incorporate these perspectives into the analysis of different employment relations phenomena. For example, studies have used GVC/GPN approaches to examine the role of labour agency in structuring global networks[8] and vice versa (e.g. Rainnie *et al.* 2011; Taylor 2010), the increasing casualization and feminization of employment in such networks (e.g. Barrientos and Kritzinger 2004), the implications of firm upgrading for labour (Barrientos *et al.* 2011), and increasingly, the employment relations outcomes for workers at different points along the value chain (e.g. Nadvi and Thoburn 2004). Nevertheless, the integration of network-based approaches with the analysis of work and employment remains limited as most studies have tended to focus on a narrow range of issues and outcomes.

Thus, it would appear that, while we have two new theories/frameworks that show promise, they must be developed further in ways that permit scholars to answer the variety of employment relations questions raised by continuing globalization. One fledgling effort in this direction is described here. Lakhani *et al.* (2013), for example, build on GVC theory by providing a new configurational framework for examining the employment relations implications of the various interconnections within and between firms in global networks.[9] Using GVC theory, the authors outline the ways in which each value chain configuration, given its level of explicit coordination, power asymmetry and task requirements, shapes employment systems of the next element in the chain, the suppliers.[10] They identify four employment system criteria that capture important dimensions of supplier employment relations systems (lead firm influence, skill and knowledge levels, employment stability, and national institutional influences) and show how they are likely to vary across each of the value chain configurations (market, modular, relational, captive, hierarchy) identified by Gereffi *et al.* (2005).

As shown in Table 20.1, the configurational framework suggests that different value chain configurations will lead to fundamentally different employment system configurations. In general, employment systems in value chain configurations with high explicit coordination and power asymmetry (recall from above that this is most likely where task complexity is high, codifiability is low and/or there are low supplier capabilities) will be characterized by high lead firm influence and be subject to national institutional influences from both the lead firm's home country (referred to as 'Lead' in Table 20.1) and the supplier firm's host country (referred to as 'Local' in Table 20.1), albeit to varying degrees. This is most likely to occur under captive, relational and hierarchical configurations. In contrast, employment systems in value chain configurations with low explicit coordination and power asymmetry will be characterized by low lead firm influence and will be subject to primarily local national institutional influences. Market and modular value chain configurations are expected to evidence such a pattern. Finally, task complexity is expected to be positively related to both the skill and knowledge of employees and the stability of employment, with relatively higher skilled workers and higher employment stability found in value chain configurations with high task complexity and vice versa. Thus, employees in hierarchical, relational and even modular value chain configurations are expected to be higher-skilled and hold more permanent forms of employment than employees in market and captive value chain configurations. As an example, then, the configurational framework predicts that a supplier in a relational value chain configuration and a supplier in a captive value chain configuration will have very different employment system configurations, particularly across the dimensions of skills and stability. Research from the software and call centre industries provide support for these assertions, with long-term highly skilled workers found in software development firms under relational configurations (Piore 2004) and lower skilled workers with low job security and high turnover typically found in call centres under captive configurations (Taylor 2010).

The configurational framework described above permits a better understanding of the dynamics of globalization and its effects on employment relations than previous theories

Table 20.1 A configurational framework for employment relations

Value chain configuration	*Nature of task requirements*	*Employment system criteria*			
		Lead firm influence on supplier employment relations	*Skill & knowledge of employees in the supplier firm*	*Stability of employment in the supplier firm*	*National institutional influences on supplier employment relations*
Market	Low task complexity High task codifiability High supplier capability	Low	Low	Low	Local
Modular	High task complexity High task codifiability High supplier capability	Low	Moderate	Moderate	Local
Relational	High task complexity Low task codifiability High supplier capability	Moderate	High	High	Local and Lead
Captive	High task complexity High task codifiability Low supplier capability	High	Low	Low	Local and Lead
Hierarchy	High task complexity Low task codifiability Low external supplier capability	High	High	High	Lead

Source: Lakhani *et al.* (2013).

allow, particularly for the analysis of value chains. The framework serves as a baseline tool for comparative analysis and can be used to examine a variety of different employment relations issues in the global context. As a result, the framework generates enough testable propositions for further research. It may also, in turn, aid in the development of effective practices and policy responses to address a myriad of global employment relations challenges, including but not limited to challenges surrounding the international regulation of labour standards and the implications of globalization for employment relations systems and actors, as discussed earlier. However, the framework is also limited in some ways, and the effort, while taking us forward, illustrates the challenges in developing network-based theories into useful tools for employment relations researchers in order to advance both the theory and practice of employment relations in the global economy.

Conclusion

Globalization presents employment relations actors with a variety of new challenges, while also challenging employment relations scholars to think in new ways about the interesting questions in the field. And as employment relations actors experiment with new approaches, it provides new issues for scholars to study. At a time when unions are in decline in most countries, triggering a decline in national industrial relations scholarship, globalization and regionalization stimulate the growth of comparative approaches. This chapter has provided a broad overview of some of the challenges for policy-making as well as for research. A key challenge for students is the development of frameworks that are better able to capture the nature of global inter-firm linkages. This is an exciting time for students of employment relations and we hope this chapter will stimulate the development of new research questions.

Notes

1 While globalization is multidimensional (e.g. economic, political, social, environmental, cultural, see Held *et al.* 2004), the focus of this chapter is *economic globalization* though we will, at times, touch on the other dimensions as they are inevitably interrelated.

2 Chapter 22 in this volume deals with regionalization issues in greater detail, and Lance Compa's authoritative work on NAFTA and its labour side agreement NAALC is a valuable reference (Compa 1999).

3 For more information on ratifications by country and convention, see http://www.ilo.org/dyn/normlex/en/f?p–ORMLEXPUB:1:0.

4 While the discussion here focuses on one voluntary form of regulation in particular, corporate codes of conduct, there are other voluntary approaches as well, such as international framework agreements at the company level and private social standards or multi-stakeholder codes at the industry level (Riisgaard and Hammer 2011). These approaches will be covered in detail in Chapter 22.

5 It is worth noting that initial findings from the FLA's investigation of working conditions in Foxconn factories revealed numerous violations of its own codes as well as Chinese labour laws. For the full report, see http://www.fairlabour.org/report/foxconn-investigation-report.

6 These are all voluntary certification and reporting systems that global corporations join. SA8000 was launched by a coalition of rights activists, governments, MNCs (Avon, Dole, Toys 'R' Us) and originally funded by the US government's contribution of $1.6 million. SAI sets standards for decent work and appoints inspectors, and certifies factories around the world. The AA1000 standards are a UK-based multi-stakeholder approach that also sets standards (www.accountability.org.uk). The ISO 14000 Standards related to environmental management also specify some labour issues.

7 Comparative institutional approaches do recognize the significance of inter-firm connections, for example, by examining the extent of ownership and non-ownership coordination in business systems (Whitley 1999) or the level of inter-firm cooperation (Hall and Soskice 2001). However, these inter-firm connections are assumed to take place *within* national institutional boundaries and are defining features of distinctive national capitalisms.

8 Despite the distinction made by some scholars between global value *chains* and global production *networks* (see, for example, Henderson *et al.* 2002), we use the terms 'chain' and 'network' interchangeably.

9 It is worth noting here that Lakhani *et al.* do not present their framework as a substitute for existing employment relations frameworks. Instead, they acknowledge the continuing relevance of those frameworks and offer their configurational framework as a complement to traditional theories of employment relations by focusing on the interconnections within and between firms in global value chains – the missing piece in previous theories.

10 The configurational framework focuses on employment relations in supplier firms (internal and external) rather than the lead firms (e.g. TNCs), because lead firms drive the level and type of coordination with supplier firms and as a result, it is supplier firms' employment systems which are most likely to be affected by their involvement in different configurations with lead firms.

References

Amengual, M. (2010) 'Complementary labour regulation: the uncoordinated combination of state and private regulators in the Dominican Republic', *World Development*, 38(3): 405–14.

Bair, J. and Gereffi, G. (2001) 'Local clusters in the global chain: the causes and consequences of export dynamism in Torreon's blue jeans industry', *World Development*, 29(11): 1885–903.

Bair, J. and Ramsay, H. (2003) 'MNCs and global commodity chains: implications for labour strategies', in W. N. Cooke (ed.) *Multinational Companies and Global Human Resource Strategies*, London: Quorum Books.

Barrientos, S. and Kritzinger, A. (2004) 'Squaring the circle: global production and the informalisation of work in South African fruit exports', *Journal of International Development*, 16(1): 81–92.

Barrientos, S., Gereffi, G. and Rossi, A. (2011) 'Economic and social upgrading in global production networks: a new paradigm for a changing world', *International Labour Review*, 150(3–4): 319–40.

Batt, R. and Hermans, M. (2012) 'Global human resource management: bridging strategic and institutional perspectives', *Research in Personnel and Human Resources Management*, 31: 1–52.

Blank, R. M. and Freeman, R. B. (1994) 'Evaluating the connection between social protection and economic flexibility', in R. Blank (ed.) *Social Protection versus Economic Flexibility: Is There a Trade-Off?*, Chicago: University of Chicago Press.

Bolle, M. J. (2012) *U.S.-Columbia Free Trade Agreement: Labour Issues*, Washington, DC: Congressional Research Service Report for Congress. Available at: http://www.fas.org/sgp/crs/row/RL34759.pdf.

Bronfenbrenner, K. (2008) 'The experience of organizing in the context of the global economy', in T. Hastings (ed.) *The State of the Unions: Challenges Facing Organized Labour in Ireland*, Dublin: The Liffey Press.

Brune, N. and Garrett, G. (2005) 'The globalization Rorschach test: international economic integration, inequality and the role of government', *Annual Review of Political Science*, 8: 399–423.

Charnovitz, S. (1992) 'Environmental and labour standards in trade', *The World Economy*, 15(3): 335–56.

Compa, L. (1999) 'NAFTA's labour side agreement five years on: progress and prospects for the NAALC', *Canadian Labor and Employment Law Journal*, 7: 1–30.

—— (2003) 'Assessing assessments: a survey of efforts to measure countries' compliance with freedom of association standards', *Comparative Labour Law and Policy Journal*, 24: 283–320.

Dicken, P. (2011) *Global Shift: Mapping the Changing Contours of the World Economy*, 6th edn, London: Sage.

Doellgast, V. (2012) *Disintegrating Democracy at Work: Labor Unions and the Future of Good Jobs in the Service Economy*, Ithaca, NY: ILR Press.

Dunlop, J. (1958) *Industrial Relations Systems*, New York: Holt.

Edwards, T. and Kuruvilla, S. (2005) 'International HRM: national business systems, organizational politics and the international division of labour in MNCs', *International Journal of Human Resource Management*, 16(1): 1–21.

Freeman, R. B. (1994) *A Hard-Headed Look at Labour Standards*, Geneva: International Institute for Labour Studies.

—— (1998) *What Role for Labour Standards in the Global Economy?*, Boston, MA: Harvard University and National Bureau for Economic Research/London School of Economics, Centre for Economic Performance, Discussion Paper.

Frenkel, S. and Kuruvilla, S. (2002) 'Logics of action, globalization, and changing employment relations in China, India, Malaysia, and the Philippines', *Industrial and Labor Relations Review*, 55(3): 387–412.

Friedman, E and Lee, C.K. (2010) 'Remaking the world of Chinese labour: a 30-year retrospective', *British Journal of Industrial Relations*, 48(3): 507–33.

Gallagher, M. (2004) 'Time is money, efficiency is life: the transformation of labour relations in China', *Studies in Comparative International Development*, 39(2): 11–44.

Galvin, P. and Morkel, A. (2001) 'The effect of product modularity on industry structure: the case of the world bicycle industry', *Industry and Innovation*, 81: 31–47.

Garrett, G. (2000) 'The causes of globalization', *Comparative Political Studies*, 33(6–7): 941–91.

Gereffi, G., Humphrey, J. and Sturgeon, T. (2005) 'The governance of global value chains', *Review of International Political Economy*, 12(1): 78–104.

Giddens, A. and Griffiths, S. (2006) *Sociology*, 5th edn, Cambridge: Polity Press.

Global Reporting Initiative (GRI) (2012) *Press Resources: Quick Facts*. Available at: https://www.globalreporting.org/information/news-and-press-centre/press-resources/Pages/default.aspx.

Gordon, M.E. and Turner, L. (eds) (2000) *Transnational Cooperation among Trade Unions: Philosophy, Structure and Practice*, Ithaca, NY: Cornell University Press.

Greenhouse, S. (2012) 'Early praise in inspection at Foxconn brings doubt', *The New York Times*, 17 Feb. Available at: http://www.nytimes.com/2012/02/17/business/early-praise-in-foxconn-inspection-brings-doubt.html?_r=1.

Hall, P. A. and Soskice, D. (eds) (2001) *Varieties of Capitalism: The Institutional Foundations of Comparative Advantage*, Oxford: Oxford University Press.

Held, D., McGrew, A., Goldblatt, D. and Perraton, J. (2004) *Global Transformations: Politics, Economics and Culture*, Oxford: Blackwell.

Henderson, J., Dicken, P., Hess, M., Coe, N. and Yeung, H. W-C. (2002) 'Global production networks and the analysis of economic development', *Review of International Political Economy*, 9(3): 436–64.

Hirst, P. and Thompson, G. (1999) *Globalization in Question*, 2nd edn, Cambridge: Polity Press.

Hyman, R. (1999) 'National industrial relations systems and transnational challenges: an essay in review', *European Journal of Industrial Relations*, 5(1): 94–111.

International Labour Organization (ILO) (1998) *Labour and Social Issues Relating to Export Processing Zones*. Available at: http://www.ilo.org/wcmsp5/groups/public/---ed_dialogue/---actrav/documents/publication/wcms_114918.pdf.

—— (2009) *United States Free Trade Agreements (FTAs)*. Available at: http://www.ilo.org/global/standards/information-resources-and-publications/free-trade-agreements-and-labour-rights/WCMS_115531/lang--en/index.htm.

Jensen, N. M. (2006) *Nation-States and the Multinational Corporation: A Political Economy of Foreign Direct Investment*, Princeton, NJ: Princeton University Press.

Katz, H. C. and Darbishire, O. (2000) *Converging Divergences: World-Wide Changes in Employment Systems*, Ithaca, NY: Cornell University Press.

Keller, B. (2011) *Atypische Beschäftigung und soziale Risiken. Entwicklung, Strukturen, Regulierung*. Bonn: Expertise für die Friedrich-Ebert-Stiftung. Available at: http://library.fes.de/pdf-files/wiso/08527.pdf (with S. Seifert/S. Schulz/B. Zimmer).

Kerr, C, Dunlop, J., Harbison, F. and C. Myers. (1960) *Industrialism and Industrial Man*, Cambridge, MA: Harvard University Press.

Kochan, T. A. Katz, H. C. and McKersie, R. B. (1986) *The Transformation of American Industrial Relations*, New York: Basic Books.

Kohli, A. (2006) 'Politics of economic growth in India, 1980–2005, Part 1: the 1980s', *Economic and Political Weekly*, 1 April.

Kuruvilla, S. and Verma, A. (2006) 'International labour standards, soft regulation, and national government roles', *Journal of Industrial Relations*, 48(1): 41–58.

Lakhani, T., Kuruvilla, S. and Avgar, A. (2013) 'From the firm to the network: global value chains and employment relations theory', *British Journal of Industrial Relations* doi:10–1111/bjir.12015.

Lanz, R. and Miroudot, S. (2011) *Intra-Firm Trade: Patterns, Determinants and Policy Implications*, Paris: OECD, Trade Policy Working Paper No. 114. Available at: http://www.oecd.org/official-documents/publicdisplaydocumentpdf/?cote=TAD/TC/WP(2010)27/FINAL&docLanguage=En.

Locke, R. M., Qin, F. and Brause, A. (2007) 'Does monitoring improve labour standards? Lessons from Nike', *Industrial and Labor Relations Review*, 61(1): 3–31.

Longworth, R. C. (1999) *The Global Squeeze*, Chicago: Contemporary Books.

Markusen, J. R. (1995) 'The boundaries of multinational enterprises and the theory of international trade', *Journal of Economic Perspectives*, 9(2): 169–89.

Nadvi, K. and Thoburn, J. (2004) 'Vietnam in the global garment and textile value chain: impacts on firms and workers', *Journal of International Development*, 16(1): 111–23.

OECD-WTO (2012) *Measuring Trade in Value-Added: An OECD-WTO Joint Initiative*. Available at: http://www.oecd.org/document/51/0,3746,en_2649_37431_49865779_1_1_1_37431,00.html.

Osland, J.S. (2003) 'Broadening the debate: the pros and cons of globalization', *Journal of Management Inquiry*, 12(2): 137–54.

Piore, M. J. (2004) 'The limits of the division of labour in design and the prospects for off-shore software development in Mexico', paper for The Software Industry in the Developing World Workshop, Yale University.

Porter, M. E. (1985) *Competitive Advantage: Creating and Sustaining Superior Performance*, New York: The Free Press.

Quan, X. and Chesbrough, H. (2010) 'Hierarchical segmentation of R&D process and intellectual property protection: evidence from multinational R&D laboratories in China', *IEEE Transactions on Engineering Management*, 57(1): 9–21.

Rainnie, A., Herod, A. and McGrath-Champ, S. (2011) 'Review and positions: global production networks and labour', *Competition and Change*, 15(2): 155–69.

Riisgaard, L, and Hammer, N. (2011) 'Prospects for labour in global value chains: labour standards in the cut flower and banana industries', *British Journal of Industrial Relations*, 49(1): 168–90.

Scherrer, C. and Greven, T. (2001) *Global Rules for Trade: Codes of Conduct, Social Labelling, Workers' Rights Clauses*, Munster: Verlag Westfalisches Dampfboot.

Schmukler, S., Zoido, P. and Halac, M. (2004) *Financial Globalization, Crises and Contagion*, Washington, DC: World Bank, Globalization Policy Research Report.

Scholte, J. A. (2004) 'Civil society and democratically accountable global governance', *Government and Opposition*, 39(2): 211–33.

Sisson, K. and Marginson, P. (2001) 'Soft regulation: travesty of the real thing or new dimension?', Working Paper 32/01, University of Warwick, Industrial Relations Research Unit, Coventry.

Sturgeon, T. J. (2003) 'What really goes on in Silicon Valley? Spatial clustering and dispersal in modular production networks', *Journal of Economic Geography*, 3(2): 199–225.

Taylor, P. (2010) 'The globalization of service work: analysing the transnational call centre value chain', in P. Thompson and C. Smith (eds) *Working Life: Renewing Labour Process Analysis*, Basingstoke: Palgrave Macmillan.

Traxler, F. and Brandl, B. (2010) 'Collective bargaining, macroeconomic performance, and the sectoral composition of trade unions', *Industrial Relations*, 49(1): 91–115.

Turner, L. and Cornfield, D. (eds) (2007) *Labour in the New Urban Battlegrounds: Local Solidarity in a Global Economy*, Ithaca, NY: Cornell University Press.

Turner, L., Katz, H. C. and Hurd, R. W. (eds) (2001) *Rekindling the Movement: Labor's Quest for Relevance in the 21st Century*, Ithaca, NY: Cornell University Press.

UN Global Compact (2012) 'UN global compact has expelled over 3,000 companies', 9 February. Available at: http://www.unglobalcompact.org/news/188-02-09-2012.

Whitley, R. (1999) *Divergent Capitalisms*, Oxford: Oxford University Press.

World Bank (2007) *A Guide to the World Bank*, Washington, DC: World Bank.

21 Voluntary regulation

Codes of practice and framework agreements

Michael Fichter

Introduction

Economic globalization has had far-reaching consequences for the lives of millions of people throughout the world. Directly and indirectly at their workplaces, in their training institutions or on the job market, people have been affected by dynamic restructuring processes across national borders often far removed from their immediate surroundings. The globalization process has created and spread new economic structures, exposing the existence of working conditions and employment relations that are poorly or non-regulated, underpaid and dangerous (International Trade Union Confederation [ITUC] 2011; Institute for Global Labour and Human Rights [GLHR] 2012), and giving vent to political and academic debates over a 'race to the bottom' (Kapstein 1997; Lee 1997; Drezner 2000; Chan and Ross 2003; Singh and Zammit 2004; Mosley and Uno 2007). Public awareness of the need for global labour standards to ensure collective representation of employees and collective bargaining and to prevent whipsawing and undercutting is spreading. But overcoming resistance, among both governments and businesses, and finding the ways and means of regulating the employment relationship and setting globally recognized minimum standards across boundaries have proven to be a daunting task and an uphill struggle. As was presented in Chapter 20, the growth and power of transnational corporations (TNCs), together with the complexity and fragmentation of supply chains and global production networks, combined with the heterogeneity and staying power of domestic institutional barriers, make this task even more difficult.

Despite the increasing transnationalization of labour markets, setting standards for wages and working conditions is still handled within national boundaries. Often this is primarily an issue governed by employer unilateral action or by state regulations, but where unions and employers are organized and institutionalized, wage setting is regulated by negotiated contracts between national employer and employee representatives. In other words, as economic activity became more internationalized, the embeddedness of labour in national regulatory regimes was threatened by deregulation arising from the adoption of neo-liberal policies (Waddington 1999: 2). Nevertheless, the question of setting standards for the employment relationship is no longer being addressed exclusively as a national issue, but increasingly in terms of the need for a global answer to setting standards. In his 2001 report to the International Labour Conference, ILO Director-General Juan Somavia pointed out that:

> A plethora of self-regulatory initiatives known as voluntary private initiatives (VPIs) have emerged in recent years which, while not enforced by law, may serve to

> enhance or supplement behaviour regulated by law. Codes of conduct, social labelling initiatives, certification, licensing, monitoring and social audits, as well as framework agreements between companies and ITSs [International Trade Secretariats, forerunners of the Global Union Federations] such as those noted above, are providing social signposts to guide economic activity along the entire commodity chain, from the sourcing of raw materials to manufacturing and retail. Many lead firms in these chains today are applying codes of conduct to their subcontractors. Many of the companies that have adopted codes are now finding it necessary to develop monitoring systems to check on compliance. In some cases they have found that to be credible they need to include independent verification systems to reinforce their own efforts. VPIs need to show evidence of their actual implementation. There is a new demand for ratification of companies' social policies.
>
> (International Labour Organization 2001)

Efforts of a broad array of civil society organizations (CSOs), including consumer campaigns and labour unions, to revamp the asymmetry of interest articulation in the 'contested fields' (Levy 2008) of employment relations and challenge the dominant role of TNCs have noticeably impacted the course of globalization during the past two decades. But the results up to now have been more of a patchwork than a coherent set of standards. Indeed, this is a general shortcoming of the progress of 'global governance' in which private interest governance (Cutler 2002; Haufler 2006; Bartley 2007; Conzelmann and Wolf 2008) and self-regulation schemes have a primary role while the presence of the state is a shadow (Abbott and Snidal 2009). Instead of supplementing an institutional framework of governmental legal standards, private interest governance has risen to fill a gap opened by deregulation and liberalization in the globalizing economy. Often it serves to protect hegemonic interests and dominant positions, but occasionally it can serve a broader array of interests (Cutler 2010). And, second, because of the non-governmental status of the promulgators and participants and a general lack of recourse to judicial remedy, the character of private interest governance is voluntary. In the field of employment relations, this voluntarism poses an enormous challenge in regard to implementation, even when rational self-interest – and not just good will – is the driving impetus.

This chapter will explore and evaluate three types of transnational voluntary regulations in respect to the employment relationship. Such regulations may be regarded as exemplifying the 'voluntary standards model', which has been recognized as one of four possible models of international labour standards (Block *et al.* 2001).[1] In the voluntary standards model, all policies and procedures turn on TNCs as central actors. As the literature shows (Djelic and Quack 2003), TNCs are actively and strategically shaping global governance beyond their own firm boundaries. TNCs are increasingly involved in global regulation and institution building. This is most evident in the discourses on global value chains or networks (Fichter and Sydow 2002; Gereffi *et al.* 2005; Boyd *et al.* 2007; Locke and Romis 2007) as well as on 'corporate social responsibility' (CSR) (Scherer and Palazzo 2007; Waddock 2008). Establishing voluntary labour standards involves processes in which management interacts in different ways with external actors.

For our purposes, the typology proposed by Kolk *et al.* (1999) offers a useful tool for presenting and analyzing these differences. To begin with, voluntary regulation may initially be unilaterally determined, that is, corporate-driven and corporate-controlled, directed at its own operations or at suppliers (standard-setting, compliance) and designed to notify the public of the existence of such a policy. This is generally the case with CSR. Examples of this first type of regulation are individual corporate codes of conduct covering labour and environmental issues. As a second type, voluntary regulation may also be pursued by TNCs in collaboration with external interest groups such as CSOs. In most accounts, labour unions are included in this general category of organizations that exist organizationally outside of the firms they are attempting to influence. But in contrast to other types of CSOs, labour unions have a representative legitimacy grounded in their representation of employees within the firm. Voluntary regulation that includes CSOs and possibly labour unions along with several TNCs are considered as multi-stakeholder initiatives. Finally, framework agreements between Global Union Federations (GUFs) and TNCs will be presented as a third distinct type of transnational voluntary regulation. We will return to these three types further on, and then turn to their comparative analysis in terms of the international environment; the transnational institutional setting; the actors and their interests, ideas, ideologies and identities; power resources; and strategies and actions.

Voluntary regulation in the context of global governance

Stepping back from our discussion of labour standards for a brief overview of some broader issues, we find that in the academic discourse around economic globalization, the role of private actors and regulatory regimes has been conducted using the term 'global governance'. In a definition offered by the UN Commission on Global Governance, it is:

> the sum of the many ways individuals and institutions, public and private, manage their common affairs. It is a continuing process through which conflicting or diverse interests may be accommodated and co-operative action may be taken. It includes formal institutions and regimes empowered to enforce compliance, as well as informal arrangements that people and institutions either have agreed to or perceive to be in their interest . . . There is no single model or form of global governance, nor is there a single structure or set of structures. It is a broad, dynamic, complex process of interactive decision-making that is constantly evolving and responding to changing circumstances.
>
> (Commission on Global Governance 1998: 1)

From the perspective of the international relations discipline, the discourse on global governance addresses the functionality and legitimacy of international institutions in the absence of 'government' (Rosenau and Czempiel 1995). For some authors, this is placed in conjunction with processes of 'denationalization' (Zürn 1998). In classical international regime theory,[2] which juxtaposes the anarchy of the international sphere with the sovereignty of the nation state, increasing internationalization has curtailed the capacity of states to cushion the social impacts of market liberalization and given rise to a disembedded corporate sector in a new global public domain (Ruggie 2004). In this context, the global governance discourse is often defined as being about 're-regulation' and having both an analytical and a normative dimension (Cox 1987; Brand 2003). In particular, the ongoing debates in the political science community and among students of International Political Economy (IPE) on 'global economic governance' (Schirm 2007:13) have centred on the growing power of TNCs to both shape and avoid transnational social and political responsibilities (Djelic and Quack 2003: Scherer and Palazzo 2011). Their role in the proliferation of global governance schemes has roots in both market-driven factors and in policy choices by a wide range of political actors arising over conflicts of interest. The character of such schemes and the selection and role of the actors involved have important ramifications for theoretical considerations of legitimacy and democracy (Palan 1999; Zürn 2004; Kolben 2011). Non-state actors are recognized for their role in rule-making, for their competency and resources (informational, expertise, monitoring capacity, mobilization and representation power), and above all for their contribution to the implementation of decisions (Grande *et al.* 2006). In particular, because 'the regulation of transnational socio-economic problems depends essentially on the option "governance without government"' (Müller *et al.* 2004: 69), increasing attention is being paid to the spread of such phenomena as 'public-private-partnerships' (Börzel and Risse 2005), 'global public policy networks' (Detomasi 2007), 'industry self-regulation' (Haufler 2003), 'transnational private authority' (Nölke 2004) and cooperative 'private governance' schemes (Pattberg 2005), the existence of which attests to a piecemeal process of constructing new locations of authority in a global space.

To the extent that such schemes involve the global regulation of labour, there is an overlap with the 'voluntary standards model' referred to above, in particular when concerned with TNCs and non-governmental organizations (NGOs). Certainly, academic interest in the role of these non-state actors has not ignored the issue of working conditions and the violation of human rights (Greven and Scherrer 2002). But within this broader global governance discourse, and in regard to the real-life conflicts reported almost daily, the dominant focus has been on the policies of transnational corporations and their critique. The UN Global Compact (Paul 2001), or the concept of 'ratcheting up' to higher labour standards (Sabel *et al.* 2000) may be regarded as prime examples of the approach of encouraging management to use its capacities and capabilities toward this end. Only marginal attention has been directed at issues of employment and the impact of globalization on the daily lives of employees (Amoore 2002), and neither the question of employee voice or empowerment nor the role of organized labour have been raised consistently in regard to global governance apart from the field of management and business charter (Cragg 2007: Koch-Baumgarten 2011). Moreover, research and theoretical considerations have generally treated TNCs as homogenous entities, rarely problematizing their internal power struggles and interest conflicts (Strange 1999; Fuchs 2004). Transnational activism (Keck and Sikkink 1999) has for the most part been defined in terms of consumer campaigns, non-governmental organizations and ethical investors who are involved as 'value actors motivated by principled beliefs rather than any direct stake in an issue' (Abbott and Snidal 2009: 60). Invoking 'moral authority' (Lipschutz and Fogel 2002: 117), the aim of such activism has been to place TNCs in the public limelight and bring corporate management to adhere to human rights norms and internationally recognized labour standards. In contrast, while labour unions may also be engaged as 'value actors', their pursuit of such goals is primarily motivated by their mandate to represent the material interests of employees within the firm and give them a voice in setting standards. On this level, questions of participation and empowerment become important factors for judging the outcomes of voluntary regulation of the employment relationship within the context of global governance.

> Rather than looking to international human rights campaigns for models, transnational workers' advocates might consider strategies aimed at strengthening workers' citizenship rights within democratic states-strategies that would rely less on consumer ethics and corporate codes of conduct and more on improving inspections and enforcement of labour laws around the world.
>
> (Seidman 2005: 164)

Voluntary regulation and the employment relationship in the global arena

Nearly equal to the vast number of non-governmental or partnership schemes for market and policy regulation that exist today are analyses and reports on them in academic publications. While a good majority of these publications are concerned with schemes that include references to 'labour' or 'social' issues, only a small number of publications, as a rule those focusing on a single scheme or a particular set of schemes (Organization for Economic Co-operation and Development [OECD] 2001; Kocher 2008; Schömann *et al.* 2008) actually address labour issues specifically. Abbott and Snidal (2009) have provided a 'governance triangle' consisting of states, firms and NGOs engaged in 'regulatory standard-setting' for all kinds of voluntary schemes that can serve as an initial reference. Kolk *et al.* (1999) provide a more specific typology of voluntary employment regulation schemes that is appropriate to our purpose. Although the heterogeneity of such schemes and the dynamic nature of their actual practice make their precise categorization in many cases difficult, resulting in a variety of hybrids, the following types are deemed to cover the most typical – and prevalent – kinds that are operative today.

We begin with single corporate statements and agreements. This category refers to both unilaterally drafted and published codes of conduct as well as to those agreements resulting from corporate campaigns directed at a single firm, particularly those with recognizable brand names. We also include codes developed under the auspices of business associations in this category, because it is generally the member companies that draft and then individually administer such codes. The associations have provided only assistance – infrastructure and media outlets. The second type of voluntary regulation (multi-stakeholder) involves a larger number and different types of actors. Multi-stakeholder initiatives (MSIs) are constructed to integrate competing interests groups in a regulatory structure covering either a single sector or used as a cross-sector instrument. Both of these categories of regulation are outcomes of TNC reactions, directly and indirectly, to the criticisms and pressure of civil society organisations and investors. While labour unions have been participants in a variety of 'naming and shaming' coalitions, they have not figured prominently in their development or outcomes. Rather, they have developed their own, interest-based, approach – framework agreements – to voluntary regulation, which is the third type we will explore.

The three groups of voluntary regulations are structured so that we can compare them. Following a short review of their history and of the international environment in which they exist, we will introduce the actors with their interests, ideas and power resources. From there we move on to cover the contents of the regulations, their procedures of implementation and monitoring, and their reach or field of intended applicability.

Single corporate arrangements and the employment relationship: unilateral CSR; corporate campaigns

The first appearance of corporate 'codes of conduct' is generally associated with the announcement of the Sullivan Principles in 1977. The Sullivan Principles were designed to serve as a guideline and justification for US corporations doing business in South Africa after they had been widely criticized for their acceptance of the apartheid regime (Seidman 2005). Years later, as the growth of transnational corporations and their global production networks became a major topic in the globalization debate (Klein 1999), TNCs were returned to the limelight of public attention again as leading actors. Their counterparts were mostly activists from the USA or Europe, coming together in college groups, consumer campaigns, church-supported initiatives or political organizations. In the absence of effective institutional safeguards for employees dependent for their livelihood on TNC global production and supply networks (for example, in regulation-free export processing zones), a wide array of groups have used public spaces and media presence to question the business operations of brand name commercial corporations, organize effective boycotts and mobilize broad support for their demands.

Being at the centre of the regulation controversy, growing numbers of such corporations have responded to both the scaling back of governmental market regulations and to public accusations of involvement in labour rights violations by proclaiming a unilaterally defined policy of 'corporate social responsibility' (Dashwood 2007; Taneja *et al.* 2011; Brammer *et al.* 2012; Marens 2012). Especially in the early phases of this development, such policies were little more than vague internal statements of principle designed to enhance the corporation's public image and ward off binding governmental regulations (Fuchs 2000). But faced with a growing international concern for the recognition of universal human rights (Ruggie 2007) and for the closing of the 'responsibility gap' in regard to the condition of labour in the global economy (Braun 2001: 258), corporations have signed on to the use of voluntary codes of conduct as pivotal elements of CSR (Fichter and Sydow 2002) in the hope of making a virtue out of necessity (Locke *et al.* 2009) and to enhance their 'reputation in the marketplace' (OECD 2001: 16).

The proliferation of such codes has been especially widespread in the apparel, textile and sport shoe industries which have been targeted by consumer campaigns. An OECD survey in 2001 reported that of a total of 246 codes, the highest number (23) for any single sector was found in textiles, while there were 61 in retail trade (ibid.). That study found that, while more than half of all codes included references to labour, only 13.5 per cent of them referenced ILO conventions (Table 21.1) (OECD 2001: 9). Here again it was those sectors that have been subject to public controversy that showed a 'high level of commitment' to labour issues in their codes.

The most recent review of such codes, based on case studies of some 50 corporations with both codes of conduct and framework agreements, came to the conclusion that: 'codes of conduct aim at reaffirming norms related to the broader concept of corporate social responsibility and business ethics, and thus include also references to labour standards' but that these 'are only one issue among others in codes of conduct' (Schömann *et al.* 2008: 2).

As guidelines, these codes usually contain no formal or special procedures for implementation; instead, there is an underlying assumption that they will be integrated into standard corporate operations and that existing measures will ensure that all responsible corporate sites will comply with the policies set out in the code by central management. But in the end, to achieve compliance, most codes include procedures for internal or external monitoring, the latter being more common among corporations interested in espousing transparency (OECD 2001). In the OECD survey, obligations for suppliers were included in 40 per cent of the codes, and in a more recent smaller survey the inclusion rate was 60 per cent (Schomann *et al.* 2008: 26). Other analyses in the literature on codes of conduct regularly mention the incompleteness of coverage in regard to suppliers, while at the same time acknowledging the 'upstream' prevalence of labour violations, especially where unskilled labour in developing countries is involved. To be sure, the issue of supplier adherence to a code it neither drafted nor pronounced is complex, making the boundaries of a code's application an area of inconclusiveness, even when explicitly extended in general to suppliers.

Table 21.1 The labour content of the codes

	Percentage of codes mentioning attribute *
Reasonable working environment	75.7
Compliance with laws	65.5
No discrimination or harassment	60.8
Compensation	45.3
No child labour	43.2
Obligations on contractors/suppliers	41.2
No forced labour	38.5
Provision of training	32.4
Working hours	31.8
Freedom of association	29.7
Specific mention of 'human rights'	25.0
Monitoring	24.3
Right to information	13.5
ILO Codes mentioned	10.1
Promotion	8.8
Reasonable advance notice	3.4
No excessive casual labour	3.4
Flexible workplace relations	0.7

Source: OECD.

Note: * These are calculated as: 100* (the number of codes mentioning attribute) ÷ (the number of codes citing labour).

Multi-stakeholder initiatives and monitoring auditors

In contrast to the codes with single TNC jurisdiction (sometimes with mention of suppliers), this group includes schemes with both a generally broader mandate and a broader range of parties. Multi-stakeholder initiatives, as the name implies, are composed of representatives from different constituencies, including corporations, civil society organizations, and sometimes government agencies, in which case they may be known as public-private-partnerships.[3] Whatever their organizational form, their mandate is usually defined in terms of monitoring or auditing labour conditions.

Many of these types of schemes were initiated by non-governmental organizations as models for particular industry or product standards. In some cases, such as with the Ethical Trading Initiative (ETI) or the Forest Stewardship Council (Bernstein and Cashore 2007; Overdevest 2010), membership was open to companies as well as NGOs and labour unions. The earliest instances of this type of voluntary regulation appeared in the apparel industry, the first most widely-known organization being the Fair Labour Association (FLA). The FLA was inaugurated out of negotiations initiated by US President Clinton in 1996 in the wake of reports of child labour in the industry. The FLA code has been lauded by UN Special Representative on Business and Human Rights John Ruggie, but because its policy is to work with the companies that fund it to improve their internal monitoring systems (Leipziger 2010: 220), the FLA has been widely criticized for lacking autonomy (Greenhouse 2012). Original participants including trade unions and church groups withdrew early on in favour of supporting such organizations as the Workers' Rights Consortium (WRC)[4] or the Clean Clothes Campaign[5] that are not associated with industry in the manner of the FLA.

However, the dichotomy between those multi-stakeholder initiatives that are consciously working together with corporations and those that do not is not always hard and fast. In the case of the Social Accountability International (SAI)[6] and its code SA8000, for example, representatives from the Global Union Federations have maintained their advisory role despite repeated criticisms by the labour movement of the organization's procedures and effectiveness (Wick 2005). While this code has gained broad recognition globally, providing a cross-sector standard for auditing working conditions and training both managers and workers, its usefulness has been limited due to the costs of implementation which must be borne by the facility under examination. For most small and medium-sized enterprises in the supply networks of transnational corporations, the costs are reported to be prohibitive (Leipziger 2010: 205).

Framework agreements

For international labour unionism, getting TNCs to negotiate and sign framework agreements has become one of the most important tools at its disposal for regulating the employment relationship. These global framework agreements (GFAs)[7] represent a contractual relationship between TNCs and Global Union Federations (GUFs) which afford mutual recognition of the parties to the agreement; set binding standards regarding the ILO Core Labour Standards and other ILO Conventions; provide mechanisms of monitoring and conflict resolution; and define the boundaries of application and implementation (Fichter *et al.*, 2012).

Throughout the 1990s, international unions were more focused on a political strategy aimed at incorporating ILO labour standards into the WTO sanction mechanisms (Anner 2001: Gumbrell-McCormick 2004: 44 et ff.). But when this failed, primary attention again turned to influencing labour policies in global corporations. Two overt signs of this renewed effort were the model agreement drafted by the International Confederation of Free Trade Unions (ICFTU) in 1997 (International Confederation of Free Trade Unions [ICFTU] 1997), which challenged the credibility of voluntary corporate codes of conduct, and the renaming of the sectoral International Trade Secretariats as Global Union Federations in 2002. Significantly, the number of GFA signings has increased notably since then. By mid-2012, almost 25 years after the signature of the archetype of GFAs by the International Union of Foodworkers (IUF) and BSN in 1988 (Gallin 2008), there were 85 functional GFAs, with five GUFs responsible for more than 90 per cent of them[8] (Table 21.2; see also Papadakis 2011).

Compared to the vastly larger number of TNCs operating worldwide, the group of those that have signed a GFA is still very small. But as Table 21.2 shows, they are generally among the leaders in their sector. Moreover, all of them are advocates of CSR, although their commitment varies strongly. While all of these TNCs regard GFAs as an element of their policy on corporate social responsibility, labour argues that they represent a means of globalizing labour–management relations and creating space for building and strengthening unions (Fichter, Hefen and Schiederig, 2013).

In this respect, it is important to note that the Core Labour Standards (CLS) as embodied in the ILO's Declaration on Fundamental Principles and Rights at Work (1998) are the generally recognized basis of GFA *content*. The four CLSs in turn are drawn from ILO Conventions: C87 and 98 covering freedom of association and the right to collective bargaining; C29 and C105 on forced labour; C138 and C182 on child labour; and C100 and C111 on discrimination and equal pay. References to further ILO Conventions on topics such as workers' representatives, health and safety, employee training and minimum wages are to be found in a number of GFAs as well. *Procedurally*, GFAs also provide in varying detail mechanisms and

Table 21.2 Global Framework Agreements (GFAs), 1988–2012

Global Union Federation	*Number of GFAs*	*Available at: http://www.global-unions.org/framework-agreements.html*
Building and Wood Workers' International (BWI)	18	http://www.bwint.org/default.asp?Issue—ultinationals&Language=EN
International Federation of Journalists	1	http://www.ifj.org/en/pages/international-framework-agreements
International Union of Food, Agricultural, Hotel, Restaurant, Catering, Tobacco and Allied Workers' Associations	6	http://cms.iuf.org/ http://www.global-unions.org/framework-agreements.html
IndustriALL	41	http://www.industriall-union.org/issues/confronting-global-capital/global-framework-agreements
Public Services International	2	http://www.world-psi.org/en/mne-guidelines http://www.global-unions.org/framework-agreements.html
UNI Global Union	46	http://www.uniglobalunion.org/Apps/uni.nsf/pages/gfaEn

Note: No total number is given because a few agreements have been signed by more than one GUF. Also, a few of the agreements listed are no longer operational because of TNC mergers, acquisitions and restructuring.

means for monitoring the agreement, for renewing it, and for conflict resolution. Finally, GFAs have a *spatial* dimension. They delineate the boundaries within which the GFA as an instrument for the governance of labour is applicable. With suppliers, sub-contractors and other business partners referenced in most of the GFAs (with the exception of the service sector), GFAs are generally directed at reaching beyond the formal organization of the signatory TNC to be inclusive of the more extensive realm of global production networks.

As a relatively novel policy tool for transnationalizing labour relations, GFAs speak to all these issues at the same time (Hammer 2005; Riisgaard 2005: Bourque 2008). Regarding their substantive rules, GFAs adopt the core labour standards of the ILO, which are meant to be enforced at multinational subsidiaries and – in many cases – also at joint venture partners and suppliers. As such, the ambition of GFAs is to tackle directly the consequences of cross-border production networks for labour and labour relations. For the GUFs, GFAs are a company-focused strategy for establishing their mandate to bargain and to create space for organizing as a precondition for transnationalizing labour relations. GUFs can establish an arena for continuous negotiations with management on a global scale in which they play a role in their own right. In direct confrontation with multinationals they can increase the scope for organizing for their local affiliates in that they can bring local violations directly to central management's attention, thereby bypassing deadlocks at the subsidiary level.

However, this requires an organizational capacity that is capable of connecting affiliates to each other in spite of cross-border institutional differences (e.g. in labour law, social insurance, etc.) and local political cleavages among multiple unions vying for recognition (Fairbrother and Hammer 2005). As negotiated and signed with central management, GFAs incorporate some sort of partnership approach to labour relations, because the parties usually agree on procedures for monitoring and implementing these agreements including the handling of disputes over standards violations. For the central management of multinationals, GFAs as partnership agreements bear the potential to gain credibility for their CSR policies (Egels-Zandén 2009a). And, as multinationals have a higher visibility for public monitors like NGOs and the media in various countries, an agreement with unions might ensure the pre-emptive avoidance and internal handling of possible labour standards violations without public reputation damage. For European multinationals, these and similar considerations might increase their willingness to negotiate a GFA with unions and employee representatives according to the already established traditions of labour relations at their home country locations in Europe (Preuss *et al.* 2009).

Conclusion

The foregoing selective overview, while focusing on the three basic types of transnational voluntary regulation, has emphasized the variety and heterogeneity of voluntary regulation schemes for employment relations, along with the patchwork character of their existence and implementation. But what can be learned from this development and what kinds of options may it open for the future? Is there discernible progress toward a 'global labour rights regime' as some have suggested (Hassel 2008; Thomas 2011). Answers to such questions are not easily found but some will be explored with the idea of sketching some important considerations for the future in regard to the international environment, the institutional setting, and the interests, ideas and power resources of the main actors (Egel-Zandén 2009b: 170; Niforou 2012).

The international environment is the neo-liberal framework of economic globalization: deregulation of capital controls, elimination of trade barriers and market-driven development. The ILO is the major institution in the field of labour, but in the chorus of international institutions, it is the weakest. It has virtually no power in relationship to the World Trade Organization (WTO), the International Monetary Fund (IMF) or the World Bank. While its Conventions and its Core Labour Standards (CLS) are internationally recognized norms, their application is devoid of effective sanctions. Private voluntary agreements increasingly refer to them, but their application remains a contested issue. Depending on the particular issue, namely child labour, non-discrimination or collective bargaining, the extent of their public recognition and impact may vary greatly. Over the past decades, the ILO and a broad coalition of transnational activists have been successful in mobilizing public support for banning child labour. At the same time, non-discrimination as an equally relevant principle of the CLS has generated little interest. Highly contested is the ILO's standard on collective bargaining. Despite continued efforts on the part of the global unions and their affiliates, employer resistance to union recognition and collective bargaining is still quite strong. Governments do exercise varying degrees of influence, but are often limited in their impact due to self-imposed restraints. The perceived need to compete for investments is pervasive (Scherrer and Greven 2001), driven by the basic interests of TNCs in avoiding and preventing all-encompassing regulation by government. Indeed, from an actor perspective, we can observe the dominating role of transnational corporations and their global production and service networks. Globalization has been strongly driven by the cross-border spread of production and supply through transnational corporations. This ongoing development has been linked to the organizational restructuring of business entities and production processes, often referred to as outsourcing, offshoring and fragmentation. At the same time, the construction of 'global production networks' has led to an unprecedented linking of far-flung production sites and labour markets, with economic, social and political ramifications marked by competition and interdependencies. In regard to labour standards TNCs are prone to orient toward the weakest elements of the institutional setting in the country of their operations, going beyond the local standards where necessary to secure their market and production, but also pushing for exceptions to local standards where possible and whenever given the opportunity by local authorities (for example, in export processing zones, see Jauch 2009).

Civil society organizations have been instrumental and highly successful in putting the topic of labour conditions, especially in developing countries, on the public agenda. The processes of economic globalization that gave rise to powerful transnational corporations, enhanced their mobility and enabled them to exploit labour virtually at will have also generated local and globally-linked collective protest movements that target such TNCs – particularly those with well-known consumer products and brand names – with criticism of their practices. These movements may be considered to be 'value actors', driven by moral issues and able not only to speak to the concerns of affluent consumers, but also able to mobilize public support in the name of upholding human rights and redressing labour rights and environmental violations. Their wide-ranging activities and protests have become somewhat of a counterweight to TNC excesses, reshaping the debates on globalization and making an essential contribution to the development of voluntary CSR-based standards on employment relations.

Workers are key actors, but highly atomized and in most cases, as suppliers of labour in a global market, easily replaceable. Their collective organizations, labour unions, still struggle effectively to mobilize their limited resources and develop the means of organizational cooperation essential to making the voices of labour heard more widely. Labour unions have been marginally active in coalitions of local and global protest movements. But as collective actors with a primary mandate to represent the employment interests of their members (and other workers?), their concern with labour violations far away from their place of operation has been secondary to defending what they have achieved for their members and exercising their influence within their own national institutional settings (Logue 1980). To the extent that such globalization processes as defined above have challenged this approach, unions have been more open to flanking their local and national policies with transnational union networking and support for the strategy of framework agreements to regulate the power of TNCs. Progress has been slow in coming inasmuch as labour–management negotiations go to the heart of fundamental interest conflicts over labour and production costs, working conditions, and management prerogative.

While TNC operations thrive on unencumbered market access, this is generally not tantamount to a complete absence of regulations, regardless of how their effectiveness is evaluated. What is striking as a characteristic of this international environment is the paradox of regulation: legally enforceable and comprehensive regulations with sanctions and penalties are either absent or inadequate, while an almost endless proliferation of privately agreed standards, norms, guidelines, recommendations and codes abound. Such agreements are very limited in scope, unsystematic in content, heterogeneous in their application, and even contradictory in their goals. Categorizations show both the extensiveness of the number of schemes, but also the existence of a patchwork of soft law with many gaps and weaknesses

(Abbott and Snidal 2009), especially in regard to enforcement in conflict situations. In the field of labour standards, for example, we are confronted with a patchwork of autonomous, atomized, and limited norms and rule-settings. Beyond the general framework of ILO Conventions (norms without sanctions), there is no comprehensive and legally binding global framework of reference for regulating the employment relationship. National and local institutional settings prevail, and in most cases, there is no clear definition or understanding of the inter-relatedness of local, national and global environments of regulation.

The presence and input of a myriad of civil society organizations and actors have contributed markedly to advancing the voluntary regulation of employment relations over the past two decades. Nevertheless, the effectiveness of these regulations needs to be evaluated both individually and in context with other associated or similar schemes. This holds for all of our three categories of voluntary schemes. Moreover, as is sometimes raised in the literature, there is a basic question as to the democratic legitimacy of many such schemes, both in regard to the selection, the authority and the input of the actors involved (TNC-management; NGOs) and in regard to the nature of such schemes as a possible 'privatisation of social rights' (Mund and Priegnitz 2007). Voluntary schemes are an important contribution toward a general improvement of employment relations on a global scale. But on their own, they have shortcomings, making it necessary to secure this process through its embeddedness in a public framework of comprehensive and legally binding regulations (Merk 2008:112–13). This entails the improvement of national laws and institutional settings, which would of course apply comprehensively to all businesses, not only to TNCs. But it also concerns to a certain extent a required recognition of international norms and standards which will establish cross-border 'rules that regulate capital and empower workers' (Stevis and Boswell 2008:194). In a globalized world, balanced economic development hinges on bringing voluntary regulations into line with public legal standards to provide a solid foundation for comprehensively raising the level of well-being for all.

Notes

1 The other three being the legislative model, the trade sanctions model and the multilateral enforcement model.
2 See Krasner (1982: 186), who defines a regime as 'a set of explicit or implicit principles, norms, rules, and decision making procedures around which actors' expectations converge in a given area of international relations'.
3 In one case, the authors define the International Labour Organization (ILO) as a 'co-regulating' type of public-private partnership due to the tripartite structure of this body (Börzel and Risse 2005: 202).
4 See http://www.workersrights.org/.
5 See http://www.cleanclothes.org/.
6 See http://www.sa-intl.org/.
7 Over time, the terminology has changed. At the outset, the International Confederation of Free Trade Unions labelled its model agreement a code of conduct. But soon thereafter, the term International Framework Agreement came to be generally accepted, making a differentiation between unilateral codes and union negotiated agreements more obvious. With the merger of three GUFs (International Chemical, Energy, Mining and General Workers Federation [ICEM], International Metalworkers' Federation [IMF], International Textile, Garment and Leather Workers' Federation [ITGLWF]) to form IndustriALL, the terms Global Framework Agreement or Global Agreement have become standard.
8 The five GUFs are the IUF (International Union of Foodworkers), the ICEM, the IMF, the BWI (Building and Woodworkers' International) and UNI (UNI Global Union). Agreements with TNCs are defined as GFAs when they are signed by one or more GUF, have a global reach and are based on the ILO Core Labour Standards.

References

Abbott, K. and Snidal, D. (2009) 'The governance triangle: regulatory standards institutions and the shadow of the state', in W. Mattli and N. Woods (eds) *The Politics of Global Regulation*, Princeton, NJ: Princeton University Press.

Amoore, L. (2002) *Globalisation Contested: An International Political Economy of Work*, Manchester: Manchester University Press.

Anner, M. (2001) 'The international trade union campaign for core labour standards in the WTO', *WorkingUSA*, 5(1): 43–63.

Bartley, T. (2007) 'Institutional emergence in an era of globalization: the rise of transnational private regulation of labour and environmental conditions', *American Journal of Sociology*, 113(2): 297–351.

Bernstein, S. and Cashore, B. (2007) 'Non-state global governance: is forest certification a legitimate alternative to a global forest convention?', in J. Kirton and M. Trebilcock (eds) *Hard Choices, Soft Law: Voluntary Standards in Global Trade, Environment and Social Governance*, Aldershot: Ashgate.

Block, R. N., Roberts, K., Ozeki, C. and Roomkin, M. J., (2001) 'Models of international labour standards', *Industrial Relations*, 40(2): 258–92.

Börzel, T. A. and Risse, T. (2005) 'Public-private partnerships: effective and legitimate tools of transnational governance?', in E. Grande and L. W. Pauly (eds) *Complex Sovereignty: Reconstituting Political Authority in the Twenty-First Century*, Toronto: University of Toronto Press.

Bourque, R. (2008) 'International framework agreements and the future of collective bargaining in multinational companies', *Just Labour: A Canadian Journal of Work and Society*, 12(1): 30–47.

Boyd, D. E., Spekman, R. E., Kamauff, J. W. and Werhane, P. (2007) 'Corporate social responsibility in global supply chains: a procedural justice perspective', *Long Range Planning*, 40(3): 341–56.

Brammer, S., Jackson, G. and Matten, D. (2012) 'Corporate social responsibility and institutional theory: new perspectives on private governance', *Socio-Economic Review*, 10(1): 3–28.

Brand, U. (2003) 'Nach der Krise des Fordismus. global Governance als möglicher hegemonialer Diskurs des internationalen Politischen', *Zeitschrift für Internationale Beziehungen*, 10(1): 143–66.

Braun, R. (2001) 'Konzerne als Beschützer der Menschenrechte? Zur Bedeutung von Verhaltenskodizes', in T. Brühl, T. Debiel, B. Hamm, H. Hummel and J. Martens (eds) *Die Privatisierung der Weltpolitik: Entstaatlichung und Kommerzialisierung im Globalisierungsprozess*, Bonn: Dietz.

Chan, A. and Ross, R. J. S. (2003) 'Racing to the bottom: international trade without a social clause', *Third World Quarterly*, 24(6) 1011–28.

Commission on Global Governance (1998) *Our Global Neighbourhood: The Report of the Commission on Global Governance*, Oxford: Oxford University Press.

Conzelmann, T. and Wolf, K. D. (2008) 'The potential and limits of governance by private codes of conduct', in J-C. Graz and A. Nölke (eds) *Transnational Private Governance and its Limits*, London: Routledge.

Cox, R. W. (1987) *Production, Power, and World Order: Social Forces in the Making of History*, New York: Columbia University Press.

Cragg, W. (2007) 'Multinational corporations, globalisation, and the challenge of self-regulation', in J. Kirton and M. Trebilcock (eds) *Hard Choices, Soft Law: Voluntary Standards in Global Trade, Environment and Social Governance*, Aldershot: Ashgate.

Cutler, A. C. (2002) 'Private international regimes and interfirm cooperation', in R. B. Hall and T. J. Biersteker (eds) *The Emergence of Private Authority in Global Governance*, Cambridge: Cambridge University Press.

—— (2010) 'The legitimacy of private transnational governance: experts and the transnational market for force', *Socio-Economic Review*, 8(1): 157–85.

Dashwood, H. (2007) 'Corporate social responsibility and the evolution of international norms', in J. Kirton and M. Trebilcock (eds) *Hard Choices, Soft Law: Voluntary Standards in Global Trade, Environment and Social Governance*, Aldershot: Ashgate.

Detomasi, D. (2007) 'The multinational corporation and global governance: modelling public policy networks', *Journal of Business Ethics*, 71(3): 321–34.

Djelic, M.-L. and Quack, S. (eds) (2003) *Globalization and Institutions: Redefining the Rules of the Economic Game*, Cheltenham: Edward Elgar.

Drezner, D. W. (2000) 'Bottom feeders', *Foreign Policy*, 121(Nov.–Dec.): 64–70.

Egels-Zandén, N. (2009a) 'TNC motives for signing international framework agreements: a continuous bargaining model of stakeholder pressure', *Journal of Business Ethics*, 84(4): 529–47.

—— (2009b) 'Transnational governance of workers' rights: outlining a research agenda', *Journal of Business Ethics*, 87(2): 169–88.

Fairbrother, P. and Hammer, N. (2005) 'Global unions: past efforts and future prospects', *Relations Industrielles/Industrial Relations*, 60(3): 405–31.

Fichter, M. and Sydow, J. (2002) 'Using networks towards global labour standards? Organizing social responsibility in global production chains', *Industrielle Beziehungen*, 9(4): 357–80.

Fichter, M., Sydow, J, Helfen, M., Arruda, L., Agtas, O., Gartenberg, I., McCallum, J., Sayim, K. and Stevis, D. (2012) *Globalising Labour Relations. On Track with Framework Agreements?*, Berlin: Friedrich-Ebert-Foundation.

Fichter, M., Helfen, M. and Schiederig, K. (2013) 'Transnational solidarity around global production networks? Reflections on the strategy of international Framework Agreements', in P. Fairbrother, C. Levesque and M.-A. Hennebert (eds) *Transnational Trade Unionism, Building Union Power*, London: Routledge.

Fuchs, D. A. (2004) 'The role of business in global governance', in S. A. Schirm (ed.) *New Rules for Global Markets: Public And Private Governance in the World Economy*, Basingstoke: Palgrave Macmillan.

Fuchs, P. (2000) 'Codes of conduct – neue Handlungsoption zur Re-regulierung transnationaler Konzerne 'von unten'?', in C. Dörrenbächer and D. Plehwe (eds) *Grenzenlose Kontrolle?: Organisatorischer Wandel und politische Macht multinationaler Unternehmen*, Berlin: Edition Sigma.

Gallin, D. (2008) 'International framework agreements: a reassessment', in K. Papadakis (ed.) *Cross-Border Social Dialogue and Agreements: An Emerging Global Industrial Relations Framework?*, Geneva: International Institute for Labour Studies.

Gereffi, G., Humphrey, J. and Sturgeon, T. J. (2005) 'The governance of global value chains', *Review of International Political Economy*, 12(1): 78–104.

Grande, E., *et al.* (2006) 'Politische Transnationalisierung: die Zukunft des Nationalstaats – transnationale Politikregime im Vergleich', in S. A. Schirm (ed.) *Globalisierung. Forschungsstand und Perspektiven*, Baden-Baden: Nomos.

Greenhouse, S. (2012) 'Early praise in inspection at Foxconn brings doubt', *New York Times*, 16 February.

Greven, T. and Scherrer, C. (2002) 'Instrumente zur globalen Durchsetzung fundamentaler Arbeitsrechte', in A. G. Scherer, K. H. Blickle, D. Dietzfelbinger and G. Hütter (eds) *Globalisierung und Sozialstandards*, München; Mering: Rainer Hampp.

Gumbrell-McCormick, R. (2004) 'The ICFTU and the world economy: a historical perspective', in R. Munck (ed.) *Labour and Globalisation: Results and Prospects*, Liverpool: Liverpool University Press.

Hammer, N. (2005) 'International framework agreements: global industrial relations between rights and bargaining', *Transfer*, 11(4): 511–30.

Hassel, A. (2008) 'The evolution of a global labour governance regime', *Governance*, 21(2): 231–51.

Haufler, V. (2003) 'Globalization and industry self-regulation', in M. Kahler and D. A. Lake (eds) *Governance in a Global Economy: Political Authority in Transition*, Princeton, NJ: Princeton University Press.

—— (2006) 'Global governance and the private sector', in C. May (ed.) *Global Corporate Power*, Boulder, CO: Lynne Rienner.

Institute for Global Labour and Human Rights (GLHR) (2012) *Reports*. Available at: http://www.globallabourrights.org/reports (accessed 26 March 2012).

International Confederation of Free Trade Unions (ICFTU) (1997) *The ICFTU/ITS Basic Code of Labour Practice*. Available at: http://www.icftu.org/displaydocument.asp?Index=991209513&Language=EN, (accessed 2 Sept. 2010).

International Labour Organization (2001) *Report of the Director-General: Reducing the Decent Work Deficit – A Global Challenge*, Geneva: International Labour Organization.

International Trade Union Confederation (ITUC) (2011) *Annual Survey of Violations of Trade Union Rights 2011*, Brussels: ITUC.

Jauch, H. (2009) 'Attracting foreign investment at all costs? The case of export processing zones (EPZs) and Ramatex in Namibia', *International Journal of Labour Research*, 1(1): 73–84.

Kapstein, E. B. (1997) 'Racing to the bottom? Regulating international labour standards', *Internationale Politik und Gesellschaft*, 2: 155–60.

Keck, M. E. and Sikkink, K. (1999) 'Transnational advocacy networks in international and regional politics', *International Social Science Journal*, 51(159): 89–101.

Klein, N. (1999) *No Logo: No Space, No Choice, No Jobs; Taking Aim at the Brand Bullies*, New York: Picador.

Koch-Baumgarten, S. (2011) 'Gewerkschaften und global Governance: Grenzen und Möglichkeiten einer grenzüberschreitenden Regulierung der Erwerbsarbeit', *Internationale Politik und Gesellschaft*, 2: 51–68.

Kocher, E. (2008) 'Codes of conduct and framework agreements on social minimum standards – private regulation?', in O. Dilling, M. Herberg and G. Winter (eds) *Responsible Business: Self-Governance and Law in Transnational Economic Transaction*, Oxford: Hart.

Kolben, K. (2011) 'Transnational labour regulation and the limits of governance', *Theoretical Inquiries in Law*, 12: 1–35 (online).

Kolk, A., van Tulder, R. and Welters, C. (1999) 'International codes of conduct and corporate social responsibility: can transnational corporations regulate themselves?', *Transnational Corporations*, 8(1): 143–80.

Krasner, S. D. (1982) 'Regimes and the limits of realism: regimes as autonomous variables', *International Organization*, 36(2): 497–510.

Lee, E. (1997) 'Globalization and labour standards: a review of issues', *International Labour Review*, 136(2): 173–89.

Leipziger, D. (2010) *The Corporate Responsibility Code Book*, Sheffield: Greenleaf Publishing.

Levy, D. (2008) 'Political contestation in global production networks', *Academy of Management Review*, 33(4): 943–63.

Lipschutz, R. D. and Fogel, C. (2002) '"Regulation for the rest of us?" Global civil society and the privatization of transnational regulation', in R. B. Hall and T. J. Biersteker (eds) *The Emergence of Private Authority in Global Governance*, Cambridge: Cambridge University Press.

Locke, R. and Romis, M. (2007) 'Improving work conditions in a global supply chain', *MIT Sloan Management Review*, 48(2): 54–62.

Locke, R., Amengual, M. and Mangla, A. (2009) 'Virtue out of necessity? Compliance, commitment, and the improvement of labour conditions in global supply chains', *Politics and Society*, 37(3): 319–51.

Logue, J. (1980) *Toward a Theory of Trade Union Internationalism*, Gothenburg: University of Gothenburg Press.

Marens, R. (2012) 'Generous in victory? American managerial autonomy, labour relations and the invention of corporate social responsibility', *Socio-Economic Review*, 10(1): 59–84.

Merk, J. (2008) 'The private regulation of labour standards: the case of the apparel and footwear industries', in J-C. Graz and A. Nölke (eds) *Transnational Private Governance and Its Limits*, London: Routledge.

Mosley, L. and Uno, S. (2007) 'Racing to the bottom or climbing to the top? Economic globalization and collective labour rights', *Comparative Political Studies*, 40(8): 923–48.

Müller, T., Platzer, H-W. and Rüb, S. (2004) *Globale Arbeitsbeziehungen in Globalen Konzernen? Zur Transnationalisierung betrieblicher und gewerkschaftlicher Politik*, Wiesbaden: VS Verlag für Sozialwissenschaften.

Mund, H. and Priegnitz, K. (2007) 'Soft law – second best solution or a privatisation of social rights? Some pointers for a future discussion', *Transfer*, 13(4): 671–7.

Niforou, C. (2012) 'International framework agreements and industrial relations governance: global rhetoric versus local realities', *British Journal of Industrial Relations*, 50(2): 352–73.

Nölke, A. (2004) 'Transnational private authority and corporate governance', in S. A. Schirm (ed.) *New Rules for Global Markets: Public and Private Governance in the World Economy*, Basingstoke: Palgrave Macmillan.

OECD (2001) *Codes of Corporate Conduct: Expanded Review of their Contents*, Paris: Organisation for Economic Co-operation and Development. Available at: www.oecd.org/industry/inv/corporateresponsibility/1922656.pdf (accessed 27 March 2012).

Overdevest, C. (2010) 'Comparing forest certification schemes: the case of ratcheting standards in the forest sector', *Socioeconomic Review*, 8(1): 47–76.

Palan, R. (1999) 'Global governance and social closure or who is to be governed in the era of global governance?', in M. Hewson and T. J. Sinclair (eds) *Approaches to Global Governance Theory*, Albany, NY: SUNY Press.

Papadakis, K. (ed.) (2011) *Shaping Global Industrial Relations: The Impact of International Framework Agreements*, New York: Palgrave Macmillan.

Pattberg, P. (2005) 'The institutionalization of private governance: how business and nonprofit organizations agree on transnational rules', *Governance: An International Journal of Policy and Administration*, 18(4): 589–610.

Paul, J. A. (2001) 'Der Weg zum global Compact: Annäherung von UNO und multinationalen Unternehmen', in T. Brühl, T. Debiel, B. Hamm, H. Hummel and J. Martens (eds) *Die Privatisierung der Weltpolitik: Entstaatlichung und Kommerzialisierung im Globalisierungsprozess*, Bonn: Dietz.

Preuss, L., Haunschild, A. and Matten, D. (2009) 'The rise of CSR: implications for HRM and employee representation', *International Journal of Human Resource Management*, 20(4): 953–73.

Riisgaard, L. (2005) 'International framework agreements: a new model for securing workers rights?', *Industrial Relations*, 44(4): 707–37.

Rosenau, J. N. and Czempiel, E.-O. (ed.) (1995) *Governance without Government: Order and Change in World Politics*, Cambridge: Cambridge University Press.

Ruggie, J. G. (2004) 'Taking embedded liberalism global: the corporate connection', in D. Held and M. Koenig-Archibugi (eds) *Taming Globalization: Frontiers of Governance*, Cambridge: Polity Press.

—— (2007) *Business and Human Rights: Mapping International Standards of Responsibility and Accountability for Corporate Acts*, New York: United Nations General Assembly, Human Rights Council.

Sabel, C., O'Rourke, D. and Fung, A. (2000) *Ratcheting Labor Standards: Regulation for Continuous Improvement in the Global Workplace*, New York: Columbia University, Columbia Law School, KSG Working Paper.

Scherer, A. G. and Palazzo, G. (2007) 'Toward a political conception of corporate responsibility: business and society seen from a Habermasian perspective', *Academy of Management Review*, 32(4): 1096–120.

Scherrer, C. and Greven, T. (2001) *Global Rules for Trade: Codes of Conduct, Social Labelling, Workers' Rights Clauses*, Münster: Westfälisches Dampfboot.

Schirm, S. A. (2007) 'Analytical overview: state of the art of research on globalization', in S. A. Schirm (ed.) *Globalization: State of the Art and Perspectives*, London: Routledge.

Schömann, I., Sobczak, A., Voss, E. and Wilke, P. (2008) *Codes of Conduct and International Framework Agreements: New Forms of Governance at Company Level*, Dublin: European Foundation for the Improvement of Living and Working Conditions.

Seidman, G. W. (2005) 'Monitoring multinationals: corporate codes of conduct', in J. Bandy and J. Smith (eds) *Coalitions Across Borders: Transnational Protest and the Neoliberal Order*, Lanham, MD: Rowman and Littlefield.

Singh, A. and Zammit, A. (2004) 'Labour standards and the "race to the bottom": rethinking globalization and workers' rights from developmental and solidaristic perspectives', *Oxford Review of Economic Policy*, 20(1): 85–104.

Stevis, D. and Boswell, T. (2008) *Globalization and Labour: Democratizing Global Governance*, Lanham, MD: Rowman and Littlefield.

Strange, S. (1999) 'An international political economy perspective', in J. H. Dunning (ed.) *Governments, Globalization, and International Business*, Oxford: Oxford University Press.

Taneja, S., Taneja, P. and Gupta, R. (2011) 'Researches in corporate social responsibility: a review of shifting focus, paradigms, and methodologies', *Journal of Business Ethics*, 101(3): 343–64.

Thomas, M. P. (2011) 'Global industrial relations? Framework agreements and the regulation of international labour standards', *Labour Studies Journal*, 36(2): 269–87.

Waddington, J. (1999) 'Situating labour within the globalization debate', in J. Waddington (ed.) *Globalization and Patterns of Labour Resistance*, London: Mansell.

Waddock, S. (2008) 'Building a new institutional infrastructure for corporate responsibility', *Academy of Management Perspectives*, 22(3): 87–108.

Wick, I. (2005) *Workers' Tool or PR Ploy? A Guide to Codes of International Labour Practice*, Bonn: Friedrich Ebert Foundation, Südwind.

Zürn, M. (1998) *Regieren jenseits des Nationalstaates: Globalisierung und Denationalisierung als Chance*, Frankfurt am Main: Suhrkamp.

—— (2004) 'Global governance and legitimacy problems', *Government and Opposition*, 39(2): 260–87.

22 Regional regulation

The EU and NAFTA

Monika Ewa Kaminska

Introduction[1]

Regional (economic and/or political) integration has been one of the major developments in international relations since 1990.[2] Most industrialized and developing countries are members of regional organizations or regional integration agreements. By 2000 about one-third of global trade took place within regional organizations, of which the European Union (EU) and the North American Free Trade Agreement (NAFTA) are two prominent examples (OECD 2002a).[3] Regional organizations vary hugely: they have in common the objective of reducing barriers to trade between member countries, but some go further in their political and economic functions and objectives. Whether regional integration must be understood as a challenge to globalization or as an expression of globalization will be discussed at the end of this chapter, when evaluating the impact of the EU and NAFTA on employment regulation and employment relations.

The chapter compares the two largest regional organizations: the EU and NAFTA. The first section presents integration theory and the second section discusses the two cases by outlining their institutional set-up, objectives and history. The third section compares regional arrangements and policies affecting labour standards and employment relations. Finally, the chapter presents a critical evaluation of what can be learnt from the EU and NAFTA experience for the broader theme of supranational regulation of labour standards and employment relations in a global economy.

Regional integration: general principles

The EU and NAFTA differ substantially in terms of their institutional structure, as well as aimed for and achieved levels of integration. Regional integration theory distinguishes between organizations based on intergovernmental cooperation, and those equipped with supranational institutions. The channels through which citizens and interest groups, including organized labour, can pursue their interests differ in these two models. In a regional organization governed by intergovernmental relations, national governments act as 'gatekeepers' (Hoffman 1995) and the demands of any interest group are filtered through domestic politics and aggregated at the national level (Moravcsik 1993). Organized labour and business can also formulate their respective demands transnationally, through cross-border consultations and negotiations within the regional organization, and then present them to intergovernmental forums. The governments can be more or less willing to accommodate these demands, based on their domestic situation. Within a regional organization equipped with supranational institutions, the demands of labour and business can be communicated to the government which aggregates these demands at the national level and then brings them to the international arena (as in the intergovernmental case). However, their demands can also be directly presented to supranational institutions, or become aggregated transnationally through their own international lobbies and organizations and subsequently be presented to supranational institutions. In short, international organizations with supranational governance structures present multiple layers for influencing politics and policies, and national governments are no longer the exclusive gatekeepers (Kaminska and Visser 2011). This erosion of the control by individual countries of the policies of the regional organization is enhanced when voting procedures within the regional organization change from unanimity (requiring the consent of each member state) to qualified majority voting (allowing the possibility that individual member states are outvoted).

Supranational institutions may 'exercise forms of surveillance and monitoring of member states over the implementation [of regional norms and regulation], together with the power of taking infringement proceedings against member states, and of inflicting economic sanctions on them for non-compliance' (Threlfall 2007: 288). Moreover, supranational bodies may function not only as addressees of demands but they themselves can formulate demands towards member states of a regional organization and promote regional level regulation. The role of such supranational regulatory bodies may be theorized by using the concepts of 'positive integration' or initiatives to create new regulation, and 'negative integration' or reforms that remove obstacles to integration, for instance, by disallowing certain policies of member states that are seen as hindrances to market integration (Scharpf 1999). As stressed by Aspinwall, positive integration policies are more likely to be resisted by member states because they require the adoption of new regulatory approaches and result in stronger adjustment pressures at the national level than negative integration policies which 'simply require deregulation or liberalization' (2009: 5). Here the ability of independent supranational institutions to produce pressure on defiant member states becomes important. This chapter provides important examples of this pressure, for instance when discussing the role of the Court of Justice in the EU.

As for the different stages of integration, the literature distinguishes between a trading agreement, a free trade area, a customs union, a common market, an economic (and monetary) union and a political union (Scharpf 1999). In a free trade area, only custom duties and quantitative restrictions on imports and exports between member states are removed. In a customs union, member states go further and harmonize tariff barriers and quantitative restrictions to trade with non-members but most non-tariff barriers between member states are upheld. A common market lifts restrictions on the free movement of goods, services, capital and labour. An economic and monetary union has common currency and policies with regard to economic matters. And, finally, a political union integrates areas such as defence and foreign policy and recognizes common citizen rights. These differences matter greatly for the impact of regional integration on domestic and international politics and policies, including employment regulation and employment relations.

The EU and NAFTA: differences in kind

The European Union

The European integration project was initiated by six countries which in 1951 founded the European Community of Steel and Coal and then in 1957 created the European Economic Community, which by 2012 has extended to 27 European states within the EU.[4] The creation and development of competences for EU institutions originate from the specific historical conditions in Western Europe after the Second World War, where limits imposed on the European states' sovereignty were supposed to prevent military conflicts and to ensure post-war socio-economic development (Milward 1984).

There are four EU institutions of relevance: the European Commission is the 'guardian of the treaties' and has the right of initiative in matters of legislation or policy; its 27 members come from each of the 27 member states, but they are bound by the Treaty not to act as representatives of their home countries.[5] The Council of Ministers is composed of and represents the governments of the member states and passes legislation on many economic and social issues, since the mid-1980s with qualified majority voting. The European Parliament, directly elected since 1979, has acquired a stronger co-legislative role in various Treaty revisions (Maastricht 1992, Amsterdam 1997, Nice 2000, Lisbon 2007). Finally, the European Court of Justice (ECJ) is an independent supranational body. Its rulings have a direct effect on member states in that they overrule national legislation (Weiler 1999). The ECJ has the power to implement a Treaty by 'striking down features of national systems that are deemed incompatible with the development of the single market' (Pierson 1998: 140). Arguably, the European Central Bank (ECB), founded in 1999, is the fifth institution with relevance for employment relations although it does not affect all EU member states. Its duties and responsibilities are regulated in the Treaty, and it sets monetary policy for the 17 EU member states that share the Euro currency and form the Economic and Monetary Union (EMU).[6] Although not directly involved in setting or revising employment standards, its monetary policies and policy recommendations carry a lot of weight and affect employment relations throughout the EU.

The EU is comparatively advanced in terms of the depth of its regional integration, with important steps taken in the 1980s and 1990s. From a pure customs union it has developed into a common market (the Single European Market initiative of 1986) and a monetary union (with a common currency, the Euro), realized in 1999, mixed with elements of a political union. EU citizens are granted fundamental rights to move and reside freely within the territory of the member states, seek employment, establish businesses and provide services (with some restrictions which must, however, be the same for all nationals). The high economic interdependence, and in particular the free movement of labour across the EU,[7] have generated policies to coordinate national social agendas and adopt similar minimum standards.

For decades after its creation, the capacity of the EU to regulate social policies and employment relations at the regional level remained limited. According to Marginson and Sisson (1998: 513), this was due to:

> the economic focus of the political project which led to its creation and enlargement; the narrow scope of [the EU's] competence in the field of industrial relations enshrined in the Treaty of Rome and subsequent revisions . . . the requirement to secure unanimity in the Council of Ministers for matters other than health and safety and the working environment . . . and the weakness of the social partners . . . in relation to their constituent national affiliates.

Nonetheless, over the years the EU's repertoire of employment regulation has been gradually expanding while some of the obstacles mentioned above have been reduced.

Already the founding Treaty of Rome (1957) in its Part One ('Principles') stated the Community's commitments to preserving a high level of social protection for workers. However, the Treaty's Title on Social Policy did not contain provisions for developing employment regulation at the regional level. Article 156 TFEU[8] limits the Commission's role to 'encouraging close collaboration' and 'facilitating coordination' between member states in the fields of 'employment; labour law and working conditions; basic and advanced vocational training; social security; prevention of occupational accidents and diseases; occupational hygiene; the right of association and collective bargaining between employers and workers'. Article 157 is probably the most far-reaching and states the obligation that '[e]ach member state shall ensure that the principle of equal pay for male and female workers for equal work of equal value is applied'. This principle, however, was not implemented until the mid-1970s when the ECJ ruled in favour of complaints made by private citizens and this forced member states to finally implement 'equal pay' and 'equal opportunity' in their national legislation. In later years this was widened to a more general principle outlawing discrimination on grounds of gender, race, religion, age, disability and sexual orientation. Finally, the free movement of workers, enshrined in the Treaty, has inspired an EU-wide coordination regime for social insurance rights, starting in 1971. This was gradually widened to guarantee social security benefits to migrant workers (originating from other EU states) and their families in cases of sickness and maternity, invalidity, old age and death, work accidents, occupational disease, death grants and unemployment (EU Regulation 88/2004).[9]

In the 1980s, the vision of 'a greater social dimension to the European integration project' promoted by Commission President Jacques Delors 'legitimated and provided fresh impetus to the introduction of EU measures' in the field of employment relations (Marginson and Sisson 1998: 513). Guiding social principles were included in the Community Charter of Fundamental Social Rights for Workers adopted in the form of a declaration in 1989 by all member states with the exception of the United Kingdom (this changed under Tony Blair's government). The Single European Act of 1986 (which was the legal foundation for the Single Market project) in Articles 154–155 TFEU provided for the European Social Dialogue between unions and employers (called 'the social partners') at the Community level and made the European Commission responsible for its promotion. This forum of exchange, consultation and bargaining exists in over 40 sectors, and at the intersectoral level. In the preparatory process leading to the Treaty of Maastricht (1992), where the foundations for an EMU were laid, 'social dialogue was considered important first as an institution-building process necessary as a precursor to any European industrial relations system, and second as a potential joint regulatory procedure alongside other more centralized and legalistic forms' (Gold *et al.* 2007: 9).

Crucially, the Single European Act and the Maastricht Treaty extended the use of qualified majority voting and opened the way for agreements concluded between the social partners to acquire the force of legislation. Legislation through agreements of non-governmental, transnational organizations was a 'procedural breakthrough' (Threllfal 2007) which provided an alternative way to produce EU-level employment regulation by allowing the European trade unions and employers associations to act jointly but independently of Council and Parliament. As a result, the 1990s witnessed a significant growth of EU-level employment regulations.

Article 153 states that the Union 'shall support and complement the activities of the Member States' in: (a) improvement of the working environment to protect workers' health and safety; (b) working conditions; (c) social security and social protection of workers; (d) protection of workers where their employment contract is terminated; (e) the information and consultation of workers; (f) representation and collective defence of the interests of workers and employers, including codetermination; (g) conditions of employment for third-country nationals legally residing in Union territory; (h) the integration of persons excluded from the labour market; (i) equality between men and women with regard to labour market opportunities and treatment at work; (j) the combating of social exclusion; and finally (k) the modernization of social protection systems. On (a) to (i) the EU can issue legislation, usually in the form of Directives, after consultation with unions and employers, or encourage unions and employers to negotiate their own EU-wide agreements. Examples of such Directives will be discussed below. It should be noted, however, that according to Article 153.5, EU social policy competencies do 'not apply to pay, the right of association, the right to strike or the right to impose lock-outs'. This clause has often been interpreted as a brake on EU ambitions in the field of employment relations. In recent years, trade unions and even member states have cited this clause in their criticism of ECJ, the ECB and the Commission.

On (j) and (k), the EU has developed an 'open method of coordination' among member states since 2000 – a procedure based on target setting (for instance, the reduction of poverty rates by half in 2020), peer review and benchmarking (encouraging member state governments, and non-governmental organizations (NGOs), to participate in a process of mutual criticism in order to improve policy performance). This method has also been applied to the so-called European Employment Strategy (EES), which was given a Treaty base in 1997. Article 145 obliges member states 'to work towards developing a coordinated strategy for employment and particularly for promoting a skilled, trained and adaptable workforce and labour markets responsive to economic change'. The EES is best known for its target setting (e.g. a 70 per cent employment rate by 2010, 60 per cent for women; reduction of unemployment of early school-leavers) and was revised several times in the following decade in response to disappointing results (Goetschy 2003). In later revisions of the strategy, the emphasis has been placed on finding ways to promote growth and productivity.

These developments suggest there is an ambition to insert a 'social dimension' into the European integration process. It was clearly present in the EU Charter of Fundamental Rights that began its life as a commitment of the parliaments of EU member states in 2000 and has been accepted as a legal source by the ECJ. It guarantees to EU citizens, *inter alia*, the right of assembly and association (Art. 12), the right to engage in collective bargaining and collective action (Art. 28), the right of workers to information and consultation within the undertaking (Art. 27), protection in the event of unjustified dismissal (Art. 30), fair and just working conditions (Art. 31), prohibition of child labour and protection of young people at work (Art. 32), and much more.[10]

It is important to note, however, that EU-level employment relations have not displaced national employment relations. Instead, they are supplementary in some areas where they provide a floor of rights, while in other areas they seem to constitute a straitjacket, disallowing particular national policies or policy methods, for instance, where they are deemed by the ECJ to hinder the development of the internal market (see the *Viking* and *Laval* cases, discussed below). Moreover, the EU-level and the national-level employment relations are highly interdependent. The EU must rely on national actors (governments, courts, unions, firms) to implement policies and laws; and national actors can only act or legislate in accordance with the fundamental principles of EU law.

NAFTA

NAFTA was ratified in 1993 by the governments of Canada, Mexico and the United States with the goal of eliminating barriers to trade and investment between the three member states within 15 years of its implementation in January 1994. The USA was the prime mover behind NAFTA which was to promote market liberalization and encourage capital flows across its northern and southern borders (Porter 1999) through softening or removing tariffs (border taxes) and establishing new rules of as to how and in what sectors trade would occur between the three countries. Porter (1999) claims that through NAFTA the Americans aimed to obtain a nearby low-wage location in which the labour costs of US corporations could be reduced and their competitiveness enhanced by shifting parts of their production to Mexico, with the additional benefit of stemming the tide of (illegal) immigrants from Mexico (see also OECD 2002a). Although NAFTA was ostensibly about trade policy, the implicit understanding was that, if Mexico maintained the neo-liberal reform policies which it had started in preceding years, it would gain access to the US market and be able to claim more generous US assistance (Fernandez and Portes 1998).

NAFTA facilitates the movement of people but, unlike the EU, there is no general freedom of movement. Labour mobility is limited to a temporary entry right 'without the intent to establish permanent residence' (OECD 2002b: 10) and is restricted to renewable admissions for higher skills categories and business representatives. Although certification procedures may be waived, work permits are still required (ibid.). NAFTA stipulates that measures relating to qualification and licensing requirements should not constitute barriers to trade in services (Pinera González 2000). However, unlike the EU, NAFTA member states only have the right to recognize qualifications and there is no regional qualifications framework.

NAFTA operates on an intergovernmental basis (Aspinwall 2009). Unlike the EU, it does not have an executive body with legislative initiative competences, a Parliament or a Court of Justice. Consequently, in NAFTA there are no mechanisms other than intergovernmental cooperation to promote regional-level labour standards, and channels through which organized labour can pursue its demands are very limited. There is no aspiration or agenda for promoting a social dimension to trade integration. NAFTA is most of all a precise set of trade rules (a text of more than 2,000 pages) meant to ensure binding commitments between the three countries, without escape clauses. As a result, there are no regional institutions, as in the EU, with the power to develop supplementary legislation that might modify the agreement as it evolves. Only a modest level of authority is delegated for the purposes of dispute settlement and this process is tightly prescribed, as we will see below.

Of main interest to this chapter is the North American Agreement on Labor Cooperation (NAALC), which is one of the two NAFTA side agreements (the other concerns the environment). The NAALC enumerates 11 basic labour principles, including freedom of association and the right to collective bargaining and to strike, the prohibition of child labour, forced labour and employment discrimination, as well as rights related to occupational health and safety, compensation in cases of occupational injuries, minimum employment standards, equal pay, and protection of migrant workers. There is a firm commitment to the core labour standards (the first five in the list above) of the International Labour Organization (ILO) but no common charter of citizen and worker rights to which courts can refer. The NAALC commits the three member states to the implementation of these labour standards but only within 'the framework of existing national labour legislation and institutions' (Dombois *et al.* 2003: 8). 'Each party shall promote compliance with and effectively enforce its labour law through appropriate government action' (NAALC, Art. 3). Apart from the core labour rights, the NAALC does not prohibit member states from weakening their respective labour regulations and recognizes 'the right of each Party to establish its own domestic labour standards, and to adopt or modify accordingly its labour laws and regulations'. Thus, member states retain the right to change and lower domestic labour standards. This is different from the EU where lowering labour standards requires a decision of the Council and the European Parliament or an explicit agreement between the EU social partners.

Under the NAALC the Commission of Labor Cooperation (CLC) was created as a trilateral body to implement the obligations of the three member states. It consists of a ministerial council (the three labour ministers) and an international secretariat, the activities of which are limited to administrative and investigative tasks (UNU-CRIS 2008). The CLC was given only limited decision-making, coordinating and monitoring powers, and inadequate material resources (Dombois *et al.* 2003); its findings or rulings have no direct effect in the three NAFTA states (Finbow 2006; UNU-CRIS 2008) and there is no redress for individuals. In order to submit an allegation of wrongdoing, the parties involved must first exhaust national dispute resolution mechanisms. This option allowed the national authorities multiple opportunities to find solutions to the issues before they reached the regional level. Perhaps the most interesting feature of the NAALC is that complaints can only be filed in a NAFTA member state other than the one in which the violation has allegedly occurred. For the purpose of filing such complaints, officially called 'submissions', National Administrative Offices (NAOs) have been created in the labour departments (ministries) of the three NAFTA member states. They receive and process submissions from civil society, unions and NGOs concerning non-enforcement of labour law in either of the two other countries.

Like NAFTA itself, the NAALC was largely dictated by US trade negotiators and responding to US concerns. It was designed 'to appease the U.S. labour movement', which was hostile to the NAFTA treaty (UNU-CRIS 2008: 21) because of fears that low standards in Mexico might 'trigger a massive exodus of companies and jobs south of the border' (Dombois *et al.* 2003: 6). Thus, 'in the eyes of the U.S. administration and public, the NAALC's principal objective was to subject employment relationships in Mexico to international monitoring and to force the Mexican state actually to implement its . . . labour legislation' (ibid.). At the same time, 'the Mexican government tried to exclude any possibility of foreign intervention into Mexican labour relations' (ibid.: 7). Indeed, the NAALC was not meant to restrict national sovereignty in any way, either by putting in place supranational institutions or by legally harmonizing labour and social standards. Yet, by allowing member states to monitor each other's compliance with their domestic labour laws, the NAALC was a breakthrough and introduced an element of extra-territorial control (Van Wezel Stone 1995) or foreign influence over its territory which US Congress is steadfastly rejecting in most other cases, except when it comes to the WTO.[11] Clarke (2007) has plausibly argued that the US Congress accepted NAALC following the conviction that complaints would only be directed against Mexico. This turned out to be wrong, as there have been Canadian complaints against the restriction of bargaining rights in the USA, and mostly Mexican complaints about denial of freedom of association to Mexican legal immigrants into the USA.

To conclude, compared with the EU, NAFTA's integration project is much more modest: it is limited to establishing a free trade zone and operating on a purely intergovernmental basis. To be fair, NAFTA and NAALC were never intended to develop a 'social dimension' or regional arrangement of employment relations. Within NAFTA there is a catalogue of common principles and a mechanism for resolving conflicts, but there are no transnational employment regulations or policies. Unlike the EU, there is no provision for general freedom of movement of labour nor is there a system for a cross-national transfer of social security rights of immigrant workers. Despite some advocates of regional labour regulations among US unions, these were not adopted due to the strong opposition of US business, the fears of the Canadian government of US interference in their national labour relations, and the resistance of the Mexican government, afraid that regional labour standards might undermine the country's comparative cost advantages (Finbow 2006). At its heart, NAALC is therefore a set of principles and a complaints and monitoring procedure which rarely produce effective sanctions (Dombois *et al.* 2003; Finbow 2006; Kay 2011).

Arrangements for regional labour standards and employment relations

This section compares specific EU and NAFTA policies which shape various dimensions of individual and collective labour standards and employment relations. The emphasis is on policies affecting regional employment relations and on those substantive issues that are regulated by regional institutions and policies.

Individual employee rights at work

Most EU legislation in the field of employment can be classified under individual (rather than collective) labour law. A major breakthrough was the legislation of health and safety of workers that was part of the Single Market initiative and the first social policy issue for which the unanimity voting was lifted. EU law in this area has taken the form of Directives. Under a general framework Directive, issued in 1989, employers have been made responsible, and liable, for the conditions at work and the health and safety of workers. In a number of industries (mining, fishing, seafaring, chemistry, construction), there are special regulations, often based on agreements negotiated between the European unions and employers associations.

EU anti-discrimination law has gradually expanded from its original protection against discrimination between men and women in the Treaty of Rome (1957) to protection against discrimination based on race, religion, age, disability and sexual orientation, now framed in a general 'catch all' Directive of 2002. EU legislation on equal opportunity and equal treatment has been expanded with Directives on maternity leave (1992) and parental leave (1996, revised in 2009). Individual labour law also covers the Directives obliging employers to inform their employees of the conditions applicable to their employment contract (1991); the protection of employee rights in case of collective redundancies (1992) or a transfer of ownership (2001); and ensuring payment of employees' outstanding claims in the event of employer insolvency (2008). Two pieces of EU legislation, on working hours (1993) and on workers posted to another member state (1996), have proven very controversial and will be discussed below, as they touch on collective and individual labour law.

NAFTA does not have minimum labour standards. The side agreement on labour (NAALC) provides a mechanism for the public to submit a complaint to any of the three participating countries alleging failure of one of the others to enforce its labour standards. However, only 'violations of worker health and safety, child labour and minimum wages standards could result in fines and trade sanctions' (Delp *et al.* 2004: iv). An 'Evaluation Committee of Experts' can be established to assess the issue. Ultimately, a violation can lead to the suspension of NAFTA trade advantages (Dombois *et al.* 2003), but this has never happened.

Collective representation at work

On fundamental worker rights, such as freedom of association, the right to bargain collectively and the right to strike, the EU and NAFTA take a similar position: the enforcement of these rights is first and foremost a matter for member states. Although these rights are included in the EU Charter of Fundamental Rights, the EU has been explicitly denied the competence to legislate in the area of pay, the right of association, the right to strike or the right to impose lock-outs (Art. 153 TFEU). Arguably, this is not only the prerogative of member states but also, at least in some member states (for instance, in Denmark), the prerogative of social partners themselves, who wish to keep all state interference at bay.

EU guarantees of the right to strike have recently become a matter of controversy after rulings of the ECJ in 2007 (Dølvik and Visser 2009). The *Viking* case concerned a Finnish seafarer union that had threatened industrial action against a Finnish shipping company planning to relocate a ship production to Estonia (with much lower-paid Estonian workers). The ECJ ruled, with reference to the Charter of Fundamental Rights, that there exists a right to strike throughout the EU, but that the threat of union action in this particular case was a disproportionate restriction of the freedom of establishment. The *Laval* case involved collective action by the Swedish construction workers' union to enforce a collective agreement on a Latvian company building a school in Sweden. The ECJ deemed the union action disproportionate and in breach of EU law, because no clear (national) rules on minimum wages exist in Sweden as is required under the 'Posting of Workers Directive' (see below). Understandably these rulings caused widespread anger among European trade unions. The Secretary General of the European Trade Union Confederation (ETUC), John Monks, considered the Court's rulings a 'licence for social dumping' and warned that they could fuel 'protectionist reactions' (Arnholtz 2012: 44). According to Hyman (2009: 24), the ECJ decisions featured prominently in the campaign that led to the Irish 'No' to the Lisbon Treaty in May 2008.

Such supranational interventions, either upholding or curtailing rights, do not exist in NAFTA. The provisions in a side agreement referring to collective worker rights go no further than committing the three member states to observing their national legislation related to the freedom of association, the right of collective bargaining, and the right to strike. In cases of infringements of these core rights, the weakest measures apply: '[bilateral] consultations between ministers and the agreement of programmes intended to resolve the problems identified' (Dombois *et al.* 2003: 8).

The EU and NAFTA also differ in the area of employee information and consultation rights. This reflects different institutional traditions, with many European countries having works councils (elected by the employees) with legal rights of information, consultation and, in a few countries, also codetermination rights regarding management's decisions. This is an anathema in North American labour relations (Rogers and Streeck 1995). Attempts to legislate such councils at the EU level go back to the 1970s. At the time these attempts failed in view of the large diversity of employee involvement regulations across EU member states, the massive opposition of European employers and the mighty lobby of the American Chamber of Commerce (ibid.). However, in 1994, the EU adopted a Directive on consultation and information rights in transnational undertakings, and finally in 2002 a Directive on information and consultation in national firms employing at least 50 employees. The 1994 European Works Council (EWC) Directive is generally seen as a weak piece of legislation, with many loopholes, and implemented in less than 50 per cent of the transnational firms concerned, yet it seems to have provided trade unions in EU member states with 'a new platform for cross-border information exchange and cooperation' (Arrowsmith and Marginson 2006: 246). It has also served as a springboard for negotiating so-called 'transnational framework agreements' with multinational companies, mostly on issues of collective worker rights, labour standards outside Europe, and corporate social responsibility. The 2002 Directive has helped to establish minimum rights regarding information and consultation in national firms in countries such as Ireland and the UK, and in a number of countries in Central and Eastern Europe, where these rights did not exist, or pertained only to the decreasing segment of unionized firms.

NAFTA and EU also differ very strongly in the role of regional union organizations (and employers organizations) within the integration and policy-making process. NAFTA lacks any regional level union structures embracing North American labour.[12] If there is cooperation across the US-Mexican border, it is mostly with unofficial unions and opposition groups within the Mexican labour movement. The official Mexican unions, which carry a 'corporatist' legacy of cooperation with the Mexican state and party in government, have been resistant to any regional-level solutions that might threaten their monopoly of local labour representation (Gitterman 2003). Transnational collective bargaining does not exist in NAFTA.

Regional-level union representation in post-war Europe is as old as the oldest European Community organizations (Haas 1958). The ETUC was founded in 1973 as a regrouping of some older organizations (Ebbinghaus and Visser 2000: 780–5). At present, 83 national trade union centres from all 27 EU member states and 9 other European countries, as well as 12 European industry federations, are affiliated with the ETUC, which claims a total of 60 million members, including retired workers. Its counterpart on the employers' side is BusinessEurope, the European regional organization of employers. Together with some smaller employers organizations, the ETUC and BusinessEurope are involved in the European Social Dialogue which has, since the Treaty revision of Maastricht (1992) and Amsterdam (1997),[13] obtained the right to co-legislate on social policy matters. The regional social partners have to be consulted by the Commission on social policy issues and, if they wish, can negotiate agreements which can either be the basis for EU legislation to be passed by the Council and Parliament or may be implemented 'in accordance with the procedures and practices specific to management and labour and the member states' (Art. 155.2 TFEU). Such 'autonomous agreements' have been reached on telework (2002), work-related stress (2004), harassment and violence at work (2007) and inclusive labour markets (2010).

Employee experience of work

A variety of EU Directives address issues connected with the employee experience of work. Central is the Working-Time Directive (1993, revised in 2003), which has proven very controversial and is currently being renegotiated between ETUC and BusinessEurope. Its main provisions are a maximum working week of 48 hours, a minimum daily rest period of 11 hours and annual paid holidays of at least four weeks. It is possible, however, to derogate from particular aspects of this regulation by means of collective agreements. When the UK adopted the Directive in 1998, after ending its opt-out on EU social policy, it negotiated a transitional right to grant individual employees the possibility to express in writing that the maximum of 48 weekly hours did not apply to them. When this clause expired in 2003, the UK allowed the clause to continue, but the European Parliament rejected this compromise. In 2009, the Parliament also rejected a Council compromise in which the UK gave up its opposition against regulation on agency workers but would be allowed to continue its exceptional position in working time regulation. The issue has stalled since and it is unlikely that the current negotiations on the European Social Dialogue will lead to an agreement any time soon.

Based on framework agreements, the EU has issued Directives on parental leave (1996, revised in 2009), part-time work (1997) and fixed-term employment (1999). In 2009, after ten years of negotiations, the EU issued a Directive on work in temporary work agencies, in which unions gained the principle of 'equal treatment' of agency worker compared with workers in user firms, and the agency business gained recognition and the abolition of restrictions existing in many EU member states. In this case the UK negotiated a three-months delay in applying these rules to agency workers.

Perhaps the most controversial piece of EU legislation is the Directive on the posting of workers which addresses the problem of low pay and substandard working conditions of workers posted by foreign firms and agencies. In the 1990s, the posting of workers from Portugal, Ireland, the UK and Central and Eastern Europe to building sites in mainland Europe was seen as a threat to national standards and wage floors by the construction unions in the receiving countries. After intense lobbying and a coalition with employers in construction, themselves under threat of low-wage competition, the 'Posting of Workers Directive' was passed in 1996 and allowed member states to declare minimum employment rights pertaining to a particular industry mandatory by law or collective agreement with binding effects on non-organized employers. At the time the understanding was that, like other EU Directives, this was a 'minimum rights' Directive, which could be improved upon through national law or collective bargaining (Dølvik *et al.* 2013). The ECJ rulings in the *Laval* and *Viking* cases have rejected this interpretation and made implementation of the Directive very problematic in countries without minimum wage legislation or a practice of making collective agreements legally binding on non-organized employers. Attempts at re-regulation have failed and unions now seek recourse to national solutions which must, however, pass the test of the ECJ (ibid.).

In contrast, NAFTA has no regional standards on working time, work–life balance, non-standard contracts or the posting of workers. Some of these matters are regulated in the national labour laws of the USA, Canada and Mexico, and could become a target in the complaints procedure of NAALC, but no concrete examples are known.

Employment relations, welfare and politics

With the establishment of the EMU, trade union leaders became anxious to gain some influence over the policies of the European Central Bank (ECB), in particular regarding a too strict interpretation of its Treaty-based task of preventing inflation. They succeeded in establishing a 'Macroeconomic Dialogue', initiated by the Council, the Commission, the ECB and the social partners in 1999 to improve information and coordination between the different stakeholders. Unlike the Social Dialogue, it cannot set targets, conclude agreements or issue recommendations. The European unions have tried to strengthen the Macroeconomic Dialogue along with their own role in wage policy coordination, but with little result. The ECB's interpretation of the Macroeconomic Dialogue as an informal forum for exchange of views has prevailed. European employers have resisted EU-level collective bargaining and refused to participate in union attempts at wage policy coordination.

In March 2011, 25 of the 27 EU Member States signed the so-called 'Euro-Plus Pact', which in earlier editions was called the 'Competitiveness Pact' or the 'Pact for the Euro'. The UK and the Czech Republic refused to sign, but other non-Euro members such as Sweden, Denmark and Poland went along with it. This Pact, which is supposed to foster competitiveness and employment, and reduce sovereign debts, recommends, *inter alia*, lowering the level of centralization in wage bargaining, the abolition of indexation mechanisms, and restraint on public sector wages. Significantly, although the pact gives the Commission and the Council far-reaching monitoring powers, these were not discussed in the Macroeconomic Dialogue or in other EU forums where trade unions are present, but were directly negotiated between governments, under strong pressure from Germany and the ECB. Predictably, the European unions have criticized the 'Euro-Plus Pact', which they see as an infringement of national (and social partner) sovereignty in matters of pay and collective bargaining, and they reject the retrenchment and austerity logic that underlies the pact.

NAFTA has no equivalent of the Macroeconomic Dialogue involving the governments, central banks or non-governmental organization. Only in Mexico would there be a 'corporatist legacy' on which such initiatives could build, but the structural reforms that the USA wanted and that NAFTA institutionalized make the return to such practices unlikely. Vertical pressures on member states' labour rights, emerging from regional policies, as in the above case, are absent in NAFTA. To the extent that such pressures exist, they are generated through competition between the three states, horizontally, with the USA in a dominant role.

The global economy and the impact of the EU and NAFTA on employment relations

How do the EU and NAFTA compare in terms of their impact on labour standards and employment relations in their member states? What lessons can be drawn from their experience for the broader theme of regional regulation of employment relations in the global economy? The answer must start with acknowledging the differences in institutional development and ambitions of the EU and NAFTA. NAFTA is a trade agreement, while the EU is also a customs union and a common market that includes a monetary union and incorporates elements of a political union. Most important from the perspective of employment regulation is the common market (for goods, services, capital and labour). A common market between countries with different employment standards opens the prospect of a 'race to the bottom' and 'downward policy competition', and much of the EU's legislation on minimum employment standards (health and safety; working hours, work–life balance, atypical work, information and consultation within companies) is meant to address this issue, not through harmonization of standards across member states, as was the initial approach before the 1980s, but by creating a common floor of minimum rights. This approach, and ambition, are entirely missing in NAFTA. The issue of downward pressure on employment standards and the loss of well-paying jobs, resulting from the freedom of capital (and products) to move across borders, has been addressed by a set of common minimum principles (basically those of the ILO) and the establishment of a procedure to enforce compliance with national labour standards, where they exist.

Have these varying approaches been effective? Has the EU successfully established a European floor of rights and standards? While EU social policies are sometimes rightly seen as 'a saga of high aspirations and modest results', in many areas – health and safety, non-discrimination, migrants' rights, work–life balance issues, and even working hours – EU legislation on employment standards has moved beyond 'lowest common denominator policies' and 'the combined impact of what has been passed is not trivial' (Pierson 1998: 129–31). However, the social policy ambitions of the EU have significantly lowered, starting in the 1980s when attempts to harmonize conditions across EU member states were abandoned (except in the case of non-discrimination and health and safety legislation) resulting in a much more flexible approach which allows national opt-outs and variations in policy implementation. For instance, with regard to areas such as working hours, information and consultation rights of employees, or the rights of atypical employees, the evaluation of their effectiveness depends not only on how the EU Directives have been implemented in each of the member states (Falkner *et al.* 2005), but also whether they are actually enforced in practice, especially in firms with no or weak trade unions. This can be very problematic, given the EU-wide decline in unionization and the weakness of unions in many EU member states.

Streeck (1995: 424) has characterized the post-Maastricht EU approach to employment regulation as neo-voluntarist: trying 'to do with a minimum of compulsory modification of both market outcomes and national policy choices, presenting itself as an alternative to hard regulation as well as to no regulation at all'. Since 2000, this trend towards legal flexibility has been further intensified by the growing conviction of EU policy-makers that regulation should not place too heavy burdens on industry, in particular, on small and medium-sized firms.

With regard to NAFTA, the NAALC complaints procedure has been criticized for procedural shortcomings, the slow processing of complaints (it takes on average two years to process a submission), the weakness of potential and actual sanctions which has seriously affected its effectiveness (Dombois *et al.* 2003; Finbow 2006; Kay 2011), and for the poor compliance of member states, even regarding core labour standards (Scherrer and Greven 2001). Most studies of the NAALC functioning therefore evaluate the practical and legal outcomes of the submissions rather negatively (Ayres 2004). The decline in submissions, after an initial surge directly after the start of NAFTA, has been attributed to a widespread disappointment with the poor results ('submission fatigue') (Dombois *et al.* 2003). Based on a large survey, Kay concludes that 'the NAALC is woefully inadequate as a tool for redressing labour rights violations across the (North American) continent' (2011: 444). All her respondents, with the exception of those of the official Mexican unions, agreed on 'the NAALC's lack of enforcement mechanisms' (ibid.) and 'a general feeling among union leaders and strategic decision makers that, with minimal enforcement mechanisms, the NAALC yields few concrete results in terms of directly improving wages and working conditions' (ibid.: 445). The conclusion is that NAFTA's side agreement looks very much like a failure, which may explain why US unions, which were initially the major force behind the side agreement, have continued their opposition to NAFTA.

What are the effects of the regional organization on the organized actors in employment relations? Has regional integration contributed to regional cooperation among trade unions? Has it increased their capacity to influence outcomes? Undoubtedly, the power of unions has declined on both sides of the Atlantic. But has this decline been intensified or, instead, moderated by regional integration? We would argue for the latter. By institutionalizing a social dialogue at the supranational level, however feeble, the EU has set an example for the cooperative conduct of employment relations and for the legitimacy of union involvement, even though the EU has been far from consistent in valuing the voice of labour. And even NAFTA, on a much smaller scale, has indirectly encouraged transnational union cooperation (which had been foreign to all three national labour movements) through the complaints procedure of its side agreement.

In the EU, the concentration of power at the regional level has triggered the creation of regional organizations of unions and employers, some with a mandate to negotiate on behalf of members. The fact that European social partners have been willing and able to negotiate EU framework agreements and take responsibility for their implementation has been interpreted as the start of EU collective bargaining. However, the process is more akin to standard setting by means of 'shadow legislation', and the employers' willingness to partake tends to depend on the possibility of avoiding or pre-empting hard legislation (Visser 2006).

EU Directives, too, have triggered transnational union coordination. For instance, the 1994 EWC Directive has brought together union representatives from different countries and engaged the European sectoral federations. Some have seen in the EWCs the precursors of transnational collective bargaining (Marginson and Sisson 1998), but European employers steadfastly reject such projects. In its Social Agenda 2006–2010, the European Commission proposed an optional framework for transnational collective bargaining in sectors and companies. This was welcomed by the ETUC, but BusinessEurope argued against any governance tool that facilitates bargaining above the national level. The Commission duly dropped the proposal (Keune and Warneck 2006). Some EWCs and union federations have nonetheless succeeded in concluding international framework agreements with European and non-European multinational companies, in which they seek stronger enforcement of international labour standards (Müller *et al.* 2011). The Posting of Workers Directive is an example of legislation which, in spite of or rather because of its defects, has inspired transnational union cooperation. For example, although attempts to establish a European Migrant Workers Union failed, in its place a service point for migrant workers run in co-operation with Polish unions has been established by the European Federation of Building and Wood Workers which is the most active union in these matters (Dølvik *et al.* 2013).

In NAFTA, there are no regional organizations that can be lobbied. Of course, regional cooperation among unions might also develop without supranational institutions that can be targeted or asked for help, but it is more difficult. Yet, the complaints procedure in the NAALC has had the unintended consequence of bringing about novel forms of cross-border cooperation of unions and NGOs. As a consequence of the NAALC allowing complaints only to be filed outside of the home countries, 'a union with a grievance in the U.S. must file a submission with the NAO in Mexico or Canada (or both). This procedural rule . . . provides an incentive for unions to collaborate on submissions across borders' (Kay 2011: 433). These attempts to regionally enforce core labour rights and improved health and safety standards have led to the creation of cross-border networks of labour unions and human rights organizations (Stillerman 2003) and promoted a kind of 'legal transnationalism' (Kay 2011) around social issues such as freedom of association and the rights of migrants. Kay concludes that, although limited and disappointing in its immediate and short-term legal effects, the NAALC potentially carries long-term social effects by bringing an unprecedented degree of internationalism and regionalism into the North American union movement.

How can the examples of employment regulations in the EU and NAFTA be evaluated within the broader context of globalization? The rise of regionalism in the 1990s has been seen as an indicator of or a challenge to globalization, potentially inhibiting trade liberalization on a world scale, as embodied in the World Trade Organization (WTO) (OECD 2002a). Regional integration might indeed serve 'as a form of resistance to globalization and as a platform where alternative norms and practices can be developed' (Hurrell 2007: 131). For this reason, proponents of a stronger social dimension to global trade have praised regional integration, especially the EU model, and advocated it as a bridge between national and global social policies, arguing that it is easier to develop and enforce common standards among a smaller group of countries with similar democratic credentials and levels of economic development (Yeates and Deacon 2006).[14]

However, as is clearly exemplified by the EU and NAFTA, regional integration has not primarily centred on social policy but on trade integration and gaining economic advantages in global markets. NAFTA can be seen as the response to US decline in manufacturing in global markets and the attempt by US firms to gain low cost production sites nearby. The 'Single Market' initiative of the EU 'ratified a "move to the market", that was a reaction against the poor economic performance of the 1970s and against the activist state intervention associated with it' (Hall 2007: 63). It moved the EU significantly beyond the Treaty of

Rome by forcing member states not only to remove non-tariff barriers to trade but also to eliminate national policies that inhibited intra-Community competition. Opening up their markets to each other was seen as a way to reduce regulation and make Europe fit for global competition. This was politically possible because of a confluence of liberalization preferences of the governments of Britain, Germany and France (Moravcsik 1998) and a remarkable ideological standpoint of the European Commission, presenting a more flexible market as the answer to Europe's underperforming economies and its stagnating integration process (Eichengreen 2007: 345). This analysis is consistent with Stubbs and Underhill's conclusion that regional integration is not an alternative to or hindrance of globalization, but rather 'a way of taking advantage of some of the forces set in train by the process of globalization' (1999: 289). Thus, it might be argued that, in the EU, the regional, supranational level rather than the nation state has become the 'appropriate and viable level to reconcile the changing and intensifying pressures of global capitalist competition on the one hand with the need for political regulation and management on the other' (Hurrell 2007: 131). The same argument cannot be made for NAFTA, as competences (whether on trade policy issues or on social and employment issues) have not been relocated to the regional level.

Whether the EU has succeeded in reconciling the dual pressures of global competition and upholding employment rights, and presents something akin to 'fair globalization' (ILO 2004), is open to debate. EU social policies are often seen as a model for the world (Deacon 2007; ILO 2004), and the European Commission is keen on presenting it that way. Within the EU, scholars are divided between those who see the EU as a 'vehicle of social regulation of the internationalising labour market' and those who dismiss EU employment regulation as a 'vehicle for liberalisation' and 'a matter of form rather than substance' (Hyman 2001: 290). This chapter has tried to show that both views are one-sided and that European integration has been both 'a mechanism promoting market-building and a means to counter its negative effects by promoting social regulation' (Visser and Kaminska 2009: 25). The free trade zone NAFTA is, not surprisingly, weaker on either side of this balance: the agreement leaves both market making and (compensatory) social regulation to the three member states, and provides only minimal solutions for distrust in each other's willingness to uphold globally recognized standards.

Notes

1 This chapter is based on earlier work: Visser and Kaminska (2009) and Kaminska and Visser (2011).

2 Of the 94 agreements registered at the World Trade Organization (WTO) in 1999, 87 have been ratified since 1990 (OECD 2002a).

3 Other examples include MERCOSUR in Latin America, Association of Southeast Asian Nations (ASEAN) in South-East Asia, South African Development Community (SADC) in Southern Africa and the Economic Community of West African States (ECOWAS) in Western Africa (Kaminska and Visser 2011).

4 The member states of EU (F= founding member; year of later accessions in brackets): Austria (1995), Belgium (F), Bulgaria (2007), Cyprus (2004), Czech Republic (2004), Denmark (1973), Estonia (2004), Finland (1995), France (F), Germany (F), Greece (1981), Hungary (2004), Ireland (1973), Italy (F), Latvia (2004), Lithuania (2004), Luxembourg (F), Malta (2004), the Netherlands (F), Poland (2004), Portugal (1986), Romania (2007), Slovakia (2004), Slovenia (2004), Spain (1986), Sweden (1995), United Kingdom (1973). As of 2013, Croatia will be the 28th member state.

5 The Treaty (Art. 225) states: 'Member States shall respect their [the Commissioners'] independence and shall not seek to influence them in the performance of their tasks.'

6 With the exception of Denmark and the UK, which negotiated an opt-out from the Maastricht Treaty which laid the foundations for the Economic and Monetary Union (EMU), EU member states which have not yet joined the euro are bound to do so, though no time-schedule has been set.

7 With the exception of Ireland, the UK and Sweden, all the 'old' member states negotiated temporary restrictions, up to seven years, on the freedom of movement for workers from the new member states that joined in 2004 and 2007.

8 TFEU stands for Treaty of the Functioning of the European Union and is the consolidated version of the Treaty since the latest changes made in Lisbon in 2007, which came into force in 2010 after having been ratified by all member states. All references to Treaty articles refer to this consolidated version as published in *Official Journal of the EU*, 30-03-2010 (http://www.consilium.europa.eu/documents/treaty-of-lisbon).

9 A *Regulation* is a form of secondary EU law (the Treaty itself being primary law), with immediate effect in member states. A *Directive* is another, more flexible instrument of secondary law and must be 'transposed' (i.e. incorporated in national law) within three years of its acceptance by the Council and Parliament.

10 Charter of Fundamental Rights of the European Union, signed in Nice, France, in December 2000. See: www.europarl.europa.eu/charter.

11 Think of the US refusal to recognize the International Criminal Court or the refusal to ratify ILO Conventions 87 and 98 on the freedom of association and the right to collective bargaining.

12 Traditionally, the so-called 'international U.S. unions', affiliated with the American Federation of Labor and Congress of Industrial Organizations (AFL-CIO), also organize workers in Canada in the same occupations and crafts, though their share in Canadian union membership has continued to decline. Today, these unions represent only a very small percentage of Canadian union membership.

13 Originally, this co-legislative role did not include the UK, which had 'opted out' of the Social Policy Agreement signed by the other (at the time 11) member states and annexed to the Maastricht Treaty. The British 'opt-out' was ended after Labour's victory in the UK general election of 1997, and the Agreement was included in the Treaty revision negotiated in Amsterdam in 1997.

14 This argument has its variant within the EU, where proponents of a stronger social policy have sometimes argued that the Southern and Eastern enlargements have made it more difficult to agree on higher standards, as they have increased the internal heterogeneity in terms of economic development, democratic tradition, social policy standards and employment relations (Scharpf 2002).

References

Arnholtz, J. (2012) *Slowing Down Social Europe? The Role of Coalitions and Decision-Making Arenas: Report 4: The Posting of Workers Issue*, Copenhagen: FAOS, Research Paper 125.

Arrowsmith, J. and Marginson, P. (2006) 'The European cross-border dimension to collective bargaining in multinational companies', *European Journal of Industrial Relations*, 12(3): 245–66.

Aspinwall, M. (2009) 'NAFTA-ization: regionalization and domestic political adjustment in the North American Economic Area', *Journal of Common Market Studies*, 47(1): 1–24.

Ayres, J. (2004) *Power Repertoires Under NAFTA: Reassessing Contentious Transnationalism*, Ontario: Carleton University, Department of Political Science, CGPE Working Paper 04-07.

Clarke, C. (2007) 'Assessing the impact regionalism has on labour rights and employment standard', paper presented to the 48th International Studies Association Annual Convention, Chicago, 28 February–3 March 2007.

Deacon, B. (2007) *Global Social Policy and Governance*, London: Sage.

Delp, L., Arriaga, M., Palma, G., Urita, H. and Valenzuela, A. (2004) *NAFTA's Labor Side Agreement: Fading into Oblivion? An Assessment of Workplace Health and Safety Cases*, Los Angeles, CA: UCLA, Center for Labor Research and Education.

Dølvik, J. E. and Visser, J. (2009) 'Free movement, equal treatment and workers' rights: Can the European Union solve its trilemma of fundamental principles?', *Industrial Relations Journal*, 40(6): 491–509.

——, Eldring, L. and Visser, J. (2013) 'Setting wage floors in open markets: the role of the social partners in Europe's multilevel governance', in S. Evju, J.E. Dølvik and J. Malmberg (eds) *Regulating Transnational Labour in Europe: The Quandaries of Multilevel Governance*, Cambridge: Cambridge University Press.

Dombois, R., Homburger, E. and Winter, J. (2003) 'Transnational labour regulation in the NAFTA: a problem of institutional design?', *International Journal of Labour Law and Industrial Relations*, 19(4): 421–40.

Ebbinghaus, B. and Visser, J. (eds) (2000) *Trade Unions in Western Europe Since 1945*, Basingstoke: Palgrave Macmillan.

Eichengreen, B. (2007) *The European Economy Since 1945*, Princeton, NJ: Princeton University Press.

Falkner, G., Treib, O., Hartlapp, M. and Leiber, S. (2005) *Complying with Europe: EU Harmonisation and Soft Law in the Member States*, Cambridge: Cambridge University Press.

Fernandez, R., and Portes, J. (1998) 'Returns to regionalism: an analysis of non-traditional gains from regional trade agreements', *World Bank Economic Review*, 12(2): 197–220.

Finbow, R. G. (2006) *The Limits of Regionalism: NAFTA's Labour Accord*, Aldershot: Ashgate.

Gitterman, D. P. (2003) 'European integration and labour market cooperation: a comparative regional perspective', *Journal of European Social Policy*, 13(2): 99–120.

Goetschy, J. (2003) 'The European Employment Strategy, multi-level governance and policy coordination: past, present and future', in J. Zeitlin and D. M. Trubek (eds) *Governing Work and Welfare in a New Economy: European and American Experiences*, Oxford: Oxford University Press.

Gold, M., Cressey, P. and Léonard, E. (2007) 'Whatever happened to social dialogue? From partnership to managerialism in the EU employment agenda', *European Journal of Industrial Relations*, 13(1): 7–25.

Haas, E. B. (1958) *The Uniting of Europe: Political, Social and Economic Forces, 1950–1957*, Stanford, CA: Stanford University Press.

Hall, P. A. (2007) 'The evolution of varieties of capitalism in Europe', in B. Hancké, M. Rhodes and M. Thatcher (eds) *Beyond Varieties of Capitalism: Conflict, Contradictions, and Complementarities in the European Economy*, Oxford: Oxford University Press.

Hoffman, S. (1995) *The European Sisyphus: Essays on Europe, 1964–1994*, Boulder, CO: Westview Press.

Hurrell, A. (2007) 'One world? Many worlds? The place of regions in the study of international society', *International Affairs*, 83(1): 127–46.

Hyman, R. (2001) 'The Europeanisation – or the erosion – of industrial relations?', *Industrial Relations Journal*, 32(4): 280–94.

—— (2009) *Trade Unions and "Europe": Are the Members Out of Step?*, London: London School of Economics and Political Science, Europe in Question Discussion Paper Series, 14.

ILO (2004) *A Fair Globalization: Creating Opportunities for All: Report of the World Commission on the Social Consequences of Globalization*, Geneva: International Labour Organization.

Kaminska, M. E. and Visser, J. (2011) 'The emergence of industrial relations in regional trade blocks: a comparative analysis', *British Journal of Industrial Relations*, 49(2): 256–81.

Kay, T. (2011) 'Legal transnationalism: the relationship between transnational social movement building and international law', *Law and Social Inquiry*, 36(2): 419–54.

Keune, M. and Warneck, W. (2006) 'An EU framework for transnational collective bargaining: an opportunity for European trade unions?' *Transfer: European Review of Labour and Research*, 12(4): 637–41.

Marginson, P. and Sisson, K. (1998) 'European collective bargaining: a virtual prospect?', *Journal of Common Market Studies*, 36(4): 505–28.

Milward, A. (1984) *The Reconstruction of Europe, 1945–51*, Berkeley, CA: University of California Press.

Moravcsik, A. (1993) 'Preferences and power in the European Community: a liberal intergovernmentalist approach', *Journal of Common Market Studies*, 31(4): 473–524.

—— (1998) 'Europe's integration at century's end', in A. Moravcsik (ed.) *Centralization or Fragmentation? Europe Facing the Challenges of Deepening, Diversity and Democracy*, New York: The Council on Foreign Relations.

Müller, T., Platzer, H-W. and Rüb, S. (2011) 'European collective agreements at company level', *Transfer: European Review of Labour and Research*, 17(2): 217–28.

OECD (2002a) *Regional Integration Agreements*, Paris: Organization for Economic Cooperation and Development.

—— (2002b) *Labour Mobility in Trade Agreements*, Paris: Organization for Economic Cooperation and Development, Paper of the Working Party of the Trade Committee, TD/TC/WP(2002)16/Final.

Pierson, P. (1998) 'Social policy and European integration', in A. Moravcsik (ed.) *Centralization or Fragmentation? Europe Facing the Challenges of Deepening, Diversity and Democracy*, New York: The Council on Foreign Relations.

Pinera González, C. (2000) 'Mexico's free trade agreements: extending NAFTA's approach', in S. M. Stephenson (ed.) *Service Trade in the Western Hemisphere: Liberalization, Integration and Reform*, Washington, DC: Organization of American States/Brookings Institution Press.

Porter, T. (1999) 'The North American Free Trade Agreement', in R. Stubbs and G. R. D. Underhill (eds) *Political Economy and the Changing Global Order*, 2nd edn, Don Mills, Canada: Oxford University Press.

Rogers, J. and Streeck, W. (1995) 'United States: lessons from abroad and home', in J. Rogers and W. Streeck (eds) *Works Councils: Consultation, Representation, Co-Ordination*, Chicago: University of Chicago Press.

Scharpf, F. W. (1999) *Governing in Europe: Effective and Democratic?*, Oxford: Oxford University Press.

—— (2002) 'The European Social Model', *Journal of Common Market Studies*, 40(4): 645–70.

Scherrer, C. and Greven, T. (2001) *Global Rules for Trade: Codes of Conduct, Social Labelling, Workers' Rights Clauses*, Münster: Verlag Westfälisches Dampfboot

Stillerman, J. (2003) 'Transnational activist networks and the emergence of labor internationalism in the NAFTA countries', *Social Science History*, 27(4): 577–601.

Streeck, W. (1995) 'From market making to state building? Reflections on the political economy of European social policy', in S. Leibfried and P. Pierson (eds) *European Social Policy: Between Fragmentation and Integration*, Washington, DC: The Brookings Institution.

Stubbs, R. and Underhill, G.R.D. (1999) *Political Economy and the Changing Global Order*, 2nd edn, Don Mills, Canada: Oxford University Press.

Threlfall, M. (2007) 'The social dimension of the European Union: innovative methods for advancing integration', *Global Social Policy*, 7(3): 271–93.

UNU-CRIS (The United Nations University Institute on Comparative Regional Integration Studies) (2008) *Deepening the Social Dimensions of Regional Integration*, Geneva: International Institute for Labour Studies.

Van Wezel Stone, K. (1995) 'Labor and the global economy: four approaches to transnational labor regulation', *Michigan Journal of International Law*, 16(Summer): 987–1028.

Visser, J. (2006) 'More holes in the bucket: twenty years of European integration and organized labour', *Comparative Labour Law and Policy Journal*, 26: 477–521.

—— and Kaminska, M. E. (2009) 'Europe's industrial relations in a global perspective', in J. Visser (ed.) *Industrial Relations in Europe 2008*, Luxembourg: Office for the Official Publications of the European Commission.

Weiler, J. H. H. (1999) *The Constitution of Europe*, New York: Cambridge University Press.

Yeates, N. and Deacon, B. (2006) *Globalism, Regionalism and Social Policy: Framing the Debate*, Bruges: United Nations University Comparative Regional Integration Studies, UNU-CRIS Occasional Papers 2006-6.

23 International regulation

The ILO and other agencies

Keith D. Ewing

Introduction

On 22 November 2011, the International Labour Organization (ILO) published the Report of a High Level Mission to Athens (International Labour Office 2011). This followed a reference to the ILO's Committee of Experts in 2011 by the Greek Confederation of Trade Unions (GSEE) about the austerity measures introduced in response to the financial crisis that had gripped their nation (ibid.). These measures were taken following the decision of the Heads of State and Government of the Euro Area to offer support for the Greek economy. In order to activate that support, the Greek Ministry of Finance agreed a package with the European Commission, the European Central Bank and the International Monetary Fund (IMF) (the Troika), in the course of which the Greek government undertook not only to reduce public sector pay, but also to reform the legal framework for wage bargaining in the private sector. This would be in addition to minimum entry level wages, a new control system for undeclared work, the extension of probationary periods, the increase in the use of part-time work, and the 'recalibration' (*sic*) of rules governing collective dismissals.

The GSEE was concerned that the latter violated a number of obligations of the Greek government arising under a wide range of ILO Conventions, leading the Committee of Experts to conclude that such was the complexity of the matter that the government of Greece should be invited to avail itself of the technical assistance of the ILO, and to accept a high level mission 'to facilitate a comprehensive understanding of the issues', before the Committee proceeded to assess the impact of the austerity measures on the ratified Conventions (International Labour Office 2011: 4). The High Level Mission (HLM) was composed of ILO officials and produced a report that made sobering reading, highlighting the decentralization of pay bargaining, the changing nature of employment from permanent to flexible forms of engagement, and the swingeing cuts in public and private sector wage rates. Quite apart from their implications for workers as a whole, the measures were said to have a disproportionate impact on women, who were more likely to bear the brunt of the move to flexible employment arrangements, and who were more likely to be employed in the public sector where 30,000 job cuts were taking place.

At the heart of the austerity measures, however, was the desire to secure an 'internal devaluation', defined to mean 'a sharp reduction in wages and consequent living standards' (ibid.: 16), as an alternative to a currency devaluation which was not possible for Greece as part of the Eurozone. The 'internal devaluation' was designed to enhance Greece's competitiveness in the international economy, and would be achieved by 'fundamentally revising the way the collective bargaining system functioned, especially at sectoral level' (ibid.). The system operating in Greece was one where the national agreement set minimum terms and conditions for workers across all sectors. Sector agreements could then make specific provision in individual sectors to improve upon the national agreement, while enterprise agreements in turn could build upon the provisions of the sectoral agreements in individual enterprises where the circumstances so justified. Apart from imposing severe pay cuts by law and invalidating any terms in collective agreements that made provision for the contrary, the austerity package also provided that both sector and enterprise-based agreements could make provisions less favourable than those contained in the national agreement.

Under the new law, moreover, ad hoc associations of employees could negotiate these latter arrangements where there were no trade unions. This last provision was a response of the Greek government to the concerns of the Troika that enterprise-level agreements were not sufficiently widespread. This was because there were very few trade unions at enterprise level, with enterprise agreements applying only to organizations with more than 50 workers, and with Greek law requiring a minimum of 20 persons to establish an association. The glimpse that this provides of the Troika demanding so-called labour market reforms regardless of legal obligations to the contrary is more explicit in the High Level Mission Report's discussion on the impact of the austerity measure on employment policy. Expressing concern about rising levels of unemployment in Greece, the HLM noted that members of the Eurozone had ratified ILO Convention 122 (Employment Policy Convention 1964) which calls for full, productive and freely chosen employment, and also the coordination of economic and social policies. But although recognizing the acute difficulties facing Greece, in a telling passage, the HLM reported being 'struck by reports that in discussions with the Troika employment objectives rarely figure' (ibid.: 63).

The report of the HLM was duly considered by the Committee of Experts in 2012, and a number of findings were made expressly about the compliance by Greece with international labour standards, and by implication about the role of the Troika in ensuring that it operated within a framework of legality (ILO 2012a). We return to these findings below. In the meantime, there are a few more fundamental questions to address first. Thus, what is the ILO and what does it do? What are international labour conventions and how are they supervised? To whom are they addressed and to whom do they apply? Why do international labour conventions matter and why should we care if they are observed or not? What are the legal consequences of any failure to comply with the obligations they create? At that point we can return to the report of the HLM and the Conclusions of the Committee of Experts, and assess the implications of international labour standards for the unfolding drama in the Eurozone. The latter represents perhaps one of the greatest challenges to the living conditions of working people for at least a generation, and as such presents a stern test for the institutional relevance and practical effectiveness of the ILO (as well as other organizations).

ILO: Purpose, procedures and problems

Like most great creations, the ILO had a long gestation, with government interest in international labour standards beginning to emerge in the late 1880s. At the initiative of the Swiss, an international conference met in Berlin in 1889 to produce detailed recommendations about child labour, the employment of minors and women, and Sunday work (Ewing 1994). The Berlin conference led to another in Brussels in 1897, to 'study the principles on which an international labour office should be built' (ibid.), leading in turn to the formation of the International Association for Labour Legislation in 1900. It was the International Association that was responsible in 1905 and 1906 for the first international labour standards, dealing with night work by women, and the use of white phosphorous in the production of matches. How this gradual evolution would have continued – and at what pace – without the intervention of the First World War is uncertain. But what is certain is that the experience of war was a major catalyst for the creation of a permanent agency for the regulation of labour standards. So too was the Russian Revolution of 1917, leading one prominent speaker to reflect at the plenary session of the Versailles Peace Conference that: 'There are two methods of making the revolution that we feel is happening throughout the world – the Russian and the British method. It is the British method that has triumphed in the Labour [Chapter of the Treaty of Versailles]' (Stewart 1969).

The ILO Constitution

The ILO was formed in 1919, its certificate of birth to be found in the Labour Chapter of the Treaty of Versailles. The first of three objectives set out in its Constitution (ILO 2012b) was the political goal of peace and stability, said to be impaired by conditions of labour 'involving such injustice hardship and privation to large numbers of people as to produce unrest so great that the peace and harmony of the world are imperilled' (ibid.). Even in 1919, however, there was also a clear economic objective, in the sense that there was a concern about what would now be referred to as social dumping. Thus, the Constitution provides clearly that 'the failure of any nation to adopt humane conditions of labour is an obstacle in the way of other nations which desire to improve the conditions in their own countries' (ibid. and see Box 23.1). In other words, standards should be raised to the level of the

BOX 23.1 The Declaration of Philadelphia

The founding principles of the ILO were re-affirmed by the Declaration of Philadelphia in 1944.

The Declaration was an important reminder of the continuing importance of the ILO in the post-war era and an important renewal of enduring principles, including 'labour is not a commodity'. At the heart of the Declaration, however, is the commitment that:

> all human beings, irrespective of race, creed or sex, have the right to pursue both their material well-being and their spiritual development in conditions of freedom and dignity, of economic security and equal opportunity.

Moreover, the central aim of national and international policy must be 'the attainment of the conditions in which [the foregoing] shall be possible', while

> all national and international policies and measures, in particular those of an economic and financial character, should be judged in this light and accepted only in so far as they may be held to promote and not to hinder the achievement of this fundamental objective.

After the Second World War the ILO became an agency of the United Nations, then with 50 members, and now with 185 member states.

best, a principle that seems directly to contradict the 'internal devaluation' approach now being adopted by the Troika and the Greek government. But it is not only about politics and economics: there is also the commitment to 'social justice', a term that appears twice in the preamble.

Members of the ILO participate with other countries in the structures created by the Constitution, to ensure that the foregoing constitutional objectives are met. The most important of these structures is the International Labour Conference, which meets annually in Geneva, the official seat of the ILO. The International Labour Conference is responsible for making Conventions and Recommendations to give effect to the ILO's constitutional mandate to improve working conditions relating specifically to:

> the regulation of the hours of work including the establishment of a maximum working day and week, the regulation of the labour supply, the prevention of unemployment, the provision of an adequate living wage, the protection of the worker against sickness, disease and injury arising out of his employment, the protection of children, young persons and women, provision for old age and injury, protection of the interests of workers when employed in countries other than their own, recognition of the principle of equal remuneration for work of equal value, recognition of the principle of freedom of association, the organization of vocational and technical education and other measures.
>
> (ILO 2012b)

There are in fact now 189 Conventions passed by the International Labour Conference since the first Convention gave effect to the historic campaign for the eight hour day (Hours of Work Convention 1919). The ILO Constitution provides uniquely that each member state is to be represented at the International Labour Conference by representatives of trade unions, employers and governments, the annual Conference being seen by some early pioneers as the 'Parliament of Labour'. It is an essential feature of this practice of tripartism that trade union and employer representatives are not bound to follow the lead of their government in ILO proceedings, and that by the Constitution they are entitled to act independently. Although now taken for granted, at the inception of the ILO this was seen to be 'an almost revolutionary novelty and an astonishing break with the tradition of international conferences' (Phelan 1936: 4). Once approved by Conference, a Convention will come into force only when ratified by a minimum number of countries, and even then it will be binding on member states only if they ratify it. But once ratified, an ILO Convention gives rise to binding obligations under international law, a point emphasized by the HLM in its report relating to Greece (International Labour Office 2011: 63).

Once the International Labour Conference makes a Convention, the ILO Constitution requires each member state to bring the instrument 'before the authority or authorities within whose competence the matter lies, for the enactment of legislation or other action'. There is no duty on the part of a government to ratify a Convention, even though it may have voted for it at the International Labour Conference; and there is no duty on the part of a national Parliament to introduce implementing legislation, even where the government of the country in question has ratified the Convention (Ewing 1994). So although there may be 189 Conventions at the time of writing, Greece, for example, has ratified only 70, which according to Hepple (2005) puts Greece at the higher end of obligation compared to the other ILO member states. There are 189 Conventions and 185 member-states, which means that if all the Conventions were ratified by all the Member States, there would be 34,587 ratifications, though it is true that some of the Conventions have been withdrawn and others have been replaced. Nevertheless, there are only just under 8,000 ratifications, with some countries (such as the United States and China) having ratified very few, and with some Conventions having attracted very few ratifications.

The Constitution also makes provision for a Governing Body of 56 members (said to perform the executive functions of the ILO), and the International Labour Office (said to be the secretariat controlled by the Governing Body). The former 'takes decisions on ILO policy, decides the agenda of the International Labour Conference, [and] adopts the draft Programme and Budget of the Organization for submission to the Conference' (ILO 2012c). By virtue of the principle of tripartism, 28 of the 56 members of the Governing Body are representatives of government, with 14 being representatives of trade unions and another 14 being representative of employers. Some 10 of the 28 government positions must be occupied by countries deemed to be countries of 'chief industrial importance', namely Brazil, China, France, Germany, India, Italy, Japan, the Russian Federation, the United Kingdom and the United States. Crucially, the trade union and employer representatives on the Governing Body are elected only by the workers' and employers' delegates respectively, for three-year periods. It is an important responsibility of the International Labour Office not only to prepare documents for the International Labour Conference, but also to assist governments to implement decisions of the Conference.

The International Labour Code

ILO Conventions cover a wide area of activity, though some are now regarded as being more important than others and to be the subject of special supervision. The core Conventions each relate to four core principles, namely freedom of association, the abolition of forced labour, the prohibition of child labour, and the elimination of discrimination. The importance of these core Conventions was enhanced by the ILO *Declaration on Fundamental Principles and Rights at Work of 1998*, which has been signed by all ILO Member States (ILO 1998). Not only does this reaffirm the commitment of the Member States in question to these fundamental principles, but it has set in train a process of more regular scrutiny of Member States on their compliance with the principles and the offer of greater support from the International Labour Office to help them meet their obligations. The Declaration also set in train a process whereby the International Labour Office sought to increase the level of ratifications of core conventions on which the fundamental principles are based. It was, moreover, the catalyst for the making of ILO Convention 182 (Worst Forms of Child Labour Convention 1999).

Beyond the core, there are three distinguishing features of the International Labour Code. The first is its *scope and range*, having grown since the first Convention in 1919 to cover a large number of work-related questions. Many of these provisions are universal in the sense that they apply to all (subject to specified exceptions) workers. This includes Conventions dealing with minimum wage fixing machinery, working time and holidays, occupational health and safety, and termination of employment. Other provisions are targeted on the special problems faced by particular groups of workers, with a particularly large number of instruments dealing with the rights of seafarers, and other prominent measures addressing the particular vulnerabilities of home-workers, part-time workers and now domestic workers. And apart from dealing with employment rights, a number of important instruments deal with labour administration and labour policy, covering matters as diverse as labour inspectorates, tripartite consultation between government, trade unions and employers, and the promotion of 'full, productive and freely chosen employment' (ILO Convention 122 (Employment Policy Convention 1964)).

But while the scope and range of the International Labour Code are impressive, this is to be balanced against concerns that there are *too many instruments*, many of which are of little relevance to many of the countries to which they are addressed (Hepple 2005). This is thought to be particularly true of some of the more normative and prescriptive provisions, which set standards that in some cases may now be ambitious for large developed countries, never mind small developing countries. But although there is some merit in this concern, in truth, it is really only a problem if it is thought that all standards ought in principle to be ratified by all member states. Although ratification is always welcome, this is of course an absurd position. There is no reason, for example, why landlocked states with no shipping industry should ratify the maritime conventions. The challenge for those responsible for the International Labour Code is thus to draft standards that are suitable for both the developed and the developing world. But without denying the universality of workers' rights, it would be a grave mistake to draft a code in the expectation that it would or should be universally applied. What is possible in the developing world should not constrain what is appropriate in the developed world. The International Labour Code should set standards rather than have standards reflect prevailing practices.

Notwithstanding the above, a third feature of the International Labour Code is its *flexibility*. Indeed, this is a feature of the code required by the ILO Constitution, which provides that in framing any Convention or Recommendation, the International Labour Conference must take into account the conditions prevailing in some countries and make necessary modifications to the Convention in question. In some early Conventions – notably Convention 1 (Hours of Work [Industry] Convention 1919), this was done by making modifications for specified countries, which effectively means regulating on a country-by-country basis. The preferred method nowadays is to use promotional rather than prescriptive conventions. The difference between prescriptive and promotional regulation can be illustrated by the difference of approach to be found in Convention 1 (Hours of Work [Industry] Convention 1919) and the most recent Convention 189 (Domestic Workers Convention 2011), where the former provides that:

> The working hours of persons employed in any public or private industrial undertaking or in any branch thereof, other than an undertaking in which only members of the same family are employed, shall not exceed eight in the day and forty-eight in the week.
>
> (Convention 1 1919)

The latter in contrast provides that member states must take measures to ensure that certain objectives are met, without always prescribing what these measures are. It is undoubtedly the case, however, that strategies of this latter kind allow for – and, indeed, may even encourage – variation in the standards applicable in different member states.

Although some concerns about the current state of the International Labour Code may be overplayed, this is not to deny that the code is in need of overhaul and 'modernization' (though not in the deregulatory sense with which that latter term is sometimes associated). It is already the case that some of the existing international labour conventions have been updated and replaced, while others have been consolidated. But still others may now be anachronistic in some parts of the world in view of changing social values. A good example of this is Convention 89 (Night Work [Women] Convention [Revised] 1948), which prohibits women from being employed at night in any industrial undertaking.[1] It is important to stress that 'overhaul' and 'modernization' should not be synonymous with retreat, the changing global economy presenting new regulatory imperatives, including the need for new standards to enable trade unions more effectively to operate transnationally as well as nationally when dealing with global corporations. This means not only the right to organize on a transnational basis, but also the right to bargain collectively on a transnational basis and the right to take coordinated collective action on a transnational level. These are imperatives of globalization for which only limited provision is currently made (Ewing 2001).

Supervision and enforcement

It is one thing for a country to ratify a Convention, but another matter altogether to ensure that it complies with the Convention in question. So how do we ensure that commitments voluntarily entered into are kept, given that there are now almost 8,000 ratifications? The starting point is the procedure under Article 22 of the ILO Constitution whereby each member state must make an annual report to the International Labour Office on the measures it has taken to give effect to the provisions of Conventions to which it is a party. In order to ensure that the International Labour Office is not presented with boxes full of self-serving reports written by government officials, copies of the national reports must also be communicated to representative employers' and workers' organizations in their territory, so their comments can be considered by the ILO supervisory bodies in the consideration of national reports. Reflecting the number of ratified conventions, the cycle of supervision does not now take place on an annual basis as provided by the Constitution, but every two years for the eight core Conventions referred to above and every four years for the other Conventions.

Under the Constitution the task of scrutinizing these reports falls to the Governing Body, though clearly with the increase in the number of conventions and the increase over the years of the number of member states, this would now be impracticable. Since 1926, supervision has been conducted by the Committee of Experts, a group of 20 eminent jurists appointed by the Governing Body for renewable three-year terms, with a mandate to operate with 'independence, objectivity and impartiality', being drawn 'from different geographic regions, legal systems and cultures'. Although the work of the Committee of Experts is greatly to be applauded for its bold interpretations of ILO Conventions, this is a system of supervision and scrutiny that is not without its problems. In the first place, it depends on member states complying with their obligations to submit reports, to do so in good time, and to do so in sufficient detail. The Committee reports on problems encountered at this stage every year: in 2012, for example, it was reported that requests had been made for 2,735 reports. Putting to one side the challenge of scrutinizing on this scale, the Committee noted that it had received only 1,855 reports, which is a fairly typical response when compared with other recent years (ILO 2012a).

In addition to this reporting compliance rate of only 67.8 per cent, it was also noted that 11 countries had failed to produce any reports for two years or more, the Committee commenting that 'it is likely that administrative or other problems are at the origin of the difficulties encountered by governments in fulfilling their constitutional obligations' (ibid.). It is nevertheless the case that the countries in question (Chad, Djibouti, Equatorial Guinea, Grenada, Guinea, Guyana, Kyrgyzstan, Nigeria, Sierra Leone, Somalia and Yemen) are among those with the most to hide and among those where support from the Office is most needed. Where reports are submitted, they are usually late, the Committee reporting in 2012 that only 35 per cent of reports were submitted on time, and that only 38 countries were able to submit all their reports on time (ibid.). Although this was an improvement on previous years, the Committee was still concerned about this low level of timely reporting, which was said to disturb 'the sound operation of the regular supervisory procedure' (ibid.). A final problem encountered by the Committee is that it often needs to seek additional information from member states, though again requests for information are often ignored, seriously impeding the work of the Committee.

In carrying out its constitutional duties, the Committee of Experts provides authoritative interpretations of the International Labour Code, and makes findings about whether member states are complying with Conventions they have ratified. In performing these tasks, the Committee generally takes a wide approach to the law, and it is by the process of interpretation that the right to strike, for example, has emerged as a protected aspect of the right to freedom of association. Although not expressly recognized in any international labour convention, the right to strike has been created by the ILO Committee of Experts in its construction of ILO Convention 87 (Freedom of Association and Protection of the Right to Organize Convention 1948) (Creighton 1994). As a result, there is now a rich and detailed jurisprudence about the scope and content of the right to strike and the minimum standards relating thereto that should be guaranteed by every ILO member state (Gernigon *et al.* 1998). This, however, brings us to another problem, which is that of compliance with the Observations and Conclusions of the Committee of Experts. The reports of the latter contain the same Observations made in relation to the same issue in the same country, sometimes for year after year. In the case of the United Kingdom, for example, the Committee has been commenting adversely on the legal restrictions on the right to strike since 1989 (Novitz 2000) and despite 13 years of Labour government, its concerns remain largely unaddressed.

The report of the Committee of Experts is submitted to the International Labour Conference and considered by the Conference Committee on the Application of Standards. This, however, is a tripartite committee unlike the Committee of Experts, and in examining the report of the latter, the Conference Committee will select particularly serious cases for examination. Cases of special concern will be highlighted in special paragraphs of the Conference Committee's General Report (ILO 2012d), and although this may seem a rather weak outcome after what will have been a long process of comment, criticism and condemnation, some governments will lobby anxiously to avoid a special paragraph (Ewing 1994). In 2012, however, the system of supervision was thrown into crisis by the conduct of the employer representatives on the Conference Committee. Having accepted for many years that the right to strike is protected by ILO Convention 87, employer representatives at the ILO have now taken strong exception to the reading of such a right into the latter Convention by the ILO Committee of Experts. They have also taken strong exception to the growing recognition of the latter Committee as a quasi-judicial body, particularly as ILO Conventions and their interpretations by the Committee of Experts are being used increasingly by national and regional courts throughout the world, to the evident alarm of employers. It has been suggested that employers are seeking to take advantage of their powerful position in the global economy to weaken workers' rights (Novitz 2012).

ILO: Renaissance, revival and relevance

The foregoing account barely conceals a number of problems for meaningful international labour standards, suggesting to some that in a rapidly changing world the ILO is stuck with an operational model of declining relevance. First, is the problem of a large number of standards being ignored by those who made them, in the sense that they are not being ratified, and the level of ratification varies greatly between member states. Second, is the problem of compliance with ratified standards, since many governments undermine the supervision process by not submitting fully to its modest demands, and by not complying with the findings of the supervisory bodies. Third is the problem that this gradual decline in effectiveness raises questions of institutional relevance in a world characterized by the globalization of capital, labour and trade, in which new trading blocs are being created (such as the European Union [EU] and North American Free Trade Agreement [NAFTA]), and in which power is moving from the nation state to the transnational corporation, whose demands developing countries appear powerless to resist. The contradiction facing the ILO is how to make labour standards part of the currency of the global economy, at a time when a commitment to these standards appears to have been eschewed by the great bulk of its member states.

ILO standards and globalization

Facing up to these difficulties, the ILO has undergone a remarkable renaissance. At the heart of this renaissance are two key documents in which the ILO seeks to confront the challenges of globalization. It ought to be said at the outset, however, that this process of institutional renewal has not been without its critics (Alston 2004). Part of the process has seen an emphasis on securing support for the eight core Conventions, characterized by some as a 'retreat to the core'. Associated with this move has been an emphasis on 'promotional' activity to encourage higher levels of ratification and compliance with these standards, in contrast with the traditional forms of standard-setting and the traditional forms of supervision and enforcement. But although these criticisms have been forcefully made, they appear wide of the mark (Langille 2005). As we will, see the process of concentrating on the core is having impressive results, which will enable the ILO to move to a second layer of important standards. It is also the case that there is nothing new in promotional activity, because many Conventions are promotional rather than prescriptive. In any event, the promotional work of the ILO is in addition to its traditional standard setting activity (with an important new Convention relating to domestic workers made in 2011) with the supervisory bodies continuing to perform their traditional role of holding governments to account in changing circumstances.

The first of two important documents setting out the new vision and priorities for the ILO is the *ILO Declaration on Fundamental Principles and Rights at Work* adopted by the International Labour Conference in 1998 (ILO 1998). This commits member states to respect and promote principles and rights relating to freedom of association and the effective recognition of the right to collective bargaining, the elimination of forced or compulsory labour, the abolition of child labour and the elimination of discrimination in respect of employment and occupation. Member states are required by the Declaration to commit to these principles as a condition of membership of the ILO, whether or not they have ratified the Conventions on which they were based. At the time the Declaration was adopted, there were seven such Conventions (two each relating to freedom of association, forced labour and discrimination, and one relating to child labour). In 1999, ILO Convention 182 (Worst Forms of Child Labour Convention 1999) was adopted and added to the list. It is to be emphasized, however, that this does not address all forms of child labour, but only those falling within the following four categories: slavery and forced labour (including child soldiers), prostitution and pornography, the use of children for illicit activities (such as drug trafficking), and any work likely to harm the health, safety or morals of children.

Although the 1998 Declaration makes reference to the *Declaration of Philadelphia* of 1944 (see above, Box 23.1), it is nevertheless a greatly diluted version of the latter. As already pointed out, the 1998 Declaration was criticized by some as a 'retreat to the core' on the part of the ILO because of the narrowness of the subjects addressed, there being no reference to wages, working time or health and safety. But while there may be substance in these latter concerns, the very limited scope of Convention 182 and the inability to include other forms of child labour reveal the political difficulties in reaching a consensus even on core labour standards.[2] So although not quite a fresh start, there is much to be said for depth as well as breadth of coverage, in the sense that there is no point pumping out new instruments every year if both new and existing instruments are being ignored. It is thus an important feature of the *Declaration on Fundamental Principles and Rights at Work* that active steps are now being taken to promote universal ratification of the core Conventions, and that a follow-up procedure has been established to enable the ILO to provide 'technical cooperation and advisory services to promote the ratification and implementation of the fundamental Conventions' (ILO 1998). This approach has had impressive results, with the core Conventions in 2012 having between 150 and 175 ratifications each.

The *Declaration on Fundamental Principles and Rights at Work* provides one of the cornerstones of the more recent *ILO Declaration on Social Justice for a Fair Globalization*, adopted in 2008 (ILO 2008a). The latter is said to build on two Declarations (of 1944 and 1998) and to express 'the contemporary vision of the ILO's mandate in the era of globalization' (ibid.). Claiming to be 'a powerful re-affirmation of ILO values', the 2008 Declaration is said to reflect 'the wide consensus on the need for a strong social dimension to globalization in achieving improved and fair outcomes for all' (ibid.). There is, however, an air of unreality about this document and its inspiration from the *Declaration of Philadelphia* of 1944 which was addressed to a very different world, rebuilding after war, with many fewer independent states (50 in total), committed to different social and economic values. It is true that the preamble to the *Declaration on Social Justice and a Fair Globalization* recognizes that globalization has led to inequality, high levels of unemployment and poverty and the growth of unprotected work and the informal economy. But it is also true that the Declaration is noteworthy for its failure fully to acknowledge the problems created by two of the great engines of the global economy: the increasing mobility of both capital and labour, and the exponential rise in the power of transnational corporations or multinational enterprises (MNEs).

Addressed to member states, the *Declaration on Social Justice for a Fair Globalization* is nevertheless rooted in four principles or strategic objectives adapted from the *Declaration of Philadelphia* and elsewhere. These are respectively:

- Promoting employment by creating a sustainable institutional and economic environment.
- Developing and enhancing measures of social protection – social security and labour protection – which are sustainable and adapted to national circumstances.
- Promoting social dialogue and tripartism for a range of specified purposes, including the implementation of the strategic objectives.
- Respecting, promoting and realizing the fundamental principles and rights at work, deemed to be necessary for the realization of all the strategic objectives.

Documents such as the Declaration of 2008 clearly invite scepticism, which can be overcome only by results. Here, provision is made for a follow-up mechanism and there is much emphasis on promotional activity and technical support to realize these objectives. Otherwise, however, there are two stand-out provisions in the 'Method of Implementation' section of the Declaration. The first is an intention to reach beyond the core, 'with a view to achieving a progressively increasing coverage of each of the strategic objectives', with 'special emphasis' not only on core labour standards but also on those regarded as 'most significant from the viewpoint of governance covering tripartism, employment policy and labour inspection' (ILO 2008a). The other is the acknowledgement that if labour standards are to be part of the currency of globalization, it can only be by developing 'new partnerships with non-state entities and economic actors, such as multinational enterprises and trade unions operating at the global sectoral level in order to enhance the effectiveness of ILO operational programmes and activities' (ibid.). As we will see, however, this latter form of engagement is not without its difficulties.

ILO standards and transnational corporations

The commitment in the *Declaration on Social Justice for a Fair Globalization* to develop new partnerships with non-state entities is an important recognition of the shifting patterns of power in the global economy. There may be little point in addressing the strategic objectives to states alone, if states feel constrained by the demands of MNEs to offer hospitable labour laws that are at best indifferent to international labour standards. It is indeed a weakness of the ILO system that it has not done more to confront the MNEs and their responsibility to observe decent standards. True, the ILO pioneered the *Tripartite Declaration of Principles concerning Multinational Enterprises and Social Policy* in 1977 (ILO 1977). But this is the softest of soft law, setting down standards of behaviour drawn mainly from a number of ILO Conventions, though it is true that the latter are embellished with additional expectations. However, enforcement is a major problem. The only procedure established under this Declaration is one where a request may be made to the International Labour Office for guidance on a point of interpretation of the Declaration, which is careful to emphasize that it is not designed to provide an opportunity to challenge domestic laws. There is no complaints machinery and no follow-up to ensure that companies are complying with the terms of the Declaration.

In one sense, it seems difficult for the ILO to impose obligations on companies to which the latter have not consented. The ILO is an organization of states, not corporations, and its reach to the latter depends ultimately on the willingness of states to address MNE activity as a specific problem and to create a framework for this to be done within national law or practice. This indeed has been done by the Organization of Economic Co-operation and Development (OECD), an organization of the world's wealthiest countries. In 1976, the OECD produced guidelines for multinational enterprises, which were significantly revised in 2000 and most recently in 2011 (OECD 2011). Through these guidelines, the OECD member states have addressed a number of concerns about the role of MNEs, including their role in the political and industrial relations systems of host countries, as well as their need to respect human rights generally. So far as the industrial relations chapter is concerned, there has been a clear expectation since 2000 that MNEs will observe the core ILO Conventions, the commentary on the OECD Guidelines noting that the latter 'echo relevant provisions of the [ILO *Declaration on Fundamental Principles and Rights at Work*, 1998] as well as the 1977 ILO Tripartite Declaration of Principles concerning Multinational Enterprises' (ibid.).

An important feature of the OECD is the procedure established for dealing with complaints. Each member is required to establish a National Contact Point (NCP) to which complaints may be made about non-compliance with the Guidelines by a company which has a connection with the country in question (Department of Business, Innovation and Skills 2009). This connection may arise because the country in question is either the home or the host country. In the United Kingdom, the NCP is based in the Department for Business, Innovation and Skills, a location that has given rise to criticism and calls for change to make the arrangements more independent (Joint Committee on Human Rights 2009). But although there have been complaints by non-governmental organisations (NGOs) about the effectiveness of the guidelines in relation to alleged human rights abuses by MNEs (ibid.: 28–9), the procedures relating to the employment and industrial relations chapter of the guidelines have been quietly impressive, at least in the United Kingdom (Blackburn and Ewing 2009). The procedure in recent years has seen the appointment of an ACAS (Advisory, Conciliation and Arbitration Service) arbitrator to mediate complaints brought by national trade unions or global union federations, and these have invariably produced agreed settlements of the disputes involving companies such as British American Tobacco, Unilever and G4S (Department of Business, Innovation and Skills 2012). In the last case, mediation under this process was instrumental in securing the negotiation of a global framework agreement between the company and a number of trade unions (Blackburn and Ewing 2009; Ewing 2011).

Global framework agreements are covered elsewhere in this book (Chapters 20 and 21). But if the role of the OECD is an example of ILO standards being adopted and applied by other inter-governmental agencies, the increasing interest in global framework agreements is an example of their privatization. The first such agreement is thought to have been concluded in 1994 between French hotel chain Accor and the International Union of Foodworkers (IUF) (Wills 2002), since when the number of such agreements has steadily increased (Ewing 2007). These agreements vary in content, but at their heart is an undertaking on the part of the MNE to comply with ILO core principles at least. In some cases the agreements include additional undertakings, whereby the companies in question will seek to ensure that their suppliers also comply with such standards. Typically, there will also be a procedure for independent monitoring of the agreements to ensure that the undertakings are met. But although widely applauded, their importance should not be exaggerated.

Whilst global frame work agreement are an important and fascinating development, they are also a reminder of the weakness of states and their inability or unwillingness to enforce core labour standards in their territories. In the first place, these agreements operate in a legal vacuum though the best view at the moment is that they are unlikely to be legally binding (Ewing 2011). Serious questions have been raised about the possibility that such agreements might be enforceable in the US courts, but at the present time there is thought to be only one agreement to which a US multinational is a party (Coleman 2010). While the International Labour Code currently recognizes a right to organize at transnational level, it does not recognize a right to bargain at transnational level. To the extent that such international framework agreements exist, they are an indulgence by the companies in question, in response to trade union pressure and reputational security. Second, it is to be emphasized that such agreements cannot displace the state's responsibility for core labour standards, if only because of the tremendous strain on trade union resources that they entail. There are thousands of multinational companies and now less than a dozen global union federations, the latter operating in an environment of ever shrinking memberships and ever declining resources at a time when the need for their support has never been greater. So although there is a strong case for space to be made in the International Labour Code – or in revised OECD Guidelines for MNEs – to facilitate the making of global framework agreements, it is implausible to think that such agreements can be a meaningful substitute for the responsibility of governments.

ILO standards and international trade

One of the other problems with ILO standards being adopted by agencies other than the ILO and by private parties such as transnational corporations and global union federations is that there is no ILO role in the process of supervising the application of these standards. The danger is that we end up with multiple diluted constructions of what these principles mean, an issue that also arises in another context where these standards are making an appearance outside the formal structures of the ILO. The issue here relates to the increased use of social clauses in bilateral trade agreements, particularly those involving the United States and now the EU. The EU of course had developed its own social model for its own internal market of 27 member states (as of 2012), some aspects of which were inspired at least in part by ILO standards. But as was pointed out in the introduction to this chapter, and as will be considered further in the conclusion, that model is now under severe strain as a result of the crisis facing the euro and the austerity measures introduced in response. It is now plausible to contemplate the EU having a different relationship with the ILO, which becomes less a source of inspiration, and more a source of restraint for public policy developments (Ewing 2012).

Many of the regional and bilateral agreements that have emerged since the 1990s are recorded on the ILO website, where they appear to be applauded for providing 'minimum commitments for the protection of human rights at work', and 'referring to specific international labour standards adopted by the ILO' (ILO 2012e). Although, as we shall see, these agreements typically provide for a mutual commitment to ILO standards, there is a certain unreality about them, an unreality reinforced by the lack of any ILO involvement in their supervision and enforcement, unlike earlier proposals for a social clause (Chin 1998). Since 1994, the USA has negotiated at least 12 such agreements (with countries such as Australia, Korea, Morocco, Peru and Singapore). Under the terms of the agreements both parties 'reaffirm their obligations as members of the International Labor Organization (ILO) and their commitments under the *ILO Declaration on Fundamental Principles and Rights at Work and its Follow-up (1998)* (ILO Declaration)'. Each party also undertakes to 'strive to ensure' that 'certain labor principles and internationally recognized labor rights are recognized and protected by its law'. The 'internationally recognized labor rights' to which these provisions apply are defined to mean:

> (a) the right of association; (b) the right to organize and bargain collectively; (c) a prohibition on the use of any form of forced or compulsory labor; (d) labor protections for children and young people, including a minimum age for employment of children and the prohibition and elimination of the worst forms of child labor; and (e) acceptable conditions of work with respect to minimum wages, hours of work, and occupational safety and health.
>
> (ILO 2012e)

The unreality relates to the fact that, despite being the driving force behind these agreements, the United States has not ratified some of the Conventions at the core of the agreements in question and nor have some of its trading partners (Ewing 2003). Although the United States claims that federal law is broadly consistent with ILO standards, there is a long line of decisions of the Freedom of Association Committee that would suggest otherwise. As indicated in Box 23.2, it is possible to make a freedom of association complaint against a country even though the country in question has not ratified any of the freedom of association

BOX 23.2 The Freedom of Association Committee

In addition to the normal process of supervision by the Committee of Experts, additional provision is made specifically in relation to freedom of association. Since 1951 complaints may be made to the Freedom of Association Committee, a tripartite committee appointed by the Governing Body.

The Freedom of Association Committee receives complaints from trade unions (or employers) alleging a breach of the freedom of association principles, whether or not the country in question has ratified the freedom of association conventions. Strictly speaking, the Freedom of Association Committee does not hear complaints about breaches of the freedom of association conventions, but about breaches of the freedom of association principles, which are deemed to be binding on all member states by virtue of membership of the ILO. In practice there is little difference between the ILO principles and the ILO Conventions.

The Committee will be composed of three members and being tripartite incomposition has representatives from governments, employers and workers. On receiving the case and after giving the government and any other interested party an opportunity to respond, the Committee will produce a report and indicate what needs to be done to remedy the matter. This is a much used procedure, and is a useful way of bringing into the ILO system the concerns of trade unions in countries which have not ratified Conventions 87 or 98, and so are not subject to the normal process of supervision. Trade unions in countries that have ratified Conventions 87 and 98 also use the procedure.

conventions. This tactic has been used frequently by US unions and has led to a number of rulings of the Freedom of Association Committee which has criticized the extent to which US labour law (1) denies the right to freedom of association to public sector workers (ILO 1993); (2) denies trade union officials access to workplaces while trying to organize workers with a view to securing certification as a bargaining agent (ILO 1992); and (3) denies workers the right to strike by allowing lawful strikers to be permanently replaced (ILO 1991). In an important complaint citing a number of companies that had permanently replaced lawful strikers, the Committee said that:

> The right to strike is one of the essential means through which workers and their organizations may promote and defend their economic and social interests. The Committee considers that this basic right is not really guaranteed when a worker who exercises it legally runs the risk of seeing his or her job taken up permanently by another worker, just as legally. The Committee considers that, if a strike is otherwise legal, the use of labour drawn from outside the undertaking to replace strikers for an indeterminate period entails a risk of derogation from the right to strike which may affect the free exercise of trade union rights.
>
> (ILO 1991: 92)

A number of bilateral agreements have also been negotiated by the European Union, with the so-called 'new generation agreements' also making reference to labour standards. These standards are included in the agreement between the EU and South Korea in recognition of 'the value of international cooperation and agreements on employment and labour affairs as a response of the international community to economic, employment and social challenges and opportunities resulting from globalization'. Apart from a commitment to consult and co-operate on trade-related labour and employment issues of mutual interest, the parties also acknowledge the ILO Declaration of 1998 and commit:

> to respecting, promoting and realizing, in their laws and practices, the principles concerning the [following] fundamental rights: (a) freedom of association and the effective recognition of the right to collective bargaining; (b) the elimination of all forms of forced or compulsory labour; (c) the effective abolition of child labour; and (d) the elimination of discrimination in respect of employment and occupation.

Unlike the US agreements, there is no reference here to wages, hours or health and safety, though there is an additional commitment 'to effectively implementing the ILO Conventions that Korea and the Member States of the European Union have ratified respectively'.

There is an air of unreality here too: although EU member states generally have high levels of ratification, South Korea (a member of the ILO since 1991) has ratified only 24 Conventions, and only four of the eight fundamental Conventions (though it is reported that there are plans to ratify two more, a process acknowledged in the free trade agreement). But a commitment to observe the principles relating to freedom of association and collective bargaining seems hard to swallow in the light again of recent jurisprudence of the Freedom of Association Committee in relation to South Korea. Several such cases have concerned precarious or migrant workers who have been denied basic trade unions rights, in one of the cases it being alleged that the workers in question were 'left unprotected' in relation to:

> (1) recurring acts of anti-union discrimination, notably dismissals, aimed at thwarting their efforts to establish a union; (2) the consistent refusal of the employer to bargain as a result of which none of the unions representing those workers have succeeded in negotiating a collective bargaining agreement; (3) dismissals, imprisonment and compensation suits claiming exorbitant sums for "obstruction of business" in case of industrial action; (4) physical assaults, court injunctions and imprisonment for "obstruction of business" aimed at preventing dismissed trade union leaders from re-entering the premises of the company to stage rallies or exercise representation functions.
>
> (ILO 2008b)

But although there are concerns about the extent to which ILO standards are fully respected in South Korea, there are equally concerns about the fragile nature of these rights in the EU at the time this free trade treaty was being negotiated, a matter to which we return below. While the increasing visibility of ILO standards is thus to be welcomed, there is a nagging doubt that these treaties are being concluded by governments who commit themselves to standards they do not comply with and have no intention of complying with. In the case of the United States, full compliance with ILO Conventions 87 and 98 would require legislative change, which has constantly been blocked by an unwilling Congress.

Conclusion: the ILO in the age of austerity

One of the partners not referred to in the ILO *Declaration on Social Justice and a Fair Globalization* is the courts, though it would be a major step forward if ILO Conventions could be enforced by such bodies. The role of domestic courts in the enforcement of international treaties is largely a matter of domestic constitutional law, though in recent years there has been a growing willingness on the part of courts in different parts of the world to engage with ILO Conventions (Ewing and Hendy 2012). More important, the European Court of Human Rights (ECtHR) has also looked closely at ILO Conventions when interpreting the right to freedom of association in Article 11 of the European Convention on Human Rights. In the immensely important decision in *Demir and Baycara v Turkey* [2008] ECHR 1345, the ECtHR held that the right to freedom of association includes the right to bargain collectively, a conclusion reached by having regard to ILO Conventions, the Council of Europe Social Charter and the EU Charter of Fundamental Rights. Having thus held that Article 11 was to be informed by ILO standards, the Court addressed the 'absence of the legislation necessary to give effect to the provisions of the international labour conventions already ratified by Turkey', and found that there had been a breach of Article 11 (ibid.: para 156) (Ewing and Hendy 2010).

This brings us back to Greece and the Age of Austerity, which has confronted the ILO with a compelling new challenge to its relevance and vitality, a challenge to which so far it is responding well. When the situation in Greece returned to the ILO Committee of Experts in 2012, the Committee was informed by the Report of the High Level Mission, but inadequately informed on all issues it seems, making a number of direct requests to the Greek government for more information on a number of questions. The Committee did, however, examine the complaints under ILO Conventions 100, 111 and 156 (dealing with equal pay, discrimination and family responsibilities respectively), concerned with the 'exponential growth of part-time work and the significant increase in rotation work', and in particular the 'dramatic increase of the number of full-time contracts of employment that had been unilaterally converted by the employer into rotation contracts'. The disproportionate impact of the crisis on women was 'reportedly exacerbated by the inability of the labour inspectorate to effectively address equality cases', while 'delays in the administration of justice also discourage women from having recourse to the courts'. But despite highlighting serious concerns about the impact of the austerity measures on equality, at this stage the Committee was content to report findings, summarize the HLM Report, and seek further information (ILO 2012a).

On freedom of association, in contrast, the Committee found that there had been a breach of both ILO Conventions 87 and 98, and expressed the fear 'that the entire foundation of collective bargaining in the country may be vulnerable to collapse under this new framework' (ibid.). This was because 90 per cent of the (private sector) workforce was employed in small enterprises, in a system where trade unions cannot legally be formed in enterprises with less than 20 employees. In these circumstances:

> granting collective bargaining rights to other types of workers' representation which are not afforded the guarantees of independence that apply to the structure and formation of trade unions and the protection of its officers and members is likely to seriously undermine the position of trade unions as the representative voice of the workers in the collective bargaining process.
>
> (ibid.)

The 'risk' that 'the entire foundation of collective bargaining in the country may be vulnerable to collapse', was reinforced 'given that the abolition of the favourability principle set out [in legislation of 2010 and 2011] has the effect of nullifying the binding nature of collective agreements, in breach of an ILO principle that collective agreements should be binding'.

These findings are crucially important, suggesting that the Troika (the IMF, the European Commission and the European Central Bank) were imposing conditions on Greece in breach of Greece's obligations under international law. Indeed, it seems that these institutions were wholly indifferent to some if not all of these obligations, the HLM being 'struck by reports' in relation to obligations under ILO Convention 122 (Employment Policy Convention, 1964) 'that in discussions with the Troika employment objectives rarely figure' (International Labour Office 2011). But not only does such conduct appear to breach ILO standards, *it may as a result* also lead more seriously to a breach of EU law, and the direct obligations of the European Commission and the European Central Bank under the Treaty on European Union (TEU). By virtue of Article 2 of the latter, EU institutions are expected to uphold 'the values of respect for human dignity, freedom, democracy, equality, the rule of law and respect for human rights', in a society in which pluralism, non-discrimination, tolerance, justice, solidarity and equality between women and men prevail'. Similar values are rehearsed in Article 3 which proclaims an obligation on the part of the Union to 'combat social exclusion and discrimination, and shall promote social justice and protection, equality between women and men, [and] solidarity between generations'.

More important is TEU, Article 6, which provides that the Union recognizes the rights, freedoms and principles set out in the EU Charter of Rights, now said to have 'the same legal value as the Treaties'. Article 12 of the EU Charter of Rights provides in turn that everyone has a right to freedom of association, said to imply 'the right of everyone to form and to join trade unions for the protection of his or her interests'. Article 12 of course corresponds directly (if not word for word) with ECtHR, Article 11, relevant in view of the splendid flowering of the latter in *Demir and Baycara v Turkey* [2008] ECtHR 1345 where the Court held – having regard to ILO Convention 98 – that the right to bargain collectively was protected by ECtHR, Article 11. If (as EU law requires) Article 12 of the EU Charter is to be read consistently with the ECtHR, Article 11, and if the ECtHR, Article 11 is to be read consistently with ILO Convention 98, the implications are as enormous as they are obvious. Following the report of the ILO HLM in 2011 (International Labour Office 2011) and the ILO Committee of Experts in 2012 (ILO 2012a), it means that the austerity plan for Greece is utterly illegal. Such are the potential consequences of the new forms of engagement with ILO standards, and such is the importance of the traditional role of the ILO supervisory bodies.

Notes

1 Although ratified by a number of EU member states, this fell foul of the principle of equality in EU law, with the result that it had to be denounced by those EU member states by which it had been ratified.

2 As it is, the *Declaration on Fundamental Principles and Rights at Work* expressly:

> stresses that labour standards should not be used for protectionist trade purposes, and that nothing in this Declaration and its follow-up shall be invoked or otherwise used for such purposes; in addition, the comparative advantage of any country should in no way be called into question by this Declaration and its follow-up.

References

Alston, P. (2004) ' "Core labour standards" and the transformation of the international labour rights regime', *European Journal of International Law*, 15(3): 457–521.

Blackburn, D. and Ewing, K. D. (2009) *Any of Our Business? Human Rights and the UK Private Sector*, Memorandum submitted by the International Centre for Trade Union Rights to the Joint Committee on Human Rights, HL 5-1I, HC 64-1I, 2009-10, Ev 250.

Chin, D. (1998) *A Social Clause for Labour's Cause: Global Trade and Labour Standards: A Challenge for the New Millennium*, London: Institute of Employment Rights.

Coleman, S. (2010) 'Enforcing international framework agreements in the US courts: a contract analysis', *Columbia Human Rights Law Review*, 41(2): 601–34.

Creighton, W. B. (1994) 'The ILO and the protection of Freedom of Association in the United Kingdom', in K. D. Ewing, C. A. Gearty and B. A. Hepple (eds) *Human Rights and Labour Law: Essays for Paul O'Higgins*, London: Mansell.

Department for Business, Innovation and Skills (2009) *The UK National Contact Point for the OECD Guidelines for Multinational Enterprises*, London: BIS. Available at: http://www.bis.gov.uk/assets/biscore/business-sectors/docs/u/09-1352-uk-national-contact-point-for-oecd-guidelines-multinational-enterprises.pdf. (accessed 10 July 2012).

—— (2012) *The UK National Contact Point: Cases*, London: BIS. Available at: http://www.bis.gov.uk/policies/business-sectors/green-economy/sustainable-development/corporate-responsibility/uk-ncp-oecd-guidelines/cases (accessed 10 July 2012).

Ewing, K. D (1994) *Britain and the ILO*, 2nd edn, London: Institute of Employment Rights.

—— (2001) 'Trade union rights in the twenty-first century', *WorkingUSA*, 5(1): 19–42.

—— (2003) 'The price of free trade', *Employment Law Bulletin*, 9(7): 69–79.

—— (2007) 'International regulation of the global economy – the role of trade unions', in B. Bercusson and C. Estlund (eds) *Regulating Labour in the Wake of Globalization*, Oxford: Hart Publishing.

—— (2011) 'Global framework agreements in context: UK and US', *International Union Rights*, 18(2): 10.

—— (2012) 'Was the bailout of Greece legal?', *Morning Star*, 29 May.

—— and Hendy, J. (2010) 'The dramatic consequences of Demir and Baycara', *Industrial Law Journal*, 39(1): 2–51.

—— and Hendy, J. (2012) 'Giving life to the ILO – two cheers for the SCC', in F. Faraday, J. Fudge and E. Tucker (eds) *Constitutionalising Labour Rights in Canada: Farm Workers and the* Fraser *Case*, Toronto: Irwin Law.

Gernigon, B., Odero A. and Guido, H. (1998) 'ILO principles concerning the right to strike', *International Labour Review*, 137(4): 441–81.

Hepple, B. A. (2005) *Labour Laws and Global Trade*, Oxford: Hart Publishing.

International Labour Office (2011) *Report on the High Level Mission to Greece (Athens, 19–23 September 2011)*, Geneva: ILO.

International Labour Organization (1977) *Tripartite Declaration of Principles Concerning Multinational Enterprises and Social Policy*, Geneva: ILO.

—— (1991) *Committee on Freedom of Association, Report No 278, Case No 1543 (United States)*, Geneva: ILO.

—— (1992) *Committee on Freedom of Association, Report No 284, Case No 1523 (United States)*, Geneva: ILO.

—— (1993) *Committee on Freedom of Association, Report No 291, Case No 1557 (United States)*, Geneva: ILO.

—— (1998) *Declaration on Fundamental Principles and Rights at Work*, Geneva: ILO.

—— (2008a) *Declaration on Social Justice for a Fair Globalization*, Geneva: ILO.

—— (2008b) *Committee on Freedom of Association, Report No 359, Case No 2602 (Korea)*, Geneva: ILO.

——(2011) *Report of the Committee of Experts on the Application of Conventions and Recommendations (Report III(1A)*, Geneva: ILO.

—— (2012a) *Report of the Committee of Experts on the Application of Conventions and Recommendations (Report III(1A)*, Geneva: ILO.

—— (2012b) *Constitution and Standing Orders*, Geneva: ILO.

—— (2012c) *Governing Body*, Geneva: ILO. Available at: http://www.ilo.org/gb/lang--en/ (accessed 10 July 2012).

—— (2012d) *Conference Committee on the Application of Standards*, Geneva: ILO. Available at: http://www.ilo.org/global/standards/applying-and-promoting-international-labour-standards/conference-committee-on-the-application-of-standards/lang--en/index.htm (accessed 10 July 2012).

—— (2012e) *Free Trade and Labour Rights*, Geneva: ILO. Available at: http://www.ilo.org/global/standards/information-resources-and-publications/free-trade-agreements-and-labour-rights/lang--en/index.htm (accessed 10 July 2012).

Joint Committee on Human Rights (2009) *Any of Our Business? Human Rights and the UK Private Sector*, HL 5-1, HC 64-1, 2009-10.

Langille, B. (2005) 'Core labour rights: the true story (reply to Alston)', *European Journal of European Law*, 16(3): 409–37.

Novitz, T. (2000) 'International promises and domestic pragmatism: to what extent will the Employment Relations Act 1999 implement international labour standards relating to freedom of association?', *Modern Law Review*, 63(3): 379–93.

—— (2012) 'The Committee of Experts and the right to strike: a historical perspective', *International Union Rights*, 12(2): 20–1.

OECD (2011) *Guidelines for Multinational Enterprises*, Paris: OECD. Available at: http://www.oecd.org/document/28/0,3746,en_2649_34889_2397532_1_1_1_1,00.htm (accessed 10 July 2012).

Phelan, E.J. (1936) *Yes and Albert Thomas*, London: Cresset Press.

Stewart, M. (1969) *Britain and the ILO: The First Fifty Years*, London: Her Majesty's Stationery Office.

Wills, J. (2002) 'Bargaining for the space to organize in the global economy: a review of the Accor-IUF trade union rights agreement', *Review of International Political Economy*, 9(4): 675–700.

Index

Locators shown in *italics* refer to tables, figures and boxes.